MAN AS MAN

MAN as MAN

The Science and Art of
ETHICS

REV. THOMAS J. HIGGINS, S.J.

LOYOLA COLLEGE
BALTIMORE, MARYLAND

THE BRUCE PUBLISHING COMPANY
MILWAUKEE

Imprimi potest: David Nugent, S.J., Provincialis
Nihil obstat: John A. Schulien, S.T.D., Censor librorum
Imprimatur: ✠ Moses E. Kiley, Archbishop of Milwaukee
December 7, 1948

(Third Printing — 1950)

MARIAE, MATRI DEI ET MEI

PREFACE

The best method of learning morality is study of its adequate sources — reason and revelation. Several causes, the worth of which will not be discussed, have entrusted the teaching of morality in liberal arts colleges to philosophers who must waive the help of revelation. The divorce of morality from revelation is to be regretted: the result of that divorce can easily be an unrealistic view of human life. While he continues to hope for a reunion of reason and revelation, the college moralist must be content to stress the rational basis of morality. He trusts that reason, tainted by original sin, will not be too prejudiced against his conclusions.

This volume is offered to college students with sympathetic understanding of their effort to grasp the ultimate why of human conduct. Many of the phrases used in this book were framed to answer questions of students. These questions teachers simply must answer. In a way, I look on this volume as an answer to the ex-soldier who wrote in his campus newspaper:

"The educational system of America is failing the youth of America! . . . It is fashioning sparrows and pushing them out to compete with hawks. . . . Why on earth should we be taught . . . this foolishness about honesty, truth and fair play? . . .

"If a student is majoring in law, he should be taught not only the laws but the most approved methods . . . of finding the loopholes. . . . If he is to be a doctor, he should not only learn medicine but how to milk the largest fees. . . . If an engineer, how to construct with the cheapest materials. . . . If a journalist, how to slant, alter, lie. . . . In the securities field . . . the different methods of watering stocks and duping suckers. . . .

"Let us get up petitions to remove these namby-pamby professors stumbling on their White Horse Truth, and get some good hard-headed businessmen in our colleges to teach us what we have to know to become a success."[1]

---

[1] *Time*, March 18, 1946, p. 76.

This book is addressed to believer and nonbeliever; to sophisticate and unsophisticate; to persons emerging from unspotted adolescence; to individuals warped by shock of war or obsessed by a craving for immediate material success.

To Mr. Rene Gunning, to Rev. Joseph d'Invilliers, S.J., to Rev. Atlee F. X. Devereux, S.J., members of the faculty of Loyola College, I offer sincere thanks for the time and care which they gave to the reading of the proofs of this book.

THOMAS J. HIGGINS, S.J.

Loyola College, Baltimore
November 10, 1948

CONTENTS

BOOK II

PRINCIPLES OF INDIVIDUAL ETHICS

MAN AS MAN

BOOK ONE
GENERAL PRINCIPLES OF MORALITY

CHAPTER I

PRELIMINARY NOTIONS

I. THE IMPORTANCE OF THIS STUDY

1. There is not a single thing which is unworthy of consideration by the human mind. Everything from protocols to antipastos, from glowworms to sulfa drugs is a good of some sort, a reality, and therefore a participation in, and a reflection of, the Divine Reality. To assist ourselves in the laborious process of knowing these things, we group them together into compartments or mental brackets. But all knowable objects are not worthy of equal attention. Usually our desire and effort to know a thing are proportioned to our concept of the thing's use to us and our corresponding interest in it. Our personal estimate of a thing's value, however, may not correspond to the thing's intrinsic worth: often we prize things less or more than their objective value.

2. Apart from our ignorance or our arbitrary evaluation, there is a hierarchy of reality, a graded scale of objective value for the simple reason that some things have more reality, more perfection than others. Hence some things are more worthy of estimation than other things. Thus, inorganic substances, like nitrogen, are inferior to, and subserve, vegetation: oats, rye, and timothy are inferior to, and support, brute animal life. Brutes, in turn, exist for the use of man who finally is subordinated to, and exists for, God. Evidently the objective worth or nobility of the thing to be known must impart a corresponding value to one's knowledge of it. Hence the closer any given thing approaches to man and the nearer man and the things of man approximate God, by that much are they more noble and deserving of investigation.

3. The subject of this study is man. The entire man is studied, man as man — not a partial aspect of him, not a view of certain fields of

3

human activity interesting to specialists but of no concern to the rest of men, but rather those elementally human things which touch all men; those universal enduring values which are of worth to us not because we are physicians, housewives, barbers, or accountants, but solely because we are men. Other disciplines may purport to make good engineers, good dietitians, good speakers, good jurists; ethics intends to form good men. Not everybody is interested in being a good dentist, machinist, or beautician. Dentists, machinists, and beauticians can cease to be such, or at least can forget at times their professional capacity, and no great harm is done. We shall never cease to be men, however, nor may we, without grave hurt to ourselves, ever seriously forget we are men.

4. Moreover, while there are other sciences which, like psychology, consider the total man, this study takes that aspect of the total man which is of most penetrating consequence. Ethics answers the two vital questions of our existence: What is man for? What is he to do to accomplish what he is for? Hence ethics should be of peculiar interest to all men as having a distinctive nobility and importance surpassing all natural sciences except that which deals directly with God, the apex and end of all things.

II. WHAT IS MAN?

5. Before explaining ethics as the science of man as man, we must first make clear what man is. Modern science describes man in various ways — as *homo sapiens,* the erect and comparatively hairless animal closely related to the ape; as an extremely complicated chemical formula not yet worked out to its last constituent; as a species of electron-proton complex; as a reflex mechanism; as an assemblage of stimulus-response relationships; as a psychoanalytical *ego* motivated by *libido* or basic physiological drives. Man may be all these but he is much more. For an adequate description of man we turn to the valid findings of the other branches of scholastic philosophy which we accept as conclusively established in their proper place.

6. The clearest picture of man is had by a summary of what he is in the light of Aristotle's four ultimate causes — material, formal, efficient, and final. Man, a unified whole like any other living thing, is a composite being, a complete substance formed from the coalescing of two widely differing constituents. One of these is the material element, the undetermined and determinable part of him. Loosely this is called his body; but strictly this material element must be conceived not as a body, organized and quickened into a living thing, but as a mass of matter, inert, unshaped, as yet undetermined to be any specific thing. This is man's material cause.

7. By union with a formal, or determining, cause, this material element is determined to be a definite thing, is vivified into a human body so that the resultant of this union is a rational animal. This formal cause, or soul, is a vital principle, the ultimate internal reason why man can perform acts of a vegetative, sentient, and rational nature. This principle of life is a simple, spiritual, incomplete substance endowed with immortality. It likewise has two faculties: one cognoscitive, called intellect; the other appetitive, called will. While there are in man a variety of appetites deriving from the complexity of his nature, all of these appetites must, to insure the unity of his being, be naturally subordinate to one supreme appetite, the will. By his will he seeks his proper good as man. Since he is essentially different from all other created things, he seeks his proper good in a characteristically human way; that is, illumined by rational knowledge, he seeks it freely. Unlike other natural substances, which are bound by an inner compulsion to definite, ineluctable modes of action, man, at least in certain of his actions, is free. When all the prerequisites for one definite action are at hand, the human will is not already determined to act but has freedom of choice: it may act or refuse to act, or choose another act.

Thus we learn from psychology that the *intrinsic causes* of man are his material body and spiritual, free, and immortal soul.

8. Man's *extrinsic causes* are his efficient and final causes. Cosmology and theodicy prove that all contingent beings, of whom man certainly is one, ultimately owe their origin to a necessary, infinitely perfect Person, who, as first cause of the universe, produced all contingent beings by a unique kind of efficient causality, creation. God the Creator, then, is the ultimate efficient cause of man.

9. The ultimate final cause of the universe is likewise God. This is understood of two different things and is applicable to two distinctly different sets of activity: (*a*) on the part of God, the motive moving Him to create; and (*b*) on the part of creatures, the goal in which all their activities rest.

What moves God to create cannot be some finite good He is to acquire from creation. God is not to be imagined as a celestial contractor who invests in a universe which is to give Him an income, supply Him with something He lacks. Being infinitely perfect, He has all things; being immutable, nothing can be added and nothing taken away from Him. Since He cannot acquire He can only give. The reason, then, why He creates is *His own infinite goodness.* Good is diffusive of itself — it tends to share itself. God creates because, loving His own infinite excellence, He desires to communicate something of that infinite reality to things outside Himself. However, He is not compelled to do this, for, being infinitely perfect, He is likewise free. Therefore, the ultimate motive of divine activity in the universe is the infinite goodness and liberty of God.

10. Regarding the end toward which all created activity must tend, a distinction is made between an end which is to be acquired and an end-result which is to be produced. The end to be acquired is God, who is to be possessed according to the capacity of each thing. God, therefore, is the absolutely ultimate end of all things. The end-result in which the universe's activity is to culminate is the *extrinsic glory of God.* This is a created thing. It is not the motive inducing God to create but God cannot create without willing it because an inescapable law of order demands that all created activity conclude therein.

God's *intrinsic glory* is the knowledge and praise which He has in the depth of His own Being, of His own infinite excellence. A dim resemblance to this is the extrinsic glory rendered Him by the works of His hand. This is twofold, namely, the fundamental glory of God and the formal glory of God. God communicates finite reality to his creatures which manifests the goodness of the Creator. All created things from the simplest atomic structure to the most complex animal are patterned after, and in every way are dependent on, God. Since each is something and does something imitative of the Divine Being and His infinite activity, each shows forth something of God's excellence. This manifestation of the divine excellence constitutes the *fundamental glory of God.* Every creature by its mere existence and activity renders God this glory.

11. But a creation, no matter how beautiful, which would merely reflect but never consciously acknowledge the bounteous Creator, would be a very imperfect imitation of the glory God has in Himself. It would be a symphony no ear but God's would hear, a loveliness that would ravish no eye but its Maker's. Hence God enlarges the diffusion of Himself by making intelligent beings, images of Himself with intellect and will, who not only manifest the divine reality communicated to them but acknowledge it, and freely and intelligently subordinate themselves to Him. This is the *formal glory of God*. This must be the over-all end to be produced by a universe in which created intelligences exist; and as man is part of the universe, the apex and mouthpiece of visible creation, the final and absolute end of human activity is rendering God this extrinsic glory. Creation will have given God His glory and fulfilled the divine purposes for it when finally nonintelligent things shall have fittingly subserved created intelligences and these in turn are perfectly subordinated to God so that He is all in all.

This essential delineation of man we legitimately postulate; it is proved elsewhere. Upon it as on a foundation stone rests the structure we rear in this study.

III. WHAT IS ETHICS?

12. Ethics is an odd word. Like metaphysics, physics, and the now obsolete optics, it has come into the English language by way of scholasticism. It is a transliteration into English of the Greek ἠθικὰ, which means *moralia* in Latin and in English, "morals." Since the ultimate root of ἠθικὰ is ἦθος, which means *mos* in Latin, or customary ways of action, there are those who say morals are merely conventions, changeable customs which vary with time and place. Hence, to them, ethics is not a true science, but merely the historic record of fashions in human conduct in vogue among various peoples and in different times. Such persons admit that there are "mores," but emphatically deny that there are universal, immutable laws of morality everywhere valid. We shall establish that ethics is vastly more than a discussion of mores — that it is a true science based upon laws as valid as the laws of physics, chemistry, and astronomy.

13. The word *ethics* is sometimes used in the sense of a code of honor, of accepted and customary procedure in some given field of human activity. Thus people speak of legal or medical ethics. We mean much more for we use the term in the most universal sense, as applying to all men, not merely as a code one must live up to under penalty of offending against good taste or arousing the displeasure of fellow practitioners, but as a rule of conduct to be observed by all under risk of incurring the ultimate of human evil.

14. In the biological sciences one arrives at a scientific knowledge of the crayfish, the eel, or the ape by a systematic study of their characteristic activities. So, too, we study man as man by an investigation of his characteristic activity. Evidently man has a peculiarly distinctive act. Since he has a nature specifically different from all other beings, there must be an activity proceeding therefrom which is characteristically human. This distinctive human act is the act which proceeds from man's characteristic faculty in a distinctly human way, that is, it proceeds freely from man's will illumined by rational knowledge. It is the deliberate free act.

15. Psychology considers the *physical* nature of these acts, that is, their physiological and psychic perfection, without further referring them to a good of absolute value. Ethics considers their *moral* aspect. Moral means not merely what proceeds from man's characteristic faculty but especially how such things are directly related to man's over-all good. Hence the moral aspect of the deliberate act will be its relationship to that absolute value. It will have *moral rectitude* when it promotes that absolute value; it will have *moral turpitude* when it is destructive of that value. What this absolute value is we shall show in due course. Ethics, then, is defined as the *philosophic science which establishes the moral order of human acts.*

16. A *science* is a systematized body of truths with a proper subject matter and a particular point of view. The subject matter of ethics is man's free acts and its point of view, their moral rectitude or turpitude. That *ethics* be a philosophic science it must (*a*) treat of the *ultimate* causes of human conduct; (*b*) base its conclusions on *unaided reason*. On this latter point it differs from moral theology.

17. *Morality* is dealt with by both moral theology and ethics. Moral theology treats the whole range of morality; ethics does not. Divine grace and the sacraments are not subject matter of ethics, but both have a wide and most pertinent bearing on morality. Moral theology contemplates man as supernaturalized, as elevated to a supernatural destiny, and bases its conclusions on both reason and divine revelation. Ethics prescinds from man's supernatural status and dignity. Its conclusions are drawn not from revelation but from reason. Thus, a moral theologian in showing the heinousness of positive contraception relies chiefly upon divine authority as revealed in Genesis in the story of Onan, whom "The Lord slew because he did a detestable thing."[1] The ethician, on the other hand, makes no appeal to authority but proves the malice of this action on purely natural grounds.

Moral theology clears up certain doubts which unaided reason might not be able to solve. We might not know for certain that lewd thoughts and desires are morally wrong if Christ had not said, "Whosoever shall look upon a woman to lust after her, hath already committed adultery with her in his heart."[2]

In the field of morality, however, the function of revelation is chiefly confirmatory. It gives the mind the all-satisfying certitude which comes from infallible authority. It is the anchor that holds reason to its moorings when passion would sweep it loose. That man's weakness made such confirmation morally necessary, we shall show in due place (see § 337).

18. No science which contradicts reality can be a true science. Since the word of God contains an unerring picture of reality, no conclusions of ethics may contradict what God has revealed. If ethical conclusions legitimately deduced from certain premises conflicted with the word of God, God would contradict Himself; He is the Author of human reason and revelation. A real conflict between ethics and moral theology is impossible.

Since ethics is confined by the limits of natural reason, it cannot tell the whole truth about man as man. Hence, a realistic treatment of ethics requires supplementation from revelation. Thus, no student should be left under the impression that man's end is merely *natural* beatitude, that in his magnanimous man Aristotle describes the highest ideal of human conduct.

19. Ethics, unlike ontology, is not a *speculative* science, an investigation undertaken for the sake of knowledge alone. Like chemistry, it is a *practical* science because its end is both knowledge and action. Like logic, it is also a *normative* science for it does not summarize what human conduct *is* but sets forth the standards of what it *ought to be.*

20. Above all, ethics is an art. An art is a systematic application of knowledge resulting in acquisition of skill in the production of

---

[1] Gen. 38:10.
[2] Matt. 5:28.

some desired result. Ethics is the art of human living and its end-product should be ease in being the good man in every circumstance. Only a barren pedagogy would permit the student to be content with a take-it-or-leave-it explanation of the laws of moral behavior. As logic aims at giving the student skill in producing correct acts of the intellect, ethics should give the student skill in performing good acts of the will. Even at the risk of being called "exhortatory ethics," this science must aim at the extirpation of vice and the fostering of virtue. The purpose of ethics, then, is to teach a man how to live aright that by right living he may attain the full stature of his ultimate perfection. Ethics, therefore, is a way of life — the good life.

21. Some would find a difference between ethics and morals. They regard ethics as a scientific evolvement and demonstration of morality. Morals they describe as that code of human conduct which each one by natural inclination sets up for himself. Thus a man speaks of his neighbor as a person of loose morals, meaning that he has a flexible, easygoing code.

A distinction between ethics and morals is unnecessary. Just as the average, normal person holds with natural certitude most of the fundamental truths of philosophy, similarly he knows the basic truths of morality. Mothers are the first teachers of ethics. One of the chief concerns of the child of eight at the cinema is to find out whether a given character on the screen is a "good guy" or a "bad guy."

22. It is an observable fact that all men — except, of course, the sophisticated few who do violence to the light of their intellects — differentiate between human acts that are good and human acts that are bad. Every nation and people have distinguished between good men and bad men. All languages have words to express virtue and vice. People likewise think there are some acts which a man ought to do because they are good and some which he ought to avoid because they are bad. Those who do good are regarded as deserving praise; those who do evil, as rightly deserving censure.

Ethics accepts these facts and sets out to render our natural certitude concerning them, formal scientific certitude. Without resorting to subtle distinctions or employing unnecessary technical language, which may obscure rather than clarify, this study will show that ethics is our common sense knowledge of morality put into systematic form and not, as some beginners complain, common sense mystified.

23. Our study proposes to establish what orderly human conduct is and it falls into three main parts: *general ethics,* which studies the principles underlying all morality; *individual ethics,* which examines the particular good or evil acts man is to do or avoid as an individual; and *social ethics,* which explains what is good or evil conduct for man as a *social being.*

The fundamental principles of general ethics are simply the answers to these three central problems: (1) What is the good in which human activity should terminate? (2) What is the ultimate explanation of the difference between good and bad acts? (3) Why must a man do good and avoid evil?

READINGS

St. Thomas, *Summa Theologica,* I–II, 9, 4; 58, 1; 80, 1–3.

——— *Contra Gentiles,* III, 17 ff.

Aristotle, *Nicomachean Ethics,* I, 1–4.

Billot, L., S.J., *De Deo Uno Et Trino,* pp. 249–252. Romae, Universitas Gregoriana, 1935, ed. 7.

Catholic Encyclopedia, "Ethics," V, 556; "Morality," X, 559.

Cathrein, Victor, S.J., *Philosophia Moralis,* pp. 1–22. Friburgi Brisgoviae, Herder, 1915, ed. 10.

Coppens, Charles, S.J., *Moral Philosophy,* pp. 3–8. New York, Schwartz, Kirwin and Fauss, 1924.

Cronin, Michael, *The Science of Ethics,* Vol. 1, pp. 1–29. Dublin, Gill and Son, 1909.

Donnelly, Phillip, *Theological Studies,* 1941, Vol. 2, pp. 53–83; 1943, Vol. 4, pp. 3–33.

Messner, J., *Social Ethics,* trans. J. J. Doherty, pp. 3–52. St. Louis, Herder, 1949.

Ross, J. Elliot, *Ethics,* pp. 11–28. New York, Devin-Adair, 1938.

Sullivan, Joseph, S.J., *General Ethics,* pp. 1–10. Worcester, Holy Cross College, 1931.

CHAPTER II

THE END OF MAN

I. MAN'S SUBJECTIVE END

24. Moral rectitude necessarily implies order; moral turpitude, disorder. To determine what is good and orderly and what is evil and disorderly in human conduct we must find a fundamental principle of order. This principle can only be some *end,* because order is the fitting together of many things unto a given end. What fits in is orderly and conduces to the end; what does not fit in is disorderly and leads away from the end. As we cannot say that ticking is good for a watch, growth for a plant, or reading for a horse until we know what a watch, a plant, and a horse are for, so we cannot say that any human act is good or bad until we know what *man is for.* If we are mistaken on this elemental point, our entire system of morality will founder in grievous error.

In § 11 we postulated that man exists for God. As part of creation, man must give God glory. This is an end that he has in common with the universe — an end that is absolute and ultimate. Come what may, God will accomplish this purpose by and in creation. But has not man an end proper to himself, exclusively his, a distinctly human good toward which his human acts tend? If human nature is distinct from all other natures, has it not its own specific end — which of course is subordinate to the end of all things? The first problem of ethics, then, is, *Has man a peculiar and distinctively human purpose?*

A. What Is an End?

25. End is the most elementary of the causes. Without an end nothing would be caused, nothing contingent ever exist; for the end is *that on account of which anything begins to be.* The end is always a good, that is, something which is capable of conferring some suitable perfection, some advantage, some value. Once a good is apprehended as such and is sought, it becomes an end. Initially, then, the end is the mental representation of some object or result conceived as desirable; intermediately steps are taken to accomplish it; ultimately the end is the possession of the good sought.

26. Hence in any accomplished end we distinguish (*a*) *the end which* (*finis qui*), that good for the production or attainment of which means are taken — this is the objective end, the real *res appetita;* (*b*) *the end for whom* (*finis cui*), the person or subject for whom the good is to be procured; (*c*) *the end by which* (*finis formalis*), the act by which the desired good is attained, the *adeptio rei appetitae.* It cannot exist without the objective end. The two coalesce to form one integral end.

27. It is characteristic of an end that (*a*) *it is sought for on its own account* precisely because it is apprehended as good. Thereby it differs from *pure means,* which is sought only that a true end may be attained. However, a particular good may be sought both for its own sake and also as a means of attaining some further good. Hence there are proximate ends, intermediate ends, and ultimate ends. Moreover (*b*) *other things are sought on account of the end.* What we conceive of as leading to the desired object we seek solely that we may secure it. Finally (*c*) *end is first in the order of intention, last in the order of execution.* First is the mental representation of the desired result, then the ordering of means, and last of all the satisfaction of desire in the possession of the end obtained.

B. Has Man a Distinctive End?

28. To the question whether man has a distinctive end Aristotle answers: "Are we then to suppose that while carpenter and cobbler have certain works and courses of action, man as man has none but is left by nature without a work? Or would one rather hold that as eye, hand and foot and in general each of his members has manifestly some work; so too the whole man as distinct from these has some work of his own?"[1] His assertion is proved in these considerations: (*a*) *Man acts for an end in all his human acts.* Man's characteristic act proceeds from his will. The will acts solely for good but a good sought is an end. (*b*) *In man's human acts there must be some end*

---

[1] *Ethics,* I, 7, 1097b.

which is final, otherwise we have the contradiction that man could never start to will and could never cease to will. Since end is first in intention, if there were no final end, man could never begin to will. Since end is last in execution, if there were no final end, man would go on willing ad infinitum. (*c*) *Man can have but one final end.* The ultimate end of anything is that which fills up the measure of its capacities; beyond it there is nothing which that thing may achieve or tend to achieve. (*d*) *The last end of all men is one and the same.* Since all men have the same nature, they must have the same end. Unity of nature demands unity of end.

C. *Kinds of Human Ends*

29. To demonstrate man's distinctive end we distinguish between end of work and end of agent. (*a*) *End of work* is that result in which an activity by its nature terminates. Applied to things naturally one it is that perfection toward which nature by intrinsic impulses directs the being. Thus the end of the eye is seeing; of the feet, locomotion. (*b*) *End of agent* is that purpose chosen by a free agent for the realization of which this activity is performed. An airplane, whose end of work is to fly, can be used to carry mail; laughter, whose end of work is the outward expression of inward delight, may be used to conceal pain or embarrass one's listener.

Our inquiry is solely into man's end of work. We are not concerned with the particular purposes to which diverse individuals may shape their lives but only with that good which nature sets before each to realize.

30. An end of work may conceivably be either intrinsic or extrinsic. (*a*) An *intrinsic end of work* is a good realizable within the nature of the being itself. An *ultimate intrinsic end* is that crowning state of perfection and completeness which is attained by the proper exercise and fullest development of the being's natural capacities. (*b*) An *extrinsic end of work* is a good realizable outside the nature of the thing itself. The *ultimate extrinsic end* of a thing naturally one is the well-being of that superior thing to which it must contribute by Nature's ordinance. Thus a plant, over and above its own well-being, serves as food for brutes; brutes, in turn, are intended for the use of man.

Man's end of work is his ultimate internal good, because, although his completed and perfected nature must ever be subordinate to God, there is no ultimate good *outside* man's nature which man can achieve. He can offer God no true good or even utility; God has everything.

31. What, then, is that peak of well-being to which the finite nature of man may aspire? To the pantheist it is absorption into the absolute but pantheism has been thoroughly rejected elsewhere. To Schelling,[2] Hegel,[3] Von Hartmann,[4] and Wundt[5] it is the evolution and perfection of the race as a race to which the good of the individual is thoroughly subordinated. But it is contrary to the immortal worth of the individual, the image of God, to exist for the utility of any thing.

THESIS I. Man's end of work or ultimate internal perfection consists in the adequate satisfaction of his rational appetite.

32. God's purpose in creating the universe is the communication of His divine reality to, and the manifestation of the same in, created beings. Each contingent nature has a principle of activity whereby it moves to its appointed destiny — a limited participation in, and a manifestation of, the divine excellence. The creature's own good is identified with the divine purpose. To insure the creature's movement toward the divine purpose, the Creator implants in each a natural appetite for its proper good.

33. *Appetite,* then, is the tendency of a natural agent toward some action for the securing of some good. This motion may be conscious or unconscious, vital or nonvital. We distinguish appetites as elicited and innate. (*a*) An *elicited appetite* is the tendency toward a good apprehended by previous knowledge. Thus, a hungry squirrel seeks acorns. (*b*) An *innate appetite* is the tendency toward a truly fitting good springing from the very nature of the being and operating with or without previous knowledge. Thus, a salmon tends to spawn, a parent bird to defend its young, a man to preserve his life, molecules and atoms to enter into chemical combinations with other molecules and atoms.

---

[2] F. Schelling, *Saemmtliche Werke,* Vol. I, pp. 313 ff. Stuttgart, 1856.

[3] G. Hegel, *Werke,* Vol. VII, pp. 312 ff. Berlin, 1833.

[4] Edward von Hartmann, *Phänomenologie des sittlichen Bewusstseins,* pp. 710, 711, 870. Berlin, 1879.

[5] Wilhelm Wundt, *Ethics — The Principles of Morality and Departments of Moral Life,* trans. Washburn, Chap. 2, p. 87. London, Swan and Sonnenschein, 1901.

When the natural appetite of a being is filled to capacity, the being is complete and perfected. It has the fullness of well-being intended by nature.

PROOF

34. *Man will be internally perfected only when his rational appetite is adequately satisfied, because:*

1. As a created nature, man will be perfected only when his appetitive capacity is completely satisfied. As long as there remains anything unacquired which his nature naturally tends to, he cannot be perfected.

2. As this rational nature, he exhausts his appetitive capacity only when his will is satisfied. Although man has many appetites, these must be subordinate to one dominant appetite; otherwise he is not a unitary whole but a heterogeneous mass of disparate things. This dominant appetite must be his rational appetite, which alone is characteristic of him.

35. Corollary I. Since the state of being perfectly satisfied is called *perfect happiness,* all men seek it by natural impulse, even though they may disagree as to the objects the possession of which will make them perfectly happy.

Corollary II. In all his human acts, a man seeks his happiness, if not consciously, at least interpretatively (cf. § 69).

II. MAN'S OBJECTIVE END

36. What will fully satisfy man's rational appetite and make him happy? Man's perfection is attained only through *the possession of some object.* Since happiness is perfection, it cannot consist in mere potency, that is, the capacity to do, receive, or have something pleasant done to one. It must be an act, for act is the perfection of potency. But an act must have an object. Man cannot be perfectly happy unless he is happy about *something.* What, then, is that thing?

37. Some men, bewildered by present unhappiness, despairingly conclude that we can never know what will make us happy. *But the object of our happiness must be knowable.* Although man's pursuit of this object is in virtue of an innate appetite and although he himself did not select it as the object of happiness, nevertheless, his quest cannot be a blind following of instinct as is the case in lesser natures but it must accord with his free nature; that is, it must be a conscious tendency, a quest illumined by knowledge.

38. Hence arises the *second great problem of ethics,* namely "What will make all men happy?" What is man's *summum bonum,* his highest good? This is the riddle of the ancients. Here is a point of radical departure. A good deal of the clash of opinion on various problems of ethics shown in subsequent sections can be traced to a disagreement on this fundamental question. The chief answers that have been given now will be considered.

39. 1. *Finite external goods.* A tremendous number of people of all ages either because they cannot grasp that man has an immortal soul, or because they are completely engrossed in getting their happiness *now,* maintain, or at least act as though they did, that money, fame, and worldly power can make us perfectly happy. This belief is false because the object which sates our craving for happiness must (*a*) *exclude the possibility of unhappiness* (unhappiness often accompanies possession of these things in abundance); (*b*) *give us all we can desire* (even a great abundance of these things often leaves much to be desired); (*c*) *not of itself make us unhappy* (these things are often the very root of their possessor's misery).

40. 2. *Corporal beauty and bodily well-being.* The Epicureans held that man's highest good is the maximum of bodily well-being and the minimum of bodily pain. No combination of beauty, health, and strength, however, can constitute the perfect human good because man's body is only a part of him — and the inferior part at that. Since man is more excellent than the brute, his highest good must pertain to that wherein he excels the brute.

41. 3. *Pleasure.* The Hedonists, whose prototype is Aristippus, contend that the primary object of the will is pleasure. Complete happiness is complete pleasure.

Bentham says: "In all this chain of motives, the principal or original seems to be the last internal motive in prospect: it is to this that all other motives in prospect owe their materiality: and the immediately acting motive its existence. This motive . . . is always some pleasure, or some pain; some pleasure, which the act in question is expected to be the means of continuing or producing: some pain which it is expected to be the means of discontinuing or preventing."[6]

The cynic Hobbes constantly advocates a similar self-interest. "We all

---

[6] Jeremy Bentham, *An Introduction to the Principles of Morals and Legislation,* Chap. X, § 2, pp. 101–102. Oxford, Clarendon, 1917.

measure good and evil by the pleasure or pain we either feel at present, or expect hereafter."[7] With sardonic humor he sums up his doctrine of unmitigated selfishness, "Felicity is a continued progress of the desire from one object to another."[8]

For Spinoza "blessedness is nothing but the peace of mind which springs from the intuitive knowledge of God."[9] Butler,[10] too, is a pious hedonist. J. S. Mill says plainly, "pleasure and freedom from pain are the only things desirable as ends."[11]

All of these men confuse the state produced in the subject with the object producing that state. Pleasure is the necessary consequence of having attained the beatifying object; therefore it cannot be that object. As pleasure is a subjective quality, it cannot be the prime object of the will for these two reasons: first, pleasure can be had only *after* some object has been first attained. Second, the primary object of the created will must be something outside itself. Only the divine and necessary Will has within Itself its own end. One cannot be happy without pleasure, but happiness is not adequately identified with pleasure.

42. 4. *Knowledge, love, or virtue.* The Stoics held that virtue or wisdom was the sole good of man. These, however, are subjective and as such cannot be completely satisfying because their ability to satisfy depends on the object known or loved. The will's object must be outside itself.

43. 5. *Man himself.* Kant postulates a God who is merely the disinterested spectator of human life, the indispensable orderer and harmonizer of the physical universe.[12] Taking its cue from Kant who plainly says that man is an end unto himself,[13] a perverted

---

[7] Thomas Hobbes, *Philosophical Rudiments Concerning Government and Society,* Chap. XIV, 17. Molesworth's English edition of Hobbes, Vol. II, p. 196. London, 1841.

[8] *Leviathan,* Chap. XI, *ed. cit.,* Vol. III, p. 85.

[9] Benedict de Spinoza, *Ethic,* trans. White-Stirling, Appendix IV to Proposition LXXIII, p. 241. New York, Macmillan, 1894.

[10] Joseph Butler, *The Analogy of Religion Natural and Revealed to the Constitution and Course of Nature,* Chap. II, pp. 133–134. New York, Franklin, 1840.

[11] John Stuart Mill, *Utilitarianism,* p. 17.

[12] *Critique of Practical Reason,* trans. T. K. Abbott, pp. 221–222. London, Longmans Green, 1898.

[13] "That in the order of ends, man (and with him every rational being) is *an end in himself,* that is, that he can never be used as a means by any (not even by God) without being at the same time an end also himself, that therefore humanity in our person must be *holy* to ourselves, this follows now of itself because he is the subject of the moral law,

humanism considers man as an absolute being. This may be understood of man the individual or man the race.

The individual. The Prussian Nietzsche held that "life itself is *essentially* appropriation, injury, conquest of the strange and weak, suppression, severity, obtrusion of peculiar forms, incorporation, and at the least, putting it mildest, exploitation."[14] To him "'exploitation' does not belong to a depraved or imperfect and primitive society; it belongs to the *nature* of the living being as a primary organic function; it is a consequence of the intrinsic Will to Power, which is precisely the Will to Life."[15] Pushing this notion to its logical conclusions he evolves his theory of the superman according to which any act is lawful to him who has the will to power. As men have or have not this will to power they are supermen or slaves. Hence "there is a master-morality and a slave-morality":[16] a code of ruthless action befits the superman, a corresponding code of humility the slave.

The race. A perfect nation or a perfect human race is the destiny to which human acts are to be directed. This is the philosophic underpinning of totalitarianism. Since the twentieth century is acutely conscious of man's social character it is understandable how the emphasis has shifted from the individual as absolute to the race as absolute.

But man — neither individual nor race — cannot be his own end because that which is its own end is absolute. If man were happy in the possession of himself, he would be a necessary, all-sufficient being. But he can never be other than contingent. God alone is absolute. Therefore the object of human happiness must be *something outside the human will,* something beyond humanity itself. "Development of personality" may express the purpose of life provided one correctly understands personality as a contingent thing limited by equal claims of other humans and an absolute dependence on God. Later we shall have to note some of the grim and unlovely consequences of the racist and totalitarian idea.

---

in other words, of that which is holy in itself, and on account of which and in agreement with which alone anything can be termed holy. For this moral law is founded on the autonomy of his will. . . ." *Ibid.,* p. 229.

[14] Friedrich Nietzsche, *Beyond Good and Evil,* trans. Helen Zimmern, p. 199. New York, The Modern Library, 1937.

[15] *Ibid.,* p. 200.

[16] *Ibid.*

THESIS II. The sole object capable of satisfying our rational appetite is God. Man possesses God by an act of perfect knowledge and love.

PART I

44. From an analysis of the human appetite we conclude that the only thing capable of satisfying it is God, the uniquely necessary and infinite Person whose existence and attributes are established in theodicy. Only when man possesses God is he perfectly happy. St. Augustine expresses this fact when he says: "Thou hast made us for Thyself, O God, and our hearts are restless until they rest in Thee."[17]

Explaining how God is the end of all things, St. Thomas says, "Things are ordained unto God not as to an end for whom something is to be acquired but that they in their own way may acquire from Him Himself."[18] Man gets God from God by knowing and loving Him perfectly.

45. PROOF. *God is the only object capable of satisfying our rational appetite, because:*

1. The human will has (*a*) an innate appetite for all good because good is the formal object of the will — it does not seek merely this or that particular good but all good, good in general; (*b*) an elicited appetite for all good because the intellect can conceive of, and present to, the will as desirable a perfect good. Hence the will will not be satisfied until we shall have attained a perfect good.

2. There is only one perfect good and that is God.

PART II

46. PROOF. *Man possesses God by an act of perfect knowledge and love.*

Any being attains its final end by the highest acts of its characteristic tendencies. But the highest acts of man's characteristic tendencies are perfect knowledge and perfect love. Therefore man attains his final end by an act of perfect knowledge and love.

N.B.: Perhaps Aristotle did not appreciate the full significance of his glorious words when he wrote: "If then the understanding is

---

[17] *Confessions,* Bk. I, Chap. 1.
[18] *Contra Gentiles,* III, 18.

divine in comparison with men, the life of the understanding is divine in comparison with human life. We must not take the advice of those who tell us, that being man, one should cherish the thoughts of a man, or being mortal, the thoughts of a mortal, but so far as in us lies, we must play the immortal and do all in our power to live by the best element on our nature."[19]

III. THE NATURE AND REALITY OF HAPPINESS

47. Man's happiness in the possession of God is *beatitude,* or the full and enduring possession of a supreme and perfect good. In beatitude we distinguish three elements: (*a*) *absence of every evil* — the happy man has no positive defects, blemishes, or privations to mar the fullness of his well-being; (*b*) *presence of all good* connaturally possible — the happy man has all that his nature craves (from this absence of defect and presence of good flows the keenest delight); (*c*) *certitude that this will last.*

48. *Is beatitude an act or a state?* Beatitude must be an act because man is not perfected by having something pleasant done to him, by being the passive recipient of bliss, by having the habitual power of doing something, but rather by *his actually doing something.* Act is more perfect than potency. Aristotle says, "The good of man comes to be a working of the soul in the way of the best and most perfect excellence in a complete life."[20]

However we often speak of happiness as a state because of its permanency. The perfect good is that which lasts. We sigh for happiness as a state of rest. In happiness there will be rest from the struggle with evil. We shall cease to toil for the end but once we have achieved the end we shall not be placidly inert, the passive onlookers at the most arresting, the sublimest of spectacles, but we shall be alive and active to the very depths of our being.

49. *In what act does happiness consist?* In some act of the rational soul for therein alone can be found the perfect function of man as man. In man's final possession of God we can distinguish the act whereby man knows God, the act of the will whereby he loves God, and the resultant joy in the will because of this knowledge and love. Human happiness involves these three acts: no one could be perfectly happy

---

[19] *Ethics,* X, 7, 1177b.
[20] *Ibid.,* I, 7, 1097b.

lacking any one of them. But which of these acts constitutes the very essence of beatitude? Aristotle's explanation of the nature of happiness is that it must flow from the best and most perfect human power, operating in easy surroundings and enduring to length of days. This power he identifies as the speculative intellect.[21] St. Thomas therefore says that happiness is the contemplation of God;[22] the will acts are mere consequences. It would seem, on the other hand, that (a) man attains his last end not because of good intellectual acts but because of good volitional acts. If, therefore, the will is the dominant faculty as man moves toward his end, it may not cease to be such once the end is achieved. Otherwise man's nature would be *essentially* changed. (b) Knowledge is not an end in itself but is further ordained unto volition. We do not know merely to know, but we know in order that the object known may be embraced or rejected by the will. Therefore, the quintessential beatifying act is that of loving God.

50. Over and above the knowledge and love of God which make up his *essential beatitude,* the perfected man enjoys various minor goods. These constitute his *accidental beatitude.* Thus, for example, since man is a social being he will enjoy God not in lonely contemplation but in the company of other men.

An interesting question arises here, namely, *does the body play an essential or accidental part in beatitude?* If we lived in a purely natural order could the soul be perfectly happy without the body? Some authorities state that the soul would be in an unnatural state of separation, that, as the form of the body, it would long for reunion with the body, and hence it would not be perfectly happy unless there were a natural resurrection of the body.

Others rightly say that the resurrection of the body cannot be proved from reason, that while the soul needs the body in this life, once this life is over it can exist, operate, and be happy without the body. A spirit, by nature, must be able to exist and function independently of matter. Since the body exists for the soul, the body will have fulfilled its essential function when the soul reaches its end. Hence, in the words of St. Thomas, reunion with the body does not belong to the essence of beatitude (*ipsum esse*) but rather to the fullness of its perfection (*bene esse*).[23]

---

21 *Ibid.*, X, 8, 1178b.
22 *Sum. Theol.*, I–II, 3, 4.
23 *Ibid.*, I–II, 4, 5 *ad* c.

From revelation we have the divine assurance of a future reunion of body and soul. In the glories of a risen body we shall find the chief items of our accidental happiness.

51. An important comment must be made at this point. It must be emphasized that the beatitude just proved and described is a purely *natural beatitude,* a happiness corresponding to man's natural exigencies and capacities. It is a possession of God which man is *naturally* capable of, that is, knowledge and love of God as He is reflected in creatures. Our most perfect natural knowledge of Him can be but analytic and discursive for it is not given by nature that any creature should look upon the face of God. This discursive process would be an ascent of the mind, as described by Plato, from the individual to the universal, a step-by-step ascent up the grades of reality from a contemplation of bodily beauty to intellectual and moral beauty until we reach a Beauty eternal and immutable, the Fount of all beauty and reality upon whom all other beauties depend, while it is independent of them.[24]

Glorious as this is, there is another beatitude which, properly speaking, belongs to God alone. It is the happiness which arises from the clear, immediate vision of God. It is knowing God without any intervening medium, knowing Him as He knows Himself. This is *supernatural beatitude,* a sharing in the very life of divinity. By supreme condescension of purest love man is *actually destined* for this and this alone. No student of ethics should be under the delusion that he is meant for merely natural beatitude. Of course, in either case God alone is the object of our happiness, but there is a difference in the way God is known and attained — a very great difference. In one case we are but servants before a very kind Master; in the other we are lifted from the status of creatures to that of sons by a Friend and Father.

In his supernatural destiny, man's natural end is adequately and eminently contained. In ethics, however, we consider man's final end exclusive of its supernatural elements.

52. *Is happiness a reality* or just an unsubstantial dream? Is it an endless chase which is never climaxed by the capture of the quarry? Kant says: "Now, the perfect accordance of the will with the moral law is *holiness,* a perfection of which no rational being of the sensible

---

[24]*Symposium,* 210–211.

world is capable at any moment of his existence. Since, nevertheless it is required as practically necessary, it can only be found in a *progress in infinitum* toward that perfect accordance, and on the principles of pure practical reason it is necessary to assume such a practical progress as the real object of the will."[25] Nor does a future life hold out any more certain hope of realization. For "one who is conscious that he has persevered through a long portion of his life up to the end in the progress to the better . . . may well have the comforting hope, though not the certainty, that even in an existence prolonged beyond this life he will continue steadfast in these principles; . . . he may have a prospect of a blessed future; for this is the word reason employs to designate perfect well-being . . . which like holiness is an idea that can be contained only in an endless progress and its totality, and consequently is never attained by a creature."[26] Man, then, desires a holiness and a happiness he never achieves, a perfection "whose margin fades forever and forever as I move."[27] This we deny.

THESIS III. Happiness in the possession of God is actually realizable.

PROOF

53. *Happiness is actually realizable, because:*

1. It would be contrary to *divine wisdom* to put in us an ineluctable tendency toward an end that would not be realized.

2. It would be contrary to *divine fidelity* to lure us on by a promise which is impressed on our nature but which would not be consummated.

3. It would be contrary to *divine goodness* to stimulate us by an appetite of which we are conscious but which would never be satisfied.

IV. THE TIME OF HAPPINESS

54. According to their answer to the inevitable question, When does man have his happiness? all men fall into two categories: (*a*) those who seek happiness *now*; (*b*) those who are willing to wait for happiness *hereafter*. Here we have another aspect of the great point of departure noted in § 38. The happiness-now theory is that the only

---

[25] *Critique of Practical Reason*, p. 218.
[26] *Ibid.*, p. 220, note.
[27] Tennyson's "Ulysses."

life which counts is the here and now. There may not be another life, and, even if there is, it cannot be of much importance. Hence, if one misses happiness now, he has failed in life. The second view is that perfect happiness is impossible in this life; that whatever imperfect happiness is now obtainable must always be kept subordinate to permanent, substantial happiness hereafter.

THESIS IV. Perfect happiness is impossible in this life.

55. PROOF. The universal experience of mankind testifies that there is no one who does not experience an abundance of evil and a lack of many good things at all stages of life. Death, inevitable for all men, precludes the hope of permanently possessing any good. God is known and loved only vaguely and remissly. Our mortal happiness, therefore, must be imperfect.

V. THE PURPOSE OF THIS LIFE

56. Happiness is real and realizable. If, then, we cannot get it in this life, it must be obtainable in a future life. Hence this most important question is left: *What is the purpose of this life?*

THESIS V. Man's end of work in this life is preparation for perfect happiness hereafter. The attainment of this purpose depends on the moral character of his will acts.

PART I

57. PROOF. *The purpose of this life is preparation for happiness hereafter, because:*

1. The end of this life is either the actual enjoyment of happiness or preparation for it. This is so because man's final end is also his *chief good.* Now the chief good of any being is that toward which all things pertaining to that being tend. Hence all things human — this life included — must tend either to happiness itself or to direct preparation for it.

2. Perfect happiness is impossible in this life, as we have just proved (§ 55).

Corollary. Man disposes himself for happiness by ordering and directing his whole life to knowing and loving God, the sole object of his beatitude.

PART II

58. PROOF. *The attainment of this purpose depends on the moral character of man's will acts.*

A finite, contingent being who has not yet reached his final perfection may, if he is free, choose to reject it. Because he is free, man can perform acts which perfect his nature and acts which degrade it. It is impossible that the latter should conduce to his happiness. Therefore, if man insists on acting in a way which degrades his nature, it is impossible that he arrive at perfect happiness or even at a state approximating it. Therefore his attaining a state of preparation for beatitude depends on the moral perfection of his will acts.

59. N.B. What constitutes adequate preparation for beatitude? Is there further opportunity for preparation after death? Neither of these problems can be solved by reason with certainty. However, revelation unmistakably tells us that the sole disposition requisite for beatitude is the state of sanctifying grace at death; that there is one mortal life and one death. Hence the practical meaning of life is reduced to this: the necessity of dying in the state of sanctifying grace.

60. Corollary I. Mortal life is essentially a probation.

Corollary II. Man's ultimate intrinsic end, his beatitude, is not absolutely but only *conditionally* decreed by God. The ultimate end of the universe, the glory of God, has been absolutely decreed. Even with regard to those who fail to win their happiness, God will work His purposes and obtain His glory.

Corollary III. Moral values have supremacy over all else in life. Every activity or happening in the life of every man has enduring meaning and value only in so far as it leads him to his final end. For upon his judicious use of this life depends the character of his future life. Hence, as a prudent man, he must endeavor to use the things of life in so far as they lead to a happy life hereafter and should abstain from whatever hinders the accomplishment of life's purpose. One cannot exaggerate the seriousness of human life.

Corollary IV. Except the perpetual loss of beatitude, there can be no greater misfortune than ignorance of the meaning of this mortal life. The pall which hung over Hellenic civilization when it was at its height arose from doubt and uncertainty about life's meaning. Euripides sums it up in the lines:

O'er all man's life woes gather thick;
Ne'er from its travail respite is.
If better life beyond be found
The darkness veils, clouds wrap it round;
Therefore infatuate fond to this
We cling — the earth's poor sunshine-gleam:
Naught know we of the life to come
There speak no voices from the tomb
We drift on fable's shadowy stream.[28]

Like doubts and uncertainty are producing a similiar pessimism among modern men.

Corollary V. While civilized pessimism originates in ignorance or uncertainty about life's meaning and purpose, more proximately it springs from the frustration of desires and the problem of pain. Pain baffles the unwise. They fail to discern a divine instrument of probation in the so-called miseries of human existence. As we shall see in our discussion of merit, God gives beatitude only if it is deserved. We prove our deserving chiefly by the endurance of difficulty. As gold and silver is tried in the furnace, so a man's soul is tried by tribulation. Moreover, from pain we learn that we were not made for the things which pass. It weans us from a love of creatures and teaches us to rest our hope in the Eternal alone. If in this life we unfortunately find repletion and satisfaction in honor, publicity, human love, wealth, or in any of the obvious objects of human striving, we soon forget and cease to strive after the One Thing for which we were made.

---

[28] *Hippolytus,* 190–198.

READINGS

St. Thomas, *Summa Theologica,* I–II, 1–5.
———— *Contra Gentiles,* II, 46; III, 16–22, 24–53.
Aristotle, *Ethics,* I, 5–10; X.
Brosnahan, Timothy, S.J., *Digest of Lectures,* pp. 23–28. Baltimore, Murphy, 1913.
Catholic Encyclopedia, "End of Man," IX, 582; "Highest Good," VI, 640.
Cox, Ignatius, S.J., *Liberty, Its Use and Abuse,* Vol. I, pp. 12–32. New York, Fordham University Press, 1936.
Donat, Joseph, S.J., *Ethica,* Vol. I, pp. 9–62. Oeneponte, 1920.
Farrell, Walter, O.P., *A Companion to the Summa,* Vol. II, pp. 1–20. New York, Sheed and Ward, 1945.
Leibell, J. F., ed., *Readings in Ethics,* pp. 171–191. Chicago, Loyola University, 1926.

Meyer, Theodore, S.J., *Institutiones Juris Naturalis,* Vol. I, pp. 33–63. Friburgi Brisgoviae, Herder, 1906.
Miltner, Charles, C.S.C., *Elements of Ethics,* pp. 25–49. New York, Macmillan, 1932.
Nivard, Marcel, S.J., *Ethica,* pp. 3–35. Paris, Beauchesne, 1928.
Rickaby, Joseph, S.J., *Aquinus Ethicus,* Vol. I, pp. 1–38. London, Burns and Oates, 1892.
———— *Moral Philosophy,* pp. 3–27. London, Longmans Green, 1919.
Ross, J. Elliot, *Ethics,* pp. 61–71. New York, Devin-Adair, 1938.
Sullivan, Joseph, S.J., *General Ethics,* pp. 35–63. Worcester, Holy Cross College, 1931.

CHAPTER III

THE HUMAN ACT

61. How does man achieve happiness? Only by a succession of his own contingent acts. What kind of acts? Since he has a distinctive nature and end, he must have a distinctive act whereby alone that end is attained. We call this *the human act*. Human acts alone constitute the field of ethics. But before we can study human acts from their moral aspect, we must first know the physical nature of the human act.

I. THE PHYSICAL NATURE OF THE HUMAN ACT

A. What Is a Human Act?

62. *Not every act of man is a human act.* Man has a complex nature. He is the agent of actions which are the same as those of (*a*) *minerals* — he is subject to the same laws of physics as stones and rocks: should he stumble on the coping of a roof, he would fall to the ground like any loose tile; (*b*) *plants* — like them he digests food and grows; (*c*) *brutes* — like them he experiences the sensations of cold, heat, general well-being. These are not human acts because they do not proceed from man's characteristically human faculty, they confer no perfection which is distinctively human. The human act must proceed from the human faculty.

63. The will is man's dominant faculty, but *not every act of the will is a human act.* There are spontaneous indeliberate reactions of the will to good and evil proposed by the imagination. These are not human because man is not master of them. He can be master only of those acts of which he has previous knowledge. These are *voluntary* acts, that is, acts proceeding from the will together with knowledge of the purpose of the act. This knowledge is not mere accompaniment; it is also a cocause of the act.

64. *Is man master of all his voluntary acts?* Man is master of all but one, namely, that highest act whereby he will embrace his Supreme Good. When the intellect adequately presents to the will the Perfect Good, the will will be unable to reject it. This act will be perfectly voluntary because there will be full knowledge, approbation, and willingness. It will not, however, be free. By his very nature man will be determined to elicit this act: this act is The End of the will. The created will is not free with respect to its End; it is free only as regards the means to The End. However, since this act will not take place in this life, and since ethics deals with the proper ordination of human acts toward their last end, it suffices here to say that man is master of his voluntary acts, that voluntary acts are free acts.

The human act, therefore, is *a free, deliberate act.* Of this act man is fully master. The act of which man is master is the *act of man as man.* In this respect his act differs from that of other visible created things.

65. Three elements enter every human act: (*a*) motion of the will; (*b*) previous intellectual knowledge of the purpose of the act; (*c*) freedom. This question arises concerning the first element, *Is a velleity a human act?* The term "velleity" is applied to these two situations: (1) It refers to an inefficacious wish, the tendency of the will toward some externally unrealizable object merely as an object of inner complacence. Thus a small boy who would like to thrash a bigger boy may gloat over an imaginary picture of such a triumph. All these are human acts. Our secret desires, even our daydreaming, present moral problems. (2) Velleity also refers to a situation in which the mind perceives the object to be unattainable so that the will refrains from any act. "I should like to be a great saint but this is utterly beyond me." Where there is no motion or intention of the will no human act is possible. However, this absence of volition, resulting from the indolence of the will, is quite different from the case where one wills not to act. "I would hate you if that were not wrong." This is a negative will act, so called because its object is a negation.

If either the second or third element is totally lacking, a man's act is *involuntary.* An involuntary act may be performed without knowledge of the purpose of the act, as when a stroller inadvertently taps the pickets of a fence as he passes. It may be done with knowledge against the choice of the will, as when a man emerging from ether talks ridiculously but is unable to control his speech.

Between the fully deliberate, or voluntary, act and the indeliberate, or involuntary, act stands the very real but elusive *semideliberate* act. The semideliberate act lacks the completeness of knowledge or free choice requisite for the human act. Thus, when one is half asleep he may not be fully aware of what he is doing; or when a person is exposed to a very vivid enticement he may yield partial consent.

How the voluntariness of our acts is affected by a variety of factors is discussed in the second part of this chapter.

B. The Object of the Human Act

66. The deliberate will act has to have an object. As you cannot know without knowing something, so you cannot will without tending to some object. It is this object which gives the will its specific character not only psychologically but ethically. We do not evaluate the will act by its subjective intensity or remissness but by the thing willed. This object may be either direct or indirect.

67. 1. *Direct object of the will.* This immediately terminates the will act. It can be anything or everything for there is no limit to the will's capacity to act. What *immediately* terminates the will act may be (*a*) some object involving no external activity, such as a man's love or hatred for his employer; (*b*) the action of some other faculty placed at the will's command, such as the freely chosen act of eating one's dinner or singing a song. This is an *imperate act* and is physically distinct from the *elicited act of the will.* If nothing further is sought than the exercise of that faculty, as when one goes merely to walk or swim, that activity is the will's object. If the imperated act moves to some object proper to itself, as when the mind sets out to learn a geometric theorem or the hands attempt to seize a piece of fruit, the object to be attained by the imperated faculty is likewise the will's direct object. The imperate act and the elicited act of the will, though physically distinct, constitute a volitional unity: the imperate act is the means chosen by the will to attain its desired object.

However, *the truly human act is always and only the inner elicited act of the will.* It alone is free. Imperate acts are spoken of as free because they result from the will's free choice. Without the will they could not be called free.

68. 2. *Indirect object of the will.* This is an effect which is not intended but is foreseen, at least confusedly, as following from what is directly intended. Thus, I take a horn away from a noisy child and he cries. I foresee but do not intend his crying. Should I intend it, it would become a direct voluntary object.

To be called voluntary in any way, an unintended effect must be known to some extent. Unintended effects which are not knowable have no measure of voluntariness. Noe's drunkenness was probably wholly involuntary because he had no means of knowing how the wine would affect him.

The indirect object is called *voluntary in cause* for its voluntariness is to be sought in its cause, the directly willed action of which it is the effect.

C. Kinds of Human Acts

69. In terms of the completeness of an act we distinguish: (*a*) the *perfect voluntary* act, in which there is full knowledge and freedom of consent; (*b*) the *imperfect voluntary* act, also called semideliberate, in which there is incomplete deliberation or consent.

The voluntary act is a volitional motion toward some object, the production of some effect. It is aptly termed intention. From the point of view of the object sought we distinguish: (*a*) *positive intention,* which is directed toward a positive action; and (*b*) *negative intention,* whose object is the omission of an act.

From the point of view of the influence of the will in the production of an effect we have the following intentions: (*a*) *actual intention,* a will act which here and now produces this effect; (*b*) *virtual intention,* a will act which has been placed and has been physically interrupted but morally continues and produces this effect; (*c*) *habitual intention,* a will act which has once been placed and never revoked but has been so interrupted that it no longer influences this effect as an act but merely as a habit; (*d*) *interpretative intention,* a will act which is not actually placed but would be if it were thought of and hence is considered as productive of an effect.

The following example will illustrate the four types of intentions: I walk to town to buy my father a certain brand of tobacco (*actual intention*). On the way I get into conversation with a friend and forget why I am going to town but in **virtue** of my previous intention to obey my father I continue on my way (*virtual intention*). In town my friend invites me to have a drink. On her deathbed I had promised my mother never to drink. I never revoked this promise. I have forgotten it. But it has formed in me the habit of not drinking. I refuse the invitation because of this habit (*habitual intention*). When I get to the store I buy my father a different brand of tobacco because I find an extraordinary bargain. I prudently interpret that such would be my father's intention if he knew this (*interpretative intention of my father*).

Finally, brief mention must be made here of the qualifications, good, bad, and indifferent. They are not applied to the physical aspect of the human act: they are applied to its moral aspect.

D. Responsibility

70. From the free physical nature of the human act we are able to draw an immediate quasimoral conclusion regarding responsibility, or imputability. An act is imputed when it is charged or ascribed to one as its responsible agent. The person who is responsible for an act must answer for its consequences, that is, assume blame if these consequences are unsatisfactory or receive credit if these are satisfactory.

THESIS VI. Man is responsible for his human acts.

71. PROOF. Man is responsible for those acts of which he is master. But man is master of his human acts. Therefore man is responsible for his human acts.

N.B. All men agree that we are chargeable for the acts under our control. Our human acts attach themselves to us and are ours in a peculiarly personal way. They are the stuff out of which our human destiny ultimately is composed. What is accredited to us or blamed on us depends upon the objects of our will acts.

II. THE MODIFICATION OF THE HUMAN ACT

72. The voluntariness of our acts depends on intellectual knowledge and free consent. Responsibility is proportionate to voluntariness. Therefore, whatever hinders or enhances the will's freedom or the mind's knowledge will likewise affect one's responsibility for acts performed under such modifying influences. There are four such modifying factors: ignorance, passion, habit, and violence.

A. Ignorance

73. *Ignorance* is absence of knowledge in one capable of knowledge. What is said here regarding ignorance applies to error, mistake, inadvertence, or whatever may be the name used to designate a modifying factor of the human act proceeding from the intellect.

Ignorance is an obstacle to voluntariness because one does not will what one does not know. Hence, if I walk off with my neighbor's handbag thinking it to be my own, I do not will to take *his* bag. Does ignorance then release one from all responsibility? This depends on whether one's ignorance is voluntary or involuntary.

74. Considered as a privation in the human agent, ignorance is invincible or vincible.

1. *Invincible ignorance* is wholly involuntary, unavoidable either absolutely or relatively. It is not the result of conscious and willful neglect. This person is ignorant because, despite the care and diligence proportionate to the circumstances, the knowledge is beyond his grasp. What constitutes proportionate care and diligence depends on the importance of the matter, the age, mental development, and even the health of the individual. *There is no responsibility in the case of invincible ignorance.*

2. *Vincible ignorance* is voluntarily induced either by an actual act of the will whereby we choose to be ignorant (affected ignorance), or by conscious failure to obtain required knowledge within our grasp. In the case of vincible ignorance there exists a previous obligation to know which has been slighted in whole or in part. If no effort has been made to obtain the knowledge, the ignorance is crass; if a feeble but inadequate attempt has been made, the ignorance is simply vincible. The essential difference between invincible and vincible ignorance consists in this: in the former there is no previous obligation to know; in the latter such an obligation must exist.

Acts performed through vincible ignorance are chargeable to us, not as directly willed but as *voluntary in cause*. They are the necessary and foreseeable results of voluntary neglect. The degree of culpable responsibility depends on the culpability of our causative negligence.

75. As regards the object of our ignorance we distinguish between ignorance of law and ignorance of fact.

1. *Ignorance of law* is lack of knowledge concerning the existence of the law or of the law's comprehension of the case. In civil law

ignorance of the law generally does not excuse one from the consequences of an act contrary to the law. To admit such an excuse as valid, the courts would have to determine whether the person actually were ignorant of the law and if such ignorance were culpable. Since the gathering of conclusive evidence regarding these points would present virtually insurmountable difficulties, the courts must concern themselves with external conformity or nonconformity to the law presuming it is the duty of all to know the law.

In the case of any law binding in conscience, a person's ignorance must be judged according to the principle set down above.

Where a law prescribes the conditions for the validity of an action, even invincible ignorance of the law will not render the action valid if the requisite conditions have not been fulfilled. Even though a layman were totally unaware that civil law requires the signature of two witnesses for the validity of a will not written in the testator's own hand, nevertheless his ignorance would not validate a typewritten but unattested document.

2. *Ignorance of fact,* taken as the correlative of the above, is lack of knowledge concerning some circumstance pertinent to the application of the law. Thus, John, knowing he cannot marry a married woman, attempts marriage with Eleanor, thinking her single. As far as conscience is concerned, such ignorance must be adjudged as is ignorance of the law. In American law ignorance of facts is a recognized defense where knowledge of certain facts is essential to a civil offense, but no defense where a statute makes an act indictable, irrespective of guilty knowledge.

B. Passion

76. Because he has an animal nature, man has natural, instinctive tendencies toward or away from what he apprehends as sensible good or sensible evil. These motions can and do interfere with the free play of the will. An intense motion of this kind is called a *passion,* that is, a vehement movement of the sensitive appetite toward sensible good or away from sensible evil accompanied by a more or less noticeable change in the bodily organism. Thus, under stress or fear the face pales and the heart beats rapidly; in anger the arteries dilate, adrenalin is secreted, and blood rushes to the face and brain. It is because the body undergoes these changes that these motions are called passions.

Passions differ from sentiments, which are the elicited acts of the will. One may have a passion of love and a sentiment of love, a passion of hatred and a sentiment of hatred, and so forth. Passion blends with sentiment, and sentiment stirs up passion because the sensitive appetite and will are rooted in the same vital principle, the human soul.

77. *Varieties of passion.* Psychologically passions stem from a fundamental motion which we call sensible love — the yearning for union with that which pleases the sensitive appetite. Because of a difference in the object sought for or avoided, two types of passions are distinguished, concupiscible and irascible. (*a*) In the case of *concupiscible* passions, no special difficulty attends the attainment of good or the avoidance of evil. They include the passions of desire, joy, aversion, sadness, and hatred. (*b*) In the case of *irascible* passions, there exists such a special difficulty. They include passions of hope, fear, daring, despair, and anger. For the purposes of ethics, a simple division is made into: (1) motions toward sensible good, called *concupiscence,* (2) motions away from sensible evil, called *fear.*

78. *Concupiscence.* By concupiscence we do not mean a tendency to sexual pleasure nor a general inclination to moral evil but simply any motion of the sensitive appetite toward a good strong enough to cause a reaction in the rational appetite or in the external faculties. We distinguish between antecedent concupiscence and consequent concupiscence.

1. *Antecedent concupiscence* is a sensible motion aroused by an object pleasing or displeasing to the appetite without any premeditation or incitement by the will. Thus, struck by a snowball, I flare into resentment and profane language. The word antecedent does not refer to the action performed under the influence of the sensible motion — in this case the profane language — but to an act of the will accepting or approving the sensible motion.

2. *Consequent concupiscence* is a sensible motion deliberately aroused by the will or concomitantly stirred by a strong tendency of the will. Thus, I may deliberately work myself into a rage against one whom I greatly dislike, or a deep sentiment of love for one of the opposite sex may arouse carnal desire.

79. Concupiscence affects responsibility for our acts in the following ways:

1. *Antecedent concupiscence diminishes the freedom of the will.*

First, it increases the inclination of the will toward one particular object. For perfect freedom, the will should not be inclined by any influence outside of the illuminating intellect more one way than another. Second, passion renders calm deliberation more difficult. Under its influence the mind is partially befogged.

2. *Antecedent concupiscence may destroy the freedom of the will.* Experience clearly shows that extremely violent passion, an over-whelming feeling of pleasure at the presence of some object, may make a man incapable of reasoning. Hence, acts performed under the influence of such passion would in themselves be blameless. But a man may well be antecedently blameworthy in that he is not the master of his passions. Passion in an adult of sound mind is hardly strong enough, of itself and wholly without the will, to effect any considerable outward action. If passion does overwhelm an adult, the reason is that the will for a long time has been yielding its supremacy to passion and permitting it to range unchecked.

3. *Consequent or stimulated concupiscence,* far from lessening re-sponsibility, increases it, or better, is a sign of the will's intense inclination toward its object. The will and the sensitive appetite are rooted in the same soul. Hence, when the will's desire for some object is so intense that it arouses a similar vehement motion in the sensitive appetite for the same object, we conclude that the will act is exceedingly strong. Thus, should a man deliberately beat his enemy with a strap and in so doing get into a towering rage, such rage is a manifest indication of the ferocity of his hatred.

4. *Evil actions foreseen as the result of stimulated concupiscence are indirectly voluntary and imputable.* The reason is that they are foreseen, at least confusedly, as effects flowing from a directly voluntary act.

The chief practical result of the study of ethics should be the formation of the reasonable man. Nothing is more reasonable than that passion always be under our control. Neither the delight of forbidden pleasure nor the difficulty of what is reasonably enjoined should deter us from fulfilling our duty. Hence the chief moral end of education is the acquisition of self-control. Our passions are like children or horses — they will run away with us if they are not constantly kept in check. Over and above the habit of temperance, of which we shall speak in due time, we must practice self-denial. We practice self-denial when, upon due occasion, we refuse the sensitive appetite even what it might lawfully have, so that in the time of temptation it will have learned to yield to the dictates of reason.

80. *Fear.* Fear, specifically as an irascible emotion, is the withdrawal of the sensible appetite from some sensible evil difficult to avoid. As an impediment to the voluntary act, we take it in the generic sense of being any motion of the appetite away from evil. It includes the specific passions of aversion, hatred, sadness, fear, and despair.

People are constantly subject to a variety of fears. Of these some are totally negligible. These we merely disregard. Others move us to action. These we call *grave fears,* that is, they are induced by the apprehension of serious danger and consequently are efficacious of some action. The danger may be *absolute,* that is, such as would affect the ordinary, constant man, for example, imminent death or loss of limb. The danger may be relative, that is, such as is to be avoided by a particular person at a particular time. Thus, a small boy who is afraid of the dark might disobey his parents when told to go to bed.

81. *How does such fear affect the voluntariness, or freedom, of our actions?*

1. Extreme fear can develop into hysteria, at which stage, one is no longer able to reason. Thus a woman, frightened by a man coming in the window of her apartment, kills him although he mistakenly thinks that he is entering his own place.

2. Actions performed under the influence of ordinary grave fear are *voluntary acts and hence are imputable.* The knowledge and freedom sufficient for a human act is present. Thus, to avoid chastisement for losing a two-pound box of sugar, a boy steals another box from the grocer. Stealing the second box is apprehended as the lesser of two evils and is chosen as an efficacious means of avoiding a worse evil. Therefore, it is a truly volitional act and is imputable.

3. There is a lessening of responsibility when fear perturbs and excites the mind rendering a calm, reasoned decision difficult. In a case like this there usually is a nonvoluntary element, reluctance, an inefficacious wish that we did not have to do this thing. Thus, to save his property a man perjures himself, reluctantly, wishing some other means were available.

4. Although fear is never an excuse to do that which is everywhere and always wrong, fear of extreme evil, nevertheless, usually exempts us from immediate compliance with human law for the human

legislator is rightly considered as not wishing to impose too grievous a burden. Sometimes, however, the human legislator can demand the heroic: thus even under threat of death, a priest is forbidden to reveal the secrets of the confessional, a captured soldier to betray information vital to the security of his nation. In such instances, however, the human legislator is merely reiterating the prohibition of the Natural Law.

5. Positive law invalidates or declares rescindable certain acts performed under pressure of grave fear unjustly imposed by some external, rational agent. The reason is not that such acts are not voluntary but that otherwise the law would be approving an injustice and the common good would suffer. Vows, wills, renunciations, and marriages are invalid under these conditions; oaths and many contracts are rescindable.

C. Habit

82. Habit requires a longer explanation than would be feasible here. It is treated in Chapter IX (see § 310). As an obstacle to the human act it operates as does antecedent concupiscence.

D. Violence

83. Violence is an abuse of force, applied from without and tending to compel a reluctant agent against his choice. No amount of force can directly touch the elicited act of the will. Not even God can force the will and at the same time leave it free. Violence, then, affects our imperate acts, that is, actions of (a) the external faculties, such as being compelled to sign a perjurous affidavit at the point of a gun; or of (b) the imagination and sensitive appetite, such as being tempted by the evil one to commit a sin of thought against one's will.

84. Two problems at this point arise, responsibility for acts performed under duress and resistance to violence.

Concerning *responsibility* there are three important considerations. First, under any kind of stress one can and always must withold *internal* consent to what is wrong. Should there be consent, it would be voluntary though with proportionately diminished responsibility. Second, where violence is *irresistible,* neither the moral nor the positive law holds us responsible for the external act. Third, where the external pressure is not *irresistible,* responsibility is diminished in proportion to the force brought to bear and the acquiescence of the will.

Is any *further external resistance* demanded beyond the resistance of the will? (*a*) If the oppressor alone does the wrong and the oppressed is but a spectator, as in a robbery, no resistance is demanded. (*b*) If some passive kind of participation in a wrong act is required of us, we must offer enough resistance to prevent internal consent or obvious scandal. (*c*) If a threat of force is employed to induce one *actively* to perform an act always and everywhere wrong, one may not comply irrespective of the consequence. Thus, prisoners of the G.P.U. given a choice between masturbating and a bloody beating had to choose the beating.

READINGS

St. Thomas, *Summa Theologica,* I–II, 6, 7, 17.

Aristotle, *Ethics,* III, 1–2.

Brosnahan, Timothy, S.J., *Digest of Lectures,* pp. 18–22. Baltimore, Murphy, 1913.

Catholic Encyclopedia, "Voluntary Acts," XV, 506; "Human Acts," I, 115; "Intention," VIII, 69; "Ignorance," VII, 648; "Passions," XI, 534; "Fear," VI, 21; "Concupiscence," IV, 208.

Cronin, Michael, *The Science of Ethics,* Vol. I, pp. 30–46. Dublin, Gill and Sons, 1909.

Holaind, Rene, S.J., *Natural Law and Legal Practice,* pp. 71–94. New York, Benziger, 1899.

Rickaby, Joseph J., S.J., *Aquinus Ethicus,* Vol. I, pp. 232–244.

——— *Moral Philosophy,* pp. 27–31.

Sullivan, Joseph, S.J., *General Ethics,* pp. 10–33. Worcester, Holy Cross College, 1931.

CHAPTER IV

MORALITY

WHAT IS MORALITY?

85. We have described the act which leads to happiness — the human act which forms the subject matter of ethics. We turn now from the physical aspect of the human act to its moral aspect which is the peculiar point of view of ethics. As we have already seen (§ 15), the *physical aspect* is limited to those realities or properties of the human act necessary to make it man's characteristic act. We prescinded from any further relation to something of absolute value. The *moral aspect,* then, is the over-all relation of the human act to something of absolute value. By absolute we do not mean absolute in itself, as God is absolute, but absolute and final *to man;* we refer to that supreme, enduring value whose presence in man spells total success for him, whose absence total failure. As the free deliberate act is *the act* of man, so its morality is *the paramount aspect* of that act.

86. Up to the present, men have agreed that morality has to do with some such absolute value, but the impact of evolutionary doctrine on modern thought has resulted in the denial of all absolute values, especially in the field of morals. However, it is not within our province to give a general refutation of this philosophy of perpetual change for every branch of scholastic philosophy shows the existence of unchanging realities and of universal truths which are valid always and everywhere. Our demonstration of man's last end is an instance in point. In the course of this chapter we shall show the absurdity of ever-changing morality.

87. Assuming, then, that there is an absolute value in human life and that morality is the relation of conduct to that absolute value, we ask what that value is. It must be that which is supreme as far as man is concerned: it must be that for which the whole man exists.

Man is not a necessary, all-sufficient being but a created being, contingent and dependent. Hence he exists for the accomplishment of some *end*. Therefore, man's *absolute value* is the *end* for which he exists, and his supreme business is directing himself toward that end. The word *moral*, then, pertains to whatever has a direct bearing on man's perfect happiness, and the moral aspect of his human acts will be the direct relationship of these acts to his final end.

88. Man, however, does not necessarily attain his final end, perfect happiness. All things less than man by physical compulsion move toward their appointed ends. Not so man because he is free. He can choose to work out his destiny or he can refuse. His good acts conduce to his final end; his bad acts lead away from it. But why is a good act right and a bad act wrong? Here arises *the third great problem of ethics*, namely, *What is the ultimate difference between moral good and moral evil?* Is its source nature or convention? To give a satisfactory explanation we shall show (*a*) what good and evil are; (*b*) why some human acts are good and some evil; (*c*) what the specific difference is between the goodness and badness of human acts; (*d*) to what different things the designation moral good and evil applies.

I. GOOD AND EVIL

A. The Nature of Good

89. It is said that the concept *good* is so simple that it defies exact definition. However, typical of modern thought, a novelist writes: "Good is what helps us or at least does not hinder. Evil is whatever harms us or interferes with us according to our own selfish standards."[1] A modern ethician says: "To men everywhere it feels bad to be in severe physical pain, to be shut away from air or food. It feels good to taste an appetizing dish, to hear harmonious music. To say that these experiences are good or bad is equivalent to saying that they *feel* good or bad. This is the bottom fact of ethics. Different experiences *have different intrinsic worth* as they pass. They need nothing ulterior to justify them. The bad moments feel bad, and no sophistication can deny it. In the last analysis, all differences in

---

[1] Marjorie K. Rawlings, *Cross Creek*, p. 151. New York, Scribner's, 1942.

value, including all moral distinctions, rest upon this disparity in the immediate worth of conscious states."[2]

90. In the first sentence of his *Ethics,* Aristotle says that the good is that at which all things aim.[3] He did not mean that there is some one thing to which all things tend but whenever a being desires, it desires only good. Hence, in an *a posteriori* sense good is whatever satisfies appetence. Thus, light is the good of a plant, water of a fish, happiness of a man.

The good, then, implies a relation between (*a*) a being or faculty seeking something, and (*b*) an object called good because it is capable of satisfying that appetite. But why is this object capable of satisfying appetence? Solely because it is something which suits, fits in with, or bestows a suitable perfection on the being or faculty seeking. This quality of goodness, or capacity to satisfy an appetite, is the object itself. Therefore, we formulate this *a priori* definition of the good: *The good is that which is suitable or fitting.*

But what is suitable and desirable to a given thing? First its own entity: every being is good to itself. But here we do not have reference to its minimum essentials but to the fullness of its being, that is, the full complement of the perfections proper to it. All things desire their perfection, which consists of all those elements that make it what it is fully capable of being and which render it capable of faultless action proportionate to its place in the hierarchy of things.

B. Kinds of Good

91. Every real being is good to itself. This goodness is *absolute goodness,* its partial or total perfection, considered without reference to anything distinct from it. Every real being is also good to some other beings. This goodness is its *relative goodness.* There are three types of relative goodness, the perfective good, the delectable good, the useful good.

92. 1. *Perfective good* affords a suitable perfection. This is good in the true and more proper sense. Appetite is aroused because of the want of a suitable perfection or the presence of an imperfection. The perfective good supplies this want, for it is that which is desirable and fitting to supply an absent perfection or remove an imperfection. Thus, food is a perfective good considered not as something enjoyable

---

[2] Durant Drake, *Problems in Conduct,* pp. 75–76. Boston, Houghton Mifflin, 1935.
[3] *Ethics,* I, 1, 1094a.

but as something which is taken into an organism for growth, work, and the maintenance of the vital processes. Once perfective good is had it becomes a perfection of the appetent being: more of reality has been added to it.

93. 2. *Delectable good* arouses a suitable delectation. Because of the absence of some perfection or the presence of an imperfection appetite can experience so keen a disquiet that the removal of this uneasiness becomes an object of appetence. The quiescence of appetite — its passing from a state of dissatisfaction to one of content — is suitable and desirable. What is the explanation? Goodness is fullness of being. But appetite of itself cannot satisfy itself. Its satisfaction depends on the possession of some object external to it, some perfective good. When this good is attained, the appetent being capable of cognition experiences a delight, a subjective satisfaction in the possession of the desired object. Thus a well-cooked dinner satisfies hunger and gives enjoyment. In so far as this perfective good yields satisfaction and pleasure it is *delectable good*. By metonomy the pleasure and satisfaction is also called delectable good. It is in this sense that we generally understand the term, namely, the satisfaction of the conscious appetite by the acquisition of some perfective good.

Every perfective good produces suitable satisfaction unless the appetent being is distracted by a more powerful delight or dissatisfaction. Delight naturally attaches to perfective good. This is nature's inducement to conscious beings to seek the fullness of their being in their proper perfective goods.

94. 3. *Useful good* is a means to what is desirable for its own sake. It is fitting only in that it is a *means* to delectable and perfective good. It is good only by extrinsic denomination. Thus to a man who has lost the sight of an eye, a painful surgical operation is a good solely because it is the only way of healing his eye.

95. *Summary*

Perfective good is good in itself and of itself. It is good in itself because it is something desired; it is good of itself because it is suitable. The practical problem of morality will be to discern what man's true perfective goods are; the order and measure in which they are to be sought; and, above all, actually to strive for them.

Delectable good — pleasure — is good in itself but not of itself. It is good in itself because it is desired for its own sake; it is not good of itself because appetite cannot satisfy itself. This must come from perfective good.

The great moral problem is learning not to make delectable good the chief object of appetite; not to prize it above perfective good. To do so is unreason; it is to live by emotion.

Useful good is neither good in itself nor of itself. It is desired solely as a means to true good. The moral difficulty here is confounding the useful with the perfective; the degradation of perfective good to the role of the merely useful.

Lamentable confusion of thought inevitably follows upon failure to distinguish the perfective, the delectable, and the useful. The denial of this distinction by nineteenth-century utilitarianism is summarily put by Herbert Spencer, "the good is universally the pleasurable."[4] The consequences of this denial in daily living are always tragic and enormous.

96. A perfective good considered as that which in itself is suitable to any unitary nature or a faculty of that nature is called a *natural good*. The natural goods of man, sought in the way that is natural to man, that is, as objects of deliberate choice are called *moral goods*.

97. In complex beings with many conscious appetites and hence goods corresponding as objects of appetite we distinguish real good and apparent good. (*a*) *Real good* perfects the whole being as such: it is suitable to a unitary nature or to a faculty of that nature duly subordinated to that nature. Thus a moderate meal is suitable to man's taste, to his appetite, to the whole man. (*b*) *Apparent good* is desired but does not perfect the whole being. It is suitable to some faculty but not as that faculty is duly subordinated to the unitary nature. A piece of poisoned liver may appeal to a dog's taste but it may kill him.

98. Among all perfective and real goods is the *Supreme Good,* the good which is suitable in the highest degree, the good which completely satisfies all appetence. Since an end is a good sought for itself, man's final end must be his supreme good. Aristotle terms this *Eudaemonia* (*a*) which consists in complete well-being of life and its activities; (*b*) which is desirable in itself always and never on account of anything else; (*c*) which suffices man in all his essential relations and is beyond comparison with other goods; (*d*) which is found in

---

[4] *The Data of Ethics,* p. 30. New York, D. Appleton, 1898.

his specific and distinctive function. It is the highest energizing of man's rational life in conformity with the laws of its excellence, and the essential delight following therefrom. Such is beatitude considered from the standpoint of the good.

99. *What precisely is man's supreme good?* (*a*) The supreme perfective good of man is God, knowable, lovable, glorifiable. God known, loved, and glorified is man's supreme delectable good. (*b*) The supreme perfection of man is his perfect act of intellect and will possessing God in perfection. (*c*) Man's supreme pleasure is the delight consequent upon the act of possessing God.

C. Evil

100. Evil is understandable only in terms of good, for evil is the lack of goodness. We saw that there is absolute goodness, the perfection which a thing has in itself; so, also, there is absolute badness, a want of reality that belongs to the thing. Thus we speak of a bad tooth, a bad soldier. Just as a thing conferring some reality on another is good for it, so also a thing depriving another of reality is bad for it. Thus the boll weevil is bad for cotton; cats are bad for birds.

101. Badness, whether absolute or relative, is not a mere lack. If badness were just a lack of reality, everything but God would be bad because God alone lacks no reality. Badness, then, is the want of something that *ought to be present*. A dog is not a bad dog because he has no horns, but he would be a bad dog if he had no legs. Hence evil is a privation, the absence of good which ought to be present.

102. What is this privation of good? Is it an entity or a nonentity? Just as some people erroneously regard moral good as the remote or mystic, so they look on evil as a positive thing, something repulsive like a wart or hideous birthmark. In as much as evil is said to inhere in, to belong to, some actual being it is said to be positive. But evil as evil — the privation of good — cannot be a positive thing for two reasons: first, every positive entity is good. It has real being. Good and being are identical. Second, if evil were a positive thing, God, being the ultimate cause of all positive beings, would also be the cause of all evil, moral evil included, but this would involve in God the contradiction of willing and forbidding the same thing under the same aspect.

103. Evil, the privation of good which ought to be present, is not natural to any being. Hence it is brought about by some cause which destroys or hinders the perfection in question. But all efficient causes are real beings and, as such, good. Therefore evil is caused by good — but not directly. Only good can be the object of appetite. What is intended is a good, but the production of a particular good may bring along with it a privation which is evil. Thus the cat's dinner is the mouse's death. Evil, then, is sought only under the guise of good. Men seek evil not as evil but as apparent good.

104. *Physical* evil is the privation (or what causes the privation) of a natural good in a unitary being. *Moral* evil is the privation (or what causes the privation) of goodness in human acts. But what moral suitability should be present in the human act? From what we have proved about man's last end and the relation of morality to it, we may assert here that in order to be suitable, the human act must have rectitude, it must be directed to that end. Thus moral evil is the privation of the rectitude which the moral act should have.

But is this the ultimate explanation of human evil and human goodness? May we not ask why some acts have rectitude, and why others lack it? The answer to these questions is to be found in the analysis of human good and human evil. The solution is given in Part II.

II. THE STANDARD OF MORAL GOODNESS

105. What makes the *right* act good and the *wrong* act bad? What is the cause of goodness in some acts, badness in others? After the problem of man's end, this is the most fundamental question in ethics. The answer is: the relationship of the act to some yardstick of morality technically called a *norm of morality*.

106. A norm is a rule of measurement, an authoritative standard. In the National Bureau of Standards is a bar of platinum-iridium which is the standard for all linear measures. Similarly a norm of morality is a standard to which a human act is compared and enables us to determine if it is good or bad.

107. A norm of morality may be (*a*) *subjective*, that is, existing in the human agent and giving him moral guidance in the placing of his human acts; (*b*) *objective*, that is, existing outside the human agent in the order of objective reality. Here we encounter one of the most far-reaching controversial issues in ethics, namely, *is morality purely subjective?* Does it depend entirely on the viewpoint of man, individual or collective, so that rules of morality are nothing "more than a series of convenient arrangements"[5] or the expression of social customs founded on emotion, which change with time and place? Or is morality objective, rooted in reason, and founded on principles as valid as those which underlie physics or astronomy?

108. Thus, the problem which has vexed moral philosophers through all the conflict of ethical discussion is this: What is the norm whereby we measure the morality of our actions? What is that thing by comparison to which the human act is not only called, but truly made, good or bad?

Schools of moral thought have often derived their names from the answers they give to this basic problem. Let us classify and evaluate the most noteworthy among them.

A. Utilitarianism

109. Utilitarianism includes all those systems which hold that the morality of an act consists in its utility to serve as a means to some end. John Stuart Mill explains: "the creed which accepts as the foundation of morals, utility or the greatest happiness principle, holds that actions are right in proportion as they tend to promote happiness, are wrong as they tend to promote the reverse of happiness. By happiness is intended pleasure and the absence of pain; by unhappiness, pain and the privation of pleasure."[6]

Note that these systems do two things. First, they deny the great distinction among perfective, delectable, and useful goods. For them the Useful is the Good and the Good is what is useful. Perfective good is only a form of the useful. Jeremy Bentham says: "Pleasure is in itself a good; nay, even setting aside immunity from pain, the only good: pain is in itself an evil; and, indeed, without exception, the only evil; or else the words good and evil have no meaning."[7] Second, the vast majority of these hold that happiness, the final end of man, is some kind of temporal felicity. Hence those actions are good which conduce to the attainment of temporal happiness; those are bad which hinder it. Two types of utilitarianism can be distinguished, individual and social.

---

[5] Vincent Sheean, *Personal History*, p. 310. Garden City, Doubleday, Doran, 1935.
[6] John S. Mill, *Utilitarianism*, pp. 9–10.
[7] Jeremy Bentham, *Principles of Morals and Legislation*, Chap. X, § 2, p. 102. Oxford, Clarendon, 1907.

110. 1. *Individual utilitarianism or egotistic hedonism.* This doctrine is concerned with the greatest possible pleasure of the individual. Hence that which promotes personal happiness is good: that which produces pain or discomfort is bad. The good which constitutes this personal happiness ranges from purely sensual pleasure to the delight consequent upon the possession of God.

Democritus (460–370 B.C.) was the first of the ancient Greeks to teach that delight (εὐθαμία) is the highest good. This he identified with equable and imperturbed temper of mind (συμμετρία) to be obtained by moderation and limitation of desire.

Aristippus (435–354 B.C.) held that the supreme good is the present pleasure of the body. Hence the only cognizable good is that smooth motion of sense which everybody knows as pleasure. But good is transient. Therefore, seek the pleasure of the moment without troubling yourself about a dubious future.

Epicurus (341–270 B.C.) taught that pleasure is the sole, ultimate good and pain the only evil; that no pleasure is to be forgone except for its painful consequences and no pain to be suffered except as a means to greater pleasure. However, the pain and pleasure of the mind are far more important than that of the body. The wise man can finally strike a true balance of pleasure over pain by keeping his mind freed from disturbing fears for the future. This Horace re-echoes in his *nil admirari*. How this tranquil state is to be had by exorcising away one's dread of the vengeance of the gods and the fear of death is ingeniously set forth by Epicurus.

Hobbes was the first outstanding writer of Christian times to return to the pagan concept of the good. "Everyman, for his part, calleth that which pleaseth and is delightful to himself, good; and that evil which displeaseth him. . . . And as we call good and evil the things that please and displease; so we also call goodness and badness the qualities or powers whereby they do it."[8]

The encyclopedist Diderot[9] and Helvetius,[10] the materialists, Holbach and Feuerbach,[11] and many others have gone far beyond Hobbes and

---

[8] *Human Nature,* Chap. VII, 3. Molesworth's English edition, Vol. IV, p 32.

[9] *Oeuvres de Denis Diderot,* "Pensees Philosophiques," Tome 1, pp. 197–278; "De L'Interpretation de la Nature," Tome II, pp. 139–224. Paris, Briere, 1821.

[10] *De L'esprit,* pp. 99–113. Paris, Lavigne, 1845.

[11] Ludwig Feuerbach, *The Essence of Christianity,* trans. Marian Evans. Boston, Houghton Mifflin, 1881, 2 ed.

Engels, the shadow of Karl Marx, gives his reaction to Feuerbach's book, "Then came revived the doctrines of Democritus and Aristippus in a stark, crude form. Man is nothing but matter; his so-called mental activities do not differ essentially from sense impressions. He seeks bodily pleasure and flees from bodily pain. What produces the former is good; what entails the latter is bad. This is outright sensualism. Holbach's[12] advice on how to choose among pleasures and how to give passion its head is worthy of Lucretius Carus, the disciple of Epicurus.

111. 2. *Social utilitarianism or altruism*. According to this theory, the happiness of mankind is the norm of morality so that actions are good or bad in so far as they advance or impede the common felicity. The chief originator of this solution seems to be Pufendorf. He taught that God gave man the kind of nature He pleased.[13] God laid on man, as the supreme law of his nature, sociability:[14] what conforms to this prescription is good, what contravenes it is bad.

According to Bentham,[15] an act is good in so far as it promotes the greatest amount of pleasure for the greatest number of people (and animals too!). "This (the Greatest Happiness Principle)," Mill reiterates, "being, according to the utilitarian opinion, the end of human action, is necessarily also the standard of morality; which may be accordingly defined, the rules and precepts of human conduct, by the observance of which an existence such as has been described might be, to the greatest extent possible, secured to all mankind; and not to them only, but, so far as the nature of things admits, to the whole sentient creation."[16]

Comte, who coined the word "altruism" (from the Provençal *altrui*, "other"), demands such devotion to neighbor and to humanity as a whole that we cease to love ourselves.[17] One's egoistic acts, if not bad, are only amoral. "Live for others:" he said, "such is the supreme formula of positive ethics."[18] Since Wundt maintains that the end

---

Feuerbach's *Essence of Christianity*. With one blow it . . . placed materialism on the throne again. . . ." F. Engels, *Ludwig Feuerbach*, p. 28. London, Lawrence, 1934.

[12] *La Morale Universelle,* Tome 1, pp. 75–79. Paris, 1820.

[13] Samuelis Pufendorfii, *De Jure Naturae et Gentium*, Lib. I, Cap. II, § 6, p. 18. Amstelodami, Hoogenhuysen, 1688.

[14] *Ibid.*, Lib. II, Cap. III, § 15, pp. 142–144.

[15] *Morals and Legislation*, pp. 2 and 310.

[16] John S. Mill, *Utilitarianism*, p. 17.

[17] John S. Mill, *The Positive Philosophy of Auguste Comte*, pp. 124–125. New York, Holt, 1875.

[18] L. Levy-Bruhl, *The Philosophy of Auguste Comte*, trans. Frederic Harrison, p. 319. New York, Putnam, 1903.

of human acts is the progress of culture,[19] it follows that for him only that act is good which advances culture. Marxist Communism, while envisioning ultimately an earthly paradise, sets up a most variable and pliable norm. At the present time it is this: whatever helps the proletariat in its class struggle is good; whatever retards the solidarity of the working classes is bad.

112. 3. *Egotistic altruism.* Herbert Spencer combined social and individual utilitarianism, a reconciliation of egoism with altruism, upon a background of evolution. "If the maxim — 'Live for self' — is wrong, so also is the maxim — 'Live for others.' Hence, a compromise is the only possibility."[20] Whereas some evolutionary writers reject the utilitarian theory of balance of pleasure over pain for some more objective end such as the preservation of the human race or just "quantity of life," Spencer is both an evolutionist and a utilitarianist. To him the absolute end is not increase or quantity of life but the purest pleasure of life, life without any admixture of pain. He says: " . . . if we can call good the conduct conducive to life, we can do so only with the implication that it is conducive to a surplus of pleasure over pain . . . no school can avoid taking for the ultimate moral aim a desirable state of feeling called by whatever name, gratification, pleasure, happiness."[21]

Spencer hopes society will some day reach an ideal stage wherein the perfection of life will consist in the greatest possible happiness of each and all. Governing this ideal condition is Absolute Ethics, the primary rule of which will be this: those actions are simply or perfectly good "which produce pure pleasure — pleasure unalloyed with pain anywhere."[22]

Now we are merely progressing toward this ideal state so that the present meaning of life, as we may learn from the conduct of the lower animals, is a continuous adjustment of internal relations to external conditions, that is, the adaptation of the organism to its environment. Conduct which promotes this adjustment brings relative pleasure and is relatively good; conduct which hinders this adjustment brings pain and is bad. The code which regulates such conduct is Relative Ethics.

---

[19] Wilhelm Wundt, *Ethics — The Principles of Morality and Departments of Moral Life,* trans. Flag-Washburn, Chap. 2, Sect. 4, p. 90. London, Swan Sonnenschein, 1901.
[20] *Data of Ethics,* p. 219.
[21] *Ibid.,* pp. 45–46.
[22] *Ibid.,* p. 261.

Since we are only partially evolved and adjusted to our social surroundings, perfect happiness is out of the question. Hence our conduct is partially good and partially bad. There are too many conflicts between a man's self-regarding and his other-regarding impulses. Practically, then, the best conduct we can achieve is "the least wrong" or "the relatively right."[23]

But as evolution proceeds and as man adjusts himself more perfectly, he will rise from the low level of perverted egoism to the perfect level of an ego-altruism. As the individual tempers his egotistic tendencies he will find greater and greater pleasure in serving society until all men will place the general interest above private interest. At this point the millennium will have been reached and Absolute Ethics will displace Relative Ethics. Adaptation will be complete; pain will be nonexistent and every act will yield the purest pleasure. In that blessed state a man following his egoistic impulses will also promote the common good for there will be perfect harmony between his self-regarding and his other-regarding impulses. The great instrument which will reconcile egoism with altruism is Sympathy, which is sharing the joys and sorrows of others.[24] As evolution takes its course, sorrow must decrease until such time as we find the most unalloyed pleasure in doing good to others.

113. 4. *The pessimism of Schopenhauer.* According to Schopenhauer, because this present world is the worst conceivable, positive happiness is inconceivable. The best we can achieve is the absence of pain, which "is positive, and makes itself known by itself; satisfaction is negative — simply the removal of the former."[25]

As life is essentially suffering, and as the misery of life is only increased by intellectual progress, the supreme end of life is the negation of life, the denial of the will to live. For "Peace, Rest and Bliss dwell only where there is no where and no when."[26]

To Schopenhauer there are two levels of morality. One is ordinary virtue built upon sympathy whose purpose is to diminish misery by compassion. Since the sole springs of human conduct are egoism, malice, and compassion, and since morally good conduct is impossible

---

[23] *Ibid.*, p. 261.

[24] *Ibid.*, pp. 244–257.

[25] Arthur Schopenhauer, *The Basis of Morality*, trans. A. B. Bullock, p. 173. London, Swan Sonnenschein, 1903.

[26] *Parerga und Paralipomena*, Vol. II, Chap. 3, 30, p. 46. Berlin, 1862.

from egoism and malice, compassion alone remains.[27] Hence only those acts are good which, tending to alleviate the sufferings of others, proceed from compassion.

However, in ordinary virtuous or sympathetic conduct some trace of the fundamental error of the will to live remains. Hence one does not rise to the truest reaches of morality until he shall have achieved the completest asceticism or self-mortification for "true salvation, deliverance from life and suffering, cannot be imagined without complete denial of the will."[28] This entails the turning away from the illusory pleasures of life, the repression of the sexual instinct.[29] Though he denies that suicide is a crime and seems to praise Hume's essay on suicide, he does conclude that it is morally objectionable.[30]

114. *Criticism of utilitarianism.* Utilitarianism is correct in its contention that an act is good if it leads to happiness but its notion of happiness is false.

1. Its fundamental error is its misconception of man's end. Utilitarianists either hold the "happiness now" theory or the theory that the individual or humanity is an end in itself.

2. Its second error is confusion of useful, delectable, and perfective. Happiness is not merely the delectable: good and useful are not adequately synonymous.

3. It establishes a norm which is inconstant and variable. However, a standard whereby other things are measured should be unchanging to be reliable. A variable standard is no standard. The modern heirs of utilitarianism readily admit this acknowledging that moral values and standards are in a state of perpetual flux, but a relativistic, ever-changing morality we shall show to be absurd.

B. Intuitionism

115. Shaftesbury (1671–1713) was the first modern to transfer the origins of morality from the realm of reason to the realm of emotion. Moral acts are sentiments, affections, emotional tendencies to good or evil. "Since it is therefore by affection merely that a creature

---

[27] *Basis of Morality*, pp. 171–172, 200.
[28] *The World as Will and Idea,* Durant's edition of "The Works of Schopenhauer," p. 238. Garden City, 1928.
[29] *Ibid.,* pp. 330–363.
[30] *Essay on Suicide,* Durant's edition, pp. 432–437.

is esteemed good or ill, natural or unnatural, our business will be to examine which are the good and natural, and which the ill and unnatural affections.[31] The proper instrument of discrimination is a moral sense,[32] distinct from reason and possessed by all men, which no rationalization can argue out of existence. "Sense of right and wrong therefore being as natural to us as natural affection, and being a first principle in our constitution and make up there is no speculative opinion, persuasion or belief, which is capable immediately or directly to exclude or destroy it."[33]

Subsequent writers explain this faculty in various ways. Rousseau[34] said it was the heart, the seat of emotion, so that we distinguish right from wrong by sensible attraction to the good and sensible aversion from evil. Herbart[35] said this faculty was a kind of moral taste and that ethics is but a branch of aesthetics.

Reid calls it "an original faculty" whereby we "perceive certain things to be right, others to be wrong."[36] This perception is intuitive, analogous in its operation to that of the senses so that our common sense discriminates right from wrong in much the same way as vision distinguishes red from blue or taste tells bitter from sweet. "All moral reasoning rests upon one or more first principles of morals, whose truth is immediately perceived without reasoning."[37] For "if the rules of virtue were left to be discovered by demonstrative reasoning, or by reasoning of any kind, sad would be the condition of the greater part of men. . . . As virtue is the business of all men, the first principles of it are written in their hearts in characters so legible that no man can pretend ignorance of them."[38]

Adam Smith, though he did not assume the existence of a specific moral faculty,[39] held that moral judgments rested on a *feeling of propriety*. To him virtue or morality is propriety, and propriety is

---

[31] *An Inquiry Concerning Virtue and Merit*, Part II, Sec. 1, found in *Characteristicks of Men, Manners, Opinions, Times*, Vol. II, p. 22, 1711.

[32] *Ibid.*, Part III, Sect. 1, *ed. cit.*, Vol. II, p. 41.

[33] *Ibid.*, p. 44.

[34] *Emile*, trans. Foxley, Bk. IV, pp. 250–252. New York, Dutton, 1933.

[35] *Allgemeine Praktische Philosophie*. See Johann F. Herbart *Sämmtliche Werke*, Vol. 8, pp. 4–212. Leipsig, 1851.

[36] *Essays on the Active Powers of the Human Mind*, p. 236. Edinburgh, Bell, 1788.

[37] *Ibid.*, p. 241.

[38] *The Works of Thomas Reid*, collected by Sir Wm. Hamilton, Vol. I, p. 481. Edinburgh, Maclachlan and Stewart, 1863.

[39] *The Theory of Moral Sentiments*. Dugald Stewart's edition, pp. 479–480. London, Bell, 1880.

the nice and delicate fitting of sentiment and emotion to all situations of life, pleasant or unpleasant. The basis of propriety and hence of morality is sympathy[40] which is the inclination to share the joys and sorrows of others.[41] This is the norm of morals.

Those acts, then, are good which produce sympathy and hence approbation in others; those are bad which provoke antipathy and hence condemnation in others. However, since those who judge the value of actions may be depraved or prejudiced, and since the danger of prejudice is greatest when one passes judgment on the value of his own acts, an appeal is made to the impartial and disinterested spectator.[42] Hence Smith's axiom, Always act in such a way that the impartial onlooker can sympathize with, and approve of, you. The conscientious man "has been . . . under the constant necessity, of modeling, or of endeavoring to model, not only his outward behaviour, but, as much as he can, even his inward sentiments and feelings, according to those of this awful judge."[43] From this, it was an easy step, historically, to the view that public opinion or Mrs. Grundy is the norm of morality. And Mrs. Grundy survives in the phrase, "What will the neighbors think?"

116. *Criticism.* Since certain points of morality are evident, one can readily see why men assume them to be true. It does not follow, however, that they have no justification in reason or that such justification is impossible. To say that morality stems from emotion is to deny the order of man's nature, according to which appetite should follow reason. Since the moral act is *the* act of man conducing to his last end, there is little wonder that it is accompanied by emotion, but to say that it is all emotion is a denial of his rational nature. Hence, intuitionism is unacceptable, because:

1. The existence of a moral sense distinct from reason is gratuitously asserted.

2. Such a norm is purely subjective and is at best a declarative or manifesting norm but by no means an objective and constituent norm. If we say that this act is good because it agrees with my feeling or sense of morality, a further question must be asked, namely, Why does this act agree with my moral sense? If no further and objective reason can be given, then we are blindly following a subjective instinct which

---

[40] *Ibid.*, pp. 1–9.   [42] *Ibid.*, pp. 192, 205.
[41] *Ibid.*, p. 4.   [43] *Ibid* , p. 206.

is unworthy of man. However, if a further reason is offered, this will be the norm of morality rather than the so-called moral sense.

3. Such a norm is variable and therefore subject to the changes of time, place, and circumstances.

C. Kant's Autonomous Reason

117. According to Kant there is a moral law, as awe inspiring as the starry heavens, which is completely independent of any nonhuman lawgiver. This law consists of dictates of the Practical Reason — categorical imperatives — whereby one must do this and avoid that. Reflecting on these categorical imperatives, Kant found in them the notes of universality and necessity. Whence do these come? Not from outside me, thought Kant, because outside me all things are singular and contingent. Therefore, they must come from within me — from my rational nature as rational. Hence these categorical imperatives cannot be subordinated to anything outside man. Therefore he called them Autonomous. Man has his own law within himself and is an end unto himself.[44] In Kant's view, God exists not as a supreme lawgiver and judge of human conduct but as a kind of Divine Atlas, propping up the physical universe and making it go, so that those who obey the dictates of the Autonomous Reason may have their happiness.[45]

Do *these dictates of reason* form the norm? Not quite. The one rational thing which is simply good is good will. A good will is good not through what it effects nor through its fitness for any given goal but simply through willing it is *good in itself*.[46] How does it become such? Materially when one wills what duty prescribes. But this is not enough for one may will what the law prescribes out of mere natural inclination or expectation of personal advantage. The morally determining element of the will act, then, is its motive. The will act becomes simply good when its motive is solely that of duty done for duty's sake. Now duty is the necessity of acting from respect for the law.[47] Law and law alone can determine the human will. Neither this nor that particular prescription of law but law in general — this alone is to serve the will as a principle.[48]

How, finally, does one determine that a given act possesses this

---

[44] *Critique of Practical Reason,* trans. Abbott, p. 229.
[45] *Ibid.,* p. 222.   [47] *Ibid.,* p. 16.
[46] *Ibid.,* p. 10.   [48] *Ibid.,* p. 18.

required conformity to law? Only when one can reasonably will that his motive for acting can be converted into a universal law, for the dictates of reason must be addressed to all rational beings as such. Therefore, Kant frames this most fundamental of all imperatives: so act that thy maxim may become a universal law. This is the fountain-head whence all particular imperatives are to be derived. He illustrates his principle by promise breaking and lying which must be wrong because one could never will that his motive (to extricate himself from a difficulty by a lying promise) should ever become a law for all men.[49] Such a law would be worthless and self-destructive.

118. Criticism.

1. No one can deny that duty done for duty's sake is noble and praiseworthy, but we cannot admit that only such acts are good. A man who follows his conscience out of desire for eternal beatitude, or out of fear of losing it, acts well, though not perfectly. Not every self-regarding motive is reprehensible.

Kant appears unable to distinguish good that we must do from good that we are counseled to do. We are seldom obliged to do the heroic, but whoever, over and above the call of duty, does the heroic through self-sacrifice or the pure love of God, assuredly does what is eminently good. An act of this kind is, in fact, better than one done for duty's sake. Certainly no one would claim that a girl is obliged to surrender all her earthly goods and prospects to devote herself to the service of the aged and poor, but all mankind would call such an act good.

2. What is the exact meaning of his ultimate imperative, namely, act only on that maxim whereby thou canst at the same time will that it should become a universal law? From his examples of deceitful promises, suicide, neglect of talents, etc., we gather that each moral law must be thoroughly self-consistent, that it may not contradict and destroy itself, that it must be applicable universally to human nature as such, and hence that reasonableness is the soul of law. To this one can agree. But Kant's over-all principle has universal application only *if all good is obligatory*. When we apply it to supererogatory works it becomes absurd. A man could will to quit society for the sake of divine contemplation, but he could never will that all men do the same. An individual may virtuously choose to be a celibate,

---

[49] *Ibid.*, p. 19.

but a universal law of nature enjoining celibacy would be evil. Simeon Stylites sitting on his pillar was an object of awe and veneration, but it would be impossible for the entire human race to imitate him. These courses of action are morally good, but only on condition that they do not become universal laws.

3. Have the Kantian dictates of autonomous reason objective validity? Inasmuch as they are proffered as embodiments of reasonableness, and as reasonableness to be such must be valid for all rational beings, they would appear to be objective. Kant indeed says they are valid for all men.[50] He deduces them ultimately from the autonomy of the will, and freedom, he says, is the key which explains the will's autonomy.[51] But what objective reality has the freedom of the will for Kant? The freedom of the will, the immortality of the soul, and the existence of God are postulates of Kant's practical reason, assumed but unprovable. We carefully note that what Kant calls practical reason is the will[52] demanding obedience to moral law: what we call intellect, he calls the speculative or pure reason. But are these postulates known by the intellect? Kant says no: "The above three ideas of speculative reason are still in themselves not cognitions."[53] If there be any reality behind them we do not know and we cannot know. Kant plainly says: "The question then: How a categorical imperative is possible can be answered to this extent that we can assign the only possible hypothesis on which it is possible, namely, the idea of freedom; and we can also discern the necessity of this hypothesis, and this is sufficient for the exercise of reason, that is, for the conviction of the validity of this imperative, and hence of the moral law; but how this hypothesis itself is possible can never be discerned by any human reason."[54] Again, "Reason would overstep all bounds if it undertook to explain how pure reason can be practical, which would be exactly the same thing as to explain how freedom can be possible."[55]

If, then, the dictates of the practical reason are deduced from the freedom of the will, and if the intellect cannot validate the freedom of the will, how can these dictates be validated? If the basis on which they rest are unprovable assumptions, why are not also they?

The root of the difficulty is Kant's epistemology, according to which

---

50 *Ibid.*, p. 105.
51 *Ibid.*, p. 65.
52 *Ibid.*, p. 60.

53 *Ibid.*, p. 232.
54 *Ibid.*, pp. 81–82.
55 *Ibid.*, p. 79.

the intellect can know only the appearances of things, the phenomena, but it can never penetrate to the thing as such, the nouomena.[56] As a consequence, Kant has handed on to modern life a God-idea which is only a hollow shell, the content of which is whatever anyone chooses to make of it. He has done the same for moral principles; the words and the formulae remain but their content and meaning are the sport of individual whim.

D. Is the Norm Man's Last End?

119. Some scholastic authors contend that since a good act leads to man's last end, the last end is the norm of goodness. The argument may be put in the following syllogism:

> Human acts are means to the ultimate end.
> But means derive their goodness from the ultimate end.
> Therefore human acts derive their goodness from
> the ultimate end.

That human acts are means arbitrarily chosen to the end, we deny. That human acts are such that of their very nature they ought to be chosen as means to the end, we admit. Applying these facts to the minor premise, we admit that means arbitrarily chosen derive their goodness from the end; but we deny that those things which must be chosen as means derive their goodness from the end.

In other words, the human act is not good because it leads to beatitude, but because it is good, it leads to man's end. Before the act is actually ordered as a means to man's end, it already has a fundamental goodness, a *bonitas primitiva,* as St. Thomas says.

E. Moral Positivism

120. To solve the problem of the norm of morality we should first determine whether the difference between moral good and evil is natural or arbitrary. The difference is natural if it derives from the nature of things so that this act is good and that bad whether one likes them or not. Just as a circle or a triangle is what it is not by the will or choice of anyone so a good act is good not because someone has labeled it good but because eternal truth makes it good. The difference between moral good and evil is artificial if it is dependent on someone's free choice and designation. The system which rejects

---

[56] *Ibid.*, p. 70.

the natural distinction between moral good and evil is *moral positivism*.

121. Occam,[57] Gerson,[58] and Pufendorf[59] taught that there is no intrinsic necessity why one act should be good and another evil: all moral distinctions depend on God's good pleasure. Descartes piously avers that just as the three angles of a triangle equal two right angles for the sole reason that God wants it that way, so, too, all differences of good and evil depend on his arbitrary will.[60] Hobbes said that the notions of right and wrong cannot exist before law determines them.[61] This law can only be the law of the State. [62] For Rousseau the social contract is the origin of morality.[63] St. Lambert points to public opinion as the norm of morals.[64]

Following the lead of Comte, the modern positivist holds that ethics is not a system of *a priori* principles but the record of how men actually conduct themselves.[65] As the physical scientist examines the phenomena of nature to discover the physical laws of nature, so the moralist by a similar objective study of human behavior will arrive at moral laws.[66] These laws fluctuate from generation to generation. Hence moral distinctions derive from the practice and custom of people. "Custom," says Paulsen, "forms the original content of duty."[67] "Customs," says Dewey, "constitute moral standards."[68] There are

---

[57] *Super IV libros sententiarum*, Lib. II, q. 19, ad 3 dubium. Lugduni, 1495.

[58] *Tertia pars operum Joannis de Gerson*, LXI, E and F, Joannes Knoblauch, 1514, cf. Suarez, *De Legibus*, Lib. II, c. 15, n. 3.

[59] *De jure naturae et gentium*, Lib. I, c. 2, § 6.

[60] *Meditationes de prima philosophia*, "*Appendix continens objectiones* etc.," Resp. VI, n. 6 et 8. Amstelodami, Blaviana, 1656. In French, *Oeuvres de Descartes*, edites par Cousin, Tome deuxieme, "Objections et Responses," pp. 348, 349, 353. Paris, Levrault, 1824. In English, *The Philosophical Works of Descartes*, trans. Ross-Haldane, Vol. II, pp. 248–250. Cambridge, University Press, 1912.

[61] *Leviathan*, Chap. XIII. Molesworth's English edition of Hobbes' Works, Vol. III, p. 115.

[62] *Ibid.*, Chap. XVII, *ed. cit.*, Vol. III, pp. 157, 158.

[63] Jean Jacques Rousseau, *The Social Contract*, Bk. I, c. VIII, p. 18. London, Dent, 1935.

[64] *Principes des moeures chez toutes les nations ou Catechieme Universel* par (Jean Francois, Marquis de) St. Lambert, Vol. I, Sect. XXIV et XXV, pp. 126–136; Vol. II, dialogue premier, pp. 17–22. Paris, Agasse, 1798.

[65] L. Levy-Bruhl, *The Philosophy of Auguste Comte*, trans. F. Harrison, p. 307. New York, Putnam, 1903.

[66] L. Levy-Bruhl, *La Morale et la Science des Moeurs*, pp. 97–128. Paris, 1903.

[67] Friedrich Paulsen, *A System of Ethics*, trans. Thilly, Vol. I, p. 345. New York, Scribners, 1903.

[68] John Dewey, *Human Nature and Conduct*, p. 75. New York, Holt, 1922.

only mores — rules of conduct founded on metaphysics are an offense to modern enlightenment.

Thanks to Comte and Durkheim,[69] ethics has become but a branch of sociology. Following the master's lead, Nordau says: "If individuals had been able to live alone morality could never have come into being. The concepts of Good and Bad characterize those actions which society feels to be beneficial or harmful to itself."[70]

Whence do mores arise? From the emotions of the group, says Westermarck[71] — those of approval and disapproval. Hence the *Encyclopedia of Social Sciences* defines morals as "the sum of taboos and prescriptions in the folkways by which right conduct is defined. Right conduct is what the group approves of, wrong conduct what the group disapproves of."[72]

Evolutionary ideas have accelerated the trend of modern thought to the inevitable position where custom is of rubbery flexibility. Just as people have sloughed off the Puritan prohibition against Sunday cooking and some persons have taken to bathing in the almost nude, so the man of tomorrow will free himself from whatever he finds inconvenient in our presently accepted code. As Levy–Bruhl placidly confesses, "being positive, this morality will be relative."[73] One prize-winning author[74] calls ethics parontology (from παρῶν, *to become*) — the science of things that are about to be. The clever ethician is the one who can best predict the shape of the new mores.

THESIS VII. There is a natural difference between moral good and moral evil.

122. We contend that some acts have that in themselves whereby they must always and everywhere be suitable or unsuitable to men and hence are good or evil in themselves and cannot be anything else. Their goodness or badness comes from no factor external to them but solely from themselves. Such acts are intrinsically good or evil.

---

[69] Emile Durkheim, *"Determination du fait moral," Bulletin de la Societé francaise de philosophie,* Vol. VI, pp. 113–212, 1906.

[70] Max S. Nordau, *Morals and the Evolution of Man,* trans. by M. A. Lewenz of *Biologie der Ethik,* p. 83. New York, Funk & Wagnalls, 1922.

[71] Edward Westermarck, *The Origin and Development of the Moral Ideas,* Vol. I, pp. 5–20; Vol. II, p. 738. London, Macmillan, 1912.

[72] "Morals," Vol. X, p. 643, reissue of Nov., 1937.

[73] *The Philosophy of Auguste Comte,* p. 307.

[74] Henry Lanz, *In Quest of Morals,* Chap. IV, pp. 163 ff., Stanford, Calif., Stanford University Press, 1941.

They are so by their very nature. Therefore nature draws the line between moral good and evil.

We do not say that every good act is intrinsically good and every bad act intrinsically evil. There is an extrinsic source of morality but this is not the sole or fundamental source. An act or omission may be wrong only because the law forbids it, for example, failure to report income. Remove the law and such failure is no longer wrong. But there are some acts which, though they were never commanded by law, would always be good; and others which, though no law forbade them, would still be wrong.

123. To avoid serious confusion one must sharply distinguish between the concepts of goodness and obligation. *Goodness* is suitability, what fits in with, affords a proper perfection to a nature. *Obligation* is moral determination to one act or course of action, the constraint of the will to observe a fixed rule. Hence, the fundamental notion of morality, or human goodness, is suitability, not obligation. Because certain acts are entirely fitting, the law makes them obligatory; because certain others are entirely unfitting, the law forbids them and not vice versa. No custom, no lawgiver — not even God — can make what is entirely unfitting to men — such as blasphemy or masturbation — obligatory or even permissible.

PROOFS

124. 1. There is a universal and unshakable conviction among men that certain acts, such as parricide, mass murder of the innocent, betrayal of one's country, are always and everywhere wrong; that other acts, such as filial reverence, mercy to the afflicted, fidelity to one's word, are always and everywhere good. What is always and everywhere good or evil is so not by human convention but by the very nature of things.

2. Nature herself discriminates between moral good and moral evil because *there are natural moral goods.* This is clear for man has natural goods. He has appetites for life, food, the opposite sex, knowledge, society. These appetites are natural because: (*a*) all men have them; (*b*) man has bodily organs allied to certain appetites which have no purpose other than to serve as instruments for the satisfaction of these appetites; (*c*) without some of them life would be impossible. Therefore the goods which satisfy these natural appetites are natural goods. When these natural goods are sought consciously, under reason's direction, and in accordance with man's last end, they are *natural* *moral* goods, that is, they belong to man as man and are designated by nature.

125. Corollary I. *Some actions, independently of any will, human or divine, are of their very nature morally good or bad.*

Corollary II. *There is an unchanging difference between moral good and evil because of the nature of things.*

126. N.B. I. Not all morality is immediately intrinsic and directly founded on the nature of things. Much is extrinsic, based on precept, but this, as we shall see, has validity only inasmuch as it is rooted in principles intrinsically and eternally true (cf. § 249 ff.).

N.B. II. People's ideas on certain moral issues may change: (*a*) One generation may erroneously look upon card playing, horse racing, gambling, dancing, drinking, and the like as *totally* wrong. A subsequent generation may repudiate this view. (*b*) Social customs may change that which constitutes a proximate occasion of sin. Thus a manner of dress, provocative when first introduced, may cease to allure when people have grown used to it. (*c*) Positive ill will, followed by a wish to justify one's wrongdoing, will sanction as right what is truly wrong as is seen in the modern approval of divorce.

F. The Norm of Morality Is Human Nature

THESIS VIII. The norm of morality is man's rational nature adequately considered.

127. We have consistently rejected every purely subjective norm of morality for two reasons. First, such a norm would make each man the norm of his moral acts. Hence there would be as many norms as there are men. Consequently there would be no norm. Second, a moral standard without objective validity would be nothing other than the blind following of impulse. Advocacy of such a theory is subversion of man's rational nature. Therefore, the norm of morality must be objective.

128. An objective norm may be manifesting, constitutive, and obligating. (*a*) A *manifesting norm* designates an act as good, another bad but it does not make them so. The universal testimony of mankind is such a norm. It tells man that ordinary drunkenness is wrong but it does not tell why. This is the function of the constitutive norm. (*b*) A *constitutive norm* is that criterion by relation to which an act is *made* good or bad. Our sole inquiry is: what is the constitutive norm of morals? (*c*) An *obligating norm* not only distinguishes the good from the bad but also enjoins the doing of good and the avoidance of evil. Suitability must not be confused with obligation.

129. That the nature of man is man's norm of morality can be seen from the following: an act is good because it confers a perfective good on the human agent; an act is bad because it deprives him of a good that he should possess. The first confers a perfection because it is suitable; the second deprives him of a perfection because it is unsuitable. Whether an act is suitable or unsuitable can be determined by comparison with man's nature. The nature of man, therefore, is the constitutive norm of the goodness and badness of his actions.

We follow the same line of reasoning in appraising things other than human acts. Should an egg have the fragrance of a lily? That depends on the nature of an egg. If I ask the owner of a pet shop, "Is spinach and celery good for my pet?" he will reply, "What kind of a pet have you?" If I ask, "Is peanut butter good for a lizard?" to give a sensible answer, he will compare peanut butter to the nature of a lizard. In determining human goodness we do just that.

130. *What is human nature?* A nature is an ultimate principle of activity, the source of a being's operations. Contingent natures are destined for ends to be attained by proper activity. When we say man's rational nature is the norm of his acts, we do not mean to say that just as we have a platinum-iridium bar measuring a standard foot to which all other foot measures may be compared, so also we have a concrete ideal human nature, as Plato seems to have held.[75] By rational nature we understand the *reality* underlying that collection of notes which is found in every human being and which mark him off as a man. Although this reality does not exist in the abstracted way in which philosophers conceive it, yet it is most real and actual. It is common to all men, though actually it is united to the individual characteristics of each person.

131. *What is human nature looked at adequately?* We might be led astray if we said the norm of morality is man's rationality exclusively considered. Man is a very complex being in whom are many complicated elements fused to form a unitary whole. He is virtually vegetative and sentient but formally rational. Hence the norm is not a partial aspect of his nature but its totality. Therefore, an adequate

---

[75] *Phaedrus,* 247. Whether Plato really held this doctrine on universals or merely had it imputed to him by Aristotle is disputed. According to St. Augustine, Plato was referring of the *ideae exemplares* in the Divine Mind.

account of human nature must take into consideration his essential relations, intrinsic and extrinsic. The extrinsic relations of man must be included because he is not an isolated being but by nature a being who comes into contact with other beings.

132. *What, then, is a complete view of human nature?*

1. *Intrinsically and essentially* man is a composite, the inferior part of which must be subordinated to the superior element. Otherwise the order of his unitary nature will not be preserved. Such order requires that the vegetative and sentient be *subordinate* to the rational. Vegetative and sentient goods can be proper objects of the appetite of the entire man because man is by nature vegetative and sentient and the reasonable fostering of these goods can indirectly promote his rational life. However, excessive attention to man's lower needs disturbs the order of his nature and hence is harmful to the entire man. On the other hand, actions which directly promote his rational life may be bad for the entire man if, sought to excess, they do not take into account the reasonable demands of the lower man. Such would be long hours of study which impair a person's health. Hence, a primary need of man is due subordination of part to part to ensure the welfare of the whole.

133. *2. Extrinsically yet essentially* man is a contingent, social, and proprietary being. (*a*) As a *contingent being,* man is a creature essentially and completely *dependent* on the one necessary Being. Whatever violates man's necessary dependence on God is a bad or unsuitable act. (*b*) As a *social being,* man is intended by nature to develop and attain his last end in the company of his fellow man. This relationship is one of equality except where the common good demands that an individual participate in God's authority and thus be superior to some of his fellows. (*c*) As a *proprietary being,* man is intended by nature to have dominion over irrational creatures which are meant to be pure means to assist man to attain his end. Since God cannot abdicate His absolute dominion over these things, man is the *steward* of all visible creation. Whatever tends to make these things ends in themselves or to make man their absolute lord is contrary to an essential disposition of human nature.

If, therefore, a human act disturbs any one of these relationships, that act is unsuitable to human nature and bad. To be morally good, the act must promote one of these relationships and at the same time must not disturb any of the other three. Hence the following

expression: *Bonum ex integra causa; malum ex quocumque defectu:*
Good results from a totally good cause; evil from any defect in
the cause.

PROOF

134. The norm of morality is man's rational nature adequately
considered, because:

1. The norm of morals must be *that by comparison to which a
human act is seen as perfecting or degrading man as man.* Since
moral goodness is man's unique perfection, his perfection as a unified
whole, then the norm of morals will be that standard to which the
human act is compared to determine whether or not it perfects man
as man, as a unitary whole.

2. This standard of comparison must be man's *rational nature.*
(*a*) Every nature is a principle of action. Hence, to determine whether
an act proceeding from this nature is suitable to it or not, we must
compare the act to the nature. (*b*) Man's nature is rational.

3. The standard is the *totality* of man's rational nature. Man's
nature is complex. Therefore, if his total nature were not the norm,
one would not measure the act as good or bad for man as man,
the total man.

Corollary. Since evil is the privation of good, what indicates the
good indicates the evil. Since a morally good act is one which duly
perfects human nature, so a morally bad act degrades human nature.

G. The Ultimate Norm of Morality

135. The norm of morality which we have established, namely
human nature, is a proximate norm. We can scarcely conceive of
a closer relationship than that between a nature and its actions. But
human nature is not the ultimate explanation of morality, for human
nature, not being self-sufficient, does not fully explain itself. The ultimate norm, then, will be the last assignable reason why human nature
is precisely what it is. This is the Divine Nature, of which every
created nature is something of an imitation. The Divine Nature, as
archetype and exemplary cause of all created being, is the last reason
why any nature is what it is.

The natures of things are not, as Occam contended, dependent on
God's arbitrary will. God does not compose essences as a child makes
castles of sand according to his fancy. Essences are fixed and im-

mutable. The divine will must follow the law of the Divine Being, which here means that the divine will depends for its act upon the object which the divine intellect presents to it. Nor does the divine mind make up its object; it presupposes it. This object can only be the Divine Nature. Therefore, as the proximate norm is human nature, so *the ultimate norm is the divine or supreme nature.*

Independent morality, or the theory that moral distinctions have no relation to God, is absurd. Morality is based upon the nature of things, and the nature of things upon the nature of God, the Fount of all reality. The experience of mankind, especially of ancient Greece and Rome and contemporary modern life, shows that where due regard and respect for God decays, true morality withers.

III. THE SPECIFIC DETERMINANTS OF MORALITY

136. We sometimes speak of an act as good because of the skill with which it is performed; for example, we call a song good or a race good meaning that the singer sang well or that the runner ran expertly. But acts of the will are good or bad not because of the ease or difficulty wherewith they issue from the agent but because of the object willed (§ 66). The human act is good when one wills a good object, that is, one that conforms to human nature. The relation of the object willed to the norm of morals makes the act *generically* good or bad. But the act is not only generically good or bad. It has a *specific* goodness or badness. An act of almsgiving adds a specifically different moral luster to a person than an act of obedience. Perjury degrades a man in a peculiarly different way from adultery. We shall learn what these varying grades of moral good and evil are in our discussion of virtue and vice. Our present question is: *What explains the specific morality of the act?* The answer, simply put, is: (*a*) what a man does, and (*b*) why he does it.

137. Upon closer examination of the term of the will act, that is the complete end or good known and willed, we discover these elements contributing to the morality of the act: (*a*) *the act as it is in itself* (sometimes called the object in the more restricted sense); (*b*) the act as modified by certain *moral circumstances;* (*c*) *the motive of the doer* (often called the end of agent). The first two constitute the what of the will act; the third the why.

138. These three elements are the sources of the act's morality or *its specific moral determinants:* they are the factors which determine not only the conformity or nonconformity of the act with the norm but also the specific nature of its conformity or nonconformity. These elements do not constitute a new norm; they are the reason why the act has its specific relation to the norm.

In order that an act may be good, both what a man does and the reason why he does it must conform to the norm. If one or the other factors does not accord with the norm, the whole act is bad according to the axiom, *good results from a totally good cause; evil from any defect in the cause.*

A. The Moral Object

139. The determinants of morality are more easily understood from examples than definitions. This is particularly true of the object. We may describe this element in simple terms by calling it the action in the abstract, that is, action stripped of its motive and circumstances, and say that ethics and law deal with moral acts such as lying, murder, theft, etc.

140. We may also consider the analogy between the moral object and the "end of work" described in § 29. An end of work is that result in which an activity by its nature terminates. This applies primarily to physical actions. Applied to moral acts, it means that moral result in which the human act naturally culminates. This moral result bears a single relationship to the norm of morality. It must be single because the moral act, like a physical thing, cannot specifically be two things; it can only be one. Thus, taking the life of an innocent person, whether by stabbing, shooting, or strangling, is one moral result in which the human act ends. We designate the result by a single label, murder. Another act may terminate in compliance with a superior's order, another in relief of a neighbor's want. The former is an act of obedience, the latter an act of charity.

141. The moral object may be identified with a single physical act such as an interior act of the love of God or hatred of one's enemy. Usually a series of physical acts constitutes one will object. This is a unit because there is a single relation between the norm of morality and the object known and willed by the agent. "Taking what belongs to another against that person's reasonable will" is a single moral result; it has one specific relation to the norm, and to it we apply the single term of stealing. Many distinct physical acts may be involved, for example, influencing others, signing a check, changing records. But we are not so much interested in the physical character and number of these actions as in the result in which these actions terminate and *the relation which this result has to the norm of morality*. This result, desired, achieved, or only approved, standing in a definite relation to the norm of morality, is the *moral object* of the will act. This morally specifies the will act and gives it its first status in the moral order. It is the moral core of the human act, *its primary moral aspect*.

142. The relation between this moral result, or moral object, and the norm may be one of conformity, difformity, or neutrality.

1. The relation may be one of *conformity* either because:

a) The moral object and hence the will act so conforms to the norm that its contradictory is positively out of accord with the norm, for example, love of God, obedience to one's parents. Such actions are intrinsically good.

b) The moral object — and hence the will act — does not so conform to the norm that its contradictory would *of itself* positively degrade human nature but solely because it is that commanded by a prescription of positive law, for example, payment of income tax or compliance with military draft. Such acts are good but not intrinsically good.

2. The relation may be one of *difformity* either because:

a) The result is an abuse of the faculty from which it proceeds and hence is always out of accord with the norm, for example, a lie, masturbation, or blasphemy. Such will objects are *intrinsically* evil.

b) The result, while not an abuse of a faculty, contravenes some positive law and thereby is out of accord with the norm. If the law which forbids this act ceases to be a law, the act is no longer bad, for example, the eating of meat on Friday or failure to register for the draft.

3. *Neutrality.* Sometimes neither the object nor its contradictory is out of accord with the norm. Such acts of their nature are *morally indifferent,* for example, riding a bicycle, taking a Sunday walk, walking rapidly or slowly.

There are moral objects, therefore, which are good, bad, and indifferent. To will a bad object is always morally evil no matter how good the motive may be. To will a good object does not necessarily make the act good — the motive must also be good. In the case of an indifferent object, the morality of the action must be judged from the motive (cf. § 151).

B. Moral Circumstances

143. *What* a man does morally depends primarily upon the substantial relation of the act to the norm. The moral quality of an act, however, may be further affected by *moral circumstances,* that is, those accessory conditions which modify the substantial morality which the act already possesses. To strike one's brother is worse than hitting a stranger; to pray for ten minutes is better than to pray for five.

Accidental circumstances may surround an act which in no way affect its morality, for example, to steal with the right hand or the left, to save the life of a Frenchman or an Englishman. Only those circumstances are moral which modify the *moral status* of the act. This modification can only be accidental for the substantial morality of the act depends on its moral object. Moral circumstances do not give the act its first and essential morality but merely modify what morality it already possesses.

144. The phrase, "circumstances alter cases," should be carefully understood. There are certain physical concomitants which change an act indifferent in itself into one that is good or bad. To walk in the morning is indifferent in itself. For a child to walk when he ought to be in school is wrong. The circumstance of time certainly alters the case. It is not, however, a moral circumstance of the act but pertains to its moral substance. It is a decisive factor making the act disobedience. A moral circumstance is never the altering factor that makes the act substantially good or bad.

145. Moral circumstances can alter the status of the human act in two ways: (*a*) They can change the species of the act. To an act which is already good or bad from its object they can add a new relationship to the norm, or give it a new moral angle. To touch a girl immodestly is a violation of chastity; if the girl is a blood relation, the guilt of incest is added. (*b*) Within the same moral species, circumstances can increase or diminish the goodness or badness of a human act. To cheat the railroad of a single fare is wrong; to cheat it of five fares is worse.

146. To categorize moral circumstances, authors have borrowed from the Latin rhetoricians the following: *quis, quid, ubi, quibus auxiliis, cur, quomodo, quando.*

Quis, or *Who* — the status of the agent. An agent may be married or single, a parent or a stranger. These circumstances will sometimes make a difference in the moral quality of the act.

Quid, or *What* — the status, that is, the quality or quantity, of the material object of one's will act. Whom did I detract — my sister or a mere acquaintance? What did I take — five bonds or five pieces of blank paper?

Ubi, or *Where* — circumstance of place. A murder in a church is worse than a murder in a railway station.

Cur, or *Why* — The motive of the agent will not be included under the mere circumstances; it will be treated in the next section.

Quando, or *When* — circumstance of time. A brawl on Sunday is worse than a brawl on a weekday.

Quomodo, or *How* — circumstance of manner. One may be uncharitable with greater or less anger. One may extort information by cruelty which can be greater or less.

Quibus auxiliis, or *Means* — An act may be performed by means of force or guile.

C. The Motive

147. The motive is the reason for acting, that good, freely chosen by the agent, which he wishes to accomplish by an act. It is the original source of the whole act because an act, with its object and circumstances, is the means taken to accomplish the end in view. Since end is first in the order of intention, it is the first and most important moral element in the human act. No man is better than his motives.

Motives are not usually single and simple but multiple and complex. This is one of the reasons why self-examination is so difficult. There are proximate and ultimate motives as in the case of a person giving alms to obtain a favor from God. The proximate end is to relieve one's neighbor, the ultimate end is to dispose God to grant the favor sought. All our motives must be at least implicitly reducible to the absolutely ultimate end of all human activity, the glory of God.

Several motives each of which is sufficient to move the agent are referred to as partial motives. A primary motive is one of two motives which would move the agent without the other; the other is a secondary motive.

148. How the motive influences the morality of an act is clear from the following:

1. If the motive coincides with the object, as in giving alms to relieve another's necessity or playing a game for the sake of mere recreation, the action's morality is adjudged from its object.

2. If the object is morally indifferent, as running, the action will be good if the motive is good, as in running to help put out a fire in a neighbor's house; the action is bad if the motive is bad as in running to steal or assault. A good end ennobles an indifferent means — which is poles apart from saying that the end justifies the means.

3. If the object is bad, *no amount of good intention will render the act good*. No one may perjure himself to escape unjust condemnation. The will may never will evil. However, such an act is not as evil as an act in which the motive is also bad.

4. If the object is good and the motive bad:

a) If there is only one motive and that bad, the entire act is vitiated. All actions chosen as a means to an evil purpose, though good in themselves, are tainted by such motivation. If I visit a sick man to discover where his valuables are kept so that I might later steal them, such a visit is part of my act of theft.

b) If there are several motives, one good and one bad: (1) If the bad motive is grievously wrong, even though it is only a secondary motive, the entire act is vitiated. For example, if a man were to assist a woman in a tangled legal predicament, his chief motive being one of kindness yet accompanied by a base hope of seduction, the entire act would be wrong. The agent is thereby turned completely away from God his last end. (2) If the bad motive is only secondary and merely venially wrong, the whole act is not vitiated. In this there are really two moral actions, a substantially good act with an evil concomitant. For example, if I make a substantial donation to charity out of true pity for the afflicted and at the same time experience a feeling of vain complacency, such vanity does not destroy the substantial goodness of my act.

SUMMARY

149. 1. *What is a morally good act?* The good is the suitable. Once we have established man's end, we may say that the suitable human act is the right act, one properly directed to man's end. Having set up the norm of morality, we see that the act is right because it befits human nature adequately considered. Formally, rectitude is the correct relation of the act to the attainment of the end; goodness, the relation of conformity of the act to human nature. But that which is good is always right and vice versa. Finally, consideration of the specific determinants of morality showed us that the good act befits man's nature and is this particular good act when the will tends to this totally fitting object, that is, one that conforms to human nature both in its moral object and circumstances as well as in its motive.

150. 2. *What is a morally evil act?* It is an act that lacks the suitability it should possess. In such an act the agent wills what is unbecoming his human nature. This unsuitability may be either in his motive or in the act itself. Whoever so acts is not tending to his last end.

An act is *grievously evil* when the agent wills what is so unbecoming his nature that he is completely turned from his last end. He chooses a created, apparent good and subordinates himself to it as to a last end. Such an act is a total denial and complete overthrow of the prime order of his nature.

An act is *venially evil* when it is directed away from his last end but does not destroy his habitual tendency to it. It is not total subversion of his nature.

151. 3. *What is a morally indifferent act?* It is an act that has neither rectitude nor wrongness, one that has a neutral relation with respect to the norm, for example, digging, running, whistling. These acts, in themselves, or viewed in the abstract, are neither morally good nor evil. However, in the concrete there are no morally indifferent acts.

All truly human acts as they happen are good or bad. This is clear from an analysis of man's intention. A man intends what is morally good or morally bad or morally indifferent. To intend moral good is a good act; to intend moral evil is a bad act; to intend the morally indifferent must be either a good or bad act. The morally indifferent is sought either reasonably or unreasonably. When a person seeks it reasonably, he is directing his act at least interpretatively toward his last end. The act then has proper rectitude and must be good. If he seeks the morally indifferent unreasonably, his act is not directed toward his last end. The act lacks rectitude and is wrong.

IV. THE EXTENSION OF MORALITY

A. Direct Objects of the Will

152. To how many things may the term moral good and evil apply?

1. Moral goodness and badness primarily inhere in the elicited act of the will. The act may be desire, love, hope, content, or their op-

posites, and even if it is in no way externalized, it is still *the moral act* because it alone is the free act (§ 67).

2. An imperate act of any faculty placed in obedience to the will's command is also called good or bad. It is so called only by extrinsic denomination for, strictly speaking, only the will act is good or bad. However, in common parlance it is the external act, such as heroic rescue or theft, which is called good or bad rather than the will act imperating them. The reason is that the external act, as the immediate object of volition, gives moral character to the will's inner act. Besides, in divine and human laws it is the external acts which are emphasized.

153. Though physically distinct, the inner act of the will and the imperate act of some other faculty form one moral action, the controlling factor of which is the will act. Thus, if the will decides on an act which is good or bad, a man is worthy of praise or blame even though the act is prevented. Thus, a woman who has offered to be a blood donor and is refused certainly has a charitable intention. A young man who has determined to see a lewd show but is prevented from entering the theater is guilty not of seeing a lewd show but of intending to do so.

It may be argued that once a man has resolved to commit an evil act, he may as well go through with it even though in the interval between his evil resolution and its execution his conscience bids him to desist. It may be argued that since he is already guilty of a wrong act of the will, he will be no worse off if the external act is performed. This is fallacious because: (*a*) The most general principle of morality, as we shall see, is that a man must avoid evil as far as he can. If he stops before the external act is accomplished, he has avoided the evil of the external act — he is guilty only of a bad internal act. (*b*) Many bad external acts result in scandal or injustice to others. If a bad external act is not accomplished, there is no obligation to repair scandal or make restitution. (*c*) Positive law, civil or ecclesiastical, can punish only for the external act.

What, then, does the external act add to the inner act of the will? Morally, it adds nothing essential. However, it does add an accidental fullness of perfection because the intention is realized. Greater effort and intensity of will is required to externalize the act; there is longer and more intense dwelling on the good or evil. The difference between the will act realized and the will act unrealized is merely quantitative, that is, one of degree.

B. Indirect Objects of the Will

154. The direct object of the will whether internal or both internal and external makes the will act good or bad. Does the indirect object, the voluntary in cause, affect the will act? Is the will act made good or bad because of foreseen but unintended effects?

Unintended good effects do not affect the will act. If one foresees that certain good effects will follow from his will act but one does not intend them, these effects do not add to the moral goodness of his act. He has not willed good when he could have done so; he has not done good as far as he could.

I may do a notable kindness to a sick man, which has the further effect of relieving the anxiety of his wife. If foreseeing this effect, I do not also intend it because I do not care whether she is relieved, I cannot be credited with doing her a charitable deed.

155. What of bad unintended effects? *Is the will act bad merely because some evil but unintended effects result?* An act in itself innocent may become bad when all the following conditions are present: (*a*) some evil effect is foreseen at least confusedly as resulting from it; (*b*) one is free to place or not to place the act; (*c*) *there is an obligation to omit the act precisely to avoid this evil effect.* To prevent scandal or immediate co-operation in another's evil act one is forbidden to do various things innocent in themselves (cf. § 668 ff.). To proceed to do them is to be guilty of wrongdoing.

156. But many evil though unintended effects may follow from one's will acts. Must one, therefore, refrain from acting whenever an evil though unintended effect will follow, according to the axiom that one must avoid evil as far as he can? We are to avoid evil unintended effects *as far as we can.* However, if one had to avoid every act which had any sort of evil effect, one would be reduced to almost complete inactivity. To determine, therefore, when a will act that is followed by a bad effect is permissible, we make use of the principle of double effect.

157. *The Principle of Double Effect.* A will act followed by two effects, one good and one bad, is permissible under the following conditions:

1. *The initial voluntary act must itself be good,* for the will can never directly tend to evil.

2. *The good effect must follow as directly as the evil effect.* This sequence is not one of time but of causality, that is, the evil effect cannot be the cause of the good effect. If it were, the agent would have to will the evil effect directly to attain the good. Evil, however, may not be willed under any circumstances, irrespective of the good that may be obtained.

3. *There must be a proportionately grave reason for placing the act* and permitting the evil effect. It would not be reasonable to allow a grave evil for a relatively insignificant good.

4. *The evil effect must never be intended,* otherwise the will would directly tend to evil.

Points 1 and 4 above are not difficult to understand and apply. The heart of the principle is contained in 2 and 3. Unless one can grasp how two effects can follow with equal directness from one act and what would constitute a sufficiently grave reason for allowing some effect, he cannot apply this principle.

158. The following is an example of the application of the principle of double effect. A pregnant woman is suffering from a cancer of the womb. May a surgeon perform a surgical operation which will remove the cancerous womb and at the same time result in the death of the unborn child?

First condition. The initial act, the removal of the cancerous womb, is not a morally bad act. It is justifiable mutilation, so designated according to the principle that a part may be sacrificed to save the whole.

Second condition. Two effects follow from this act: a good effect, the correction of the mother's dangerous pathological condition; and a bad effect, the death of the child. Both effects follow with equal directness because the surgical operation removes the womb both with its cancer and its foetus. It would be different if the surgeon were to kill the foetus in order to afford the mother relief. In this case the evil effect would be directly intended as a means to the good effect.

Third condition. There is a sufficiently important reason for allowing the child to die, namely, saving the life of the mother.

Fourth condition. The surgeon does not intend the child's death but merely permits it.

READINGS

St. Thomas, *Summa Theologica*, I–II, 18; 19; 20; 54, a. 3; 94, a. 2.
———— *Contra Gentiles*, III, 129.

Aristotle, *Ethics*, II, 5–6; IX, 8.

Adler, Mortimer J., *A Dialectic of Morals*, Review of Politics. University of Notre Dame, 1941.

Catholic Encyclopedia, "Altruism," I, 329; "Categorical Imperative," III, 432; "Epicureanism," V, 500; "Hedonism," VII, 187; "Indifferent Acts," I, 116; "Utilitarianism," XV, 241.

Cathrein, Victor, S.J., *Philosophia Moralis*, pp. 69–125. Friburgi Brisgoviae, Herder, 1915, 10 ed.

Cronin, Michael, *The Science of Ethics*, Vol. I, pp. 87–168. Dublin, Gill, 1909.

Frins, Victor, S.J., *De Actibus Humanis Moraliter Consideratis*. Friburgi Brisgoviae, Herder, 1894.

Gredt, Joseph, O.S.B., *Elementa Philosophiae*, Vol. II, pp. 333–343. Friburgi Brisgoviae, Herder, 1937.

Janet, Paul, *Theory of Morals*, trans. Chapman, pp. 309–352. New York, Scribners, 1898.

Miltner, Charles, C.S.C., *Elements of Ethics*, pp. 117–143. New York, Macmillan, 1932.

Nivard, Marcel, S.J., *Ethica*, pp. 47–97. Paris, Beauchesne, 1928.

Rickaby, Joseph, S.J., *Aquinus Ethicus*, Vol. I, pp. 48–83.

———— *General Metaphysics*, pp. 93–165. London, Longmans Green, 1930.

———— *Moral Philosophy*, pp. 31–41; 177–189.

Shallo, Michael, S.J., *Scholastic Philosophy*, pp. 162–166. Philadelphia, Reilly, 1926.

Urraburu, J. J., S.J., *Institutiones Philosophicae*, Vol. II, pp. 417–508. Romae, 1891.

CHAPTER V

DUTY AND LAW

159. We began our explanation of what human conduct ought to be by establishing the ultimate principle of orderly human action, namely, that final end of happiness to which man's conduct should tend. We saw that since some of his acts do not tend thither, since there are right acts and wrong acts, it was necessary to find a basic principle of differentiation between the good and the bad. This we found to be the norm of morality, human nature in its essential relationships.

From consideration of the end and of the good it is clear that man *can* be happy. The next inquiry might be: *how* does man become happy, that is, what are the specific good acts which lead to happiness, what are the specific bad acts which prevent happiness? These particular questions, however, are as yet out of place because one final constituent of basic morality has not been explained. The notions of the end and of the good must be complemented by the notion of obligation for these three, end, good, and obligation, are the pillars upon which morality rests.

Just as all men see that there are good acts and bad acts so also they acknowledge some kind of compulsion to do the good and avoid the evil. Even the rudest person has a code which commands that certain good things must not be left undone, certain evil things avoided, under penalty at least of being an evil person. Men call this compelling force duty, or moral obligation. All human beings are conscious of it except the few who do violence to their reasonable nature. Upon what objective basis does this universal conviction rest? What is it that demands that a man do good and avoid evil?

160. This brings us to the next great problem of ethics which we may put in terms of the word "ought." The word "ought" may express wishful thinking, as when we say, "Our team ought to win tomorrow."

It may mean what is expedient, as when a wife says to her husband, "We ought to go to your boss's party." It may signify a logical necessity, as when Lincoln's cabinet probably said to him after Chancellorsville, "Since Hooker is so incompetent, he ought to be replaced." When ought is used in an ethical sense it does not signify propriety nor merely hypothetical or logical necessity but absolute necessity. When we say, "Fathers ought to support their children," we mean that without qualification they are compelled to do so. To this ought, no "ands," "ifs," or "buts" are attached. It is categoric and necessitating.

A threefold problem arises: (*a*) Whence comes this necessity? (*b*) Where is it found? (*c*) What is its nature?

I. THE SOURCE OF MORAL OBLIGATION

Note carefully that we are not asking how man arrives at an adequate knowledge of obligation or how blameworthy the absence of this knowledge would be, but rather what the thing is in itself. This we learn only by knowing its cause. Hence our first question means: From what source does obligation arise? What would automatically entail the cessation of obligation if it ceased to exist itself?

A. The Unsatisfactory Answer

161. *The force theory.* Hobbes held that all moral distinctions and hence obligation arise from the law of the State which is purely an accumulation of physical might.[1] Spencer says that evolving man was first conscious of an internal restraint, the foreseen usefulness or harmfulness of a proposed act;[2] later, as he began to lead a less simple life, an external pressure was brought to bear upon him, the fear of political, religious, and social penalties. Out of this dread of social consequences has evolved the notion of moral obligation.[3] This in turn will disappear the higher man mounts in the moral scale.[4]

The statement of Holbach, that "moral obligation is the necessity of doing or avoiding certain actions in view of the well being we seek in social life,"[5] is elaborated upon by modern sociologists who say

---

[1] Thomas Hobbes, *Leviathan*, Chaps. XIII and XVII, Molesworth's English edition, Vol. III, pp. 115, 157–158. London, Bohn, 1841.

[2] Herbert Spencer, *Data of Ethics*, pp. 120–121.

[3] *Ibid.*, p. 126.

[4] *Ibid.*, pp. 127–128.

[5] *La Morale Universelle*, Tome I, p. 2. Paris, 1820.

that what people experience as moral obligation is fear of the coercive power of society. Because the group resents certain actions, it forbids them. If indirect coercion is sufficient to induce conformity to its taboos, well and good. If not, the dominant group forces its will upon the nonconformers. The boldest upholder of the theory of social coercion is Holmes, who says law is physical force, a "statement of the circumstances in which the public force will be brought to bear upon men through the courts."[6]

162. Criticism. If a man goes counter to his nature and acts like a brute, force may be necessary to bring him to reason. However, it is a subversion of human nature to hold that man should be directed to his final end primarily by physical compulsion. This is to deny the freedom and dignity of his nature, to make a mere brute of him.

163. According to Kant, the obligation of observing the moral law originates in man himself. He reasons that only that will act can be simply good which is posited without hope or fear of anything consequent thereupon. Hence, to be good the will cannot be determined by anything outside itself. Therefore it is autonomous. "What else," he asks, "can the freedom of the will be but autonomy, that is, the property of the will to be a law unto itself?"[7] And Kant is the first discoverer of this principle. "Looking back now on all previous attempts to discover the principle of morality, we need not wonder why they all failed. It was seen that man was bound by duty, but it was not observed that the laws to which he is subject are *only those of his own giving* . . . and that he is only bound to act in conformity with his own will; a will, however which is designed by nature to give universal laws."[8]

Man, then, is a legislator obligating himself to live in accord with his nature.

164. Criticism. The authoritative commands of morality cannot originate in man. If the autonomous reason is the sole source of morality, man is both a superior who imposes a command and an inferior who is bound by it. But in a contingent being, there is no self-binding principle. Only the Necessary Being whose end is wholly

---

[6] O. W. Holmes, Jr., *Holmes-Pollock Letters,* ed. M. O. Howe, Vol. II, p. 212. Cambridge, Mass., Harvard University Press, 1941.
[7] *Critique of Practical Reason,* trans. Abbott, p. 65.
[8] *Ibid.,* p. 51.

in Itself can compel Itself to act in conformity with Its nature. Man is neither a necessary being nor an end unto himself. Therefore, moral obligation originates outside of man. Reason discovers and enunciates it but reason cannot be identified with it.

165. *The theory of essential order.* Vasquez[9] seems to hold that the objective order of our human nature, apart from or antecedent to any divine command, compels us to do good and avoid evil. Janet says: "Moral obligation is based on the following principle: 'Every being owes it to himself that he should attain to the highest degree of excellence and of perfection of which his nature is capable'. . . . It is not because a higher power desires our good that it is incumbent on us to seek it; it is because we inevitably desire it ourselves."[10]

166. *Criticism.* Order — the disposition of means to an end — imposes a hypothetical obligation on the mind, that is, "you must do good and avoid evil if you wish to attain your final end," but it is not sufficient to obligate the will. The will can be bound only by some orderer. To say that this orderer is human nature is to say that a contingent nature can bind itself categorically. This is impossible as we have seen.

Our answer to the problem of the source of obligation is as follows: *The ought of duty or moral obligation arises only from the compelling will of a superior embodied in moral law.*

B. *The Eternal Law*

167. Law essentially involves two things, order and necessity.

1. *Order.* This is the intelligent and efficient disposition of means to a chosen end. Thus the canons of art indicate the orderly process to be followed to produce some aesthetic effect. The laws of grammar point out the means we must use to speak intelligibly. Military, civil, and ecclesiastical law manifest the order men must observe to secure the purposes of the armed forces, the State, and the Church.

2. *Necessity.* True law compels obedience to the order prescribed. A process indicated for the attaining of an end can become true law only when a superior makes it obligatory.

168. Military, civil, and ecclesiastical law are instances of human

---

9 *Commentariorum, ac Disputationum in Primam Secundae S. Thomae, Tomus Secundus,* q. 90, disp. 150, cap. 3. Ingolstadii, 1606.

10 Paul Janet, *Theory of Morals,* trans. M. Chapman, pp. 170, 173. New York, Scribner's, 1898.

activity, order, and law in defined and limited fields. Is there an all-inclusive activity, order, and law?

There is certainly a universal activity and order — *the order of the universe*. When God created the universe, He had in mind some supreme and focal purpose which the entirety of creation — angels, planets, stars, rocks, men, brutes — was to accomplish. As part of this general scheme of things, He had in view more particular ends which particular classes of creatures and individuals themselves were to attain. The means whereby this general end and all particular ends were to be achieved were patent to Him. The sum of these means converging upon this grand purpose — the activity of a universe pointed toward one supreme end — we call the order of the universe.

Does God will that this order be necessarily carried out? If so, there is a universal law, and the divine guidance and compulsion of creatures unto the end of the universe constitutes *The First Law*, the prototype and source whence all other law must proceed.

THESIS IX. There exists in God an Eternal Law directive of all creatures unto the end of the universe.

169. Law may be considered as existing in three ways: (*a*) *actively,* as it exists in the mind of the legislator — a pattern of order — and in his will — the determination that this order be executed; (*b*) *passively,* as it exists in the minds of those who are to obey it; (*c*) *significatively,* as it exists in some external sign, some book, tablet, or inscription, whereby it is conveyed to its proper subjects.

St. Augustine defines the Eternal Law as *the mind and the will of God commanding the natural order of the universe to be observed, forbidding it to be disturbed.*[11] It is law in the *active sense* and consists in the decree of the divine intellect devising the means that make possible the attainment of the divine creative purpose and in the decree of the divine will making mandatory the following out of this order. All things that are moved must be subject to the Prime Mover.

170. An adumbration of this doctrine is apparent in ancient classic philosophy. In *Oedipus the King,* Sophocles speaks of laws ordained on high, without mortal birth, deathless.[12] In the *Antigone* he says, "No man can override the unwritten and undying laws of the gods."[13]

---

[11] *Contra Faust.,* Lib. XXII, cap. 27.

[12] *Oedipus Tyrannus,* 863–869.

[13] *Antigone,* 454–455.

In the *Gorgias,* Plato quotes Pindar, "Law is king of all, of mortals as well as immortals."[14] In almost the very words of Augustine, Cicero teaches that a divine eternal law rules the universe which is the mind of God commanding and forbidding: *Quae non tum denique incipit lex esse, cum scripta est, sed tum, cum orta est. Orta autem simul est cum mente divina. Quamobrem lex vera atque princeps apta ad jubendum et vetandum ratio est recti summi Jovis.*[15]

171. PROOF. *There exists in God an Eternal Law,* because:

1. (*a*) There eternally exists in the mind of God the pattern of action required of creatures for their co-operation toward creation's purposes. God has a purpose in creation and He knows what creatures must do in order that this purpose will be realized; otherwise He would not be infinitely wise. (*b*) There eternally exists in God's will the efficacious decree that this activity of creatures be forthcoming. God must will both the purpose of creation and the means of achieving it; otherwise creatures and not God would be supreme.

2. This act of God's mind and will constitutes a law for it is the norm of action whereby creatures are properly necessitated to act toward the common end of the universe and are restrained from action contrary thereto. It is an Eternal Law for whatever is in God must be eternal.

172. But it is objected there can be no Eternal Law because: (*a*) there are no subjects existing from eternity, (*b*) nor is there an eternal promulgation or outward sign manifesting the law.

In answer to the first objection we say that while there is no community of subjects *actually* existing from eternity, nevertheless, following the decree of creation, it does exist as known and *preordained* by God.

In answer to the second objection we say that there certainly can be no terminative promulgation, no actual manifestation of law to creatures until such time as they begin to be. Such terminative promulgation is requisite for a law existing passively. Is such promulgation requisite for a law existing actively, that is, in the mind of the legislator? In the case of a human legislator, such promulgation is necessary, but not in the case of the Divine Legislator. The reason is that after the human legislator has determined to enact a law, he may change his mind during the interval between his decision and

---

[14] *Gorgias,* 484 b.
[15] *De Legibus,* Lib. II, n. 4.

actual promulgation. Hence such a determination is regarded as an intention to frame a law, which intention does not acquire the fixity of law until it is outwardly signified to those to whom it pertains. With God, the Divine Legislator, it is different. He is unchangeable. Therefore, once God has absolutely determined to legislate, the thing is done — nothing more is required for a law in the active sense. God will not alter his determination and the terminative promulgation infallibly will occur at its appointed time.

173. Corollary I. *God absolutely wills the end of the universe* — the divine extrinsic glory, which is the communication of reality by God to creatures according to their capacity to receive it and the manifestation and acknowledgment of the same by creatures. This is the primary decree of God's will pertaining to creation and in it every species of obligation is rooted. Paley[16] rightly derives obligation from the divine will but mistakenly deduces it from the divine will to reward the observers of the law and punish its violators. Certainly the predominant motive why most men keep the law is fear of punishment and hope of reward, but the meting out of punishment and rewards are but subordinate ends to God — they are but means to the primary end, the maintenance of universal order.

Corollary II. *God wills that all things act according to their kind.*

Corollary III. *Moral obligation exists.* A compulsion befitting his nature is imposed on man to co-operate with God's purpose.

II. WHERE MORAL OBLIGATION IS FOUND

A. The Existence of a Natural Law

174. Law, in the sense just established, extends to every created thing. To produce its effect, the Eternal Law must issue from the Divine Legislator and be received by all who are to be governed by it. How then is it communicated? It is communicated *naturally,* that is, in the way that accords with the make-up of each. Any other way would be a frustration of the divine purpose.

The natural way whereby God impresses His mind and will on creatures is through principles intrinsic to them. Experience shows us that beings operate through their own internal principles. Hence God does not steer His creatures toward their destined ends by

---

16 William Paley, *The Principles of Moral and Political Philosophy,* Vol. I, Bk. II, Chaps. II and III, pp. 57–62. London, Faulder, 1791.

means of some external force, as a child pushes his sailboat. These internal principles are nothing other than the being's nature equipped to attain its destiny. Hence every creature is subjected to, and participates in, the Eternal Law *naturally*.

175. Concerning the Eternal Law as it has been communicated and now exists within the creature two questions arise. The first is this, What is this divine guidance which the creature receives? This impress of the divine mind must constitute the specific law of each creature's nature. Those directives, naturally given to it and moving it to its allotted end in the universe (which is also its own supreme good) cannot be other than the law of its nature.

The second question is, How does the law so communicated compel creatures? The general answer must be, again, *naturally*. In irrational beings the law functions blindly, through instinct: the divine compulsion brought to bear is sheer physical necessity. A set of necessary tendencies ineluctably move these beings to observe the order divinely appointed for them. These tendencies give rise to constant and uniform modes of action which men express in convenient formulae known as the *physical laws* of the universe. However, since law is a function of reason and as these beings have no reason, the impress of the divine mind and will upon them can be called law only metaphorically.

176. The Eternal Law cannot operate in man as a blind impulse. Such a mode of operation would contradict human nature, whose chief glory is self-direction. True, we have an innate appetite for beatitude, but it functions rationally, that is, through our intellect which is endowed with the power to judge what is orderly and must be done, what is disorderly and must be left undone. The mind of man must clearly mirror the Eternal Law for man.

Therefore the Eternal Law's compulsion of man cannot be physical. It can only be moral, that is, manifested to his reason and imposed on his free will. An Eternal Law prescribes a course of conduct for him and while he has the physical freedom to act otherwise, nevertheless the categoric need of conforming to the mandates of the law is made clear to him. The Eternal Law, in so far as it operates by appeal to reason and through moral necessity and in so far as its purpose is the maintenance of *man's* part in the universe, is called *Moral Law*. This alone is law in the true sense of the word.

177. From the foregoing it is evident the Eternal Law exists and operates *in man*. As it so exists we call it the *Natural Law*. It is law in the passive sense and is defined by St. Thomas as the rational creature's participation in the Eternal Law.[17] It is simply man's knowledge that certain conduct is necessarily good, certain other necessarily evil; that God commands the former and forbids the latter.

Since angels, oxygen, trees, cats, etc., have a part to play in the universe and are legislated for in the Eternal Law one could speak of the natural law of angels, oxygen, trees, cats, etc. So also we speak of a natural *moral* law for men. However, since our interest is solely in the divine law as it touches man, we appropriate the term "natural law" and apply it to man alone.

We wish to prove, therefore, that in human reason there exists a genuine reflection of God's mind and will concerning man, to which we give the name, the Natural Law. Herein man finds moral obligation.

THESIS X. The Eternal Law applies to man and is proposed to his reason. As it exists in the mind of man it is aptly called the Natural Law. Its injunctions constitute the specific law of human nature.

PROOF OF PART I

178. *The Eternal Law applies to man* for he is a creature.

PROOF OF PART II

The Eternal Law is proposed to man's reason for God must deal with man according to man's rational nature.

PROOF OF PART III

The reproduction of the Eternal Law in the mind of man is "de facto" called the Natural Law. That this is an apt designation is clear from Proof IV.

PROOF OF PART IV

The Eternal Law's injunctions for man constitute the specific law of human nature because:

1. Directives naturally given to a class of beings and compulsorily guiding it unto its peculiar end in the universe are the specific law of that nature. They constitute a law because they indicate activity

---

[17] *Sum. Theol.*, I–II, 91, a. 2.

necessary to an end and fittingly compel the beings toward that end. They constitute a specific law because each nature, each class of beings, has its characteristic end to fulfill in the universe.

2. The directives for man in the Eternal Law naturally indicate what men are to do to play their characteristic part in the universe and impose on them a moral compulsion to act accordingly.

179. Corollary I. Moral obligation is embodied in the very law of man's nature which proposes a scheme of orderly conduct to his intellect and obliges his will to observe it.

Corollary II. We may now define law in the words of St. Thomas as "an ordination of right reason promulgated by him who has the care of the community for the common good."[18]

"An ordination of right reason" means: (*a*) a competent directive proceeding from the mind of a legislator as the reasonable means of attaining a common end; (*b*) a command issuing from the legislator's will that the directive be obeyed. In that law begets a true obligation it differs from a mere *counsel.* "For the common good" means that the end of law is the effective direction of a perfect community toward a good common to all the members. Every movement toward an end is of course toward some good. Here it is a good for many, to be obtained from the collective effort of many, and when obtained shared by many. Hence law differs from *precept,* which is given to an individual or a group of individuals. "Promulgated" means that since the ordination of reason is actually to direct, it cannot remain hidden in the breast of the lawgiver but must be so externally proposed that it readily comes to the knowledge of those it is to direct. Hence, promulgation is the authoritative manifestation of the law as binding. "By him who has the care of the community," means that to ordain authoritatively unto an end belongs to him in whose care the end is. To regulate unto the end of the community belongs either to the whole community or that individual or moral person legitimately acting for the community.

180. Modern legalism which is almost wholly positivistic contends that nothing can be called law which does not issue from a supreme *visible* authority capable of enforcing its commands.[19] Hence the Natural Law which is not enforced as such by visible authority is not to be called law but at best "moral principles."

---

[18] *Sum. Theol.,* I–II, 90, 4.

[19] Thomas E. Holland, *Jurisprudence,* p. 54. Oxford, Clarendon, 1937, 13 ed.

Certainly only that is *positive* law which proceeds from visible authority, but we shall show that all positive law, to deserve the name of law, must be founded on the Natural Law. While the authority of God is invisible, it is nonetheless genuine and effective and is the true source of all visible authority.

B. In What the Natural Law Consists

181. To the Eternal Law as it pertains to man, constituting *the law* of his nature and existing in his cognizance, we have given the name, the Natural Law. What exactly is this thing? What is there in the mind of man which deserves the name of law?

THESIS XI. The Natural Law consists in practical universal judgments which man himself elicits. These express necessary and obligatory rules of human conduct which have been established by the Author of human nature as essential to the divine purposes in the universe and have been promulgated by God solely through human reason.

182. When we say the Natural Law consists in universal judgments we do not mean the law is just a psychological act of man. Obviously our emphasis is upon the content of these judgments as revelatory of the Eternal Law.

Just as man formulates principles of knowledge, such as the principle of contradiction, and mathematical and physical formulae, so also he forms judgments concerning his moral behavior. Reflecting upon the world about him, he arrives at general conclusions regarding human action, such as, Children must obey their parents. These judgments express two things: (*a*) an ideal of human conduct; (*b*) an obligation to follow the ideal.

These judgments, then, are a law because they convey to man a pattern of action and an obligation to conform thereto, both of which originate in a Supreme Legislator, the Author of his nature. We must note, though, how differently each of these proceeds from the Divine Legislator.

183. 1. *The ideals of conduct.* Does God arbitrarily command certain acts which He might have forbidden? Are these basic rules of conduct framed by the whim of some supramundane authority on etiquette? Not at all. What these rules command or forbid does not depend on God's free choice; it ultimately arises from the nature of things. For example, the obligation of reverence for parents arises from an essential relation of human nature (cf. § 133). But all essential human relations, all created essences are what they are and are unchangeably such because they are so many possible imitations of the divine nature (cf. § 135). God's will cannot change the essences of things. Even if, by an impossibility, God were to order otherwise two and two would always make four, blasphemy would be evil. In His governance of the universe, God is not like the artist of Donald Duck or Porky Pig, contriving by caprice; rather, He follows a law of order which is the immutable order of His own Divine Nature. Hence the ideals of conduct, embodied in the Natural Law, depend not on the divine will but on the divine nature.

These ideals of human conduct concern *activity which necessarily promotes or frustrates man's last end*. When we proved that there is a natural difference between good and evil (cf. § 122), we saw that an action intrinsically good of its nature perfects man, that an action intrinsically evil degrades man. At that point of our investigation we discerned in such acts logical necessity touching the mind but not the will. Logical necessity means that a man ought to do thus and not thus if he wishes to be reasonable, if he desires his last end. But suppose that he does not wish to be reasonable, that he is not concerned with attaining his last end? Law then intervenes imposing obligation.

184. *2. Obligation.* The Divine Legislator commands man to be reasonable: he orders man to attain his final end. A true necessity falls not merely on the mind but on the will, on the total man, to frame his conduct in accordance with these ideals.

Knowing that certain acts necessarily perfect man, God must command man to do them; knowing that others degrade man, He must forbid man to do them. Once God determines to create man, He has no choice but to prohibit murder, injustice, lying, and the like, for human nature cannot but be degraded by such acts. Since God absolutely wills the end of the universe and efficaciously desires man's good, He must convey to man not merely the desirability of doing what is good and avoiding what is evil but He must obligate him to act accordingly without, however, physically constraining him.

185. What God so wills constitutes *the most necessary and obligatory norms of conduct*. They are necessary because they either enjoin goods so fundamental that the minimum fullness of human well-being is impossible without them or forbid evils which are totally subversive of human well-being.

The Natural Law, then, is simply nature moving us to those real goods without which we cannot be happy, forbidding those apparent goods which destroy happiness. The particular contents of this law flow directly from human nature, ultimately from the divine nature of which ours is a reflection. Its obligatory character comes from the will of God commanding that every creature shall act according to its kind.

186. *How has God promulgated this law,* that is to say, how has God so manifested it that man recognizes it as an authentic pattern of behavior to which the Divine Lawgiver demands conformity? Rhetoricians answer that it is inscribed in the heart of man. This is metaphorical speech which means that God enunciates this law through our nature, that is, *the sole instrument of promulgation is human reason.* The promulgation of the Natural Law has two aspects. On His part, God gives man the light of reason, which is endowed with the power of correctly formulating these necessary rules of conduct. On his part man makes use of reason to set up a moral code for himself. From training and observation, the mind readily formulates these principles, at least in general outline. It does not find them in any codex or book of law, nor written on tablets of bronze or granite, nor in any external sign. No archaeologist is going to unearth from some prehistoric city an original copy of this law. It exists in the mind of God and in the enlightened moral consciousness of the race.

187. Cicero has well said that the Natural Law is right reason.[20] In summary, then, (*a*) the Natural Law is *virtually* the human intellect endowed with the power of formulating judgments as to what a man must and must not do. (*b*) *Formally* the Natural Law consists in these judgments. They are a true law existing in man's consciousness whereby he regulates and measures his behavior. It is law in the passive sense. (*c*) *Fundamentally* the Natural Law is the objective reality giving validity to those judgments — that essential order of human nature explained in §§ 130–133 now made obligatory by the will of God commanding.

There is a mild point of controversy here. Is the Natural Law the judgments (*b*) or the realities (*c*) behind the judgments? When we

---

[20] *De Re Publica,* III, 22.

say it is the judgments we mean judgments possessing objective validity. Hence the issue is one of words, not realities.

188. PROOF. *The Natural Law consists in practical universal judgments, elicited by man himself, and expressive of the essentially necessary and obligatory rules of human conduct because:*

1. The Eternal Law, as it pertains to man, must be promulgated to him naturally. For the law of his nature must be disclosed to him in a way that befits that nature.

2. The only natural way in which the Eternal Law can be promulgated to him is that he himself elicit practical, universal judgments which express the essentially necessary and obligatory rules of human conduct because:

a) The natural way of promulgating law to man is through his reason;

b) It is not natural that God implant judgments in his mind;

c) Nature has not written this law in any natural *external* sign for man to read.

Hence the only way remaining is that *man himself elicit judgments revelatory of this law.* This truly befits a being whose chief dignity is self-direction toward his last end. These judgments must be practical, universal, and expressive of the essentially necessary and obligatory rules of human conduct; otherwise the law is not *promulgated.*

3. The Eternal Law naturally promulgated is called by men the Natural Law.

III. THE INTIMATE NATURE OF DUTY

189. We have shown that moral obligation originates in the Eternal Law of God and is found in the Natural Law. We now consider its nature.

Obligation involves these four elements: (*a*) one who obligates, namely, God absolutely willing the final purposes of the universe; (*b*) one who is obligated, namely, man — his free will which bears the burden of duty; (*c*) that to which one is obligated or the sum total of commands and prohibitions which must be laid on man that he fulfill his part in the universe; (*d*) obligation, or duty, looked at in itself or formally. Our final inquiry here is: *What is the essential definition of duty?*

190. Moral obligation is a form of necessity, and necessity is a determination unto one. Obligation, then, is a relation. One term of the relation is the free will of man bound to do or omit some act. What is the other term? What is that to which the free will so bound is determined? Since the necessity here involved is final and moral we have a free being determined unto an end which categorically must be reached. What is that end or good for the sake of which duty compels the free act or omission? This is the other term of the relation of obligation.

191. The problem may be discussed in more concrete terms as follows. In the dictates of the Natural Law we recognize a categoric necessity: children must reverence their parents: parents must refrain from adultery. Why are they so compelled? Because they thereby live according to the nature given them. But why must they lead reasonable lives? Because God so commands. Why does God so command? Because this act or this omission is necessarily connected with that end which God has decreed must simply be attained. Is this end our beatitude? No, *de facto* some do not attain beatitude. What, then, is that ultimate goal which man must reach by God's decree? It is giving external glory to God. Among all ends and goods that may be proposed to man only one is supreme, unique, ultimate, and absolutely must be attained. God has decreed that all creatures must give Him external glory and He will obtain it both from the just who attain beatitude and the unjust who do not. The divine goodness communicated to man will be fittingly manifest, and God will be all in all.

192. The necessary way of accomplishing his unalterable purpose in the universe is for man to perform good acts and refrain from evil acts. Since doing good and refraining from evil are necessary means to an absolutely obligatory end, these means are also obligatory. The reason is that whoever is determined to an end is likewise determined to the unique means conducing to that end.

Moral obligation, therefore, is the necessity, imposed by God and manifested to man, of performing or refraining from acts which inevitably conduce to or hinder the attainment of the absolutely ultimate end of man.

193. It is not necessary that man perceive the connection between his act or omission and the glory of God in order that he be actually obligated. He may at first see only the nexus between the act or omission and its suitability to his nature. In this case he is not adequately conscious of obligation. If, however, he once perceives that God truly desires the act or omission, he then becomes adequately subject to obligation even though he has only a confused knowledge of why God wants it. This, of course, requires knowledge of God, at least as the Supreme Lawgiver. Whether a man can without fault lack this knowledge of God and hence this knowledge of moral obligation, is one of the first questions of *special ethics* (cf. § 332).

194. N.B. I. From the foregoing we see how moral good — that which is perfective of human nature — is transformed by law into duty. Not every good, however, is always obligatory. Affirmative laws always bind, not in the sense that they press us every moment of our lives but when the occasion arises for their observance. Some kinds of good, that is, of supererogation, never become obligatory.

195. N.B. II. We also see how moral evil — that which degrades man — becomes sin, the deliberate violation of God's will commanding us unto our good. Sin alone is wrong and unnatural. In the truest sense it is the sole evil for by it alone can beatitude be lost. The world is full of merely physical ills — pain, hunger, disease, death. These things, however, are not contrary to nature; they come by defect of nature, the inevitable falling short of beings who do not possess the plenitude of reality. But the flouting of the divine command by sin is no mere shortcoming or lack of further perfection. It is a positive turning against nature. It alone is a breach of Eternal Law. It is the one thing which defeats nature's purpose and disturbs the order of the universe. However, as we shall presently see, this check is only temporary. God, through the sanctions attached to His law, can undo the evil of sin.

READINGS

St. Thomas, *Summa Theologica*, I–II, 90–94.
———— *Contra Gentiles*, III, 111–114.
Catholic Encyclopedia, "Natural Law," IX, 76; "Law and Morality," X, 560; "Duty," V, 215; "Obligation," IX, 54.
Cathrein, Victor, S.J., *Philosophia Moralis*, pp. 147–164. Friburgi Brisgoviae, Herder, 1915, ed. 10.
Cronin, Michael, *The Science of Ethics*, Vol. I, pp. 203–244; 597–622. Dublin, Gill, 1909.
Holaind, Rene, S.J., *Natural Law and Legal Practise*, pp. 41–51; 61–66. New York, Benziger, 1899.

LeBuffe, Francis, S.J., *Outlines of Pure Jurisprudence*, pp. 32–48. New York, Fordham, 1924.

Leibell, J. F., ed., *Readings in Ethics*, pp. 301–326. Chicago, Loyola, 1926.

Maritain, Jacques, *The Rights of Man and the Natural Law*, pp. 58–64, trans. Anson. New York, Scribners, 1943.

McKinnon, Harold R., *The Higher Law*. Berkeley, Calif., Gillick, 1946.

Messner, J., *Social Ethics*, trans. J. J. Doherty, pp. 52–74. St. Louis, Herder, 1949.

Nivard, Marcel, S.J., *Ethica*, pp. 106–135. Paris, Beauchesne, 1928.

Rickaby, Joseph, S.J., *Aquinas Ethicus*, Vol. I, pp. 264–285.

——— *Moral Philosophy*, pp. 115–132.

Suarez, *De Legibus*, L. 1, c. 12; L. 2, cc. 1–7.

CHAPTER VI

SANCTION AND MERIT

196. No law is an end in itself; it is but a means for the securing of some further necessary good. Thus the Natural Law is promulgated as the set of necessary directives whereby God is to secure from man the ultimate purpose of human existence. As this end which the law is designed to achieve has been absolutely willed, so also the lawgiver must categorically will observance of the law. However, law is proposed to a free being who is capable of disregarding it. Some effective means, therefore, are necessary to assure satisfactory observance of the law and adequate attainment of the purpose of the law. A reasonable motive for observance of the law is reward for obedience and punishment for disobedience. Whatever measure of due observance is finally lacking will be compensated for by the infliction of just penalties whereby the end absolutely desired will be attained. Hence, there can be no complete consideration of law without a discussion of that good in which the observance of the law naturally issues and of the evil which attaches to the violation of the law. We shall consider first the sanction of the law and then its reward.

I. SANCTION

197. *What is a sanction?* The word *sanction* derives from the Latin, *sancire,* which means to render holy and inviolate, to consecrate. Technically, to sanction means to affix to the law definite rewards and punishments in order to insure observance. In ordinary use the punitive rather than the premial element is connoted. A sanction is either (*a*) the decree of the lawgiver assigning a reward for observance and a punishment for violation; or (*b*) the reward promised or the punishment threatened.

198. Sanction has an immediate and an ultimate end.

1. The immediate end of sanction is to provide efficaciously for the law's observance. Before a person decides to keep the law or violate it, he sees that punishment awaits the offender. The threat of punishment is expressly intended to be an effective motive to induce persons to observe due order. Hence the first purpose of sanction is to promote observance of order and prevent violation of the law. *Sanction is a preservative of moral order.*

Considered from this aspect, sanction is a stimulant or corrective for man's inconstant will. The threat of punishment which we know will be carried out serves as a moral prophylaxis. A person who has run afoul of the law and incurred its penalties is not so eager to embark on further violations. Then, too, the punishment of the guilty is a deterrent to others. However, it would not be just to pick out one and punish him merely to frighten others from violation.

The immediate end, or preservative aspect, of sanction has to do with the good of the subject, for sanction serves as a *corrective* for the individual and a *deterrent* for the community. This because the observance of the law and the good of the indivdual are identified.

2. The ultimate end of sanction is the realization of the final purpose of the law, that is, man's rendering to God the glory He desires from him. Consequent upon man's free determination either to obey or disregard the law, sanction provides for the stabilization of objective justice by giving the observer the reward promised and by meting out adequate punishment to the violator. Therefore *sanction is finally a restoring or a vindication of moral order.*

199. Materialists, atheists, and many of our so-called advanced thinkers scoff at the notion of punishment as a relic of the dark ages or a hangover from old-fashioned, hell-and-brimstone religion. They contend that the threat of punishment is unworthy of human dignity and that henceforth "men are to be emancipated from heaven and governed by love alone." Others, while admitting that the corrective aspect of sanction has some value, vigorously denounce the idea of retribution. If you say God is so good, they cry, how can He take delight in human pain. Just as man may not take vengeance, neither may the Supreme Lawgiver.

Such persons forget that man's universal craving for retributive justice is a natural inclination, which is in itself good. Man instinctively recognizes that they who do evil must suffer evil in return. Vengeance, however, is forbidden the individual man because he is unable temperately and impartially to right the wrongs done him. But our instinct says that someone must — someone who is sufficiently impartial and competent. If this were not the case, man would have an essentially evil instinct. Our nature, however, can have no such flaw.

Second, such individuals blind themselves to the malice in every serious violation of the Natural Law. They fail to see how evil it is for man to reject the Creator's will, to prefer a creature to the Creator, and by such choice despise the Creator. This is dishonoring an infinitely lovable Person and the overthrow of essential order.

Nor must we anthropomorphize God as seeking petty vengeance upon the despisers of His commands. His punishment is not vengeance: it is vindication of order. As Universal Provider and Ruler, God has the infinite knowledge, power, and perfect equity to do what no human could do, namely, restore perfectly the balance of moral order disturbed by wrongdoing. God not only can do this but He must — His infinite sanctity demands that no creature prefer himself to the Creator and benefit thereby. In vindicating order, God does not will evil. He wills the punishment conditionally before the law's violation; after the violation He wills it absolutely, *not however as an evil, but as a good,* that is, a necessary restoration of order. Men, blinded by pride and passion, may not conceive the necessity for restoration of the moral order violated by sin. One must contemplate the infinite goodness of the Creator and the utter dependence of the creature to appreciate this fundamental truth.

200. As the preservative function of sanction has to do with the good of the subjects, so its vindicative (not vindictive) function pertains to the good of the lawgiver, the establishment of perfect justice, and the attainment of creation's purpose. Both of these aspects of sanction are natural and essential. Which is the more important?

If we consider the immediate good to be effected, the prevention of moral evil and the preservation of the moral order here and now, the preservative function of sanction would appear of first importance. But since man is prone to evil, no sanction is absolutely efficacious as a deterrent of evil. There must be recompense for man's lapses: the divine glory which these actions did not render must be realized. Therefore, bearing in mind the final purpose of creation, we see that the vindicative function of sanction is paramount. Only as a restorative of order is sanction completely efficacious, for it is only by equitable apportionment of rewards and punishments that creation's purposes are ultimately obtained. Revelation alone tells us there will be a day of general judgment given over to vindicative justice. Reason, however, acclaims it only right and fitting that there be some final reckoning, a righting of wrongs, and an acquittal of debts so that at some future time there will be a final and irrevocable equilibrium of perfect justice.

201. *Kinds of sanctions.*

1. By reason of its *efficacy,* a sanction is: (*a*) *sufficient,* when it constitutes a motive sufficient of itself to induce the subject to obey the law; (*b*) *insufficient,* when of itself it is not sufficient to induce obedience.

2. By reason of its *proportion to merit and demerit,* a sanction is either just or unjust. It is (*a*) *just* when there is true proportion between the observance of the law and the reward, between the violation of the law and the punishment. "To make the punishment fit the crime" is not a mere saying but an ideal of distributive justice. (*b*) A sanction is *unjust* if such proportion does not exist.

A *perfect* sanction is both sufficient and just. Such a sanction promises a good which outweighs any evil resulting from observance of the law and threatens punishment surpassing any advantages gained by violation of the law.

3. By reason of its *origin* a sanction is (*a*) *positive,* that is, established by the free will of some legislator, for example, fines, imprisonments, excommunications; (*b*) *natural,* that is, the inevitable result of actions conforming to or contravening the Natural Law.

202. *Has the Natural Law appropriate sanctions?* There are three main spheres, or orders, of moral activity: individual, social, and universal. In each order there are corresponding sanctions.

1. *The individual order.* This is the moral order of man's activity in regard to his personal individual good. The law of this order is that the appetites of the individual must be subject to reason. To enforce this order, nature establishes appropriate sanctions — approbation of conscience and tranquility, or disapproval of conscience and remorse; health of mind and body or diseases; the freedom of self-control or slavery to concupiscence. Every city hospital bears eloquent testimony of the existence of such sanctions. The man who gives full rein to his passions must pay the price nature exacts.

2. *The social order.* Man is a social being and from the necessity of living in the company of his fellow man, a multifarious activity arises. The law which governs these activities is that man must do unto others as he would have them do unto him.

Here, too, nature applies her sanctions such as domestic peace or strife; friendship and neighborly relations or enmities and friction; prudent management of public resources or national bankruptcy; prosperity and peace in national relations or war, penury, and social disturbances. Love begets love; hatred, hatred. As you sow, so shall you reap.

Many people, however, believe only in such sanctions. They say that if they observe the physical laws of their nature they will be rewarded with good health; if they are industrious and work hard they will achieve success, perhaps riches; if they are neighborly and keep the law of the State, they will be secure and well thought of. But a mere Horatio Alger view of life is not complete; temporal success and happiness is not an end in itself; it is only a means to the true end of man which is everlasting beatitude.

3. *The universal order.* This is the complete moral order of *man as man* in relation to his *last end*. It is supreme and contains within itself all other relations. Its law is that every man is obliged to seek his last end.

What are the sanctions of this order? Are they one or many? Are they like those mentioned above, halting and imperfect?

THESIS XII. The Natural Law has a perfect sanction, realizable only in a future life and consisting in the perpetual loss or attainment of beatitude.

PROOF OF PART I

203. *The Natural Law has a perfect sanction,* because its Author is infinitely holy, wise, omnipotent, and just.

1. Since He is wise and holy, He must attach *some sanction* to His law; otherwise He is indifferent to the law's observance. His infinite sanctity forbids that He be indifferent to that which concerns His external glory.

2. Since He is wise and omnipotent, He will employ means sufficient in themselves to assure the purpose for which the law was promulgated. Hence the sanction of the Natural Law is *sufficient.*

3. Since He is just, His rewards will be proportionate to man's observance of the law; His punishment, to man's violation of the law. Hence the sanction of the Natural Law is *just.*

PROOF OF PART II

204. *The perfect sanction of the Natural Law is realizable only in a future life* because experience amply testifies that the sanctions of the Natural Law in this life are imperfect. Many observe the Natural Law and receive no reward; others constantly flout it and suffer no punishment.

PROOF OF PART III

205. *The perfect sanction of the Natural Law is the perpetual attainment or loss of beatitude,* because it is the sole sufficient sanction and it is adequately just.

1. *The sole sufficiency of this sanction.*

a) A sufficient sanction offers as a reward a good that outweighs any advantage to be had by breaking the law. Only beatitude is such a reward.

b) The sufficient sanction must threaten a penalty greater than any evil which may come from keeping the law. Since death sometimes is necessary for observance of the law, the only evil conceivably greater is the perpetual loss of beatitude. Besides, if violators of the law are some day to attain perfect happiness, no other sanction can possibly deter them from evil. They may sin with the assurance that some day all will be well with them.

2. *The justice of this sanction.*

a) It is *most natural* that observance of the Natural Law, which is intended solely as a means to man's last end, should result in perfect happiness and that those who refuse to obey the law should not obtain their last end.

b) There is *just proportion* between good acts and the attainment of beatitude and bad acts and the loss of beatitude. The first is evident because good acts, of their nature, must terminate in man's ultimate perfection.

It is argued, however, that there is no proportion between bad acts and the perpetual loss of beatitude. We answer that God must fix a limit beyond which the probation of man may not be protracted. Otherwise God might have to wait forever upon man's good pleasure, which is impossible since God is Master of man.

At the conclusion of this probation a man is either (*a*) substantially in a state of accord with the Natural Law or (*b*) substantially in a

state of rebellion against it. In the case of the former, he is substantially prepared for beatitude, which must be an eternal possession
for unless he has no fear of losing it, he could not be completely
happy. In the case of the latter, a man is to be either (1) annihilated,
(2) granted another probation, (3) admitted to beatitude, (4) given
a temporal punishment after which he will be admitted to beatitude,
(5) eternally deprived of beatitude.

The first possibility is rejected because annihilation frustrates God's
purpose in creating this man. Thereby God would forever be deprived
of the glory He decreed to obtain from this individual. The second is
absurd in the supposition that the man has come to the end of all
probation. The third is contrary to the justice and holiness of God.
He cannot grant beatitude to one who is a rebel against Him. The
fourth is inadequate. Turning from an infinite good constitutes an
infinite evil. No temporal punishment is adequate for an infinite
wrong.

206. N.B. I. God is not *unjust* in punishing with eternal pain bad
acts that were but momentary in their execution. The reason is that
the guilt of sin is measured not by the duration of the act but by
the grievousness of the act. Every seriously sinful act of man is a total
turning away from his last end which is infinite good. Now natural
equity demands that each one be deprived of that good against which
he acts, for thereby he shows himself unworthy of it. Second, each sin,
being a rejection of the divine will, is contumelious of an Infinite
Person. Hence its guilt is infinite, and it deserves an infinite penalty.
But since pain cannot be infinite in intensity, it can only be everlasting in duration.

N.B. II. Nor is the decreeing of such punishments contrary to
divine *goodness*. God does not delight in these as an evil to man but
He wills them as a good required by the order of the universe. Order
demands that no one enjoy the divine good who is unworthy of it.
The person who violates the Natural Law proves himself unworthy
of the divine good; hence order demands that he should not enjoy it.
Punishment is the withholding of good from one who is unworthy.

N.B. III. The *sanctity* of God demands that He deny beatitude to
one who ultimately rebels against His law. The reason is found in
the necessity for God's concurrence in the acts of contingent beings.
The sinner denies that God is his last end. Therefore, if God were
to concur in the perpetual happiness of the unrepentant sinner, He

would co-operate *forever* in a lie, for He would approve the false-hood that something other than God can be man's last end.

The man who concludes his mortal probation in a condition of serious sin has chosen some creature and rejected the Creator as his last end. Since the opportunity of changing that choice by repentance has passed, God must accept as irrevocable the choice the sinner has made. Since the sinner has irreparably chosen something other than God, it is now impossible that he should ever have God. God accepts as final the sinner's fateful choice. Since the sinner is hardened in evil, God cannot communicate beatitude to him for he has no capacity to receive it.

N.B. IV. It is objected that the threat of the loss of beatitude does not induce all men to observe the law and hence is an inefficacious sanction. We reply that as a motive it has everything necessary to induce observance and that it is only *per accidens* inefficacious be-cause: (*a*) men refuse to advert to the existence of the sanction; or (*b*) they do not think the imposition of the sanction is imminent.

N.B. V. Reason cannot give a certain answer to a number of important questions on this problem. For the whole truth one must turn to Revelation. The following, for example, are some questions and the answers that are obtainable only from Revelation. (*a*) What constitutes immediate preparation for entering upon one's final beatitude? Possession of sanctifying grace. (*b*) What moral state entails loss of final perfection? Death in the state of unforgiven mortal sin. (*c*) How many probations is a man granted? One and only one.

II. MERIT

207. The notion of merit might have been introduced at the end of the treatise on good by establishing that man's good actions will ultimately terminate in a deserved reward and that therefore man's supreme good is an object of merit. Merit, however, is included in our treatment of law because it becomes more understandable when considered in conjunction with law and the sanction of the law.

Even the most uncivilized men know that man is a responsible being, the master of his acts (at least of some). Consequently they understand why his bad acts deserve denouncement and should be punished, why his good acts are worthy of praise and perhaps should be rewarded. What is the basis of this universal conviction? In treating sanction (§ 205) we demonstrated that the ultimate of blame and punishment that can be imposed on man is loss of beatitude. What is the ultimate praise and reward that can be bestowed on him? As there are natural punishments for evil conduct culminating in the supreme punishment of the loss of beatitude, are there likewise natural rewards for good conduct terminating in an ultimate reward which consists in the attainment of beatitude? This is the problem of the present section.

208. Man's attainment of beatitude may be viewed under two aspects. First, it may be regarded as a natural climax of a good life. A man performs such and so many good acts acquiring thereby such human perfection that he connaturally attains to a state of ultimate perfection. This ultimate good is the natural crown of many particular good acts. Second, we may look on man performing his good acts as one freely fulfilling an onerous obligation which is of advantage to the Supreme Lawgiver and consequently is deserving of a suitable return from Him. Has this second view objective validity? Is beatitude bestowed on man as a reward? Do man's good works entitle him to a reward which may not be denied him? Can man merit; must God reward?

209. Although the question is a familiar one, it is replete with difficulty. Revelation has familiarized us with the notion of eternal reward. Considering man as elevated by grace to a supernatural status and hearing the clear and oft-repeated promises contained in Scripture of a forthcoming reward, it is easy for us to conclude that the relationship of true merit can exist between God and His adopted sons. But if man were not raised to a supernatural plane, if he were never to become a *filius Dei* (son of God) but were to remain merely a *servus Dei* (servant of God), could man merit? To understand the difficulty let us first see what merit is.

210. *Merit* is that quality in a free act which renders the agent deserving of some reward. We also speak of a merit as any free act possessing this quality. Merit can also be used to designate either reward or punishment. It is commonly restricted to the former and the term "demerit" is used to signify the latter.

211. Three conditions must be fulfilled for the human act to be meritorious.

1. The act must be *free:* the agent must be the master of his act. Only on this condition may the act be called imputable, that is,

truly belonging to the agent and rendering him deserving of praise or blame. Necessary acts are not meritorious. No dog, horse, or any animal may receive a reward in the true sense.

2. The act must benefit another, bestow on him some *favor* or *utility*. The agent, however, must not be bound in justice to confer the good because of benefit or reward already received.

3. The recipient must *freely accept* the favor. Thus, if someone does me a favor, for example, cuts my lawn without my knowledge or presumed consent, I am not strictly obliged to give him anything in return. If this were not the case, I could become the victim of unlimited imposition. Acceptance can be explicit or implicit and can be signified in different ways, for example, contract, mutual understanding, silence, or even the very nature of things.

When all three of these conditions are simultaneously present an act deserves reward. What is the reason for this? Is it something exclusively within the act itself or may it also be something outside the act? To answer this question we must distinguish between condign merit and congruous merit.

212. 1. *Condign merit* alone is merit in the strict sense. It exists when the act is in some way equal to the reward: the act itself, in the estimation of both God and men, entitles the agent to proportionate reward. Note that we say "in some way." The most obvious case is that of *strict justice;* of such sort is all condign merit between man and man. The refusal to concede a reward so due is a violation of commutative justice and involves a consequent obligation of restitution. However, not all condign merit urges from justice. It can be founded on a promise given and the need to be faithful to it.

2. *Congruous merit* is merit by analogy. It exists when the reward proceeds from the generosity of the giver, while the intrinsic value of the act is not proportionate to the reward. For example, in a competition, only one prize may be offered, but the runner-up may come so close to winning that a prize is also given to him. For extraordinary services to the State great generals have been granted pensions and gratuities. Rewards given because of congruous merit are not due by way of strict justice. The conferring of such rewards may be based on some kind of equity, distributive justice, gratitude, or friendship. Withholding them is not a violation of commutative justice, although it may offend against decency or gratitude or involve personal discrimination.

213. The main difficulty now is clear. How can man do good to God since God is already all good? How can man benefit the infinite God who already has all things? If no benefit is conferred, no relation of merit is possible. The answer is that while man cannot add to God's intrinsic perfections, he can give God external glory by obeying His law. But how can man ask a reward for giving God what actually belongs to God? All that man is, all the external glory which man's good acts can proffer, is God's possession. Why should man be rewarded for rendering God His due? The answer is, that, although God has a pre-emptive claim to all of man's activities, man can merit if God wills to reward man for fulfilling his obligations. We shall prove that God does so will and hence that *man can merit*.

214. *What can man merit?* Man can merit beatitude, the only good really worth earning. If, then, man can merit beatitude, is it by congruous or condign merit?

How can man attain beatitude by condign merit if all condign merit is based on strict justice and if strict justice cannot exist between God and man? It is true that commutative justice cannot exist between God and man because: (*a*) it presupposes equality and independence between the two parties and (*b*) the object matter of commutative justice (§ 308) consists of goods which of themselves could belong to either one or other of the parties. But there is no equality between the finite and the Infinite; contingent being depends absolutely upon the Necessary Being. Furthermore, God has prior claim of absolute ownership upon whatever man can make, effect, or possess. Hence the relation of commutative justice cannot exist between man and God. Therefore, can man's merit before God be merely congruous merit? No, we shall prove it to be condign, based not on justice but on the divine fidelity.

THESIS XIII. Man can condignly merit beatitude from God. This merit rests not on justice but on God's fidelity.

215. In a condignly meritorious act we distinguish between remote exigency and actual exigency for a reward. The *intrinsic value* of the act as a benefit to another constitutes *remote exigency; acceptance* by the one benefited of an act that has been *performed* constitutes *actual exigency* for a reward.

To prove the relation of condign merit between man's good acts and beatitude we must show first *their remote exigency for beatitude.*

Man's final end is a double good, a divine good, the glory of God; and a human good, man's happiness. By perfecting himself man glorifies God: man benefits God and God in turn benefits man. But man can attain his final end only by his morally good acts. There is true proportion, then, between these acts and the divine glory and human happiness. They are the sole and necessary means whereby God obtains from man what He desires. The root of merit, then, is the intrinsic value of human acts. An additional but not essential feature of merit is that keeping the law and rendering God glory is onerous and difficult.

216. Remote exigency for a reward becomes *actual exigency* when these two conditions are fulfilled: (*a*) God must will to reward good acts with beatitude. If God so wills and man performs good acts, they are the meritorious cause of beatitude — the divine promise is a necessary condition. (*b*) Man must be on good terms with God when he performs the good deeds and when he claims the reward of beatitude. A person who is completely turned from God, his final end, can claim no reward from God, certainly not a reward of perfect union with Him.

PROOF OF PART I

217. *Man can condignly merit his beatitude,* because:

1. A fundamental exigency for beatitude as a reward attaches to morally good acts. 2. God has promised so to reward good acts.

The truth of (1) is established in the second paragraph of § 215; (2) is proved by the fact that the divine promise is implicit in the voice of nature calling men to their beatitude. God has implanted in us an ineluctable tendency to beatitude and imposes on us an inescapable obligation of doing what conduces to attaining it.

Since there is something in the act itself proportionate to the reward, the merit is not congruous but condign.

PROOF OF PART II

218. *This merit rests not on justice but God's fidelity.* Merit between man and God is based either on justice or on God's fidelity. There is no other conceivable basis. It cannot be based on justice because God cannot be bound to man for whatever man has or can have already belongs to God. To hold that God is bound to man

would imply that some sort of equality existed between Creator and creature, but this is impossible. Therefore, merit between God and man rests on God's fidelity.

219. If God has promised a reward for obedience to His law and man obeys it, God necessarily is obliged to give him beatitude. God does not owe man this reward in justice. God cannot be so bound: this would entail the subordination of God to man. Rather, because of His divine perfection, God must be faithful to His promises and the order He established in the universe. Let us suppose, however, that the impossible did happen and that God withheld the reward, would wrong be done? Yes, but no injustice would be done to man, for man has no rights before God; there would be the greater disorder of God failing to act in accordance with His divine attributes.

220. In § 213 we called the glory of God an "external benefit" given by man to God for which man is rewarded with beatitude. How is man's submission to the divine will a good as far as God is concerned? It adds no intrinsic perfection to God nor is it useful for the acquisition of such. The universe and all the glory it renders God could cease and God would be perfectly happy and unchanged. Hence Suarez, though admitting that some call the glory of God His "extrinsic good," mildly deprecates the use of the term with reference to God, because "among men these extrinsic denominations would not rightly be called a good unless they were useful for what is internal; since, therefore, this glory affords God no utility, it cannot properly be called any good of his."[1]

Is it not haggling over words to restrict the term good to internal perfections and to that which conduces to their attainment. Provided we realize the significance of our speech, why cannot we call a thing good which is completely external and can in no way be an intrinsic perfection of the person to whom it is attributed? The word would be used analogically, just as terms are used that we apply to both God and creatures. The inadequacies of language force us to call such a thing good. After admonishing us not to call God's glory an extrinsic good, Suarez proceeds to denominate it a *bonum quoddam honestum et decens Dei Majestatem*[2] (a befitting good of a sort, becoming the majesty of God) which God can intend and acquire. While this can in no way affect God, it is something — a divine advantage — de-

---

[1] *De Gratia*, L. VIII, c. L, no. 13; *editio Bert.*, tom. IX, p. 312.
[2] *Ibid.*

manded by the nature of things and which God in creating cannot renounce. It is the very last result in the whole concatenation of produced causes and results: the fact that God is known, loved, and glorified.

Comparison of the tenuousness of this divine advantage to the tremendous reward of beatitude reveals the boundless munificence of God. By way of intrinsic good God gets nothing, man everything; God gives all, man nothing. Because man is primarily the beneficiary of creation, St. Thomas says: "God seeks His glory not on account of Himself but of us."[3] As Cajetan explains, this does not mean that we are the ultimate end of the creative act but they for whose *utility* God seeks His glory.

Who then is the ultimate beneficiary of creation? In the sense that internal benefit is gained, it is man; in the sense that perfected man must be subordinated to God, it is God. The divine operation must of necessity ultimately terminate in God; otherwise He is less than His handiwork.

---

[3] *Sum. Theol.,* II–II, 132, a. 1, ad. 1.

READINGS

St. Thomas, *Summa Theologica,* I–II, 87; 21, a. 3–4; 114.
———— *Contra Gentiles,* III, 139–145; IV, 91–93.
Catholic Encyclopedia, "Sanction," XIII, 428.
Cronin, Michael, *The Science of Ethics,* Vol. I, pp. 544–558. Dublin, Gill, 1909.
Donat, Joseph, S.J., *Ethica,* Vol. I, pp. 109–122. Oeniponte, 1920.
Nivard, Marcel, S.J., *Ethica,* pp. 135–142, 170–174. Paris, Beauchesne, 1928.
Rickaby, Joseph J., S.J., *Aquinus Ethicus,* Vol. I, pp. 253–260.
———— *Moral Philosophy,* pp. 159–176.
Sullivan, Jos., S.J., *General Ethics,* pp. 105–107, 171–178. Worcester, Holy Cross College, 1931.

CHAPTER VII

THE PROPERTIES OF THE NATURAL LAW

221. Having established the existence of a Natural Law with a perfect sanction and a fitting reward, we now inquire whether it has any permanent characteristics. There are three distinct problems. Is this law one and unchangeable for all men of all times? Or is it rather a set of flexible directives that may be discarded or replaced as varying circumstances may suggest? Is it a code whose tenets all normal men readily come to know? Or is morality something of itself so obscure and elusive that men can have no certain knowledge of it? Is it both so explicit and comprehensive as to assure adequate guidance for the whole range of human conduct? Or is it only a broad outline the further particulars of which must be supplied from some other source? Three distinct questions are here raised.

I. DOES THE NATURAL LAW ADMIT OF CHANGE?

222. The doctrine of perpetual change is prominent in modern philosophy. Nothing remains the same, everything changes. Ramifications of this formula are found in modern ethics. Just as man is the product of slow evolution, so too are moral directives. The code that sufficed for us as we were emerging into the subhuman ape that walked erect was quite different from the moral norms acceptable to the cave man of the late Pliocene Age. According to Durant Drake, "morality is not static but a set of experiments, being gradually worked out by mankind, a dynamic, progressive instrument which we can help ourselves to forge."[1] The relativist Lanz maintains that "moral principles change, not because the social and economic conditions compel them to change but because under different conditions they logically mean different things and practically call for different pat-

[1] *Problems of Conduct*, p. 38. Boston, Houghton Mifflin, 1935.

terns of behavior. . . . The old formulas, which we still regard as holy commandments . . . become empty words because they no longer fit the trend of time."[2] Evidently, if human nature is gradually changing into something different, then the fundamental laws governing human conduct must change too. Contrary to this most prevalent modern opinion we establish *Thesis XIV*.

THESIS XIV. The Natural Law is one, universal, and both intrinsically and extrinsically unchangeable.

223. 1. *Unity.* There is one body of moral truths. This fact can be established by two proofs:

a) Although the law contains many commands and prohibitions, all of these are derived from, and are reducible to, one principle (§ 236). The fact that there is disagreement as to how this fundamental rule of life is to be expressed does not invalidate this argument.

b) All men possess the same specific nature and are destined to one ultimate end. Since the end is one, the ordination unto that end is likewise one. The Natural Law is the outward expression of that one ordination.

224. 2. *Universality.* The law is not only one in itself but it binds all men imposing on each the same obligation of observing the due order leading to man's last end. The reason is that all men have the same specific nature and tend to the same end. While the law may not actually obligate this or that individual because of insanity or lack of development, nevertheless, each, inasmuch as he is a human being and has an intellect, falls under the law at least as its potential subject.

Furthermore, all human acts of every individual are governed by this law. There are no areas of personal or public conduct which lie outside the jurisdiction of the Natural Law. Every human act as a motion toward a particular good can be such only if it is also a motion toward the supreme good. Man seeks his happiness in each human act. But what governs man's motion to his last end is the Natural Law.

Under the same conditions of person, place, time, and circumstance the same rule of conduct holds for all men.

225. 3. *Immutability.* Let us distinguish between the changeable and unchangeable in morals. Subjective changes, even on the part

---

[2] Henry Lanz, *In Quest of Morals*, pp. 161, 162, 166. Stanford University Press, 1941.

of large groups, are common enough. In Massachusetts in 1700 cooking on Sunday was a sin; slaveholding, however, was permissible. In 1840 the vast majority of American colleges frowned on dancing as the invention of the devil. Card playing, smoking, drinking, horse racing were sins to many Evangelicals whose grandchildren ridicule the notion. Such subjective changes do not concern us.

Objective changes, however, are also possible. Social custom may change a proximate occasion of sin into a remote occasion. The ordinary man now is not lasciviously affected by women wearing shorts. People have become accustomed to them. In 1905 such dress would have been a proximate occasion of sin. Again, positive law commanding or forbidding under pain of sin may be revoked. The very rigorous laws of fasting are an example.

The *genuine* commands and prohibitions of the Natural Law cannot be changed. To this objective body of moral truth nothing can be added, nothing taken away. A projected change in the law would be made either by addition or loss of binding force.

226. 1. *Addition.* If the law were changed by addition, some new and fundamental rule of conduct would be added. Certainly by study and reflection we can learn more about the law, but no one will discover new fundamental commands or prohibitions. This is quite contrary to Bertrand Russell's recent statement: "Perhaps when we know more we shall be able to say that the best sexual ethic will be quite different in one climate from what it would be in another, different again with one kind of diet from what it would be with another."[3] Even though we move into an atomic age of the most unforeseen developments, we shall not need a new moral code. The Natural Law concerning man's behavior to the State was valid though inapplicable in the days before States existed. So too were its precepts concerning international relations when these were of the sketchiest sort. If completely undreamed-of circumstances of life unfold, so too will nature's precepts concerning them. These will not be new precepts. They will always have been in nature's code. The fact is that the occasion for their application will never have arisen before.

227. 2. The more likely way that we may conceive of a change taking place in the Natural Law is that it lose its binding force even

3 Bertrand Russell, *Marriage and Morals*, p. 6. New York, Liveright, 1929.

though the conditions of persons and circumstances remain unchanged. The change would be either intrinsic or extrinsic. If the change were *intrinsic,* the law would break down from within. The precepts would cease to exist because it had become useless or harmful. Thus "the Everlasting's canon against self slaughter"[4] or adultery would lapse because neither of these prohibitions any longer promoted human welfare. An *extrinsic change* would be one initiated by the lawgiver. He might *abrogate* the law, that is, render it null and void in its entirety; he might *derogate* from the law, that is, cancel a part of it while the remainder retained its force; or he might *dispense* from the law, that is, exempt some individual or individuals while the law continued to bind everyone else.

Our position is that the Natural Law will never lapse of its own dead weight nor has God, the Supreme Lawgiver, the power to cancel the law in whole or in part nor even to dispense one individual so as to render good or at least permissive what the law forbids.

To some this may be an extreme point of view. It contradicts all modern opinion which does not admit the existence of a Natural Law. It also apparently contradicts the older scholastics and theologians who held that the Natural Law is immutable in its primary precepts but admits of a few rare exceptions in some of its secondary precepts. This, however, is but a dispute about words.

228. The basis of our position is this: *the Natural Law forbids only actions intrinsically evil and commands only actions intrinsically good.* Unless one clearly grasps (*a*) the precise meaning of each precept and (*b*) the nature of an intrinsically evil action, he may conclude that exceptions to the law are possible.

229. 1. Difficulty arises because the Natural Law is expressed in general formulae which do not designate the precise limits of the law. Some have the impression that the law commands or forbids what it does not intend to command or forbid. We formulate the law, "Thou shalt not kill." This does not mean that all bloodshed is wrong but only the shedding of innocent blood on human authority. We say, "You must not take the property of another." Not every instance of the taking of another's property is wrong, but only that which is contrary to his *reasonable* will. We have the formula, "Deposits are to be returned," but this does not express the exact sense of

---

[4] *Hamlet,* Act 1, Scene 2.

the law, namely, that deposits are to be returned when justly and reasonably sought. When each precept is expressed in exact language it will be evident that no exceptions are permitted. However, the briefer formulae are in general use, because they are simple and apply to the vast majority of cases.

230. 2. Sometimes a difficulty arises in the formulation of a particular precept because one does not always understand what an intrinsically evil act is. We may distinguish two types of evil acts: (*a*) Some acts are in themselves so totally destructive of human good that they are never tolerated. Lying, blasphemy, perjury, and masturbation are such acts. (*b*) There are others which are not good but are not in themselves so completely destructive of human good as never to be permissible. Divorce and polygamy are cases in point. Both of them render difficult, but do not frustrate, the ends of matrimony.

That the Supreme Legislator for a grave reason and under controllable circumstances could tolerate the latter practices as the lesser of two evils is conceivable. A grave reason would be some pressing supernatural good and circumstances would be controllable if special providence would fend off the evils normally resulting from these practices. God, the Universal Provider, could exercise such providence. Since man cannot, it would always be wrong for him to assume these practices of his own accord. Since the attainment of created ends is ultimately the care of God, He could permit man to take the more difficult rather than the less difficult means to the end of a natural institution. Man could not take it upon himself to do this. Thus the will object which is intrinsically evil is not "plurality of wives" but "plurality of wives without divine permission." It is the latter which the Natural Law forbids and to which there is no exception.

231. *The matter remaining the same, the Natural Law is always unchanged.* Every act intrinsically evil must always be forbidden. But certain acts which otherwise would be intrinsically evil are not such and do not fall into the category of evil acts because of an act of God's supreme dominion. When God told Abraham to slay Isaac, the Israelites to take the precious vessels of the Egyptians, Osee to take to himself an adulterous woman, He was not permitting a violation of the laws against murder, theft, or adultery. As master of life He could end Isaac's life in the manner He chose; as owner of all things He could dispose of the Egyptians' goods; as custodian of matrimony He could cancel a previously existing matrimonial bond.

Hence the acts commanded were neither murder, theft, nor adultery. Therefore they were not prohibited by the law. If the matter is changed, the law does not apply.

232. At this point we note a tremendous difference between Natural and positive law. In the latter, the lawgiver determines the matter of the law; in the Natural Law, the matter determines the law. A state may decree that driving a car at a speed greater than forty miles an hour is a civil offense. Because adultery is of its nature wrong, it has to be forbidden by the Natural Law. In positive law, the matter remaining the same, the law can be nullified. For example, a state may void its speed laws. In the Natural Law, however, the matter remaining unchanged, no change is possible in the law. What objectively is adultery must forever be forbidden.

Occam[5] is certainly an adversary when he says God may, if He chooses, permit actions which contradict any natural precept. Scotus[6] held that the precepts on the first tablet of the Decalogue were immutable; those on the second admitted of exception. Durandus[7] held that God could dispense from the affirmative precepts.

PROOF OF PART I (Thesis XIV)

233. *The Natural Law is intrinsically immutable,* because its prescriptions cannot in whole or part become useless or harmful.

1. Whatever becomes useless or harmful ceases to be binding and hence to be law. It would no longer promote the common good.

2. That the precepts of the Natural Law cannot become useless or harmful follows from the fact that they express essential relationships of human nature. Relations flowing from the essence of a thing can no more change than can the essence itself. A change in an essence would argue a change in the Immutable Essence of God in which created essences are founded.

PROOF OF PART II

234. *The Natural Law is extrinsically immutable,* because God must always forbid what is intrinsically evil and command what is intrinsically good.

---

[5] *Super IV libros sententiarum,* Lib. II, q. 19, ad 3 dubium.

[6] *Sum. Theol.,* IV, 94, a. 5. Vol. 4, pp. 614–617 (Doctor, Oxon. 3, disp. 37). Romae, 1902.

[7] *Super sententias Petri Lombardi* etc., Lib. I, distinct. 47, quaest. 4, pp. 92–94. Paris, Roigny, 1539.

1. The matter of the Natural Law is intrinsically good and evil acts. If God must always command one and forbid the other, He cannot possibly change the law.

2. The sanctity of God and the absolute need of His upholding the order of the universe forbid that He should ever cease to prohibit what is intrinsically evil and command what is intrinsically good. The unseen Lawgiver fixes His law once and forever: He does not return to amend it.

II. IS THE NATURAL LAW EASILY KNOWN?

235. The Natural Law, as a code levied on all men, must be adequately promulgated. How effectively has this been done? Do all men with sufficient correctness form these universal practical judgments regulative of human conduct? Is there ignorance of the law? Is any of this ignorance inculpable? Since all the precepts of the law are not equally easy to grasp, we classify them according to the clarity of the objective evidence giving them validity.

236. 1. *Primary principle.* All the precepts of the law are reducible to a single formula. In the past, especially toward the close of the eighteenth century, many writers have tried to sum up all moral obligation in one compact phrase.[8] Hobbes' dictum was: "Every man ought to endeavor peace, as far as he has hope of obtaining it; and when he cannot obtain it, . . . seek, and use, all helps, and advantages of war":[9] This is another way of saying: "Self-preservation is the first law of life." Pufendorf's summation is: "Every man . . . should cultivate and preserve toward others a sociable attitude which is peaceful and agreeable to the nature and end of the human race."[10] Fichte says: "Do at each time what thou art determined to do or always fulfill thy destination."[11] Destination according to Fichte appears to be the subordination of all things to one's Ego which constantly moves toward absorption into infinitude — which it will never completely accomplish. Comte says: "Live for others."[12] According

---

[8] See Neubauer in *Wirceburgenses,* Tractatus de Legibus, Vol. 5, c. 1, a. 4, pp. 216–222. Paris, 1880.

[9] *Leviathan,* Chap. XIV. Molesworth's English edition, Vol. III, p. 117.

[10] *De jure naturae et gentium,* Lib. 2, c. 3, § 15.

[11] Johann G. Fichte, *The Science of Ethics,* trans. A. E. Kroeger, p. 159. London, Keegan Paul, 1897.

[12] Levy-Bruhl, *The Philosophy of Auguste Comte,* p. 313.

to Liberatore the ground principle of Thomasius is: "Do what makes the life of man as long-lasting and happy as possible: avoid the opposite."[13] We have already commented on Kant's doctrine: "Act only on that maxim which you can will to become a general law" (see § 117). Herbert Spencer submits: "Every man is free to do what he wills, provided he infringes not upon the equal freedom of any other man."[14] According to Lanz, "the highest law of morality may be expressed in the form of the norm: Be free, or negatively: 'Do not be a slave to forces which tend to compel you to act as they command.' "[15]

The falsity, or at least the inadequacy, of these summations is clear from our explanation of morality. Some have presented the truth but in too vague a fashion as Epicurus when he said, "Follow nature," or the Stoics advising us, "Live according to nature."

Some scholastics have summed up moral obligation as follows: "Love God as your end and everything on account of Him," or "Live comformably to human nature considered in all its essential aspects."[16] Berti says: "All the precepts of the natural law are reduced to two, love of God and one's neighbor."[17] Meyer puts it: "Observe the right order of rational nature sanctioned by God."[18] However, no one better resolved it philosophically or expressed it more aptly than St. Thomas: "Good is to be done and sought for, evil is to be avoided."[19] Like Suarez[20] we may syncopate the phrase of the Angelic Doctor and thus epitomize the whole law: "Do good and avoid evil."

This principle does not mean that every possible good must be done but every good the omission of which would be evil. Reason tells us that any human act which is necessary for man to obtain

---

[13] Matt. Liberatore, *Institutiones Philosophicae*, Vol. III, ed. 5. Neapoli, Giannini, 1871. *Ethica*, n. 102, p. 119.

[14] *The Principles of Ethics*, Part IV, Chap. 6, n. 272, Vol. II, p. 46. New York, Appleton, 1898. Though he offers this as a supreme principle of justice yet in view of his social philosophy one can take this as his over-all principle of morality. Compare Appendix A of the same work, pp. 437–439 of Vol. II and his *Social Statics*, Chap. 6, 1, pp. 67–68.

[15] Henry Lanz, *In Quest of Morals*, p. 148.

[16] Cited by T. Brosnahan, *Adversaria Ethica*, p. 97. Woodstock, 1902.

[17] Jo. Laur. Berti, *De Thelogicis Disciplinis*, T. 2, lib. 20, c. 4, prop. III, pp. 6–7. Venetiis, 1750.

[18] T. Meyer, *Institutiones Juris Naturalis*, Sect. 1, Lib. 3, c. 2, a. 6, Vol. I, p. 253.

[19] *Sum. Theol.*, I–II, q. 94, a. 2.

[20] *De Legibus*, Lib. II, c. VII, n. 5.

the proper goods and the end of human life must be performed; that any act that prevents him from obtaining the same is forbidden.

This principle holds the same primacy in the order of moral truth as the principle of contradiction does in the order of speculative truths. In the latter the subject is something immediately known and from a consideration of the subject we necessarily infer the predicate. In this first principle of the moral order the subject is not something immediately known but once a person, however young, comes to know, either through his own efforts or the instruction of others, what moral good and moral evil are, he immediately forms the judgment that good is to be done and that evil is to be avoided.

237. 2. *Secondary principles* are those conclusions which immediately or by ready inference follow from application of the primary principle to the essential needs and situations of human life. Since good is to be done, parents must rear their children; children must reverence their parents. Since evil is to be avoided, one must not steal or commit murder.

238. 3. *Tertiary principles* are those more difficult conclusions which by a more involved process of reasoning are deducible from the primary and secondary principles and for which the evidence is not so strikingly clear. Thus we shall prove divorce on human authority, dueling, and *all* lying intrinsically evil.

THESIS XV. No man whose reason is developed can in any way be ignorant of the primary principle of the Natural Law; nor is invincible ignorance of the secondary principles possible although at times he may be inculpably ignorant of some tertiary principles.

239. Since infants, the feeble-minded, and the insane are incapable of forming true judgments, they are not subject to moral obligation. However, the average man, whose reason is developed by normal individual effort and assisted by normal parental and social influence will infallibly arrive at certain knowledge of the primary principle of the Natural Law. Invincible ignorance of it is impossible. Nor will a man ever lose his knowledge of this principle unless he loses the light of reason.

PROOF OF PART I

240. *No man whose reason is developed can in any way be ignorant of the primary principle of the Natural Law.*

1. The universal experience of mankind proves this. No one has ever become so depraved as to accept that evil is to be done and good avoided. No man has ever sincerely said with Milton's Satan, "evil, be thou my good."[21] No thinking man has ever actually believed the natural is to be avoided, the unnatural to be done. While depraved men have considered the unnatural to be natural, no one contends on principle that the unnatural is to be done.

2. There is also an *a priori* proof. If invincible ignorance of the primary principle of the Natural Law were possible, this contradiction would follow. The normal man would be equipped with everything necessary to attain his end and at the same time he would *not have knowledge* of the most fundamental norm for attaining it.

Moreover, the formal object of the will is the good and man has an innate tendency to his own good. To contend that a normal person could ever fail to perceive that good is to be done and evil avoided, is to say that the human mind can know no moral truth. This contention is one step removed from universal scepticism.

PART II

241. *No man of developed reason can be invincibly ignorant of the secondary principles of the Natural Law.*

When a child reaches the use of reason, he does not at once know the secondary principles of the Natural Law, that is, those moral truths which immediately follow from the application of the primary principle to the facts of life. Rather, in the course of normal mental development he gradually gains this knowledge so that by the end of his formative years he has a sure grasp of the commands and prohibitions contained in the Decalogue. Failure to attain this knowledge is due to moral perversion for which he is blamable.

242. Much has been said against this position. Ethnological facts are cited to prove whole people's ignorance of the fundamental laws of morality. "The lowest races" have no religion,[22] not even a name for divinity.[23] Darwin[24] and Bridges[25] said the Fuegians had no

---

[21] *Paradise Lost*, Book IV, 110.

[22] Lord Avebury, *Marriage, Totemism and Religion*, p. 138. London, Longmans Green, 1911.

[23] Charles Darwin, *The Descent of Man*, Part I, Chap. III, pp. 93–94. New York, Appleton, 1886.

[24] Charles Darwin, *Journal of Researches Into the Natural History and Geology of the*

knowledge of God. They should have said they saw no evidence of such knowledge. So sacred did these primitive people regard their religion that they jealously guarded it from all strangers. Years later missionaries[26] who won their confidence found them true monotheists.[27]

Again evidence of ignorance is offered which is not ignorance of Natural Law but false application of the law. Thus, a barbarous people knowing that theft is forbidden, steal from strangers under the impression that this is not theft.[28] Others, knowing well that they should honor their parents and not kill, put their parents to death under the mistaken idea that this is not murder but rather the conferring of a needed favor on them.[29]

243. But what of civilized men who are intellectually keen about everything except moral matters? To such sophisticates the term amoral is often euphemistically applied. Are they blamelessly ignorant of the secondary principle of the Natural Law? Let us consider those who once had a clear knowledge of these principles and have willfully allowed their knowledge to become distorted. This results when conscience is throttled. One leads an evil life and yielding to passion forms habits contrary to right reason. The protests of conscience are gradually stilled, and because of the desire for self-righteousness, the mind is

---

Countries Visited During the Voyage of H.M.S. Beagle (Round the World, Under the Command of Capt. Fitz Roy, R.N.), pp. 214–215. London, Murray, 1845, 2 ed.

[25] Thomas Bridges, "Manners and Customs of the Firelanders," *A Voice for South America,* Vol. XIII, p. 181 ff. London, 1866.

[26] Ivan Kologriwof, S.J. (ed.), *God, Man, and the Universe,* p. 263. London, Coldwell, 1937. Wilhelm Schmidt, S.V.D., *Der Ursprung der Gottesidee,* Vol. II, pp. 876 ff., 917 ff. Münster, Aschendorf, 1929.

[27] Andrew Lang's change of opinion is noteworthy. In his *Myth, Ritual and Religion* (Vol. I, pp. 34–39. London, Longmans Green, 1887) he espoused the view of Tylor that the first form of religion was a mere animism which excludes any notion of morality and a Supreme Being. After reading the reports of the Benedictines of New Norcia, Western Australia, and pursuing his own investigations of Australian aborigines, Bushmen, Adamanese, Zulus, North American Indians he reached the conclusion "that there are two chief sources of Religion, (1) the belief . . . in a powerful, moral, eternal omniscient Father and Judge of men; (2) the belief . . . in somewhat of man which may survive the grave." (*The Making of Religion,* p. 301. London, Longmans Green, 1909, 3 ed.) Long ago Plutarch denied that any traveler has come across a city destitute of temples, gods, or sacrifices (*Adversus Coloten,* c. XXXI). The more patiently ethnographic investigation is pursued and the evidence sifted, the more the conclusion is reenforced that there are no peoples without religion. See Wilhelm Schmidt, *op. cit.,* Vol. II.

[28] Edward Westermarck, *The Origin and Development of Moral Ideas,* Vol. II, Chap. 28, p. 20. London, Macmillan, 1917, 2 ed.

[29] *Ibid.,* Vol. I, Chap. 27, p. 390.

perverted to assent that no wrong is being done. Evidently such ignorance is most culpable.

Could a man, because of exposure to false doctrines and bad example in his youth, be invincibly ignorant of the moral law and at the same time be intelligent in other matters? Billot[30] seems to think so. Others say that a man might be a mathematical genius and yet a moral moron.

This is not admissible. First, there would be no defect in the mind of such a person. The mind is not composed of parts, one of which knows financial truth, another aesthetic truth, still another moral truth. If the mind can know some truth, it can know all natural truth. If then it functions normally in other respects, we cannot say that its failure to understand moral truth is due to some intellectual incapacity.

Second, these moral truths are obvious. Since the minds of these persons are shown to be normal by their grasp of other truths, the cause of their ignorance must lie in the will. Thus if a man knows languages very well but is totally ignorant of mathematics, the reason is not that he is incapable of understanding mathematics but that he is not interested in, or dislikes, the subject. So also, if an intelligent person does not know simple moral truths, the reason must be attributed to the will. No one has better expressed this fact than St. Paul: "As they liked not to have God in their knowledge, God delivered them to a reprobate sense."[31]

Therefore, even the victims of perverted rearing are blamable, though with diminished guilt, if they do not know the obvious truths of the Natural Law. The normal mind, as long as it is normal, does not confound the natural with the unnatural, the obviously evil with the good. It is able to differentiate between good and evil and even in the midst of untruth arrive at truth.

PROOF OF PART II

244. *No man of developed reason can be invincibly ignorant of the secondary principles of the Natural Law,* because, otherwise the Natural Law would not be sufficiently promulgated.

1. If the Natural Law were insufficiently promulgated, God would be guilty of folly or inefficiency. The Natural Law is law directive

---

[30] *Etudes,* December, 1920, Vol. 165, p. 515 ff.
[31] Rom. 1:28.

into man's last end, but it could not be such if it were inadequately promulgated.

2. The sole instrument chosen by nature to promulgate the Natural Law is man's intellect. Therefore, the mind eliciting the judgments which form the outstanding precepts of the law must be *naturally infallible*. If it were not, man would not be participating in the Eternal Law. Hence, if man through no fault of his could be ignorant of these principles, there would be a defect not in his willing co-operation but in his very nature, in his intellect. If his intellect is deficient, the Natural Law cannot be promulgated to him.

PROOF OF PART III

245. *A man of developed reason may at times be inculpably ignorant of some tertiary principles of the Natural Law,* because under certain conditions knowledge of them would be a moral impossibility.

1. One is inculpably ignorant if knowledge is morally impossible.

2. Since the tertiary principles are conclusions of rather involved processes of reasoning, the ordinary person who grows up in surroundings where these conclusions are commonly rejected would not have the opportunity and ability to arrive at the truth. Thus he might conclude that divorce and polygamy are allowable. Such ignorance would not be incompatible with nature's purposes because the ends of human life could be sufficiently attained despite it.

III. IS THE NATURAL LAW SUFFICIENT?

246. The Natural Law is not sufficient to direct man in the infinite variety of problems which he encounters. Since the tertiary principles of the Natural Law are not always readily discovered, some authority is needed to declare them. Moreover, the Natural Law does not explicitly indicate how its precepts apply to all cases. If it were left to each individual to decide what concretely constitutes theft, assault, defamation of character, or perjury, chaos would easily result. Therefore, further refinements of the Natural Law are necessary to prevent conflicting opinions and insure harmony among men. Thus, since the Natural Law does not specify in detail how the citizen is to support the State, some other law must. Finally, there is need of some temporal sanction for the enforcement of the Natural Law over and above that which it provides. The law which supplements the Natural Law is *positive law*.

247. *What is positive law?* Positive law is a rule of action freely established by a competent authority for the common good and promulgated not in the nature of the subject but in some external sign, oral or written. This competent authority can be human or divine. Divine positive law proceeds from God, the Author of the supernatural order, but since ethics is primarily concerned with the natural order, our treatment will be restricted to human positive law.

How does positive law differ from Natural Law?

1. The *matter* of Natural Law consists of acts intrinsically good or evil; the matter of positive law is also and chiefly acts intrinsically indifferent.

2. The obligation of Natural Law arises from God's will hypothetically necessary. If God decrees to create man, He must make obligatory the precepts of the Natural Law. The obligation of positive law derives from the free will of a human lawgiver.

3. The *promulgation* of Natural Law is effected by nature and the unaided intellect; of positive law, by some external sign expressly chosen for the purpose.

4. As to *source,* Natural Law proceeds from God immediately as the Author of nature; positive human law, from man immediately, from God mediately; positive divine law, from God the Author of the supernatural order.

5. As to *extension,* Natural Law applies to all men; positive law does not necessarily apply to all. Natural Law is immutable and inseparably bound up with human nature; positive law is not.

THESIS XVI. An inadequate Natural Law must be supplemented by positive law based on the Natural Law.

PROOF OF PART I

248. That the Natural Law is inadequate and must be supplemented from some positive source is proved in §§ 245 and 246.

PROOF OF PART II

249. *Positive law must be based upon the Natural Law,* because otherwise it would not lead man to his last end.

1. All law must lead man to his last end. All things in the universe

less than man are for man and were created to assist him in the prosecution of his last end.

2. The *sole* norm indicated by nature directing man to his last end is the Eternal Law naturally promulgated to man. Any other law would not lead him to his last end.

250. *Positive law is based on the Natural Law* in either of two ways: (*a*) the matter of a positive law may be the same as that of the Natural Law, or (*b*) where the matter is different, the obligatory force of positive law is derived from the precept of the Natural Law that the laws of legitimate rulers are to be obeyed. Therefore positive law may be declarative and determinative.

1. Positive law is *declarative law* inasmuch as it commands or forbids what is commanded or forbidden by the Natural Law, or more clearly applies the Natural Law to specific cases, or enjoins what is necessarily deducible from the Natural Law as requisite for good living. Both the content and the binding force of such law comes immediately from the Natural Law and is positive only in its mode of promulgation and the special sanction — if any — which attaches to it. Such is the moral law — not the liturgical law — given to Moses on Mount Sinai as well as the common law defining fornication, perjury, robbery, homosexuality, and providing civil penalties for the same. The greater part of the criminal codes of nations is but a more definite enunciation of the Natural Law.

2. Positive law is *determinative law* which enjoins what is not an evident deduction from the Natural Law. It is human authority commanding or forbidding actions in themselves morally indifferent but whose presence or absence are here and now deemed necessary or useful to the common good. An example is the provision of our Constitution that the function of sovereignity be distributed among three coequal and mutually interchecking departments of government. While the Natural Law commands that the State be financially supported, it does not determine that this should be done by a levy on real estate or by a tax on income or on the sale of merchandise. Any further discussion of positive law is the province of special ethics.

READINGS

St. Thomas, *Summa Theologica,* I–II, 94–96.
——— *Contra Gentiles,* III, 122.
Cathrein, Victor, S.J., *Philosophia Moralis,* pp. 171–182. Friburgi Brisgoviae, Herder, 1915, ed. 10.

Meyer, Theodore, S.J., *Institutiones Juris Naturalis,* Vol. I, pp. 237–262. Friburgi Brisgoviae, Herder, 1906, ed. altera.
Miltner, Charles, C.S.C., *Elements of Ethics,* pp. 81–89. New York, Macmillan, 1932.
Nivard, Marcel, S.J., *Ethica,* pp. 144–152. Paris, Beauchesne, 1928.
Rickaby, Joseph J., S.J., *Aquinus Ethicus,* Vol. I, pp. 283–287.
—— *Moral Philosophy,* pp. 144–152.
Suarez, *De Legibus,* L. II, cc. 8, 13, 14, 15.

CHAPTER VIII

CONSCIENCE

251. Thus far we have treated of the Natural Law in general, the objective norm of morality. We now turn to a consideration of the norm within man which distinguishes right from wrong, the subjective norm of morality.

One of man's greatest gifts is self-direction. He is equipped for this function with intellect, which enables him to discern the true way to his ultimate destiny. This faculty guides him in two ways. First, it sets up a moral code by disclosing those general principles of morality we called the Natural Law. However, in addition to knowledge of these general principles, man must understand the application of the law to particular circumstances. Herein lies the second moral function of reason, namely, the ability so to apply the law to the daily happenings of life that one can discern right acts from wrong acts. This moral guidance a man must supply for himself. Only his own mind tells him which of his actions are right and which wrong. We give the name conscience to reason fulfilling this function of moral guidance.

252. *What conscience is not.* Conscience is not:

1. *Consciousness,* or intellectual awareness of our own internal acts.

2. *Intellect,* or the light of reason. Conscience and intellect are most intimately connected since intellect is the potency, or faculty, of which conscience is the act. By metonomy the name of one is used for the other.

3. *Synteresis,* or habitual knowledge of moral principles. Conscience is not a habit but an act.

253. *What moral conscience is.*

1. *In a broad sense* conscience includes all intellectual acts which discern the goodness or badness of a concrete human act either past, present, or future.

Concerning past or present acts conscience acts as witness or judge testifying, or adjudging, that what I am doing or have done is worthy or unworthy. Thus, preparatory to confession, a Catholic examines his conscience, judging which of his past acts are morally bad. A man may feel the sting of remorse for years after doing a particularly base or sordid deed. In the very act of wrongdoing one may experience an uneasy conscience. The tranquillity of conscience following our good acts is the perception of the spiritual delectable good consequent upon acts that truly perfect us. We give the name *consequent conscience* to the moral judgment concerning what we have done or are doing. Its function is to testify, approve, accuse, or excuse. Since it follows the human act which it judges, consequent conscience cannot serve as the moral guide to that act.

254. 2. *In the strict sense* conscience is the last practical judgment concerning the moral goodness or badness of a human act here and now to be performed. Conscience, as guide, is not concerned with past or present acts but only with future acts. It is not concerned with acts of the remote future which may never present themselves for decision. Conscience is called a practical judgment because it is concerned not with speculation but with action. It is, however, a practical application of speculative truths already possessed. It is called the "last" judgment because it immediately precedes the resolution of the will to act or not to act. It is that immediate intellectual light shed upon the proposed act without which the act would not be a human act. We call it *antecedent conscience.*

Immediately prior to the will's free determination, the mind elicits a judgment — which is conscience — informing the agent that the act he contemplates or its omission is one of the following: (*a*) necessarily good and commanded, and hence to be done; (*b*) good but not commanded, better than its opposite and therefore counseled; (*c*) bad and therefore forbidden; (*d*) neither commanded nor forbidden, to be done or omitted as one chooses.

This practical judgment is not intuitive. It is the result of a reasoning process, the conclusion of an implicit syllogism. The major premise is some universal law, a precept of the Natural Law, or an edict of positive law. The minor is the enunciation of a pertinent fact applying the universal truth of the major to this particular act. The conclusion is the dictate of conscience. The following is an example:

Stealing is wrong.
But changing the figures on this check is stealing.
Therefore changing these figures is wrong.

Usually this is an instantaneous process. It is only in obscure and difficult cases that one is aware of a formal process of reasoning.

255. There is no need to demonstrate that *antecedent conscience* is the moral guide of our individual acts. It is simply that knowledge absolutely requisite to make the will act a human act. There can be no dispute that this judgment of conscience is the necessary guiding light of the will.

Three closely related problems arise concerning this judgment: (*a*) Is there an obligation to act in accordance with it? (*b*) What degree of certainty is sufficient to induce moral obligation? (*c*) How does one arrive at such a degree of certainty?

I. THE OBLIGATORY FORCE OF CONSCIENCE

256. *Conscience may be correct or incorrect.*

1. Conscience is *correct* when it conforms with the law. The major of one's reasoning process is the enunciation of a valid law, the minor is a correct application of this law to this concrete case. Hence the resultant dictate of conscience is true.

2. When conscience misrepresents the law or pertinent facts it is *erroneous*. Either that which has been apprehended as law is not law or the law has been wrongly applied. The failure of conscience to conform to the law may be due to invincible or vincible error. (1) Invincible error is error which cannot be avoided despite the care and diligence which a good and prudent man should give. For example, a working minor might think he can secretly hold back part of his wages from his father; a mother might imagine she can appropriate to general family use a gift of money expressly intended for one child only. (2) Vincible error is error which can be avoided with effort commensurate with the importance of the matter. Examples are the refusal of some people to see any wrong in cheating a railroad or public utility or in petty stealing from a department store.

257. As the law commands, forbids, and allows, so does conscience. What obedience must we give to it?

THESIS XVII. Whenever conscience commands or forbids, it must be obeyed both when it is correct and when it is invincibly erroneous. A vincibly erroneous conscience must be corrected.

PROOFS

258. *A correct conscience must be obeyed,* because it is nothing other than the moral law applying to this particular case.

259. *An invincibly erroneous conscience must be obeyed.*

If a man is not obliged to follow an invincibly erroneous conscience, he is not obliged to follow a correct conscience. Precisely because the error is invincible a man has no means of detecting it. Hence he cannot distinguish between a correct conscience and an invincibly erroneous conscience. Both are the same to him. Hence if he must obey in one case, he must obey in the other.

The same conclusion follows from a consideration of the will act. The will act becomes good or bad inasmuch as it embraces an object, not as the object is in itself, but as the object is presented by the intellect as good or bad.

260. *A vincibly erroneous conscience must be corrected.*

One is obliged to attain necessary truth as far as he can. But whoever acts with a vincibly erroneous conscience has not attained necessary truth as far as he can. Therefore, whoever acts with a vincibly erroneous conscience has failed to fulfill an obligation. Therefore, a vincibly erroneous conscience must be corrected.

261. Corollary. Since conscience is the subjective norm of morality, each one is obliged to see to it that his conscience corresponds with the objective norm, the law. Hence, with industry commensurate with one's years, training, and state of life, one should learn what his moral obligations are — both those he has in common with all men and those applying to himself as an individual. This duty is especially urgent when moral doubts arise and persist. Then a person must investigate what the moral law is and how it applies to himself. To fail to take reasonable measures to solve such doubts is equivalent to assuming a state of affected ignorance, which is quite blameworthy.

II. THE REQUISITE QUALITY OF CONSCIENCE

262. Every correct conscience is a particular declaration of the moral law. But when does one *know* that his conscience represents the moral law? Three states of knowledge are possible. One may be

(a) *absolutely certain,* that is, have no fear that one's judgment is wrong; (b) *prudently certain,* that is, have no *reasonable* fear that the opposite is true; (c) *doubtful,* that is, be unable to form a certain judgment.

263. Therefore (a) a *certain conscience* is a moral judgment one adheres to without any fear of the opposite being true. (b) A *prudently certain conscience* is a firm assent in moral matters against which no positive probability militates. It represents a state of mind distinguishable from strict certitude and mere probability. In strict certitude all fear of the truth of the opposite is legitimately excluded: mere probability is accompanied by a reasonable fear of the truth of the opposite whereas prudent certitude excludes all *reasonable* fear of error. This is also called broad moral certitude and seems to participate in the nature of both certitude and probability: of certitude because firm assent is rendered; of probability because all fear of error has not been excluded. Objectively it is the highest kind of probability; subjectively, it is firm assent given where error is not absolutely impossible though it rarely occurs. (c) A *doubtful conscience* is an assent rendered to one of two contradictory moral propositions with a reasonable fear that the rejected proposition may be equally true. One may buy a ticket to a show guessing that it may be clean but fearing that it may not. Which of these three types of moral judgment is required for a morally good act?

THESIS XVIII. It is always wrong to act with a doubtful conscience. A prudently certain conscience suffices for upright action.

PROOF OF PART I

264. *It is always wrong to act with a doubtful conscience,* because by so acting one does not avoid evil as far as he can.

1. Whoever acts with a doubtful conscience has a serious suspicion that his act is wrong.

2. We are obliged to avoid evil as far as we can. Unless we remove the reasonable suspicion that our act is wrong before proceeding to act, we are not avoiding evil as far as we can. The reason is that whoever wills to act regardless of this suspicion, must will the law's violation, which is always wrong. If a man about to discard a cigarette packet suspects that it contains a cigarette and does not resolve his doubt,

he cannot throw away the packet without willing to throw away a cigarette.

265. Corollary I. *A person in doubt must investigate before acting.* A person with a doubtful conscience who acts without investigation does wrong. If direct investigation yields no solution, one may not proceed to act. The dictum of common sense — in doubt never act — also applies to the realm of conscience. However, if one is compelled to act under such circumstances, he has the equivalent of a perplexed conscience, which is treated in § 268.

Corollary II. By acting with a doubtful conscience one assumes the specific guilt of the sin about which he was in doubt.

PROOF OF PART II

266. *A prudently certain conscience suffices for upright action.*

If one is always wrong when he acts with a doubtful conscience, must one have a certain conscience? The strict moral certitude of epistemology cannot be demanded.

Strict certitude is not requisite for human acts. If action had to be suspended until such certitude were attained, man would be reduced to almost complete inactivity. Therefore, a prudently certain conscience suffices, because it excludes all reasonable fear of wrongdoing.

267. From the standpoint of one's habitual mode of forming his conscience, four types of conscience may be distinguished, namely, scrupulous, perplexed, lax, and tender.

1. *Scrupulous conscience.* Scrupulosity is a habit of mind inclining one to judge for slight reasons that moral evil exists where actually it does not. Scrupulous persons refrain from many innocent acts. In performing good acts they are tormented often by a false conscience which makes them feel that they are doing wrong; after the act they constantly worry whether or not they did wrong. They are so troubled over the past that confession becomes a torment. They can become so haunted by the constant thought of wrongdoing or of unforgiven sin that they lose peace of mind. Scrupulosity, however, should be carefully distinguished from remorse over a wicked past.

The scrupulous person should first be made to realize that he is suffering from a form of abnormality. Scrupulosity may be the result of a naturally indecisive temperament; it may be a symptom of a mental disorder; it may be due to some physical disturbance; or it may be a special trial sent by God. Second, this person should blindly submit to a prudent adviser and boldly follow his advice. He then should endeavor to act as other good people act convincing himself that what is right for them is also right for him. It is important that he constantly exercise himself in hope and confidence in God.

268. 2. The *perplexed conscience* is somewhat like the scrupulous conscience. However, unlike the scrupulous conscience, it does not connote a state of doubt but only a single instance. The perplexed conscience is one to which two alternatives are proposed and both seem evil. Thus, one may be torn between the duty of not lying and the duty of parental loyalty. If he defends his father he lies; if he does not defend him he is disloyal. One is never obliged to do evil. If duties seem to conflict, one should do what appears to be the better act. If one cannot obtain advice, he should choose what seems most reasonable in the circumstances, that is, the farthest removed from evil. While the layman may not know the theologian's rules for settling one's conscience, the intelligent person follows the maxim, "I do the best I can."

269. 3. *Lax conscience.* Laxity is a habit of mind which inclines us to avoid obligation for trifling and insufficient reasons. Thus, many people think there is no obligation to find the owner of lost articles; some unmarried people consider petting harmless, and some married people see no wrong in contraceptive birth control. A lax conscience is the result of too frivolous an attitude toward life, constant desire to avoid the unpleasant, the shirking of responsibility, deliberate and affected ignorance of the moral law. The truly lax conscience is at least an unconscious rejection of the law and if logically pursued leads to the conclusion that there is no such thing as wrongdoing. In the eyes of the lax person everything he does is natural and right simply because he does it. The voice of conscience is stifled to the point that the person may go to the length of sinning against the light.

270. 4. *Tender conscience.* A person of tender conscience is inclined correctly to be aware of the smallest elements of moral evil. Too often this type of conscience is confused with the scrupulous conscience. For example we may call a man scrupulously honest when we mean that he is exactly honest. A scrupulous conscience is a false conscience; a tender conscience is exact and true.

III. THE SOLUTION OF DOUBTS

271. We have seen that every dictate of conscience must be prudently certain. Man arrives at certain moral judgments by the direct method and the indirect method. In the case of the direct method, both the moral law and the pertinent facts are clear and certain. A householder, for example, knows with certainty he must discharge his debts as soon as he can conveniently do so. Let us say that he owes his grocer five dollars. He receives his pay check, and he has the money to pay the debt. He at once knows with certainty that he must discharge his debt without undue delay.

The direct method is the ordinary procedure for the normal person. Frequently he experiences no special difficulty in forming his conscience with certainty. His difficulty is obedience to conscience.

272. But occasionally the normal person, and very often the scrupulous person, encounters a doubt which prevents the immediate formation of a certain conscience. Thus one may be uncertain of the moral law. For example, one may be uncertain about the obligation of restoring stolen goods received in good faith, or whether a husband may invalidate a vow taken by his wife. Many people have only confused knowledge of some moral principles. Or again one may doubt about the existence or nature of a fact capable of applying the law to a particular case. A man knows that he should not appropriate another's property but he may be uncertain whether the article which he is about to put into his bag belongs to himself or a stranger. Certainly if one knew all the facts which enter into a given case and knew all the laws which touch upon it, he would have immediate certitude as to the course to follow. No doubt could be possible because *objectively* nothing in morals is doubtful. Objectively either a law is or it is not; either this is a pertinent fact or it is not. But because the human mind is so often incapable of arriving at the truth with certainty in a complex and involved situation, subjectively one is left in doubt.

When after due investigation our knowledge of the moral law or of pertinent facts does not lead us to an immediate and certain conclusion, recourse is had to the *indirect* or reflex method. Doubts of conscience are practical obstacles to a good life and moral science offers a means of solving these doubts. This method of evolving a certain dictate is called indirect or reflex because when all direct available knowledge fails to produce certainty one has recourse to a further set of principles, or a process of reflection in the hope of attaining certainty.

273. All doubts of conscience fall into one of two categories. Unless the nature of these two categories is understood and a clear-cut difference is noted between them, one will not be quite competent to solve his personal doubts because the categories are governed by entirely different principles.

274. 1. *Doubt about appropriate means to fulfill obligation.* We have reference here to the situation in which a person has a definite and certain obligation of *efficaciously attaining some determined end* but is in doubt about the means to attain the end. His problem is not merely whether the contemplated act is good or bad but, first, whether it will be the appropriate means to his end. The goodness or badness of his act will depend on whether it is a fitting or unfitting means to the end.

Doubts of this type are solved by this reflex principle: *One must always choose the safer means.* Hence, where an obligation must be safeguarded and two means present themselves, one more probably efficacious than the other, one must always choose the more probable means. The validity of this principle is clear from the following cases.

a) *Means necessary to salvation.* Salvation is an end which must be insured beyond possibility of doubt. Of the means at hand, those must be chosen which most surely lead to this end. Hence, though there is a probability that an infidel might save his soul without becoming a member of the Church, he cannot rest upon such a probability but must take the safer course and enter the Church.

b) *Validity of an act.* If a person doubts whether there is a diriment impediment to a contemplated marriage, he cannot marry on the strength of the probability that no impediment exists; he must choose the safer course of making an investigation and consulting proper authority. If he does not do this, he takes the chance of contracting an invalid marriage.

c) *Safeguarding rights certainly existent.* A hunter may not fire at what probably is a beast but which might be a man. If I owe a man ten dollars and have two bills, one probably genuine, the other certainly genuine, I may not endanger the discharge of that debt by giving in payment what is merely probably genuine. A physician must choose between two doubtful remedies that which more probably will restore his patient to health; an agent, overseer, or lawyer must take that course which more surely will protect their principal's interests; a judge or juryman must choose the solution which is more probably just.

THESIS XIX. If a person has an absolute obligation to attain some determined end and is in doubt as to the means of fulfilling this obligation, he must follow the more probable argument and choose the safer means.

PROOF

275. The absolute obligation of attaining an end extends to the choice of means toward the end. If certain means exist, they must be chosen. If certain means do not exist and one must choose among those available, one must always choose what appears more apt. To choose what appears less apt is unreasonably to endanger attainment of the end. Therefore, in any doubt as to the means of fulfilling such an obligation, one must always follow the more probable argument and choose the safer means.

Corollary. Whoever solves such a doubt by following the less probable argument does wrong.

276. 2. *Doubt about the goodness or badness of an act.* We have reference here to the situation where a person has no obligation of attaining a determined end but is in doubt as to the *liceity or nonliceity, the sinfulness or nonsinfulness, of the act.* In the first type of doubt considered, obligation exists and the doubt concerns the means of fulfilling it. In the second type, the doubt is *whether an obligation exists.* There are six different theories on the latter.

a) Rigorism. Whenever a doubt arises as to the presence of moral obligation, a person is under moral obligation until he becomes *certain* of the contrary. The principle of rigorism is: "Law obliges until its nonexistence is certain." Hence man must act upon the supposition that he is morally obligated until the argument for freedom from obligation is certain. Thus in a national crisis a youth weighs the thought: have I a moral obligation to volunteer for military service? According to rigorism he must volunteer unless he is certain he should not.

b) Tutiorism. This is a mitigated form of rigorism. According to this theory moral obligation is present unless I am *most probably* certain that it is not. Its principle is: "Law obliges unless its nonexistence is most probable." Moral obligation exists until I have a most probable argument for freedom from it. Hence in the example given, the youth would have to volunteer unless he were most probably certain that he should not.

c) *Probabiliorism.* Moral obligation exists unless the argument against it is more probable. Its principle is: "Law obliges unless its nonexistence is more probable." Hence the youth would have to volunteer unless the argument for staying home were more probable than the argument against it. This doctrine had some rabid adherents in the seventeenth century but it has long since been entirely abandoned.

d) *Equiprobabilism.* Whenever doubt arises, moral obligation is presumed to exist. It ceases to bind only by an equally probable argument to the contrary. Its principle is: "Law obliges unless its nonexistence is equally probable as its existence." One becomes free from obligation only when the argument for freedom is equally as good as the argument for obligation. Hence the youth is not obliged to volunteer if the argument for staying home is as good as the reason for volunteering.

e) *Probabilism.* Moral obligation binds only when its existence is certain. Its principle is: "A doubtful law does not oblige." When the argument against obligation is based on solid probability, there is no law and no obligation even though the argument for obligation has a greater probability. Thus, as long as the youth had a solidly probable reason against volunteering he was free to stay home even though the argument for volunteering was more probable.

f) *Laxism.* Moral obligation vanishes in the presence of any reason against it. The principle is: "Law does not exist when there is the slightest reason to doubt its existence." Even a tenuous and trifling argument in favor of freedom from obligation is sufficient to excuse one.

The doctrines of rigorism and laxism are patently false, the former because it demands the morally impossible of human nature; the latter because it is equivalent to a denial of the moral law. Of the remaining four we choose to defend probabilism.

THESIS XX. In solving doubts of conscience in which the sole act, one may follow a genuinely probable opinion against obligation even though there is a more probable opinion for obligation.
point at issue is the goodness or badness of one's contemplated

277. Probabilism holds that if an obligation is doubtful, one may disregard it even though the argument for obligation is more probable than the argument against it. This does not mean that we may do what is *probably right* but may be more probably wrong. To believe so would be a serious misunderstanding of probabilism. No one may do what is probably wrong. What we do must be *certainly right*. What probabilism does hold is that when we act on the principle that a doubtful obligation is no obligation we are certainly right.

Probabilism is based on these epistemological truths: (*a*) what is probable cannot be certain, what is certain cannot be probable; (*b*) probability is ultimately subjective; (*c*) in a conflict of probabilities, the most probable proposition does not destroy the probability of the opposite proposition; the less probable one may objectively be the true one.

278. A *genuinely probable opinion* is one to which a sincere and prudent man may reasonably assent. If there is reliable evidence, he must necessarily assent; but if reliable evidence is lacking, he is free to choose either of two probable alternatives, provided he has reasons which are genuine, comparable, and practical. A genuine reason is one which has a sound basis and is neither frivolous nor ridiculous. It may be intrinsic, that is, an argument from the nature of the case, or extrinsic, that is, an argument from the word of a competent authority. It is comparably probable when it remains not unlikely after examination of opposing reasons. It is practical when it has taken into account the actual circumstances of the case.

When, therefore, a genuinely probable opinion indicates that there is no obligation, the person is free, the reason being that the law imposing obligation is here and now a doubtful law and *a doubtful law is no law*.

PROOF

279. Probabilism is valid because *an uncertain law can induce no obligation*.

1. A law against which a genuinely probable opinion militates cannot be certain, for certitude and probability mutually exclude each other.

2. If an uncertain law could beget a certain obligation, the effect would be greater than its cause, since obligation is the effect of law.

A person therefore is free to disregard an uncertain law even when a more probable opinion favors its existence.

280. The truth of this demonstration can be made evident by this illustration. I am asked to give blood to a cousin who is critically ill. On the one hand piety and charity incline me to assist a kinsman in distress. On the other, to do so I will have to sacrifice important business; besides I am not sure whether my health warrants it. I probably have no moral obligation to give the blood; it is more probable that I have such an obligation. In such a conflict of probabilities one could not justly tell me that I *must* give the blood.

If a person comes to me for advice and relates a story involving similar conflicting probabilities, I could not rightly tell him that he had to do what was only of uncertain obligation. It would be wrong of me to convert an uncertain obligation into a certain obligation. I could tell him he was under no obligation. If, therefore, I could justly give such advice to another, I can morally follow such a way of acting myself.

Probabilism offers a sure and ready solution to the anxieties of conscience. Provided my reason is worthy of an honest man, I can readily reach a certain dictate of conscience. Compared with other systems, it has this practical advantage: where they demand a more probable or equally probable argument, probabilism merely asks for a genuinely probable reason. In many cases to seek a more probable or equally probable reason would only prolong one's doubt. We have no nicely balanced moral scales to assay the value of probabilities.

Probabilism, like any other principle, may be abused. If a person imagines probabilism to be a license to pare one's obligations down to the barest minimum and converts it into a clever scheme whereby a certain conscience can be rendered probable and obligation avoided, he is not a probabilist but a laxist. The probabilist readily recognizes certain obligation. Probabilism is not an instrument to blunt the keen edge of obligation. Nor is it to be used for the daily formation of one's conscience; it is reserved for the crisis of doubt.

The function of probabilism is to cut the knot of doubt and rigidly expose the extent of one's obligation. It does not pretend to counsel the better course of action. If one chooses he may assume as obligations what are only probably obligatory: one may be as strict as he chooses on himself but he may not impose uncertain obligations upon others as though they were certain.

READINGS

St. Thomas, *Summa Theologica,* I, 79, a. 13; I–II, 19, a. 5–6.

Ballerini-Palmieri, Vol. I, pp. 145–160. Prati, Giachetti, 1889.

Catholic Encyclopedia, "Conscience," IV–268.

Davis, Henry, S.J., *Moral and Pastoral Theology,* Vol. I, pp. 64–115. New York, Sheed and Ward, 1936.

De Lehen, F., S.J., *The Way of Interior Peace,* p. 268 ff. New York, Benziger, 1888 (trans. from German).

Healey, Edmund. F., S.J., *Moral Guidance,* pp. 27–35. Chicago, Loyola University, 1942.

Koch-Preuss, *Handbook of Moral Theology,* Vol. I, pp. 182–202. St. Louis, Herder, 1919.

Leibel, J. F. (ed.), *Readings in Ethics,* pp. 342–354. Chicago, Loyola University, 1926.

Noldin-Schmitt, *Summa Theologia Moralis,* Vol. I, pp. 208–258. Oeniponte, Rauch, 1938.

Sabetti-Barrett, *Compendium Theologiae Moralis,* pp. 35–73. Neo Eboraci, Pustet, 1920, ed. 29.

Slater, Thomas, S.J., *Manual of Moral Theology,* Vol. I, pp. 57–79. New York, Benziger, 1909.

CHAPTER IX

VIRTUE AND VICE

281. Ethics is not only a science; it is also an art. The supremely important result of the pursuit of both the science of ethics and the art of ethics is that one perform morally good acts and avoid evil acts. It is one thing to learn from the science of ethics what orderly human conduct is; it is another and a better thing to be skilled in the art of ethics so that we not only can do good and avoid evil but also that we acquire facility and, if possible, perfect ease in the same.

We have laid down the fundamental objective principles of the science of ethics, the norm of morality, and the Natural Law. There are also subjective moral principles, namely, conscience or intellect, discerning the lawful and the unlawful, and the will choosing good or evil. These faculties can be conditioned for permanent facility in performing certain types of acts. If this is not done, the human agent experiences difficulty in performing requisite acts. Since habit, super-induced on intellect and will, gives man a readiness, even an ease, in doing good or evil, it is called a subjective coprinciple of morality.

I. HABIT

282. In the most general sense, habit is a quality whereby the existence or operation of a substance is permanently affected for better or worse. Habits which affect the existence of a substance are entitative habits, such as shape or color. Those which affect its operation are operative habits. Ethics is concerned exclusively with operative habits, and these are called simply habits.

A. The Nature of Habit

283. Habit is a stable quality superadded to a faculty whereby the faculty's capacity to act in a variety of ways is canalized to produce readily and easily a particular kind of act. Habit is difficult to change and in this respect it differs from *disposition,* which changes easily. Moods come and go; habits abide. Habit differs from faculty because habit presupposes an initial potency which it perfects. One cannot have the skill of a swimmer or gymnast if he is unable to move his limbs. Both habit and faculty are immediate principles of action but faculty is a natural endowment whereas habit is the acquisition of the agent. Habit adds an intrinsic perfection to faculty. Hence it is a real modification of the agent's nature which abides with him in the intervals between one occasion for its exercise and another. The skill of an eloquent pleader or a fine surgeon remains with him even when he is playing cards or fishing. Finally, habit differs from mere custom or routine, which of itself involves no skill or facility. One may be accustomed to going to bed every night at ten or seeing a movie every Friday, but there is no skill or added potency in such routine.

284. A faculty which acts in only one way cannot be modified by habit. Water will not boil faster if it has been boiled ten times before. Habit belongs to living things. It has two distinguishing features. (*a*) It presupposes *activity illumined by knowledge.* Physiological activities which are not governable by reason, such as the beating of the heart and the circulation of the blood, are not habits. However, certain vegetative and sensitive activities can be sufficiently controlled by reason so that we rightly speak of good hygienic habits of eating and rest. Although brutes have ways of acting which resemble habits, habit is more properly a perfection of the rational nature because (*b*) *it operates under the direction of the will.* While seals and elephants may be trained to repeat certain acts, these acts are not habits in the true sense because animals have no will. Essentially habit is something usable at will. In man those habits which become mere reflex actions are routine. They are not habits ethically speaking for the acts which proceed therefrom are not human acts and have no moral significance.

B. *The Value of Habit*

285. Habit has as *its end product a particular act easily done, well done, perfectly done.* The permanent ability to do this is well named a second nature. Habit understood in the wider meaning of custom or routine has also very practical advantages. William James aptly remarks: "The great thing is to make our nervous system our ally instead of our enemy. For this we must make automatic and habitual, as early as possible, as many useful actions as we can and guard against growing into ways that are disadvantageous to us. The more of the details of our daily life we can hand over to the effortless custody of automatism, the more our higher powers of mind will be set free for their proper work. There is no more miserable human being than one in whom nothing is more habitual than indecision and for whom the lighting of every cigar, the drinking of every cup, the time of rising and going to bed and the beginning of every bit of work, are subjects of express volitional deliberation."[1]

One of the ends of education is the formation of proper psychological habits and the avoidance of undesirable ones. Everyone should have a system of daily living. It should not be a rigid plan but should admit of reasonable exception. Advantageous as these routines are, the less voluntary they become, the more they recede from the ambit of ethics.

C. The Origin of Habit

286. Once an act is completed, its effect on the agent is not terminated. A sort of residue, which is the tendency to repeat the act, remains in the agent. Hence habit is the act continued. Habits are caused by the repetition of the same kind of act. Ease in accomplishment comes in no other way than by doing a thing often. Aristotle puts it: "Men become builders by building and lyre players by playing the lyre; so too, we become just by doing just acts, temperate by doing temperate acts, brave by doing brave acts."[2]

The initial acts of a habit are performed with difficulty, fitfully perhaps, and by special effort. If one or other of these acts is done excellently it is due to chance — beginner's luck — and is not reproducible at will. Drudgery and repetition intervene between the first act and accomplished execution. Practice alone makes perfect. Habit is a living thing which feeds on acts and the more frequently and intensely the act is performed the deeper the habit is implanted.

Psychologists offer these valuable suggestions for the development of good habits: (a) To break off a bad habit or to implant a new one begin with as intense and determined an initial effort as possible for great starting power is needed to overcome the inertia of nonmovement. (b) Never allow an exception, permit no small deviations from your resolve, until the new habit is securely rooted in your life.

---

[1] William James, *Principles of Psychology*, Vol. I, p. 122. New York, Holt, 1923.
[2] *Ethics*, II, 1, 1103a.

(c) Seize every first possible opportunity to act on every resolution formed and on every emotional prompting in the direction of the habits desired.

As habits grow by repeated acts of the same sort, so they are diminished by contrary acts. Unexercised, a habit languishes, disintegrates, and finally passes away. One forgets a language he no longer reads or speaks: the habit of chastity is utterly wrecked by constant unchaste acts.

287. The *ethical habit* is skill in the performance of moral acts. As it is important for man to acquire corporal and psychological habits which make for efficient daily living, so it is eminently worth while for him to cultivate habits of ethical conduct. Ethical habits reside in man's moral faculties and are of two general kinds. Habits which perfect the moral faculties and are productive of acts conducing to man's last end are called *virtues*. Habits which degrade man and incline him to activity leading him away from his last end are called *vices*. Virtue and vice play a large part in the loss or attainment of beatitude and may not be lightly passed over in any ethical treatise.

II. VIRTUE

288. Two of the most fascinating and oft discussed questions among the ancient Greek philosophers were: (a) *What is virtue?* and (b) *Who is the virtuous man?* Virtue derives from the Latin, *virtus,* which means "power." This word in turn comes from *vir,* or "man."

289. In its most general sense, virtue is the excellence of a thing according to its kind, its due perfection. It is the virtue of the ear to hear, of the legs to walk. So, on the contrary, vice is a flaw, a lack of due perfection. But virtue is more than a mere power to act — it is potency to *work well.* "Every virtue," says Aristotle, "both brings into good condition the thing of which it is the excellence and makes the work of that thing to be well done; e.g., the excellence of the eye makes both the eye and its work good . . . therefore, the virtue of man will be a state of character which makes a man good and makes him do his own work well."[3] Therefore, virtue is a habit perfecting man as man and inclining him to do well the good acts of man. St. Augustine calls this a good habit consonant with our nature;[4] and St. Thomas, a good operative habit.[5]

---

[3] *Ibid.,* II, 6, 1106a.

[4] *De Diversis Quaestionibus,* LXXXIII, q. 31.   [5] *Sum. Theol.,* I–II, 55, a. 2.

Virtue is a principle whence good acts easily flow, the power *to choose well* what befits a man. Man is a being subject to rule and his perfection lies in conformity to that rule. Human evil consists in nonconformity with the rule by going too far or not going far enough. Virtue consists in conformity with the rule by striking the midpoint between excess and defect. This is the *auream mediocritatem* (the golden mean) which Horace[6] applies both to human desires and literary composition. "We often say," Aristotle remarks, "of good works of art that it is not possible to take away or add anything, implying that excess and defect destroy the goodness of works of art, while the mean preserves it; and if virtue is more exact and better than any art, as nature also is, then virtue must have the quality of aiming at the mean."[7]

290. Some authors speak of a mean in intellectual acts so that a judgment falls short of the mean by false negation and exceeds it by false affirmation. The mean, however, exists only for activities subject to the choice of the will. There is no mean for an activity moved by necessity toward its proper object. The intellect is necessitated by objective evidence to affirm truth. Since every judgment affirms or denies the identity of two objective concepts, there is no middle ground between an affirmation and a denial of identity. Hence a judgment is good or bad solely in that it is true or false.

The mean in our will act is not a thing of mathematical exactness, the center of two equidistant extremes. It is that mean which *objectively,* here and now is the best for this particular agent. Thus, virtue in the control of our emotions means that one does not check them too much or too little but permits them to be aroused at the right time, toward the right object, with reference to the right people, from the right motive, in the right measure. In observing justice toward our fellow man there is a clearly recognizable mean. We act justly toward him when we give him what is his own, no more, no less. But in the control of self, the mean of virtue varies from person to person and circumstance to circumstance. What would be temperate drinking for one man would be excessive for another. What then determines the mean of virtue? Right reason as employed in the varying circumstances of life by a man of practical wisdom. The chief obstacle to such wisdom is our bias for the pleasant.

[6] *Odes,* Bk. II, Ode X; *Ars Poetica,* 25–31.
[7] *Ethics,* II, 6, 1106b.

291. The virtuous man, therefore, is endowed with habits that incline him to act readily in accord with right reason. He is thereby correctly ordered to his last end and supreme good. He is *the good man*. But how do we recognize the good man, that is, *what habits must a man possess in order to be truly good?*

292. The answer to this question depends upon one's fundamental view of morality, upon what one sets up as the norm of morality. To Kant the good man is one who obeys the dictates of reason from the sole motive of duty. But there is no point in restating doctrines already refuted (§§ 105–121). Let us rather turn to the Greek philosophers who so earnestly studied this question and so carefully expounded the idea of virtue.

Socrates taught that virtue is knowledge and vice is ignorance. "Those who knew," he says, "what were just and righteous acts would prefer nothing else, while those who did not know them could not do them if they would."[8] In this he is followed by Plato the whole theme of whose Meno is that virtue is understanding. In the *Protagoras* Plato says: "No man voluntarily pursues evil, or that which he thinks to be evil. To prefer evil to good is not in human nature."[9] The Stoics, emphasizing the need of overcoming difficulty, said the good man was the brave and enduring man. Horace, expressing the doctrine of Epicurus, sums up all virtue in his famous phrase, *nil admirari:*[10] the wise man is one of undisturbed mind, cushioned against the shocks and surprises of fate by unfailing tranquillity.

The opinion of Socrates is not a mere literary museum piece. Modern literature often re-echoes the opinion of the old sage. Understanding makes human relationships, says a certain Gubsky, meaning that to get along with a man all that is required is that one know him thoroughly. *What then are good habits of mind? Do they suffice to make a man unqualifiedly good,* i.e., totally good, correctly ordered to his last end?

III. INTELLECTUAL VIRTUES

293. The intellect may be endowed with a number of good habits assisting both its speculative and practical activities. The following virtues may be distinguished.

1. *Intuition* is insight into, and facility for, grasping self-evident

---

[8] Xenophon, *Memorabilia*, III, c. IX, 5.   [9] *Protagoras*, 358b.   [10] *Epist.,* I, 6, 1.

truths. This virtue enables man to arrive at truth without the effort of discursive reasoning.

2. *Wisdom* is the ability to understand realities in the light of ultimate causes.

3. *Science* is the ability to grasp conclusions in some specialized department of knowledge such as mathematics, chemistry, or physics. These three habits perfect the speculative activities of the intellect. The following two perfect the practical activities of the intellect.

4. *Art* is the ability to choose efficient means to effect external productions: knowledge of how to make things whether useful or artistic.

5. *Prudence* is the ability to discern the true ends of human conduct and to fashion means proper to effect these ends.

Intuition, wisdom, science, and art are *merely* intellectual virtues; they confer a facility for intellectual activity and thereby make the subject good, but since the supreme good of human life is not attained by merely intellectual activity, these habits do not make one unqualifiedly good but good only in a restricted field. Thus, one may be a good metaphysician, mathematician, or sculptor without being a good man.

294. Since prudence directly and of itself correctly orders man toward his supreme good, it is not only an intellectual virtue; it is also a moral virtue rendering a man unqualifiedly good. The prudent man is therefore a good man. But does the good man require anything more? Socrates says *no*. He cannot conceive how a man can know what his true good is and fail to embrace it.

But the Socratic theory contradicts human experience. Men do act contrary to their better judgment; the sinner knows he should be doing better. Ovid expresses this universal experience: *Video meliora proboque: deteriora sequor.*[11] Besides, if Socrates were right, there would be no such thing as sin, for no one could do evil willfully. Hence no one could be blamed for being wicked because he could always offer the excuse that he did not know better. St. Thomas masterfully explains how it is possible for the sinner to turn his back on the light of reason.[12]

If a man is to be completely equipped to walk with readiness in the way of the moral law, other habits than those that perfect the

---

[11] *Metamorphoses*, VII, 20.
[12] *Sum. Theol.*, I–II, q. 77, a. 2.

intellect are required. The appetitive faculties must be habituated to obey the voice of reason. Hence from a consideration of merely intellectual virtues we pass to moral virtues.

IV. MORAL VIRTUES

A. Moral Virtues in General

295. What we referred to above as virtue in general we shall now call *moral virtue*. Moral virtue is any habit operating under the direction of the will *directly* ordering man to his last end. Since human acts must be subject to the will, since man's last end is attainable only by good volitional acts, any permanent source of good conduct must be will-directed and conducive to perfect happiness. Since it is the will's function to obey right reason, moral virtue gives man readiness to act in accord with reason. Since that which is reasonable leads to the last end, the person who possesses moral virtue is unqualifiedly, totally good.

296. *Is moral virtue one or many?* There are as many moral virtues as there are specifically different morally good acts, and there are as many of these as there are specifically different moral objects which it befits a man to attain. As these are actually numerous, there are many virtues but all are reducible to four main categories or *cardinal virtues*. We are indebted to Greek thought for the division, to St. Ambrose[13] for the name, which comes from Latin, *cardo,* a "hinge." That there are four and only four cardinal virtues is proved as follows:

To be steadily prompted to morally good acts in all circumstances, man must be assisted by good habits dwelling in those potencies whence the human act proceeds and in those which tend to oppose the will's dominion. Hence a habit must reside in each of the following:

1. *The mind.* To act well, the will first must be illumined by the mind presenting a true good to it. Hence the mind must be habituated to discern true good from apparent good. The mind, skilled in recognizing the reasonable thing to do in all particulars of human conduct, possesses the virtue of *prudence.*

2. *The will.* Man's will does not require a special habit to assist him to seek his own good, for innate impulse urges him to do this. However, man's will requires a special habit to dispose him to respect the

---

[13] *Expositio Evan. secundum Lucam,* Lib. V, n. 49. Migne, *P.L.,* XV, 1734.

good of his fellow man and to act reasonably toward him. This habit is the virtue of *justice*.

3. *The concupiscible appetite.* In dealing with self, however, a man may be disordered by the importunities of his sensitive appetite. Hence, a good habit must reside in the concupiscible appetite restraining it within the bounds of reason from wanton pursuit of sensible good. This habit is *temperance,* which moderates the concupiscible appetite.

4. *The irascible appetite.* A similar habit must reside in the irascible appetite and restrain man from acting unreasonably in the face of difficulty and danger. This is *fortitude*.

297. The person, then, who by patient striving has acquired a perfect synthesis of the moral virtues of prudence, justice, temperance, and fortitude is the good man. He is habitually good. He is recognizable by the fact that in all situations he promptly, uniformly, and pleasurably does what is reasonable. It is the effect of good habit to do the right thing *promptly; uniformly,* because virtue is permanent; *pleasurably,* because what we do well and skillfully we do with pleasure.

298. There is a mutual relationship between the moral virtues in their perfect state. The person who is perfectly just is also truly prudent, temperate, and courageous. The reason is that no real virtue can be had without prudence, and prudence is impossible without justice, temperance, and fortitude. The presence of prudence implies that one's appetites are in proper order. Since man's moral judgments reflect the order or disorder in his appetites, no one can constantly make prudent judgments if his appetites are not in order.

Imperfect virtues are inclinations to right conduct resulting from natural temperament or virtues in their unformed state. They are not interconnected like perfect moral virtues. However, it is generally true that any serious attempt to develop one virtue is accompanied by growth in the other virtues. Likewise, serious collapse of a virtue often brings with it a breakdown of other virtues. A woman who surrenders to unchastity will often become unjust, untruthful, and intemperate. A drunken man will steal to satisfy his cravings, forget his family, his honor, and his obligations.

B. Moral Virtues in Particular

299. 1. *Prudence* is the ability to discern the becoming ends of human conduct and the morally good act in all the contingencies of life.

Though it resides in the intellect, it is a moral virtue for it is subject to the supreme dominion of the will. It orders man to his last end and makes clear the golden mean of the other virtues. It points out the path of justice, the measure of temperance, the limits of fortitude. Without prudence, courage becomes recklessness, patience degenerates into apathy, modesty into prudery, and meekness into pusillanimity.

The acquisition of prudence does not so much depend on one's intellectual ability as on the strength of one's will steadily focusing the mind on the true ends of life. An ignorant man, even a person of low intelligence, can be quite prudent, for, through the influence of the will he may not permit his mind to be distracted from the genuine purpose of life. Contemplating and evaluating those ends which alone are worthy of human endeavor, such persons can devise efficient means of attaining them. Brilliant persons who pursue ignoble ends possess shrewdness or sagacity but not prudence.

300. 2. *Temperance* is that virtue which restrains within the bounds of reason the sensitive appetite seeking its proper pleasure. Nature attaches a commensurate pleasure to all our activities. However, bodily pleasures are so vivid and alluring that they can diminish the appeal of purely spiritual pleasure. There is a danger, therefore, that we may seek bodily pleasure unreasonably. Hence, not only must the mind be endowed with prudence to discern between real good of the spirit and an apparent good of the body, but, to ensure reasonable action, the bodily appetite must be restrained lest it overwhelm both mind and will. The virtue of temperance is the means of moderating our concupiscible appetites.

There is no danger that man will sin by defect as far as the satisfaction of bodily pleasure is concerned. No one is so apathetic to his bodily urges that he requires a special virtue to help him seek his bodily good. Nature has taken care of this by the strength of our bodily drives.

Of all sensible pleasures none are greater than the pleasures attending those acts whereby life is conserved and new life is begotten. To conserve life we need food and drink, but an excessive indulgence in them is opposed to the Natural Law. This disorderly tendency is the capital vice of gluttony against which temperance inculcates *abstinence,* or moderation in food, and *sobriety,* or moderation in drink.

Nature attaches the greatest of all sensible pleasure to that activity whereby her own purpose, namely, the continuance of the race, is immediately attained. Reproduction is a good not primarily of the individual but of the race. This pleasure, therefore, may be enjoyed only as nature dictates. Nature's dictum is this: venereal pleasure is allowed only between those two who are conjoined in legitimate matrimony. That the monogamistic conjugal union is the *sole* instrument intended by nature for human reproduction will be set forth in special ethics (cf. § 731, Corollary). Hence any other use of the reproductive function or indulgence in its attendant pleasure is a grave deordination against nature's purpose.

However, the sexual impulse is so urgent that one is inclined to follow it regardless of the limits set down by reason. This sexual drive is the capital vice of lust, and against it temperance prescribes *chastity*. The all-inclusive law of chastity may be summarized thus: to seek or willfully to enjoy any venereal pleasure is a serious wrong for the unmarried, or for the married apart from a natural act with one's lawful spouse.

301. 3. *Fortitude* is that virtue which inclines a man to act reasonably despite the prompting of his irascible appetite. The irascible appetite moves toward an arduous good or shuns a difficult evil. In either case it may easily miss the mean of virtue. Therefore, when we are inclined to avoid a danger which we ought to face, fortitude enables us to meet it. Or, more rarely, when we would injudiciously expose ourselves to harm, fortitude tempers our boldness. Its function is to restrain our fears and moderate our rashness. It seeks a golden mean between cowardice and rashness, moderating our internal motions of fear and recklessness and our external acts of flight and aggression. There is a special moral fitness in the *reasonable* endurance of evil or the conquest of difficulty, even the most arduous. Not every suffering of hardship or display of courage is moral virtue. To be virtue it must be in accord with reason, that is, for a worthy end. Evil men in pursuit of crime may act bravely and perseveringly but no one may rightly ascribe this to the virtue of fortitude.

With Plato[14] we may aptly compare the sensitive appetite to a team of horses one of which, spirited and straining ahead, needs to be checked. This is appetite striving for pleasure and requiring the rein of temperance. The other is dull and lagging and needing to be urged

---

[14] *Phaedrus*, 253D–256.

on. This is appetite, beset with fears, that must be enspirited by the goad of fortitude. Fortitude is the moral stimulus which enables us to overcome our fears.

302. There is an evil which some men fear more than death, namely, dishonor. As fortitude enables us to cope successfully with the fear of death, a special kind of fortitude, namely *magnanimity*, disposes us to deal reasonably with dishonor.

Magnanimity is that virtue which inclines a man to great deeds and hence to act reasonably in the face of great honor or dishonor. It is the reaching out of the soul for what is truly great. Relatively, it is a great thing to use a trifle excellently but absolutely speaking it is a great act to use a grand thing magnificently. Of all human goods external to man, the greatest is honor. It is nearest to virtue; it is the testimony of virtue; it is that which is paid to God Himself; it is the highest prize for which men strive.

As a man is called brave because by facing death he does what without qualification is difficult, so a man is called magnanimous because, by bearing great honor reasonably, he does what without qualification is great. What the magnanimous man seeks is the great deed, but since great honor inevitably follows from his action, the perfection of his virtue is manifest in his attitude toward honor.

303. Aristotle weaves a picture of the magnanimous man which represents the noblest summit attained by Greek philosophy. "The magnanimous man," he says, "being by hypothesis worthy of the greatest things, must be of the highest excellence since the better a man is, the more he is worth, and he who is best, is worth most; it follows, then, to be truly magnanimous a man must be good, and whatever is great in each virtue belongs to the magnanimous. . . . This virtue, then, is a kind of ornament to all the other virtues in that it makes them better and cannot be without them; and for this reason it is a hard matter to be really and truly magnanimous for it cannot be without thorough goodness and nobility of character."[15]

When honor inevitably comes his way, the magnanimous man will not be wrongfully affected because he will rightly consider it his due. On the other hand, he will not be saddened by disgrace; he will contemn it for in his case there are no just grounds for it. For "as regards wealth and power, good or bad fortune of every kind, he will bear himself with moderation, fall out how these may and

[15] *Ethics,* IV, 3, 1123b.

neither in prosperity will he be overjoyed nor in adversity unduly pained."[16]

Do some minor strands of error find their way into the elaborate tapestry woven by Aristotle? We find these details: "He is the sort of man to do kindnesses but he is ashamed to receive them." "Such men remember those they have done kindnesses to but not those from whom they have received them." "It is characteristic of the magnanimous man to ask no favors at all, or very reluctantly . . . to bear himself loftily toward the great and fortunate . . . never to go where others are chief men . . . to be remiss and dilatory except where some great honor or work is concerned . . . to be candid in his likes and dislikes . . . his contempt for others makes him a bold man . . . neither is his admiration greatly excited for nothing is great in his eyes."[17] St. Thomas[18] makes a loyal and able defense of Aristotle, but one cannot help concluding that Aristotle lived in pagan surroundings where there was little charity, humility, and simplicity. While the magnanimous man, Aristotle excogitates, is a noble and commanding figure, he is a far cry from the reality who actually walked this earth, the Perfect Man, the model of all human excellence, in whom is found the perfect synthesis and exquisite tempering of all the virtues, Jesus Christ, our Lord.

304. There is a lesser form of magnanimity which helps the more ordinary man to persevere in doing good despite discouragement. Human respect and fear of ridicule can be a powerful deterrent to upright conduct. Men have been ashamed to worship God with due frequency because they feared derision. Young men have been lured from the way of chastity because they could not endure the mockery of their friends. Magnanimity gives one the courage to disregard the empty yawping of others and undisturbedly to cling to virtue.

Fortitude provides a strong defense against severe and protracted temptations. The human will is fickle and grows tired of repeated resistance and will yield merely to have the struggle done with. Fortitude steels us to hold out, to continue saying *no* despite our moral weariness. It must be said here, however, that no amount of fortitude or of any natural virtue is enough for victory. The tempted man inevitably falls unless rescued by the supernatural aid of God.

---

[16] *Ibid.*, IV, 3, 1124a.
[17] *Ibid.*, IV, 3, 1124b.
[18] *Sum. Theol.*, II–II, 129, a. 3, ad 5.

The commonest way we manifest our fortitude is by reasonable endurance of the ordinary difficulties of life. This is *patience*. It is the passive counterpart of the boldness of fortitude. Every man has much to suffer, and he bears it well or ill in proportion to the steadfastness of his will. But such steadfastness is impossible unless he constantly bears in mind that mortal life is the proving ground of virtue whereon nothing happens by chance but all is governed by an infinitely wise Providence. All hardships befall us with divine permission, and they are intended for our ultimate good. The troubles of life are the component elements of the complete problem each one must cope with and solve in order to gain eternal beatitude.

305. 4. *Justice*. From Aristotle's time on, the word *justice* has been used in a general and particular sense.

a) In a *general* sense justice is the equivalent of virtue or sanctity so that its contrary injustice is the same as vice. Hence, it is all the virtues rendering all the actions of a man conformed to law and thereby making the man just. In this sense Scripture calls Joseph a just man. Justice always connotes an equality of some sort. Here it is an equality between one's actions on the one hand and the law and one's last end on the other. Thus Aristotle says that the violator of the law is unjust and the keeper of the law just.[19]

b) As a *particular virtue* compared to virtue in general, as a part to the whole, justice is that moral habit which regulates our conduct toward other men. As prudence, temperance, and fortitude perfect a man in regard to himself, justice perfects him in regard to others. Since justice tends to establish equality and since equality supposes two terms physically distinct, one cannot be just to oneself. Hence we define the cardinal virtue of justice as *the constant and perpetual will to render to another his due*.

The word *constant* indicates a *habit* of the will. *Perpetual* does not mean that the just will is always in act but that it is ready to respect another's right not merely for a time but always. *Due* means that which belongs to another by *strict right*. Things which are due in a broader sense such as from fitness, decency, and need, are not the object matter of justice but of some allied virtue such as veracity, fidelity, gratitude, natural charity, friendliness, and equity. Justice deals only with things due by right. The word *another* may refer to one totally separate from oneself or to one only partially distinct.

---

[19] *Ethics*, V, 1, 1129a.

From this distinction three principal relationships to others are possible. Upon them the three great divisions of justice are founded.

306. 1. *Social justice*. This is the virtue which moves the individual as a member of a natural community — family, State, the race at large — to promote the common good of that community. As a social part of a social whole he is not adequately distinct from the community, and this quasi-identification with the community is the source of his obligation to it. Justice demands that the part contribute its due share to the whole. Social justice, then, envisions an equilibrium of duty toward the social whole which each social part must maintain. A man is *socially just* when he constantly renders the common good what it exacts of him.

No special term is used to designate the kind of justice existing between the individual and the family or the race at large. The kind of justice which binds the individual to the State is called *legal justice,* because law determines what the common good of the State requires. Although the common good of the State can evoke the practice of very many virtues, legal justice is not virtue in general (§ 305); it is a special virtue. Though its material object touches many virtues, it has a distinct formal object, or motive, namely, the promotion of the common *civic* good. The end of social justice is primarily the common good; the means, the reasonable subordination of the individual good to the common good.

307. 2. *Distributive justice*. Distributive justice is the counterpart of social justice. As the individual is obligated to the community — family, State, race — so the community is obligated to the individual. What a natural society *owes* the individual is determined by distributive justice, which envisions an equality between the social whole and the social parts. There must be a fair disbursement of common advantages and a sharing of common burdens — all proportioned to the needs, abilities, and merits of individuals. The communistic slogan, "from all according to their abilities: to each according to his needs," is an expressive summation of distributive justice. Since the obligation belongs to the total community as such, it will be exercised by the community's head — by the father in the family, by the legitimate authorities in the State. Distributive justice, then, is the virtue which inclines the head of a natural community to promote the social good of the individual. It is violated by favoritism and partiality. When distributive justice takes the form of meting out punishments for offenses against the common good it is called *vindicative justice* (§ 200). The end of distributive justice is the social good of the individual, his well-being as a member of the community.

308. 3. *Commutative justice.* Strict justice involves two things, (*a*) parties adequately distinct, (*b*) an object which actually belongs to someone by right. Consequently social and distributive justice are not strict justice. First, as far as social justice is concerned, the individual is not completely distinct from the community. Second, society demands that something which it does not yet possess become its property. The same is true of the individual under distributive justice. Since only commutative justice involves distinct parties and since its object actually attaches to one by right, it alone is strict justice, and the definition of justice given above (§ 305) alone applies fully to it.

Commutative justice maintains equality between individuals. This does not mean that all individuals should have equal possessions but that the possessions of all are inviolable.

The word *commutative* comes from the Latin, *commutatio,* an "exchange." Man is constantly exchanging things which he owns — money, service, goods, abilities — for things which his neighbor owns. Commutative justice secures a proportionate equality in these dealings. The object of this type of justice is not the common good but the good of the individual, *mine* and *thine.* The good of the individual is not a subjective estimate but an objective reality. The mean of commutative justice is an exact and objective thing, the mine, the thine, the his. In the discussion of right the further ramifications of this problem are taken up.

309. Since the fundamental requisite of justice is that each one have what is his, restitution is necessary for violations against commutative justice. When that which belongs to a man is unlawfully withheld or taken from him, the equality of justice demands that it be returned to him.

Restitution, however, does not enter into social or distributive justice. Thus, if a citizen withholds something due the State through social justice, though he does wrong, it cannot be said that he is keeping public property in private hands. At the bidding of the law he has failed to convert to public use some of his private property but he has not stolen public property. So, too, with distributive justice. The rewards and emoluments which a citizen may have a claim to from the State do not become his until the State gives them to him. He may have what ancient Roman jurisprudence called a *jus ad rem* but he does not as yet have a *jus in re*. The latter is a right in or over one's own object. Such a thing is truly a person's property. The former is a right to demand of another that something become one's own. The thing is not yet the person's property but he can demand that it become his. Thus, before a veteran receives his bonus he has a *jus ad rem* to the money from the government; after he receives it he has a *jus in re* to it.

If an obligation imposed by social or distributive justice has been neglected and the opportunity for fulfilling it passes, that particular obligation lapses; however, if an offense is committed against commutative justice, the obligation of restitution always *remains*.

V. VICE

A. Vice in General

310. As virtue is the inclination to act in accord with our rational nature, vice is the contrary habit disposing us to act against it. As good acts are the products of virtue, evil acts are the product of vice. Vices are formed the same way that virtues are formed, that is, by repetition — repetition of evil acts which becomes, in turn, a partial cause of further sinful acts. A man is called good or bad, virtuous or vicious, in so far as he possesses virtue or vice, but he is adjudged guilty or innocent in so far as his act is good or bad. Guilt is chargeable not to the vice but to the act.

Vices, like virtues, may become mechanical, involving no deliberation and consent. The vicious do evil, it is said, by second nature. Thus the question arises, "How responsible is a man for evil acts committed under the influence of a vice?" (*a*) If a person adverts and consents to a bad act, he is responsible for it, despite the presence of a vice. (*b*) If a person does not advert to a bad act as he performs it, the act is not chargeable to him as a wrong but the habit is imputed as a wrong if it is voluntary. A vice is voluntary when it has been knowingly contracted or when one neglects to break it as far as one can. It becomes involuntary when one sincerely renounces it by a definite will act. The sincerity of such a will act is manifested by the practical means one takes to implement his resolve. If no means are later taken to break a grave vice, one is guilty of grave neglect. If some measure of diligence is used, even though insufficient, one is not guilty of grave neglect.

B. Vice in Particular

311. Vice, as evil, is the deprivation of good — the absence of virtue. Hence each vice is specifically differentiated in terms of the virtue of which it is the absence. Since virtue conforms to the golden mean, vice either falls short of it by defect or goes beyond it by excess.

Holding that a special virtue derives from every special kind of human good or human difficulty, the scholastics, following Aristotle, evolved the particulars of morality upon a framework of virtue and vice. All human conduct is made to fit into this pattern.

312. 1. *Vices contrary to prudence.* Prudence involves (*a*) constant contemplation of the sole and true end of human life; (*b*) wise ordering of the details of life unto that end. Opposed to the former is *prudence of the flesh,* which is a repudiation of the true end of life and the substitution of the enjoyment of mere temporal goods for it. The ability to secure these things cleverly is a counterfeit of true prudence. Akin to this is *oversolicitude for the future,* which is reproved in the "Sermon on the Mount." "Be not solicitous therefore saying, What shall we eat or wherewith shall we be clothed. For after all these things do the heathens seek. Seek ye first the Kingdom of God and all these other things shall be added unto you."[20] These two are bad through excess.

As to the wise ordering of means to life's end, one errs by *negligence,* if he fails to take the proper moral means to an end; by *precipitation,* if he allows himself to be carried away by the impulse of the moment; by *inconsideration,* if he acts without taking due account of all the circumstances of a case; by *inconstancy,* if, after having determined upon the proper course of action, he changes his mind influenced by disorderly affection and abandons it. These errors are bad through defect.

313. 2. *Vices contrary to temperance.* There are no vices contrary to temperance except those of excess. These are *gluttony,* which is excess in food; *insobriety,* excess in drink; *unchastity,* excess in sexual pleasure. The disordered inclination of the appetite for food and drink is often called the capital sin of gluttony. It is called a capital sin because such sins are a source of other sins. In the quaint phrase of St. Thomas,[21] the daughters of gluttony are five: inept mirth, un-

---

[20] Matt. 6:31–33.
[21] *Sum. Theol.,* II–II, 148, a. 6.

cleanness, buffoonery, much talking, and dullness of mind for intellectual things. How intemperance in drink so easily leads to quarreling and unchastity is a matter of daily experience. The uncurbed appetite for sex is called the capital sin of lust. Developing the phrase of Aristotle that "intemperance most of all destroys prudence,"[22] St. Thomas[23] enumerates the effects of this capital vice as blindness of mind, inconsiderateness, headlong haste, inconstancy, selfishness, hatred of God, love of this world, and a horror or despair of the world to come.

The proper scope of temperance is the pleasures annexed to the senses of taste and touch. Many other pleasures both sensitive and psychic are regulated by virtues allied to temperance. Of these the chief are meekness, modesty, and humility. (*a*) *Meekness* is the virtue which enables man to control anger. The vice opposed to meekness is irascibility, better known as *anger,* or the disorderly inclination to anger and revenge. It is rightly set down as a capital vice for from it proceed brawling, turbulence of spirit, contumely, clamor, indignation, and blasphemy. (*b*) *Modesty* must not be confused with chastity. Chastity regulates venereal pleasures; modesty is that external decorum which tempers all of one's external motions —dress, speech, deportment — according to the reasonable demands of time, place, and person. It is the outward splendor of chastity and one of its surest safeguards. Much of what is called *immodesty* may well be unchastity, such as wantonness in carriage, dress, gesture, and speech. The vices opposed to modesty are *insolence* in external behavior, *hypocrisy* by excess, and *clownishness* by defect. (*c*) *Humility* is the virtue which restrains man's natural tendency for self-exaltation. This virtue is founded on a true estimation of self. It is not incompatible with magnanimity because the truly humble recognize that of themselves they are nothing and can do nothing but with divine assistance they may accomplish even the greatest things. The contrary vice is *pride,* the inordinate seeking after excellence, which St. Augustine describes as the love of self even to the contempt of God.[24] In a certain true sense, this is the fountainhead of all vices.

314. 3. *Vices contrary to fortitude.* The special function of fortitude is the regulation of fears and actions in time of danger or adversity. It is possible that one's fear may be so slight that he does not take

---

[22] *Ethics,* VI, 5, 1140b.   [23] *Sum. Theol.,* II–II, 153, a. 5.   [24] *City of God,* XII, 13.

adequate precautions to prevent harm. Aristotle takes note of this possibility remarking: "A man would be mad or insensate if he feared nothing at all, neither earthquakes nor waves, as they say of the Celts."[25] Persons without normal fear are few. There possibly are some people who through pride, sheer stupidity, or prolonged exposure to danger feel no fear of it but they are the exception. No special name is given to their insensibility. Fearlessness is a misnomer. The fearless man has an inward dread of death but conceals it by showing no outward sign of fear.

Excessive fear is far more common than lack of fear. This is the vice of *timidity*. It is detrimental to soundness of mind and is the cause of many neuroses. It results in acts of *cowardice*. Thus one may prefer acts against chastity, justice, sobriety, religion, etc., to avoid the thing feared. The vice of excess opposite to cowardice is *temerity*. It is unreasonable boldness in the presence of danger.

In categorizing the virtues regulative of the irascible motion, the scholastics aligned four virtues with fortitude, namely, magnanimity, magnificence, perseverance, and patience. To the greatest of these — *magnanimity* — presumption and ambition are opposed by way of excess. *Presumption* is the attempting of great things which are beyond one's power; *ambition* is the inordinate seeking after great honor. One falls short of magnanimity by *pusillanimity*, the refusal to undertake great things which are commensurate to one's ability.

Magnificence is the virtue of making great expenditures for great works. This virtue is eminently proper where its object is honor to God. Aristotle remarks: "Those expenses are most honorable which relate to the sacrifice of the Deity."[26] One acts counter to golden mean of this virtue by *extravagance*, which is needlessly lavish spending, or by *parsimony*, which is the unreasonable restriction of expense.

Perseverance inclines man to continue in doing good and to overcome protracted and troublesome difficulties. The excess of this virtue is *stubbornness*, or continuing to act when it is no longer reasonable to do so. The defect of perseverance is *inconstancy*, or the desisting from action when it is reasonable to continue.

Patience inclines man to endure the ordinary difficulties of life without yielding unduly to sadness. Its opposite is *impatience*, probably the commonest of human failings.

---

[25] *Ethics*, III, 7, 1115b.   [26] *Ibid.*, IV, 11, 1122b.

315. **4.** *Vices contrary to justice.* Whoever constantly violates justice is the unjust man. The unjust act may be contrary to social, distributive, or commutative justice. Only those who exercise social authority can violate distributive justice. Social justice may be violated both by those who command and those who obey. The chief obligations arising under distributive and social justice are related in social ethics.

The epithet, unjust, is more properly applied to the person who constantly acts contrary to commutative justice. Commutative justice is violated by withholding or taking from another that which is rightly his. Every infringement of justice is the overriding of some other's right. Hence acts of injustice are designated in terms of the right violated. That people can and do form vicious habits contrary to commutative justice is clear from the number of thieves, calumniators, adulterers, etc., found in any large community.

VI. CHARACTER

316. We have seen that virtue is the disciplined, perfected ease of acting as a reasonable man. It consists in those habits of mind and will which enable one at every turn to do good and avoid evil. It is the harmonious synthesis of prudence, justice, temperance, and fortitude whereby one is adequately equipped, as far as human endeavor can achieve it, to attain life's great purpose. It is the summit of human greatness in this life. Virtue, then, is the mortal goal of human striving; character is the means to this goal.

317. *Character* comes from a Greek word meaning a "seal," an impression made in some substance such as wax or clay denoting ownership. Hence a characteristic is an individualizing trait, a significant quality distinguishing this thing from all others.

Every man is endowed by nature with individual characteristics of body, mind, and will. The general disposition of the whole man is determined by these complex factors. We call it temperament. Temperament may incline one toward mechanical skills or literary art, pugnacity or kindliness, boldness or timidity, and so on. At birth, however, temperament is unformed. It is pliable and awaits an imprint that it will bear permanently. The impression is or should be made by the will playing its role of mistress of the human faculties. The impression of will on temperament gives character, which distinguishes a man morally from other men.

As reason develops, the will either assumes its function of domination — and that for good or evil — or it surrenders its primacy and follows the natural bent of the lower appetites, giving passion a more or less free reign and being motivated merely by whim, fancy, or the opinions of others. A person's character is weak or strong in so far as the will exerts a weak or strong effort in self-formation. The wax of disposition receives a good impression if the pressure of the will is heavy and constant; a poor impression, if light and intermittent. If a man's will is weak, lower tendencies are strong and a particular one usually plays a dominant role. Such a person receives his moral designation from his prevailing passion. Thus we call him a man of irascible or gluttonous character.

318. If a man's will is strong, his character will be good, provided his moral principles are correct; if a strong-willed person's principles are incorrect, his character will be vicious. But rarely do we find a man who is totally good and never one who is totally bad. Hence the strong and good man has a bias toward a particular virtue so that he will be described, let us say, as a conspicuously honest man or a charitable man or even a meek man — for there can be a constant, strong tendency toward the quieter, less assertive virtues. And the same applies to the strong and vicious man. He will be characterized as rapacious, proud, or domineering.

The person who has attained perfect virtue is one in whom all the virtues coexist in harmony. He is not conspicuous for this or that virtue because in him no one moral quality towers above another. This indeed is beauty — sublime unity amid fascinating variety. Such a person has a perfect character.

319. Although there has been but one perfect character in the history of man, it is worthy of special comment because it remains forever the concrete pattern after which all human goodness is modeled. It is the true ideal of human endeavor, for virtue constitutes the enduring value of life. The self-mastery and self-perfection resident in virtue are a good more desirable than wealth, power, artistic ability, athletic prowess, and the like. These things — though they are commonly the object of intense human striving — do not necessarily make one more a man. The opposite is often the case.

320. Virtue is power. First it is power for oneself. It is man's best equipment. It gives strength against "the slings and arrows of outrageous fortune." It alone gives assurance of some measure of happi-

ness now and promise of happiness hereafter. Any acquisitions other
than virtue are of little worth. Second, it wields an influence on
others which no man may disdain. Parents who are outstanding not
so much for beauty of body or grace of personality as for nobility of
character leave the most effectual impression upon their children.
How enduring can be the result of even a single man's virtue is
seen among the founders of religious orders. Even evil and careless
men are desirous of virtue's name for no indictment is more terrible
than the simple statement, "He is not a good man."

321. How is virtue attained? First, by willing to acquire it. This
does not mean ineffectually wishing for it but actually seeking it by
submitting ourselves to the rigorous control of will. The will can
overcome the inertia of temperament or the tenacity of acquired defect.
It can produce virtuous habits contrary to natural inclination. Will
power can change timidity into courage, irascibility into sweetness,
lust into continence. There is no limit to the virtue one may attain;
with divine assistance, a man can make of himself what he chooses.

322. But such determination is impossible without a deep appreciation of virtue. No one makes strenuous efforts to possess something
he does not highly value. It is precisely because most men have
a more vivid appreciation of the comforts of life, or prestige, good
times, and the like, that they desire these rather than virtue. Therefore, man must not only discover the value of virtue; he must
constantly revert to it to appreciate it. If he does not, it will elude
him and he will lose his desire for it.

Nor is it enough to appreciate virtue and know what it is. One
must also know himself. Men have always applauded Socrates for
his admonition, "Know thyself."[27] Knowledge of self is not only
acquaintance with the fundamentals of human nature and the moral
law; it is deep understanding of one's own peculiar abilities, tendencies, failings, and lapses. Without it, man can make little progress
in the attainment of virtue.

323. It is one thing to appreciate — perhaps from afar — the attrac-
tiveness of moral beauty, it is another thing to resolve to attain it.
It is still quite another thing to be faithful to such a resolve. Character
comes not only from willing but from doing. One must act, act, act.
Virtue comes from doing virtuous things.

---

[27] Plato, *Protagoras*, 343B; *Phaedrus*, 229E.

But man is powerless to accomplish anything in this respect without the divine help of grace. This, however, belongs to the realm of the supernatural. Suffice it to conclude this subject with the pithy advice of St. Ignatius Loyola who says that we are to do and act as though everything depended on our own effort and to pray and hope for God's help as though everything depended on Him.

READINGS

St. Thomas, *Summa Theologica,* I–II, 49, 53, 61, 65, 84; II–II, 47, 123, 141.

Aristotle, *Ethics,* II, 6; III, 6–10; V, 1; VI, 5 ff.

Cathrein, Victor, S.J., *Philosophia Moralis,* pp. 126–147. Friburgi Brisgoviae, Herder, 1915.

Cronin, Michael, *The Science of Ethics,* Vol. I, pp. 559–596. Dublin, Gill and Son, 1909.

Davis, Henry, S.J., *Moral and Pastoral Theology,* Vol. I, pp. 253–258. New York, Sheed and Ward, 1936.

Holaind, Rene, S.J., *Natural Law and Legal Practice,* pp. 151–165. New York, Benziger, 1899.

Leibell, J. F. (ed.), *Readings in Ethics,* pp. 207–291. Chicago, Loyola University, 1926.

Nivard, Marcel, S.J., *Ethica,* pp. 97–105. Paris, Beauchesne, 1928.

Rickaby, Joseph J., S.J., *Aquinus Ethicus,* Vol. I, pp. 149–195.

—— *Moral Philosophy,* pp. 41–108.

BOOK II

PRINCIPLES OF INDIVIDUAL ETHICS

CHAPTER X

RELIGION

SPECIAL ETHICS

324. In an overview of general ethics, this fact stands out pre-eminently: a man ought to attain his final end — glorify God and be eternally happy. To accomplish this he ought to lead a life in keeping with his nature, a reasonable life. This he does by obeying the Natural Law. Our study of morality, then, is completed by study of the contents of this law.

325. The Natural Law is but nature properly inclining us toward the natural and necessary goods of human life. One way to explain these particulars of the law is to determine the definite goods toward which nature impels man and the contrary evils from which she restrains him. This is the method of the older scholastics, who neatly and adequately arranged the particulars of morality on a framework of the virtues and vices.

326. The modern but not necessarily better method is this. Since the formal effect of law is obligation, our general inquiry is: What are the *particular* obligations of the Natural Law? The answer is given by special ethics, which is divided into two parts. The first is *individual ethics,* which treats man's private obligations in three general groups — his obligations toward God, toward self, and toward his fellow man. The second is *social ethics,* which studies man's obligations as a social being.

However, while the major aspect of law is obligation, it is not its sole aspect. To imagine that morality is only obligation, that the moral life is a dolorous burden of restrictions, is a dour and false view of reality. Law not only commands and forbids; it also concedes. Nature is no Simon Legree nor even a spoil sport. She makes liberal allowances. Some of these positive law may restrict, but others are so sacred to the individual that no human power may deprive him of them. When nature commands, she urges us toward our real and compelling good. When she forbids, she is restraining us from the deceptive appearances of good, which pursued would entail the loss of all good. When she concedes, she is a wise parent giving us an ample field whereon to exercise our natural freedom. We shall examine first, what nature commands, forbids, and concedes the individual with respect to God, himself and his fellow man.

327. *Duties to God.* In a true sense, all moral obligations are duties to God, because He is the Author of the moral law and the beginning and end of all things. In many cases, however, God is the object of our moral obligation only mediately and indirectly. By duties to God we refer solely to obligations which have God as their direct object. Whatever these duties prove to be, we may conveniently group them under a single heading — Religion.

I. WHAT IS RELIGION?

328. There can be no denial of the fact that there is such a thing as religion. The term is familiar, and greatly variegated phenomena are classified under it. But what really is religion? Is it a blind instinct or emotion devoid of rational basis; a perception of the infinite (Max Miller);[1] an awareness of another world of spirits; morality touched by emotion (Matthew Arnold);[2] the opium of the masses (Marx)?[3] Before we can determine what obligations, if any, are imposed by religion, we must first know what the true nature of religion is.

329. To the overwhelming majority of mankind who conceive of religion as some kind of direct connection with God, the atheist replies — Absurd, there is no God. For an Infinite Person he substitutes blind, physical forces. There is no need to repeat here the demonstrations of natural theology proving that a necessary and infinitely perfect Being exists who is the Creator and provident Ruler of the universe; it will suffice here to say with the Wise Man: "Only the fool hath said in his heart there is no God."[4] There is scarcely a greater perversion

---

[1] F. Max Miller, *Lectures on the Origin and Growth of Religion,* Lect. 1, pp. 21–22. New York, Scribner's, 1879.

[2] Matthew Arnold, *Literature and Dogma,* Chap. 1, p. 21. London, Smith Elder, 1873.

[3] Karl Marx, *Selected Essays,* "Criticism of Hegelian Philosophy of Right," trans. H. J. Stenning, p. 12. New York, International Publishers, 1926.

[4] Ps. 52:1.

of the human intellect than denial of the existence of God. Foremost among modern atheists are communists, who not only vigorously propagate atheism but endeavor to root out all hitherto existent forms of religion and in its place substitute blind devotion to the party.

Agnostics claim that we do not have sufficient grounds for asserting that God exists; pantheists maintain that everything is but an emanation from one absolute thing wherewith everything is ultimately identified; deists admit that God made the world but cannot be bothered to look after it. From all these, because of their errors concerning the Deity, can come only false notions of religion.

Against this background of faith versus reason, we find four outstanding false views on religion. (a) Religion is emotion — a feeling of abasement before an ideal infinitely above us, of personal exaltation as we move toward, and participate in, the perfection of this idea. Schleiermacher is the voice of pietistic Protestantism when he defines religion as a *feeling* of the absolute dependence of man on the infinite.[5] (b) Religion has man as its object; this is the view of humanitarians. For Comte, religion is an expansive philanthropic devotion to mankind.[6] With Feuerbach[7] it is a fierce turning from God to divinize man. With Hegel and Schelling it becomes an adoration of the State as the Absolute Thing.[8] (c) Religion is ethics. One is religious if he keeps the moral law, but in that law there is no explicit command to worship God. This is another of Kant's legacies to the modern world. For him, religion is the sum total of the unprovable hypotheses one must assume to explain the moral law.[9] (d) Religion originated in devotion to departed ancestors,[10] and has evolved into vague emotional curiosity regarding the ultimate mysteries of this world.

[5] Friedrich Schleiermacher, *Reden über die Religion.* See his *Sämmtliche Werke,* Vol. I, pp. 174, 184. Berlin, Reimer, 1843.

[6] Levy-Bruhl, *The Philosophy of Auguste Comte,* IV, 3, pp. 333–342.

[7] "We have shown that the substance and object of religion is altogether human: we have shown that divine wisdom is human wisdom; that the secret of theology is anthropology; that the absolute mind is the so-called finite subjective mind . . . there is no other essence man can think, dream of, imagine, feel, believe in, wish for, love and adore as the absolute, than the essense of human nature itself." Ludwig Feuerbach, *The Essence of Christianity,* trans. Marian Evans, p. 270. Boston, Houghton Mifflin, 1881, 2 ed.

[8] See § 820, footnotes 8 and 9.

[9] Immanuel Kant, *Religion Innerhalb der Grenzen Blossen Vernuft.* See Rosenkranz's edition, Vol. X, pp. 184 ff. Leipsic, Voss, 1838.

[10] Herbert Spencer, *Principles of Sociology,* Vol. I, p. 440.

330. *The true concept of religion.* There is a dispute over the etymology of the term religion. Cicero derives it from *relegere,* which means to treat carefully, to reread. He says, "Those who carefully took in hand all things pertaining to the gods are called *religiosi,* from *relegere.*"[11] This is an unlikely derivation, for religion existed long before complicated ritual. St. Augustine first thought it comes from *religere,* "to recover." "Having lost God through neglect we recover Him and are drawn to Him."[12] This view appears to be too subjective, too colored by the saint's own experiences. Lactantius derives religion from *religare,* "to bind." "We are tied to God and bound to Him by the bonds of piety."[13] This seems most acceptable. Some persons who accept this derivation add this further refinement: there is an objective bond of dependence of man upon God; man's faculties recognize this and deliberately rebind man back to God. This seems to be a complication more pious than sound. Whatever the merits of these arguments, there is a bond between God and man which determines the nature of religion.

331. *The elements of the bond between God and man.* This bond is physical and moral. (*a*) It is *physical* because it is a bond of origin. All things outside of God ultimately owe their existence to God the Creator. As contingent beings, they are constantly and immediately dependent on divine conservation and co-operation. This physical bond is due to the efficient causality of God. (*b*) The bond between God and man is also *moral.* God is not only the exemplary cause, the pattern after which man is made, but He is man's last end. God operates upon man's mind and will as final cause and supreme legislator. Therefore, God is man's beginning and end, upon whom man is totally dependent always and in everything. This is the basis of religion; and the sum total of the truths pertaining to the nature of God, the nature of man, and the relation of man to God constitute *theoretical religion* or the dogmas of natural religion.

But religion is not mere theory. From God's complete dominion and man's utter dependence, certain corollaries of action follow with inexorable logic. Man must conduct himself with due subjection to God: his voluntary subjection of self to God constitutes *practical religion.* Our ethical problem, then, resolves itself to this: by what

---

[11] *De Natura Deorum,* II, 28.
[12] *De Civitate Dei,* X, 3.
[13] *De divin. Institut.,* IV, 28; Migne, P.L., VI, 537.

specific acts must man manifest his dependence on God; what are the particular tenets of natural practical religion?

II. KNOWLEDGE OF GOD

332. Man's first specific obligation is to know the *one true* God. Man's subjection to God must accord with his nature: it must be a reasonable subjection, but man cannot reasonably submit to what he does not know. He must seek his last end, God, rationally; and this presupposes knowledge of God. Polytheism — which sets up creatures or fictitious beings as gods — does not satisfy this obligation. Through inculpable ignorance one could be a polytheist for a time, but ignorance of the one true God over a long period must be culpable, for constant obedience to the Natural Law results in knowledge of its author. Absence of knowledge of the author of the Natural Law over a long period argues to constant violations of the law. The reason for not knowing God is not lack of evidence to convince the mind but refusal of the will to recognize a Lawgiver who demands control of passion.

From knowledge of the one true God, one advances to knowledge of His chief attributes — power, divinity, and infinity. The latter naturally follows from the former. This knowledge need not be precise and scientific: the realization that God is of supreme excellence and might suffices. We shall prove that man must hope in God, worship Him, and love Him above all things — knowledge of God's chief attributes is necessary to arrive at these conclusions.

333. How is this knowledge acquired? Two ways are conceivable: reason and revelation. Natural theology is the study of God by means of reason. Divine revelation is direct communication of God to man. It may be objected that divine revelation, because of its supernatural character, lies beyond the scope of ethics. The answer is that although the relationship between them is indirect, it is sufficiently pertinent.

334. *What is divine revelation?* It is the manifestation of truth by God to man. Divine revelation may be either natural or supernatural.

1. *Natural* revelation is the manifestation of truth on the part of God to man which is due human nature. It is the action of God whereby man is so internally constituted and so externally and natur- ally assisted by God that man may attain any truth within the grasp of his intellect. We roughly but correctly enough say the natural way

for God to communicate to man is through the world of nature wherein God has written the truth about Himself for man to discern.

2. *Supernatural* revelation is the action of God manifesting truths to man via formal speech. Speech is the act of communicating thought to another by arbitrary objective signs. Between God and man this is something supernatural, that is, it is not due to man's nature nor is it necessary for his development nor the prosecution of his natural end. This is what usually is meant by the term divine revelation.

335. *Is divine revelation possible?* Rationalism not only denies the fact of revelation but even its possibility. However, no proof has yet been adduced to show that God cannot do what man can do, that is, communicate His thoughts by words and signs. If such an impossibility did exist it would arise either on the part of God, or of man, or it would be due to the truth to be revealed.

Revelation could not be impossible as far as God is concerned. Being omniscient, God knows revealable truths; being omnipotent, He can devise and execute the means of presenting these truths to man so that man can know with certainty that God is speaking to him.

As for man, by nature he is able to discover truths through his own industry and from the instruction of another. Indeed, the one instructing may be an infinitely perfect Person. In fact it is but fitting that a finite mind should agree with the pronouncements of an infinite mind, that man should be able to recognize God speaking to him.

Finally, any truth which is not strictly a mystery can be proposed to, and accepted by, the human mind. Whether there are mysteries or whether these are revealable does not pertain to this investigation.

Divine revelation, then, is possible. Granted that it is possible, a hypothetical obligation arises from the Natural Law.

THESIS XXI. If God makes a supernatural revelation, the Natural Law commands man to accept it.

PROOF

336. The Natural Law commands man to accept the manifestation of One who (*a*) can neither deceive nor be deceived; (*b*) speaks precisely in order that He may be believed; and (*c*) has the right to speak and exact assent. Man would act contrary to his nature in rejecting manifest truth authoritatively proposed. Since God knows all things and cannot lie, since He has the right to speak and exact man's assent, since He would not speak unless He desired man's assent, it follows that if He were to make a revelation, the law of man's nature would oblige him to accept it.

Corollary I. From nature man has a hypothetical obligation to accept divine faith, that is to say, in the event of divine revelation, the Natural Law compels us to believe.

Corollary II. If a doubt arises concerning the existence of a divine revelation, the Natural Law obliges man to make suitable inquiry; otherwise he would be culpably ignorant of the will of the Supreme Legislator.

337. *Did God actually make a supernatural revelation?* Apologetics offers irrefutable evidence of supernatural revelation. Since one of these demonstrations is actually an ethical argument, it is given in general outline.

The truths of natural religion—both theoretical and practical — are of utmost importance to man; therefore he should come to know them early in life, with facility, and with certitude. Because of man's intellectual sloth and preoccupation with the necessities and pleasures of life, these truths must come easily or not at all. Again, man should have a reasonably good understanding of them early in life. Good habits are best formed in youth, but this is impossible without early knowledge of the truths of natural religion. Finally, unless man holds these truths with certitude, he will not lead an upright moral life: there could hardly be a greater impediment to the attainment of his final end than doubt about these fundamental realities.

Unaided by divine revelation, most men will not acquire the truths of natural religion *easily*. These truths are rather abstruse, appeal little to the imagination, and therefore are difficult to grasp. The ordinary man will not learn these things *early in life*. They are not only difficult to grasp, but youth is so distracted and subjected to such strong emotions that he has little inclination to consider them, let alone pursue them on his own initiative. Finally, it is clear from history that only a few men of unusual ability have come to know these things *late in life,* and even their findings were not unmixed with serious error. The most civilized nations of antiquity, lacking such a revelation, have held gross and fantastic errors in matters of religion and morality. A few outstanding men like Plato, Aristotle, Cicero, and Vergil had a fair knowledge of these truths, but even their conclusions were unhappily mingled with error.

In view of the above facts, we conclude that God must super-naturally reveal to man those religious and moral truths which man could discover for himself. However, there is no absolute necessity for such a revelation: man does have the capacity to discover these truths; but actually man will not do so unaided because of weaknesses which render him prone to error. God is infinitely generous. His beneficence is not limited to giving man only the bare requisites of human exist-ence; He also bestows on man those things which make for fullness of life. Even though man by folly and sin blinded himself to religious truth within his grasp and thereby practically put this truth beyond his grasp, God gives him the light of divine revelation. Theophanies and supernatural revelation are by no means incompatible with natural religion and ethics.

III. HOPE IN GOD

338. After knowledge of God, religion demands hope. Hope is the confident expectation that God will ultimately admit us to beatitude and consequently that He will grant us in due time the means necessary thereunto.

Without hope, beatitude cannot be realized, for beatitude is an arduous good, attainable only by constant exertion and the conquest of difficulties. The enticements to ignore the Natural Law are so alluring and obedience to the Natural Law so exacting that man could scarcely undertake to keep the law or to persevere long in such an attempt without steadfast hope of reward. Without hope of attaining his end one could not reasonably strive for it. Our present happiness is hope.

Hope is not self-confidence — reliance on one's own virtue; hope rests in God. Man's attainment of his end depends not only on his own good will but especially upon the assistance of God. Man, conse-quently, must reasonably expect that this divine aid will be forth-coming. He must hope for the guidance of Divine Providence and especially an effective remedy against his disordered concupiscence.

IV. THE WORSHIP OF GOD

A. The Individual and Divine Worship

339. Equity demands that we accord everyone his due. Does man give everything that is directly due to God by knowing Him and hoping in Him? No. In addition, the practically unanimous voice of mankind, attested to by the religious activities and experiences of man through the ages, demands worship — the formal and explicit acknowledgment of man's subjection to God. This men regard as the very core of religion.

340. *What is worship?* Worship means "worthship," the state of being worth something. Persons are the most excellent beings of which we have experience. A person deserves honor, that is, recognition of his excellence. Honor is more than mere knowledge, for it implies an act of the will referring such knowledge to another as that other's extrinsic good. Honor does not add to one's essential excellence; it is the external adornment of personality.

If the person is of superior excellence, as, for example, a father or ruler, *reverence* is also due him. Reverence is the acknowledgment of another's superior dignity and power coupled with a desire of not displeasing him. Superior excellence enjoins fitting subordination on the part of inferiors. As honor is due to all men, whether inferior, equal, or superior, precisely because they are men, so reverence is an added tribute to those who are superior among men. Reverence is not something useful, it does not supply a need — what admiral really needs the dipping of a flag or the firing of guns — but since dignity is worthy of recognition, order requires that man does not withhold it.

341. As it is fitting for man to honor and reverence created personalities, so he must duly recognize the Uncreated Person. Man gives honor to God by *divine worship,* which is the recognition of God's infinite excellence together with submission of ourselves to Him. Worship involves a fourfold submission: (*a*) *praise and reverence* unto God's infinitely perfect nature — this is adoration, which would be due to God even on the impossible assumption that we were not dependent on Him; (*b*) *thanksgiving* to the Benefactor from whom man receives all things; (*c*) *propitiation,* since man is constantly conscious of transgressions against the Supreme Lawgiver and hence desires to regain his favor; (*d*) *petition* for further benefits from God from whom alone all benefits come.

Any act of divine praise, thanksgiving, propitiation, or petition entails three acts on man's part: (*a*) an act of the mind recognizing God's infinite excellence and judging it worthy of respect by submission to it; (*b*) an act of the will ordering that some fitting token of respect be shown; (*c*) actual manifestation of respect — this may be external, such as bowing the head, bending the knee, or saying a vocal prayer; or it may be purely internal, such as a simple act of submission of the will.

342. The commonest form of divine worship is *prayer*. Prayer is conversation with God. Even apart from the dictates of religion, this ascent of the mind and heart to God is absolutely necessary for man to reach beatitude. Prayer is the efficacious instrument which disposes God to grant what we need for happiness. Its importance in man's moral life cannot be exaggerated. The man who does not know how to pray does not know his own misery and dishonor.

The most solemn and complete act of divine worship is *sacrifice*. Described in simple terms, sacrifice is the offering of a gift to God. Man, the creature, instinctively realizes that when he comes formally into the presence of his Creator he must bear with him a gift as the supreme token of his respect. This gift is some material thing of value: it is a symbol of God's supreme dominion over all things, especially over man, for whom it is substituted. To signify its return to God's exclusive possession, the gift is destroyed or altered in some way.

The method of honoring God which we have described is *direct divine worship*. Some persons, even of those who admit the one true God, claim that *indirect worship suffices*. It is their contention that submission to the Natural Law releases one of the obligations of religion. As long as one leads a good clean life, there is no need of special religious observances. But one does not fully keep that law unless he offers God explicit worship for one of the particulars of the law is thus enunciated:

THESIS XXII. The Natural Law commands each individual to render internal and external worship to God.

343. Every man, capable of reasoning, from time to time must acknowledge within himself his complete dependence upon God and give external testimony of his dependence by suitable acts of praise, thanksgiving, propitiation, and petition. Since God is the ultimate and sole source of all benefits accruing to man, man has the never-ending obligation of thanking Him for His benefits and asking for further blessings. Since God is the Supreme Lawgiver and man is constantly transgressing the law, man has the recurring need of regaining God's favor. What remains to be proved is the need of explicit praise and reverence, that is, adoration.

PROOF

344. The Natural Law forbids man to be indifferent to or to contemn God, because he is essentially and absolutely dependent on Him as Creator, Conserver, and Co-operator. Now man would contemn or at least would be indifferent to God if he failed to render interior adoration and exterior worship to Him.

1. *Interior adoration.* If man does not acknowledge his total dependence on God, his intellect violates its natural inclination for truth; if man does not freely subordinate himself to God, his will acts as if it were independent.

2. *Exterior worship.* First, interior worship will fail if it is not externalized. Second, since man is made of body and spirit, the body too by external worship must acknowledge man's total dependence on God. God, the absolute Lord, has a right to all the activities of man, his complete servant.

B. Society and Divine Worship

345. The obligation of divine worship does not only bind man as an individual; it also binds him as a social being. Religion is not confined to the hidden recesses of the soul or the privacy of one's room. It bears a social character and obligation.

THESIS XXIII. Man must unite with his fellow man in offering God the homage of society.

By this thesis we understand that the State and the family as natural institutions have an obligation to render God external worship and that the individual must have part in such religious observances. This we call *public worship*.

PROOF

346. *Man must unite with his fellow man in offering God the homage of society,* for the family and State are natural institutions immediately dependent on God as Cause, Conserver, and Guide. Just as the individual must recognize and acknowledge his complete dependence on his Creator, so too the family and State must acknowledge a similar dependence. As the family and State are moral persons, their obligations can be fulfilled only by acts of individuals.

1. That God is the *Cause* of family and State is proved in social ethics (cf. §§ 705, 738, and 817).

2. He is also *Conserver*. The well-being of family and State depends on man's observance of the Natural Law. As God is the Author of this law, He is the Conserver and Preserver of State and family.

3. Finally, God is the Guide of the family and State. Human authority directs these institutions to the attainment of their well-being; this authority, however, is delegated by God, the supreme Lord of the universe and is a participation in His divine guidance. This is proved in social ethics, §§705 and 862.

347. Corollary I. From the need of external worship of God, the need of liturgy, or ritual, follows. Liturgy, or ritual, is the natural outgrowth of repeated religious observances. The decorum and reverence attaching to religious worship demands that the words, actions, costume, appurtenances, gestures, and even posture, belonging to worship be defined carefully by custom or law and not left to hasty improvisation of the moment.

Corollary II. A man cannot be a good man if he does not worship God, for to fail to do so is to spurn one of the most patent dictates of the Natural Law. This attitude of neglect is *practical religious indifference.*

348. Abundant evidence for the acceptance of this obligation is furnished by the history of religions. Among all peoples there has been worship regulated by authority.

Where the family is the only social institution, the time and manner of fulfilling this obligation, as well as the necessity of individual participation, is to be regulated by the head of the family. Families did fulfill this duty. Among many people the head of the house was also the family priest until this function was absorbed by State or Church.

Where the State alone exists, that is, where there is no separate religious authority, the responsibility for public worship falls to State law. Where the Church exists, that is, where there is a distinct and separate religious authority, individual and familial participation in worship is to be regulated by that authority.

If God supernaturally intervenes and indicates a particular mode of divine worship, the Natural Law commands all men and all States to worship in this manner.

C. Manner of Worshiping God

349. The Natural Law indicates only the broadest outline of the mode of worshiping God. But there is a vast array of systems by which the one true God is worshiped. Does the Natural Law say anything concerning them? Does it leave each man free to choose whichever he fancies? Does it command him to accept what civil or parental authority dictates?

Every system of worship has a body of dogmatic truths. A creed is necessary. Religious worship cannot be mere ritual and emotion; to be worthy of God and man it must have an intellectual basis. In so far as a method of worship is also a system of religious dogmas, the Natural Law does contain precepts directly pertaining to them.

In commanding man to worship Him, God cannot oblige him to accept falsehood: man is obliged only to accept truth. Hence the Natural Law says that man is to worship God by that system of rites which is founded on the truth and the truth alone.

350. There is a most prevalent notion to the effect that all religions are equally pleasing to God and useful to man. This is called *dogmatic religious indifference*. Since it represents God as pleased with error and implicitly asserts that error is as good as truth, it must be rejected. All known religious systems contradict one another on various points of doctrine. Consequently all cannot be right. Therefore God cannot be pleased with all religions, and it is false to say one religion is as good as another. On the other hand, all of the religions cannot be wrong, for if they were, God would receive nothing but false worship, which is absurd.

Certainly if God desires to be worshiped in a particular manner, He must intervene with supernatural revelation, for as we have said, the Natural Law does not give the details pertaining to divine worship. To prove that God did make such a revelation is beyond the province of ethics.

D. Sins Against the Due Worship of God

351. Sins of defect against divine worship are classified as irreligion; those of excess, as superstition.

1. *Irreligion* is lack of reverence for God. It includes the following:

a) *Practical religious indifference* — failure to worship God when the proper occasion demands it.

b) *Tempting God* — any word, act, or omission whereby man endeavors to test one of God's attributes. It is a serious want of reverence to doubt God's power and to challenge Him to manifest it.

c) *Blasphemy* — contumely directed against God or creatures precisely because of their relationship to God. This is dishonor to God and grave perversion of human nature. To the ancient Greeks it was the worst human crime.[14] So great was the reverence of the ancient Jews for the name of God that they carefully refrained from using the proper name of God, "I am who am," and substituted in its stead, "The Lord."

Even if contempt of God is not intended, it is still irreverence to use God's name as a mere exclamation or expletive. Ordinarily, frivolous and profane use of God's name is not a serious wrong. It is a serious wrong, however, to use the name of God in cursing. In cursing, one deliberately asks God to wreak evil upon another. The name of God is dishonored by being associated with a serious sin against charity.

A person who has contracted the habit of using blasphemous language is obliged to rid himself of it. Even though he does not directly intend to be contemptuous of God, his evil habit dishonors God and scandalizes others.

d) *Perjury* — the violation of an oath. There is a vast difference between a mere lie and a lie under oath, for in an oath God is called upon to witness the truth of what is said. An oath is assertory when God is asked to confirm the truth of an assertion; it is promissory when He is asked to confirm a promise or resolution.

Two conditions are required for the validity of an oath: (*a*) the intention to swear and (*b*) a proper external formula. Three conditions are required for lawful swearing: (*a*) truth, (*b*) judgment, and (*c*) justice. According to the first condition, truth, one cannot ask God to witness a falsehood. According to the condition of judgment, one must have a sufficient reason for swearing and must take an oath with proper reverence. Last, the condition of justice means that in a promissory oath, one may promise only what is morally lawful.

e) *Violation of a vow.* A vow is a free promise made to God concerning a good which is possible and a *greater good* than its contradictory. A vow is not a mere promise or resolution; it is a self-imposed obligation which binds one through the virtue of religion. It is truly

---

[14] Cf. Sophocles, *Oedipus Tyrannus*, 883–893; Plutarch, *Alcibiades*, XXIII.

an act of worship. No one is required to make any vow, but once a vow is made, the Natural Law obliges fulfillment. While one may bind himself by the extra tie of religion to that which already is obligatory, for example, chastity, the matter of a vow is usually not obligatory.

352. 2. *Superstition* is either giving a creature honor which belongs to God alone or giving God false or unsuited worship. Noteworthy among such crimes are the following:

a) *Idolatry* — explicit tribute of divine worship to a creature. History shows that no other moral evil has had such a degrading influence on man.[15] It is the most heinous sin against divine worship.

b) *Divination* — the endeavor to learn the *free future* from a source other than God. Since God alone knows what men will freely resolve to do in the future, the attempt to learn it from a creature is implicit tribute of divine honor to that creature. Man's insatiable curiosity has led him to seek for this knowledge in countless ways — consultation of oracles; inspection of cards, the entrails of men or beasts, the palm of the hand, the bumps on one's head; study of dreams; the flight of birds and the stars; messages from the spirits of the dead; use of a ouija board. To use seriously any of these means in an attempt to learn the free future or to consult a person who seriously believes that he or she has this power is always a grievous wrong. To attempt to learn the future from things in which one only half-believes or from persons who do not take themselves seriously is a venial wrong. To play with these things for recreation is not sinful but may be dangerous.

c) *Vain observance* — the use of means which neither naturally nor by divine authority have the power to produce the effects expected of them. In thus attributing to a creature a power which it does not possess, there is at least an implicit invocation of the creature as God. People have sought knowledge through charms, spells, the drinking of certain potions; they have resorted to talismans to ward off evil and bring good luck — a man once wore a horse chestnut in his left hip pocket during the time of his wife's pregnancy to insure the birth of a boy.

The malice of divination or vain observance cannot be adequately understood without reference to certain facts of revelation. There is a personal devil, Satan, the enemy of God and of mankind whose purpose is ever the dishonoring of God and the eternal ruin of men.

---

[15] Cf. Romans 1:18 ff.

Every act of divination or vain observance seriously intended contains an implicit invocation of Satan's aid. If a desired result cannot be obtained from a creature's natural powers, and if God does not see fit to grant it extraordinarily, then to choose means which are not naturally calculated to effect it, is an appeal for Satan's aid. To ask this help is to dishonor God, for everything which Satan does is directed to God's dishonor and the harm of men. Consequently, the person who believes that a desired result will *infallibly* follow from such unnatural means is always guilty of grave wrong.

If the effects to be produced by vain observance are marvelous, the practice is called *magic*. The use of magic is quite prevalent among barbarous tribes. If a wonder-worker or sorcerer endeavors to wreak evil on his neighbor, he is guilty of an additional violation against justice or charity. Instances of the evil eye — or hexing, as the Pennsylvania Dutch call it — have been found among us as late as 1926.

There are certain silly superstitious practices which people observe for the sake of good luck or fear of bad luck. Many of these are only slightly wrong, because people do not *infallibly* expect good or bad luck from them. Through invincible ignorance, some persons see no harm in them. Others, however, comply with these practices not because they put real credence in them, but because they would be uneasy or nervous if they disregarded them.

If all superstitious intent is excluded, it is not wrong to investigate the occult powers of nature in order to widen the field of human knowledge. For example, knowledge of the influence of the mind on the body and of the body on the mind has led to progress in medicine. Again, the workings of the subconscious mind, hypnotic influence, the communication of thought directly from mind to mind (mental telepathy) may be legitimate subjects of psychological research. Scientific investigation may demonstrate that a number of seemingly marvelous or even supposedly preternatural effects have a purely natural cause. Investigation of these and similar phenomena requires utmost prudence, for experience has shown that rash dabbling may prove disastrous to health, morality, and supernatural faith.

The most prevalent of present-day forms of vain observance is *spiritism,* which is nothing more than ancient necromancy (the evocation of the spirits of the dead) in modern setting. While most spiritistic mediums may be laughed at as frauds and spiritism may be considered just another shady way of making a living contrived by shrewd individuals who exploit and play upon the gullibility of their fellow man, not all the phenomena of modern spiritism may be dismissed as hokum. Some truly genuine effects are wrought. While the explanation of some of these effects may be traced to occult but natural causes, others are undoubtedly of preternatural origin — which can be due only to diabolical intervention.

353. Since religion is so basic a need of man, and since so many modern men have abandoned belief in, and the practice of, supernatural religion one can logically expect in our time a growing increase in superstitious practices. Man must have some religion, and when he rejects one revealed by God, he will fashion a substitute of his own contriving. How poor and crude such substitutes are, becomes quite clear in times of war and calamity. Then the old dark gods emerge from the jungle and primitive superstitions reappear. Our age of advanced thinkers, the intellectual heir of eighteenth-century rationalism, has returned to astrology, dream books, and numerology.

V. THE LOVE OF GOD

354. The obligation of loving God usually is included in the obligation of worshiping Him. Some element of love must enter the act of worship. Most ethicians gloss over this topic — some, because of their false notions of God; others, because they feel that the subject should not be treated apart from revelation. Men might be confused by the meaning of a love of God, which is distinct from, and higher than, acts of divine honor and reverence. They readily see that they must love their parents, wives, and children and how they must express their love; but they might not understand how they could love a Pure Spirit, invisible to them, unless God had revealed Himself by assuming human nature in the Incarnation. However, even if God had not appeared among men in the likeness of man, the Natural Law, nevertheless, would indicate a distinct duty of loving God.

355. *What is love?* In the widest sense, love is the motion of an appetite toward an object apprehended as good and hence as desirable. While many appetites seek divers goods, our discussion is restricted to the intellectual appetite. Now this prosecutive motion of the will varies as does the reason motivating it, which may be twofold: (*a*) *the will may strive to subordinate the object sought to the agent's*

good. Such an object is not loved for its own sake; love for it is a qualified love, because the object is sought as a means to the good of the subject. This is *love of desire.* Thus, a person may love oysters, good wine, or even a person who is extremely useful to him. (*b*) *The will may wish good to the object loved.* This is always a person who is sought for his own sake. This is *love of benevolence,* in which the object is loved absolutely, that is, for himself. We do not say "for himself alone," meaning to the exclusion of the good of the one loving. While we may conceive of one who loves another more than he loves himself, even in that case there is love of self. Is love, then, basically selfish? The exaggerated altruism of the nineteenth century, teaching that man's final end is the subordination of the individual to the good of society, exhorted man to love his fellow man with a love which excluded self. This has caused great befuddlement. Certainly all men admit that the noblest love is that which is least self-centered, yet there is a love of self which is laudatory because it is orderly. This the altruist confused with selfishness which is despicable because it is disorderly. Mere selfishness is not wrong but selfishness which is exaggerated and unreasonable is.

356. Aristotle contends that all love — even love of benevolence and friendship — stems from love of self.[16] The reason is that the basic principle and final purpose of all love is union between the one loving and the object of his love, but the person loving is more at one with himself than with any person outside himself. Now friendship is the loftiest kind of love, yet we never speak of a man being friendly to himself. He has for himself that which is deeper than friendship. By friendship we strive for union with other people, but a man is related to himself by something more fundamental than union — it is the relation of unity itself, and unity goes deeper than union for it is the very principle of union. Therefore, as unity is the principle of union, so love of self is the principle of love. A man then loves others in so far as he wishes them to be at one with him and himself with them.

357. Is it incorrect to say that benevolence whereby we love another for his own sake must flow from love of self? No, for love of self is the ground of every human impulse. The transition from self-regarding love to benevolence occurs in this way. Because I desire that

---

[16] *Ethics,* VIII, 5, 1157b.

another be one with me, my love goes out to him. He is an *alter ego,* my other self; hence I put him in my place and wish good to him accordingly. Thus, maternal love, which can be so self-effacing, has its roots in love of self, because mothers see in their progeny the continuation of their own personalities; and so they crave for themselves, continued in their children, not only the advantages they enjoyed but especially those they themselves missed.

358. The crown and flower of benevolence is *love of friendship,* which is a love of mutual benevolence between equals. This includes benevolence, mutuality of benevolence, a certain equality, communion of all things.

1. *Benevolence* is involved for the one loved is loved for his own sake.

2. There is *mutuality of benevolence* in love of friendship, that is, there is an interchange of goods. The one who loves wishes to endow the one loved with all of his goods, and vice versa. Hence it is a love which is expressed not so much by words as by deeds. This characteristic peculiarity of friendship St. Thomas[17] calls a communication of life, that is, those goods which are proper to lover and beloved are mutually exchanged. Because brutes cannot share in what is proper to man, namely, rational life, this kind of love cannot exist between man and brute.

3. The mutual interchange of goods demands *a certain equality,* at least of nature, so that the giving and taking of what is proper to each is possible. Because of this harmony of nature, a mutual attraction, or sympathy, of one to the other is possible. This harmony does not imply that the two are exactly alike but more often that one complements the other. Each receives the richness and fullness of life possible to him precisely through this interchange of goods. This is most evident in the love of husband and wife.

4. Since the final end of love is the completest union possible, love exacts a *communion of mind, heart, and all things,* each giving to the other all that he can and that the other is capable of receiving. In perfect love there are no secrets, no reserves, no holding back a part of one's self or goods: there is as full a giving as possible. Perfect love is perfect self-surrender. Love seeking such union begets the desire to be near and enjoy the physical presence of the one beloved. Hence unrequited love cannot perdure: there is no lasting love of friendship

---

[17] *Sum. Theol.,* II–II, 23, aa. 1, 5.

without a mutual giving and receiving. The culmination of love is the intensest joy in the possession of one's beloved.

359. *What kind of love must man have for God?*

1. *Man must love God with a love of desire.* Since God is man's last end, man will have his supreme good only when he possesses God. Since man cannot help desiring his perfect happiness, he must desire God. In such a love, man loves God for man's sake.

2. *Man must love God with a love of benevolence.* God must be loved for His own sake and not merely because He is good for man. If man loved God merely with a love of desire, God would ultimately be subordinated to man's good. But it is repugnant to the order of nature that God, the end of all things, should be subordinated to any thing whatever. Hence God should be loved absolutely and for His own sake.

3. *Man must love God more than he loves himself.* The reason is not precisely because God is of an excellence superior to man, for then a man would be obliged to love above self all men who are better than himself — which is not true. The reason is subtler, for it is grounded on the principle that love of self is man's primary impulse plus a consideration of God's infinite perfections. Now a man can love his neighbor, because his neighbor is one with him in nature. But in many ways his neighbor fails to be one with him; there are many things in himself which he does not find in his neighbor. Therefore, man loves his neighbor less than he loves himself. While God is utterly distinct from man, every perfection which is in man is also in God and to an infinite degree. Hence God is to be loved above self. A friend is an *alter ego* but lesser; God is an *alter ego* but greater and is therefore more lovable than self. All of which comports with the conclusion already established that man's perfect happiness, had by loving God, is subordinated to the divine glory.

We do not mean that God must be loved with the utmost intensity or emotion of the appetite. The intensity of the will's love for an object depends both on the adequacy of one's knowledge concerning the object and the presence of a concomitant drive of the sensitive appetite toward the same object. Thus a man's most intense love goes forth to a fellow man — a wife, a parent, a child, because he can know them intimately and they can powerfully appeal to his imagination and senses. God, however, as a pure spirit, does not appeal to the sensitive appetite. Hence it is only the will, illumined by fitful intellectual knowledge, that seeks Him; not the total man. However, when God finally is presented to the will by fitting knowledge, man will be drawn to Him with irresistible force.

Since will acts are nobilitated by the excellence of the object sought, an act of the love of God for his own sake is the supreme moral act of which man is capable.

360. 4. *True love of friendship is naturally impossible between God and man,* for there is no natural equality between God and man. Without equality of nature, lover and beloved cannot share what is *proper* to each. Only when God lifts man to a level above his own nature and makes him a partaker of the divine nature is this love possible. God effects this divinization of man by the infusion of sanctifying grace, which lies beyond the field of ethics.

361. 5. *How does man fulfill the precept of loving God?*

a) Man fulfills this precept negatively by not hating God as, for instance, Lenin did when he said, "I hate God as I do my personal enemies."[18] Hatred can also be leveled against the divine attributes, as when a hardened sinner reviles divine justice. A greater abomination than hatred of God is impossible to conceive.

b) Indirectly, one loves God by every act of the service of God. Whenever anyone observes the law of God, he renders God an external good, he gives Him glory, he makes God manifest in his own moral act.

c) Over and above such implicit love, as occasion demands, man must make explicit acts of love of which God is the direct object.

---

[18] Cf. Delaye-Schumaker, *What Is Communism?*, p. 83. St. Louis, Herder, 1938.

READINGS

St. Thomas, *Summa Theologica*, II–II, 81–100.
——— *Contra Gentiles*, III, 114–120.
Boylan, M. Eugene, O.Cist.R., *This Tremendous Lover*, pp. 51–64. Westminster, Md., Newman, 1947.
Castelein, A., S.J., *Institutiones Philosophiae Moralis et Socialis*, pp. 217–230. Bruxelles, Societé Belge de Libraire, 1899.
Catholic Encyclopedia, "Adoration," I, 151; "Blasphemy," II, 595; "Cursing," IV, 573; "Divination," V, 48; "Idolatry," VII, 636; "Indifferentism," VII, 759; "Oaths," XI, 176; "Occultism," XI, 197; "Perjury," XI, 696; "Religion," XII, 748; "Superstition," XIV, 339.
Coppens, Charles, S.J., *Moral Philosophy*, pp. 82–93. New York, Schwartz, Kirwin, Fauss, 1924.

Cronin, Michael, *The Science of Ethics,* Vol. II, pp. 1–46. Dublin, Gill, 1909.

de la Boullaye, H. Pinard, S.J., *L'Etude Comparée des Religions.* Paris, Beauchesne, 1922.

Janet, Paul, *Theory of Morals,* pp. 472–485, trans. Chapman. New York, Scribner's, 1898.

Karrer, Otto, *Religions of Mankind,* pp. 84–109. New York, Sheed and Ward, 1936.

Langan, J. T., S.J., *Apologetica,* pp. 6–15, 339–373. Chicago, Loyola University Press, 1921.

Lattey, C., S.J., *Revelation.* London, Catholic Truth Society, 1923.

Leibell, J. F. (ed.), *Readings in Ethics,* pp. 432–449. Chicago, Loyola University Press, 1926.

Morrison, Bakewell, S.J., *The Catholic Church and the Modern Mind,* pp. 134–162, 272–305. Milwaukee, The Bruce Publishing Co., 1933.

Rickaby, Joseph J., S.J., *Aquinus Ethicus,* Vol. II, pp. 110–196.

――― *Moral Philosophy,* pp. 191–201.

Ross, Eva J., *Social Origins,* pp. 71–104. New York, Sheed and Ward, 1936.

CHAPTER XI

DUTIES TO SOUL

362. Since man must love God more than himself, his particular duties to God are of first importance. Since he is to love himself more than his fellow man, certain duties to himself are next in importance. We shall now consider these duties. Man's first duty to himself is to attain his final end, his ultimate perfection. This is immediately evident from what has been established in general ethics regarding the end of man and the sanction of the Natural Law. Since this life is but a preparation for another life wherein ultimate perfection is granted or denied us, at the age of reason man must begin to strive for self-perfection. Man must make of himself what he can according to his ability and his opportunities. This is summed up in the phrase, *a man must love himself with a well-ordered love*. This he does in a general way when he directs his entire life to the attainment of beatitude.

More specifically, a man loves himself reasonably when he secures certain internal goods of soul and body as well as a number of external advantages. Since the spirit is of prime importance, we must know what spiritual perfection a man must acquire to assure beatitude. Man's ultimate perfection is directly promoted by the activity of his moral faculties, particularly by his will constantly embracing his real good, refusing merely apparent good. An essential prerequisite is that the intellect present to the will truth, that is, that which objectively is man's real good. The problem then reduces itself to this: a man must cultivate his intellect to the extent that he is sure of knowing his real good, and he must train his will so that he will readily choose the same.

I. TRAINING OF THE MIND

363. From our explanation of the Natural Law and of man's obligation to obey his conscience, it is clear that reason is man's supreme

directive. "Follow reason"—this is one of nature's first laws. But before reason is prepared to lead, it must properly fulfill its natural function, which is not proficiency in logical gymnastics or mental legerdemain; nor is it readiness to wisecrack, criticize, and devise arguments: reason is prepared to lead when it possesses the truth. The so-called trained mind, in which truth and error are inextricably intertwined, is a human instrument of doubtful validity. Only the mind which has a clear, unwavering grasp of fundamental truth is a reliable guide.

364. The inevitable effect of erroneous principles of action is failure. From error must come disorder and chaos. With reference to material things this scarcely needs demonstration. The airplane manufacturer who uses faulty theories of aerodynamics may turn out scores of planes, but they will not stay long in the air. An engineer whose fundamental mechanics are awry may construct roads, bridges, and apartment houses; but in a short time the roads will buckle, the bridges will sway and fall, and the apartment houses will be unsafe for habitation. The same is true in moral matters the only difference being there is a longer interval between the acceptance of error and the inevitable confusion. In the nineteenth century, Nietzsche taught the superman theory; in September, 1939, Hitler and the Wehrmacht gave a concrete demonstration of domination and spoliation. From Darwin some men took the theory that man is only an animal; now more and more men are living purely animal lives. In the sixteenth century, for the first time in the history of Christianity, it was denied that matrimony is a sacrament of the New Law. The leaven was slow to work but today the full fruit of that denial can be seen in our sordid story of trial marriages and bargain divorces. You cannot sow the wind without some day reaping the whirlwind.

Just as we may unconsciously take on the accent or copy the grammatical mistakes of those with whom we associate, so we can absorb their erroneous thoughts. Such intellectual disease is as contagious as smallpox. Two causes operate to make this danger very real: one is as old as humankind; the other, bright as a new penny, is disguised as the offspring of human progress. The first is prejudice; the second, intellectual license.

365. *Prejudice,* or judging from insufficient evidence, is the subordination or even the very substitution of wishing for thinking. While the mind must necessarily accept the truth presented to it, yet it can be and is turned from the truth by undue influence of the will. As man's supreme faculty, the will can unduly dominate the mind. Thus, in solving a problem to which a conclusion has not yet appeared, the will can direct and fix the mind's attention on reasons leading to a preferred conclusion and keep it from full consideration of opposite reasons. Even if the truth is evident the will can turn the mind from it by having it advert to frivolous reasons contrary to the truth. This is more easily done when one is dealing not with facts and happenings but with universal ideas. The will so acts because without sufficient reason it prefers one opinion to another. It arbitrarily fixes upon one conclusion and orders the mind to find justifying reasons for it. This is usurpation of the function of intellect, enslavement of it, and deprivation of its prerogative of being led solely by objective evidence.

366. The will can arbitrarily select one opinion rather than another for the following reasons:

1. The opinion *conforms to passion*. A person indulges in illicit pleasure. The will seeks self-justification and influences the mind to regard the object of such passion a real good. Many who practice artificial birth control cajole themselves into holding that their act is laudable.

2. The opinion promises something *more useful to one's temporal advantage*. A man who cares little for beatitude, to be enjoyed hereafter, is deeply concerned over the apparent goods of fortune, power, and enjoyment. Thus, to gain a political victory or to save himself from jail he will think it right to perjure himself.

3. The opinion is *more popular*. Living in a democracy, people can readily make an unconscious transition from public opinion as the norm of political decision to public opinion as the criterion of moral ideas. Thus, if a Gallup Poll discloses that 63 per cent of the people favor divorce, then divorce is acceptable. Fashion can dictate not only the cut of one's clothes but the style of one's ideas. Despite the spread of literacy, it is easier for most people to accept ideas ready made for them than undergo the labor of thinking. If the people of my circle consider this public figure a villain, he must be so. If the nice people of my community get drunk at parties or commit adultery, there cannot be much harm in this.

4. The opinion is a *racial or religious misconception*. To one reared in the atmosphere of the Ku Klux Klan, a given opinion can be wrong

solely because it is held by Catholics. The proposal of a German is anathema to a Frenchman, and vice versa. To an anti-Semite a man stands condemned of being a knave and a trickster merely because he is a Jew.

367. *Intellectual license* generally parades itself as liberalism, as the opposite of prejudice. It is the creed of so-called broad-minded men, of the advanced and tolerant thinker; and it comes to this: You can think what you please. Seek truth for truth's sake but truth is simply what you think is true. Truth is not reality made manifest to the mind; it is the mind pronouncing its subjective view of reality; or worse still, the mind creating reality. For objective reality and objective evidence, personal whim ultimately is substituted. This is subjectivism gone wild in the field of intellect. It stems from the notion that man is the measure of all things. Hence each one is free to doubt, affirm, and deny what he pleases. Of course, if a man is sincere, he will not deny the existence of facts, for facts have a hard and stubborn quality. But in the field of universal ideas, each one is his own master. From this, one is naturally driven to relativism, the ultimate epistemological absurdity, the mind's last stop before out and out repudiation of the rational faculty. If reality is always shifting, if the same thing can be true to you and equally false to the next, then there is no moral order; what was moral truth to Hector and Achilles is not so to Dewey and Einstein; what is moral truth to these will not be so to the supermen of the twenty-fifth century.

368. An immediate corollary is that one may deny any revealed truth which he cannot understand. Because of all the mud that has been slung at revelation by so-called modern science, the taunt of obscurantism, of hindering human progress, revelation has been on the defensive for more than a century. Among those who still cling to some shreds of revelation despite the taunt of superstition, there is a vague uneasy feeling that with science in the saddle, revelation must give way whenever the two contradict.

This attitude is founded on two false premises: (*a*) there is no obligation to accept the totality of revelation; (*b*) revelation and reason can contradict each other. If God made a revelation, one is obliged to accept all of it. God's infallible word underlies every revealed truth. If His word is rejected in one instance, it is implicitly rejected in every other instance. Nor can there ever be a true conflict between reason and revelation because all truth rests in God, the exemplar of all things. In God no contradiction is possible. There may appear to be conflicts between discoveries of science and God's word. This happens either because God's word is not understood for what it really is or because something is claimed to be a natural truth which objectively is not.

369. It is a rare man who is able to break entirely free from the bonds of prejudice and escape the pitfall of believing that his own mind is the measure of truth. This ability comes from submission to long, rigid discipline and an earnest and unbiased quest for truth. It is that mental perfection which a liberal education aims to foster. The attainment of such mental perfection is not obligatory on all men. What, then, is the minimal perfection of mind demanded by the Natural Law? To achieve his end a man has to know who he is, what he is, and what he is for. This means that he must have a knowledge of God, at least as his Maker — the Supreme Being to whom he is responsible — the primary and secondary precepts of the Natural Law; and those particular obligations incumbent on him as this individual.

THESIS XXIV. The Natural Law obliges every man to cultivate his mind to the extent at least that he understand the moral duties common to all men and those special ones pertaining to his state of life.

PROOF

370. Whoever is absolutely obliged to attain to an end is likewise obliged to obtain the means necessary to that end. But man is absolutely obliged to attain his last end, and knowledge of his common and individual moral duties are a necessary means to that end. Therefore man is obliged to know his common and individual moral duties.

II. TRAINING OF THE WILL

371. The order of man's nature is maintained when man avoids false principles and possesses moral truth. What essential good must he then procure as regards his will?

1. When the mind presents moral truth, man's real good, the will is obliged to accept it. As nature ordains that the mind illumine the will, she likewise commands that the will follow its guidance. Therefore, if a person disregards the voice of reason, he does not act in conformity with his nature. The essential order of his nature demands the *compliance of his will with the dictates of right reason.*

Every sin is a sin precisely because it is a revolt against reason. A morally evil act is possible only if reason is disregarded. The axiom, "Follow reason," is about as fundamental a law as "Do good and avoid evil." As was said in the treatise on virtue (§ 299), every man must habitually act in accordance with right reason, that is, man must practice prudence. Otherwise, he is exposing himself to the loss of beatitude.

2. *The will must exercise its natural dominion over the other faculties.* This means (*a*) that the will keep the mind steady and unwavering in the pursuit and retention of moral truth; (*b*) that no subordinate appetite be permitted to seek an apparent good to the detriment of man's real good. Morally man is a unitary whole when the will is mistress of the faculties, the custodian of the integrated personality. If animal appetites divert man from his real good, the essential order of human nature is again violated. Man, then, must practice temperance and fortitude.

III. SELF-MASTERY

372. To preserve the ability of the reason to enlighten and the ability of the will to guide, man must ever strive for mastery of his sense appetites. To prevent passion from disturbing the due order of his rational nature, he must give special attention to the control of anger and the use of right reason in eating, drinking, and sex.

A. Control of Anger

373. *Anger* is the prosecutive motion of the irascible appetite, whose purpose is the total destruction of evil leveled against the agent. Its immediate end is the warding off of the evil threatened; its ultimate end, once evil has been done, is the total eradication of that evil by the infliction of compensatory punishments upon the evildoer.

Anger in itself is good and is necessary for man. For self-preservation, he must protect himself from harm; again, it is reasonable that evildoers be punished. Righteous indignation is called for at times as a just protest against injustice or when it is the only way of correcting those for whom one is responsible. Though anger must be controlled by reason, man tends toward unreason when he becomes angry. The tendency to unreasonable anger is the *Capital Sin of Anger*.

Anger may be unreasonable with respect to its intensity, object, and motive: (*a*) Anger is unreasonable in its *intensity* if it is out of proportion to the evil done. (*b*) Anger is unreasonable with respect to its object if the object does not deserve punishment. Effects which do not result from an evil will do not deserve punishment. Hence objects incapable of reasoning and the indeliberate faults of children should not excite anger. (*c*) Anger is wrong which arises from wrong motives such as pride, hatred, envy, and private vengeance. One must endure with patience wrongs which are purely private, for only a superior having lawful authority may punish.

B. *Right Reason in Eating and Drinking*

374. The orderly use of means is determined from the end for which they are intended. Since food and drink are the natural means of preserving life, and since the Natural Law obliges man to preserve his life, man must eat and drink. The use of food and drink is orderly if it promotes or at least does not endanger one's health and life; it is unreasonable if it imperils health or shortens life.

375. In the use of food ancient man, both civilized and barbarous, was guilty of notorious excesses. The barbarian, so often living on the edge of starvation, gorged himself unto inaction when unexpected plenty came his way. Roman society carried the cult of bodily pleasure to such an extreme that the wealthy epicure provided special rooms — *vomitoria* — where his guests could spew up one meal so that they might enjoy another banquet.[1] However, the penitential discipline of Christianity, especially its laws regarding fast and abstinence, did succeed in removing the grosser enormities of gluttony, but with the return of pagan ideas of morality there may well be a recrudescence of this brutish vice.

376. The misuse of drink is a vastly greater moral evil. Vicious as ancient man was, he was fortunately saved from worse evils by his ignorance of distilled liquors. Modern man has a special problem to solve here.

What is drunkenness? Drunkenness is voluntary and excessive imbibing of alcoholic drink to the extent that one loses the use of reason without a justifying cause. Two elements in this definition require special note: namely, loss of reason and lack of justifying cause. Loss of reason may be partial or complete. Indications of

---

[1] Juvenal, Liber I, Satire I, 142–143.

complete loss of reason are conduct that is totally different from one's normal behavior, inability to distinguish right from wrong, failure to realize that one actually is drunk.

Not every instance of the loss of reason involves moral wrong. Sleep is a natural and necessary loss of reason. However, it would be wrong if a person drank to excess and immediately went to bed because he would be incapable of being roused if he had to be. To ease the shock of a surgical operation, one is allowed to lose consciousness. The effect produced by ordinary anesthetics may also be produced by alcohol. Thus, alcohol in great quantity might be a legitimate remedy against snake bite. The essential evil of drunkenness is put down in the following thesis.

THESIS XXV. The Natural Law forbids man to deprive himself of the use of reason without a justifying cause.

377. The thesis points out an important fact, namely, the close connection between intemperance and our duties to our own soul. Some people, referring to some solitary alcoholic, may exclaim, "Poor fellow, he's harming only himself." They do not seem to appreciate the gravity of any serious subversion of nature's order even in a single individual.

PROOF

378. To deprive oneself of the use of reason without a compensating cause is patently unsuited to human nature, because:

1. All men of every age, race, and circumstance regard it as wrong;
2. Nature intends that man be self-directive. To abdicate reason even temporarily is to run counter to nature's intent. Hence nature must forbid it except when it is necessary for self-preservation.

Corollary. The same moral principle applies to the use of narcotics.

379. Over and above the essential malice stated above, drunkenness presents other evil facets. It is often the occasion of other sins such as unchastity, blasphemy, quarreling, and even bloodshed.

Again, the excessive use of alcohol is a positive detriment to health. What damaging effect great quantities of alcohol may have on the nervous system, the liver, the digestive organs; how it may lead to certain kinds of insanity, one may learn from any standard medical textbook. Drug addiction is even a more serious menace to health than alcoholism. Ethically this can amount to serious wrong because, as we shall presently prove, we have an obligation to preserve life and health. Wantonly to squander one's health and notably to shorten one's life for the sake of gratification of the senses is grave wrong.

380. Drunkenness is not only a violation of the supremacy of reason; constant excess as a rule permanently weakens the will. The alcoholic vice is a habit rooted in the body and produces a craving which the will often finds impossible to deny. This weakening of the will cannot but undermine one's entire moral fabric. How difficult it is to rid oneself of this vice once it has taken hold is expressed in the Spanish proverb — "There is no cure for the drunkard but death."

Excessive drinking is not merely a private vice; it has far-reaching social effects. Most drinking is done in the company of others as a manifestation of friendship and sociability. Drunkenness is probably the most social of all vices for men do not congregate to steal, murder, and even debauch in the same open way they do to drink. One contracts the vice from the example of another, and he in turn infects others. What appalling misery drunkenness brings into family life is only too familiar a story. More than a fair amount of sordid poverty is directly traceable to drunken parents.

The automobile has added a new aspect to the problem of drink. Even mild indulgence in alcohol makes most people incapable of driving safely. Police records everywhere testify to the tremendous damage to life, limb, and property suffered by innocent parties because of drunken driving.

381. *Prohibition* aims by law to deprive the citizens of access to alcoholic beverages. It is neither an efficient nor human remedy for the drink evil. It is not efficient because it does not work but rather induces worse evils than those it attempts to remedy. It is not a human remedy for two reasons. First, it rests on the false presupposition that all drinking is an absolute evil. There is a sober and innocent drinking which has its place in life. It is not use but abuse which makes the moral evil. Second, the human way to solve a moral difficulty is not by an attack on human freedom, that is, by violent compulsion to induce observance of the moral law. This is not the way Divine Providence treats human weakness. A free man is not made a better man either by compelling him to outward observance of the law or by depriving him of the opportunity of breaking the law. The State may take such action in matters pertaining to public and necessary order but not in matters of conscience. Such compulsion in matters of conscience would not make for the free service God expects of man. Where widespread moral difficulty exists, man's moral faculties must be appealed to and strengthened. His mind should see the reasonableness of moderation and even in some cases of abstention; his will must be strengthened to eschew all excess. "Resist the beginnings of evil," should be his principle. Legal force cannot produce free compliance: this is properly the field of divine grace.

C. Right Reason in Sex

382. Nothing is more likely to blind the mind to man's true good and destroy the dominance of will over sense than inordinate pursuit of sex and venereal pleasure. No force so frequently operates to upset the order of man's nature, that is, the subjection of lower to the higher faculties, than the uncontrolled drive of the sex appetite. Hence no man is master of himself if he cannot keep within reason's bounds this mighty impulse.

383. By sex is understood all activity which is directly related to the propagation of human life. To no other activity does nature attach a comparable pleasure, for the simple reason that the ultimate end of sex is not the individual good but the good of the race. If there were no need to propagate the race, sex would not exist. The sex drive is so strong precisely because its end is a good superior to that of the agent; otherwise the agent would not be sufficiently inclined toward a good other than his own.

Sex pleasure we call venereal pleasure. It is correct to express the problem of sex in terms of venereal pleasure because: (*a*) this pleasure exercises so universal a lure that men are conscious of it as an acute problem of morality; (*b*) here more than anywhere else there is a danger of mistaking a merely delectable good for perfective good; (*c*) men are drawn to use the sex faculty not so much because of its perfective good as by reason of the pleasure which attaches to it.

384. *What is venereal pleasure?* Pleasures of sense, especially tactile, fall into three classes: (*a*) *purely sensible* — the natural pleasure accompanying the exercise of the sense and in no way connected with sex, such as patting a baby's cheek; (*b*) *venereal* — pleasure perceived in the organs of reproduction because of activity directly tending to the reproductive act; (*c*) *sensual* — pleasure which stands midway between the first two and easily develops into the second, such as the pleasure of kissing one of the opposite sex.

Venereal pleasure may be perfect or imperfect. It is perfect in the male when there is an ejaculation of seed; in the female when there is a diffusion of vaginal glandular secretions. It is imperfect when the reproductive organ has not reached this consummated stage but is in preparation for it. A variety of acts — touches, looks, words — may produce these effects. From an ethical standpoint, it matters little whether the venereal pleasure be complete or incomplete, because the only natural reason for any incomplete act is that it issue in the complete act, that is, once a truly venereal act however slight is set in motion, it tends by the very impulse of nature, like a snowball rolling down a hill, to its completed perfection.

385. When does the enjoyment of venereal pleasure accord with nature's law? When does it transgress that law? Here again the reasonable use of a means must be determined from the end. The end of sex is the procreation of children. We do not have reference here to any haphazard procreation but to procreation under such conditions and in such surroundings as will assure that well-being of body and mind which nature designs for men. It is for nature — not men — to determine what these fundamental conditions of well-being shall be. It is for man's reason to discover them and put them in practice. We shall prove in social ethics that nature's over-all requirement for procreation and use of sex is (*a*) husband and wife united in lawful wedlock, (*b*) who in their use of sex do nothing to defeat nature's purpose of more life.

THESIS XXVI. Deliberately to seek or willfully to admit any venereal pleasure on the part of the unmarried or on the part of the married apart from one's lawful spouse or in any other than a natural way is a serious breach of Natural Law.

Venereal pleasure becomes the direct object of the will either when one sets out in quest of it, or when such pleasure spontaneously arises from an indeliberate source, the will approves and makes it its own.

PROOF OF PART I

386. *All venereal pleasure is forbidden the unmarried,* for every sexual act is forbidden them. Since a pleasure exists solely for the perfective act of which it is the concomitant, obviously if the perfective act is forbidden, so too is the accompanying pleasure.

1. *Consummated acts.* All solitary and homosexual acts are forbidden

all men because thereby nature's purpose of procreation is absolutely defeated. The unmarried may not perform the natural bisexual act because nature allows it only in lawful wedlock. It is reasonable only when it takes place under conditions which make adequate provision for the *total* well-being of offspring. Any arrangement other than lawful wedlock is detrimental to the continuance of the human race. That no exception to this general law of nature is possible is demonstrated in social ethics (confer § 707).

2. *Imperfect acts.* The only reason for imperfect acts is that they lead to, and are preparatory for the complete act. In nature's economy there is no other explanation for them. Since the unmarried may not exercise the complete act, neither may they the imperfect act.

PROOF OF PART II

387. *Venereal pleasure may be had only with reference to one's spouse.* Since only the married may willfully have venereal pleasure, and since marriage is the *exclusive* union of one man and one woman, as is proved in social ethics, venereal pleasure may be had only with reference to one's spouse (cf. § 731, Corollary).

PROOF OF PART III

388. *Venereal pleasure may be had by the married only in a natural way.* That is natural which promotes nature's end — procreation. That is unnatural which in itself defeats nature's purpose. For nature to allow what in this matter directly destroys her intent would be for her to sign her death warrant (cf. § 778).

PROOF OF PART IV

389. *All unlawful venereal pleasure constitutes a serious wrong.* To violate nature's ordinance with respect to venereal pleasure is to do that which is detrimental to the continuity of the human race.

390. N.B. I. Nothing is more indicative of the ignorance which disordered sexual passion can beget than the serious statement that fornication and self-abuse cannot be proved wrong from reason alone. The objective reasons why these are intrinsically wrong as defeating an absolute end of nature are evident enough without the added light of revelation. The difficulty lies not with the reason but with the ill will of men who do not wish to perceive these reasons.

II. The morality of veneral pleasure which is only indirectly voluntary must be adjudged from the principle of double effect.

READINGS

St. Thomas, *Summa Theologica,* II–II, 47, 148, 149, 150, 151, 158.

Aristotle, *Ethics,* VII.

Belloc, Hilaire, *Survivals and New Arrivals,* pp. 141–171. New York, Macmillan, 1929.

Bonnar, A., O.F.M., *The Catholic Doctor,* pp. 43–52. New York, Kenedy, 1939.

Cox, Ignatius W., S.J., *Liberty, Its Use and Abuse,* Vol. II, pp. 13–19. New York, Fordham University Press, 1937.

Davis, Henry, S.J., *Moral and Pastoral Theology,* Vol. II, pp. 172–224. New York, Sheed and Ward, 1936.

Farrell, Walter, O.P., *A Companion to the Summa,* Vol. III, pp. 3–60. New York, Sheed and Ward, 1940.

Hoornaert, G., S.J., *Le Combat de la Pureté,* pp. 13–173. Paris, Desclee de Brouwer, 1931.

Janet, Paul, *Elements of Morals,* pp. 260–274, trans. C. R. Corson. New York, A. S. Barnes, 1884.

Koch-Preuss, *Handbook of Moral Theology,* Vol. III, pp. 101–111. St. Louis, Herder, 1919.

Martindale, C. C., S.J., *The Difficult Commandment.* New York, Kenedy.

O'Malley-Walsh, *Essays in Pastoral Medicine,* pp. 105–119. London, Longmans Green, 1907.

Plato, *Charmides.*

——— *The Laws,* Book II; Book V, 1st third.

Sanford, Alexander, *Pastoral Medicine,* pp. 163–172. New York, Wagner, 1904.

Sutherland, Halliday, *Laws of Life,* pp. 90–107. New York, Sheed and Ward, 1936.

CHAPTER XII

DUTIES TO BODY

391. The law of self-preservation is operative in all living things. Every organism by nature tends to conserve the life and faculties with which it is endowed. Existence is the first good, and continuance in existence is a proper good of every actually existing being. All things less than man are compelled to this good as a primary end. Does this same compulsion also apply to man, or has man, as master of his activities, a freedom in this respect not accorded lower animals? Is he free to dispose of his corporeal members and even cut short his life for what seems good to him? In answering these questions, we shall consider the three general cases wherein the law of self-preservation may apply to man — suicide, self-mutilation, and care of one's health.

I. SUICIDE

392. *Suicide* literally means the killing of self. A careful distinction must be made between a direct and indirect self-destruction. (*a*) *Direct self-destruction* occurs when one's own death is the immediate object of an act of the will, as when one deliberately takes an overdose of sleeping pills to avoid the painful death of cancer. (*b*) *Indirect self-destruction* follows from an action which, by its nature and the intention of the agent, can produce some effect other than death, as when a soldier sets off a spark which blows up both himself and a large body of the enemy. In direct self-destruction life is destroyed, death is sought; in indirect self-destruction, life is not preserved, death unsought is permitted.

393. Direct self-destruction could take place upon the authority of a competent superior or on one's own authority. A competent superior authorizing self-destruction would be one who has complete dominion over the life of the person. Such self-destruction would not be an

immoral act but rather obedience to the command of a lawful superior. God is the master of life and death; hence if He inspired the act
of those martyrs who rushed to death of their own accord, they were
guilty of no wrong. Is the State also a competent superior in this
matter? Could a judge order a condemned criminal to carry out a
sentence of execution upon himself? First, there is quite a dispute
as to whether a criminal may obey such a command if given. Some
maintain that where self-inflicted death would be less painful than
the death intended by the State, the criminal may choose the former
as the lesser of two evils; others say he may not, because this act is
contrary to the essential tendency of self-preservation and there is no
compensating social good in which he shares. However, all agree
that a person is not compelled to obey such a command. But a
command which a subject is not compelled to obey is no command.
All true commands are to be obeyed. This, then, is an extrinsic
indication that the State may not issue such an order. The intrinsic
reason is that the State may command the individual to perform only
actions involving social co-operation; but self-destruction, which also
destroys one's relation with society, precludes the possibility of the
individual's social co-operation.

In self-destruction upon one's own authority the individual wills
his own destruction without the leave of God or man. This is *suicide,*
which we define as the *direct killing of one's self upon one's own
authority.*

394. *The morality of suicide.* Whether suicide is always wrong or
sometimes to be permitted depends on the answer to the question:
What is man's relation to himself and his corporeal life? Is man
steward or master? If he is but a steward, he is the agent of his
principal, God, and has no rights over the substance which has
been entrusted to him. He may use life and body, but his use of them
must accord with the will of his principal. Obviously, no steward may
on his own authority destroy his trust. If man is master, then despite
his natural urge of self-preservation, he may decide that under certain
intolerable conditions life is no longer desirable. Thus, a general who
loses a crucial battle, or a ship's master whose vessel is foundering
because of his blunders may prefer death to life with dishonor. Does
the free nature of man argue such self-mastery? Of course, such self-
mastery would not be completely independent, but it would be the
same sort of participated dominion which man has over brutes.

God has given man a limited dominion over beasts so that he may kill them without fault. Has he a similar dominion over himself? If a farmer decides how long his hog is to live, may he decide the same for himself?

THESIS XXVII. Suicide, whereby man kills himself upon his own authority, is always forbidden; but indirect self-destruction or exposure to danger of certain death is allowable for a sufficiently grave reason.

PROOF OF PART I

395. *The Natural Law forbids suicide* as intrinsically evil, because it is an invasion of God's exclusive dominion. For man to do what belongs to God alone is to pervert the essential order of human nature.

Suicide trespasses upon God's exclusive dominion, because:

1. It is an act of perfect dominion over one's life; destruction of a thing is the ultimate act of dominion.

2. God has dominion over man's life, for God is man's efficient cause and last end.

3. This dominion is exclusively God's so that it cannot be shared by man. If man were granted such dominion over himself, then God *alone* would not be man's final end, and man, the creature, would be an end unto himself. But no creature is an end unto himself.

Corollary. Man is but the steward of his corporeal life and of all his faculties.

396. The intrinsic evil of suicide is clear also from a consideration of the truth, that, since God is the Maker and Last End of man, man belongs totally and essentially to God, he is the property and servant of God. It is contrary to right reason to hold that one who is essentially the servant of another should determine how long he is to serve and when he is to receive the reward of his service. By suicide man overturns right order.

397. When man by suicide invades God's exclusive rights, of what in particular does man deprive God? Since God owns man absolutely, man cannot say his life is his own to do with as he chooses. He must use it as God through divine law directs. What God expects of man and has an exclusive right to exact is this — the moral fruits of man's mortal life. By morally good acts man gives God extrinsic glory. How much extrinsic glory is due from each and for how long a time it is to be rendered are matters for God to determine. Therefore, when man by his own act shortens his life, he is acting the part of God, and deprives God, at least temporarily, of that to which God is entitled, namely, further moral fruits of mortal life, a definite amount of extrinsic glory expected of probationary man.

398. It may be argued that life is a gift given to man without his asking for it; and because it was unasked for, it may be relinquished at will. This conclusion is contrary to the nature of the gift of life, for life must be retained at the good pleasure of the donor.

Suicide as an escape from overwhelming personal disaster, an evil life, misery, frustration, or dishonor, far from being an act of fortitude, is an act of cowardice It is a refusal to accept a severe test sent us by God. Persons who take their lives under such circumstances have a fundamentally false view of life, namely, that happiness in this life is man's last end.

Suicide as an escape from being a burden to others also manifests the erroneous conception that the purpose of life is temporal felicity. The aged, broken, chronically infirm, and seemingly useless serve at least this praiseworthy function, namely, that they afford others magnificent opportunities for practicing the moral virtues. God has promised eternal beatitude to those who feed the hungry, clothe the naked, shelter the homeless. How could such virtues be exercised if God did not permit appropriate opportunities?

It is lawful to wish death, that is, orderly death in conformity to the plans of Divine Providence, but we may not wish to kill ourselves.

PART II

399. Men sometimes embark on a most hazardous enterprise whence death is surely or most likely to ensue. The timid onlooker calls it suicide. And it is suicide if self-destruction is intended. But even if they do not intend their death, if they are merely resigned to accept it if it comes, are they justified? Does the law of self-preservation, the fact that they are stewards of their mortal life, demand that they take every means to save their lives and avoid every proximate danger of death? No, for reason may allow, sometimes demand, exposure to imminent peril. The morality of such acts must be judged by the principle of double effect.

PROOF

400. *Exposure to danger of certain death is justified* if all of the following conditions are verified:

1. The action from which result the bad unintended effect of death and some other good effect must itself be morally good or at least indifferent.

2. The effect other than death must be morally good, as when a man plunges into icy water to save a drowning skater. If this effect be treason, adultery, revenge, or the like, there can be nothing good about the action.

3. The intended good effect may not be caused by one's death. If it were, then one would first have to intend one's death, which is always wrong. Hence the good intended must follow from the act of exposure as immediately as does death. If exposure to death has one and only one immediate effect, namely, self-destruction, one cannot intend it without intending suicide. In such cases, the principle of double effect does not apply.

4. There must be reasonable proportion between the good intended and the evil permitted, namely, death. Death is allowed only for a gravely compensating reason. This reason could be a spiritual good, for example, avoidance of a proximate occasion of serious sin; or some notable material benefit to one's neighbor or the community.

II. MUTILATION AND STERILIZATION

401. Since man is but the steward of his corporeal life, he must take every reasonable precaution to preserve life and the integrity of his body. He cannot wantonly dispose of his faculties.

Bodily integrity is disturbed by *mutilation,* which is the destruction and usually the removal of some member of the human body. Strictly speaking, mutilation involves the loss of some bodily function. Hence the removal of a small portion of one's finger or external ear does not constitute a grave mutilation.

Mutilation is never allowable except for the sole reason of saving one's life. That integrity of body must be preserved is obvious from all that has been said. That an exception may be made in order to conserve life is also clear, because it is reasonable that a part be sacrificed to maintain the whole.

402. *Are there any other exceptions?* St. Thomas denies that mutilation for the sake of a spiritual good is lawful. "Spiritual good can be procured by means other than the cutting off of a member because sin lies in the will. Therefore in no case is it allowed to cut off a member for the sake of avoiding any sin whatever."[1]

Ever since modern science has discovered easy, effective, and fairly painless means of destroying the human sex faculty, heated controversies have raged concerning the morality of those procedures known as sterilization. A very old problem in a new guise has revived.

403. *What is sterilization?* A sterile person is one who is not fertile, who lacks the power of reproduction. Sterility may be the result of unformed organs or of a natural defect in or malformation of reproductive organs. It may be a natural cessation of fecundity because of age or it may be artificially induced. Modern sterilization is of the latter type. It renders a human being incapable of reproduction through surgical or medical means. In the male it is usually achieved by vasectomy, or the severing of the seminal ducts. In ancient times, it was done by castration, which is still practiced on brutes. Castration is the removal of scrotum, testicles, and seminal glands. Except in the rarest instances castration made sexual intercourse impossible; this modern sterilization does not do. The female is sterilized by the operation called salpingectomy, or the severing of the Fallopian tubes. From the standpoint of the motive for sterilization, four types may be distinguished, therapeutic, punitive, contraceptive, and eugenic.

1. The purpose of *therapeutic* sterilization is the health of the individual. The removal of cancerous Fallopian tubes, ovaries, womb, or injured testicles would fall in this category. It is said that sterilization may be an effective remedy for tuberculosis. If sterilization should prove to be the proper remedy for any serious ailment, it would become legitimate mutilation, because it is just to sacrifice a part for the good of the whole.

2. *Punitive* sterilization is inflicted by the State as a punishment for crime. The argument runs that since the State can take life as a just punishment for crime, *a fortiori* it can inflict the lesser evil of mutilation. This argument is sound, and the sole point of investigation here is whether sterilization is an apt sanction. Would this particular mutilation measure up to the requirements of an effective sanction?

---

[1] *Sum. Theol.,* II–II, 65, 1.

404. It appears that sterilization does not. Any proposed sanction to be effective must have its *deterring* value. The threatened punishment must have some power to keep prospective evildoers from crime. The fear of losing the procreative power might have some deterring effect upon peoples like Mohammedans and Chinese, who have a strongly developed sense of progeny; but sterilization to most criminals might be a rather welcome procedure, because it does not prevent sexual intercourse but rather prevents the inconvenient result of offspring. A sanction must have a *remedial,* or reformative, aspect; but since sterilization rather grants the criminal more freedom for sexual indulgence, scarcely any criminal will be improved by sterilization. Furthermore, sterilized people often experience an unhappy increase of libido. Finally, a sanction should exact *expiation* from the wrongdoer. Since sterilization involves little personal hardship, and since it takes from the offender a power he is just as pleased to be rid of, the expiatory value of sterilization is next to nothing. Sterilization, therefore, is a very inept instrument for law enforcement.

3. *Contraceptive* sterilization is induced to prevent conception. The person's sole motive is avoidance of parenthood. It is not unheard of that a surgeon on the occasion of a Caesarean section will ligate or sever the Fallopian tubes so that the woman may continue sexual relations without risk of pregnancy. The mutilation in these circumstances is voluntarily accepted, although such operations have been performed without the knowledge and consent of the patient. May one for contraceptive reasons undergo sterilization?

4. *Eugenic* sterilization has as its object the prevention of conception for the evolvement of a more perfect race.

405. *Eugenics.* "Eugenics," in the words of Francis Galton who coined the term, "is the study of agencies under social control that may improve or impair the racial qualities of future generations either physically or mentally."[2] It is the outgrowth of organic evolution. Natural selection, or the law of the survival of the fittest, brought man to his present level of development, but now it no longer serves him because so many of the fittest perish in war and so many of the unfit,

---

[2] Cited by Paul Popenoe, *Applied Eugenics,* p. 147. New York, Macmillan, 1918. Popenoe is here probably improving on Galton's definition — "Eugenics is the science which deals with all influences that improve the inborn qualities of the race; also with those that develope them to the utmost advantage." Cf. Sir Francis Galton, *Essays in Eugenics,* p. 35. London, The Eugenics Society, 1909.

on account of the humanitarianism of the past century, are so cared for that they too can readily propagate. The race is deteriorating because not enough superior people have sufficient progeny and too many tainted parents are passing on defective inheritance to their children.

The race cannot be substantially improved by improving the environment in which people live. Acquired characteristics are not transmissible. The germ plasm which passes from parents to progeny is not capable of modification. So, to that age-old problem which Euripides in his *Hecuba* expresses by the question, "Is it the parents or the education?"[3] the eugenist answers vociferously that it is the parents. A man is a superior man if he comes of superior stock; he is unfit if he comes from poor stock. And that is the end of it.

Since unaided nature cannot effect the improvement of the race, the co-operation and intervention of human intelligence is required. This eugenics will supply by carrying out this simple program: let the superior element in the community, the bearers of good germ plasm, do the propagating; let the defectives, the bearers of bad germ plasm, stop propagating.

406. There is no danger to the race from the unfit who are now institutionalized, for the opportunity to propagate is taken from them. But it is financially impossible to segregate all potential parents of defectives. Since so many must be at large in society, let society protect itself from them by taking from them the power to propagate. Let the defective willingly submit to sterilization, but if he will not, the State should have the power to compel him.

407. Legislative bodies have listened to the arguments of eugenists, and it is not surprising that Nazi Germany, so loud a protagonist of the theory of superior and inferior races, should have taken extreme measures in this regard. It not only legislated that very numerous categories of the mentally diseased be sterilized, but thoroughly carried out the program. Up to January 1, 1944, thirty-two of our states had passed sterilization laws. Of these, four were declared unconstitutional. Of the remainder, only the Californian law has drastic provisions. In two thirds of these states these laws are practically moribund.

408. The end envisioned by eugenic legislation is admirable. Every State is interested in the birth of sound, healthy children. Taxpayers ought not be saddled with the support of the unfit if this reasonably

---

[3] *Hecuba*, line 599.

can be avoided. Nor is an individual justified in begetting children, if he foresees that he will have to turn them over to others for support.

But are the means advocated — voluntary or compulsory sterilization — equally good? Two questions are involved. One is scientific: Is sterilization a certain, sound, and efficient means of securing a better race? The other is moral: Does such sterilization accord with the moral law? To the first question a reply will be made presently. The second question is answered in the following thesis.

THESIS XXVIII. Voluntary contraceptive sterilization and eugenic compulsory sterilization are forbidden by the Natural Law.

PROOF OF PART I

409. *Voluntary contraceptive sterilization is contrary to the Natural Law,* because it is unjustifiable self-mutilation and it partakes of the nature of positive contraception, which is intrinsically wrong.

1. *It is unjustifiable self-mutilation.* The only reason justifying mutilation is the integrity and well-being of the entire body. Man is not absolute master of his body; he is only its custodian. A custodian may destroy something of what has been entrusted to him only if it is necessary for the whole. But in contraceptive sterilization, this justifying reason is not found.

2. *It partakes of the nature of positive contraception.* By positive contraception one intends and effectively hinders by artificial means the union of sperm and ovum. That positive contraception is intrinsically wrong is proved in Social Ethics, § 778.

PROOF OF PART II

410. *Compulsory eugenic sterilization is contrary to the Natural Law* because it is unjustifiable invasion of the State upon the integrity of the citizen's body and it partakes of the nature of positive contraception.

1. *It is unjustifiable invasion by the State upon the integrity of the citizen's body,* because the State has no direct right over the faculties of citizens who are guiltless of crime.

a) Direct dominion over an individual's faculties belongs solely to the individual. To contend that the State has a similar, even a superior, dominion, as laws of sterilization imply, is a gross subversion of nature's purpose. Nature gives each one his faculties for *his own perfection*, not the convenience of his fellows. These are his possessions in the strictest sense of the word. It is unjust to deprive a guiltless person of even one of his faculties. What nature alone gives, nature alone can take away. This is evident with respect to life; it is likewise evident with respect to limb and faculty. The common good may determine how one is to *use* a faculty at times; however, it can never deprive an innocent man of a faculty.

b) Even the individual himself has not complete dominion or unrestricted right over his members. He has the right to *use* them in accordance with the law of nature for the development of his total personality; he does not have the right to damage or destroy them except when the good of the whole man is at stake. *A fortiori* the State does not possess this right except *per accidens* where the State would inflict on the guilty a just and proportionate punishment.

2. *Compulsory eugenic sterilization partakes of the nature of positive contraception.* It is calculated to permit sexual relations but in such wise that their primary end is frustrated.

411. *Is sterilization scientific?* Eugenists, who see in sterilization a necessary means of racial betterment, grow very impatient when ethicians say it is contrary to the moral law. Convinced that sterilization is a sure and easy way to a most desirable good, they accuse moralists of obscurantism, of narrow-mindedness, of blocking the onward progress of science. But is sterilization scientifically sound? In other words (*a*) is sterilization founded on certain truths of science or on merely probable theories; (*b*) can sterilization of defectives reduce the number of the unfit?

In answer to the first question, it may be pointed out that eugenists have assumed as certain, basic principles which others hold only as probable. They have mistaken theory and conjecture for principle and fact. Claiming that eugenics rests upon a sure substratum of progressive evolution, Popenoe states that what is inherited — *the germ plasm — is incapable of improvement or deterioration.*[4] But how could there have been progressive evolution, if improvements achieved by one generation could not have been transmitted to another? The noted geneticist Jennings[5] is inclined to think that the germ plasm may deteriorate through injury to the genes. Again, Goddard, to

---

[4] *Applied Eugenics*, p. 74
[5] H. S. Jennings, *Genetics*, pp. 190–191. New York, Norton, 1935.

reach the conclusion that feeble-mindedness is purely hereditary, uses only the method of counting noses: as evidence of feeble-mindedness, he adduces the merest hearsay and blithely ignores the factor of early environment. Cameron says, "Turning . . . to the data which have already been accumulated upon the problem of inheritance in the field of human behavior, one must rapidly gain the impression that little of it is fated to withstand the closer scrutiny of more exact procedure."[6]

412. According to Pratt, "eugenical sterilization presupposes a proven and universally accepted law of heredity. As a matter of fact no such law exists. Our theories about heredity are constantly changing."[7] At one time all thought tuberculosis and cancer were hereditary. Now we know better. When Koch denied that tuberculosis was hereditary, he was publicly ridiculed and it took many years, even for the world of science, to be convinced of the nonhereditary character of that disease.

But let us assume for the sake of argument that the eugenist's contention is correct as stated by Popenoe,[8] that it is a man's nature and not his nurture that is responsible for his character. The fundamental law of eugenics may then be stated: superior stock will breed superior children; inferior stock will breed inferior children. But upon what scientific basis does one discriminate between superior and inferior stock? According to Conklin, "mankind is a mongrel race."[9] Jennings notes "from vigorous and efficient parents may be produced offspring which are weak and inefficient. From defective parents may be produced offspring that are normal."[10] The truth of the latter fact is shown even in Goddard's doleful family tree of the Kallikaks.[11] R. A. Fisher, in his endeavor to refute the findings of Punnett (see § 417), admits that not more than 11 per cent of the feeble-minded derive from feeble-minded parents.[12] A. F. Tredgold reviews the figures of numerous authorities and concludes with this

---

[6] D. E. Cameron, *Objective and Experimental Psychiatry*, p. 362. New York, Macmillan, 1941, 2 ed.

[7] *Journal of Social Hygiene*, May, 1925, p. 262. Cited by George Worthington in "Compulsory Sterilization Laws."

[8] *Op. cit.*, p. 24.

[9] Edwin G. Conklin, *Heredity and Environment*, p. 425. Princeton, Princeton University, 1915.

[10] H. S. Jennings, *op. cit.*, p. 298.

[11] H. H. Goddard, *The Kallikak Family*. New York, Macmillan, 1935.

[12] *Journal of Heredity*, December, 1927, Vol. XVIII, p. 530.

summation: "I think it may be said that in England somewhere between 5 and 15 per cent, probably taking aments as a whole round about 10 per cent of the total number, are the offspring of a defective parent or parents."[13]

413. The gene theory — Jennings cautiously observes that the gene has not yet been demonstrated microscopically[14] — affords a fairly satisfactory explanation of these facts. According to this theory, genes are the determinants of the traits and tendencies of the new being and are received in equal proportion from sperm and ovum. Whenever a defective or low-grade gene from the sperm unites with a low-grade gene from the ovum, the result is a defective characteristic. Jennings thus sums it up: "Superior individuals are the result of particularly fortunate combinations of genes, inferior ones the result of unfortunate combinations."[15] Many normal people, fit in every way to propagate, are carriers of defective though dormant genes. But just who are such carriers genetics cannot say. Perhaps all men are.

414. Numerous scientific facts have been established concerning heredity. However, just what can be transmitted by heredity, how heredity really operates, what fundamental law underlies it — all these questions have not been answered by science. Certainly each individual has inherited traits from a number of ancestors, and certain of his own traits will be found in a definite number of his descendants, but no one knows in what particular descendant any particular set of characteristics will be found nor how they will be combined. The study of family histories reveals genius and idiocy, strength and weakness mingled in rather bewildering ways. The age-old problem of nature versus nurture, of heredity versus environment is still an unresolved question. Haldane says, "If you suddenly exchange all the babies in a Kentish village and a South African kraal, it is quite likely that the standard of civilization of the village would go down and that of the kraal go up, *but I don't know*."[16] That "I don't know" rather neatly sums up current knowledge on superior races. It is unscientific, therefore, to base so radical a measure

---

[13] A. F. Tredgold, *A Text-book of Mental Deficiency*, p. 29. Baltimore, Wood, 1937, 6 ed.

[14] H. S. Jennings, *op. cit.*, pp. 158–159. Cf. also D. E. Cameron, *op. cit.*, p. 364.

[15] H. S. Jennings, *op. cit.*, p. 298.

[16] J. R. Baker and J. S. B. Haldane, *Biology in Everyday Life*, p. 110. London, Allen and Unwin, 1933.

as deprivation of generative power upon a series of guesses and probabilities.

415. While the eugenist must admit that his science cannot determine what superior stock is, he is sure he knows what inferior stock is. To the question, "Who should be sterilized?" the eugenics catechism answers, "Such criminals, paupers, insane, feeble-minded, epileptics, rapists, and other defectives who can be proved to have inherited such defects as to make them incapable of leading normal lives, and who unless sterilized, are likely to transmit their defects to their children."[17] To determine who the degenerate are, a eugenic classification of six categories has been drawn up: (1) the infectious and contagious, such as the tuberculous, syphilitic, and leprous; (2) the perverted, such as homosexualists, rapists, drug addicts; (3) the wayward and habitually criminal; (4) the deaf, blind, and deformed; (5) psychotics; (6) the feeble-minded, who range from idiots, imbeciles, morons to the backward child. To be degenerate in a genetic sense, these unfortunates must have defects which are not acquired but are truly inherited. Genetics insists that acquired traits cannot be transmitted.[18] It is conceded that persons who fall in the first four categories have defects acquired either by birth, infection, or evil living.

416. Concerning the fifth category, we do not find agreement among authorities as to the origin of mental disease. Landman says that "the causes of mental disease are still an unsolved mystery."[19] Strecker denies that psychiatrists are hopelessly groping for these causes. "Inheritance," he says, "is an important predisposing cause, but its importance has been grossly exaggerated. The Mendelian law is rarely applicable to human disease."[20] A standard textbook of psychology states: "Heredity is often mentioned as a possible cause of mental disorders, but the evidence is not entirely conclusive. Certainly no one has scientific grounds for concern about his own mental health merely because there is a case of psychosis in his family."[21] Myerson thinks that two psychoses are hereditary diseases but that they are not handed on indefinitely because the disease will either kill off the stock or there will be a

---

[17] *A Eugenics Catechism*, n.d., p. 7. New Haven, American Eugenics Society.
[18] Cf. D. E. Cameron, *op. cit.*, p. 368.
[19] J. H. Landman, *Human Sterilization*, p. 146. New York, Macmillan, 1932.
[20] Edward A. Strecker, *Fundamentals of Psychiatry*, p. 15. Philadelphia, Lippincott, 1947, 4 ed.
[21] Shaffer, Gilmer, Schoen, *Psychology*, p. 466. New York, Harper, 1940.

final recovery.[22] Groups of children born of psychotic parents have been compared to groups born of normal parents. While nervous disorders have been found in both groups, the incidence of nervous disorders is slightly higher among children born of psychotic parents. What tentative conclusion may be drawn from such comparisons? It seems to be that the predisposition to mental disease found in the children of psychotics consists in this, that under the strains of modern life, the chances are slightly greater that they will develop mental disease than will the offspring of normal parents. A similar susceptibility to certain physical ills is found in many families. The careful scientist does not call this susceptibility a hereditary disease.[23]

417. The greatest pother occurs with respect to the feeble-minded. Eugenists have been frightening us with the claim that feeble-mindedness is on the upswing. Since only a small fraction of the feeble-minded can be institutionalized, it is argued that society must be protected by sterilization. Yet only 11 per cent of the feeble-minded have defective parents, and feeble-minded parents do beget normal children. Suppose we admit, again for the sake of argument, that all feeble-minded adults are carriers of defective genes, and suppose that eugenics had its way and sterilized them all — which brings us to the second question. How efficiently can sterilization improve the race?

If all the feeble-minded of this generation were prevented from propagating, there would be a reduction of feeble-mindedness in the next generation, due to the fact that 11 per cent of the feeble-minded are born of feeble-minded parents. However, for every feeble-minded person, there are thirty apparently normal carriers of defective genes. Hence, in the next generation there will be a large number of feeble-minded persons born of such parents. In addition, there will be those who will become feeble-minded from prenatal, delivery, and infantile accidents. There will still be carriers who will be reproduced at such a rate that it would take between two and three thousand years to reduce the number of feeble-minded from one in a thousand to one in ten thousand.[24] Sterilization of defectives, therefore, is scarcely an efficient instrument of race improvement.

---

[22] Abraham Myerson, *Psychology of Mental Disorder*, pp. 117–118. New York, Macmillan, 1927.

[23] Gregory Zilboorg, *Mind, Medicine, and Man*, pp. 68–69. New York, Harcourt, Brace, 1943.

[24] R. C. Punnett, *Journal of Heredity*, Oct., 1917, Vol. VIII, p. 465.

418. The argument so often advanced to legislators on behalf of sterilization laws has been an economic one, namely, that the defective, once sterilized, need no longer be kept segregated in a public institution. But this is a view both shortsighted and cruel. To turn loose upon the community such persons — especially women — of low intelligence and irresponsible tendencies would give a tremendous impetus to the spread of venereal disease. In the long run the latter would cost the State more than the upkeep of the feeble-minded.

The menace to society from increased feeble-mindedness has been greatly exaggerated. "The high birth rate [of defectives], the threatened swamping of the normal population — these are myths."[25] The marriage and birth rate for defectives is lower than that found in the general population: the sterility and death rate for defectives is definitely higher. "All the statistics and the biological trends indicated by the marriage rate, birth-rate, death rate, divorce rate, and fertility rate indicate that these groups are not increasing and, if anything, are declining."[26] Furthermore, society is adequately protected by segregation of those incapable of competent self-direction.

419. There is a sensible eugenics which consists in observance of the laws of sound hygiene and above all the moral law. The chief reason for human deterioration is disregard for the moral law. If a man disregards the specific law of his being, there is little reason for wondering why his being should suffer. The race can be improved only by improvement of the individual, and the most powerful factor that makes for the improvement of the individual is divine grace. But here again we enter the field of the supernatural.

Eugenics is another sign of the prevalent "happiness now" attitude of mind. Eugenists fail to see that "happiness hereafter" is purchasable by self-sacrificing care of the unfortunate. Divine Providence permits the unfortunate to be among us to give man an opportunity to exercise that charity which deserves the kingdom of heaven. They scarcely deserve that kingdom who would rid us of the inconvenient presence of unfortunates by violating nature's law.

---

[25] Abraham Myerson, "Summary of the Report of the American Neurological Association Committee for the Investigation of Sterilization," *American Journal of Psychiatry,* Vol. 92, No. 3, p. 619, November, 1935.

[26] *Ibid.,* p. 617.

III. CARE OF HEALTH

420. The law of self-preservation also obliges every man to use all *ordinary means* to preserve life and health. The reason is that failure to do so is equivalent to destroying life. Extraordinary means, however, are not generally obligatory. Extraordinary means would be anything which would impose a relatively intolerable burden, such as excruciating pain or expense notably beyond one's means. Occasionally, for the well-being of others dependent on him, one may be obliged to use extraordinary means to preserve his life and health. Such a person might be a sovereign or the father of a large family of small means.

READINGS

St. Thomas, *Summa Theologica*, II–II, 64, 5; 65, 1.

Betten, F. S., "The Morality of Sterilization," *The Catholic Mind,* October 22, 1933.

Catholic Encyclopedia, "Suicide," XIV, 326.

Corpus Juris, "Suicide," Vol. 60, pp. 995–999.

Davis, Henry, S.J., *State Sterilization of the Unfit.* London, Burns, Oates, Washbourne, 1931.

D'Eschembault, Antoine, *Eugenical Sterilization,* pp. 72–147, 1937, 2 ed.

Koch-Preuss, *Handbook of Moral Theology,* Vol. III, pp. 9–85. St. Louis, Herder, 1919.

Jennings, H. S., *Genetics,* pp. 179–265. New York, W. W. Norton, 1935.

Landman, J. H., *Human Sterilization.* New York, Macmillan, 1932.

LaRochelle-Fink, *Handbook of Medical Ethics,* pp. 131–155. Westminster, Md., Newman, 1932.

McFadden, Charles J., O.S.A., *Medical Ethics for Nurses.* pp. 214–253. Philadelphia, Davis, 1946.

Miltner, Charles, C.S.C., *Elements of Ethics,* pp. 199–214. New York, Macmillan, 1932.

Ruland, Ludwig, *Foundations of Morality,* pp. 291–339, trans. T. A. Rattler. St. Louis, Herder, 1938.

Sutherland, Halliday, *Laws of Life,* pp. 108–142. New York, Sheed and Ward, 1936.

CHAPTER XIII

ON CERTAIN EXTERNAL ADVANTAGES
TO THE INDIVIDUAL

421. In considering man's obligation of loving himself with an orderly love, we have seen that he must procure definite goods of soul and body. Are the goods enumerated sufficient for the good life? The experience of the race says no. No man is sufficient unto himself. To secure that degree of well-being and self-perfection which lies within his grasp, the individual depends on others. He requires what we may call a favorable milieu or environment. Unless his surroundings are favorable, it will be more difficult for him to lead a life worthy of a human being. Therefore, for moral reasons, man must provide himself with certain external advantages: he must utilize a minimum of certain external spiritual and material goods.

I. WHAT ARE THESE ADVANTAGES?

422. Five external advantages to the individual may be enumerated.

1. *Good name* — the esteem of our fellow man externally manifested whereby one is praised and honored for the excellence that is his. The point of particular reference here is the reputation of being a good man.

2. *Personal liberty* — freedom from external coercion in the use of one's goods and faculties; it is the status of not being the property or chattel of another.

3. *Friendship*. Over and above the ordinary ties of domestic life, one of the most prized external advantages is mutual esteem and affection for an equal.

4. *Amusement* — legitimate recreation of mind and body, the relaxation of one's powers in the enjoyment of delectable good.

5. *Material resources* — a source of material goods helpful to one's temporal life, such as money, land, or the equivalent.

II. HOW NECESSARY ARE THEY?

423. We do not say that all these things are of equal value to men or that all of them are necessary for all men and in all circumstances. Some men may dispense with one or other of these. A few heroic men of extraordinary virtue like Simeon Stylites may do without practically all of them and lead a moral life. The point is that normally speaking a certain minimum of these things is necessary for the ordinary man in order that he keep the moral law. The reason is that without this minimum of external advantages he will not preserve his dignity and avoid the proximate occasions of moral evil. The need of these things in normal circumstances is clear from the evil consequences which result when they are absent.

1. A good name is a help to the practice of virtue as a bad name is a hindrance. The man of evil reputation very often concludes that he might just as well live up to a bad name. Evil persons seek the company of persons of damaged reputation who may develop a resentment and desire for revenge on those of good reputation. Besides, as a man must seek virtue, so he must seek a good name, which stands closest to virtue and is its mirror.

2. Compulsion to wrongdoing is easily brought to bear on those who are not free. The outstanding evil of slavery is that the slave is made to do his master's bidding no matter how immoral. Freedom, on the other hand, comports with the independence of human nature.

3. A man bereft of true friendship loses that solace of human companionship so helpful to weather the crises of life; he is without that moral support and encouragement which is one of the benefits of friendship. The lonely man can sink into sordid vices.

4. Nature does not intend that man be without delectable good. Mind and body suffer deeply when deprived of a minimum of pleasure. If a man is deprived of legitimate satisfaction, he will seek it in forbidden ways.

5. Without a minimum of material resources, a man lacks many means of intellectual and moral improvement. Because man has a natural inclination for these things, the abjectly poor will be willing to seize them unlawfully — they will commit crimes against chastity, truthfulness, loyalty, and the like to secure them. One of the surest breeding grounds of crime is abject poverty.

III. IN WHAT MEASURE ARE THEY TO BE SOUGHT?

424. The Natural Law commands man to acquire the minimal amount of these external advantages necessary for the fulfillment of his common and individual obligations. Failure to observe this command is to be guilty of sloth.

May one seek these things beyond the minimum prescribed by the Natural Law? Nature does not restrict man to bare essentials; however, in the pursuit of that which is not necessary, man may not sacrifice virtue. These external advantages must always be regarded not as good in themselves but only in so far as they are means to the end of man. Possession of them does not constitute perfective human good, for no man is *eo ipso* a better man because he owns five hundred acres and is respected for his honesty. These are useful goods. These things may seem to be perfective goods because men have a strong urge to secure them. But what is less than man and external to him can only be a useful good — a means to man's real good. However, these advantages do exercise so powerful an influence over most men that there is always danger that they will not be used with right reason and that they will be sought as ends in themselves.

IV. THE DANGER OF EXCESS

425. 1. In the matter of praise a man may be guilty of excess by seeking it for reasons which are unworthy of praise, or from the evil whose opinion is not worth having. A man may desire the reputation of being a good man but may not be willing to practice the virtue which alone deserves it. Hence he may hide his vice under a mantel of virtue, which is hypocrisy. Or one may seek fame and reputation in many things solely for the love of such honor. This is an inordinate self-exaltation, which can lead to great excesses of pride.

2. Loving liberty, a man may be too independent and unwilling to show reverence and obedience where it is properly due from him. True freedom does not mean that man is entitled to think, say, and do as he chooses. One may not seek a freedom which is incompatible with his state in life. Liberty can degenerate into outright license. One can never be independent of God.

3. Too many friends or the wrong friends can be a stumbling block to man's real good. One may not sacrifice moral ideals or upright

conduct to acquire or retain the friendship of any man. Too many vices have a social origin: too many bad habits are assimilated from bad company.

4. The axiom, "virtue stands in the middle ground," is nowhere better illustrated than in the case of pleasure and material goods.

It is easy to confuse pleasure and happiness and to conclude that all happiness is to be found in pleasure. Pleasure is the result of some really or apparently perfective action; happiness is the combination of the truly perfective good and the legitimate pleasure which accompanies it. If pleasure is sought for its own sake, one is little concerned whether it is the apparently or truly perfective good. The great delusion of life is founding happiness upon the pleasure of apparently perfective good.

5. The good man is content with a modest competence. This thought the Book of Proverbs expresses: "Give me neither beggary nor riches."[1] One may seek a surplus of material goods in an orderly and virtuous manner, but the quest presents no little difficulty. Avarice can grow unrecognized; it is fed by what one has accumulated and may develop into a craving which knows no bounds. It is a pernicious delusion to believe that a man should ambition always to increase his income. Few tremendously great fortunes have been amassed by their original owners without violations of justice and charity. And once attained, great wealth can be an even greater occasion of sin than abject poverty. For the very wealthy man has at hand the ready means to satisfy his every whim and concupiscence.

V. PRACTICAL CONCLUSION

426. Because all of these advantages are external to man, they cannot truly be called good in themselves; they are useful goods, the common sense means to man's perfective good. As Ignatius Loyola[2] expressed it, all other things upon the face of the earth are to help man attain thereunto (that is, to his last end). The reasonable way to use any instrument is to employ it in so far as it helps to attain the end for which it was made and to stop using it whenever it no longer serves our purpose. This is the way a mechanic uses the tools of his trade.

---

[1] Proverbs, 30:8.

[2] Joan. Roothaan, S.J. (ed.), *Exercitia Spiritualia Sancti Patris Ignatii De Loyola,* no. 23, p. 35. Taurini, Marietti, 1928.

No carpenter will continue to saw, merely because he likes to use a saw, when further sawing will ruin his work. However, when it comes to honor, freedom, friendship, pleasure, and wealth, men too easily invert the order of right reason, and look on helps to the good life as the good life itself, and hence will seek these things in unreasonable measure and cling to them even though by so doing they frustrate the purpose for which these things were made. The fascination of trifles obscures the good.[2] Hence, one must cultivate the virtue of prudence so as to discern the true value and purpose of these things, and above all the virtue of temperance so as not to be excessive in their use. No sounder advice was ever given the human race than this admonition in the Sermon on the Mount: "Seek ye first the kingdom of God and His justice and all these things will be added unto you."[3]

---

[3] Wisdom 4:12.
[4] Matthew 6:33.

READINGS

St. Thomas, *Summa Theologica,* I–II, 2, 4; II–II, 114; 132, 1; 168, 2, 3, 4.
———— *Contra Gentiles,* III, 121, 133.
Aristotle, *Ethics,* VIII–IX.
Catholic Encyclopedia, "Wealth," XV, 571; "Glory," VI, 585.
Cathrein, V., S.J., *Philosophia Moralis,* pp. 251–252. Friburgi Brisgoviae, Herder, 1915, 10 ed.
Cox, Ignatius, S.J., *Liberty, Its Use and Abuse,* Vol. II, pp. 35–37. New York, Fordham University Press, 1937.
Meyer, Theo., S.J., *Institutiones Juris Naturalis,* Vol. II, pp. 50–51. Friburgi Brisgoviae, Herder, 1900.
Plato, *Republic,* I, IV.
———— *Laws,* I, II, V, IX.
Rickaby, Joseph J., S.J., *Aquinus Ethicus,* Vol. II, pp. 272–276; 375–381.

CHAPTER XIV

OUR FELLOW MAN

---

427. Having viewed the individual's obligations toward God and himself, we shall now consider his obligations toward his fellow man. We sum up man's obligations to God in the phrase, God must be loved above all things. We sum up his obligations to himself by saying that man must love himself with an orderly love. Can man's obligations toward his fellow man be similarly epitomized in the word *love?*

I. SENSIBLE AND INTELLECTUAL LOVE

428. We have seen in § 355 that love is the motion of the appetite toward an object apprehended as good. Love may be either sensible or intellectual.

1. If the act of cognition presents to the appetite a *particular sensible good,* we call the desire for this good *sensible love.* A brute animal loves itself with a sensible love. This love is completely self-regarding: it embraces self as self and self alone. And this is the first kind of love of self; it is a love which every man possesses.

A man loves another man with a sensible love when his imagination represents this person as agreeable to his sensible nature and when he consequently seeks him with more or less intensity of sense appetite or emotion. It is a spontaneous attraction in which the intellect plays little part. Teen-agers adore the current screen or radio sensation, and that is the end of it.

2. If our intellect presents an object to us not merely as this particular desirable object but also as representative of an entire class of lovable objects, we call such a tendency of the will *intellectual love.* Thus, one can love this nun, not because of her personal attraction, but from an appreciation of her devotedness, and in loving her he implicitly loves all nuns.

Over and above sensible love of self, a man has, if he is a decent man, an intellectual type of love whereby he loves himself, because he appreciates the excellence of his nature. Such intellectual love overflows from self to one's fellow man, because he too shares that nature. Such love is not mere love of self; it is also love of race, the milk of human kindness, philanthropy.

II. IS MAN OBLIGED TO LOVE HIS FELLOW MAN?

429. 1. Does the Natural Law command sensible love of others? Since the motions of our sensitive appetite are not wholly under the dominion of the will, the Natural Law makes no positive command in this regard. Negatively, however, it forbids the voluntary pursuit and exhibition of such sensible love as will proximately conduce to moral evil. Man's natural likes and dislikes must be disciplined by right reason so that he will not offend against his fellow man in thought, word, or act.

2. Reason apprehends our fellow man as possessing the same goodness, the same fundamental excellence, as ourselves. Since man must love himself because of the excellence of his nature, he must likewise love all in whom that excellence is found. This will be an intellectual love founded upon an appreciation and esteem of common excellence.

Therefore, man must love his neighbor as himself. This does not mean that he must love him with the same intensity as he loves himself but with the same quality of benevolence, wishing him the same goods temporal and divine as he wishes himself. Man's love of self is stronger than his love of neighbor, because, if love springs from likeness, much more does it arise from identity. The love which he has for himself is to be the pattern of the love he has for his fellow man.

However, many may not understand how any tendency of the appetite toward a desirable object can be called love. To them, the term is restricted to an *intense* motion toward an object especially dear, such as natural affection. To avoid confusion, therefore, let us, in this context, substitute the expression "good will" for the word "love." Man's moral obligations to others are summarized in the following thesis.

THESIS XXIX. The Natural Law commands man to accord his fellow men the same quality of good will which he has for himself.

PROOFS

430. The Natural Law commands man to accord his fellow man the same quality of good will which he has for himself because his fellow man has the same dignity of nature and final end as himself. A man must wish good to himself because of the excellence of his nature. Since all men share this same excellence, all must be accorded similar good will.

This conclusion is also demonstrable from the social nature of man. Unless this good will is obtained, social life is not possible.

431. This command of the Natural Law is expressed in the homely proverb, *Do unto others as you would have them do unto you.* This is a principle of human conduct that cannot be removed from human consciousness. What does a man wish that his neighbor should do to him? *Whatever is needful that he and his neighbor should live together as human beings.* Here we again distinguish man the individual from man the social being. What social man expects of his neighbor is set down in social ethics. As one individual to another, we expect our neighbor to leave us undisturbed in what is our own. This is the fundamental law of justice from which juridical duties stem. Therefore, man's first obligation toward others is to observe his juridical duties. All other duties may be called nonjuridical. Juridical duties come first; then nonjuridical duties.

READINGS

St. Thomas, *Summa Theologica,* II–II, 23, 1; 25, 1.
La Farge, John, S.J., *The Race Question and the Negro.* New York, Longmans, Green, 1945.

CHAPTER XV

JUSTICE AND RIGHT

432. Requisite to a clear understanding of our obligations to our fellow man and the nature of justice is a knowledge of rights, for it is the province of justice to preserve and regulate rights. In our study of rights, four chief points will be considered, namely, their nature, origin, relative components, and essential properties or attributes.

I. WHAT IS A RIGHT?

433. Everybody is familiar with the concept of a right in civil law. According to Bouvier's *Law Dictionary*, a right in general is a well-founded claim;[1] and when a given claim is recognized by civil law, it becomes an acknowledged claim or legal right enforceable by the power of the State. Is it true that a right is not a right until the State has begotten it by legislative decree or confirmed it by decision of a tribunal? Jurisprudence and the legal sciences recognize only legal rights. It is for philosophy to determine if there be a further and ultimate explanation of the nature of a right.

434. Etymologically, right is that which is straight, not crooked. It is opposed to wrong — that which does not conform to a given standard. Whatever leads to a given end is straight and right; what leads away is wrong. Thus we speak of right and wrong conduct as leading or not leading to man's last end. Because law points out the right direction to be taken to achieve the ends of the State and of the universe, it is called in German *recht,* in French *droit,* and in Latin *jus* — all of these terms are used primarily to express the notion of right and also to denote the idea of law. This is readily understandable because whoever keeps the law does right, whoever violates the law does

---

[1] "Right," p. 1072. Ed. 1934.

wrong. However, in English "a right" does not mean a law; it refers either to things possessed or to subjective right.

435. 1. *Right referring to things possessed* designates certain things, both material and immaterial, which belong exclusively to me. These things I call "mine." What belongs to my neighbor in like manner is "his." "Mine" and "his" appertain to us and are made sacred to us by a subjective element called a right. By metonomy, "mine" and "his," as the objects of rights, are also called rights or, better, objective rights. Thus a man has a right to life, to a watch, to a walk in the public park. Life, a watch, a walk in the park are called rights because they are objects of subjective rights. Objective rights, then, are either possessions belonging to the individual by the bond of right, or actions, omissions, or any advantage he may enjoy because of right.

436. 2. A *subjective right* is a legitimate and inviolable power whereby one vindicates something for himself as his own. It is a *power,* that is, a faculty or capacity in virtue of which a person *can* do something in contradistinction to a duty in virtue of which a person *ought* to do something or owes something. Where duty constricts human freedom, right confirms or enlarges it. A right is a *legitimate* power, that is, one may act or not act in a given way so that the act or its omission is not wrong or evil. Thus a right to fish a stream does not mean I have the skill and strength to fish but that if I choose to fish my act is good. A right is an *inviolable* power, that is, it is more than a license or permission; it carries with it true security from undue interference. Right first supposes something to be already mine or allows that something to become mine. Its function, then, is to protect me in what is mine. Thus, the right to fish not only permits me to fish but also protects me from being stopped if I choose to fish. If there were no possibility of anyone despoiling me or of preventing me from enjoying what is mine — in the unrealizable situation where all would clearly know what belonged to each other, and where perfect good will existed — rights, or legitimate powers, would still exist, but there would be no need of invoking immunity on their behalf. But right renders inviolable man's just possessions. Right *vindicates something for man as his own.* Right sets up a bond of legitimacy and immunity between a man and some object in virtue of which this object falls under his exclusive control. This extends not only to what actually belongs to a man but also to what he may demand should become his. Hence it is a capacity not merely of doing or not doing, of having or holding something, but also of exacting from others. What may be done, omitted, held, or exacted because of right, that is, what things a man can call his own or make his own, constitute objective rights.

437. What now is the exact nature of this power? Whence this legitimacy and inviolability? Is this legitimacy something physical, something coextensive with my skill and ability so that, for example, because I *can* swim therefore I may? Is this inviolability the force of the individual which wards off aggression, or, in last analysis, the strong arm of the law compelling respect for that which belongs to others? Or is this power perhaps essentially moral? It is a moral legitimacy if it is a grant not of physical power but of freedom to use physical power in accord with moral law. It is a moral immunity if it operates upon the moral faculties of others, informing them that this thing is another's and binding them not to interfere under the penalty of doing evil. If it is a moral power, it enters the realm of morality; if it is a purely physical power, it is divorced from morality.

438. Hobbes said that anything is our right which we may wish to make our right. He writes: "In the natural state of man, a sure and irresistible power confers the right of dominion and ruling over those who cannot resist, insomuch as the right of all things that can be done adheres essentially and immediately unto this omnipotence thence arising."[2] Kant equates right with the power to compel,[3] and explains this power as physical power. On the contrary, with the vast majority of mankind we hold to the definition of right found in our next thesis.

THESIS XXX. Right is a moral power imposing a duty or obligation in conscience to respect it.

439. Holland speaks of right as a moral power but he regards this power to consist in the force of public opinion. "Thus," he says, "if, irrespectively of a man having or not having the force or persuasion to carry out his wishes, public opinion would view with approval, or at least acquiescence, his so carrying out his wishes and with dis-

---

[2] *Rudimentary Philosophy Concerning Government and Society*, Chap. 1, n. 14. Molesworth's Eng. ed., Vol. II, p. 13.

[3] In his *Metaphysische Anfangsgründe der Rechtslehre* (1797) Kant says: *Recht und Befugnis zu zwingen bedeuten also einerlei.* (Right and the power to compel mean the same thing.) Immanuel Kant's *Sämmtliche Werke*, ed. Hartenstein, Vol. 7, p. 29 E. Leipzig, Voss, 1868.

approval any resistance to his so doing; then he has a moral right to so act."[4]

We attach a further meaning to the moral power, which is the essence of right. A man's right binds the minds of his fellow men to recognize the object of his right as something peculiarly attaching to him, and it obligates their wills not to do anything which will interfere with, nullify, or make void what is his. A person who interferes commits a *moral wrong*.

PROOFS

440. 1. There is an unshaken conviction among men that rights persist even when they have been overriden by physical force, that rights exist even in those who have not the physical power to exercise or protect them. Nothing is more repellent to men's common sense than the contention that might makes right. If right is not a physical force, it must be a moral power.

2. Right is a moral power, because it appeals to the intellect and constrains free will. Men could not live together unless they respected the possessions of one another. What demands this respect is right. This demand for respect cannot primarily be force or threat of force, for man is not a brute. Hence an appeal must be made to man's mind to recognize the possession of another; and his will, under the penalty of being guilty of wrong must be constrained not to interfere with another's possession. This alone befits the dignity of man. When he fails to act reasonably in this regard and interferes with that which belongs to another, only then may force be used against him.

441. Corollary I. For every right of a man there is a corresponding juridic obligation, or debt, on the part of some other individual. Otherwise right imposes no obligation in conscience and is but a vain and empty permission.

Corollary II. That right is a legitimate moral power is deducible from the proposition just proved. This point becomes more evident in the discussion of the origin of right and the object of right.

II. THE ORIGIN OF RIGHT

A. The Ultimate Source of All Rights

442. We noted above that in the Latin, French, and German tongues the same word is used for right and law. There is good reason for

---

[4] Thomas E. Holland, *Jurisprudence*, p. 86. Oxford, Clarendon Press, 1937.

this because *the basis of every right must be some law*. Right begets obligation, it places a moral bond on the free will of another, but the only thing capable of imposing obligation and binding free will is law. One man cannot truly obligate himself — self-binding is no binding. Nor can man morally be obligated by his fellow man as such, because all men as men are equal. Nothing other remains than the will of some superior made manifest by law.

The great question now arises: What is the nature of the law from which rights derive? Is this law a supreme accumulation of physical force, which depends for its power of enforcement solely upon an irresistible power to compel? Or is it a moral law which imposes moral obligations and depends on moral sanctions?

443. To the Positivistic School this is an idle question, because there is no law but the law of the State, which ultimately is physical force. Positivism is a development of the political philosophy of Hobbes, who was imbued with the Calvinistic notion that man is naturally selfish and corrupt and amenable only to coercion. Man originally was antisocial and had a right to all things he had the skill to pursue and the brawn to hold. In such a primitive world, right is force. But a condition like this cannot last long for it means war of all upon all. So for self-preservation, men give up their original mode of existence for an artificial thing called society, or the State. Upon entering society, all cede their rights to the State, which becomes the depositary of all right and whose law is the norm of good and evil actions. This law alone now concedes or extinguishes rights. Since the rights originally given to the State by man were equivalent to physical force, the State is now the wielder of this combined might, and actually one's rights extend only so far as the State can enforce its writ. There is no moral law different from the law of the State because all morality derives from the decree of the State. The State is omnipotent and possesses a supreme right limited solely by its own current and accidental weakness.

Positivism underrates and distorts human nature. We have already shown that the norm of morality is not the law of the State — that might neither of the individual nor of the State can constitute the essence of right. Furthermore, to say that the law from which rights issue is but the combined might of all men living in community is to claim that man is to be directed not by moral obligation but by brute force — which is unworthy of human nature.

444. Kant maintains a complete cleavage between justice and morality.[5] For him there is nothing ethical about a strict right. Therefore the juridical order of Kant differs from his moral order as to origin, end, scope, and obligation.

1. *Origin.* Morality proceeds from internal legislation,[6] the dictates of the autonomous reason. Justice depends on the external legislation of the State; outside the State, right and justice do not exist.

2. *End.* The end of morality is internal liberty, that is, without external coercion and without consideration of the utility or nonutility of his act, a man willingly obeys the dictates of reason out of the sole motive of duty. The end of justice is external liberty.[7] Where many live together, their conflicting liberties must be reconciled; and so from the general notion of external freedom, Kant deduced his concept of right which, as we said, is the power to coerce (§ 438). Every man is compelled to cede so much freedom that his fellow man may be equally free. What each is to cede, how much external freedom each is to have, is settled in a mechanical way by the law of the State, whose purpose is to establish that condition of affairs wherein the acts of one are reconciled to the acts of every other according to a universal law of freedom.[8] No man can trespass upon the right of another but each has the right to any line of conduct which does not injure, that is, limit the liberty of another.

3. *Scope.* Justice deals only with external acts, which are subject to coercion. Hence a judge in applying juridic law is not concerned with one's motive: all he looks for is conformity with law — legality. Morals deals with internal and external acts. Its primary concern, however, is that definitely internal thing — motive. It is only indirectly concerned with justice: that is, it is a dictate of reason that one observe the juridic order.[9]

4. *Obligation.* Moral precepts bind in conscience, but laws of justice of themselves do not. They rely for their enforcement upon the coactive

[5] Immanuel Kant, *Die Metaphysik der Sitten, Erster Theil. Metaphysische Aufangsgründe der Rechtslehre.* Koenigsberg, 1797. This contains his philosophy of right and law. It has been translated by W. Hastie as *The Philosophy of Law,* see pp. 9–58. Edinburgh, Clark, 1888.

[6] *Ibid.,* p. 23.

[7] *Ibid.,* p. 14.

[8] "Right, therefore, comprehends the whole of the conditions under which the voluntary actions of any one person can be harmonized in reality with the voluntary actions of every other person, according to a universal law of freedom." *Ibid.,* p. 45.

[9] *Ibid.,* pp. 20–24.

power of the State. Morality is essentially autonomous; justice essentially heteronomous.

445. We shall shortly demonstrate (§ 448) that Kant is wrong in completely divorcing rights from morals. He is also wrong in contending that all rights are deducible from the need of reconciling conflicting claims to freedom. The right of a parent to the love of his child follows from the very personal relation between them and has nothing to do with the general freedom of all. If right is an immediate derivative of freedom, then one could freely surrender any right. But there are inalienable rights no one can give up. A child could not give up its right to support, nor could a man surrender his right to avoid the proximate occasions of sin.

Nor is it correct to say that the object of a right is only an external act amenable to coercion. An internal act may also be the object of right. A husband has a right to the love of his wife and vice versa; parents, to the love and respect of their children. But none of these can be subjected to coercive force.

Some writers[10] describe as pernicious Kant's statement that one has a right to do whatever will not injure his fellow man. They allege, for example, that one could never acquire a right to hate God, kill himself, or commit solitary sins of impurity. In a certain sense this objection is valid but let us give Kant his due: these acts, according to him, have nothing to do with justice — the Kantian laws of justice do not touch them — but Kant would not therefore say they were allowable. To him they belong in another category entirely, they are forbidden *ex alio capite,* that is, by the dictates of the autonomous reason.

446. Reacting strongly against the *a priori* theories of Kant, Savigny[11] and the Historical School offer a purely empirical explanation. Rights, according to them, have their origin in the customs of the people. Before the acceptance of a custom by the people and before the confirmation of custom by the advent of public law, men had no true rights. They had the foundations of rights, but no real rights existed until first custom and then law rose to guarantee, approve, and protect them. Rights are empirically evolved by men living in community in much the same way as speech, public manners, and art.

It is true that some rights result from custom just as some laws

---

10 See M. Cronin, *Science of Ethics,* Vol. I, p. 648.

11 Karl von Savigny, *The Vocation of Our Age,* trans. Abraham Hayward, p. 30. London, Littlewood, 1831, 2 ed.

result from custom but custom as such, that is, mere practice apart from the will of the lawgiver, can beget neither law nor right. That note of moral obligation which is present in every law and right can come only from the will of a lawgiver. A custom receives the force of law only by the approval, tacit or explicit, of the lawgiver.

THESIS XXXI. The juridical order is a constituent of the moral order.

447. We maintain the *sacred oneness* of all human activity under the governance of one supreme moral law. Every human act, whether purely internal or also externalized, self-regarding or other-regarding, either advances a man toward his final end or withdraws him from it. Therefore all human acts, whether legal or moral, juridical or ethical, fall under the moral law guiding man toward his end.

The *juridical order* is the total system of rights and justice, that is, juridical laws which define or confirm rights, and juridical duties to respect the rights of others, and rights themselves. Justice is "the constant and perpetual will to render to each his due."[12] It includes commutative, legal, and distributive justice. The end of justice is to regulate our dealings with *others* and to establish this equality among men that each one has that which is his own.

The *moral order* includes whatever is directly related to man's last end — the sum total of norms, laws, obligations, human faculties, and acts whereby man's last end is attained. This order stands in contradistinction to the physical order, that is, all those activities, laws, and the like which are not directly related to man's last end.

PROOF

448. *The juridic order is part of the moral order,* because rights and the laws creating them are subject to the Natural Law. Since the Natural Law regulates the moral order, man's activity toward his last end, whatever falls under this law belongs to the moral order.

Juridic laws are subject to the Natural Law because all positive laws are subject to it. For the Natural Law commands men to live in society; otherwise they would not reach the due perfection of their nature. Since society flows from the Natural Law, so must those things necessary for the maintenance of society chief among which is the power of society to make laws.

---

[12] *Sum. Theol.*, II–II, 68, 1.

449. Corollary I. Right is totally a moral power both as to its legitimacy and its inviolability.

Corollary II. What is unjust is always immoral. What is immoral is not always illegal, that is, forbidden by positive law. What is illegal is also immoral except for the violation of a purely penal law.

Corollary III. There can never be a right to that which is immoral. For the moral law cannot grant that which is destructive of itself.

B. The Natural Source of Some Rights

450. The question now arises, With what immediacy do rights flow from the Natural Law? It is clear that some rights come directly and immediately from civil law, for example, the right of suffrage. Are all our rights of this character? Provided positive law conforms to Natural Law, does the Natural Law leave it to positive law to create and determine all rights so that a right is not a right which the civil law does not grant? Or do some rights arise immediately from the Natural Law, which are of prior validity to any right conceded by positive law and which no positive law can wholly abolish?

451. As the legal profession and juristic writers dislike to recognize as law anything other than positive law, so too they think the term *right* should not be applied to anything but legal rights. Pound claims, "The seventeenth-and-eighteenth-century theory, however, confused the interest, which exists independently of law, and legal right, the creature of law. It confused the interest, which the law recognizes in whole or in part and seeks to secure with the right by which the law gives effect to the interest when recognized and to the extent of the recognition. Natural rights simply mean interests which we think ought to be satisfied. It is perfectly true that neither law nor state creates them. But it is fatal to all sound thinking to treat them as legal conceptions."[13]

452. However, natural rights are not merely interests which *we think* ought to be satisfied. They have a most objective existence, for they represent the most fundamental of human goods without which a reasonable life is impossible. They are rights in a prior and more sacred sense that civil rights. They preceded all other rights and they directly emanate from that law upon which all law, to be law at all, must be founded. Sanctions surround these rights which, while they

---

[13] Roscoe Pound, *The Spirit of the Common Law,* p. 92. Boston, Marshall Jones, 1931.

appear to operate ineffectively and spasmodically, will eventually produce the most evenhanded justice. It is scarcely justifiable arrogance
to delimit the terms "law" and "right" to civil law and legal right, nor
does the ability to distinguish between "natural" and "positive" conduce
to unsound thinking. It is the opposite that may well be claimed.

**THESIS XXXII. Independent of any positive law, there exist
natural rights which are direct concessions to man from the
Natural Law.**

453. A positive right is one that proceeds from positive law, human
or divine; a natural right proceeds from the Natural Law.

Nature not only endows man with certain powers — vegetative,
sentient, and intellectual — but also gives him freedom in exercising
them. This freedom of exercise means two things. First, man is
accorded a proper sphere of independence wherein to exercise these
powers and thereby seek the perfection proper to rational life.
This freedom, however, is not absolute but it is conditioned by the
counterclaims of other beings equally free and by his status as a
contingent being who has not reached his final perfection. It is the
freedom of one who is responsible for the right use of freedom;
perfect happiness is to be granted or denied him in so far as he wisely
or unwisely uses his freedom. Second, since man has the responsibility
of attaining final perfection, he is not to be interfered with in the
reasonable pursuit of it.

To say that nature gives each man his proper field of free activity
and makes him secure in the pursuit of means to his final end means
that nature has endowed him with certain rights.

454. These rights preserve the sacredness of the human person. Every
man is a person — a rational, self-active, and independent being. As
self-active, he is the master of his actions, that is, he is the ultimate
responsible agent of what he does. As independent he is a complete
whole, that is, he is not part of any other being, nor inferior to any
other man in the essentials of his nature and his end. It is the sub-
limity of this destiny — participation in an infinite good — which confers on him a unique and inviolable dignity. To prevent him from
attaining that destiny is to treat him not as a person but as a thing.
To secure this destiny he must attain a number of internal and external goods. Therefore, just as his person is inviolable, so also is that
which belongs to him. In commanding that the person and its neces-

sary adjuncts be respected, nature is conferring natural rights. These are the safeguards wherewith nature renders the human person inviolable.

Not all human rights are connatural; some are acquired. Connatural rights are those which one possesses because of the mere fact of actual existence. Such are the rights to life, liberty, happiness, good rearing. Acquired natural rights are conferred by the Natural Law because of some fact other than that of mere existence. Such is the right to the fidelity of one's spouse, to the love of one's child.

PROOF

455. 1. Every law must confer at least the right of security to observe it.

Since there is a Natural Law, it must give men the right to keep it in peace.

2. Unless the Natural Law immediately granted men moral inviolable powers to vindicate things as their own, men would be denied by nature the essentials of human existence. Without such moral powers, a man's physical faculties would be of little use to him; for, if other men could without moral fault and whenever it pleased them hinder his use of them, deprive him of the fruit of them, take away his life, members, liberty, or goods, he could not live as a man.

Now the essentials of human existence are necessary means to man's destiny. It would be absurd to say that nature summons man to his destiny and that she herself neglects to give him the means necessary for attaining it.

These moral powers then must exist. Moral inviolable powers immediately granted by nature are natural rights.

Corollary. Prior to any positive law, men are in possession of genuine rights.

C. The Equality of Natural Rights

456. *Does nature give all men the same natural rights?* Let us first see if nature gives all men the same things. Certainly she must give all men the same *essential* things, because she cannot give actual existence and withhold anything that necessarily belongs to human nature. It is equally evident, however, that nature does not give the same *accidental* things to all — some have fleeter feet, others more vivid imaginations, others more brilliant minds, etc.

Since that which makes right at all possible is the protection of the law, our question is, Are the things of every man equally sacred in the eyes of the Natural Law? Indubitably. The possessions of a rich man or a native are no more inviolable than those of a poor man or a foreigner. Therefore, as all men are essentially equal, that is, endowed with the same nature and destined to the same end, so they likewise possess the same rights immediately deriving from human nature.

But each individual is not equal in every way with every other individual with respect to natural rights. Men are equal as to nature and destiny and hence as to the number and sacredness of the rights flowing therefrom. But here the equality ends. These rights do not have in every individual the same extension, content, and opportunity of exercise. Nature does not distribute all her gifts evenly. As each personality differs from every other, so too do the *contents* of the rights deriving from these personalities. Thus the right to a livelihood or to an education will extend to a larger amount of particular goods in the case of those who have greater needs and greater capacities. A Negro stevedore has the same natural right to a livelihood as a king, but the actual goods that form the content of this right will vary in either case. So also, the right to an education for the brilliant son of a university professor and a crippled moron will not extend to the same disciplines and instruments of education.

However, in every case the natural right of the individual must embrace a certain minimum of goods. What that minimum calls for will depend on a variety of circumstances, personal and social. To keep a man from that minimum is practically to suppress the right. This no man — not even the State — can do. Some persons are endowed by nature with an abundance far beyond this minimum. However, there is no reason why everyone must receive physical powers of the exact same quality or be given the same opportunity to use them. Justice does not demand that all have exactly the same things but that each be secure in what he does have. Hence we may say that the natural rights of all are equal as to kind, number, and inviolability; but not as to content, quantity, and scope of exercise.

III. THE RELATIVE COMPONENTS OF RIGHT

457. A right is a relation. We shall now consider the factors involved in this relation.

What is a relation? The term *relative* is opposed to the term *absolute*. The absolute is that which denies or at least prescinds from connection with another. The relative is that which is connected with another. Hence a relation is the connection between one thing and another, or that which makes a being a relative being.

Every relation involves (*a*) a *subject,* which bespeaks a relation to another; (*b*) a *term,* to which the subject is referred; (*c*) a *foundation,* or reason why the subject is referred to the term.

Right is not a logical but a real relation, for it exists independently of one's thoughts. While it is not a material, tactile thing, it is most actual and real, being a suprasensible moral thing.

For clarity and convenience, the three elements of a relation will, in the case of right, be divided into the following five: the subject of the relation of right we shall call the *subject party;* the term will be divided into the *matter* and the *object-party;* and the foundation, into the *ground* and the *title.*

A. The Subject Party

458. The subject party is the one in whom the right is vested, the one possessing the moral power involved in a right. The question here is, Who or what can possess rights?

THESIS XXXIII. Only persons possess rights.

459. We have defined a person as a rational, self-active, and independent being. The term *person* here applies to (*a*) *natural person,* an individual human being and (*b*) *moral person,* a collection of human beings or even a collection of interests to which by a justifiable fiction of law the condition and unity of personality is attributed.

Children, the insane, and all others incapable of exercising rights have rights in virtue of their human personality which others must safeguard on their behalf. To have actual rights, however, one must actually exist, for a power without a subject in which to inhere is not a power.

460. Animals and all other inferior beings have no rights since they are not persons and exist solely for the utility of man. Hence men have no obligations *to* brutes although they have obligations *about* brutes. Man has an obligation to himself to treat brutes in a becoming way — he cannot visit upon them unreasonable anger; he cannot treat them with wanton cruelty lest being cruel to brutes he become cruel to man; nor can he abuse the bounty which the Creator puts at his disposal. Bentham,[14] however, claims brutes have rights just as men have.

Some prove the proposition under discussion by an appeal to obligation. Rights, they say, come from moral obligation; but since man alone is subject to moral obligation, only he can have a right. This argument seems more pious than valid, for whereas God certainly has rights, He has no obligations.

PROOF

461. *Only persons have rights,* because moral inviolability does not attach to the things which pertain to brutes. Moral inviolability is the essence of right. If then, brutes — which come next to man in the hierarchy of being — enjoy no such inviolability, only persons have rights.

Brutes cannot have moral inviolability, because being totally material and mortal, they must subserve man, the immaterial and immortal. The reason for their existence is man's utility. Beings whose very substance is subordinated to the utility of some other beings are merely things.

B. The Matter of a Right

462. The term of the relationship of right includes two things, the personal term and the material term. (*a*) The *personal term* is the person who has the juridic obligation to respect the right: this is the object party of whom we treat in the next section. (*b*) The *material term,* or better, the matter or object of right, is the "just thing," that which one may do, hold, or exact, that over which or in regard to which a person has a right. Two chief questions may be raised here: *What can be the object of right?* What can a person claim as his own?

1. Negatively

It is of fundamental importance to establish that no person, moral or individual, can own another person.

THESIS XXXIV. The matter of a right can never be a person.

---

[14] *Morals and Legislation,* p. 310. Oxford, Clarendon, 1907.

463. No one can have a right *in the person* of another. A person, as a person, cannot be subordinated as a mere means to another. The State may have a right over the goods of a citizen or over certain of his activities, as in time of war. One individual may have rights over the actions of another, as a father over a child or a master over a servant; but no one, neither individual nor State, can have such rights over a human being as to consider and treat that person as his own, that is, to do with him as he pleases, as he would do with his goods or chattels.

PROOF

464. *No person can be the matter of a right,* because a person cannot be made to serve the mere utility of another. An attempt to do so would militate against the essentially natural equality of all persons and the reason for the existence of rights, namely, to secure the independence of the human person.

Corollary. Absolute servitude whereby one person becomes the chattel of another, is contrary to the Natural Law. Even limited servitude, whereby one's total activities are permanently put at another's disposal, does not befit the dignity of human personality (cf. § 504).

2. Positively

465. In the following chapters, we set forth the chief items which can attach to the individual because of commutative justice. These form the object of right in the strict sense. What the individual may claim from society because of distributive justice and what society may claim from him because of legal justice are objects of right in a less strict sense. Their precise nature is explained in social ethics. It is sometimes said that man has a right to the assistance, friendship, benevolence, truthfulness, gratitude, and fidelity of his fellow man. That is using right in a loose sense. These do not represent juridic claims of the individual but rather duties of his fellow man toward him springing not from justice but from other virtues roughly classified under charity.

C. The Object Party

466. The object party is the person or persons in whom resides the juridic duty corresponding to a given right. As has been stated (§ 441), a right could not be a moral power unless it gave rise to this moral obligation.

This obligation is first *negative:* one must do nothing which will make void or interfere with the right of another. It is *positive* when (*a*) one has bound oneself by an agreement in justice to perform certain acts, for example, a lessee to pay his rent, a judge to administer justice; (*b*) the Natural Law demands an act necessary to save the life of a fellow man, such as giving food to a starving man (cf. §§ 548–550); (*c*) one has become liable to restitution.

467. *Restitution.* If a person upsets the equality between man and man by a violation of commutative justice, he must restore the balance of justice by restoring the injured party to that condition of right which was his before the injury. What belongs to our fellow man remains his even though by force, fraud, or accident it has passed from his actual control. The Natural Law must demand its restoration to him; otherwise it would contradict itself. For on the one hand, by granting a right it would forbid his spoliation: on the other hand, by tolerating its unlawful passage from him, it would approve his spoliation.

Violations of distributive justice do not entail such an obligation. What a citizen may claim by reason of distributive justice is not yet his. Public authority certainly errs in withholding from him what it should grant him; however, when the opportunity of granting his claim has passed, no obligation of restitution remains. Something that ought to have been given him was never granted: he was not despoiled of what already was his. The same is true of violations of legal justice.

468. The obligation of restitution arises (*a*) *from the possession of another's goods.* Whether a man knows that the goods belong to another or mistakenly thinks that he has justly acquired them, makes no difference. In either case they still belong to their rightful owner and must be returned. No one can enrich himself by another man's goods. The obligation of restitution also arises (*b*) *from the infliction of damage.* Unjust damage caused by an evil act demands reparation.

D. The Ground and Title of Right

469. The third relative component of right is its *foundation.* The foundation is the reason why a given relation exists. What is it that endows a person with the moral power of right over this matter? What is the objective reason why he has this right? To answer these questions we must distinguish between the ultimate reason, called the *ground* of right, and the proximate reason, called a *title*.

470. The *ground* is the fundamental basis upon which a right rests: it is its ultimate cause and principle. In § 442 we saw that this must be some law: every right ultimately proceeds from some law.

Law, however, may be called the foundation of right only in the broad sense. Law considers rights only in the abstract: it is concerned with general classes of acts. In seeking the origin of a particular concrete right, we find that over and above the general law conceding a right, something more is required for the existence of this right. Thus, a law of primogeniture could state in general terms that the oldest surviving legitimate son will succeed to the entailed property of his father. In order that John Brown enter upon this entailed property as heir, over and above the general provisions of the law, the *fact* that he is his father's oldest legitimate son must be verified. The fact of his primogeniture is the proximate reason why he acquires this property right. Such a concrete fact is called a title.

471. A *title* is some contingent particular fact which is the immediate cause why this particular right inheres in this person.

Obviously, not all goods and advantages can belong to each individual. Some persons have rights to some things; others to other things. How do these individual rights arise? Law is not enough. Besides the law which states the general conditions under which it grants the individual a right, these conditions must be verified. Between the law and the actual right, the fact applying the law must intervene: this fact is the concrete reason bringing the law into effect in a particular case and demonstrating the existence of this right. This fact is a title. Through the medium of title, law confers this actual right. *Every right, therefore, is actuated in the concrete by some fact called a title.*

Here a logical process is always involved. The following is an example:

Whatever a man legitimately buys must be acknowledged as his.
But John Smith legitimately bought this field.
Therefore, this field must be acknowledged as his.

The major premise enunciates a general law — the foundation of Smith's right. The minor states a fact — the pertinent fact which is his title to the right. The conclusion is an affirmation of his particular right.

This fact can be either (*a*) the mere fact of a man's existence, which is the title to all *connatural rights,* or (*b*) some further contingent or historical fact as in the case of *acquired rights.* The Natural Law acknowledges that from the fact of matrimonial consent, of generation, of donation, various concrete rights ensue. It is a fundamental function of civil law to determine which facts give rise to or extinguish civil rights.

IV. THE ESSENTIAL PROPERTIES OF RIGHT

472. A property is that characteristic of a thing which, though not constituting its essence, is invariably found with it. What are the properties of right? Some say inviolability is such a characteristic, but we have shown it to be more. It is of the essence of right and enters its essential definition. There are but two properties of right, limitation and coactivity.

A. Limitation

473. Limitation is that quality in a right whereby its scope and exercise are restricted to given boundaries. The law that grants the power of right will also determine how far that power may extend. There are no sky-blue rights. I cannot go beyond what is mine; my neighbor, beyond what is his. Rights are finite. They are necessarily such because they flow from human personalities which are limited both in themselves and their powers, obligations, and needs. Just as in the body the exercise of one organ is delimited necessarily by the exercise of the other organs and the good of the entire body, so in the juridic order the rights of one individual are limited by the counter-claims of the others and the needs of the common social good.

In the past there have been periods of undue emphasis either upon the rights of individuals or of society. Thus, misinterpreting the Natural Law, the encyclopedists and revolutionary philosophers of the eighteenth century attributed to the individual exaggerated rights which denied the just claims of society. The social aspect of man's nature was sadly overlooked. The particular result of such liberalism is that the State must stand by while the strong and cunning oppress the weak. State totalitarianism is the opposite extreme. It holds that the State has a right which knows no limit, that the individual has no prior and inalienable rights which society is bound to respect and protect. The truth, however, lies midway between the extremes. A most pressing modern need is the accurate statement of the individual's debt to society and of society's obligation to the individual.

474. The problem of conflicting rights is an ever-present phenomenon. How are such conflicts resolved? Civil law has very definite procedures. However, we are not concerned with the legal processes involved; we are seeking a moral principle whereby one may settle his own conscience before having recourse to external authority.

THESIS XXXV. A true conflict of concrete rights is impossible, and in an apparent conflict the actual existing right is determined by an examination of the relative factors in each conflicting claim.

475. A conflict of rights may be either of these two situations. (*a*) One person may claim the moral power to do a certain thing and another may claim the moral power to prevent him. Thus, Jones claims a right of way over his neighbor's farm; the neighbor claims the right to stop him. (*b*) Two persons may claim the same thing. Thus, Brown and White produce deeds to one and the same piece of land.

476. In the concrete there can never be a conflict of actual rights. Of two contradictory claims, only one can represent an objectively existent right. If this were not the case, there *would be a contradiction in the Natural Law*. All rights ultimately stem from the Natural Law, but if there were an actual conflict of rights the Natural Law would be ratifying or commanding two contradictory things.

477. In the seeming conflict between two rights, the practical difficulty is to determine which one is the actually existent right. Some say the stronger right always prevails. This reply is not too helpful and is open to misinterpretation. Right here might be construed to mean the stronger force. The question is not whether one right is stronger or weaker but rather which is the actual right. The actual right is discovered by examination of each claim in the light of the five relative components of right.

478. The most important component to be examined is the foundation of a right, that is, its ground and title. The ground of right is law. Hence, to interpret right, one must know the limitations implicitly contained in the law. A minor living with his father might argue that because he worked for his wages they belong to him alone, not knowing that in the case of working minors the right to wages belongs not to the minor but to his father. A conflict thus arises because one believes that a law grants him a right which it does not concede. Again, one must recognize that there are certain circumstances in which a right once conceded may be suspended in its actual exercise. I may have a right to use my boat for purposes of recreation, but if at the moment I wish to use it to fish, a man is in danger of drowning and my boat is the only means of rescue, my right to use it for fishing is temporarily suspended. An adequate knowledge of the Natural Law, of the conditions and circumstances wherein rights may be exercised, would obviate many quarrels over conflicting rights.

479. Again it may not be clear that a given fact is sufficient title to a right. Thus, I may wonder if as a quite distant blood relation I am entitled to a share of the estate of an intestate decedent. Or it may not be clear whether a fact capable of creating title has actually taken place. For example, *A* demands of *B* the return of five dollars. *B* says *A* gave it to him; *A* says it was only a loan. One of the great sources of obscurity and conflict is this — did this pertinent fact take place?

480. A scrutiny of the matter of each conflicting right might reveal which is the existing right. The matter is some personal good, and the closer the good is to the subject and the greater his need of it, the stronger is the bond of right attaching it to him. This good may be the necessary means of fulfilling an inescapable duty or a good so necessary that it simply cannot be surrendered. The right which binds such a good to a man is an *inalienable right* before which every alienable right in another gives way. As there is an objective hierarchy of goods, so there is a corresponding order of preference. Rights, then, which concern goods of the soul will generally be preferred to those which concern the body; the common good is preferred to an individual good; a more necessary good to one less necessary.

481. An examination of the subject and the object party will generally yield little in deciding a conflict of rights, for justice ought not to be a respecter of persons. Where a solution is given from a consideration of one party's subjective status, piety or charity rather than justice decides the issue. However, one's peculiar condition, such as extreme danger of death, gives rise to rights. Thus the right of a baker to demand money for the bread he just baked yields before the right of a penniless starving man to live.

What is true of rights is likewise true of conflicting juridic duties.

B. Coactivity

482. Coactivity is the power of using force to protect the object of our right. Coaction is the actual employment of such force. That right does not consist in brute force or coaction has already been shown in the refutation of Hobbes. Hegel held that right is the power to use force: he identifies right with coactivity.[15] He is mistaken for two reasons: First, coactivity presupposes a right existing prior to itself so it cannot be right itself. Thus, when I say I have a right to defend my home from violence, I mean the home is mine, I already have a right to it. Second, there are some true rights which cannot be secured by any resort to force. A husband has a right to the love of his wife, but he may not use force to make her love him.

It is easy to see how one can mistakenly identify right with force, because in everyday life, force is constantly allied with right. The police answer the violence of criminals with clubs, bullets, and prison bars. Armies exist to vindicate a nation's right to live. Force gives security in our rights. *How moral then is the alliance of force with right?* Few laws of conduct are of more basic importance than this: *man must be made to respect what belongs to another.* How? First, by an appeal to moral obligation. Man's free and spiritual nature demands this. Whoever denies man's spiritual nature implicitly holds that man is to be ruled only by physical force. The grim, humorless resort to all-compelling force exerted by the Soviets is the logical outcome of their belief that man is simply matter determined by iron forces.

The use of force is reasonable only when men cease to act as men and despise the appeal of moral obligation. When men act as brutes, they may be coerced as brutes, for the Natural Law allows man in defense of right to counter force with force.

1. The Legality of Force in Defense of Right

483.

THESIS XXXVI. It is lawful to use force to defend certain rights. This is in essence a moral power distinct from the physical ability to coerce. The exercise thereof is normally entrusted to the civil government.

This thesis answers three questions: Is there a lawful power of

---

[15] G. Hegel, *Philosophie des Rechts*, § 94. *Werke*, Vol. VIII, p. 133. Berlin, 1833.

defending right with force? What is the nature of this power? Who can exercise it?

484. No one will deny that the Natural Law must allow force in defense of right. Without this power, our rights would be almost useless owing to the malice and cupidity of men and their proneness to disregard moral obligation. This power does not go with every right because some rights of their nature cannot be secured by force.

485. *What is the nature of coactivity?* Is it a moral license, or is it identified with one's physical ability to coerce? We shall prove that it has a moral aspect, though in its use physical power is involved. In any event, coactivity must be distinguished from that essential note of every right, inviolability, which is moral immunity from interference. Coactivity permits (*a*) *defense* — when a right is threatened, one may repel the aggressor — and (*b*) *reparation* — after an injury has been inflicted, one may forcefully compel restitution. The purpose of co-activity, then, is such a defense and vindication of right as will secure the equality of justice, that is, that each one have what is his own or, if it be taken from him, that it be returned. Coactivity does not, however, empower a man to exact vengeance or to punish the unjust.

Coactivity does not attach to all rights: those which possess this added property are *perfect rights:* those which do not are *imperfect rights.* This does not mean that in the essential quality of right — moral inviolability — an imperfect right is inferior to a perfect right. Both equally place a moral bond on the will of another. Whoever violates the bond of an imperfect right is guilty of injustice.

A right is called perfect because it is fully implemented, that is, it has all the means requisite to maintain itself, one of which is physical force. *Per accidens* an imperfect right is not so fully implemented, and this, not because the matter of such a right is of lesser value but because as a spiritual good or an internal act it is not amenable to force.

Rights enforceable by physical might can spring from commutative and legal justice but not from distributive justice. Piety forbids the latter. It is a grave disruption of the natural order if a member of a natural society raises a violent hand against the head to secure that which has not actually passed into his possession.

486. *Who possesses this power?* The obvious answer is the one who has the right. This power accompanies right. Hence the enforcement of rights flowing from legal justice belongs solely to the head of the State. As to rights springing from commutative justice, though the power of coercion primarily resides in the individual, the public welfare demands that this right be *exercised* on his behalf by the civil government. When public authority cannot or will not protect the individual, when the immediacy of the danger is such that recourse to police protection is impossible, then the individual must exercise this power for himself.

PROOF OF PART I

487. The first part is proved in § 484.

PROOF OF PART II

Coactivity is in its essence a moral power, because the right of defense is possessed by those bereft of sufficient strength to coerce. To say that the sick and aged, children and women have no right of defense because their physical strength is not equal it, is to say that might is right.

If then the right to invoke force is distinct from one's physical power and can exist without it, it must be a moral power.

PROOF OF PART III

488. *The exercise of coactivity in the defense of rights springing from commutative justice is normally entrusted to the civil government,* because the reasonable conduct of social life demands it.

Peace and order would be impossible if every man could immediately invoke force whenever his rights were imperiled. It is the natural duty of the State, as the guardian of the juridic order, to protect these rights. Hence, only when an appeal to the State would be impossible or useless may an individual forcibly protect his rights.

2. How Much Force May Be Used?

489. Only that amount of force may be used which is requisite to safeguard the right from violation or to repair an injury already committed. The harm arising from recourse to force cannot be greater than the evil involved in the disturbance of right. However, the ultimate of violence — the death of another — may sometimes be the only means available. May one go so far?

THESIS XXXVII. Under the conditions of blameless self-defense, the Natural Law allows a man in defense of life and rights equivalent to it even to slay an unjust aggressor.

Although the rights discussed here will not be proven to exist until we finish Chapter XVI, we may reasonably presuppose their existence. We also presuppose that it is impossible for the individual to invoke the aid of the State in the protection of his right.

490. *The conditions of blameless self-defense.*

1. *Unjust attack.* One must be the victim of an unjust aggressor. It does not matter whether the assailant is formally, that is, deliberately or culpably, or only materially, unjust, such as a madman or a drunkard. A person who is justly assailed, such as an escaping criminal pursued by police, may not repel such an assault with violence.

2. *Actual aggression.* That a prospective assailant should only think of attacking one does not constitute a condition of blameless self-defense; he must actually intend and in some way initiate the attack. It would be destructive of peace if man were allowed to resort to force on mere suspicion or the remote prospect of danger. On the pretext of imaginary danger to himself, man would constantly be doing violence to his neighbor. However, at times it will be difficult to determine when an attack has begun. Certainly one may defend himself before his attacker is breaking down his door. Some make too fine a distinction between an assailant's actions which are only "means preparatory to aggression" — which would not as yet justify violent defense — and his "acts which are part of his aggression." There is considerable merit to DeLugo's statement[16] that the assailant's attack begins with his intention to harm. If a person knows that this is an *efficacious* intention, he may consider that he is in danger. An intention is efficacious if something is done to execute it. Hence, if a person is morally certain that someone has determined to attack him and has taken measures to carry out his plan, the attack has begun, and it may be violently repelled. This of course must be interpreted in the light of the remaining conditions.

3. *Last resort.* There must be no other means of self-protection. If the danger can be averted by calling for help, by frightening the assailant, by fleeing, one must do so, provided, of course, that no tremendous difficulty such as exile or a reputation for cowardice would result.

4. *No more force than is necessary to repel the danger.* To inflict

---

[16] "Wherefore if he (the aggressor) has made ready his weapons or done anything else to carry out his determination to kill you, his attack upon you has begun and you can defend yourself." *De Justitia et Jure*, Disp. X, Sect. 7, No. 157.

further harm upon the assailant after his attack has been effectively checked is to take vengeance. This is allowed to no individual. If an assailant can be stopped by wounding him, it is wrong to kill.

5. There is a great dispute concerning the intention one may have. Many, following the opinion of St. Thomas[17] that only public authority can intend the death of an individual, say that a person may never intend the death of the aggressor, only self-defense. They consider this an evident application of the principle of double effect. Others, following DeLugo,[18] hold that death as death may be intended, not as an end gladly sought but as a *necessary means* to self-defense. Since death as death is a physical, not a moral, evil, it may be intended as a necessary means to some proportionate good end. Certainly death may be intended by God; certainly by the State; why not also by an individual?

It would seem that cases may arise in which the principle of double effect will not apply. There are defensive actions which have but one end of work — death. If one chooses the act, he cannot but intend death. Thus, in a death struggle, one may manage to get his pistol to his enemy's head. To fire a pistol directly against a man's head has only one end of work — that man's death. Hence, if one intends to pull the trigger, he cannot but intend to kill. To insist that one may intend only the "quiescence" of the other party is to beget needless scruples and to utter just so many words. However, the validity of our thesis does not depend on the outcome of this dispute: it does not rest on the principle of double effect but on the principle that it is moral to counter force with adequate defensive force.

PROOF

491. The Natural Law must permit *legitimate* defense of life and rights equivalent thereunto, otherwise the grant of right is delusive. Now the slaying of an unjust aggressor is *sometimes* a legitimate means of defending life and similar rights. By *sometimes* we understand whenever the conditions of blameless self-defense are verified. Death of an assailant under these conditions is a means of legitimate defense because *in the conflict of rights arising the right of the innocent party prevails*. If this were not so, the right of the assailant would become more sacred precisely because of his crime; and the innocent

---

[17] *Sum. Theol.*, II–II, 64, 7.
[18] *De Justitia et Jure*, Disp. X, Sec. 6, No. 149.

party, placed in danger of death or spoliation by the crime of the guilty party, would be compelled to prefer the good of his assailant to his own. This conclusion is contrary to right reason.

Our argument is confirmed by the laws of all nations justifying blameless self-defense. It also accords with the declarations of the Roman Pontiffs.

492. *Rights equivalent to life.* The loss of material goods of great value, personal liberty, chastity, and integrity of limb are commonly likened to loss of life. The least of these is material goods of great value. If by these we mean what is necessary to support life or maintain one's state in life, they may well be comparable to life itself. A further reason for the violent defense of them is added, namely, the common social good. If men were not allowed to defend these goods in this manner decent people would be at the mercy of robbers and bandits. Personal liberty, chastity, and integrity of limb are much closer to a man and can more readily be called his than external material goods.

493. *Defense of the right to reputation.* The defense of one's reputation presents a particular problem. It is not quite accurate to say that force is a totally inept means of defending one's reputation on the ground that one is material and the other immaterial and that consequently there is no proportion between them. Reputation is a perfect right in the sense that one can invoke the coercive power of positive law to defend it. But what can the individual do without recourse to law? He certainly may not kill a detractor or calumniator *after* the offense, for such an act would be mere vengeance. So, too, if the calumniator should refuse to restore the good name of another even under the threat of death, the carrying out of the threat would be equivalent to vengeance.

May one use force *beforehand* to prevent a loss of honor? If the prospective dishonoration is to take the form of violence to one's person, such as slapping one's face or pulling one's hat down over one's eyes, it may be repelled by force. It is lawful to answer force with force. If the assault upon one's honor is to be done by word alone, one cannot kill or maim the traducer, because (*a*) beforehand it is difficult to say how serious such an injury is going to be; (*b*) granted we are sure the worst sort of damage is to follow, *such an injury is not irreparable.* A good name may be recovered. If life and limb are endangered, one may use the utmost of violence, for otherwise the injured party would suffer an irreparable loss. Since the calumniated party does not suffer an irreparable loss, it is not equitable that he resort to irreparable damage as a means of safeguarding his right. (c) To allow the defense of honor by shedding blood would be destructive of public peace. Honor is a most variable and subjective thing; if one could resort to arms to defend his honor, slight resentment might result in death.

However, today when men do not habitually carry lethal weapons, to say that one may not silence a calumniator by a good beating is to deny men a protection which decency demands. In the circumstances this measure of force is an apt means of security.

494. What the Natural Law allows a man to do to defend his life and equivalent rights, the law of charity permits him to do on behalf of others.

Man is allowed to defend life by taking life. But is he compelled to do so? For the vast majority of people, such means are extraordinary and abhorrent. The strict obligation of preserving life extends only to the use of ordinary means. However, a person may be so necessary to the State or his family that he would be obligated to take such extraordinary means to save his life.

495. The Natural Law allows the use of force in the defense of certain rights, yet in revelation we are *counseled* not to use force. "Blessed are the meek for they shall possess the land."[19] "If anyone shall strike thee on the right cheek, turn to him the other also."[20]

The virtue whereby man restrains his desire for revenge and the use of violence is meekness. In the matter of meekness, we may distinguish as follows between that which is obliged and that which is counseled.

1. Man is obliged to have under the control of reason all motions of anger, all manifestations of irascible passion. He is counseled sometimes to forego the natural right of using force in preserving rights.

2. Man is obliged to refrain from private revenge and personal retribution. He must forgive injury and insult to the extent that he does not will evil to anyone, even to one who has wronged him. He is counseled generally to repay evil with good. "Love your enemies: do good to them that hate you."[21]

3. The defects of other persons must be endured with patience. It is counseled that injustice be tolerated.

---

[19] Matt. 5:4.   [20] *Ibid.*, 5:39.   [21] Luke 6:27.

The virtue of prudence enables man to discern the admonitions of counsel. However, when the attack upon one's rights constitutes proximate danger of consent to sin unless forcible resistance is made, there can be no question of submission to injury. Thus, the victim of a rape must exert all force possible to drive off her attacker, for there is danger of consent to the sexual act.

READINGS

St. Thomas, *Summa Theologica*, II–II, 57; 67; 73, 1–3.

Aristotle, *Ethics*, V.

Bouvier's Law Dictionary, Baldwin's edition, "Right," p. 1072. Cleveland, 1934.

Catholic Encyclopedia, "Right," XIII, 55; "Self Defense," XIII, 691.

Cicero, *De Officiis*, Bk. I.

Corpus Juris, "Self Defense," Vol. 57, p. 107; "Slaves," Vol. 58, pp. 745–768.

Cronin, Michael, *The Science of Ethics*, Vol. I, pp. 623–651. Dublin, Gill, 1909.

Davis, Henry, S.J., *Moral and Pastoral Theology*, Vol. II, pp. 284–323. New York, Sheed and Ward, 1936.

DeLugo, *De Justitia et Jure*, Disp. 1–3.

Haas, Francis J., *Man and Society*, pp. 25–63. New York, D. Appleton-Century, 1930.

Holaind, Rene, S.J., *Natural Law and Legal Practise*, pp. 265–286. New York, Benziger, 1899.

Holland, Thomas, *Jurisprudence*, pp. 82–125. Oxford, Clarendon, 1937, 13 ed.

Rickaby, *Moral Philosophy*, pp. 244–251, 208–213.

Ritchie, David G., *Natural Rights*, pp. 78–116. London, Swan and Sonnenschein, 1895.

Ryan and Boland, *Catholic Principles of Politics*, pp. 13–28. New York, Macmillan, 1940.

Suarez, *Opusculum*, VI, Sect. 6, ed. Berton, Vol. XI, pp. 527–549.

Vermeersch, A., S.J., *Quaestiones de Justitia* (ed. altera), pp. 1–13, 142–187. Bruges, Beyaert, 1904.

CHAPTER XVI

OBJECTS OF NATURAL RIGHT

496. In an explanation of justice and right, three elements may be distinguished: (*a*) a man's possession; (*b*) the law which make his possession inviolable; (*c*) the immunity or secure enjoyment resulting from law, which is right. We have already considered *c*, the nature of right. We have shown its origin in *b*, Law. We shall now consider *a*, the object of right, or man's possession. The purpose of our investigation will be to determine the chief things which the Natural Law guarantees a man as an individual. The objects of right pertaining to man as a social being are taken up later.

I. LIFE AND LIMB

497. That life and corporal members belong to the individual is so obvious that it need not be demonstrated. No human agency may directly deprive him of these unless his malicious conduct makes loss of his life or limbs necessary to preserve similar rights of others or of the State. If he is innocent of crime, the taking of his life by homicide or the invasion of his bodily integrity by mutilation is grave injustice.

The summary formula, *Thou shalt not kill,* is not an adequate statement of nature's prohibition. Homicide is the direct taking of innocent life upon human authority. This is always and everywhere wrong because it is destructive of the natural equality existing among all men and is an invasion of God's exclusive dominion over human life. The morality of indirect killing is judged by the principle of double effect as in the case of indirect suicide (§ 399). While men generally recognize the heinousness of homicide, they endeavor, on convenient occasions, to avoid guilt on the claim of justifiable killing.

A. Euthanasia

498. To mask an ugly deed behind a euphemism is an age-old escape. The killing of the aged, the incurably ill, or the mortally wounded on the battlefield to bring an end to their misery is not an act of kindness but murder. Even if the painfully wounded ask for death, their request may not be acceded to on the pretext that *volenti non fit iniuria.* For more is involved than their own right to life: the superior right of God's supreme dominion is the first consideration. Doctors and nurses have a contractual obligation to use all ordinary means to keep their patients alive. Deliberately not to do so, or positively to hasten death partakes of the malice of murder. Nor may doctors use the bodies of their patients as guinea pigs in order to experiment with uncertain drugs when surer remedies can be used. When there are no sure remedies, a doctor may test the curative value of a newly discovered drug provided there is no risk to the patient.

B. Dueling

499. The common sense of mankind has finally abated a practice which until the end of our American Civil War constituted a serious moral evil that was tolerated and even approved by intelligent men. A duel is a fight with lethal weapons on private authority and by previous appointment. It is wholly and intrinsically wrong. An invasion of God's supreme dominion over life, it partakes of the malice both of murder and suicide. The principal in a duel deliberately endangers his life without a reasonable cause and by private authority attacks the life of his opponent.

The vicious custom of dueling arose in the early seventeenth century from a distorted notion of gentleman's honor. An insult demands satisfaction, but a duel is no substitute of satisfaction. Satisfaction is the retraction of wrong done. But the challenger, far from receiving a proper amend, allows the challenged to maintain his insult by force of arms and gives him an opportunity to perpetrate on him a more grievous wrong. After an unretracted insult honor can no longer be defended; only the opportunity for vengeance remains.

C. Abortion

500. The destruction of the human foetus is a most serious issue in modern ethics. The foetus is destroyed in two ways, by foeticide and abortion. Foeticide is the direct killing of the foetus in the mother's womb, after which it is expelled. This is murder just as truly as is infanticide. Abortion is *the expulsion of a living and non-viable foetus from the womb*. Since the foetus cannot live outside its mother until the completion of the twenty-eighth week of pregnancy, removal of an inviable foetus from the womb is equivalent to destroying it.

Abortion may be spontaneous, such as a miscarriage brought about by accident or disease. This would not be a human act, unless, of course, a person had been guilty of culpable neglect. An abortion is induced when it is the result of intentional interference with the foetus. A distinction must be made between directly and indirectly induced abortion.

In a *direct abortion* one intends the expulsion of the nonviable foetus and takes measures to effect it. Direct abortion is wrong whether it is sought as an end in itself — such as avoiding the consequences of moral evil — or whether it is reluctantly undertaken as a means to a good end — such as saving a pregnant woman's life. It is a direct attack upon innocent human life and is always murder.

501. It is argued that foeticide and abortion are allowable because a foetus, not being a person, has no rights. This contention is fallacious. The morality of the problem has no relation to the dispute as to the time when the rational soul is infused into the embryo. The likeliest opinion is that this occurs when, after fertilization, a distinctly new living thing is formed. Actually, abortion is not resorted to until the foetus is fairly well formed and is certainly informed with a rational soul; but even if it were invoked in the early stages of gestation, the act would still be destructive of a human person. The reason is that there is direct and unbroken continuity of life from the fertilization of the ovum to the development of the embryo, foetus, infant, child, youth, and man. Any distinct and living organism, fundamentally capable of intelligence, is a human person and remains such as long as it possesses life. Every adult was once a foetus: the foetus is the first stage in the development of the human person.

It cannot be maintained that if a difficult pregnancy endangers a mother's life, the foetus as the cause of this condition becomes an unjust aggressor and hence forfeits its right to life. A foetus cannot be an aggressor — neither formally, because it is incapable of volition, nor even materially, because its existence is not the result of its own choice but of the will act of others.

It is claimed that since the mother's life is endangered by child bearing, her right to life is prior to that of the child's. The answer is that neither the mother nor the foetus has prior rights to life: they have equal rights to life, because each is equally a human person. The right of the foetus is just as sacred as that of the mother's. Any action intentionally directed against the life of either is homicidal.

It is exceedingly difficult to arrive at a decision in some actual cases, and in serious emergencies the solution may appear to be abortion to save the mother. The argument that an unborn baby will be missed less than a woman in her prime may seem quite compelling. Praise-worthy as the physician's intention may be, he is never justified in saving one life by directly taking another. He may argue that necessity knows no law — that he cannot stand by and see his patient die because he fears to use this last means. It is true that necessity knows no law in the sense that no man can be blamed for not doing the impossible, but no matter how dire one's necessity, an act intrinsically wrong is never justified. Moral evil may not be willed that any good, however great, may be obtained.

502. Too many intelligent and otherwise respectable people approve so called *therapeutic abortion.* In the overwhelming majority of cases this is direct abortion, but every direct attack upon the life of the foetus is a crime irrespective of the motive and permission by law. It is cynically said that an abortion is criminal if only one doctor signs for it but it is therapeutic if three sign for it. Unfortunately, too many medical practitioners consider the procedures of the healing art a kind of sacred cow removed from any higher law of morals. To these, what-ever will effect a desirable medical end is good and beyond moral reproach. We have seen, however, that the Natural Law is the over-all law of human life and acts.

503. In *indirect abortion,* some medical treatment is administered or a surgical operation is performed for a serious purpose other than abortion but abortion results. An example would be the removal of a cancerous pregnant womb. The morality of such acts must be adjudged according to the principle of double effect. *Hastening of birth* after the completion of the twenty-eighth week of pregnancy is allow-able for a proportionally grave reason. The foetus then is capable of living outside the womb.

II. LIBERTY OF PERSON

504. It is not too surprising to find that Aristotle not only justified but also approved absolute slavery as something intended by nature. He says, "He who would participate in reason enough to apprehend reason but not to have it is a slave by nature."[1] The medieval scholastics, seeing serfdom as an everyday fact of social existence, repeated without criticism the arguments of Aristotle favoring slavery. However, liberty of person is not merely a desirable advantage, a helpful condition of life which may be accorded or denied him as circumstances permit; it is a strict right, as we have shown in § 464.

A question arises as to the morality of limited servitude. In limited servitude a man's services are wholly and perpetually handed over to a master in return for care and keep. A person who has so bound himself would still retain all his essential human rights to life, sustenance, fair treatment, marriage, and, if married, cohabitation. While this state is less becoming the dignity of man's independent nature, yet in theory it seems that a man might be sentenced to such a life for crime or that he might freely contract for it if he felt unable to provide for himself.

Slavery, however, inevitably involves such abuses that it must be condemned. There is always the danger that the slave will be treated as a thing; his chances of intellectual and moral development are almost nil; he has no redress against injustice; he can be bent to any immoral purpose of his master. Slavery begets a slave mentality and a slave morality which has pernicious effects on slaves and slaveholders.

III. INTELLECTUAL AND MORAL INTEGRITY

505. Integrity, positively, is a condition of wholeness; negatively it is the absence of defect. A being or faculty is said to possess integrity if it actually or potentially has those things which naturally complete it. Intellectual and moral integrity means that, unimpeded by his fellow man, a man may use his specifically human powers and direct them toward their proper objects — his mind to truth and his will to moral goodness. His fellow man may not maliciously place any obstacle in the way of his mind's quest for the true and his will's appetite for the good. Otherwise he could be prevented from proper development and

---

[1] *Politics,* Bk. I, 5, 1254b.

final perfection. Without access to truth and to moral goodness, man could not live as a man.

506. Man's right to *intellectual integrity* is violated by depriving him of the use of his mental faculties without his consent; by teaching him false doctrines; by making him the victim of false promises; by unduly deceiving him.

507. Man's right to *moral integrity* is violated in the following ways:

1. *By compelling him to act against his conscience.* Immunity from such compulsion is generally called *freedom of conscience.* What does this right involve? Under penalty of moral guilt the will must obey the dictates of conscience even when it is invincibly erroneous. No power may compel man to do what conscience says is wrong. When conscience dictates that a given good act is to be done, a person must be free to do it, except when the act would militate against the common good or the equivalent good of another individual. In such a case, a man may be restrained from acting, but he may never be forced to perform an act forbidden by conscience. This right is *inalienable,* for no man can surrender it since it is necessary in order to fulfill the absolute duty of avoiding evil. It is *indefeasible,* that is, it may not be taken away by any authority, for to do so would be to deprive the individual of an essential means to his last end. This is the right which masters, employers, military commanders, and the like violate when they command those under their charge to violate the negative precepts of the Natural Law.

2. *By depriving him of the necessary means of moral development.* Those to whom is entrusted the care of children, orphans, prisoners, and servants, dwelling with them day and night, must afford them suitable opportunities to cultivate their spiritual life. A law which would forbid religious instruction to children under eighteen years of age would not be a law but a moral injury. Pastors, teachers, and parents have a contractual obligation in virtue of their office to assist their charges by the good example of their lives. Bad example on their part violates not merely charity but justice.

3. *By exercising undue hypnotic influence.* Hypnotism is a somnambulistic state artifically induced wherein the patient's mind is passive but alert to the suggestions of the hypnotist. The patient's exercise of free will is impaired during such a trance but it is not clear how complete the control of the hypnotist is. Many claim that a hypnotized person will refuse to execute commands which he

considers immoral when he is fully conscious. Others say that if the trance is deep enough, a hypnotized person will yield to any suggestion.

Hypnotism is not intrinsically wrong. As one may temporarily surrender the use of reason for a just cause, so also one may temporarily yield the exercise of his free will for a good reason. Hypnotism is said to have a definite curative value for people with alcoholic, gambling, and suicidal tendencies which they seem unable to resist.

Hypnotism is wrong if by means of it one (a) suggests immoral acts; (b) attempts to learn the free future; (c) endeavors to maintain a permanent hold on the patient's will.

One may submit to hypnotism if he has a grave reason and takes proper precautions which include obtaining a reputable hypnotist and having a reliable witness.

IV. HONOR AND REPUTATION

508. Every man is made to the image of God and is destined for perfect happiness. Every man deserves recognition of and respect for the excellence of his nature. This is a connatural right. Every man, irrespective of his wealth, ability, or social standing, possesses the dignity of being a man and to think of, speak to, or act toward him as though he were not a man is to deprive him of the honor he is entitled to by nature.

Over and above his native dignity, by industry or even by accident a man can acquire other perfections which bring additional honor. He may win credit for being a skilled architect or eloquent speaker; he may be honored as a father by his child; he may be respected as a civil superior by citizens; he may be revered for heroic virtue. All such honor acquired by a man's activity is a distinct advantage and of perceptible value to him. He may justly claim it as his own because it is the result of his effort. To prevent him from acquiring this honor is usually an injustice: to deprive him of acquired honor violates his strict right.

The practice of virtue is the most praiseworthy activity of man. For there is nothing a man can do that is more becoming a man than to act virtuously. A man is to be honored not only for *being* a man but also for *acting* as a man. By acting as a man, one is entitled to *reputation* or a good name. Reputation is the right of all men. It belongs to the truly good man as the natural outcome of virtue. It also belongs to the man who is only apparently good until his conduct shows that he is not. All men are to be judged good until they prove themselves otherwise. The peace and good order of society demand this attitude. If a man's reputation is genuine, his right is absolute and it cannot be taken from him against his will. If a man's reputation is only apparent, his right to it must yield to the common good, the protection of an innocent party, and his own correction and ultimate good.

509. A man's right to honor and reputation is violated by rash judgment, contumely, and backbiting.

1. *Rash judgment* is a *firm* assent of the mind whereby one judges another guilty of moral evil for insufficient reasons. It differs from rash suspicion, which does not involve firm assent. By judging rashly, man offends against his neighbor's right that he be well thought of until his misconduct forfeits good opinion. The evil consists in the will, upon insufficient grounds, compelling a *certain* judgment to the detriment of another. Justice demands that man be esteemed neither more nor less than his conduct warrants.

2. *Contumely* is the dishonoring of a person in his presence either by omission or commission. It is the contemptuous refusal to accord a man the honor which the occasion calls for, or it is open insult. Contumely is a violation of justice because it deprives one of what is due him; it is a violation of charity because it involves contempt of his person. As an offense against justice, it demands restitution; the honor denied a person must be given to him.

3. *Backbiting* is the dishonoring of a person in his absence. It takes two forms, calumny and detraction.

a) *Calumny* is false accusation of evil whereby a man's reputation is lost in whole or in part. Justice demands that the lie be retracted.

b) *Detraction* is the revelation of a true but hidden sin of another without a justifying reason. A man does not forfeit his good name except by open misconduct. Many people fail to see the injustice of detraction. They argue that if a man does wrong, he has ceased to be virtuous to the extent of his wrongdoing and thereby loses the accompaniment of virtue which is good name. Therefore, to take away the good name of such a person is not injustice, because a good name no longer belongs to him. The argument is patently erroneous. Secret wrong does not destroy one's reputation, because if a man possesses something — say money or reputation — he has a right to keep it until his retention of it would become an injustice to another; but the retention of a good name by one who secretly sins does not as such involve an injustice to another. Therefore, the hidden faults of others must remain secret until a reason arises for their revelation. Such a reason might be the person's own amendment, the protection of his fellows, the safeguarding of the common good.

To assess the amount of harm done by detraction, consideration must be given not merely to the defect revealed but also to the character of the detractor, the standing of the detracted, and the character of those to whom it is revealed. Since justice is violated, reparation must be made as far as possible. The truth may not be denied, but the detractor can at least endeavor to repair his victim's good name by extolling his good qualities.

V. FRIENDSHIP

510. Generically, friendship is the love of mutual benevolence. Where some special tie such as blood or marriage unites persons, we speak of *natural affection*. The virtue of piety governs this relation. In more ordinary usage, friendship means that bond of mutual esteem and good will which unites persons who are not related by blood or marriage. Friendship has this meaning here.

Aristotle points out that the motive of friendship may be the good, the pleasant, or the useful.[2] In other words, man loves his friend for what he is — the good that is in him — or for the pleasure he affords him or the utility he finds in him. Friendships based on the latter two motives are egotistic outlets of self-love, for therein it is not the friend that is loved so much as one's own pleasure and utility. These are shallow, transient things, for such a friend may quickly cease to please or to be useful. When one values his friend and wishes him well for his own sake, and when these feelings are reciprocated, only then is true and permanent friendship had. True friendship is not passive. It must be fostered by habitually friendly acts; otherwise it languishes and eventually dies. Nor is it the mere acceptance of favors and affection. Aristotle said, "It is more characteristic of a friend to do well by another than to be well done by, and to confer benefits is characteristic

---

[2] *Ethics*, VIII, 2, 1155b.

of the good man and of virtue."[3] This idea has been more succinctly expressed by Christ, "It is more blessed to give than to receive."[4] The core of friendship is mutual well-doing, and the more excellent the benefits interchanged by friends, the nobler their friendship. To what heights of human grandeur it may rise was told for all time by Horace when he mourned for his dead friend Vergil as the *dimidium animae meae*,[5] the other half of his soul. Friendship is a rare and precious thing. It is not born in a day. Like true human excellence, it is the product of time and the constant exercise of virtue. It can flourish only between persons of true moral excellence.

511. Man has a connatural right to seek friends as the due development of his social nature. The good man has need of friends — virtuous companions, few in number, who share activities they mutually like and whose association is a help to virtue, giving life its pleasant flavor. To deny him friends is to deny him the most excellent of external goods. Once he has acquired a friend he has a right to keep him, not to be parted from him by the invidious or malicious acts of a third party. The invasion of this right is *mischief-making,* which consists in talk, not necessarily bad in itself, but bad in that it turns a man from his friend.

Is detraction a greater sin than mischief-making? To this question St. Thomas replies: "Sin against the neighbor is more grievous, the greater the harm done to the neighbor thereby. Harm again is greater, the greater the good destroyed. Now among exterior goods friendship stands preeminent, since 'none can live without friends,' as appears by the Philosopher. Hence it is said: 'Nothing can be compared to a faithful friend.' In fact, the good name that is destroyed by detraction is especially needed for this, that a man may be accounted fit for friendship. And therefore mischief-making is a greater sin than detraction and even than contumely because a friend is better than honor and it is better to be loved than be respected."[6]

[3] *Ibid.,* IX, 9, 1169b.
[4] Acts 20:35.
[5] *Odes,* Bk. 1, Ode 3.
[6] *Sum. Theol.,* II–II, 74, 2.

READINGS

St. Thomas, *Summa Theologica,* II–II, 64, 65, 66, 73, 74.
Bouscaren, T. Lincoln, S.J., *Ethics of Ectopic Operations.* Milwaukee, Bruce, 1944, 2 ed.

Bouvier's Law Dictionary, articles on murder, homicide, manslaughter, self-defense, abortion, liberty, undue influence, alienation of affection, libel, slander.

Catholic Encyclopedia, "Abortion," I, 46; "Calumny," III, 190; "Detraction," IV, 757; "Duel," V, 184; "Euthanasia," V, 630; "Homicide," VII, 441; "Honor," VII, 462; "Infanticide," VIII, 1; "Reputation," XII, 776; "Slander," XIV, 35.

Cathrein, Victor, S.J., *Philosophia Moralis,* pp. 273–277. Friburgi Brisgoviae, Herder, 1915, 10 ed.

Corpus Juris, "Homicide," Vol. 29, pp. 1045–1112; "Libel and Slander," Vol. 36, pp. 1134–1289; "Liberty," Vol. 37, p. 159.

Cosgrove, S.A., and Carter, P. A., article on abortion, *American Journal of Obstetrics and Gynecology,* Sept., 1944.

Holland, Thomas, *Jurisprudence,* pp. 167–174, 183–187. Oxford, Clarendon Press, 1937, 13 ed.

Jarrett, Bede, O.P., *Social Theories of the Middle Ages,* pp. 94–121. Westminster, Md., Newman, 1942.

LaRochelle-Fink, *Medical Ethics,* pp. 91–130, 156–170. Montreal, Catholic Truth, 1943.

Leibell, J. F., ed., *Readings in Ethics,* pp. 487–493, 505–512. Chicago, Loyola, 1926.

Leo XIII, *Social Wellsprings,* ed. Joseph Husslein, S.J., Vol. I, pp. 91–139, 167–204. Milwaukee, Bruce, 1940.

McFadden, Charles J., O.S.A., *Medical Ethics for Nurses,* pp. 126–270. Philadelphia, Davis, 1946.

O'Malley-Walsh, *Essays in Pastoral Medicine,* pp. 48–59. New York, Longmans Green, 1907.

Ritchie, David G., *Natural Rights,* pp. 119–134, 135–156. London, Swan and Sonnenschein, 1895.

Sutherland, Halliday, *Laws of Life,* pp. 260–270. New York, Sheed and Ward, 1936.

CHAPTER XVII

PROPERTY

I. THE PROBLEM OF PROPERTY RIGHTS

512. Can men own material goods? Can the power of personality which is right be legitimately extended so as to include portions of the physical world? If so, what is the nature of that right?

That men of all ages have made and enforced claims called property rights is a matter of historic record. However, men's theories and practice regarding such rights have altered from time to time, and contemporary man's views of property have been jarred to their depths by the impact of ideologies denying what the past four hundred years have taken for granted. It is of consuming importance, therefore, clearly to establish what the Natural Law commands, forbids, and allows in this respect; because, while these are not the most sacred of human relations, yet they absorb a major share of man's attention. There is scarcely any aspect of life, any phase of human activity, that the problem of property rights does not affect. The key to the peace of tomorrow lies in a sound knowledge and prudent application of these principles by all nations.

513. At the root of the problem is the concept of ownership. The least that men understand by ownership is not merely the use of a material object but possession guaranteed by law; the most, such a juridic tie to the thing that even though it pass out of the actual control or possession of the one who claims it, the law still recognizes it as attaching to him. Hence we define ownership as the *control of a material object in one's own interest in accordance with law.*

1. *Control.* This is the right to possess, enjoy, and determine the disposition of a thing. It may be plenary or partial, as we shall explain.

2. *In one's own interest.* In itself, ownership is an exclusive control. A man so imprints the mark of his personality upon a thing that

henceforth it attaches to him, and all others must respect his right to control it. Without this feature of exclusiveness there would be no objective distinction between mine and thine in the matter of property. A person who controls property in the interest of another is a *trustee,* not an owner.

3. *Material object.* The object of this right is some material thing, or what is reckoned as such, external to the agent and capable of being exclusively controlled. Certain common things such as air, sunlight, the high seas are in most respects naturally incapable of appropriation. The term *material object* extends here to an enormous range of things — not merely tangible objects, such as land, houses, movable goods, but also the services of another man; a variety of activities, such as a right of pasture; a right to hunt; to fish; to cross a neighboring property; to have access to light, air, water; to have the support of land or buildings; to enter upon dignities, offices, priviliges; less tangible things such as franchises, copyrights, and patent rights.

4. *In accordance with law.* The right of ownership stems from the command of law that the owner of a material thing shall be secure in his possession and use of that thing. But law does not undertake to protect any and every use of that thing. The Natural Law cannot countenance immoral use, nor the positive law illegal use. The doctrine that an owner may do absolutely what he pleases with his possession is an aberration of economic liberalism. Law must fit ownership into its reasonable place in the total scheme of human rights. Hence it is for law to designate what the scope of ownership is, who is to exercise it, how exclusive and permanent an owner's control is, and when ownership itself must cede before some higher right.

That the Natural Law subordinates the right to own to the right of other men to live we shall show in Thesis XL. Charity dictates that superfluous goods are to be given to the needy. The State has a right of *eminent domain.* This must not be confused with the State's own right of owning things. It is its superior power of jurisdiction to (*a*) regulate the uses of property in conformity with the demands of the common good, and (*b*) in certain eventualities to appropriate private property. The justifying circumstances of the latter are the clear need of the common good and the payment of fitting recompense.

514. *Divisibility of ownership.* Ownership, put in simple terms, is the control of material things. It may be partial or plenary:

1. *Partial ownership* is a right to either the fruits, use, or substance

of a thing. The following are examples. First, a man may be entitled to gather for himself the oranges grown in a grove without being the proprietor of it. He is a usufructuary and his right is that of usufruct. Second, from the proprietor of a building a lessee may acquire defined rights to the use of that building. His right is that of a user only. Third, the existence and duration of the rights to the fruits or use of things usually depend upon agreement with one who retains the right to the *substance* of the thing.

2. *Plenary ownership* is a right to the fruits, use, and substance of a thing. It permits one to hold, use, gather the fruits of, change, alienate, or destroy the thing. Plenitude of control is permanent control. The thing is not merely for the owner's temporary advantage but so long as he remains the owner he determines even its future disposition. Ownership is not delimited by time but solely by law.

Perfect dominion, or *absolute ownership,* is the right of plenary control. Imperfect dominion, or *qualified ownership,* is a right merely to the substance or to the use or to the fruits or to the use and fruits. The English word *owner* signifies primarily one who has perfect dominion; secondarily, when it refers to imperfect dominion, it means the one who has the right to the substance of the thing. We shall use the word in its primary meaning.

515. *Who can own?*

1. *Negative communism* denies that anyone may own anything, neither the individual nor groups of men nor the State. Everything should be completely open and common to all comers. This is flat denial of all ownership. Such absurd chaos would result if this dream were reduced to practice that it may be doubted if anyone outside of an insane asylum holds this opinion. *Therefore, some kind of ownership must exist.* The concept is a valid one.

We distinguish then private ownership and communal ownership. (*a*) *Private ownership* is ownership by the individual. According to it, the individual has the right of absolute ownership so that from the control of objects owned he can exclude all other men. (*b*) *Communal ownership* is ownership by a group of men, a tribe, or a State. The right does not reside in any individual but in the moral person, the group.

The great issue is *the validity of the concept of private ownership*. Until a hundred years ago the right of the individual to own was taken for granted, just as the conviction of ancient man that the earth was flat. Since the time of Karl Marx, a system of property holding once universally accepted has been widely and vehemently denounced and the right of the individual to own either in whole or in part has been vigorously denied.

Communism maintains that the State or its equivalent absolutely owns everything. Any form of private holding even in the consumers' goods is robbery of the community. This is the system which the original Bolsheviks unsuccessfully attempted to introduce into Russia.

2. *Socialism* distinguishes between *consumable goods,* that is, goods which may be used only and which may not be employed to produce further wealth, and *capital goods,* such as land, mines, factories, ships, invested money — anything capable of yielding profit or additional wealth. The individual may own consumable goods but he may not own productive goods. Then who shall own productive goods? The answer varies according to the brand of socialism.

a) The *socialist* says that the State organized in democratic form shall own all sources of productive wealth and shall see to the distribution of all goods produced. The followers of Henry George, known as *agrarian socialists,* while allowing the individual the ownership of some productive goods, deny that he may own the soil as the primal source of human wealth.

b) The *syndicalist* says these goods shall be owned, managed, and distributed exclusively by syndicals, or labor unions. The goods and tools of a given trade belong to a corporate union and the affairs of the unions shall be governed by subordinate councils democratically selected, over which shall be a general council possessing supreme power. Some syndicalists deny the need of the State and would abolish it by force. These are the *anarcho-syndicalists.* Others claim that the State has supreme jurisdiction over the people as consumers but not as producers. These are the *guild socialists.*

516. For the past hundred years men have lived in an economic system which accurately enough goes by the name of capitalism. Stripped of unessentials, this is a system of private owners operating for personal profit. The present outcry against capitalism arises from the very great evils which have grown up with it; and modern man, because of his accentuated social consciousness and of the amazing multiplication of means of communication has become more and more aware of economic injustices. He wants something done about them.

The evil may be boiled down to this: a vast portion of the wealth of the world has become the property of a few owners and the effective control of it has gotten into still fewer hands. The absorbing business of the actual directors of human affairs is a ceaseless, undercover struggle for such economic control. From time to time the heat of struggle rises beyond the boiling point and armed conflict breaks out among the principal nations, and quickly the whole world is involved.

With the few owning, or at least controlling, so much, the great mass of common men until now have had no effective protection against such undue concentrations of wealth. While the common man in some civilized communities has had a shadowy political freedom — he has been allowed to vote — yet in no community has he economic freedom. He is without security, because he is not the owner of sufficient goods to insure him a steady income. He is dependent on a wage which may cease without warning. From time to time serious dislocations in business and industrial life occur, resulting in complete or partial stoppages in the supply and distribution of exchangeable goods. In these crises the common man is the chief sufferer for his income is the first to be affected. When these crises are prolonged, a vast number who are willing and able to work can find no gainful employment and become dependent for subsistence upon the State.

The evil also shows itself in this way. During the past few generations there has been a multiplication of material comforts unparalleled in the history of mankind but relatively few enjoy them. This new wealth has not been equitably distributed. On the one hand, there are many who fulfill no useful social function and yet have every luxury; on the other hand, there are far too many who are deprived of the necessities for decent living.

Among the proffered solutions to the problem, two stand out notably, communism and socialism. Both hold that the root of the evil is private ownership itself: only when it is sufficiently curbed or totally abolished will men begin to make right use of material goods.

II. THE SOLUTION OF COMMUNISM

A. What Is Communism?

517. Communism is not just a single social or economic tenet proposed as an answer to the problem of property rights. It is a complete philosophy, an entire way of life, purporting to explain the whole of the universe by resurrecting old philosophic doctrines to which it adds the most modern of trimmings.

The ideological founder of modern communism was Karl Marx (1818–1883), whose writings are intimately linked with the materialistic teachings of the nineteenth century. The practical founder of communism was Lenin, whose revolutionary victory in Russia in 1917 made Marxist communism the official philosophy of one hundred and eighty million people occupying one sixth of the land surface of the earth. *What is Marxist communism?*

518. 1. *Dialectic materialism.* As a general philosophy, communism is a species of dynamic materialism. Nothing exists but matter in motion; therefore all reality must be explained in these terms. Matter is eternal, and its perpetual evolution into newer and higher forms gives us the history of reality. This is a species of evolutionary materialism.

The Marxist method of philosophizing is an offshoot from the dialectic of Hegel, who propounded a form of idealistic pantheism according to which the mind makes reality, and all thought is but an emanation from, and a manifestation of, one absolute idea. Hegel's philosophic procedure consists of thesis, antithesis, and synthesis. Thesis is the statement of an idea; antithesis is the denial of that statement; and synthesis, the denial of the antithesis. Hegel's fundamental epistemological contention is that every concept of its very nature contains its contradictory. Consequently, the mere positing of an idea, the thesis, necessarily brings into existence its antithesis; and the affirmation of the antithesis in turn demands its negation, which is the synthesis. This method Hegel called the dialectic. Utterly rejecting the idealistic content of Hegelianism, Marx took over the method of dialectic of Hegel and set it in operation to explain a purely materialistic universe. Hence the name dialectic materialism.

519. 2. *Explanation of nature.* Since nothing exists but matter in motion, the ultimate reason for all things is found in the communist's cosmology. Here the Marxist philosopher discovers an objective dialectic of thesis, antithesis, and synthesis. This he does not invent; he finds it already existing in nature. Hence the material universe — that is, all reality — is summed up in these three laws:

a) The unity of opposites, or thesis. Every particle of matter which is a unified whole has existed from eternity and is an objective unity of opposites, a composite of contradictory, mutually antagonistic elements. This contradiction is productive of motion since each element reacts against its opposite. Thus, matter is essentially autodynamic.

b) The law of negation, or antithesis. Because of this inherent contradiction and because of the motion resultant therefrom, each reality tends to its own negation but in such a way that it necessarily results in the increase of reality. Thus, the grain of wheat is negated, it dies in the soil but by that very negation it tends to reproduce itself a hundredfold. It is this law of negation which accounts for all the *quantitative increase* of reality.

c) The law of transformation, or synthesis. But how explain qualitatively new realities? This is effected by transformation, that leap in nature which Marxism borrowed from contemporary evolution. The process of thesis and antithesis goes on in nature over a long period of time, but all the while the evolutionary forces of nature have been at work, the usual process is suddenly halted, nature makes a leap, and, presto, a new and higher form of reality emerges. Thus is explained the emergence of life from inanimate matter and thought from unconscious life.

520. 3. *Marxism and man.* In the psychology of communism, man is nothing more than matter in a highly complicated state of development. He is the product of nature's leap from the brute level. If one knows enough physics and chemistry, he can reduce man to so many physical and chemical formulae. Man's mind is but matter delicately spun and subtly arranged: it can be totally explained in terms of physiology and neurology. Man's will is an amalgam of animal appetites, and since it is determined by its social environment *it cannot be free.* Denial of freedom of the will is an essential point in communistic philosophy.

When man first emerged from the brute state, he lived a primitive existence with but a crude form of social life. *In this stage there was no private property.* Everything was common to all: there was no question of mine and thine. But, by degrees, the craftier and the stronger began to set aside for their own exclusive use what originally had belonged to all and claimed these things as their private property. This was robbery, and this initial robbery is the cause of all man's present woes. For this beginning of private property set up the first division of men into classes — those who have, the capitalists, and those who have not, the proletariat.

521. 4. *Marxism and the State.* Before the robbery of private property was perpetrated, the State and civil government did not exist. Those who had stolen the common goods of all men sought means to confirm and secure their spoliation so they invented the State with its laws and armed force. The sole purpose of this artificial creation was to maintain the institution of private property and keep the masses in subjection to the masters.

522. 5. *Marxism and religion*. Religion existed before private property and began from primitive man's fear of the elements — thunder, storms, floods, and the like. He personified the forces of nature and by prayer and sacrifice attempted to placate these forces and make them favorable to him. Upon the rise of the property-owning classes, the proprietors saw in religion another means of maintaining their dominance. They became the bulwark of religion and the supporters of the priests, because from now on religion would teach the masses its duties to the classes. The people were to be taught to be patient in suffering and want and above all their attention was to be distracted from the robbery done them in private property by holding before them an illusory hope of a better life beyond the grave. To Marx's axiom, "Religion is the opium of the masses,"[1] Lenin adds, "I hate God as I do my personal enemies." Lenin writes: "In cradling with a hope of celestial recompense him who labors all his life in misery, religion teaches patience and resignation. As for those who live from the labor of others, it teaches them to practice beneficence here, thus offering them an easy justification for their existence as exploiters and selling them cards of participation in celestial felicity at a reduction. . . . Religion is a clumsy sort of spiritual whiskey in which the slaves of capital drown their human being and their revenge for an existence little worthy of man. But the slave who has become aware of his condition and has risen to battle for his emancipation has already come half-way toward being a free man. The awakened worker of today leaves heaven to the priests and bourgeois hypocrites and turns toward the conquest of a better existence here on earth."[2] Again he writes: "The struggle against religion must not be confined to an abstract preaching of ideals. The struggle must be firmly bound to the concrete action of class action, even aiming at the total dis-

1 "Critique of the Hegelian Philosophy of Right," *Selected Essays of Marx*, trans. H. J. Stenning, p. 12. New York, International Publishers, 1926.

2 *New Life*, No. 28, Dec. 16, 1905. Translation also found in V. I. Lenin, *Religion*, pp. 11–12. London, Lawrence, undated.

appearance of the social roots from which religion takes its source."[3]
His summation is: "Atheism is a natural and inseparable part of
Marxism."[4]

523. 6. *Marxism and history*. The history of the world is the story
of the class struggle — the endeavor of the masses to overthrow the
capitalists and the capitalistic effort to keep the masses enslaved. The
ultimate determining factor in every historic event or movement is a
purely economic one. All great changes in history can be reduced
to the human effort for food, living space, and riches. Whether men
realize it or wish it, economic forces over which they have no control
are moving them to a newer and a higher plane of evolution; namely,
communism. The force which rules human progress is economic
determinism.

524. 7. *Marxism and economics*. *Das Kapital,* the Bible of communism, a treatise on economics published by Marx in 1867, undertakes to prove how wealth is accumulating into the hands of a few
capitalists because of capitalism. The poor grow poorer and the rich
richer. The instrument producing this accumulation is what Marx
styled the *surplus-value theory*. Historically this has been a famous
argument to demonstrate the exploitation of the workman at the
hands of his employer. However, since the communistic State now
pays all the wages in Russia, nothing is heard there of surplus value
in official communistic circles.

Marx made an *adequate* distinction between the use value and the
exchange value of material objects. Use value is the suitability of a
thing for serving human needs. This utility derives from the physical
and chemical properties of the object. Exchange value is the aptitude
of a thing for common use, that is, exchange or barter with other
articles of merchandise. Thus, if one razor can be bartered for ten
pounds of soap, their exchange value is the same no matter what their
use value.

An article receives its exchange value solely from the amount of
human labor expended on it.[5] The Marxian reason is this: as exchange
value is suitability for common use, and as the sole element common

---

[3] *The Proletariat,* No. 45, May, 1909. Translation also found in V. I. Lenin, *Religion,*
p. 19.

[4] V. I. Lenin, *Religion,* p. 5.

[5] Karl Marx, *Capital,* Modern Library Edition, p. 46. New York, Cerf and Klopfer,
1936.

to all merchandise is the amount of labor expended on it, the commutative value of a thing must be measured by the human labor which went to make it. Hence two kinds of merchandise embodying the same amount of labor should have the same market value. But since all workmen are not equally industrious or skillful, how can one determine and measure this labor content? Marx set as the standard that amount of time which the ordinarily diligent and skillful workman working under ordinary conditions requires to produce any given article useful to society.[6]

From these excogitations Marx proceeds to show how the workman is defrauded by his employer. When the worker hires himself to a capitalist, he turns over to him his *labor capacity*. This as an object of contract has two values utterly distinct. There is the *use value of labor,* its power to produce further wealth, and the *exchange value of labor,* that is, the price of the necessities of life ordinarily required to sustain the laborer, or the production cost of his energies.[7]

According to the surplus-value theory, the capitalist gives the worker the exchange value of his labor when he gives the worker only what he can live on. But for the use value of his labor, the further values which the laborer's toil creates for him, he gives nothing at all. This is surplus value which the employer keeps for himself. Thus, in three days the laborer may produce goods equivalent to the value of what is needed to sustain him. For this work alone he is paid. For the value produced in the other three days no remuneration is made him. This is the fundamental injustice whereby the poor get poorer and the rich get richer.[8]

525. 8. *Revolution.* To remedy these and other injustices inherent in the capitalistic system it is idle to appeal to law or the capitalists' sense of justice. There will be no justice until the whole basis of society is rearranged, root and branch. The essential evil is private property and its twin defenses, the State and religion. But these can be swept away only by violence and world-wide revolution. The one communistic commonwealth now existing is always in peril until the whole world joins the revolution. Class warfare, therefore, must be intensified to such a pitch that everywhere there will be a rising of the masses who will take over all private holdings, destroy all bourgeois forms of government, and root out all religions. In

---

[6] *Ibid.*   [7] *Ibid.,* pp. 189–190.   [8] *Ibid.,* pp. 197–254.

their stead is to be substituted the *dictatorship of the proletariat*. How is this to be done?

526. 9. *Communistic morality*. The methods employed by Marxism to establish the dictatorship of the proletariat involves a discussion of communistic principles of morality. In an address given at the Third All-Russian Congress of Communistic Youth in 1920, Lenin gave the chief tenet of Marxist ethics: "Is there a communist morality? The bourgeoisie frequently reproach us communists with having no code of ethics. It is only a maneuver to throw dust in the eyes of the people. In what sense do we deny ethics? We deny them in the bourgeois sense, according to which morality flows from the statutes of divinity. We say with assurance that we do not believe in God and we know full well that under the name of God it is in reality the clergy, proprietors and bourgeoisie who speak in order to defend their interests as exploiters. . . . We deny all morality borrowed from concepts exterior to class or even to humanity. *Our morality is entirely subordinated to the interests of the proletariat and the needs of the class struggle.*"[9]

Clearly, then, all means are allowable which further the class struggle. Hence the Marxist norm of morality may thus be stated: any act is good which furthers the revolution; any act is bad which hinders it. Any stick will serve to beat the capitalistic dog. What means are practicable for the forwarding of the revolution, which the communist must call good?

a) Liquidate the enemies of the revolution. It is not wrong to kill counterrevolutionaries. Because the kulaks of the Ukraine resisted the collectivization of their farms, five million people died in 1932 of a man-made famine.

b) Lying and deception are valid means of promoting the cause. Tell the world there is a terrestrial paradise under communism. Since democracy holds such a spell over men's minds, parade the Russian State as thoroughly democratic: point to its constitution and elections as evidence of democracy.

c) Organize the world for revolution. Let each country be partitioned into divisions and sections over each of which will be an agent responsible for the growth of communistic doctrine and practice. The initial step is to organize communistic cells in factories, work-

---

[9] For another translation of the same speech, see *Religion* by V. I. Lenin, London, Lawrence, pp. 55–56.

shops, labor unions, youth movements, national organizations of influence. This must be done unobtrusively by setting up innocent stooges under cover of whom communistic influence can more safely operate. Smear the national army and navy and all manifestations of local patriotism. Teach class hatred. Where people are not conscious of it, make them aware of it. Organize strikes, turn strikes into riots, riots into civil war. Spread and organize atheism. Endeavor to suppress all religions, but so as to maintain an appearance of fairness do not close all the churches. However, the spread of atheism must be subordinated to the class struggle.

d) The practical test of morality for a good communist is blind adherence to the party line even if this line changes overnight and involves any sort of contradiction. The expediency of the moment and the sacredness of the cause may dictate the immediate abandonment of one policy and one set of friends for the acceptance of an opposite policy and the throwing overboard of principles hitherto deemed essential.

e) The ideal communistic man is a thoroughgoing atheist, fanatically devoted to the cause, and therefore hard working and industrious. He is blindly obedient to direction, willing to say or do anything which will advance the cause. He is lustful — for man is only organized matter — and gregarious — for men and women are equal.

f) The pattern of the ideal communistic woman follows the same lines. She is the equal of man in every respect. Whatever job he can hold she too may strive for. She will not be bound down by demands of home, husband, and children. The care and education of children will be a public charge: the individual family will cease to be the economic unit of society. Since she will have utter sexual freedom, both prostitution and monogamy — which is but legalized prostitution — will both disappear. Marriage will never be a yoke about her neck, for divorce can be had for the mere asking.[10]

527. 10. *The dictatorship of the proletariat.* Just as the Russian masses in 1917 were induced by Lenin with his cry of Peace, Bread, and Land to overthrow their masters and establish the Soviet Union, so the proletariat the world over by the skillful conduct of the class

---

[10] In 1944, the Russian State made divorce almost impossible for the common people. That this was prompted by reverence for the Natural Law is more than doubtful. It was chosen as the practicable means to insure a sufficiency of young for the armies of tomorrow.

war are to rise and seize the property and power of the ruling classes. For a time after this universal revolution, the dictatorship of the proletariat will assume the function of the State — not a national but an international State. The sole purpose of this dictatorship will be the leveling and destruction of all class distinction. This is effected by wiping out all private property. Once religion, property, and class distinction have been eradicated, men will become so psychologically renewed, uplifted, and purified by the dictatorship that eventually the dictatorship will cease to be needed. For the dictatorship is only an intermediary stage, to be achieved perhaps at the cost of much suffering and hardship. It is a necessary path leading to the next great level of mankind's evolution which will be pure communism.

528. 11. *Pure communism* is conceived as the earthly millennium — the material paradise. It will be distinguished by the following:

a) *Absence of an organized institution of government.* Under the dictatorship, men will have been purged of all selfish notions of profit and money. They will be so accustomed to give first consideration to the common good and so socially adept that they will be able to live without the aid of government.

b) *Complete absence of all classes.* With private property abolished, there will be no more haves and have-nots, no more employer and employed. True equality and fraternity will flourish in all things. No one will even be inclined to exploit another. In such universal love and brotherhood, the lamb will truly lie down with the lion. Nor will there even be any distinction between mental and physical labor, which was so distasteful in the old bourgeois world. The absolute equality of all is at length achieved.

c) *Great abundance of material wealth and comfort.* After the Armageddon of the revolution and the strain and hardship of the dictatorship, the horn of plenty of pure communism will come. The face of the earth will have been renewed by a material Pentecost. The exploitation of the many for the sake of the favored few will all be over — no more anarchy of production; no strikes, lockouts, depressions, crises, or war. Society will be so organized that all waste will be eliminated. An efficiency never before attained by man will minister to the wants of all. Since poverty will have disappeared, so too will crime. The great law will be: from all according to his ability, to each according to his needs. Every avenue to education and culture will be accessible to each. Everybody will be an officer.

B. Refutation of Communism

1. Summary Refutation

529. As a complete philosophy of life, Marxism clashes with scholastic philosophy on very many issues. Since we may legitimately suppose that the scholastics have demonstrated their conclusions satisfactorily, let it suffice as a general criticism to indicate the points of difference.

a) The fundamental tenet of materialism — all things are matter — is refuted by the proofs for the existence of spiritual substances. Theodicy demonstrates the existence of an eternal, necessary Being who is an infinitely perfect spirit. In cosmology the impossibility of matter existing from eternity is shown. Furthermore, matter in motion is impossible without a Prime Mover who is Himself unmoved. The Marxian law of opposites violates the principle of identity and the principle of contradiction. Its law of transformation violates the principle of causality, according to which no effect is greater than its cause.

b) Rational psychology disproves the Marxian view of man, for man has an immaterial, spiritual soul which is immortal, and he has a free will.

c) In social ethics the Marxian view of the State is proved false on the grounds that the State is a natural institution demanded by the Natural Law for the well-being of man (cf. § 817).

d) Theodicy and the treatise of ethics on religion refute the atheism of communism.

e) Universal economic determinism is a gratuitous assumption and false history. The economic has not been the ultimate factor in historic changes: it explains much but not all. This point lies beyond the field of ethics, but it is pertinent to note that the religious wars and the rise and spread of Christianity and Mohammedanism cannot be accounted for on purely economic grounds.

530. *f*) The surplus-value theory of Marx contains these fallacies:

(1) There is no adequate distinction between use value and exchange value. Use value is the good that the thing is to the one who has it; exchange value is the good that it would be to another. Another person will want it precisely because of its suitability to his needs. The greater the utility of a thing and the scarcer it is, and hence the more urgent the want it satisfies, the greater will be its exchange value. But utility comes from the physical and chemical properties of a thing — its use value. Hence the law of exchange value is still the

ratio of supply (utility and quantity) to demand — the social estimate of the equation, D/S.

(2) Therefore it is false to say that exchange value derives from *labor alone*. A thing has commutative value only when it is *useful* to someone who *wants* it, and the latter wants it not because of the labor expended on it but because of its suitability to his needs. Are fifty bushels of potatoes, grown in a stony field which a farmer spent countless hours tilling, of greater value than one hundred bushels which a more fortunate neighbor produced from a more fertile field with considerably less toil? It may be that the same number of hours were spent in making a Stradavarius violin as that of a crossroads' fiddler — but who would bother to inquire?

When Marx applies his theory of value to labor capacity, *his* distinction between use and exchange value breaks down. Employers hire or do not hire workmen on the basis of their usefulness and normally pay them accordingly. To say that the exchange value of labor capacity is measured by the cost of the necessities of life to sustain the worker, borders on the absurd when applied to skilled labor or great talent. Who would rate the market value of Caruso's voice on the basis of the food he ate?

The finished, marketable article receives its utility and hence its exchange value from these sources: (1) the raw materials; (2) the inventor who devised it; (3) the workmen who made it; (4) the men who risked their money to commercialize the product; (5) the management that oversees its production and distribution. Since each contributes a share, each should receive a just and proportionate return. While Marx was wrong in saying that the workman's labor created the entire commercial value of a product, he was right when he said the workman was unjustly paid. The workman of his day did not receive his due. The reason was not private property but the failure of owners of private property to fulfill the obligations entailed in the owning of property. Dominated by that tenet of liberalism which held that a man can do as he pleases with his property, society made no attempt to interfere with the injustice done to the workman. The rise of labor unions in great measure has corrected this inequity; and an increasing social consciousness, as evidenced by recent legislation, is rapidly defining the nature and extent of the social obligations that go with the ownership of property and effecting a consequent fairer distribution of the burdens and rewards of co-operative activity.

g) Violent revolution and the hatred of class for class militate against love of neighbor.

h) The norm of morality is not utility to serve the revolution. On many points the stark, objective exposition of communistic doctrine is its effective refutation.

2. *Specific Refutation*

THESIS XXXVIII. Communism is forbidden by the Natural Law.

531. By communism in the proposition we understand that politico-economic system founded upon evolutionary materialism which denies all rights to private property.

PROOF

The Natural Law forbids a politico-economic system which (1) denies man a natural right, (2) is based upon a false concept of human nature and human equality; is opposed to (3) true human liberty, (4) the peace and good order of society, (5) the well-being of the family, (6) man's possession of a legitimate abundance of material goods. But communism is such a system. Therefore it is forbidden by the Natural Law.

1. Man's right to private property is proved in Thesis XLI.

2. Man has a spiritual, immortal soul whose ultimate perfection is had not in a material millennium but in perfect happiness in another life. Men are equal only in the possession of a common nature and destiny. Actually, men do not have equal abilities, potencies, rights, and duties. Nature has made women quite different from men. To disregard these natural differences is provocative of enormous social disorder.

3. We shall prove that to deprive man of the right to own productive goods is restriction of his liberty (§ 535). *A fortiori* in the system which does not permit ownership even of consumable goods, there is no hope of his resisting tyranny. When all the sources of production are in the hands of the dictatorship of the proletariat which also owns and distributes all consumable goods, the controllers of that dictatorship could never be removed from power. The individual is then completely at the beck and mercy of his governors.

4. Since natural competition for place and position will be gone,

there will be bitter strife for the better positions. This will give rise to quarrels, factions, fraud, corruption, confusion, and the liquidation of rivals. Distribution of goods according to needs alone would inevitably result in jealousy and contention and would establish that inequality which the system seeks to remove. These inequalities of place and of goods received will rightly be ascribed to the system. Complaints, disturbances, and despotic repression will follow.

5. We shall establish in social ethics that nature prescribes that the family and its members be immediately subject to the care and providence of its natural head, the father. The care of the aged and the sick and the rearing of the young are primarily family concerns, but in this system these functions will belong immediately to the State.

6. That communism is not productive of a legitimate abundance of material goods is proved in §§ 536–537. Suffice it here to quote a firsthand witness, Barmine, a former high Soviet official: "Lenin's idea of socialism rested on two major assumptions: that under a collectized economy production would rise very much higher than it can under capitalism; and that the exploited wage workers would get the main benefit of this increased production, exploitation having ceased. The Soviet economic system, together with Stalin's totalitarian political regime, have refuted both these assumptions."[11]

III. THE SOLUTION OF SOCIALISM

532. The experiment of communism has been made. Its unadulterated doctrine has been adopted as the official program of Russia, and gigantic efforts have been made to put it in practice *in toto*. Communism has failed to this extent: while productive wealth is in the hands of the Soviet government, private property still exists; the workman is paid wages, based not upon personal or familial needs but on his skill, industry, and usefulness to the employing State. Despite the ease of divorce and the temporary character attributed to the marriage tie, the family persists. Belief in God and a need for religion has not been wrested from the people. The equality of all citizens, dreamed of by the original Bolsheviks, has never materialized. The Russian people have exchanged one set of masters for another. The place of the old aristocracy has been taken by the communistic party, which in 1944 numbered no more than four million members. This cleavage of ruler

---

[11] Alexander Barmine, *One Who Survived*, p. 313. New York, Putnam, 1945.

and ruled will continue, for Russia's present rulers are making their places of privilege safe for their children after them. The original communistic program runs counter to the plain dictates of the Natural Law in too many instances ever to succeed as such. The revolutionary, come to power, has to turn reactionary himself to the extent that he must invoke the observance of the Natural Law to secure the peace and stability of his regime. The success achieved in erecting a monolithic State has been done at the grim sacrifice of human liberty. In concentration camps there are ten million dissidents. No one is free to leave Russia: only a select few who leave behind a family as hostages insuring their return ever cross the border. Russia is a vast regimented camp obeying absolutely the nod of one, all-powerful warden. No evidence of a superior economy or a prosperity over-shadowing that of capitalistic countries is in evidence; all prewar indications were to the contrary. The Russian soldiers who invaded their western neighbors in 1945 were amazed at the superior standards of living they found there. Enough time, however, has not elapsed to prove experimentally that this economy cannot produce its vaunted abundance.

533. The existence and the recent military success of the com-munistic State has given great impetus to the spread of the *socialistic* idea. Allowing the individual to own a home, chattels, and consumable goods, socialism avoids the grim extremes of communism. It demands that all productive wealth be the sole property of the whole nation and be managed for the good of all. It has been repeated to people so often that they accept as demonstrated the charge that private owner-ship of the sources of wealth is the cause of their economic troubles. Let the State then take over all land, mines, factories, machinery, raw materials, transportation, utilities, communications, banking facilities — whatever is capable of producing revenue. The State will then regulate production and distribution to the rational needs of the people and manage business and industry for the betterment of all its citizens. The lure of a State-planned and State-owned economy is most potent today. The little man is desperate for some change that will better his lot, and he has a childlike confidence in the power of government to heal every human ill. No government is adverse to an increase of power: Caesarism is latent in every governing body. The prospect of such control over all business is a heady stimulant to all who hope for

an active part in that control. The world is watching the socialistic experiments of many western nations.

THESIS XXXIX. Socialism or State ownership of all productive wealth is impracticable on a large scale.

534. We shall later prove that the individual has a right to own productive goods. This nature allows. However, we are not now decrying socialism as the violation of a natural right. For it is conceivable that men could forego the exercise of this right if all men were reasonable, if all men would control their greed, if each would contribute his due share to the common good. This would have been the normal thing if man had not committed original sin. In a state of original justice, men could have entrusted to the community the exercise of their right to own property. Even today we do find instances of the surrender of this right as in religious communities and in selected groups of families the members of which are willing to have common possessions. There are sufficient safeguards to the individual to allow this practice. But when we pass from a closed, carefully controlled circle to one of national scale where men are not habitually reasonable, where they are inclined to feed their greed, and to shirk common responsibility, we must be realistic and bear in mind the shortcomings of a fallen race. To ask or compel all men to surrender the exercise of the right of owning productive wealth is to invite worse evils of tyranny and social unrest than the injustices which socialism seeks to remedy.

PROOF

Whether the socialistic State be organized democratically or on a totalitarian basis it would be unworkable, because (1) it attacks liberty and (2) diminishes production.

1. *Socialism Attacks Liberty*

535. Since *everyone would be an employee of the State,* the following consequences are inevitable.

a) No one may engage in business for himself.

b) Workmen may not strike against government.

c) Freedom to choose an occupation would be diminished. Since the State alone would stabilize production, it would determine the number of employees in a given industry. Once men were allocated to an industry, they would not be free to change; otherwise production would be dislocated.

d) Forced labor would be inevitable. Although some positions would be apportioned on a basis of competition, a large number of mean and disagreeable jobs would remain which no one would want. Either many of these would go unfilled and production would suffer, or they would have to be filled by forced labor. Plato moots the same problem in his *Republic*. To the necessary question, Who will do the rough work and clean up the slops? he calmly answers, "The slaves."[12]

e) A man's place of residence is fixed by his job.

f) Where the State alone owns all capital, it alone prints the newspapers and conducts the schools. Where no private capital exists, none of these things can be in private hands. Therefore freedom of press and education must vanish. If the State owns all sources of income, totalitarianism is inevitable.

g) If each man depends upon the State for his salary, the government can work its will with him by the simple threat of cutting off that salary. In practice what secures a man in his rights is productive wealth. A man's freedom of action is in direct proportion to his economic independence. The employee of an all-powerful State has only that economic freedom which the State sees fit to grant him. His economic advance would depend not so much upon individual talent and industry as upon a *fallible and quite possibly corrupt bureaucracy*.

2. Socialism Diminishes Production

536. *a*) *It destroys man's natural incentive to labor*. The fundamental motivation for strenuous labor and productive effort is personal gain. It is idle to inveigh against the profit motive: it cannot be stamped out of mankind. A man will work without sparing himself if he knows that he will get something out of his labor for himself, whether it be affluence, dignified leisure, power and influence, or a comfortable old age. He desires these rewards even more so for his family.

Strenuous labor will fall off if it is not motivated by adequate rewards. In the socialistic system one of the most deeply rooted of natural incentives is taken away. Socialism forbids all laws of inheritance. Socialists say that men should and, if they are properly

---

[12] *Republic*, II, 371, D.

educated to it, will work for nobler motives than self and family —
for the pleasure of virtue, the honor of a job well done, the satisfaction
of having served the community. Some men will work for these
motives but the ordinary man, outside of a special crisis, will do so
only when his personal interests have been secured. The naïve hope
that all men will constantly act out of these motives betrays a woeful
ignorance of man as he actually is.

537. *b*) *It discourages the spirit of commendable thrift.* When
capital is entirely in public hands it will not be conserved and fostered
as when in private hands. Nothing is so neglected as common property.
What belongs to everybody is treated as if it belonged to nobody. Men
are not and never will be so altruistic, so alert to the common good,
as to protect and increase the goods of the State with the same zeal
and interest as they look out for their own things. It is personal interest
— the hope of direct or at least ultimate gain to oneself — which
explains the increase of productive goods. If all productive goods would
be the common property of one hundred and thirty million people,
it would be little short of madness to expect all or even the majority
to take a personal interest in common property.

538. *c*) *It requires a degree of administrative ability and integrity
on the part of the State officials which is morally impossible to realize.*
The assumption of such new responsibilities would increase the difficulty of efficient government a thousandfold. The machinery of government would eventually break down from such an enormous and
complicated responsibility. If the government were to own all productive wealth, public officials would be running all farms, the manu-
facturing industry, the trades, the transportation and communication
systems. Socialism cannot guarantee public officials of such angelic
minds as would be required to administer these industries efficiently
on such a vast scale. Nor can it promise public officials of saintly
probity in sufficient quantity for such a task; it would merely multiply
the opportunity of plunder a thousandfold. Waste and inefficiency
would be canonized, for it would be protected by a government which
has no competitor.[13]

---

[13] Explaining the frequent breakdowns in Soviet industry, on page 211 of the work
cited above, Barmine writes: ". . . machinery, instead of being repaired, is used until it
is ruined, and then replaced. Thus the real cost of production of Soviet goods is higher
than in any capitalistic country, despite the fact that the workers are paid extremely low
wages. This super-exploitation should make it possible to cover most of the losses and
produce cheaply, but the incompetent bureaucratic system, wasting labor and materials,

No government should pretend to procure both the public good and the private good. We do not need an experiment to know that such an effort will fail.

539. The argument may thus be summarized: If all business is placed in the hands of government, government is either efficient or it is inefficient. Efficiency here is the cure of our economic ills with a reasonably abundant production and a smoothly flowing distribution of goods. If government is not efficient, the purpose of putting government into business is defeated. If it is efficient — and much of our argument proves that it cannot be — it could be so only at a price of inhuman tyranny — universal regimentation, espionage, forced labor, and the denial of natural rights. "Under socialism," Lenin grimly says, "all democracy withers away."[14]

IV. THE SOLUTION OF REASON

A. An Historical Conspectus

540. Neither communism nor socialism offers an acceptable answer to the great difficulty of our times which we have been discussing. However, before proceeding to give a positive answer, it may be well for us to show that historically the difficulty is not so much economic as moral. Its root is greed. Society has failed to shackle individual greed, or rather has unwisely removed the bands by which an older society once contained it.

Medieval society, as effectively as human weakness can, kept men's

---

destroys this possibility. I personally observed the same thing in several other branches of industry.

"The chief trouble seemed to be that, without competition and without free trade unions, there is no stimulus to the management to use their brains. They can afford to be wasteful and incompetent because they are not under pressure from competitors to produce better and cheaper goods, and not under pressure from workers to pay higher wages. Their problem is much simpler. When the abolished capitalistic profit is not enough to compensate for their wasteful inefficiency, they cover it by cutting down on their workers' wages. That is why, in spite of the fact that workers work as hard and harder than in capitalistic countries, the Soviet industries are unable to give them the same decent standard of living. It was a basic principle with Lenin that the socialist economy would justify its existence only if it produced more and better goods than capitalism, and thus guaranteed the workers better conditions of life. This principle of Lenin's was constantly in my mind during the following years, and out of it grew irrepressible doubts as to whether we were on the right road."

[14] V. I. Lenin, *The State and Revolution,* p. 65. New York, The International Publishers, 1932.

acquisitive instincts from running wild. Western Christendom was a completely articulated, integrated society, teleologically organized upon the basis that all human action, social and individual, was to be directed unto an otherworld aim, namely, the individual's attainment of eternal felicity. Hence, to one supreme moral code all was subject — war, business, agriculture, government. Neither statecraft, diplomacy, nor money-making were so sacrosanct as to be laws unto themselves and immune from moral governance.

541. Making due allowances for the relative scarcity of wealth and opportunities of growing rich, the comparatively undeveloped state of commerce, and the agricultural economy which prevailed, there was an active moral force in that society which kept men's avarice within the bounds of reason. Thus, trading bore a certain stigma — not because society was governed by landowners — but for the reason stated by St. Thomas: "The trader is one whose business consists in the exchange of things. The exchange of things is twofold: one natural, as it were, and necessary, whereby the commodity is exchanged for another or money is taken in exchange for a commodity in order to satisfy the needs of life. Such trading, properly so called, does not belong to the trader but to housekeepers and civil servants who have to provide the household or the State with the necessaries of life. The other kind of exchange is either that of money for money or of any commodity for money, not on account of the necessities of life but for profit; and this kind of exchange is the business of the trader. The first kind of exchange is commendable because it supplies a natural need. The second is justly deserving of blame because considered in itself *it satisfies the greed of gain which knows no limit and tends to infinity*. Hence trading, considered in itself, has a certain debasement attaching thereto, in so far as by its nature it does not imply a virtuous or necessary end. Nevertheless, gain, which is the end of trading, though not implying by its nature anything virtuous or necessary, does not in itself connote anything sinful or contrary to virtue, wherefore nothing prevents gain from being directed to some necessary or even virtuous end, and thus trade becomes lawful."[15]

542. In their quest for a just price, the guilds did much to check unlimited gain. They considered a fair price to be that which sufficed to sustain the merchant in his station in life. What went beyond was

---

[15] *Sum. Theol.*, II–II, 77, 4.

unfair. Every State had severe laws forbidding usury. All men held it a detestable thing to deprive his neighbor of the means of his livelihood. All holding of land — from king to husbandman — carried definitely defined social obligations. The theory was that the king was not the absolute owner of the nation's land but its trustee. He held it in virtue of a contract between himself and his people. He was his people's steward and could be discharged from his office for serious violation of his coronation oath. So through the entire structure of feudalism, each held land on the condition of fulfilling certain obligations — suit and service, that is, definite social, political, and military duties. No man of substance was ever allowed to forget that he had an obligation in conscience to give of his superfluous goods to the needy. The chiefest barrier to greed was the universal conviction that the absorbing business of life was not the accumulation of money but the salvation of one's soul by the observance of the moral law and that the unjust possession or the wrongful use of riches was an unsurmountable obstacle to that end.

543. This view of life and the organization of society upon this basis suffered a violent upheaval in the religious revolt of the sixteenth century. The unity of Christian life, manifested and made secure by the acceptance of one moral code interpreted by a supreme papacy, was rent by the rejection of papal authority. With the refusal on the part of many to accept this moral leadership, the once universally accepted code grew into disrepute, gradually but with ever-increasing speed.

The first cleavage came as the logical result of Calvinism. According to Calvin, one was either predestined by God to salvation from all eternity or one was marked for damnation. Nothing a man might do could alter this immutable decree. But how could one tell if he were among the saved? The Calvinist sternly and uncompromisingly answered: only by membership in the Calvinistic Church. Since, then, the Calvinist was predestined and the prime business of life secure for him, he need not worry about salvation but could turn all his energy to something else. That something else happened to be the making of money. Thus, by the end of the nineteenth century the idea that the possession of money is the criterion of a successful life had supplanted for too many individuals the older view that until one's last breath one must work out his salvation in fear and trembling.

The factor which completed the break from the traditional, otherworld view of life and has completely reoriented modern social life was the spread of the *liberal idea* to every sphere of life. It spelled the secularization of modern life. Liberalism, like every damaging error, begins with a patent, appealing truth — the freedom, dignity, and value of the individual. It forgets, however, that this freedom to be genuine must be restricted by the equally real claims of divine and social obligations. Luther sowed the seeds of liberalism by proclaiming the omnipotence of private judgment. The Scriptures do not mean what a divinely organized Church says their objective meaning is but what each individual finds them to mean for himself. With every man his own pope, the sixteenth century had what it fancied to be religious freedom. In the eighteenth century Rousseau enlarged upon the idea of individual freedom; it was introduced into the realm of politics, and the armies of the French Revolution carried the Rights of Man and their exaggerations into every country of Europe to the detriment of society. No sooner were the Napoleonic wars ended than the cry for economic freedom was heard. Feudalism was dead and buried. The old idea that land was held upon the condition of rendering public service had disappeared. The landed proprietor was not only the absolute owner of what his ancestors had held conditionally, but in the course of several centuries he had managed to obtain exclusive ownership of what had been the common lands of the village. Economic liberalism denuded property of any social tie. Its political slogan was free trade; and its cardinal principle was that property belongs absolutely and exclusively to its owner, that the owner is free to do with his property as he pleases provided only that he keep his contract. Society may in no way restrict one's use of his property nor demand that it serve a social purpose. The sole function of the State is to insure peace and enforce contracts by its police power.

544. Economic liberalism said that an employer was free to pay what he chose; exact whatever hours of labor he could get; demand as a price whatever the traffic would bear. Since the life of trade was competition, let competition be completely unshackled with no holds barred. While Darwin was saying that life is a jungle struggle wherein only the fittest survived, the mill owners of England and New England were making huge fortunes from the sweat of employees working twelve and fourteen hours a day for the barest pittance. The result of such ideas and practices was the industrial slavery of the nineteenth century; the public-be-damned spirit of the barons of industry; the adoration of property rights above mere human rights to a decent existence. Business is business and morality does not enter into it. Unbridled competition is a form of war, and since all is fair in love and war, you can use any means within the civil law to put your competitor out of business, to rig the law for your own benefit.

545. Since the solution does not lie in communism or socialism, it must be found in the equitable application of the Natural Law concerning man's ownership and disposal of material goods. What most fundamental principle underlies man's relations to these things? Upon the correct answer to this question must be based anything that is said about the use, possession, or division of material things.

In cosmology it has been irrefutably established that the relatively ultimate end of the material universe is the good of man. Nature intends that all things less than man should serve as means to his final end. The truth of this statement is evident from observation of these things and of man's needs. Hence we arrive at this primary principle: *Material goods are ordained to serve man's needs.* We shall now proceed to consider the ethical principles which derive from this cosmological truth.

B. *The Use of Material Goods*

546. The material universe is subordinate first by way of man's *use* of it. Because man *must,* he *may* use material goods. This right extends not only to the race but also to each individual. Its basis is an all-compelling need, namely, human welfare. A man cannot go on living or even continue to live in a human way without using certain material things. Since nature intends that each should live and live as a human being, she gives each the right to supply his needs by using these things and to use them undisturbed by others. This right of use and immunity in use flows from the mere fact of existence. Any further disposition, division, or possession of goods must promote this essential purpose: any arrangement that would hinder it or make its realization unreasonably difficult is forbidden by nature.

Does this mean that the individual may use anything whenever he has a mind to? Obviously not, for then there could be no order or peace among men. We must eventually establish the conditions which constitute an orderly, efficient, and peaceable realization of nature's purpose. But first let us establish nature's purpose.

THESIS XL. The Natural Law grants every man the right to use material goods in order to conserve life and secure the essentials of human living. In cases of extreme need, this right as connatural prevails over any acquired rights of ownership.

547. Goods may be classified according to a man's need of them as (*a*) *absolutely necessary goods* — those without which here and now he would die; (*b*) *gravely necessary goods* — those without which his mode of living would sink notably below the normal human level; (*c*) *simply necessary goods* — those which are useful for advancement. A person who lacks an absolutely necessary good is in *extreme need;* a gravely necessary good, in *grave need;* a number of simply necessary goods, in *common need.*

Man's right of use means (*a*) that in any sort of need he may use anything upon which no other has a claim; (*b*) in extreme need he may use any good available to stave off danger of death provided this thing is not equally needful to another in like danger who has pre-empted it. This right is so essential that any other conflicting property claim must yield to it. Therefore, to avoid imminent danger of death, one may take and use anything necessary to prolong his life and such action will not be theft. Anyone with acquired rights of ownership to such goods must cede his rights so long as the danger lasts.

May a person in grave need appropriate the property of another? He may in the following circumstances. The grave need must verge on the extreme, that is, one must be in danger of incurring grave and permanent harm such as captivity, mutilation, prolonged or incurable sickness; and the particular goods, necessary to escape this danger, are not equally needful to their owner. If, however, one's need verges on the common, one may not, because use in these circumstances would be destructive of public peace.

PROOF OF PART I

548. *The Natural Law gives each one the right to use material goods so as to secure life and the essentials of human living,* because, since nature gives the right to life and a human living, she cannot withhold the absolutely necessary means thereunto. Without the use of material goods, men cannot live as men.

PROOF OF PART II

549. *This right of use is connatural* because its title is the very fact of existence. At the moment a person begins to exist, the need and obligation of prolonging and fostering one's life commences. Hence also arises the right to anything absolutely necessary to satisfy this need and fulfill this obligation.

PROOF OF PART III

550. *The right of use conflicting in cases of extreme need with any acquired rights of ownership always prevails.* In this conflict of rights, the actually existing right will be the claim to *the more necessary good* (cf. § 480). Life is a more necessary good than property, a mere adjunct of life. Therefore the right of a man in extreme need to use property to preserve his life, destroys, for the duration of that need, any owner's acquired rights to that property.

551. Corollary I. Any particular system set up by men for the further allocation, division, and distribution of material goods must safeguard the prime intent of nature regarding them, namely, that these goods are to satisfy human needs. The purpose of such a system must be the effective, peaceable, and equable realization of this natural end.

Corollary II. Any system which would defeat or render tremendously difficult the attainment of this natural purpose or which would thwart the individual's connatural right of use is forbidden by the Natural Law. Hence we condemn:

1. Socialism and communism, because of themselves they tend to create a dearth of usable goods.

2. Overrugged individualism expressed in the Liberal creed, which holds that a man may do absolutely as he pleases with his property. In using his goods a man may not disregard every consideration other than his own needs and whims. No one may abuse or destroy these things without thought of the needs of others. No one may possess goods without accepting the social responsibility of giving of his superfluous wealth to the needy.

3. Any system which results in the concentration of wealth in the hands of the few while the great majority lack the decent comforts of human living.

C. Private Ownership of Material Goods

552. Nature commands *orderly* use of material goods, for such use alone will secure the end for which they were made. Since the number and needs of men vary from place to place, and since goods may be abundant in some places and scarce in others, it can be seen that disorder will result unless men accept and adhere to some principle which will insure orderly use.

What is this principle? Clearly the mere right to use will not suffice. Everybody cannot use everything at will. Unless certain things are set aside for the permanent and exclusive control either of individuals or of communities, incessant war or chaos will result. Ownership in some form, then, is demanded: without it orderly use is inconceivable.

553. What does nature provide regarding ownership? It is approved as necessary to rational living. What kind of ownership does she command or at least approve? Does everything belong to all men collectively and must it so remain so that no one may own anything exclusively for himself? Such an arrangement would be tantamount to the denial of ownership, for if everyone even collectively owned everything, then as owners everyone could use everything, and we are back to chaos again. But if, to avoid this difficulty, it is suggested that civil authority distribute from the common bounty what each is to have for his exclusive use, one civil government would be required for all men, which is absolutely unrealizable.

But perhaps nature assigns certain goods as the exclusive property of individuals or communities? Evidently not, because if such a division had been made, there would be evident natural signs of it but there are none.

554. But if nature directly gives nothing to any individual or community as an exclusive possession, she cannot forbid that, from her storehouse of goods, communities at least take certain things as their own. Otherwise there would be no practicable sort of ownership. The great point at issue is — does nature forbid individuals to do this? From our proofs against communism and socialism, it is clear that she does not. However, we wish to establish this position in the most positive way by showing that far from prohibiting it, nature both allows and commands it. First, then, we shall prove that the Natural Law grants the individual an indeterminate right to own — indeterminate in the sense that nature does not make him the owner of any particular things but allows him to take from the bounty she offers to all, those things of which he now becomes the owner. When, therefore, men exercise this right in order to assure orderly use of goods in the service of mankind, the Natural Law approves private ownership. For the act conforms to human nature. Second, if it is clear that the exigencies of rational living demand the exercise of this right as the only way to secure nature's purpose in an orderly and peaceful manner, private ownership is obligatory and cannot be done away with.

THESIS XLI. Not only has each man an indeterminate right from the Natural Law to acquire ownership of productive goods, but some general system of private ownership is necessary.

555. In the proof of the first part we shall show that man has a right *to acquire* the ownership of sources of material goods without specifying what in the concrete these may be. That man has the physical power to be an owner needs no proof. It is a well-established principle flowing from the free nature of man that he has a right, the moral capacity, to do anything that lies in his physical power provided it is not forbidden by natural or positive law. In the proof of the first part we will show that there can be no natural prohibition against private owning. In the second part we will show that any positive law purporting to deny him ownership cannot be a true law since it would defeat nature's purpose in providing material goods for mankind.

PROOF OF PART I

556. *Each man has from the Natural Law the right to acquire the ownership of productive goods.* Permanent and exclusive control of the source of a steady supply of material goods is an act which conforms to all the essential relationships of human nature.

1. *To human nature considered in itself.* Man has constant and recurring needs which must be satisfied by material goods and in a reasonably human way. Since he is not a wild animal, he is not to contend with his fellow man for the fulfillment of every need. Since he is not a domestic animal, his wants are to be provided for by himself. From a consideration of his free nature it follows that man is a self-provider; he himself is to procure the things he needs. But without ownership he is subject to the will, caprice, and power of others in a way that degrades the dignity and independence of his nature. Therefore, the human way for the individual to provide for his needs is by ownership of a sufficiency of productive goods.

2. *To man's relations to God.* Ownership in no way disturbs man's essential and total dependence on God.

3. *To man's relations to his fellow man.*

a) Of individual to individual. The control of goods for a man's own benefit without injury to his fellow man conforms to the due relation of one man to another. If the right of all men to use material goods in necessity is kept intact, no man injures another by taking to himself what antecedently had belonged to no one. Furthermore each is more content and peaceful, relations of one to another are better fostered when each has for himself his own stock of goods.

b) Of individual to family. Parents have the inescapable duty of supporting, educating, and rearing to maturity all their children. Children are *immediately* dependent on their parents for these things. Parents must provide not only for immediate needs but also for future needs, that is, they must provide at least for their minor children even after their own death. The fulfillment of this duty, however, is impossible unless the head of the family may own productive goods and endow his children with these.

c) Of individual to society. Private ownership is an instrument of social well-being because: nature insists that the individual provide for himself and his family and forbids that this duty be taken over by the State; every citizen should have the means of protecting himself from possible tyranny and nothing is more suitable for this than ownership of productive goods. A State will be more stable and peaceful if ownership is widely spread among its members. There is incentive to produce and conserve wealth if the rewards of personal security and ownership exist. If the production and distribution of goods is left to private initiative, the rulers of society have the leisure properly to fulfill their duty of preserving social order and providing socially necessary assistance.

d) Of man's relation to the material universe. Private ownership makes man a good steward of inanimate nature, for each one is careful to preserve and increase what is his own.

PART II.

557. *Some general system of private ownership is necessary.* Since ownership is necessary, some over-all system of ownership is requisite. In the proof of the first part of Thesis XLI we showed that men *may* own privately. Hence a system of private ownership is lawful and moral. However, that system is to be preferred which most effectively attains nature's purpose, namely, that goods serve human needs; and, if only one system actually can do this, this system must be adopted. Our second proof shows that under the unalterable impact of human instincts, needs, and defects, private ownership is the only practicable system. The Natural Law, however, does not anathematize common ownership as repugnant to human nature. The fact of the matter is that private ownership, tempered by social control, is the practicable mode of property holding, it is the one system that will work in the long run. Although individuals or small select groups may voluntarily surrender their right of private ownership, society is forbidden to abolish its exercise at large.

The preferable and obligatory system will be not merely one in which a few private owners are tolerated here and there; it will be an economy which takes its prevailing tone from a predominance of private owners. This would not prevent the State from owning certain productive goods wherever such ownership would better promote the common good.

This position is not a defense of the evils of the capitalistic system. These evils are not an inevitable consequence of private ownership; they are the result of avarice, which society has failed to check.

The evils of the capitalistic system can be traced to the centering of attention upon the individual aspect of property to the almost total neglect of its social aspect. By the social aspect of ownership is meant those obligations of justice and charity which attach to it. Justice demands that the right of ownership yield before the prior and more fundamental right of use of the State or of other individuals in certain extreme crises. Charity lays down as a precept, not as a mere counsel of supererogation, that one's superfluous goods should be used to alleviate the wants of the needy. The right of private ownership, like any other right, is not unlimited. The limitations placed on this right by justice and charity are to be enforced by wise social control. The extent of social control necessary will depend on many circumstances of time, climate, tradition, economic habits, and social development.

PROOF

558. *Some general system of private ownership is obligatory,* because only under such a system can nature's purpose for material goods be realized effectively, peaceably, and equitably.

1. *Effectively.* This is the only system which guarantees a sufficiency

of goods because: (*a*) the individual is solicitous to preserve and *increase* only what belongs to him personally. He is notoriously and incurably negligent in caring for common property. (*b*) Man's best productive efforts can be adequately motivated only by the personal appeal of a personal reward. Men will make no such efforts if no such rewards are in prospect, nor will they be much concerned over the welfare of others not connected with them by a special tie.

2. *Peaceably*. (*a*) Man has a special instinct for possession, as history attests. If this instinct which is common to all men and is deeply rooted in man's nature is frustrated, widespread and disrupting discontent will follow. (*b*) Nothing is so productive of friction and quarrels as joint ownership.

3. *Equitably*: (*a*) The free nature of man will resent as inequitable a status of constant and intimate dependence on the will of another, which any other system would demand. (*b*) The obligations of parents to children demand private ownership as the necessary means of fulfillment. It would be unfair of nature to impose the obligation and withhold the necessary means of fulfilling it.

559. Corollary. The right to acquire goods is a natural right not only in the sense that nature allows a man to own privately but also in the sense that she urges him toward it. Therefore, the contention of Hobbes, Kant, and the Juridical Positivists that property rights originate in civil law is false. Factually these rights antedated the origin of States. But the fundamental reason is that if civil law instituted private property, it could likewise terminate it by introducing collectivism. But this it cannot do without destroying the peace and order of society.

D. *The Actual Remedy*

560. No wrong is corrected by a second wrong. Truth is the only real remedy. Here the truth is to be found between the extremes of communism and socialism on the one hand and the overrugged individualism of Liberal Economics on the other. Though evil has resulted from man's failure to recognize a truth — the social obligations of private ownership — the remedy does not consist in the denial of the truth of private ownership but in a return to the forgotten truth of social duty.

The return to this truth must come as the result of enlightened social action, because of themselves men have not bridled their greed and will not. It is not enough that individuals learn the evils of greed run riot; but society must, as in the past, set up wise barriers to restrain it.

561. The first of these restraints is the sowing of economico-moral truth in the modern mind. Men must be convinced that the purpose of earthly goods is to serve human needs; that the efficient system for making goods serve human needs is ownership tempered by social use; that the moral law governs business and politics. Justice demands that all men and nations have access to the essentials of human living. Hence, it is immoral to destroy another man's livelihood or give a workman less than a living wage. Charity rejects the Darwinian notion that life is a warfare of tooth and claw for the survival of the fittest and insists upon a bond of natural fellowship uniting all men so that the fortunate will share their excess goods with the unfortunate.

562. The second change required is social legislation which retains the essentials of private ownership and at the same time removes the evil excrescences of capitalism. The need here is not merely laws against monopolistic gouging, starvation wages, and investment frauds, but the creation of social and economic conditions that will make possible three things: (1) that every man capable and willing to work be able to find gainful employment; (2) that he receive a wage which will enable him and his family to live; (3) that all men be secure in the savings which their thrift accumulates.

Reimplementation of socio-economic policy along the lines outlined above will multiply the small owner and spread ownership through society as widely as possible. A society is more stable and more likely to promote the common good if large numbers of its citizens are economically secure. In this way there will be no undue concentration of wealth in the hands of a few with the consequent ascendancy of a money power bent not on the common good but its own perpetuation. However, multiplication of small owners need not mean a return to the craft age and small business. The able and thrifty workman can be rewarded by becoming part owner of the business in which he engages.

563. To equalize the distribution of wealth, co-operative organization of society is necessary. This third point will be taken up in greater detail in social ethics. Suffice it to say here that instead of employer associations hostilely arrayed against employee associations, there ought to be occupational associations consisting of all who make their living by the same kind of work, both owner and wage earner. If such associations were wisely and justly governed for the common benefit of the whole membership, among other things, two important results would follow. First, there would be no stoppages of the incomes of workers. Second, the management of wealth would return to its real owners. The latter would remove that evil whereby a few men, strategically placed, have been able to make world-shaking economic decisions not for the general benefit but for the interest of a few.

564. Last, society must be unsecularized. All hope of lasting improvement is a febrile dream as long as the happiness-now attitude dominates men and nations. Civilized man must return to religion. Unless he does so, dark ages are inevitable. Men are callous to the rights of their fellow man because they do not give God His due. There must be a renovation of souls so that the emphasis of life will shift from material to eternal values. The individual must reorient his life to the one end of life and convince himself that greed and injustice are insurmountable obstacles to the winning of that end. When religion again impels man to recognize his true place before God, there will be a chance that justice and charity will temper man's inhumanity to man.

But here the individual absolutely needs the help of the State. Governments themselves cannot be without religion nor can they be indifferent to the individual's efforts to attain eternal beatitude. They must realign their mighty powers to assist the over-all purpose of life. They must be rebaptized and accept again the Gospel of Jesus Christ. Apart from Jesus Christ, all is darkness. Should the nations recede further from Him, night must swallow civilization.

READINGS

St. Thomas, *Summa Theologica,* II–II, 66, 2; 118, 1.

Aristotle, *Politics,* Bk. II, c. 3.

Barmine, Alexander, *One Who Survived.* New York, Putnam, 1945.

Belloc, Hilaire, *The Servile State.* London, Foulis, 1912.

—— *The Restoration of Property.* New York, Sheed and Ward, 1946.

Berdyaev, Nicholas, *The Origin of Russian Communism.* London, Bless, 1937.

Blueprint for World Conquest. Introduction by W. H. Chamberlain, Washington, Human Events, 1946.

Bouvier Law Dictionary, "Property."

Bruehl, Charles P., *The Pope's Plan for Social Reconstruction,* pp. 41–130. New York, Devin-Adair, 1939.

Burns, Emile, ed., *Handbook of Marxism*. New York, Random House, 1935.

Cahil, E., S.J., *The Framework of the Christian State,* pp. 105–220. Dublin, Gill, 1932.

Catholic Encyclopedia, "Collectivism," IV, 106; "Communism," IV, 179; "Property," XII, 462; "Socialism," XIV, 62; "Syndicalism," XIV, 385.

Cathrein, Victor, S.J., *Philosophia Moralis,* pp. 277–333. Friburgi Brisgoviae, Herder, 1915, 10 ed.

Coppens, Charles, S.J., *Moral Philosophy,* pp. 121–138. New York, Schwartz, Kerwin, Fauss, 1924.

Corpus Juris, "Property," Vol. 50, pp. 725–788.

Cronin, Michael, *The Science of Ethics,* Vol. II, pp. 113–132, 150–224. Dublin, Gill, 1909.

Dallin, David J., *The Real Soviet Russia.* New Haven, Yale University Press, 1947, rev. ed.

Dallin-Nicolaevsky, *Forced Labor in Russia.* New Haven, Yale University Press, 1947.

Davis, Henry, S.J., *Moral and Pastoral Theology,* Vol. II, pp. 225–253. New York, Sheed and Ward, 1936.

Dawson, Christopher, *Religion and the Modern State,* pp. 1–128. New York, Sheed and Ward, 1936.

Delaye, E., S.J., *What Is Communism?* trans. B. F. Schumacher. St. Louis, Herder, 1938.

Gurian, Waldemar, *Bolshevism: Theory and Practice,* trans. E. I. Watkins. New York, Sheed and Ward, 1934.

Holaind, Rene, S.J., *Natural Law and Legal Practice,* pp. 203–224. New York, Benziger, 1899.

————— *Ownership and Natural Right.* Baltimore, Hill and Harvey, 1887.

Holland, Thomas E., *Jurisprudence,* pp. 191–223. Oxford, Clarendon, 1937, 13 ed.

Kologriwof, Ivan, S.J., ed., *God, Man and the Universe,* pp. 489–578. London, Coldwell, 1937.

Leo XIII, in *Social Wellsprings,* ed. J. Husslein, S.J., Vol. I, pp. 14–23. Milwaukee, Bruce, 1940.

Marx, Carl, *Capital.* Modern Library Edition, pp. 54–79, 557–710. New York, 1936.

McFadden, Charles J., O.S.A., *The Philosophy of Communism.* New York, Benziger, 1938.

Oakeshott, Michael, *The Social and Political Doctrines of Contemporary Europe,* pp. 82–159. Cambridge University, 1939.

Pius XI, in *Social Wellsprings,* ed. J. Husslein, S.J., Vol. II, pp. 174–234, 339–374. Milwaukee, Bruce, 1942.

Sheed, F. J., *Communism and Man.* New York, Sheed and Ward, 1946.

Stalin, Joseph, *Leninism,* ed. J. Fineberg. 2 vols. New York, International Publishers.

Strachey, John, *The Theory and Practice of Socialism.* New York, Random House, 1936.

CHAPTER XVIII

PROPERTY TITLES

565. Nature endows no man with any specific material goods but merely with the right to acquire goods. Accordingly we shall set ourselves to the task of discovering what further is required to make the individual an actual owner. In the general discussion of rights we saw that an abstract right passes into the actual right to this particular thing through the medium of a contingent fact called a *title*.

A *title of ownership* is some contingent fact by which the right to own is determined in the concrete. It is the final instrument creating the moral bond of ownership between this person and this object. This may be a positive title or a natural title. (1) A *positive title* is some fact which the civil law defines as sufficient to create ownership. Thus, twenty-years use gives one a right of way over adjacent land. (2) A *natural title* is some fact valid in the eyes of the Natural Law to determine actual ownership. This title is *original* when a thing which hitherto belonged to no one now becomes the property of some owner. It is *derived* when a new owner succeeds to property previously held.

566. Since there is a natural right to own, there must be natural titles; but before discussing what facts constitute natural titles, let us find the most basic of them all. This will be the *primordial title,* which is the foundation of, and antedates every other title whether natural or positive, original or derived. By what title, then, did the first owner for the first time ever acquire ownership? This is not an historical but a juridical question because it explains the lawful origin of actual private owning — how goods offered by nature in common to all could first become the property of someone.

Absolutely speaking, the initial title to material objects is *productive causality.* This is God's title to the visible universe: the heavens and the earth are His because He made them. Man, however, cannot create. If he could make something out of nothing, that something would be his, and his act of creation would be his primordial title to it. But man can only produce changes in matter already pre-existent. From this principle of productive causality a man certainly has a right to the new values he evolves by his labor, provided the matter with which he works is his. The question of primordial title, then, reduces itself to this: How does man first come to possess those materials without which he can make nothing?

I. THE PRIMORDIAL TITLE

THESIS XLII. The natural primordial title of private ownership is effective occupation.

567. Occupation is the real and permanent seizure of a thing capable of being owned with the intent to acquire original dominion over that thing. This demands (a) *on the part of the thing,* that it be physically capable of becoming someone's exclusive property and that it now belong to no one; (b) *on the part of the occupier,* that he intend to make this thing permanently and exclusively his own and in some appropriate way signify this intention to others. Of itself, however, a mere intention to seize and acquire ownership and the expression of this will to others is not enough to make one an owner. There must be a real seizure of the thing — its effective occupation. A fisherman does not become the owner of an uncaught fish by pointing to it and telling his companions not to touch it; he must catch it. Hence, occupation is effective when the thing is actually subjected to the physical force of a person for his own proper use and service. What we cannot effectively control we cannot be said to occupy and own.

PROOF

568. The primordial title of private ownership is that fact whereby something of nature's bounty, offered to men indeterminately, may legitimately become the property of some individual. This fact can only be effective occupation. In order that things as yet belonging to nobody and capable of appropriation may pass to some private owner, effective occupation is *required.* A moral connection must be established between this object and this person which makes it evident that this thing is subjected to this person and all other persons are excluded from its ownership. But without effective occupation this is impossible. *Nothing more is required.* Since the individual has a natural right to own, he exercises this right over goods which as yet belong to no one by simply pre-empting them. Once he has effectively occupied them they are his.

569. *What can be occupied?* Man may not occupy that which is for the common good of all nor such quantities of other things which cannot be used or effectively controlled. Since everything has practically passed into the possession of some owner, occupancy is now restricted to genuinely lost articles, treasure-troves, derelicts, fish, and wild beasts. The civil law adds further refinements to this prescription of the Natural Law and usually the observance of these conditions bind in conscience.

II. SUBORDINATE TITLES

Here we briefly examine the other facts which according to Natural Law constitute true titles of ownership. Contract is reserved for special consideration.

A. Labor

570. Labor is the exercise of bodily or mental activity. It is unreasonable to restrict this term to bodily effort. It has been contended that labor is the primordial title, but this is not true in the sense that labor of itself gives one title to the material in which he works. It is true that labor, in so far as it makes occupation effective, participates in the nature of occupation.

Labor is a *natural title to its own proper fruits,* because, since man is the master of his power, he is the owner of the products of his power.

B. Gift

571. Gift is the gratuitous placing of ownership in the hands of another, or the voluntary, immediate, and absolute transfer of goods without consideration. That gift is a natural legitimate title follows from the very notion of ownership. That plenary control, which is ownership, is the power to dispose of the thing as one pleases — which surely includes giving the thing away. No higher law forbids this for otherwise a man could not fulfill many obligations of charity.

C. Hereditary Succession

572. Hereditary succession is legitimate succession to the dominion of a thing upon the death of the former owner. A person who prior to the death of the owner has the right to become the future owner is called an *heir*. Before the owner's death the heir has what the Romans called a *jus ad rem,* that is, a right to become the owner of these goods. Upon the owner's death, the *jus ad rem* becomes a *jus in re,* or a right in or over the decedent's goods. Property so transferred is an inheritance; the right of an heir is the right of inheritance. There are two ways in which one may be an heir: (*a*) by a *will* made in one's favor and (*b*) by blood relationship to the former owner. The first way is bequest; the second, intestate succession.

Any form of hereditary succession is anathema to socialists and communists. They would introduce a collectivist regime by the simple device of suppressing all hereditary succession. Does the Natural Law approve of this mode of acquiring property?

573. 1. *Bequest, or the title obtained by a will.* A *will* is the voluntary and revocable declaration of an owner concerning the final disposition of his goods to become effective at his death. How are goods actually transferred by a will? One opinion holds that the testator makes the transfer of goods at the moment of making the will but does so conditionally. There are two conditions: (*a*) that the owner not revoke his declaration before death and (*b*) that the owner die. When both of these conditions are fulfilled, the ownership of the heir which hitherto was conditional becomes absolute. According to the other opinion, the testamentary act of the testator virtually perdures until the last moment of his life, and in the moment of death his act of the will so perduring effects the transfer of dominion.

That *bequest is a natural title* springing from the Natural Law is clear for these three reasons:

a) *The nature of ownership,* which is stable and permanent dominion. Such absolute right of control is the right to dispose of the thing not only in the present but also to determine its use in the future.

b) *The need of social order and progress.* If a man could not name the persons who would succeed to his property, two consequences would follow. There would be strife and contention over his possessions at his death or, in the event that everything would go to the State, very few would bother to leave anything.

c) *The need of the family.* One of the chief reasons for private property is the well-being of the family. The Natural Law obliges the head of the family to provide not only for present but also for the future needs of his family. Hence he is to make provision for them for the time after his death by endowing them with a sufficiency of goods.

574. 2. *Intestate succession*. When a person possessed of property dies without having disposed of it by will, he dies intestate (from the Latin *intestatus,* not having made a will), and his nearest blood relations succeed according to the provisions of civil law.

The Natural Law endows the immediate family with the right to succeed to the property of one who dies intestate. Positive law provides that blood relatives become the heirs of an intestate who has no immediate family. The reason for this prescription of the Natural Law is that if the father is obliged to bequeath sufficient of his goods to his wife and children, these dependents must succeed to his property if he dies without a will. There is no need of presuming that an intestate decedent had the will to leave his property to this family, because even if he had not intended to do so, his obligation to endow his family would bind nevertheless. They are the continuation of his personality, and in virtue of that fact they become the owners of his goods. Besides, these goods were not gathered for himself alone but for himself and the continuation of himself in his family. Since as parent he is responsible for his children coming into existence, he is likewise responsible to provide for their continuance in existence and their well-being until they can fully care for themselves.

D. Accession

575. Accession is a title whereby the owner of a thing acquires a right to the products of that thing and to whatever is united to it in a supplementary way either naturally or artificially. Taken in the first sense of a right to natural products, accession is clearly granted by the Natural Law. *Res fructificat domino:* the owner is entitled to any increase of his property resulting from its own natural activities such as the yield of plants, the offspring of animals. In the latter case, positive law usually decides that in the absence of a more specific agreement between the interested parties, where the parent animals belong to different owners, the offspring belong to the owner of the female parent.

Taken in the second sense of inseparable accessory union, accession derives from positive law which recognizes four kinds: (*a*) accretion of land to land (alluvion), for example, soil carried by a river from one bank to another; (b) addition of movables to land (fixtures), for example, a tree planted on another man's land; (c) union of movables with movables (commixture or confusion), for example, mingling one man's grain with the grain of another man; (d) conversion of one man's materials into another form by a man who thinks the materials are his own (specification), for example, bread baked with another man's flour. Positive law follows the principle that the total thing belongs to the owner of the principal object. The questions, then, to be settled in law and conscience are: Which substance is of principal importance and What compensation is to be made to the owner of the accessory object?

E. Prescription

576. Prescription is a mode of acquiring (a) property or equivalent rights through long continued use or (b) freedom from juridic obligation through a creditor's nonuse of his right. In the jurisprudences founded on Roman law, the former is acquisitive, the latter liberative prescription. In jurisprudences of the English tongue, it is known as limitations.

In the acquisition of property and similar rights, prescription means that through innocent and continuous possession of a thing, a nonowner, under conditions prescribed by law, becomes its lawful owner. It is not accurate to say that the mere lapse of time extinguishes an old right or creates a new one. Only the lawgiver can erase the right of the first owner and concede his thing to the actual possessor or user.

577. The requisite conditions for prescription are five:

1. The thing must be capable of becoming private property and is *not protected against prescription by law*. Civil and canon law[1] enumerate a variety of things which may not be acquired by prescription. In the United States public property is imprescriptible: there is no adverse possession against the State.[2]

2. *A person must actually use or possess the thing as an owner.* In other words, one must so act toward the thing that other men may infer that he is the owner. One hardly acts as the owner of real property if he does not record his holdings with the proper public official. One's use or possession must be open, continuous, and peaceable. Litigation bars peaceable possession.

---

[1] Cf. *Codex Juris Canonici*, 1510.

[2] *Bouvier's Law Dictionary*, "Limitations," p. 726, col. 1. Baldwin's ed. Cleveland, 1934.

3. *The thing must be possessed in good faith.* In acquisitive prescription, possession is begun and continued without reasonable doubt concerning one's right to the thing. In liberative prescription, good faith means that the one being released from obligation is not aware of this obligation, or, if aware, does nothing to impede the right of the creditor. Bad faith, or knowledge that one is acting against another's right, cannot found a true title in the forum of conscience though it may in civil law if it is not discovered.

4. *There must be sufficient title.* Sufficient title is some fact, actual or presumed, which gives the prescribing agent fair reason to think the thing is his. He can have only an apparent title because, either the fact had some hidden flaw which prevented it from being a true title, or a sufficiently valid fact was thought to exist whereas it did not. His title cannot be a good title, because originally a right did not pass to him. Without some apparent title, good faith is impossible. If no ground of claim exists other than immemorial use, the law regards this as a presumed title.

5. *There must be a lapse of time* sufficient to justify the prudent judgment that the former owner or creditor has abdicated his right. Diverse jurisdictions indicate varying periods of time for various rights. For realty rights in this country, the time is about twenty years; for movables, about six years. Some jurisdictions grant to one who has in good faith come into possession of a particular movable, which has not been stolen from nor lost by an owner, absolute ownership against any third party.[3] This period of time, however, does not run against one laboring under an inability to sue, such as infants, married women, the insane, the imprisoned, those out of the State.

578. The Natural Law demands that States make such laws for the peace and good order of society. Without them litigation would be endless; owners unable to prove their claims because of lost documents or deceased witnesses would be dispossessed; it would be impossible to buy land or make similar contracts for nobody would risk attempting to buy things the ownership of which would always be subject to contest. The title of prescription is rather of positive law except in the case of an immemorial holding the beginnings of which are completely unknown. Such a title is of the Natural Law.

579. To avail oneself in good conscience of statutes of limitation,

---

[3] Vermeersch, *Theol. Moral.*, Vol. II. p. 339. Bruges, Beyaert, 1924.

one must distinguish between cases in which the law affects the title to property and cases in which it merely bars a legal remedy. In the former, if the old right is extinguished, one may in conscience take advantage thereof. This is clearly true in bankruptcy cases, for the lawgiver intends to give the bankrupt a fresh start in life. In the latter where the law merely limits the time wherein one may seek a legal remedy for damages one may also in conscience take advantage of them. For the fact that the injured party made no effort to seek redress when he might have done so within the allotted time is reasonably presumed to be a condonation. However, this does not apply to the nonpayment of money debts contracted for goods, services, and the like. For such is the conviction of men of upright conscience: American courts have ruled that in contracts for the payment of money there is no such thing as adverse possession of money, that the statute simply affects the remedy, not the debt.[4]

---

[4] *Bouvier's Law Dictionary*, p. 720, col. 3.

READINGS

Bouvier's Law Dictionary, articles on title occupancy, patent, copyright, trademark, gift, donatio inter vivos, donatio mortis causa, devise, bequest, will, inheritance, intestate, accession, prescription.

Brown, Ray Andrews, *Law of Personal Property*, pp. 14–34, 46–200. Chicago, Callaghan, 1936.

Catholic Encyclopedia, "Partnership," XI, 509.

Corpus Juris, "Accession," Vol. I, pp. 382–390; "Gifts," Vol. 28, pp. 617–706; "Occupation," Vol. 46, pp. 895–898; "Prescription," Vol. 49, pp. 1334–1336; "Wills," Vol. 68, pp. 381–448.

Cronin, Michael, *The Science of Ethics*, Vol. II, pp. 133–149. Dublin, Gill, 1909.

Davis, Henry, S.J., *Moral and Pastoral Theology*, Vol. II, pp. 253–265. New York, Sheed and Ward, 1936.

Holaind, Rene, S.J., *Natural Law and Legal Practise*, pp. 225–232. New York, Benziger, 1899.

Holland, Thomas E., *Jurisprudence*, pp. 216–222, 233–242. Oxford, Clarendon, 1937, 13 ed.

Jarrett, Bede, O.P., *Social Theories of the Middle Ages*, pp. 150–180. Westminster, Md., Newman, 1942.

Nivard, Marcel, S.J., *Ethica*, pp. 275–298. Paris, Beauchesne, 1928.

Valensin, Albert, *Traite de Droit Natural*, Vol. II, pp. 113–171. Paris, Editions Spes, 1925.

Vermeersch, A., S.J., *De Justitia*, pp. 329–362. Bruges, Beyaert, 1904.

CHAPTER XIX

CONTRACT

580. The most common way by which people actually acquire property rights is contract. At the same time, there is a great deal of dispute among men about the binding force of contracts. We shall now consider whether there is such a thing as a contract according to the Natural Law and whether contract constitutes a true title to property or other rights.

I. THE NATURE OF A CONTRACT

581. Writers on the civil law often experience difficulty in defining a contract, as Harriman complains: "If we seek to build up a definition of the term 'contract' which shall include all things that have been called contracts and exclude all things that have been held not to be contracts, the task is evidently impossible."[1] An old English authority cited by Holland calls contract "speech between two parties whereby something is to be done."[2] Blackstone defines it as "an agreement upon sufficient consideration to do or not to do a particular thing."[3] Justice Holmes, who sees no permanent norms of conduct in law which to him is only a rule of passing expediency, cynically says that a contract is "the taking of a risk." "The only universal consequence," he continues, "of a legally binding promise is, that the law makes the promisor pay damage if the promised event does not come to pass. In every case it leaves him free from interference until the time for performance has passed and therefore free to break his contract if he chooses."[4] However, most agree with Anson that "a contract is

---

[1] *Bouvier's Law Dictionary*, p. 227.

[2] Thomas E. Holland, *The Elements of Jurisprudence*, p. 259. Oxford, Clarendon Press, 1937, 13 ed.

[3] *Commentaries*, II–442.

[4] Oliver Wendell Holmes, Jr., *The Common Law*, p. 301. Boston, Little Brown, 1946, 40th print.

an agreement enforceable at law made between two or more persons by which rights are acquired by one or both to acts or forebearances on the part of the other."[5]

Since the province of civil law extends directly only to external acts detrimental to or promotive of the common good, civil law cannot take cognizance of every sort of agreement among men. Hence a legal contract is one which the civil law recognizes and is willing to enforce. That the law should have difficulty in determining what it should enforce is quite understandable. We are not primarily concerned with the external forum of positive law but with the internal forum of conscience. *What is a valid contract in the Natural Law and binding in conscience?*

582. Men can and do make private agreements the binding force of which is not mere fidelity but strict justice. Even though positive law may not see fit to enforce every agreement of that nature, nevertheless every free and mutual agreement between two or more competent parties concerning the transfer of a right is a true contract producing binding effects in conscience. Every agreement which is a contract passes some right and establishes some obligation in commutative justice; if no right passes, the agreement rests solely on fidelity. Our discussion will encompass (*a*) the nature of agreement, (*b*) the object of agreement, (*c*) the cause of agreement, and (*d*) the parties to the agreement.

A. The Agreement

583. Agreement is a consent, a concurrence, of mind and will. Hence, agreement is a meeting of minds and wills, a thinking and willing of the same thing by distinct parties. Consent is had when one party, called an offeror, or promisor, makes a proposal or offer expressing his readiness to be bound to a performance which in turn is accepted by a second party called a promisee. The offeror binds himself *in justice* to fulfill this proposal; and in this sense it must be accepted by the promisee, who may or may not bind himself in justice to an equivalent performance as the nature of the proposal dictates. Anything, then, that would prevent a true meeting of minds and wills would of its nature make a contract impossible, because no new bond of justice can arise between private parties except such as they willingly assume. The willing assumption of obligation demands

---

[5] *Bouvier's Law Dictionary*, p. 227.

that their minds and wills be at one concerning the proposal which lies between them. Hence to have a sufficient agreement there must be sufficient knowledge and full consent of the will.

584. 1. *Sufficient knowledge.* Unless both parties have knowledge concerning one and the same object of agreement, there can be no meeting of minds. Such knowledge is vitiated by *error* or mistake. Error may be substantial or accidental.

a) Substantial error affects the very substance of the agreement: one party has in mind one object and the other party a different object. This happens: when the error touches the very object of consent, as when I propose to buy sugar and receive salt; when it touches the kind or species of agreement, as when I take money which I think to be a gift but which the giver thinks a loan; when it touches the primary motive, the reason without which the agreement would not be entered into, as when I place an order in this store solely because I think I can get a discount for cash. *Substantial error invalidates a contract,* because without a meeting of minds consent is impossible.

b) Accidental error does not touch the substance of the thing agreed upon but only its accidental qualities. This type of error does not invalidate an agreement for there is sufficient meeting of minds. Hence it has no effect upon an unbreakable contract. If, however, one has entered a voidable contract deceived by the *guile,* or even the *innocent* misrepresentations of the other party even touching accidental points, the one deceived may seek an annulment of the agreement.

585. 2. *True and internal consent of the will.* Since a contract is a species of private law binding the interested parties and imposing obligations in justice, no one can be said to contract who does not will to accept the obligation. However, acceptance of obligation is still compatible with an intention not to fulfill it.

An essential difference between natural and civil law will be noted here. The former demands a true internal consent for a contract. The latter cannot, because men's internal acts lie beyond its scope. Justice Blackburn ruled in *Smith vs. Hughes:* "If, whatever a man's real intention may be, he so conducts himself that a reasonable man would believe he was assenting to the terms proposed by another, and that other party on that belief enters into contract with him, the man thus conducting himself would be equally bound as if he had intended to agree to the other party's terms." Holland comments on this: "The legal meaning of such acts on the part of one man as to induce another to enter into contract with him, is not what the former really intended, nor what the latter really supposed the former to intend but what a reasonable man, i.e., a judge or jury would put upon such acts."[6]

A fictitious consent — an outward appearance of consent without the internal act — is no consent. If an innocent party suffers loss because of a fictitious consent, he must be recompensed for his loss. Moreover, such a person is not obliged to accept the assurance of the other party that his consent was fictitious and has the right to exact from him the part upon which he agreed.

If a person is prevented from making a free and deliberate choice, his consent is necessarily nullified. Hence duress nullifies consent. *Duress* is defined in civil law as personal violence or imprisonment, actual or threatened, exerted by one party on the other or his wife or child. Akin to duress is *undue influence,* that is, abuse of a position of confidence or authority, so as to take unfair advantage of another's weakness of mind, necessity, or distress. This does not nullify one's consent but affords grounds for rescinding it.

Fear which takes away the use of reason nullifies a consent. Grave fear, even though it is a motive *sine qua non* of one's consent, does not of itself invalidate such consent, for the act is a voluntary one. Such fear *unjustly brought to bear* is always a reason for rescinding one's consent. In ecclesiastical law such consent is null.

586. *Consent must be mutual and externally manifested.* The consent of two parties is mutual when the consent of one is accorded because of, or with a view to, the consent of the other. If two parties would coincidentally or casually determine to do the same thing, no contractual obligation would arise. Granted this essential mutuality, it is also required that offer and acceptance simultaneously fall upon the same object and that the internal agreement of both be given outward expression.

587. The mutuality and externalization of contract demand three things:

1. There must be an unconditional acceptance corresponding exactly to the offer. A proposal to buy a building lot for one hundred dollars is not acceptance of an offer to sell the same for one hundred and twenty-five dollars.

2. Offer and acceptance must be mutual in time, that is, the offer

---

[6] *Jurisprudence*, p. 265.

must perdure until the other party accepts it. If it is withdrawn before acceptance, consent is not possible. The duration of an offer depends on the will of the offeror; it is terminated when he explicitly revokes his offer before acception. If there is no express revocation, common sense says it remains open a reasonable time, that is, that length of time after which the offer of the ordinarily prudent man would be interpreted to have lapsed.

3. Internal acceptance does not bind. Since in a contract some right passes which can be effected only by communication, acceptance must be signified by an external act. This outward expression may be writing, words, signs, or merely one's course of action. Sometimes even silence may be sufficient sign of external consent.

588. *What knowledge should each party have of the other's consent?* This is a thorny question and differing answers have been given by various civil codes. The difficulty may be put this way: at what precise time does a contract arise according to the Natural Law? Is it when the second party definitely signifies his acceptance, or only when the first party has knowledge of acceptance? English civil law chooses the first alternative and holds that an offer is irrevocable upon acceptance, which however is not a mere mental act but definitive communication of assent to the proposer. Many continental jurists demand that acceptance become known to the proposer before agreement is effected. It is more probable that the English view represents the requirements of the Natural Law. Men can communicate only by external signs. Therefore, once the offeror has expressed his mind and will in a proposal communicated to the promisee, this expression must not only stand for, but it must *be* his mind and will, as far as outward relations are concerned, until he substitute for it another sign of his mind and will. This substitution, however, would not take effect until knowledge of the change actually reaches the promisee. When the promisee joins to the mind and will of the offeror, the outward and communicated expression of his mind and will, an agreement truly is effected, even though actually the offeror has withdrawn his offer. Besides, if agreement is suspended until knowledge of acceptance has reached the offeror, why should it not also be suspended until the promisee discovers that his acceptance has reached the offeror? Thus an agreement could never be reached.

589. What *external* form should this outward manifestation of agreement take? By Natural Law the proper and sole form is true,

full, and mutual consent *externalized*. In certain contracts, positive
law demands the observance of certain formalities, or solemnities.
Failure to observe such prescribed form can make a contract null
from the beginning, as is seen in the marriage contract. As for civil
contracts lacking requisite form, they are probably valid in conscience
before a court has passed judgment on them.

B. The Object of Agreement

590. In a broad sense an object of agreement is that thing the right
to which passes hands through the contractual act. However, for the
sake of clarity, the term *object of agreement* is restricted to that which
the promisor transfers, and that which the promisee contributes is
called *consideration*. Our present discussion includes both object of
agreement and consideration. We shall attempt to discover what kind
of thing may be the object of contract.

1. The object of contract must be something which at the time
of agreement is not only physically but also morally possible of
realization, that is, it must be capable of realization without overwhelming difficulty. Hence, it must exist either *in re* or *in spe* —
either in actuality or in probability, such as newly sown crops. If the
thing is not capable of precise determination or if in the terms of the
proposed agreement it is not so determined, it must be likened to
the nonexistent.

2. It must be of some estimable value — a thing, advantage, service,
or utility which is of value to another, and whose value can be
computed. Therefore, such things as man exchanges with man in
commutative justice would be objects of contract. Anything which is
useless or requires no effort may not be the object of contract. In this
category, as an example, would be the casual pointing out of
directions to a tourist.

3. The thing must be capable of transfer and must be the property
of the one transferring it. Accordingly, one cannot contract to give
another what already belongs to him in justice.

4. That which is immoral, that is, contrary to Natural or positive
law, cannot be the object of contract. No one can give or acquire
the right to do what is sinful.

591. If an immoral act is agreed upon for a price, all agree that
no contract exists before the immoral act is performed. Both parties
are obliged to withdraw. But if an immoral act is performed, must

the price be paid? A subtle difficulty arises. Some hold that there is no obligation to pay: they contend that that which was initially invalid remains invalid. The civil law sees no difficulty here and simply refuses to entertain an action for recovery. Kent says: "If the contract grows immediately out of, or is connected with an illegal or immoral act, a court of justice will not enforce it."[7] Public justice has no other course; otherwise it would countenance and even encourage immorality. Nevertheless, most moralists now agree that the beneficiary of such an immoral act is bound to pay in natural justice. The reason is that, although the agreement was an invalid contract, yet it had the effect of estimating the price of the immoral act, not as immoral but as useful, laborious, or pleasure giving. The very positing of the immoral act brings into existence a latent contract; since the onerous part of a contract has been fulfilled, justice demands the price of it be paid.

Though the issue is not apodictically settled, the majority of men think one who has made such a bargain and had the advantage of it is a downright poltroon to renege.

From the conflicting probabilities, two practical conclusions emerge: (a) one cannot be compelled to pay the price, because it is probable that no contract exists; (b) a person who has been paid the price may keep it, because it is probable that a contract does exist.

C. The Cause of Agreement

592. In every contract there is a *cause,* that is, an immediate and *proximate* reason why a contracting party divests himself of a right or assumes a juridic obligation. Some cause is essential to every contract; otherwise, there is no rational explanation for the surrender of a right. Because it exists within the pact, this cause is intrinsic to the contract. Thus a buyer gives or promises to give a sum of money to a seller because the latter gives or promises to give him a house. The promise or the giving of the seller is the cause of the buyer's contractual act and vice versa as far as the seller's act is concerned.

In many contracts this immediate and intrinsic cause is also the impelling *motive.* Workmen enter a wage contract to obtain the salary promised. Merchants sell their goods to receive the price. However,

---

[7] *Commentaries,* Vol. 2, part 5, lect. 38, p. 466. Boston, Little Brown, 1896, 14 ed.

an impelling motive may be some more remote reason which stands outside the contract itself. For example, a builder may put up a public building for a sum of money (the cause) which nets him no profit, his motive in accepting the undertaking being prestige.

The cause of agreement may be (*a*) consideration or (*b*) liberality.

593. *Consideration.* The word consideration has come into the jurisprudence of English-speaking countries from the Latin. In that tongue it meant the compensation given the victim of an unfulfilled promise which the law did not recognize as contractual. The word now signifies the *quid pro quo* — that worth-while thing which the offeror is to obtain from the other party. This thing may be something of advantage to the offeror; it is always of detriment to the promisee. It consists of any abatement of one's right or any inconvenience which one agrees to suffer *with a view to obtaining* what the offeror proffers. It is the price which the offeror asks for the carrying out of his part of the bargain. When, therefore, something is done, promised, foreborne, or suffered by the promisee because of the promise made to him and at the instance of the offeror, that something is consideration.[8]

From what we saw in § 592, consideration is not to be confused with motive nor with the object of agreement (cf. § 590).

There also is a distinction between *good consideration* and *valuable consideration*. The former consists of natural love and affection and the latter, money or what is reducible to money value.

We now ask, *Is consideration of the essence of every contract?*

594. 1. *The Civil Law.* Blackstone defines a contract as an agreement upon sufficient consideration to do or not to do a particular thing.[9] Sitting judges reduce the elements of a contract to the bare statement — a promise for a consideration. English-speaking juris-

---

[8] American legal opinion defines consideration as "that which moves from the promisee or a third person, at the request of the promisee, to the promisor or a third person designated by the promisor, at the express or implied request of the latter, in return for his promise" (in W. L. Clark, *Handbook of the Law of Contracts*, p. 147. St. Paul, West, 1931, 4 ed.). We think, in accordance with the Roman and English view of contract, that both references to a third party should be expunged because, strictly, contractual obligations fall upon, and rights accrue to, only those who are parties to the contract. The Romans clearly distinguished between the act of contract itself and obligations which arise out of contract. Rights may arise to a third party from a contractual promise: these rights the civil law may be willing to protect but they should be considered as outside the contract itself. Since consideration is a cause of contract and intrinsic to it, the concept of consideration should not include what lies outside the contract.

[9] *Commentaries*, 2, 442.

prudence reduces all contracts to two categories: those drawn under seal, or specialty contracts, and those not drawn under seal, or simple or parol contracts. When the agreement has been drawn under seal, the law does not look for consideration; it presumes it to be present. But the presumption is rebuttable, for there are instances where agreements under seal have been nullified because no consideration was proved to exist. When the agreement is not drawn under seal, the law demands *valuable consideration.* This may not be something illegal or already due in justice. Past consideration, that is, an act performed before the agreement was entered into, is no consideration. If I promise you ten dollars for having recovered my wallet no contract exists in the eyes of the law. If I promise you ten dollars if you recover my wallet, and you do so, there is a contract. The consideration need not be adequate, that is, it need not be a commensurate return, but it must be of some value. Therefore, this general rule of civil law may be formulated: *no valuable consideration, no contract.* However, exceptional instances do exist in which the law will enforce gratuitous promises, but positive jurisprudence does not wish to call such promises contractual.

595. 2. *The Natural Law.* Can the offeror be bound in justice by agreements wherein he obtains nothing, in the broadest sense, out of them for himself? The offeror can be so bound if such is his intention. Therefore, by Natural Law we can distinguish an onerous from a gratuitous contract. In the former, consideration must exist: something must pass back to the offeror. In a gratuitous contract, obligation affects only one party: the offeror gives or promises to give; the promisee merely accepts — he neither gives nor does anything in return. Hence according to the Natural Law an agreement in which no consideration passes back to the offeror is a true contract, because a man may divest himself of a right without exacting compensation.

The civil law with good reason refuses to recognize promises as valid without consideration. If the offeror receives no benefit, and if the other party gives up nothing, may not one well question that the offeror binds himself *in justice* to perform? That he should do so for those he loves or from whom he expects affection is understandable. The cause of his transfer of right then is good consideration. But if there is no return either of affection or other value, the civil law presumes that the offeror does not bind himself in justice but in fidelity. A sound view of human nature is implied here. The fact remains, however, that men can and do bind themselves in justice without hope of return of advantage, and when they do so a natural contract arises, the cause of which is the *liberality of the offeror*. Such an agreement is binding in conscience even though unenforceable in the courts.

D. The Parties to the Agreement

596. 1. At least two distinct parties are required for a contract. No one contracts with himself, nor can a part of a corporation or moral person make a contract with another part of the same corporation. For commutative justice is always between other and other.

There may be more than one party to either side of a contract. These will be joint contractors: those who are jointly bound to fulfill the obligations of the contract are joint debtors.

2. The Natural Law demands that at the time of contract one have the free use of reason in order to be competent to contract. This excludes infants, the insane, and the drunk.

The positive law of English-speaking countries defines an infant as anyone who has not completed his twenty-first year. Recognizing that it must protect such persons from their own folly and improvidence, it holds that they are not bound to contracts which they make except those which supply necessities and that upon coming of age they may fulfill other contracts at their discretion or void them within a reasonable time. The question arises as to whether they may in conscience avail themselves of the law in their favor. Generally speaking they may, but two things are to be noticed: (*a*) they must in conscience pay for *benefits received* even through contracts void at law; (*b*) when they contract in bad faith, as when they would fraudulently misrepresent their age so as to enter a contract they intend to repudiate, they must make good the *damage sustained* by the other party. One traffics with an infant at his peril.

Up to most recent times, the contractual capacity of a married woman was practically nil, for the law looked on her civil existence as merged with that of her husband. In this country she could contract for ordinary household matters, manage her own estate, and, where a court had constituted her a feme sole trader, engage in commerce. The tendency now is greatly to enlarge the freedom of women.

3. One must be juridically free to contract; neither the Natural nor positive law places an invalidating obstacle in the way of this person

entering this contract. Thus a diriment impediment either of Natural or ecclesiastic law renders an attempted marriage contract null from the beginning. It is doubtful whether other contracts declared null by positive law are also null in conscience before a court has passed upon them.

II. KINDS OF CONTRACTS

For convenience, all contracts may be classified either as (*a*) *gratuitous,* if benefit accrues merely to the promisee or (*b*) *onerous,* if benefit and obligation devolve on both parties.

A. Gratuitous Contracts

597. Anyone, who wishes to, may divest himself of a right without receiving some compensating right in return. But is not this a violation of justice, which demands equality? No, for injustice is not done to one who willingly suffers a curtailment of what is his — *volenti non fit injuria.* But what sort of equality is demanded in the execution of a gratuitous contract? Simply that, over and above the thing freely given by the offeror, nothing of estimable value is *exacted* by him in return. Noteworthy among such contracts are promise, gift, deposit, and loans.

598. 1. *Promise.* A simple promise accepted is an offer accepted; and when the promisor has bound himself in justice to perform, there exists a true contract even though no valuable consideration is given for the promise. In practice the difficulty consists in distinguishing between a mere promise or intention to confer a favor and a promise of contract. The practical test is that men do not usually bind themselves contractually by a gratuitous promise unless they make it in the presence of deliberately chosen witnesses or through a deed or public instrument of conveyance, or fortify it with an oath. It ultimately resolves itself to this: what did the promisor intend at the time of his promise?

599. 2. *Gift,* which we have already seen to be a good title, is likewise a form of contract. It becomes binding on the conscience of the donor whenever the offer is accepted and any stipulated conditions are fulfilled. Title then passes irrevocably; and even if the beneficiary should later prove ungrateful, the donor does not have grounds in Natural Law for recovering his gift.

600. 3. *Deposit* is a contract whereby one accepts a movable of another to keep it *gratis* until the owner calls for it. The depositee is bound to safeguard the deposit with the care and skill which any prudent man would exercise. He must deliver it upon demand together with its profits and increase. If it has perished or deteriorated because of his culpable negligence, he must make good the loss. He may not use it without the owner's consent which, however, he may reasonably presume. He may even use money, provided he is certain he can repay the deposit when demanded; and he may retain any profit arising from his own industry. He is entitled to recompense for any expense undergone or damage suffered because of the deposit.

When the depositee acts for pay, the contract ceases to be gratuitous and his obligation to safeguard the thing increases proportionately. We have then the contract of *caretaking*.

601. 4. *Loans* are of two kinds, loans for use and loans for consumption.

a) *Loans for use* (*commodatum*) are contracts whereby an owner gives another *gratis* the use of a thing for a certain time with the understanding that this exact thing is to be returned. The borrower must bestow very great care on the thing, see to its ordinary upkeep, and return it at the agreed time. The lender may not seek it before the agreed time unless some unforeseen necessity may arise. If the lender is paid, the loan is an onerous contract of *letting, or lease*.

b) *Loans for consumption* (*mutuum*) are contracts whereby a thing which is consumed in its first use (*a fungible*) is given *gratis* to another with the understanding that an equivalent in kind is to be returned in due time. Thus, when a housewife loans a neighbor two pounds of butter she expects two pounds of butter in return. This differs from the first kind of loan in two ways: in the former the thing lent does not become the property of the borrower and the identical thing must be restored; in loans for consumption the thing handed over becomes the property of the borrower who cannot return the identical thing but must return its equivalent in kind.

602. Can there be a similar agreement which constitutes an onerous contract? That the borrower, in view of the benefit to himself, should freely offer a price for his borrowing and that this be accepted by the lender in no way violates justice. But can the lender *demand* a price before making the loan? He may not *in virtue of the loan itself*. In justice he may only demand the thing, because the thing lent perishes in its use. No distinction of ownership can be made between such a thing and its use; the person who owns one must own the other; hence the borrower in this case becomes the owner of the thing lent. Now the seller of such things as bread could not make two separate contracts of sale, one for the bread, the other for the use of the bread. This would be selling the thing twice, or better, selling the non-existent. Therefore, that person would also commit injustice who lent bread and demanded a double recompense — one for the bread, the other for the bread's use. It makes no difference if the borrower some-how contrived to make a profit out of his consumption of the bread. His profit would be the result of his ingenuity, and the lender, as a lender, has no claim upon the fruits of a borrower's ingenuity.

But the lender may suffer a loss because of the loan. Labor and expense may be involved; having parted with this thing, he now may lose the chance of making some other profitable contract; there may be a danger of losing the thing lent which he has to assume. These reasons, however, are extrinsic to the loan itself, but whenever anyone of them is present, he may indemnify himself for his loan by making a reasonable charge upon the borrower.

Money is a fungible, that is, it is consumed in its use. Is it lawful to take interest upon the loan of money? This question introduces the knotty problem of usury.

603. *The Nature of Usury.* The popular notion of usury derives from the civil law, which defines it as the charging of an excessive rate of interest. Moralists agree that this is wrong, but they regard this definition merely as descriptive of a fact which but serves to aggravate the inherent malice of usury. Nor does usury precisely consist in taking advantage of another's need nor in oppression of the poor. If this were so, then if a man could afford to pay an usurious tribute, it would be lawful to demand it. Reviving an opinion of Broedersen of the eighteenth century and Jannet of the nineteenth century, Hilaire Belloc defines usury as "any interest however high or low demanded for an unproductive loan."[10] It would seem, however, that as far as usury is concerned, it makes no difference whether the borrower makes a profit on his loan or not. The profit which the borrower makes from his shrewd or lucky use of money is not a just reason for demanding a share in his profit, except where the contract with him is that of partnership. If a contract is strictly a loan, the money loaned belongs

---

[10] *Essays of a Catholic*, p. 32. London, Sheed and Ward, 1931.

exclusively to the borrower. It increases for him alone, or it perishes to him. Therefore, any gain arising from that money belongs to its owner, not to its former owner, who cannot justly demand as his that which is the fruit of another's industry.

604. Usury can exist, then, only when there is a strict contract of loan, *the loan of a fungible,* and its malice consists in a party's demanding precisely because of the loan, that a greater quantity of the thing loaned be returned. A person who *lends* twenty-five dollars is unjust in asking twenty-six dollars in return. He is unjust because he is demanding back his property (twenty-five dollars) and something for the use of his property; but he is entitled to nothing for the use of his property since in this case use is identified with the substance of the thing. By demanding something more for the use of a thing which has no other use than the consumption of its substance, he is asking a price for something which does not exist. Usury, then, is the extra and unjust price asked for the use of money or any fungible which use is indistinguishable from the money or thing itself.

When the lender of money suffers no detriment in making a loan, he is entitled to nothing more in justice than the return of the money lent. Should he incur loss because of parting with the money lent, he is entitled to compensation for that reason but not because of the loan itself. This title to redress for loss sustained is extrinsic to the loan. Today money, or rather its modern equivalent, credit, is truly a capital good capable of producing further wealth. Therefore a person who parts with money on a loan loses a chance for profit, and because money lent today is genuinely risked, one may in good conscience take advantage of legal rates of interest.

B. Onerous Contracts

605. The most common type of contract is that wherein rights are mutually exchanged, where benefit and burden are assumed by both parties. The moral principles underlying these contracts are in the main those found in the contract of sale, which may serve as the exemplar of onerous contracts. Justice demands that there be a true proportion between the good transferred (or its equivalent such as a chance or hope in aleatory contracts) and the price.

606. *Sale* is a contract whereby a seller transfers the ownership of a thing to a buyer for an agreed price in money. If the exchange is not money for goods but goods for goods, the transaction is called barter.

It should be noted that an agreement to enter a future contract of sale is quite different from an actual present sale: only in the latter does ownership pass hands. The existence of one or other of these depends upon the intention of the parties. When the seller signifies his intention that a right of property, that is, not a mere *jus ad rem* but a strict *jus in re* (cf. § 572) shall pass at once and the buyer assents, then by Natural Law the contract of sale exists. It makes no difference whether the goods are sold for cash or credit; to be delivered immediately or at a future date; whether they are yet to be measured, weighed, or set apart; whether the seller has yet to complete them or further add to their value. These circumstances may be reasons for supposing that ownership has not yet passed hands, but they will not defeat an intention to do so if such an intention exists.

The precise time when ownership passes must be known to determine when the buyer assumes the risk of goods. If they become his while they are still in the possession of the seller and should they perish by chance, they perish to the buyer. If they perish because of the seller's fault he must replace them. The ordinary buyer, however, implicitly understands that they are not his until they are in his possession. In the absence of a specific agreement, positive law must determine the instances wherein seller or buyer shall assume the risk.

607. The main moral issue is: what constitutes a *real quid pro quo*? When do buyer and seller receive their money's worth? To answer this, one must first determine *what a just price is*.

Price must be measured by value received: value in turn depends on a thing's capacity to satisfy needs. This, then, is the fundamental norm: utility or capacity to satisfy human needs or desires. But since the needs of individuals vary so greatly, and since the evaluation they put upon what will satisfy these needs varies even more, how can the utility of a thing be rightly estimated for purposes of common exchange? Sometimes for the common good, positive law makes an appraisal and establishes a *legal price*. If no legally established price exists — in normal circumstances this is usually the case — common estimation is used as the estimate of value. It is the agreement of those who constantly buy or sell a given article in a given area. This estimate is computed upon a basis of the amount of demand for a thing — demand depending on utility — and the supply available. Upon this common estimation the *market price* usually is founded. However, market prices are subject to unjust manipulation, as occurs when a commodity is monopolized and an artificial scarcity created for the sole purpose of raising prices for extortionate gain.

608. This *conventional price,* based upon common estimation, may be somewhat elastic varying within a given margin so that we distinguish between a maximum price and a minimum price. To be just, the actual price of things so evaluated must fall within these limits.

This principle of justice is clearly set forth by St. Thomas: "Now a transaction designed for the common advantage of both, should not bear harder upon the one party than upon the other; and therefore the contract should proceed on the principle of equality of thing to thing. Now the quantity of a thing that serves human use is measured according to the price given for it; for which purpose we have the invention of money. And therefore, if either the price exceeds the quantity of the value of the thing, or conversely the thing exceeds the price, the equality of justice will be destroyed. And therefore to sell a thing dearer or buy it cheaper than it is worth, is a proceeding in itself unjust and unlawful."[11] Ordinarily the seller may not sell above the maximum conventional price, nor the buyer pay less than the minimum price.

609. Are there any circumstances modifying this general rule? It is contended that the *special affection* which the seller has for the article justifies him in demanding more than the maximum price. If the total charge does not exceed the true use-value of the thing to the seller, he is justified in asking more than the maximum price on the basis of recompense for the special loss he suffers in parting with the article. Again, it is argued that when some special benefit will befall the buyer, either because of his crying need of it or the exceptionally profitable use he can put it to, the seller is justified in demanding more than the maximum price. This problem involves a principle of justice of cardinal importance in commercial transactions. Every *increase of goods,* to be just, must rest on a good title, that is, a reason valid in justice. In this case, when the seller receives the maximum price he has received the commutative worth of his goods. Anything above that price is a pure increment. What would constitute a title to that increment? The need and desire of the buyer, it is answered. But these do not belong to the seller: one cannot make profit from that

---

[11] *Sum. Theol.,* II–II, 77, 1.

which belongs to another. To do so is profiteering. But it is argued that unless the buyer pays more than the maximum price, he is getting something for which he does not pay. Certainly he receives an especial benefit, but *this is not at the expense of the seller*. Therefore in justice he owes the seller no more than the maximum price. However, since he has benefited especially, he may spontaneously offer the seller a special recompense. This he does not owe in justice but he may in gratitude. Finally, when a seller of his own accord seeks out a buyer to dispose of an article immediately, a buyer is justified in giving less than the minimum price. In this instance, the buyer may be suffering a loss by accepting what is not so useful to himself as a favor to the seller. Hence according to common estimation goods so offered lose some of their commutative value.

A just price for goods such as rare and curious articles for which no legal or conventional price exists is a price which the contracting parties arrive at without deceit or undue pressure.

610. *Obligation of the buyer.* In general, the buyer may not pay less than the minimum price. Moreover, he is to pay the price agreed upon at the time and place which agreement or custom determines. In an absolute auction a just price is the highest offer made before the fall of the hammer.

Obligation of the seller. The seller may not charge more than the maximum price, and he should manifest defects. There is a difference between substantial defects and accidental defects.

1. *Substantial defects* render the articles useless for the purpose of the buyer. A doped horse would be an example. To conceal a substantial defect is to induce substantial error, which renders the contract void.

2. *Accidental defects* make the article less suitable for the purpose of the buyer. If the defect is obvious, the seller is not obliged to make reference to it; if it is hidden and inquiry is made, the seller must reveal it or abate his price proportionately. Concealment of hidden defects is just reason for rescinding a contract. The axiom of civil law — *caveat emptor* — means that the buyer is expected to notice such qualities of goods to be purchased as are reasonably supposed to be within reach of his observation and judgment; should he fail to do so, the law affords him no relief.

611. *Monopoly* is the exclusive power to sell a given commodity or service. Such exclusive control enables the controller of the monopoly to set prices. Two types of monopoly may be distinguished, natural monopoly and social monopoly.

a) *Natural monopoly* owes its existence to the peculiar nature of the marketable commodity. Examples of natural monopoly are things found only in one place, such as helium which is found only in Texas or platinum which is found exclusively in Russia; things made by a secret process, such as chartreuse; a business which demands a single control, such as a telephone system.

b) *Social monopoly* results either from the law of the State (legal monopoly) or from toleration. Thus tobacco in certain countries is sold by the State alone. A copyright or patent gives the author or inventor exclusive rights to the fruits of his work. Manufacturers may give up free competition and settle among themselves the quantity of goods to be produced and the prices to be charged. In many instances labor unions control the supply of workmen.

612. *Are monopolies lawful?* They are lawful when they advance the common good. Monopolies sometimes are necessary to build up a needed industry; to secure to the individual the legitimate fruits of his industry; to restrain immoderate and harmful production which wastes a nation's resources; to produce needed revenue.

613. *The dangers of monopoly.* State monopolies are usually set up and carried on for the common good. The State, however, may not set up so many public monopolies as would result in the practical abolition of private enterprise. This would be unjust, because it would deprive individuals of a fair opportunity to exercise their natural and legitimate initiative and thus reap the rewards of foresight, skill, and prudent management which the Natural Law provides. That the smothering of private enterprise militates against the common good is clear from our refutation of socialism and communism.

In private monopolies opportunities arise for avaricious gain because of the facility with which unjust prices may be charged. The just price here is what the price would be if there were no monopoly. To charge more than the maximum just price violates commutative justice and calls for restitution. To charge the maximum just price is not unjust; but when this is done in the sale of the necessaries of life, charity is violated because the poor are prevented from buying more cheaply. It is inequitable that the seller alone should set the price; the buyer also should have a say in determining the exchange value of commodities. The ordinary careful citizen is usually the best judge of what goods should cost the public.

The chief way in which great wealth has been concentrated into a few hands has been through monopolies wherein the savings effected by the efficiency of huge organizations have not been shared with the producers of raw materials, employees, and consumers. Incidental to the establishment and maintenance of monopolies, many other moral evils concur such as the ruin of competitors, political corruption, and bribery. Cornering the market with the result that prices violently change and many innocent people are ruined is an abomination of injustice. The sole purpose of such a maneuver is to make enormous profits as quickly as possible. The State should suppress this practice with a heavy hand. Since it is so difficult for any group to resist the temptation to exploit and abuse economic power, the State must regulate firmly and impartially all forms of monopoly.

C. Aleatory Contracts

614. An aleatory contract is a contract of chance, that is, its effects, both advantages or losses, depend on an uncertain event. Thus, I pay you fifteen dollars a year upon the understanding that you will pay my hospital expenses if I should fall seriously ill during that time. Two things are necessary to preserve the rights of both parties in an aleatory contract. First, the event on which the contract hinges must be equally uncertain to both parties. Hence it is wrong to enter such a contract and render the uncertain event certain, as when having insured his store against fire, a person sets it on fire. It is also wrong if a person enters the contract with certain knowledge of the outcome while the other party does not possess this knowledge, as is the case when one bets on a fixed horse race. The essential note of this contract — uncertainty of an event — has been destroyed. The second requisite is that the price paid be in proportion to the outcome hoped for, feared, or risked. There are four types of aleatory contracts: insurance, gaming, betting, and lottery.

615. 1. *Insurance.* Insurance is a contract whereby one party — the insured — pays a determined amount of money to another who agrees to compensate him or his beneficiary if some specified loss or detriment should happen to him. The insured is sometimes called the assured; the insurer is called the underwriter; the consideration or

money paid by the insured, the premium; the written contract, the policy; the right or interest to be protected, the insurable interest. Civil law holds that the insured must have a pecuniary interest in the event which is the object of insurance; otherwise there is no contract of insurance but one of wager. In life insurance the uncertain event is not the fact but the time of death.

The chief obstacle to justice on the part of the insurer is fraudulent concealment. This occurs when he ostensibly offers an attractive benefit in one part of the contract which is canceled in another. The chief obstacle to justice on the part of the insured is concealment of material facts. False, even innocent misrepresentation of substantial facts voids the contract. A person who receives a policy by the suppression of material facts is guilty of fraud and if insurance money is paid, restitution is absolutely necessary. If the facts concealed are such that the company would not have insured the person, all the money received must be returned less the premiums, and the company must also be paid for the maintenance of the policy. If the company would have taken the insurance but at a higher premium, the difference must be paid.

616. 2. *Gaming* is a contract wherein the rivals in a game of skill or chance agree to pay the winner a certain prize. According to the Natural Law this is a valid contract but positive law often forbids it as the occasion of many evils. Gambling, therefore, is morally permissible provided these three conditions exist: (1) The stakes belong to one and may not be required for the satisfaction of other obligations. If one genuinely risks stolen money, the winnings belong to the owner of that money. (2) There is no cheating. The rules and customs of the game distinguish cheating from legitimate deception. It is not necessary that all contestants be equally skillful, although a sense of fair play will induce the more skillful to grant odds or handicaps, which, of course, may be waived by the less skillful. (3) The constant practice does not induce bad habits such as excessive drinking, stealing, and neglect of duties.

617. 3. *Betting* is a contract wherein persons disputing the truth of a given fact or future event agree to give a reward to whoever conjectures the truth. The same principles obtain here as in gaming. The essential note of an aleatory contract — uncertainty of event — forbids one to make a bet with certain knowledge of the outcome.

However, one may take wagers as a gift if others insist on betting with him despite his protestation of knowledge.

618. 4. *Lottery* is a contract whereby out of many depositing a price, some are chosen by lot to receive a prize. One does not pay for the prize but for a reasonable chance of drawing the prize. Fraud in the selection of the prize winners invalidates the contract.

619. To many Evangelicals, gambling, betting, and lottery are sinful in themselves. This view is incorrect: each is a valid contract, and the use thereof may be legitimate recreation. However, these things are easily abused and may become an incitement to sin. They can become an absorbing passion, foster cupidity, and among the ignorant encourage magic and superstition. Witness the close connection between dream books and the number's racket. It is practically impossible that a man make his living by gambling and remain honest.

Some "hold that where the civil law forbids betting, etc., the loser can in conscience refuse to pay."[12] This contradicts man's sense of natural justice and is deservedly reprobated as welshing. If it is certain that a winner under these circumstances may keep his winnings until a court deprives him of them, why is it not equally certain that the loser pay until a court frees him of the obligation?

---

[12] Edwin F. Healy, S.J., *Moral Guidance*, p. 237. Chicago, Loyola University Press, 1942.

READINGS

St. Thomas, *Summa Theologica*, II–II, 32, 7; 77–78.

Bouvier's Law Dictionary, articles on contract, consideration, contractual obligation, sale, parties, agreement, price.

Brown, Ray A., *Law of Personal Property*, pp. 201–224. Chicago, Callaghan, 1936.

Cahill, E., S.J., *The Framework of the Christian State*, pp. 42–51. Dublin, Gill, 1932.

Carriere, Joseph, S.S., *De Contractibus*, 3 vols. Paris, Mèquignon and Leroux, 1844–1847.

Catholic Encyclopedia, "Betting," II, 539; "Contract," IV, 332; "Gambling," VI, 375; "Interest," VIII, 77; "Lottery," IX, 366; "Monopoly," X, 497.

Cathrein, Victor, S.J., *Philosophia Moralis*, pp. 334–349. Friburgi Brisgoviae, Herder, 1915, 10 ed.

Clark, Wm. L., Jr., *Law of Contracts*, pp. 1–61, 147–166, 264–278. St. Paul, West, 1931, 4 ed. by Throckmorton and Brightman.

Coppens, Charles, S.J., *Moral Philosophy*, pp. 112–120. New York, Schwartz, Kirwin, Fauss, 1924.

Corpus Juris, "Depositaries," Vol. 18, pp. 560–597; "Gaming," Vol. 27, pp. 961–1106; "Loan," Vol. 38, pp. 125–128; "Monopoly," Vol. 41, pp. 76–210.

Corpus Juris Secundum, Vol. 17, "Contracts," p. 292 ff.

Cronin, Michael, *The Science of Ethics*, Vol. II, pp. 298–353. Dublin, Gill, 1909.

Davis, Henry, S.J., *Moral and Pastoral Theology*, Vol. II, pp. 323–379. New York, Sheed and Ward, 1936.

DeLugo, *De Justitia et Jure*, DD, 18–23.

Holland, Thomas, *Jurisprudence*, pp. 257–322. Oxford, Clarendon, 1937, 13 ed.

Leibell, J. F., ed., *Readings in Ethics*, pp. 565–582. Chicago, Loyola University Press, 1926.

Restatement of the Law of Contracts, edited by The American Law Institute. St. Paul, 1932.

Vermeersch, A., S.J., *De Justitia*, pp. 363–419. Bruges, Beyaert, 1904.

CHAPTER XX

NONJURIDICAL OBLIGATIONS

620. The first way in which we observe the general precept of loving our fellow man is by being just to him. We have seen what in the main commutative justice exacts of us; the demands of distributive and social justice are presented in social ethics. Justice is the first bond that unites men: where it is lacking, their relationship is simply brutal. But justice is only a beginning of truly human order between man and man. The good man must seek the fullness of human life and the full flowering of human intercourse. To do this he must practice many virtues other than justice. These virtues we now classify in two groups: truthfulness and charity.

I. TRUTHFULNESS

621. Since men can live together in a human way only by the interchange of ideas, reason demands that the ideas exchanged be what they purport to be, namely, representations of reality, the truth. Hence man has the obligation of dealing truthfully and sincerely with his fellows. This duty is partly affirmative, partly negative. On the positive side, justice demands that we reveal to one about to enter a contract with us all that he needs to know from us for an essential understanding of the agreement. Piety demands that parents instruct their children in the moral law. Charity may require that we warn a neighbor against impending injury, about the scandalous effects of his conduct, and the like. Since there is a time for speaking and a time for keeping silent, prudence must dictate when and how much of the truth we tell our fellow man.

We are here chiefly concerned with the negative aspect of this duty which demands that we do not say what is not true. This is lying — one of the commonest of human failings. As Falstaff expressed it,

"How this world is given to lying."[1] Everybody has the general notion that lying is wrong yet extremely knotty problems arise concerning it. We may attempt to solve these problems by a scientific treatment of lying, mental restriction, and the safeguarding of secrets. To this we append a note on the positive virtue of fidelity.

A. Lying

622. Truth is a relation of conformity which may be threefold:

1. *Ontological truth* is the conformity of the object to the mind. Thus we say, "He is a true scholar or soldier," meaning that he conforms to the normally accepted idea of a scholar or soldier. Every created being, actual or possible, possesses ontological truth — that is, it has some measure of reality — and is what it is, because it conforms to the Divine Mind, which is the exemplary idea or pattern of all things. Ontological truth is simply reality knowable.

2. *Logical truth* is the conformity of the mind with the object. The mind possesses truth when it has some measure of contact with reality. This the mind has when it represents to itself the object known, as that object is.

3. *Moral truth* is conformity between one's outward expression and one's inward thought. This is the kind of truth demanded by the virtue of veracity and which is denied by lying.

623. *What is a lie?* There is disagreement about the definition of a lie. The main reason is that different moralists in different ways solve the difficulty of reconciling the concealment of truth with the general doctrine on lying and desire that their definition be consistent with the solution they offer.

Following the footsteps of Grotius[2] and Pufendorf,[3] some writers distinguish between a lie and a falsehood, contending that the former is always wrong and that the latter may sometimes be allowed. They define a lie as the denial of truth which is due and add that its malice consists in the violation of the hearer's right to the truth. If, however, the hearer — a prospective robber or murderer — has no right to the truth, or if the hearer expressly or tacitly waives his right to receive the truth, or if his right is in conflict with the stronger right of the

---

[1] *Henry IV*, Part 1, Act. V, Sc. 4.

[2] See *Hugonis Grotii Operum Theologicorum*, Tomus Secundus, pp. 466–467. Basileae, 1732.

[3] See Samuelis Pufendorfii, *De Officio Hominis et Civis*, Lib. I., Chap. X, § 8, p. 65. Cantabrigiae, 1682.

speaker to conceal the truth, then the hearer's right to the truth is suspended and one may say to him what is not true. But such a falsehood is not a lie.

624. This definition of a lie is not acceptable because: 1. If the right of the hearer is one of commutative justice, every time one told a simple lie he would be bound to restitution, that is, he would have to go back and tell the truth to the person to whom he had lied even in matters of small consequence.

2. If right is meant in the broader sense as that which is due to one from any source, then whoever has dominion over another's right could freely lie to him, as a parent to a child, the State to its citizens, God to His creatures. Undoubtedly no man has any kind of rights before God. Therefore, God could tell all manner of falsities to men without violating any right that they possess.

625. We see no reason to depart from the classic definition of St. Thomas that a lie is speech contrary to one's mind.[4] The abandonment of that definition has ever been attended with serious consequences to the virtue of veracity. Witness our own times. A lie, then, is the outward signification of what one thinks to be false or promising what one has no intention of doing. A statement or outward sign may be false in two ways: (*a*) *materially* when it differs from the objective truth without the knowledge of the speaker. Whoever speaks thus is not said to lie but to be mistaken; (*b*) *formally* when it is a deliberately intended misrepresentation of the speaker's mind. This is the lie. Objectively, one's speech may conform to reality; but if the speaker's judgment of this reality is erroneous, he can lie by saying what is true.

626. The full meaning of St. Thomas is best clarified by an analysis of speech. *Speech* is the uttering of words or the use of signs to another person capable of understanding us in order outwardly to express judgments. The purpose of serious speech is the revelation of judgments. Hence, excluded from the category of lies are all jokes which obviously are not to be taken seriously; also the singing of songs or telling of stories since the words do not represent serious judgments but rather figments of the imagination.

627. Speech is uttered *to another,* for it is the natural medium for the exchanging of ideas among men. Hence soliloquy, or talking to

---

[4] *Sum. Theol.*, II–II, 110, 1.

oneself, is excluded from this consideration. A soliloquy is necessarily conformed to the mind of the speaker. However, it may possibly be said that a man may lie to himself in soliloquizing, as follows: a man meets with a severe reverse or receives very disturbing news. He does not wish this to be so. Hence under pressure of his will he deliberately forms a judgment contrary to the truth and utters it to himself, hoping thereby to solace himself and forget the distressing fact. Such an unusual use of words is mere wishing aloud, and does not fall under our definition of speech.

628. The one to whom a person speaks must be capable of grasping what is said. Therefore, no one would say a man was lying when he talked to his dog or his horse or to a child totally incapable of understanding him. In such instances no communication of truth or falsity is possible. It would be incorrect to conclude, however, that children may be told anything one pleases. Certainly harmful truth may be withheld from children, but not by lying. They may not be told falsehoods which from the force of one's words they will rightly take to be true. A child can distinguish between fable and fact. When we purport to tell him things "for real" he does not expect a fairy tale. An example in point is the Santa Claus legend. We obtrude the story upon his belief, insisting that we are not weaving tales and commanding his acceptance — it is nothing but lying. One's intent is innocent enough, but this a fair example of the end justifying the means. This conclusion will seem preposterous to most people. It will be said that we are so used to this story; our own mothers told it to us, it is surrounded by an aura of the happiest recollections. Yet it is speech contrary to one's mind. God has never and cannot so act toward man, deluding him into accepting fiction for fact. It is a wrong way to discipline young minds — eliciting good behavior by falsehood. The motive of the good should only be the true. Because of this experience, it is difficult for the young to avoid the implicit conclusion that a lie in a good cause is perfectly legitimate. For some, the awakening is a cruel disillusionment; they cannot but be wary thereafter of the things that are told them by those whose word should be sacred.

629. *Does the intention to deceive enter into the essence of a lie?* St. Thomas says that deception pertains rather to the perfection than the essence of a lie.[5] The malice of a lie can be present where there

---

[5] *Ibid.*

is no intention to deceive. While in most instances the liar intends to deceive, yet one can and sometimes does proceed to lie even though he is aware that he is deceiving nobody. To save face, a superior may persist in denying a certain mistake, although everyone knows he made it and he is aware that everyone knows it. Masters in divorce cases know that petitioners are lying, and the petitioners lie despite the fact that they are aware of this.

630. *The malice of lying.* Why is lying wrong? Is it always and everywhere wrong?

THESIS XLIII. Lying is both extrinsically and intrinsically evil.

PROOF OF PART I

631. *Lying is extrinsically evil* in that it begets consequences inimical to social intercourse: it has bad effects on social life. Evidently it is destructive of mutual trust and good fellowship. The proper conduct of human society would be impossible if men generally were permitted to lie.

This proves that generally speaking lying is wrong. But as Milton asks, "If all killing be not murder, nor all taking from another stealing, why must all untruths be lies?"[6] Plato would have answered that a judicious lie is occasionally justifiable, for example, in dealing with enemies, to keep a friend in a fit of madness from hurting himself.[7] He allows the State to lie for the public good,[8] the legislator to lie to the young.[9] Perhaps the majority of mankind would agree with Plato. Our position, however, is that lying is wrong by its very nature, always and everywhere, without exception. Not even God may lie. Whatever God makes must be like unto Him. Whatever He does must mirror His perfections. Whenever He speaks His spoken word must correspond to His inward thought. Otherwise God would not be true to Himself. He would depart from Himself and so violate His own sanctity. This Plato admits,[10] at least to the extent that God does not need to lie. God cannot lie. As man is the intelligent image of God, the same rule of action holds for him.

---

[6] Cited by Rickaby, *Political and Moral Essays*, p. 215. New York, Benziger, 1902.
[7] *Republic*, II, 382.
[8] *Ibid.*, III, 389.
[9] *The Laws*, II, 663.
[10] *Republic*, II, 382.

PROOF OF PART II

632. *Lying is intrinsically evil* because it is wrong to use a faculty in such a way as to frustrate the natural end for which it exists. Evil is the privation of a good which should be present. No good is more fitting a faculty than the end for which nature destines it. Hence any act of a faculty which renders impossible the end for which the faculty is intended must be an evil act. In itself it is the privation of good that should be present.

Lying is an abuse of the speech faculty which renders the attainment of its natural end impossible. This end is the communication of ideas and judgments, as is clear from observation, analysis, and the common understanding of men. Remove that understanding, and speech would have no function either to convey information or to deceive. Deception by speech is possible solely because of the common understanding that speech is to convey thought.

633. *The seriousness of lying.* The inherent malice of lying is venial. Though it is an abuse of a faculty, it does not result in a grave disturbance of the order of nature. Speech has as its purpose social use, and if by a lie the hearer were deprived of some necessary truth, and that irreparably, such a result would be a grave deordination. Lying becomes a grave wrong when to the offense against veracity there is superadded a grave offense against some other virtue such as religion or justice, for example, a lie under oath or a lying attack upon another's character.

Lying is not therefore a small thing. The evil of lying is demonstrated by the shame we experience on being caught in a lie. To be called a liar is a fighting matter.

Lying is linked with most of the capital sins. One lie begets many more which are required to cover up the first. Men lie from cowardice, because they are afraid to take the consequences of wrongdoing. Injustices are covered over by high sounding words: murder is liquidation, inhuman tyranny is Bolshevic firmness. Men lie, from small-minded envy, imagining that another's good is something taken from themselves. Pride and wrongful self-exaltation prompt many a boastful lie. Lust and lying go hand in hand.

Occasional lying may develop into habitual lying. This vice may easily be contracted, especially by children who find it a ready escape from punishment, for no parents wish to think their children liars. As one grows older, lying may achieve for him an undeserved importance. For a time fabrications set the liar above the less imaginative. Finally, the unadorned truth becomes insipid to the hardened liar, and having lost sight of the distinction between the true and the false, he lives in a dream world and believes all he says. But the result is inevitably the same: the liar is found out and justly merits contempt, disdain, and distrust. What a terrible indictment of one's moral worth to have it said, "That man is an awful liar."

On the other hand, a conscientious regard for the truth is stern, uplifting, moral discipline. It is difficult, but it is a sure road to strength of will and self-mastery. Truthfulness is more than a fair indication that one practices the other virtues. There is a moral splendor in veracity which sets the truthful man apart — he is dependable. Discerning women rightly say, "I want a sincere man for my husband."

Truthfulness is not synonomous with indiscreet frankness. There are semi-idiots who boast, "I always say what I think." Such persons are usually troublemakers. Solomon judiciously observes that there is a "time to keep silence and a time to speak."[11]

B. Mental Restriction

634. For self-protection some defense from injurious revelation of the truth is required. Silence is not always the best defense, for it may be quite revelatory. How, then, can one give an answer and at the same time conceal the truth without moral fault? Those who follow Grotius say that this may be accomplished by telling a falsehood which, they claim, is not a lie. Cardinal Newman, to whom all equivocation is anathema, obliquely admits there may be extreme occasions when a lie is allowable.[12] From our preceding contention, all speech contrary to the mind is evil and never permissible. But is there not some sort of speech which is not contrary to the mind and yet protects a secret? We must further investigate the nature of speech.

635. Certainly it is not an offense against veracity to use evasive speech whereby one does not answer the question asked but proffers some irrelevant truth so that the questioner is distracted from what he is seeking. Such speech, however, is the refuge of the quick witted.

The same articulate sounds in the same language sometimes signify very different things. Hence the same group of words may convey two meanings — one intended by the speaker, the other gathered by

---

[11] Ecclesiastes 3:7.
[12] *Apologia Pro Vita Sua*, p. 360. London, Longmans Green, 1918.

the hearer. This is ambiguous speech. No one may deny that words derive their power of expressing thought not only from the literal signification assigned them but also from the circumstances in which they are used. As the written word's meaning is judged not only from the text but also the context, so too the spoken word. Thus a butcher has put away his last pound of steak for his own supper. Asked by a customer, "Have you any steak?" he answers: "No." And truthfully, for in the circumstances the question means, "Have you any steak *for sale?*" Upon these observable facts of linguistics rests the doctrine of mental restriction.

636. Mental restriction is an act of the mind delimiting the meaning of one's expression to some particular meaning chosen by the speaker. Such a meaning may or may not objectively be contained in the expression. Hence we speak of pure and broad mental restriction.

1. In *pure mental restriction* the speaker delimits the significance of his expression to a particular meaning but gives no outward clue to the same. As an outward expression it fails completely to represent the speaker's mind. It is a lie, for neither the words nor signs of themselves nor the circumstances in which they are used in any way convey the speaker's thought. Thus John has just slapped his younger brother who cries. Their mother asks, "John, did you hit him?" John says, "No," meaning to himself that he did not slap him yesterday.

2. In *broad mental restriction* the speaker delimits the obvious meaning of his expression to one particular meaning chosen by himself and yet *gives some objective clue to his meaning.* He utters words which have more than one meaning: one of these meanings corresponds to his thought; by another and more obvious meaning he endeavors to conceal his thought. Hence broad mental restriction differs from a pure mental restriction in this: in the latter the speaker's meaning exists *only* in his mind; in the former it exists also in the *speaker's expression.*

637. The most obvious form of the broad mental reservation is the use of language which literally bears several meanings, such as Abraham employed when going into Egypt he called his wife his sister. He used a Semitic word which meant both sister and female relative. He did not depart from the truth when he referred to his wife as a female relative.

But not all the meanings expressed by language are purely literal. As indicated above, contexts and circumstances can point, shade, and add new meanings to words. Thus, when John Nepomucene was

asked by the Duke of Bohemia if the Duchess had sacramentally con-
fessed to him the sin of adultery, even if she had, Nepomucene could
truly answer, "I don't know" or simply, "No." The circumstances of
his priesthood qualify his answer so that it objectively means, "I have
no communicable knowledge on this matter." So too, lawyers, doctors,
nurses, diplomats, or public officials may reply in a similar manner
when questioned by busybodies concerning a matter which falls
within the ambit of professional secrecy. A sensible listener can correctly
interpret such denials to mean that the speaker has no information to
be disclosed. Or if one who is notoriously bad pay were to ask a person
for the loan of a considerable sum, he could truthfully answer, "I
haven't got it." Truthfully, because the circumstances under which the
request was made clearly indicate that the reply means, "I have no
money to lend you." Similarly, if someone attempts to wring a natural
secret from another, the latter may answer with a flat denial. Thus,
if a person were to ask, "Didn't I hear your father choking your
mother last night?" one could answer, "Of course, you didn't." Such
denials uttered in these circumstances simply mean, "This is none
of your business."

638. Denials of this kind in other circumstances, as when the questioner has a right to ask the question, would be lies. However, these
denials are not lies when context alters their meaning. The following
are conditions which alter meaning: the speaker is safeguarding a
legitimate secret; the questioner has no right to the information he is
seeking. If the hearer is a sensible, prudent, and perspicacious person,
he will be aware of these circumstances and will correctly interpret the
speaker to mean that he does not want to tell him anything. Even
though the hearer is not capable of grasping the real meaning, the
objective situation remains unchanged. The speaker's statement still
bears a truth and imparts meaning; and although the hearer mis-
understands the meaning and is thereby deceived, this fact does not
nullify the speaker's right to his secret nor render him guilty of lying.
Even the intention to put off and deceive his hearer is not wrong,
because not every intention to deceive is morally evil. It is allowable
for a sufficient reason.

639. Constant indiscriminate use of mental reservations, however,
is forbidden for two reasons. First, the individual who indulges in
this practice constantly can easily lose his regard for sincerity and
truth and become a liar. Second, if it were allowable upon all occa-

sions, the mutual trust requisite in society would be destroyed. Hence mental restriction is an extraordinary measure which may be used only in the crisis in which some truly legitimate secret is at stake. A justifying secret is not any trifling matter; the term applies solely to those things which one reasonably fears would cause serious harm or offense if revealed. When dealing with persons from whom the information in question may not be withheld, mental restriction may not be used. Thus, mental restriction may not be used by a minor being corrected by its parents, the parties to an onerous contract, a person who is being interrogated by a judge or superior within the due limits of his authority.

640. *Mental restriction under oath.* Even in a court of law one may have an important secret to protect. One's right to guard a secret is not nullified in our American courts by the formula of the oath, "to tell the truth, the whole truth, and nothing but the truth." The reason is that this formula must be understood in the light of this natural limitation, "in so far as the law obliges me to reveal the truth." Hence a defendant at least may use a reservation to avoid convicting himself, for no one is obliged to give evidence against himself.

THESIS XLIV. A broad mental reservation is not a lie yet its unrestricted use is immoral. However, for a sufficiently grave reason it is allowable.

PROOF OF PART I

641. *A broad mental reservation is not a lie,* because it objectively represents the mind of the speaker. A restrictive statement which in nowise represents the speaker's mind is purely a mental restriction, a lie. In a broad mental restriction either the words literally, though ambiguously, contain the speaker's thought, or the words receive, from the circumstances in which they are uttered, a true reflection of the speaker's mind and as such can be understood by the discreet hearer.

PROOF OF PART II

642. *The unrestricted use of a broad mental reservation is immoral.* This was proved in § 639.

PROOF OF PART III

643. *A broad mental reservation used for a grave reason is allowable,* because it is not evil either from its object, its end, or its circumstances.

1. *From its object.* It is not speech contrary to one's mind.

2. *From its end.* The end is to conceal the truth. This can be sometimes not merely morally licit but even mandatory, for the good of an individual or of society may demand that certain secrets be kept.

3. *From circumstances.*

a) The natural evil consequences, destruction of mutual trust, is avoided because wholesale use of such restrictions is not permitted but only that restriction necessary to guard a legitimate secret.

b) The evil which actually is permitted, namely error in the listener's mind, is not a moral evil for it is not the deprivation of necessary truth but the mere absence of the information to which the hearer has no right.

644. N.B. I. Some say that words which appear to be untruthful are a legitimate self-defense against unjust verbal aggression. In other circumstances these words would be lies, but in legitimate defense they are not lies but acts of self-defense in which the deception of the hearer is not intended but merely permitted.

This is an inadequate explanation. According to that plea one might fabricate all sorts of stories in self-defense. Only those words constitute legitimate self-defense which taken with the circumstances in which they are uttered can objectively represent the speaker's mind.

645. N.B. II. Mental restriction, like probabilism, may be abused. Many so-called broad mental reservations are nothing other than downright lies. But this fact is no argument against legitimate broad mental reservation. Everyday life testifies to its existence. Of course, if one cannot conceive that it is sometimes permissible to permit another man to deceive himself, that words may sometimes be used ambiguously, that words can take on added meaning from the circumstances in which they are used, this doctrine is not for him. This is often the case with the young or unlettered who confuse a broad mental reservation with lying. If, finally, persons do not solve every sort of doubt concerning truth and veracity, let us remember that when Pilate asked Christ what truth is, he received no answer.[13] Truth, like reality, may long evade the mind's quest of it.

C. Secrets

646. A secret is a truth which a man has a right or an obligation to keep hidden. That the Natural Law may grant such a right is evident from the fact that concealment of the truth is sometimes

---

[13] John 18:38.

necessary to preserve the life, dignity, and independence of the individual. The nature of human intercourse sometimes obliges secrecy; if it did not, mutual trust would fail among men.

647. 1. *Kinds of secrets.*

a) A *natural secret* involves obligation which arises immediately from the Natural Law without convention or agreement, and its preservation is demanded by the nature of human fellowship and intercourse. The object of such natural secrecy is anyone's private affairs the revelation of which would *reasonably* cause offense or injury. Examples of the breach of natural secrets would be the revelation that a respectable neighbor, a dependable family head, had once been in the penitentiary or that a respected woman is a secret drinker.

b) A *secret of promise* involves obligation arising from the free promise of secrecy which one makes *after* learning another's secret. For example, a friend pours out his private griefs and the listener assures him that he will say nothing to anyone.

c) A *secret of trust* involves obligation arising from a pact made *before* the communication of the secret and is so accepted by the hearer. This pact may be explicit when a person says, as "I will tell you this provided you will keep it absolutely to yourself," or it may be implicit as when one consults a priest, lawyer, or other professional person.

648. 2. *Obligation of secrets.* Binding all men is the general obligation not to (*a*) pry into another's secrets as by eavesdropping, reading another's personal letters, diaries, and the like, purloining invention plans, administering a drug to a person to obtain hidden knowledge; (*b*) use secret knowledge unjustly obtained; (*c*) reveal secrets.

Concerning the first, one may read another's letters if one may reasonably presume the permission of its owner or if it is necessary to prevent a grave injustice. Those who have dominative authority may do so for the correction of those in their charge. Those who have jurisdictional authority may do so for the protection of the State. The State may drug a suspect in order to discover information essential to its protection, but it may not use information so obtained to convict him of crime.

A word of amplification is also necessary concerning the maintenance of the three types of secrets:

a) Since the *natural secret* arises immediately from the Natural Law, it binds under penalty of grave wrong when the subject matter is of serious import. If revelation causes damage or injury, justice is violated;

if embarrassment only, chagrin or offense results, charity alone is violated.

b) A *secret of promise,* which is not also a natural secret, binds in virtue of fidelity, the quality and gravity of the obligation depending on the intention of the one promising.

c) A *secret of trust* binds in justice because of an implied or explicit contract. The binding power of secrets of trust derives also from the common good. For the common good demands that people be able to seek advice and counsel in security.

649. 3. *Revelation of secrets.* The obligation to secrecy ceases *in general* (*a*) when the secret has been disclosed by other sources; (*b*) when one may reasonably presume the consent of the holder of the secret; (*c*) even though the secret is still intact, one may talk about it to another who has the same secret knowledge except, however, if the secret of the confessional is concerned.

a) If the obligation to secrecy binds only by reason of charity, a person is released when secrecy would result in grave *inconvenience* to oneself or the subject of the secret. Charity does not oblige at the cost of equal inconvenience to self. As for the protection of the subject of the secret, one may reasonably presume his consent to speak. *A fortiori* one is released when secrecy would result in injustice.

b) If the obligation to secrecy derives from justice as do all secrets of trust and some natural secrets, one is released only when grave *injury* would result to (1) oneself, (2) the subject of the secret, (3) a third innocent party, (4) the Church or State.

The revelation of professional secrets presents a delicate question. However, it seems clear enough that if *grave injury* would befall any of the above mentioned, the holder of even such a secret *may* disclose it. But *must* he? That depends on whether more good than harm would result. The violation of professional secrets would be detrimental to the common good. People certainly would be deterred from entrusting them to others if they were not held sacred. Still, there may be cases involving life and death, the security of the State, and the like in which a true obligation exists to manifest such a secret. There is one professional secret which may not be revealed under any circumstances — that of the Sacrament of Penance.

c) If one has promised to keep a secret at all costs, and this can be done without injury to another, one is bound to do so even at tremendous personal inconvenience.

650. N.B. Self-discipline is necessary to enable one to live up to his obligations as far as secrets are concerned. First, one must practice it in the matter of minding his own business and not prying into the lives of others. A man who is industriously intent upon his own concerns and the fulfillment of his obligations will have neither the time nor the energy to delve into the private affairs of others. Second, one must practice self-discipline in controlling idle curiosity. The wise man does not run after every passing fire engine nor does he itch for the latest gossip. There are many trifles the knowledge of which profits nothing. And finally, a man must practice it in learning to maintain a discreet silence. One is not equipped to administer efficiently or direct others if he can not bridle his tongue.

D. Fidelity

651. The faithful man constantly and exactly fulfills his obligations. Fidelity is a note of many virtues. Thus, the constant giving of oneself to the service of God is the virtue of devotion. The relation of servant and master requires fidelity and loyalty to the latter. Here, however, fidelity refers to constancy in carrying out promises.

652. A promise is not merely the external expression of a present resolution concerning some future course of conduct. A person who makes a resolution determines to do a given thing. A person who makes a promise determines and binds himself *to another* to act accordingly. Hence a promise is made to another, gives that person a hope of performance, and carries a moral binding force which is a guarantee of execution. This binding force may be the virtue of religion, justice, or fidelity. Thus, when an alcoholic exclaims in the company of others that he will not get drunk again, he gives voice to a resolution; when he gives his wife his word that he will not drink for a year, he makes a promise. A person who does not keep his resolution is inconstant; one who does not live up to his promises is worse — he is unfaithful. A man who outwardly promises what he has no intention of doing is not unfaithful; he is a liar.

653. A promise whose binding force is religion is a vow. As we have seen in the chapter on contracts, a promise can bind in justice whenever the promisor intends to create a true right in the promisee. We deal here with promises which bind only in fidelity. Fidelity is that moral virtue which moves us to take care that our future performances respond to our promises. As veracity demands that our words correspond to our thoughts, so fidelity requires that our deeds correspond to our words. As the good of social life demands that we speak the truth, so it requires fulfillment of promises.

654. There is tribute of moral distinction in the comment, "that man's word is his bond." It manifests a person steadfast in other respects — one on whom others can rely. But its chief praise is due to the fact that the faithful man resists what is so easy to do, namely, exempt oneself from a self-imposed obligation. A person who makes a promise, as it were legislates for himself and the extent and gravity of his obligation depends upon his original intention. It is not commendable — though human enough — to exempt oneself later, to pare down one's obligation. In as much as fulfillment of a promise lies within the control of the one who makes it, the promise-breaker is a paltry man.

The inherent malice of infidelity is that it dashes the hopes of the promisee; however, no right is transgressed. Its consequent evil is that one's promises are no longer trusted.

We are excused from keeping our promises when their fulfillment would constitute an immoral act or would be something notably greater than what we had originally bound ourselves to.

II. CHARITY

655. The apex of human perfection is found in the practice of *charity*. From justice and fair dealing, the good man rises to charity. Charity differs from justice in three ways: (*a*) Justice consists in rendering to another what is his; charity, in giving of one's own to another. (*b*) Justice when violated demands restitution; charity does not — the obligation of charity ceases when the opportunity to practice it has passed. (*c*) Except for the fulfillment of contracts, the obligations of justice are negative; while charity has its negative precepts, its inculcations are primarily positive.

656. *Charity to our fellow man.* Here we shall distinguish three types of love: love of concupiscence, love of benevolence, and charity.

1. *Love of concupiscence* (§ 355) is man's love of his fellow man solely for his own sake. Love of others solely for their usefulness or agreeableness fosters reprehensible selfishness. It is to subordinate them wholly to one's self, to fail to see the man in them. Scarcely any man is so colossally egocentric as to have no other sort of love for at least one or other of his fellows; but because too many regard the vast

majority of those with whom they deal as things to be used, mere means to their pleasure and profit, men miss out on one of the chief values of life.

2. *Love of benevolence* (§§ 355, 510) is a man's love of another person for that person's sake. This entails the procurement of that other's good. The nobler the good procured, the loftier the benevolence.

3. *Charity* is man's love of God, the Supreme Good, for God's own sake. This is our rational tendency to the supremely lovable object. Benevolence for our fellow man becomes charity when we wish and procure for him every good that leads to God. This is the most excellent kind of love: we love him for his own sake and wish him the supreme of goods.

A. The Obligation of Charity

657. We must love God for His own sake (§ 359). We must love ourselves with charity, for we must seek those goods for ourselves that lead us to God. Since our fellow man is likewise destined for God, having the same excellence of nature as ourselves, we must cherish him with the love of charity. We must love ourselves first; then our neighbor. Charity it is said, begins at home, but it must not stay there. It must go out to all men precisely because they are men.

Supernatural charity. Reason is not capable of making known to man the richness of human relations that ought to exist. Natural charity, lofty as it is, but weakly reflects the glory of supernatural charity, known only through revelation. Destined for the immediate vision of God, man is lifted from his natural status by sanctifying grace, which is a real sharing in the very nature of God. Thereby man is divinized, made the adopted son of God, and God comes to the sanctified soul and there dwells as a lover with his beloved. In a true sense God identifies Himself with man, for Christ says, "As long as you did it to one of these My least brethren you did it to Me."[14] Hence we are to love our fellow man not so much for the humanity as the divinity which is his.

What does charity require of us? In a positive way it requires essentially benevolence and friendliness to all men; beneficence to those in need; and, incidentally, gratitude. Negatively it forbids us to scandalize him or co-operate in his evil acts.

658. Charity daily urges in thought, word, and deed. Its obligation

---
[14] Matt. 25:40.

begins with *benevolence* whereby man always wishes his fellow man well, never evil. Our fellow man here means absolutely every man without exception. The same reason — a common humanity — which commands benevolence, commands benevolence to *all*. Hence no matter what a man's color, creed, nation, upbringing, or status, he may not be excluded from our good will.

Too many people forget that there are only accidental differences among men. Upon the level of our common humanity there can be no slaves or supermen, whites or natives. But two things sadly contribute to obscure man's remembrance of his humanity: an assumption of essential superiority or a remembrance of past wrongs either inflicted or endured. False pride of race, class, or family is often responsible for the attitude: "I am not as the rest of men" or the egregious stupidity that "niggers have no souls." It is easy to see how the oppressed will hate the oppressor; but the converse, so tersely put by Tacitus, is also true: "It is human nature to hate him whom we have injured."[15] The unreason of injury strives to find justification by claiming to find odious qualities in the victim.

So universal is this precept that we must love even our enemies. This does not mean we are to love them *qua* enemies, that is because they are injurious — for that would be most unnatural — but because they are men. Certainly we may hate the evil an enemy has wrought us, we may abominate his vicious characteristics, but his person is sacred: as long as a person is alive and is not irremediably confirmed in evil we may not wish him harm. Hence we may not exclude him from the general good will we are to bear all men. We must forgive his injuries to us; but so strong is our love of self, so impelling the inclination to repay evil with evil, that this precept is often the most difficult to observe. We may not be able to wipe out the memory of hideous wrong, but we must not hold a grudge nor seek private vengeance. We must even be ready to offer him the succor of charity if he is in need.

The malicious opposite of benevolence is malevolence, commonly called *hatred*. It is the wishing of evil to another. It is theoretically possible to wish harm to another as a good, that is, as preventing some greater harm, as when I hope John breaks his leg before he can run off with George's wife. But in practice this is dangerous, because man so readily rejoices at the ill fortune of others. Hatred expressed in

---

[15] *Agricola,* c. 42.

words of imprecation is *cursing*. Akin to hatred is *envy,* displeasure with the good fortune of another, which one naïvely interprets as his own loss.

B. Beneficence

659. True charity does not consist of barren good wishes. Love is manifested by deeds, and, unless it is so proved, it dies. Thus benevolence must issue forth in *beneficence* or well-doing. To whom is one obliged to be beneficent? When a similar question was put to Christ, He replied with the parable of the Good Samaritan,[16] thereby indicating nature's law that man must help anyone who is in need.

This general rule may be formulated: man is obliged by charity to supply the needs of another if he can do so without exposing himself to a like difficulty. Man's needs should be supplied because he should have the fullness of well-being. This does not mean that every whim and fancy of an individual is to be catered to but that one have what is reasonably required to live as a good man. When a person cannot supply this himself, he naturally turns to his fellow man: this is one of the basic reasons men live together in society. The obligation to help clearly devolves on one when he alone can offer assistance. However, if assisting another would place one in the same want as his neighbor's, the obligation would cease, because one may seek his own good first. The expression, "bound by charity," means a true obligation which if neglected involves moral wrong. At times charity may not merely suggest what is nice, helpful, and supererogatory; it may, like justice, impose a downright command.

The nature of the obligation of charity may be further clarified by examination of (1) the degree of one's need; (2) the responsibility of the helper; (3) the person who is in need.

660. *Degrees of need.* Three degrees of need may be distinguished:

1. *Extreme need* is spiritual when one is in immediate danger of losing his soul and *has not the means of helping himself.* It is temporal when one is in danger of losing his life or what closely approximates life.

2. *Grave need* is spiritual when one is in serious moral danger and can help himself only with great difficulty. It is temporal when temporal goods of great value such as one's fortune, status, or authority are at stake.

---

[16] Luke 10: 25–37.

3. *Common need* is a situation from which one can extricate himself unaided.

661. *Responsibility.* There is a natural hierarchy of goods: spiritual goods are to be preferred to temporal, the common good to the individual, necessary goods to unessential, one's own good to that of one's neighbor. In the application of the law of charity this rule is primary: *charity does not oblige a man to help his neighbor if doing so involves an equal detriment to himself.* Charity begins at home: it is lawful to prefer one's self. A man is obliged to prefer himself if his *necessary* spiritual good is involved. Thus, one could never risk his own salvation to save another. Nor may one commit the slightest sin to procure any benefit whatever for another. However, a person may, and sometimes should, sacrifice his own spiritual but unessential good to secure the *necessary* temporal or spiritual good of another. He may even have to postpone the fulfillment of a positive precept, as when he omits Sunday Mass to help a person who is desperately ill. As far as purely temporal goods are concerned, one may if he elects prefer his neighbor to himself. Such an act is usually consummate wisdom.

662. *The person in need.* If a person is in extreme spiritual need, any temporal good requisite must be sacrificed to rescue him. Thus even at the risk of death, one should go to an infant who would otherwise surely die without baptism. If a person is in extreme temporal need, he must be helped even at the cost of grave inconvenience. Thus, one would be obliged to pick up the victim of a hit and run driver on a lonely road, although complications with the police would result. If a person is in grave need, he must be helped but not at the cost of grave inconvenience. As for those in common need, general assistance offered from time to time suffices, as when one contributes to the support of the poor in general.

Those who are closest to us should be helped first. The order of preference is as follows: husband or wife, children, parents, blood relatives, friends, benefactors, fellow countrymen, strangers.

C. Friendliness

663. Our fellow man is not always in difficulty; how does charity require that he be treated in normal circumstances? The general answer is — with *friendliness.* Does this mean one must be a friend of all men? Since friendship can be had only with a few, it is impossible to be a friend to all. A friend is another self. There are few things more revolting than fulsome protestations of insincere regard.

There is a level though whereon all men may be said to be friends in the wider sense — the level of our common humanity. That general love which we are bound to have for all should be externalized in respect and graciousness of behavior which is due even the stranger or foreigner.

Just as men could not live in society without truth, so neither can they without the pleasure of social intercourse. As Aristotle says: "No one can spend his days in company which is positively painful or even not pleasant; since to avoid the painful and aim at the pleasurable is one of the most obvious tendencies of human nature."[17]

Therefore a man is bound by natural propriety to be pleasant, human, and agreeable in his dealings with his fellows, "unless," as St. Thomas wisely qualifies, "for some reason it be necessary at times to make others sorrowful to good purpose."[18] Put in the phrase of Newman, a man must always be a gentleman, a person who never *needlessly* gives pain. On this principle every code of etiquette should rest. Genuine good manners are a simple acknowledgment of the dignity of our fellow man.

There is a certain minimum of courtesy and good fellowship due to all men. The closer anyone is bound to me by duty, association, or blood, the greater must be these evidences of fellowship. The nature of human intercourse indicates a level of decency and humanity that must be observed by those who eat at the same table, are partners in the same firm, officers in the same outfit, monks in the same monastery, members of the same family, and so on, under penalty of being seriously at odds with the Natural Law.

D. Gratitude

664. Physics tells us that every material action has an equal and opposite reaction. Charity tells us that a kind act requires reciprocation. The return of good is an act of gratitude consisting in acknowledgment and fitting requital of a favor done. It need not be proved that those who gratuitously do good to others should receive good in return. Though all men perceive the fitness and necessity of gratitude, it is a rare virtue.

---

[17] *Ethics*, VIII, 5, 1157b.
[18] *Sum. Theol.*, II–II, 114, 2.

In a favor done two things are distinguishable: the act of beneficence and the good will prompting it. Good will is sincere — and the benefaction genuine — when it flows from a conviction of humanity, fellowship, or compassion; it is fictitious when it proceeds from a feeling of superiority, a person's looking down upon his fellow man in need. From the latter comes the saying, "Cold as charity." So too the act of gratitude must contain a sentiment of good will toward one's benefactor as well as the external act of requital.

Some people with feelings of superiority dislike being in need of a favor. Hence a favor done them may be an affront to their pride. So far from being well disposed toward their benefactor, they come in time to resent him. Samuel Johnson acridly says: "There are minds so impatient of gratitude that their gratitude is a species of revenge and they return benefits, not because recompense is a pleasure but because obligation is a pain."[19] Such people make haste to repay favors lest they be under obligation to anyone. Of these Seneca says: "If he seeks to pay too quickly, he owes unwillingly; and he who owes unwillingly, is ungrateful."[20]

But every inward acknowledgment of gratitude ought not to involve humiliation. No man is self-sufficient, no man but has a universe of wants. It is virtue to be humble and admit the poverty of our human condition. Without that, no grateful sentiment is possible.

But many people are not so high minded. They are never averse to receiving favors. Their gratitude is really the hope of future favors: it is that mother of flattery and sycophancy, as La Rochefoucauld expressed it: "Gratitude in most men is only a strong and secret hope of greater favors."[21] Robert Walpole is reported to have said: "The gratitude of place expectants is a lively sense of future favors."[22]

The least external requital that gratitude demands is an outward expression of an inward grateful sentiment. The habit of saying "thank you" is a sign of civilization. A salient feature of gratitude is opportuneness, that is, the returning of good when and in a manner in which it coincides with the benefactor's need. The perfection of gratitude means that one repays more than he received. Since the benefactor was gratuitous in giving what he was not obliged to give,

---

[19] *The Rambler*, January 15, 1751.

[20] Quoted by St. Thomas, *Sum. Theol.*, II–II, 106, 4.

[21] Duc de la Rochefoucauld, *Maximes*, No. 298, p. 108. Paris, Froment, 1823.

[22] William Hazlitt in *Wit and Humor*. See his Collected Works, ed. Waller and Glover, Vol. 6, p. 17. London, Dent, 1903.

and since the recipient to be gratuitous also must make a gratuitous recompense, it would seem that his recompense would not be gratuitous unless it exceeded the quantity or quality of the benefit received.

E. Scandal

Besides forbidding hatred, revenge, and envy, charity imposes two especial negative precepts: man may not scandalize his fellow man nor co-operate in his evil.

665. *Nature of scandal.* Many people confuse scandal with detraction — the unjust manifestation of another's sin — or with gossip. Scandal means more than misuse of the tongue.

Scandal derives from the Greek, σκάνδαλον, which means a stumbling block. One becomes a scandal or a moral stumbling block to his neighbor when he unreasonably offers him the occasion of wrongdoing. The law of benevolence obliges man to wish his neighbor every good that conduces to his last end. Since sin alone can deprive him of his final good, it is a violation against benevolence to will that another do evil or even permit him to do so when it could reasonably be prevented. The motive for avoiding scandal is clear enough, but the precise extent of this obligation requires more exact determination.

1. *One Who Gives Scandal*

666. Scandal involves two parties, one who gives scandal and one who receives it.

From the viewpoint of the one who gives scandal, scandal is any word, act, or omission which is likely to induce another to do wrong. Not every act or omission which gives scandal is evil in itself, although such acts generally are. Some innocent acts also may scandalize. Thus the fact that a temperate father keeps a stock of liquor in his home may be a scandal to his weak-willed son. The essence of scandal is inducement or enticement to sin resulting either from the mere placing of an act — such as an older brother's stealing, which results in his younger brother's stealing — or from persuasion, commanding, solicitation, or other similar means designed to lead another into evil.

In the first instance scandal is not the *cause* of another's evil act; it is the occasion. The cause is the other person's free but defective will. In the second instance the scandalizer is a *moral co-cause* or co-operator in the sin.

To be guilty of scandal it is not necessary that another person actually do wrong; one is guilty of scandal if his action constitutes an inducement to sin. Thus there is scandal in unsuccessful solicitation or in an attempt to show pornographic post cards to a young man even though he refuses to look at them.

Scandal presupposes that the will of another has not yet been determined to evil. Hence the very wicked and the one who has already made up his mind to do evil is seldom scandalized. Thus, Jones's failure to attend Sunday Mass is not a scandal to his roommate because he decided the night before that he was not going to Mass. Nor is scandal given to one who would in no way be influenced by example. Thus a cursing father is a scandal to his growing son but not to his pious wife.

667. There are two types of scandal, direct and indirect. In *direct* scandal a person intends the evil action of another. The evil action may be intended for two reasons. First, it may be willed as an end in itself, for example, a person may wish that his neighbor sin precisely because it involves his spiritual ruin or is direct dishonoring of God. Christian virgins have been judicially condemned to brothels; atheism and sexual aberrations have been taught the young with that end in view. This is the nadir of ill will to another and is aptly called *diabolical*. Usually, however, one does not desire the evil action of another as an end in itself, but as something useful or convenient to oneself. Thus one engages in lewd kissing for personal satisfaction, not for the moral harm of another. All direct scandal has a twofold malice. First, it is a violation of charity because by it we fail to render our neighbor the love due him; second, as a direct co-operator, one also assumes the guilt of the evil act of the one scandalized.

668. Scandal is *indirect* when another's evil act is not intended but foreseen as inevitable or likely. Thus, one orders alcoholic refreshments for a party although he knows Uncle George will drink too much. If the scandal-giving action is itself sinful, one is responsible for its foreseen consequences. Thus, a perjured father knows his daughter will imitate his perjury when she makes out her income-tax returns. If scandal is only indirect, one violates charity, but one does not assume the guilt of the sin which the scandalized person commits. This is an important fact, because in a matter of justice the obligation of restitution may not be imposed upon one who gives indirect scandal.

669. If a scandalous action is innocent in itself, the principles governing the voluntary in cause given in §§ 155–158 must be applied. Circumstances may oblige one to omit an innocent act precisely because scandal will follow. Thus, two doctors ought not discuss certain gynecological cases in the hearing of young people who would be venereally excited. To act in circumstances in which scandal is likely to follow, one must have a reason proportionate to the circumstances. The sufficiency of one's reason may be determined by considering (*a*) how certain and how grave the other person's wrong will be; (*b*) how close the connection is between one's act and the other's wrong; (*c*) how grave an inconvenience is involved in the omission of the act.

2. One Who Takes Scandal

670. From the standpoint of the one who takes it, scandal is the evil which one does upon the occasion of the scandal-giving action of another. Since man is amenable to suasion and is naturally prone to imitate the example of those around him, there is a certain level of scandal which is a danger to the ordinarily peccable man. However, there are two classes who have an extraordinary susceptibility to taking scandal. The sin which these commit is either pharisaical scandal or scandal of the weak.

a) *Pharisaical scandal* arises from the malice of one who wrests another's good action to his own hurt by perverse misconstruction. Thus the sight of a young couple departing for innocent recreation occasions evil thoughts and rash judgments in a busybody next door. The term is derived from the fact that the miracles of Christ were the occasion of the Pharisees' sinning against the light. Scandal of this sort should simply be spurned.

b) *Scandal of the weak* is the wrong which one commits through ignorance or frailty upon the occasion of another's good act. Thus, a wife's refusal to co-operate in her husband's sin of contraception makes him curse and swear. A tourist stopping at Havana on a Friday sees his Catholic companions eat meat and does the same, thinking it to be a sin.

671. To what extent one is obliged to avoid the scandal of the weak may be judged from the foregoing (§ 669). If the scandal flows from ignorance, the ignorant party should be instructed. Thus the tourist in Havana should be told that it is lawful to eat meat in a Spanish-speaking country on a Friday. Sometimes, though, instruction is ineffective and the scandal becomes pharisaical.

If a person is particularly weak, special consideration must be given to the problem. However, it is never permissible to do that which is intrinsically wrong to avoid even a greater sin by another. Thus, one could not steal to prevent another from committing adultery. Positive precepts necessary for salvation may never be omitted for the sake of preventing moral evil on the part of another. A wife could not neglect to have her child baptized in order to prevent her husband from blaspheming. Positive precepts not necessary for salvation, even though they bind gravely, *may* but need not be omitted to keep another from serious wrong. A girl could but is not obliged to omit Sunday Mass because her presence there will rouse the passion of a libidinous youth.

F. Co-operation

672. Co-operation is physical activity (or its omission) by which a person assists in the evil act of another who is the principal agent. Moral concurrence in the evil act of another is suasion and the like mentioned in § 666. Co-operation may be formal and material.

673. 1. In *formal* co-operation one intends the evil act of another. The person who co-operates joins the other *in his evil intention,* as when a messenger delivers an insulting note and rejoices in the hurt it causes. Formal co-operation is always wrong for two reasons. It violates charity and takes on the specific guilt of the sin in which one has co-operated.

674. 2. In *material* co-operation one does not join the principal agent in his evil intent but nevertheless assists him by an act not in itself wrong. Thus one student gives notes to another who will use them to cheat in an examination. The general law of morality is that man must avoid evil as far as he can and the specific law of charity bids him to prevent his neighbor from doing wrong to the best of his ability. May a man therefore ever have a nonvoluntary part in another's sin? Generally speaking, he may not, but at times the principle of double effect may be applied. Since the material co-operator does not intend the evil of the principal's act, whenever his own act is good or indifferent and *he has a proportionately grave reason for acting, his co-operation will be licit.*

675. Two things must always be considered. First, it must be determined whether the proposed co-operative act is intrinsically wrong. In making a decision on this point, one must bear in mind that there are simply no circumstances in which the act could be good. As this principle applies to the making of things, the question is not whether the thing made will be put to a bad use but whether it has no good use whatever. There are few such things. When the co-operative act is intrinsically evil, one may never proceed to act, irrespective of one's ostensible intention, irrespective of the pressure brought to bear on one. A person who so acts becomes a formal co-operator because, since the act has one and only one end of work and that evil, one cannot choose to do it without intending its evil end of work. Therefore one is conjoined to the evil intention of the principal agent. Even though he thought it a joke, a shipwrecked sailor could not take an active part in the religious ceremonies of pagans; the spectator of a lynching could not help pull on the rope which draws the victim off the ground even though his doing so is necessary to save himself from lynching.

The second point to be considered is whether the good one seeks by his co-operative act outweighs the evil he allows in his neighbor's bad act. Some may ask whether there can be a justifying reason for permitting moral evil since there is an obligation to prevent it. The obligation of preventing another from doing wrong derives from charity, but charitable obligation does not bind when it is disportionate to the good which will result from it.

676. In judging the sufficiency of one's reason for acting when one's co-operative act is not intrinsically wrong we distinguish three sets of circumstances: (*a*) *Where serious harm would result to Church or State,* material co-operation is never allowed, because private good must yield to the common good. Even to avoid torture or death one could not take even a material part in treason. (*b*) Where an *injustice* would be done to an innocent third party, the sole excusing reason would be threat of *equal damage* to the co-operator. One could not tell a thief where his neighbor has concealed his car unless silence would result in the loss of his own car. (*c*) Where there is no question of the first two sets of circumstances but solely one of preventing any other serious sin, the issue is decided upon the proximity of one's co-operation and the gravity of the evil to be avoided by the co-operator.

677. In terms of the proximity of one's co-operation, it may be immediate and mediate.

1. In *immediate* co-operation one has part in the very act of another's

wrong, as in fornication or adultery. In the overwhelming majority of cases immediate co-operation is intrinsically wrong and hence forbidden. An exception are those acts in which a person has a purely passive part, as in a rape to which one does not consent. It is also possible to play an immediate part in certain sins against justice. Thus under threat of death one could have an active part in a theft because the one so constrained is in extreme need and this use of his neighbor's goods becomes a unique means of saving his life.

2. In *mediate* co-operation one places an act which is preparatory to another's sin, such as selling a murderer poison. Mediate co-operation may be *proximate* or *remote* according as it approximates concurrence in the sin. It is one thing to tell a youth where he can buy pornographic post cards, another to drive him to the place of purchase, and still another to sell them to him. The ultimate of proximate co-operation is *necessary co-operation,* without which the sin could not take place.

678. If one's co-operation is quite proximate and necessary, an extremely grave reason is required. Such would be fear of probable death, serious infamy, the loss of some important organ. If co-operation is less proximate, a grave reason is required. Such would be fear of great pain or loss of a considerable sum of money. If co-operation is remote, slight inconvenience excuses. Proportionately graver reasons are required in the case of parents, teachers, pastors, and the like, who have a special obligation from piety or justice to prevent others from doing evil.

679. The general principles governing co-operation are clear enough, but they present troublesome difficulties in application. It is often difficult to distinguish formal from material co-operation (which must always be one's first consideration); and if material co-operation be established, to determine if there are sufficient grounds for allowing it. The science of casuistry takes up those cases most likely to happen — it establishes paradigms of conduct in this matter for servants, merchants, innkeepers, workmen, book publishers, and so on — and gives answers which are serviceable enough. But since the variety of human conduct is practically infinite, it does not help too much to have memorized the solution of stock cases. One repeatedly is forced to use his own judgment to decide whether one may proceed or must desist. When one cannot rely on his own prudence to apply these principles, he must seek the advise of a wise counselor.

READINGS

St. Thomas, *Summa Theologica*, II–II, 23, 26, 31, 43, 106, 109, 110.

Cathrein, Victor, S.J., *Philosophia Moralis*, pp. 252–260. Friburgi Brisgoviae, Herder, 1915, 10 ed.

Coppens, Charles, S.J., *Moral Philosophy*, pp. 97–104. New York, Schwartz, Kirwin, Fauss, 1926.

Davis, Henry, S.J., *Moral and Pastoral Theology*, Vol. I, pp. 304–352; Vol. II, pp. 380–396.

Farrell, Walter, O.P., *Companion to the Summa*, Vol. III, pp. 59–114. New York, Sheed and Ward, 1940.

La Rochelle-Fink, *Medical Ethics*, pp. 273–304. Montreal, Catholic Truth Society, 1943.

Leibell, J. F., ed., *Readings in Ethics*, pp. 528–564. Chicago, Loyola University Press, 1926.

McFadden, Charles, O.S.A., *Medical Ethics for Nurses*, pp. 254–302. Philadelphia, Davis, 1946.

Nivard, Marcel, S.J., *Ethica*, pp. 239–252. Paris, Beauchesne, 1928.

Regan, Robert E., O.S.A., *Professional Secrecy in the Light of Moral Principles*. Washington, Augustinian Press, 1943.

Rickaby, Joseph, S.J., *Aquinus Ethicus*, Vol. I, pp. 351–376, 381–398, 413–425; Vol. II, pp. 200–203, 213–222.

BOOK III
PRINCIPLES OF SOCIAL ETHICS

CHAPTER XXI

MAN A SOCIAL BEING

680. Up to the present we have considered the rights and duties of the individual man and even where we have seen him dealing with other men, his relationship to them has been that of individual to individual. We have had to touch on certain aspects of social life in our treatment of communism and socialism, but the emphasis has been upon the good or evil status of the individual. However, it is clear that man is more than an individual. He lives with other men in social groups. Not only contemporary life but all of human history emphatically testifies that men do not live isolated lives but have ever acted as members of some group. Hobbes's[1] description of the original man, a lone marauder whose hand was against every other man, has never actually been verified. Here is the fact: man has been and is social. So the moral question arises: does inclusion in a social organization impose on men duties and rights specifically different from those they bear as individuals? If so, what is their origin, nature, and extent? Before examining man's conduct as a social being, let us establish certain general truths concerning society: (*a*) its nature, (*b*) its causes, (*c*) its naturalness to man.

I. WHAT IS A SOCIETY?

681. No individual is so self-sufficient that by his own ingenuity he can fully provide for himself. Thrown completely on his own, he finds innumerable goods of the physical, intellectual, moral, and aesthetic orders completely unattainable, or attainable only with consummate difficulty. To acquire learning, bridge a river, adequately protect his family, cross the seas, or even to amuse himself, he must unite with other men: by combined and purposeful effort, advantages, otherwise inaccessible to the individual, are put within his reach. This

---

[1] *Leviathan,* Chap. XIII. Molesworth's English edition, Vol. III, pp. 112–113.

pooling of effort to secure mutual advantages results in a union to which men give the name *society*. From the way men act and speak we judge that these elements must be found in any society.

682. The idea of society implies a plurality of some kind. No one ever said that one individual constitutes a society: for association at least two persons are required. This plurality does not become a society by mere local juxtaposition. A crowd watching a fire is not a society. The plurality must be fused into some kind of union, for men understand by a society not any group however orderly but an *ordered* group, one deliberately pointed to the attainment of some definite good. Without union, order is impossible.

However, not every casual or temporary conjoining of human beings constitutes a society. When a farmer calls his neighbors for a barn-raising, they do not constitute a society. For a society is a permanent union, though not necessarily a perpetual one. The machinery of a society is not set up for the attainment of momentary or chance goods but for those whose achievement demands considerable time and are of lasting interest.

The coming together of men in a society differs from the herding together of brutes. It is a working together of human beings as human beings, a conspiration of intellect and will, a thinking and a willing of the same thing. Hence the members of a society must know in general the good which they seek by their union and the chief means conducing thereunto; and they must desire both the end and its means. The tie, then, which binds them in a social organization is moral, a tie of intellect and will.

The reason why men associate must be an end worthy of man — a real, not an apparent good. Hence associations to facilitate wrong-doing, such as Murder, Inc., or gangs of auto thieves, bear only an outward resemblance to a society. This reason is never an individual good but a *common good* — common not only in that it is the object of the striving of many but also in that it is *for* many, to be enjoyed by many in common. This purpose is sought by social or co-operative action, an orderly working of all toward the desired good, a common activity in which each plays a proportionate part. Co-operative action does not imply that all do the same things but that each has an activity helpful to the end.

683. Therefore we define a society as the *permanent moral union of two or more persons striving for a common good by co-operative* *activity.* This union is not physical but moral, and once it is set up it is regarded as possessing rights and interests similar to those of an individual. Hence it is aptly called a moral person. Because one finds in a society due subordination of part to part and of all parts to the good of the whole, a society is called an organism, a social body. It will be helpful for future explanations of particular societies to apply to the general notion of society the four Aristotelian causes, but we must keep in mind that this application is only analogous.

II. CAUSES OF A SOCIETY

684. The material cause of society is evidently the plurality, the multitude, which is socially united. The efficient cause is the one who gives the multitude the moral unity of a society, that agent whose juridical action determines the existence of a society. We say juridical action and not physical action because the effect to be produced, a society, is not a physical but a juridical unit. Hence, when treating of the origin of particular societies we shall talk not of an efficient but of a juridical cause. This cause will always be some person or persons endowed by law with the right to form a social union with this or these persons. The question of *final* and *formal* causes requires fuller treatment.

A. Final Cause

1. *The Social End*

685. The final cause is always and only *a common good*. While a common good may cover a very wide range of things — making money, improving one's aesthetic taste, marketing cattle, educating children, saving one's soul — it must always be something worthy of human striving. Men may not band together for an end forbidden by the moral law. A society must tend to make men better men, to promote human felicity.

Granted this end is worthy of men's efforts, it becomes a *common good* not merely because many seek it together, but especially because it is a source of advantage to many. If no benefits accrue to the members, there simply is no common good. But in order truly to benefit its members, a society must be a going concern, it must seek its own conservation, well-being, and improvement. For in no society could benefits be shared among its members unless it were first efficient and in good condition. But a society may seek its own aggrandizement, prestige, and efficiency to the detriment of its members. This is a perversion. No society is an end in itself; it is always of less importance than its members, because as such it is something less than man. It is a means to enable individuals to attain some human good and thereby advance to their supreme good. Societies are for men: men are not for societies.

686. But do we not say that the common good comes before the individual good? From the concept of a *common good* it follows that the thing which we call a common good can be truly good only if it benefits many. Evidently, then, what benefits many is more important than what benefits one. On the principle that the whole is greater than any of its parts, the *social good* of an individual is subordinate to the good of the social whole.

It should be carefully noted, however, that this principle is universally valid only when applied to things physically one. When it is applied to things morally one, like a society, we discover a true sense in which the human parts are greater than the social whole. For man as such is incomparably more than a society as such. Indeed, the supreme good of one man is more important than the social good of all men. For a society is temporal and mortal; a man is eternal and immortal. No man could be compelled to sacrifice his supreme good nor even to risk it, even though he would confer the most tremendous benefits on any society. However, certain societies such as Church and State are so necessary to all men, so completely equipped to promote man's real good that there never could be a true conflict in which an individual would have to choose between his supreme good and the *genuine* good of one of these societies. That which promotes the real good of these societies must eventually promote the good of the individual.

Finally, as the end varies so, too, will the nature of the society and the kind of activity requisite to achieve the end. *The end specifies the society.* Since a bridge club has a different purpose than a business partnership or a State, so will differ the form of these societies and the kind of social activity required of the members.

2. Social Activity

687. A discussion of the end of a society is incomplete without consideration of the means whereby the common good is attained. These means can only be social activity — ends are attained by proper action. What, then, is social activity? In a preliminary sense, we may call that activity social whereby a social organism of some kind is established, for example, the action of the founding Fathers writing the Constitution of the United States. Once a society has been duly erected, social activity is (*a*) the actions of the society operating as a social unit, such as Japan's signing a fisheries' treaty with Russia, or (*b*) the acts of its members performed in virtue of their particular duty or capacity to promote the common good, such as the proclaiming of Thanksgiving Day by a governor, the quelling of a disturbance by a policeman, a citizen's paying his taxes.

688. Two fundamental requirements underlie all social activity. The first is the concrete steps that the organization takes to secure its social goal. What must a golf club do to provide its members with facilities to enjoy the game of golf? How is a State to protect its citizens? Where many minds and possible opinions are involved, there must be agreement as to the means to be selected, the practical steps to be taken. Otherwise, chaos results: the social end could never be attained. Besides, as there will necessarily be a diversity of social functions, so there must be agreement as to which members fulfill the various functions. Otherwise they would not be done.

The second requirement is that a society must see to it that its various functions are fulfilled. Here difficulty is always encountered for some members will be unwilling to do their allotted share. Some may co-operate at first, but after a spurt of initial activity they lapse into inactivity. Evidently, then, since men are inconstant, there will not be a constant and efficient movement toward the common good unless the society has the power to compel continuous co-operation.

This twofold power men call *authority,* which we define as the legitimate power to direct and compel the members of a society to act in accord with the proper end of a society.

689. *How necessary is authority?* To the ordinary man this is a senseless question, but there always has been the rebel to whom the yoke of authority is heavy and who strives to throw it off. In our time Bakunin (1814–1876),[2] one of the greater gods of the social democrats, both in word and act rejected as much authority as he could. Proudhon

---

[2] See Emile de Laveleye, "L'Apotre de la Destruction Universelle — Bakounine," *Revue de Deux Mondes,* Juin 1, 1880, Vol. 39, pp. 546–582.

(1814–1865),[3] the brains of modern anarchism, denied the State much of its essential authority. Communism has woven a dream of a happy day when by natural evolution State authority will have ceased (§ 528). Among the ancients, Zeno and Carpocrates advocated a stateless society. What perhaps the modern and ancient anarchist has in mind is that the State does not constitute a true society. That question we shall resolve later. But when he decries all authority, the anarchist is actually protesting against the abuse of authority which commonly consists in rulers using the society to advance their own private interests. The great enemy of the common good is the unreasonable private good. However, in all this the anarchist is not quite sincere. When he says that he hates his rulers and would abolish all rule, he really means that he wants to rule. His abolition of authority is only a temporary expedient preparatory to his own rise to power.

690. Our contention is that you cannot have a society without authority. This seems a self-evident proposition, yet it has been at least verbally and vociferously denied.

THESIS XLV. Authority is at least an essential property of any society.

We do not say whether or not authority pertains to the essence of a society but simply that wherever you have a society there you must also have authority.

PROOF

691. Authority is an essential property of a society, because without it a society could not attain its end. A society essentially involves co-operative and constant activity toward a common end. Without some power to *direct and compel* movement toward the end, the end is unrealizable. The reasons are: (*a*) There must be harmonious agreement on the choice of social means. Otherwise there would not be order but chaos. Therefore a society must have the power to select the social means leading to the common good. (*b*) Since men are selfish, they will often be unwilling to forego their private interests for the common good. Hence there must be some power to compel

---

[3] See *La Revolution Sociale, Oeuvres Completes de P. J. Proudhon*, Vol. 7. Paris, Libraire Internationale, 1868. *De La Capacité Politique Des Classes Ouvrières*. Paris, Dentu, 1865. *De La Justice Dans La Revolution Et Dans L'Eglise*. Bruxelles, 1868, 1869, 1870.

co-operation. Since men are fickle, there will not be permanent co-operation without the power to compel. This necessary social power to direct and compel is authority.

692. Corollary I. The necessary unity of any society demands that it have *one and only one supreme authority.* This is vested in some individual person or group of persons. Whoever bears this authority is not a master but a superior. A master is obeyed by servants or slaves; a superior by subjects. A master may command what is for his own private good; a superior only what is for the common good. The obligation to promote the common good falls first upon the superior who fulfills this duty by devising and executing those particular measures conducive to the society's end. Secondarily, it falls upon subjects who fulfill their duty by obeying the directions of authority.

Corollary II. The sole kind of activity which directly falls within the sphere of social authority are external acts amenable to external direction and coercion. Social authority may not command purely internal acts, because it can neither direct, adjudge, nor compel them. However, if an internal act is necessarily involved with an external act, such as internal consent in a contract, one may be obliged to place it not in virtue of social authority but of the Natural Law.

B. Formal Cause

693. A formal cause is that determined and determining thing which converts a plurality into a society. What is that thing, analogous to the physical form in entities physically one, which makes a society a society?

Two opinions are offered by scholastic authors. According to both of these, a society is essentially a moral union: the individuals comprising a society are welded into the state of oneness. This unity is completely moral. It is caused, fostered, and preserved by activity of intellect and will. Moral union, then, being the essence of a society, what determining form gives the multitude the moral oneness of a society?

694. The first opinion contends that this is *authority.* Hence, as a being is made a man by the union of matter and a rational soul, so a multitude becomes a society when the stamp of authority is imprinted on it.

The second opinion holds that this moral union is the formal effect of a *moral and juridic bond*. The formal cause of society is a bond, because each individual in the group is united to every other individual, each to the society as such, and the society in turn to each. It is a moral bond consisting in the knowledge of, the desire for, and the striving after a common good precisely as it is common to all. It is a juridic bond, comprising the sum total of rights and duties which each member has with respect to the common end. This is aptly called the *social bond,* and once it exists and as long as it perdures, a society exists. Only when it dissolves does the society cease to be.

695. While the first opinion is easier to understand, the second seems more probable. The second opinion is preferable because we can form an essential concept of a society without including authority therein but not without including the social bond. This is clear in the case of conjugal society. Therefore, if authority does not constitute the essential form of conjugal society, it is not the formal cause of any society. Authority flows from the social bond, not vice versa. Authority is necessary that a society attain its end; it is not necessary that a society exist. Therefore, authority is an essential property of a society but not its formal cause.

III. SOCIETY A NATURAL INSTITUTION

696. The phenomenon of human association and social activity is universal. The American pioneer in his lonely farm hungered for an outlet for his social cravings. Today, Junior builds his clubhouse in the back yard; sister has her sorority; and mother her discussion club. The history of mankind is the record of the rise and fall of States. How do we explain social intercourse? Is its origin to be found in nature or the arbitrary will of man?

697. According to Hobbes, who accepted the Calvinistic view of man's essential corruption, man is arrogantly selfish, domineering, and by nature antisocial. His primitive status was one of war — not perhaps of actual incessant battle — but of insecurity, of universal hostility, of perpetual readiness to attack his fellow man. Hence Hobbes mourns that his life is "solitary, poor, nasty, brutish and short."[4] In this situation "the notions of right and wrong, justice and injustice have no place."[5] "It is consequent also to the same condition,

---

[4] *The Leviathan,* Chap. XIII, Molesworth's English edition, Vol. III, p. 113.
[5] *Ibid.,* p. 115.

that there be no propriety, no dominion, no *mine* and *thine* distinct; but only that to be every man's, that he can get; and for so long, as he can keep it."[6] This war of every man against his fellows is the result of man's desire for self-preservation. But since universal contention is really at odds with his conservation, man ought to live at peace with man. Men have agreed so to do. This covenant or social contract, which we describe at greater length when dealing with the State (cf. § 865), is the ultimate basis of all society. It is the origin of all law, right, justice, and even of all morality. Men have gotten used to this arrangement which had to be irrevocable. They cannot now rescind it. Human sociability, then, is an artificial thing, a mere human invention.

Following the lead of Spencer,[7] evolutionists contend that the social order has been evolved and established in its present state by physical laws acting with iron necessity.

698. Our explanation is that society is natural to man, not in the sense that teeth and fingernails are natural as nature's direct donation, but in this manner: man is endowed with unmistakable aptitudes and inclinations for social life by nature herself who sets before man certain goals of perfection morally unattainable without social life. Desirous of their well-being and spurred on by their human wants, men listen to the urgings of their nature and freely obey the law of nature by living in the society of their fellows.

THESIS XLVI. Man is by nature a social being.

PROOF

699. Man is by nature a social being, because (1) he has a natural aptitude for society; (2) he has a natural and compelling inclination for it; (3) outside of society he labors under the moral impossibility of attaining his proper well-being.

1. Man's aptitude for society is proved by his faculties of hearing and speech. These constitute natural equipment for social life.

2. Man's tendency to society is evident from the fact that men dislike solitude. They want to share their joys and sorrows and welcome pity and sympathy.

3. It is morally and sometimes even physically impossible for men

[6] *Ibid.*

[7] Herbert Spencer, *The Principles of Sociology*, Vol. I, pp. 3–104, 609–618. London, Williams, 1877.

to attain the fullness of well-being without social organization. First, the race could not continue without the family. As an infant and an old man, a person absolutely requires the help of others. Second, any appreciable intellectual, moral, and aesthetic development is possible only in society. Further particulars of human need are enumerated in our treatment of matrimony, education, and the State.

Therefore a tendency, inclination, and need so universally verified must be rooted in human nature.

700. N.B. I. Evolution has as yet adduced no conclusive proof for its claim that there is an unbroken continuity of cause and effect reaching from some inorganic substance to man — that by progressive steps of self-betterment this original substance evolved into man in his present state and activity. In view of the new findings of geneticists, this proof will be more and more difficult to produce. The subhuman cave man, somewhat like the original man of Hobbes preying on his fellow cave man, is scientifically as yet an unsubstantiated dream, though to be sure, he has taken firm hold in the comic strips and the Sunday supplements. The only man of whom any certain knowledge exists is a rational, social animal. Contrary to Spencer's[8] dictum, natures do not change. When man evolves into something other than a man, he is no longer man but something else. The claim that man as we know him today was once essentially different, involves a like contradiction. This discussion, however, belongs to psychology. Suffice it to say that if man does make further strides in civilization — which may well be doubted until he casts off certain prevalent but fundamental errors concerning his nature — there will be no essential change in his nature nor in the law of that nature.

N.B. II. The command of the Natural Law that men live in a social union applies to men collectively, not disjunctively. Therefore, if some individual, for the sake of contemplation or some supernatural good, were to lead a completely solitary life, he would not violate the Natural Law. Aristotle[9] well says that he who, by deliberate choice and not a mere accident of fortune, is free of all social bonds is either a very wicked man or better than man.

---

[8] *Data of Ethics,* Chap. II, pp. 8–20.
[9] *Politics,* Bk. I, 2, 1253a.

READINGS

St. Thomas, *De Regimine Principum*, Lib. 1, cap. 1, trans. G. B. Phelan as *On the Governance of Rulers*. London, Sheed and Ward, 1938.

Aristotle, *Politics*, Bk. 1, Chap. 1–2.

Bruehl, Chas. P., *This Way Happiness*, pp. 205–212. Milwaukee, Bruce, 1940.

Costa-Rossetti, Julius, S. J., *Philosophia Moralis*, pp. 404–429. Oeniponte, Rauch, 1886.

Cronin, Michael, *Primer of the Principles of Social Science*, pp. 1–39. Dublin, Gill, 1941.

Maritain, Jacques, *Scholasticism and Politics*, pp. 56–88. New York, Macmillan, 1940.

Parsons, Wilfrid, S.J., *Which Way Democracy*, pp. 77–105. New York, Macmillan, 1939.

Rommen, Heinrich, *The State in Catholic Thought*, pp. 33–90. St. Louis, Herder, 1945.

Woods, Henry, S.J., *First Book in Ethics*, pp. 177–190. New York, Wagner, 1923.

CHAPTER XXII

CONJUGAL SOCIETY

701. There are two types of society, natural and artificial. (*a*) An *artificial society* is one whose existence, end, and nature are determined by man's free choice. Here the common good will be some incidental good of man, appealing to some classes of men but not to all men generally. (*b*) A *natural society* is one whose existence, end, and nature have been determined by the Natural Law. Nature ordains man for such a society because without it he could not attain the due perfection of his nature. The common good here is an essential good of man appealing to all men generally. We shall now consider which societies are natural and how nature intends that they operate.

I. THE EXISTENCE OF THE CONJUGAL UNION

702. Every living species tends to conserve itself. For existence is the first of goods. Since nature has provided the earth and the fullness thereof as a habitation for man and subdued all lesser creatures to his utility, it must be nature's intention that the human race continue in existence.

How does nature accomplish this purpose? She must, as always, choose effective means unto her ends. Her purpose in the conservation of the human race is not merely more human life — not any sort of crippled, deficient, or moronic human beings — but more human beings who are normal and sound. For the perpetuity of the human race, it is not enough that nature endow men with the faculty of reproduction, for not any haphazard or arbitrary use of this faculty will suffice for nature's purpose. Orderly use of this faculty is requisite.

Nature provides for the orderly reproduction of brutes through the operation of blind instinct. But it is contrary to his rational dignity that man be required to co-operate blindly with nature; it is proper that his co-operation in the reproduction of his kind be by way of willing acceptance of a pattern of orderly sexual activity proposed to his reason. Therefore man's use of the power of reproduction is regulated by law. What, then, is nature's law concerning human reproduction? The first and most necessary injunction of this law is set down in the following thesis.

THESIS XLVII. The Natural Law demands a permanent union of man and woman for the proper continuance of the human race. This conjugal union is a true and natural society.

703. The procreation of new human life requires the carnal union of male and female. Does a temporary, casual union wherein fertilization is effected suffice for nature's purpose, or is a more permanent union necessary? By permanent we mean that the partners in this union live together at least until their offspring are physically, intellectually, and morally capable of a proper human living. Here we are not concerned with the question of whether this union should last until the death of one of the partners.

PROOF OF PART I

704. *A permanent union is necessary.* The Natural Law demands a permanent sexual union of man and woman because *only* by such a union can nature's purpose regarding the propagation and rearing of human beings be fittingly realized.

Casual, temporary unions do not make for sufficient propagation and fitting rearing.

1. These unions do not make for sufficient propagation because they tend to result in the sterility of the woman and the impaired physical well-being of the offspring. Furthermore, their purpose is not offspring but self-gratification.

2. They are not conducive to fitting rearing. Even among brutes, parents remain together until their young can care for themselves. No animal is as helpless and for so long a time as the human infant. Since nature intends the well-being of the young, it demands that human parents remain together until their offspring are capable of an adequate human life. Since the task of raising children is so onerous, only parents, definitely known and permanently united, can exercise that care without which the suitable physical, intellectual, and moral development of the child is impossible.

PROOF OF PART II

705. *This union is a true society*. In the conjugal union are present all the necessary elements of a society, namely, several persons working together in a stable, moral union for a common good to be achieved by mutual co-operation.

PROOF OF PART III

This society is natural. The reasons are:

1. Nature has destined men for conjugal society (*a*) *physiologically*, because men and women not only have faculties for reproduction but a strong impulse to use them; (*b*) *psychologically*, because men and women are the natural complements of one another. They are everywhere attracted to this union and see in it the natural framework on which to build their happiness.

2. That this society is morally necessary for a universal human good is proved in § 704.

706. Corollary I. *Nature forbids all transient, casual unions of the sexes* because they are *per se* destructive of her purpose regarding human propagation. The partners in every act of carnal intercourse must be prepared *beforehand* to assume complete responsibility for the possible consequences of the act, namely, adequate care of the new *person* who may result therefrom. If nature allowed the act under circumstances which do not provide this guarantee, she would countenance the deterioration of the human race. Even though these unions conceal their real identity under pleasant-sounding names, like companionate marriage, they are a blatant substitution of passion for reason, of delectable good for perfective good.

707. Corollary II. *Nature demands that sex activity be restricted to the conjugal union*. Only persons united in this society may perform the generative act. Therefore fornication is always wrong. The reason is that the indispensable guarantee of the offspring's good is the bond of this union. This is the rule of nature: no conjugal bond, no sex activity.

Is any exception possible? There is an exception to the general rule that no one may kill or take the property of another. May a similar exception be found in this matter on the ground that a particular unmarried couple will certainly educate any offspring begotten, or that their intercourse will certainly be sterile?

To preserve innocent life, there are exceptions to the laws against killing and stealing. There is no exception, however, to the law regarding the use of the sex faculty. Reason indeed demands that none be tolerated. For, to admit any exception here would destroy the general rule. To permit even one exception would be tantamount to legalizing promiscuity, because concupiscent man, as in the case of divorce, would soon use any reason as an exception. Besides, if the sex appetite could be lawfully satisfied outside of marriage, too many would abstain from assuming its burdens to the consequent detriment of the race.

708. Corollary III. The contention of evolutionists that the human race originally lived in a state of sexual promiscuity is false and gratuitous.

When the first flame of evolutionary doctrine was lighted in the nineteenth century, many were captivated by it — here at last was the all-embracing principle which explained all things. Accepting an hypothesis as a principle, the evolutionists cast about for facts to substantiate it. To fasten a purely animal status on primitive man, any and every sort of analogy was seized upon; seeming facts which pointed in the direction of evolution were pronounced indubitable facts. One of these was the alleged fact of original promiscuity.[1] An imposing array of scientific names plumped for it.

The argument ran: (1) ancient and modern primitive peoples living in promiscuity are survivals of a once universal condition; (2) there are certain customs that can be explained solely in the light of primitive promiscuity.

On the first point, later and more thorough researches show there are no substantiated instances of wholesale promiscuity, and the more scientists investigate primitive peoples, the more conclusive is the evidence that the family is the basis of social organization. Westermarck cites all the ancient and modern evidence offered and concludes: "Even if there really are or have been peoples living in a state of promiscuity, *which has never been proven,* and is exceedingly hard to believe, these people do not afford any evidence whatever for promiscuity having been the rule in primitive times."[2]

On the second point, among the customs cited are various sexual

---

[1] Herbert Spencer, *Principles of Sociology,* Vol. I, pp. 661–671.
[2] Edward Westermarck, *The History of Human Marriage,* Vol. I, p. 125. London, Macmillan, 1921.

aberrations such as prenuptial unchastity, religious prostitution, and exchange of wives. However, one can find similar instances of sexual aberration in the great cities of modern Western civilization, and by a parallel argument an evolutionist might conclude that our ancestors of three thousand years ago lived in a state of promiscuity except that the facts of history forbid such a conclusion. Modern aberrations are instances of degeneration from a loftier ideal. So too the aberrations of primitive peoples can more reasonably be explained upon the same basis.

The custom which is offered as the Achilles proof of promiscuity is that of the matriarchate, or mother right, the argument being that because descent was reckoned from the mother, therefore paternity was uncertain, and therefore a state of promiscuity once prevailed. But no proof has ever been offered that the matriarchate ever universally prevailed or that it preceded the patriarchate. Where the matriarchate flourished among primitive people, descent through the mother is reasonably explained in some cases by the fact that the new husband went to live with his wife's family and hence he was counted as a member of that family. But the best explanation is that where polygamy prevails, it is less confusing and more convenient to reckon descent from the mother than the father.

The *Encyclopedia of Social Sciences* clearly accuses evolution of missing the mark on this point and sums up the modern findings thus: "In social organizations it was shown by Starcke, Westermarck and the anthropologists in the United States that the individual family was the one ubiquitous social unit, the most primitive as well as the most persistent."[3]

Westermarck concluded his case against promiscuity, arguing that male jealousy would not tolerate a system of promiscuity. A valid enough argument. But the stronger argument is that, since promiscuity results in infertility and venereal disease, the human race could not have survived a state of original promiscuity.

II. THE NECESSITY OF CONJUGAL SOCIETY

709. From the foregoing it is clear that conjugal society is natural and necessary. It is necessary for adequate and proper propagation of the human race. The Natural Law, therefore, commands marriage.

---

[3] *Ibid.*, "Evolution, Social," Vol. V, p. 660

This command falls directly and primarily upon the race and not upon particular individuals, since propagation is primarily a good of the race, only secondarily a good of the individual. Hence this obligation directly presses an individual only when the race is in danger of dying out. Tilling the soil, gathering the fruits of the field, providing clothing and shelter are needs of the race; but it does not follow that every man should be a farmer, a builder, and a weaver. Only when there is an insufficiency of these things is the individual commanded to procure them himself. So too with conjugal society. From the way men act and have acted through history it is safe to assert that there will always be enough persons who will desire the married state and assume the function of procreation. Hence there will be little danger of this obligation falling directly upon particular individuals.

However, *per accidens,* an individual may be obliged to marry for family reasons, or reasons of state, or because otherwise he could not lead an upright life. As the Apostle says: "It is better to marry than to burn (with concupiscence)."[4]

But so vehement is the urge to procreate, so rooted in human nature is the inclination to use the faculty of procreation that one may well ask whether a man does not go counter to his nature if he refuses to marry. As we shall see in discussing the purposes of matrimony and the education of children, the conjugal tie requires practice of great virtue. Is not, then, the full perfection of one's personality, the completeness of one's natural life thwarted when one abstains from matrimony? Many authors have stated that voluntary celibacy is contrary to the Natural Law and that therefore all who are physically and socially capable of marriage ought to marry. This position we reject.

THESIS XLVIII. Individual celibacy is not contrary to the Natural Law. If it is undertaken from motives of virtue, it is a nobler state than matrimony.

710. By celibacy we understand not only abstention from matrimony but from all use of sex — perfect chastity. Some persons do not marry because of physical defect or lack of suitable opportunity; others, because of temperamental disinclination or reluctance to assume matrimonial obligations. This thesis does not pertain to virginity com-

---

[4] 1 Corinthians 7:9.

pulsorily but grudgingly borne, or assumed for selfish, ignoble reasons; but to virginity voluntarily chosen for reasons of religious worship, contemplation, or the service of mankind. As St. Thomas quotes St. Augustine: "We do not praise in virgins the mere fact of their virginity but the fact of their being virgins dedicated to God by religious continence."[5]

PROOF OF PART I

711. *Celibacy is not contrary to the Natural Law.* Celibacy would be contrary to the Natural Law if the Natural Law commanded each individual to marry. There is no such command, for (*a*) the good of the race does not require it, as proved in § 709, and (*b*) nor does the good of the individual. The precept might be necessary if celibacy were impossible to observe, but many who are prevented from marrying and others who freely choose celibacy do actually observe it. The advantages necessary for the physical, intellectual, and moral development of the individual can be secured outside the married state.

PROOF OF PART II

712. *Celibacy, undertaken from motives of virtue, is a nobler state than matrimony.*

N.B. The argument presupposes that there is a sufficiency of propagators. If this were not so, celibacy could not be chosen from motives of virtue. That this condition has held and still holds is well put in the words of St. Augustine: "The means of filling up the number of the elect abound in all nations."[6]

Celibacy, undertaken from motives of virtue, is a nobler state than matrimony because celibacy demands the subordination of a lesser to a higher good.

Celibacy essentially involves the sacrifice of a vehement bodily inclination to the pursuit of a higher good of religious worship or the common good of society in the practice of the corporal and spiritual works of mercy. As the goods of the soul are preferable to those of the body, as a strictly divine good is superior to a merely human good, as an individual good is of less account than the common good, so virtuous celibacy is a nobler state than matrimony.

---

[5] *Sum. Theol.* II–II, 152, 3.
[6] *De Genesi ad Litteram*, IX, 7.

713. Among ancient and modern people evidence abounds of celibacy, certainly of religious celibacy, being accorded greater respect than matrimony. The Romans demanded virginity of the Vestal priestesses whose prestige was beyond compare.[7] At Sena among the Gauls there were similar virgin priestesses.[8] At the time of Christ the Jewish sect of the Essenes dedicated themselves to perpetual chastity.[9] Tertullian exhorts his Christian hearers to be content with a single marriage by pointing to the chastity of the pagan priestesses of Juno and of African Ceres.[10] He cites the virgins of Apollo in Ephesus and of Egyptian Thebes;[11] he refers to the dedicates of Scythian Diana and Pythian Apollo.[12] Arnobius[13] mentions the votaries of the same Phrygian Cebele to which Lucian[14] refers. Herodotus speaks in awe of a woman consecrated to Baal in Babylon, of another sacred to Theban Jupiter.[15] The cult of Ephesian Artemis[16] and of Syrian Astarte[17] demanded eunuch priests. Passing by the tremendous tradition of Christianity, we find the Mexicans, immediately prior to the time of Cortez, compelling under penalty of death the priests and priestesses of their most sacred divinities to be celibate.[18] Chastity enjoyed peculiar honor among the Incas of Peru.[19] In India among the Jains,[20] among the Todas[21] of South India, in Ceylon among the Buddhists,[22] in Tibet[23] and China among both Buddhists[24] and Taoists[25] celibacy is

---

[7] Dionysius of Halicarnassus, *Antiquitates Romanae,* Bk. II, n. 67.

[8] Pomponius Mela, *De Situ Orbis,* Lib. III, Chap. 6.

[9] *Flavii Josephi De Bello Judaico,* Lib. II, c. VII, pp. 784–789. Geneva, Roverianus, 1611. See also Loeb's Classical Library, *Josephus,* Vol. II, "The Jewish War," II, 119–161.

[10] *Ad Uxorem,* I, 6. Migne, *P.L.,* I, 1284.

[11] *De Exhortatione Castitatis,* 13. Migne, *P.L.,* II, 928.

[12] *De Monogamia,* XVII. Migne, *P.L.,* II, 953.

[13] *Adversus Gentes,* V, 7. Migne, *P.L.,* V, 1094 ff.

[14] *De Dea Syria,* 15.

[15] I, 181–182.

[16] Strabo, XIV–1–23.

[17] Lucian, *De Dea Syria,* 50 ff.

[18] Francisco Saverio Clavigero, *The History of Mexico,* trans. Charles Cullen, Vol. I, Bk. VI, Sect. 15–17, pp. 274–277. London, Robinson, 1787.

[19] Garcilasso de Vega, *The Royal Commentaries of Peru,* trans. Sir Paul Ricaut, Part I, Bk. IV, Chap. I–VII, pp. 99–106. London, 1688.

[20] Edward W. Hopkins, *The Religions of India,* p. 294. Boston, Ginn, 1898.

[21] *Ibid.,* p. 537.

[22] Malte-Brun, *A System of Universal Geography,* corrected by James Percival, Vol. I, Bk. XLIX, p. 504. Boston, Walker, 1834.

[23] Andrew Wilson, *The Abode of Snow,* pp. 189–191. New York, Putnam, 1886.

[24] Sir John F. Davies, *The Chinese,* Vol. II, p. 81. London, Knight, 1836.

[25] *Ta Tsing Leu Lee, The Fundamental Laws etc. of the Penal Code of China,* trans.

demanded from all aspirants to true holiness and is proportionately revered. Mohandas K. Gandhi, the late spiritual leader of 300,-000,000 Hindus wrote to Viscount Wavell, viceroy of India: "We (Gandhi and his wife) were a couple outside the ordinary. It was in 1906 that by mutual consent and after unconscious (*sic*) trials we definitely adopted self-restraint as the rule of life. To my great joy this knit us together as never before."[26] Gandhi's conduct was a practical assent to the statement of St. Thomas: "If a man abstain from bodily pleasures, in order more freely to give himself to the contemplation of truth, this is in accordance with the rectitude of reason."[27]

III. THE NATURE OF THE CONJUGAL UNION

714. The nature and function of this natural society is seen in an exposition of its four causes. Of these, little need be said about the formal and material causes. In this third part we shall treat of the final cause of matrimony and the logical conclusions which follow from it. In the fourth part we shall seek the efficient cause. In the fifth part we shall examine this cause in detail. In the sixth part we shall discuss the modern evils endangering matrimony.

A. The Ends of Matrimony

715. To the all-important question, What does nature design to accomplish through matrimony? we have already (§§ 704–705) given an oblique answer. We have shown it to be a natural institution, the suitable means chosen by nature to procure a human good of universal import — the proper birth and rearing of the human offspring. But is this the only end of matrimony? Are there other goods, of less, equal, greater importance, which nature also intends?

We are not concerned with the personal motives which induce people to get married. These may be many and varied — good, bad, and indifferent. A man may enter upon the office of president of the United States for selfish and reprehensible reasons. His doing so would not alter the fact that this office had a juridical end and function fixed

---

Sir George T. Staunton, CXIV, p. 118. London, Cadel, 1810. The Taoist priest who took a wife was to be punished with eighty blows and expulsion from his order.

[26] *Time*, Sept. 4, 1944, p. 43.

[27] *Sum. Theol.*, II–II, 152, 2.

by the Constitution. So too with matrimony. While varying motives induce different people to enter upon it, nevertheless the Natural Law has already determined its end and function.

When one investigates this natural end he discovers it is not a single, simple thing. For matrimony is the natural avenue to several truly human goods. Our aim now is not only to show what these are, but to weigh their relative value in the eyes of nature.

Observation and careful analysis reveal that matrimony offers the human race three distinct blessings.

716. 1. *Mutual advantages of a life totally in common.* It is not good for a man or a woman to live alone. Both naturally crave companionship, especially of the sort that opens up to them the fullest possibilities of personal development. They perceive the great utility of casting their lots together, because their temperaments and abilities will complement one another and an agreeable harmony of life will result. The inducement is not merely the pleasure of each other's company, the protection and providence of the husband, or the home-making of the wife. Matrimony affords the opportunity of a total interchange of all human goods — physical, mental, and moral — from which a man and woman may expect what reasonable felicity this mortal life can provide.

Hence by the exchange of physical conveniences and social amenities a man and woman can rise to real communion of mind and heart — a deep, wholehearted, and affectionate love. This is more than carnal desire, a passing fire of passion; it is the decent, uplifted, and even exalted yearning of the rational appetite, nobly seeking the true good of the object of its affection, deepening and purifying itself of selfishness with the passing of the years. Where this kind of love is patiently cultivated, each shares with the other not only a common domestic economy but the loftier reaches of the spirit; each helps the other to become a better person, to acquire virtue and every advantage that leads to God, their supreme felicity. As far as personal moral benefit is concerned, matrimony is the ordinary but potent instrument whereby the adult attains his last end. Therefore, it is folly for one to choose a partner who would lessen rather than improve his or her opportunities of attaining the last end.

717. 2. *Remedy for concupiscence.* Nature has given men and women sexual faculties and a strong inclination to use them. Yet nothing is more obvious than concupiscence, man's tendency to abuse these.

That this is the immediate result of sin and the inclination to repeat sin, both revelation and experience testify. However, the fundamental cause of concupiscence is to be found in the duality of man's nature: he is both spirit and body; but the drives of the body are more compelling and alluring, and man is more inclined to satisfy his carnal urges than to restrain them in accordance with the dictates of reason. Therefore, to obviate the evils of lust, nature provides a natural, safe, and dignified means of satisfying the sex instinct. This matrimony offers in the carnal union of man and wife, which is the ultimate expression of their mutual love. Thereby two are made one flesh. The marriage act, as the ultimate expression of conjugal love, is sacred; as ordained by God, it is naturally holy.

718. 3. *Procreation and education of children*. A man and woman usually enter matrimony because of mutual love. This love finds its natural expression in the marriage act, which in turn naturally issues in the birth of a new being which must be protected, reared, and guided unto its proper perfection.

719. No labored proof is required to show that matrimony is capable of producing these three benefits and that nature intends it should do so. Also obvious is the fact that there is a clear and natural connection between these three functions of marriage. However, *which one is first and most important in nature's plan?* This is a vital question: upon its correct solution depend the essential characteristics and the fundamental laws of matrimony, so that matrimony will be one kind of thing if its primary end is the good of the spouses and quite another thing if that primary end is the good of children.

THESIS XLIX. The primary natural end of matrimony is the proper procreation and education of children. Its secondary end is the compensations of a common life chief among which are the fostering of mutual love and a remedy for concupiscence.

PROOF OF PART I

720. *The three goods mentioned in Thesis XLIX are natural ends of matrimony*. The natural ends of a natural institution constitute the goods in which its activities tend to terminate. Now the activities of matrimony tend to terminate in the compensations of a common life and the procreation and education of children. This is clear from observation and experience. That the birth and rearing of children is a natural end of the conjugal union is proved in § 704. That the compensations of a common life constitute ends of matrimony is clear from §§ 716–717.

PROOF OF PART II

721. *Among these ends, the proper procreation and rearing of children is primary* because unto this all other matrimonial goods are subordinated *by nature.*

1. All the activities of matrimony naturally and ultimately issue in the birth and rearing of children. The ultimate result of the activities of a natural institution constitute its end of work.

2. We have shown (§ 704) that the conjugal union is *necessary* for proper procreation. That for which a natural institution is necessary must be its primary end.

3. To say that nature subordinates the birth and rearing of children to the good of the spouses, is equivalent to saying that nature does not care whether that end be attained at all. From the history of civilizations, ancient and modern, wherever the notion prevails that matrimony is primarily for the good of the spouses, the race is insufficiently propagated. A declining birth rate has ever accompanied this idea. Hence, since the selfishness and weakness of men are so great, nature simply could not afford to prefer the convenience of the spouses to the propagation of the race. If the primary end of matrimony is not the birth and rearing of children, then nature has inadequately provided for the continuance of the race.

4. There is a difference of sex, and hence a mutual attraction between the sexes, and hence a need for allaying concupiscence, primarily because new human beings are to come of the carnal union of the sexes. If nature had chosen some other way for the propagation of the race — which is conceivable — there would be no difference of sex. Since the conjugal union is nature's sole provision for the carnal union of the sexes (§ 707), the primary end of the conjugal union must be the propagation of the race.

722. N.B. Nature's primary intention may not be the primary motive of the contracting parties. Sometimes it is not. As long as the intention of the parties does not exclude nature's primary purpose nor contradicts the essential characteristics of matrimony nor is immoral for any other reason, they are not at fault. Nature moves man wisely toward her appointed ends through the working of our natural instincts. Without explicit reference to nature's ultimate purposes, men follow their natural impulses and thus accomplish the purpose of nature. This is illustrated in eating. Here nature's purpose is the conservation of life. To induce eating, nature makes this a pleasant and desirable function. Man eats because he likes to, because he is hungry. Nature's purpose of conserving man's life is attained even though he seldom thinks of it. The same thing is verified in matrimony.

B. The Properties of Matrimony

723. The essential characteristics of matrimony are those qualities which flow from its nature and impart to it its recognizable, enduring form. What form, then, is the conjugal union to take? Is it one or several? Does nature offer a pleasing variety or does she insist on one and only one matrimonial system?

Since we have rejected casual temporary unions as destructive of the race and in no way measuring up to the requirements of conjugal society, there is no sense in which promiscuous unions can be called a form of marriage. Hence only these four forms of marriage are conceivable: (a) group marriage, a tie among a small closed group of men and women each of whom would have either simultaneously or successively marital rights with one another; (b) polyandry, the union of one woman with several men; (c) polygyny, the union of one man with several women; (d) monogamy, the exclusive union of one man and one woman.

724. Group marriage need not detain us. The actual practice of it is rare, being found among a few peoples such as Eskimos,[28] Todas,[29] and Australian aborigines.[30] This arrangement supposes each man in the group to have his own wife upon whom he has pre-emptive claims; it merely affords him legal toleration of access to the other men's wives under certain specified conditions, for example, when he travels he is supplied by his host with connubial comfort. It is a debased form of monogamy. Its morality depends upon the conclusions we reach concerning polyandry and polygyny.

---

[28] Waldemar Bogoras, The Jesup North Pacific Expedition, Memoir of the American Museum of Natural History, Vol. VII, "The Chukckee," Chap. XIX, pp. 602–609. Leiden and New York, Brill, 1909.

[29] W. H. R. Rivers, The Todas, pp. 522–523. London, Macmillan, 1906.

[30] B. Malinowski, The Family Among the Australian Aborigines, pp. 30–89, 113–115. London, 1913.

1. *Polyandry*

725. The practice of one woman having several husbands at the same time is quite rare and is found only among savage or degraded peoples in Tibet,[31] some places in India,[32] Africa, and the South Sea Islands.[33] Its usual form is fraternal, that is, several brothers agree to have one wife. The main reason for the arrangement is poverty; each brother being too poor to have his own wife, they agree to have one in common. Another reason is that since the husband must be away from home for a long period of time in a land where it is not safe to leave a woman alone, he agrees with other men to act as husband to his wife during his absence. In Madagascar[34] and Ashanti,[35] polyandry seems to be a special privilege accorded a reigning queen or the sisters of a king. However, it is held in abhorrence by the overwhelming majority of mankind.

THESIS L. Polyandry is contrary to the plainest dictates of the Natural Law.

PROOF

726. Polyandry is execrated by the Natural Law because it is a simulation of matrimony which renders impossible the primary end of matrimony.

1. The polyandric woman tends to become sterile.

2. The offspring of such unions will generally have to provide for themselves, because the paternity of the child can be very dubious. None of the men involved is likely to nurture and rear a child that may not be his own.

3. Such an arrangement is an inevitable source of bitter jealousy, strife, and domestic discord. No child could be properly reared in such an atmosphere.

2. *Polygyny*

727. It is by no means as unusual or abhorrent for one man to have several wives at the same time as for a woman to have several

---

[31] Andrew Wilson, *The Abode of Snow*, pp. 183–189. New York, Putnam, 1886.

[32] Rivers, *op. cit.*, pp. 515–521.

[33] Urey Lisiansky, *A Voyage Round the World*, Chap. IV, p. 83. London, 1814.

[34] Grandidier, cited by Westermarck, *History of Human Marriage*, Vol. III, Chap. XXIX, p. 151.

[35] W. Winwood Reade, *Savage Africa*, Chap. VII, p. 47. New York, Harpers, 1864.

husbands. Before adjudging the morality of polygyny let us note several facts. The first recorded instance of polygyny is that of Lamech,[36] who was also a fratricide. It has been and still is practiced by many races but never by any race enjoying a high level of civilization. It is found among people of a rude or a debased civilization, and the actual practice of it among these people is not nearly so widespread as some suppose. For polygyny is a prerogative of wealth: the ordinary man cannot afford more than one wife.

Even in the polygamous family there is an imitation of monogamy, for the man does not equally consort with all his wives but lives with a favorite. When she ceases to please him, he makes another his favorite.

Nor is polygyny so effective for reproduction as is monogamy. Wherever reliable records are kept, it is apparent that the number of male and female births is approximately equal. Where polygyny is practiced the demand for wives will exceed the supply. The older and wealthier will have plenty of wives: many of the younger and healthier men, more capable of propagating, will have none. Since the polygamous husband will live with his favorite wife, the rest of his wives will suffer neglect so that very few of them will bear the number of children they might have borne in a monogamous union.

THESIS LI. The Natural Law forbids any human authority to legalize polygyny.

728. The same evil does not inhere in polygyny as in polyandry. Hence we do not claim that polygyny — and the same holds for divorce — is intrinsically wrong, as blasphemy, perjury, and contraception are. These actions are utterly destructive of human ends. But neither polygyny nor divorce is *absolutely* opposed to the good which matrimony intends. The primary end of matrimony is still attainable despite them, though with difficulty. However, on account of the difficulties which they beget in domestic and civil life, these practices are such hindrances to the end of matrimony that the Natural Law must forbid any human power to introduce or legalize them. Therefore, polygyny and divorce, *instituted by human authority,* are intrinsically wrong and forbidden by the Natural Law.

729. But are they not of themselves, *in se,* contrary to the Natural Law? There is a tendency among modern authors — Castelein,[37]

---

[36] Genesis 4:23.

[37] A. Castelein, *Institutiones Philosophiae Moralis et Socialis,* pp. 416–417. Bruxelles, Société Belge de Libraire, 1899.

Joyce,[38] Leclercq[39] — to say that they are evil *in se*. When it is asked how God could have allowed polygyny to the Patriarchs and divorce to the Jews, they reply that God did not give a dispensation in either case, that He merely tolerated an evil in much the same way as the State might tolerate prostitution without approving it.

However, one must admit more than mere divine toleration. If polygyny is *in se* evil, the Patriarchs lived a good part of their lives in grave sin. But this is inadmissible. Their sin could not have been formal, because Holy Writ lauds their sanctity and holds them up as models of virtue. Nor could it even have been material sin. We should have to suppose that these men lived in invincible ignorance that polygyny is *in se* wrong. But in the case of holy men who received so many divine lights, inspirations, and revelations, the supposition is absurd.

Moreover, the moral code of the Mosaic law is a positive enunciation of the Natural Law. If polygyny and divorce are *in se* evil, Moses should have legislated against them. But he did the contrary. He takes polygyny for granted as an accepted institution and legislates concerning it.[40] He explicitly allows divorce,[41] to which fact Christ Himself testifies.[42]

730. It is, therefore, a plausible conclusion that polygyny and divorce are not *in se* evil. Since it is not the existence (*esse*) but the well-being (*bene esse*) of matrimony which these practices oppose, the Divine Lawgiver may, for grave reasons, permit them. This no human legislator can do. The reason for the difference is that God by his omnipotence and universal providence can do what the human legislator cannot, namely, prevent the evils usually consequent upon these practices. That God exercised this special providence seems clear, because (*a*) polygyny ceased among the Jews by the time of the Babylonian captivity; (*b*) from the time of Moses to Christ divorce

---

[38] George H. Joyce, *Christian Marriage*, pp. 22, 30. London, Sheed and Ward, 1933.

[39] Jacques Leclercq, *Marriage and the Family*, trans. T. R. Hanley, O.S.B., pp. 89–90. New York, Pustet, 1941.

[40] "If a man have two wives, one beloved and the other hated; he may not make the son of the beloved the first born, and prefer him before the son of the hated" (Deut. 21: 15).

[41] "If a man take a wife and have her and she find not favor in his eyes for some uncleanness; he shall write a bill of divorce and give it in her hand and send her out of his house" (Deut. 24: 1).

[42] "He saith to them: Because Moses by reason of the hardness of your hearts permitted you to put away your wives: but from the beginning it was not so" (Matt. 19: 8).

among the Jews never rose to be a serious social menace as it did in contemporaneous Rome and Greece. To preserve the true religion among His chosen people by allowing them to follow the marital customs of the surrounding nations appears to be a sufficiently grave reason to justify the permission. It were better that God should grant them a dispensation from the original unity and indissolubility of the marriage tie, rather than that they should take it upon themselves and thus lapse from the true religion. That this divine license does not constitute an exception to the Natural Law has already been pointed out (§ 230).

However this dispute may be settled, our contention is sound and conclusive — the Natural Law forbids *men* to introduce and legalize either polygyny or divorce.

PROOF

731. No human authority can legalize a practice which militates against the adequate ends of matrimony, for man may not lawfully hinder the essential purposes of nature. Now polygyny militates against the adequate ends of matrimony, which include the good (*a*) of the spouses, (*b*) of the children, (*c*) of the State. In polygyny there is an *essential inequity* which runs counter to the good of all three.

1. *The good of the spouses.*

a) Matrimony demands reciprocal attachment. This is impossible in a situation where a wife cannot give her whole heart to a husband for the reason that he can give her but part of his divided affections. Love of friendship can exist only between equals.

b) The polygynous arrangement lacks that equity which a permanent contract like marriage demands. Since polyandry is intrinsically wrong, a woman must give herself *exclusively* to a husband. What excuses the husband from a like exclusive giving? Polygyny does not provide a complete remedy for concupiscence for all the wives, whereas the man is artificially stimulated to more and more sexual indulgence.

c) Wherever this practice prevails, woman's condition is servile.

2. *The good of the children.*

Polygyny naturally begets discord, jealousy, and contention in the family. This must react against the proper rearing of children. Children should regard their mother as an object of reverential love, the ideal of all that is good and noble. Instead she is but a servant, a person of small consequence.

3. *The good of the State.*

Because the number of males and females born is approximately the same, where polygyny flourishes many men will have no wives. Poverty dooms to enforced celibacy many younger men who must either become eunuchs or engage in intrigue with another man's wives.

Corollary. *Monogamy* — the union of one man with one woman — is the rule of nature. Nothing more simply indicates this than the fact that the birth rate of males and females is about the same.

3. *Divorce*

732. We have established the unity of the matrimonial bond. We have already shown that a certain stability must attach to the conjugal union (§ 704). Is it absolutely and universally permanent? Does it last until the death of the spouses and admit of no exceptions in any particular case? Or, granting a general need of permanence, may we admit exceptional cases wherein the conjugal tie may occasionally be broken?

Divorce is opposed to the permanency of the marital union. It may be perfect or imperfect. (*a*) *Imperfect divorce* is a relaxation of the major obligations of the matrimonial contract without a severing of the bond. This is called a separation from bed and board. The separated parties may not remarry. (*b*) *Perfect divorce* is a severing of the bond itself and allows the parties to enter new marriages.

733. It is strongly contended today, and in many quarters taken for granted, that if a marriage has so completely failed with a decent person being reduced to misery by the infidelity, insanity, cruelty, or drunkenness of one's mate, an efficacious remedy should be provided. Since it would mean an intolerable loss of happiness for the innocent party to wait until the death of the other for the dissolution of the union, a perfect divorce should be granted.

THESIS LII. The Natural Law forbids perfect divorce upon mere human authority.

734. The Natural Law does not condemn divorce as an evil in itself which is to be always and everywhere prohibited. Divorce is not good, but, since the primary end of marriage is attainable despite it, it is not totally evil. Therefore, the Divine Lawgiver Himself may allow it as the lesser of two evils and under controllable circumstances. It has already been mentioned that He made this exception in favor of the ancient Jews. Revelation also testifies that a similar permission exists in the Church today. Thus there are circumstances wherein a pagan converted to the faith may be released from an existing marriage and permitted by the Church to remarry. The Church may also cancel the marriage of two baptized persons which has never been consummated. This severing of the bond, however, is not an exercise of mere human authority; it is done through an explicit grant of divine power.

The fact that divorce may be granted upon divine authority does not indicate that the Natural Law is subject to change. For the Natural Law does not say: "Do not grant divorces," but "Do not grant divorces unless the Supreme Lawgiver approves."

PROOF

735. The Natural Law forbids any human power to introduce into matrimony a practice which foments enormous evils.

1. *Divorce renders the primary end of matrimony more difficult to attain.*

a) A child's education requires the guidance of both parents. Both have their unique contributions for the upbringing of their offspring.

b) The child of divorced parents can scarcely have an equal love for both parents. Reverence and filial affection ought to be the foundation stone of his character, but these qualities can be destroyed in circumstances which lead to contempt or even hatred of one of his parents.

c) Divorce conduces to the avoidance of children, because the presence of a young family renders future unions more difficult.

2. *Divorce militates against the good morals of husband and wife.*

a) The possibility of obtaining a divorce tends to destroy that complete union of mind and heart between husband and wife which marriage demands. In this union there should be complete security, no fear of a future rift. If divorce is envisioned even as remotely possible, this fear will be present, at least in some degree. Such a fear may grow, give rise to suspicion, jealousy, and eventually to a desire for someone else.

b) The possibility of divorce fosters selfishness and removes a potent motive for the practice of virtue. Successful marriage demands mutual forbearance, the spirit of give and take. Where divorce is possible, the thoroughly selfish party will refuse to curb his willfulness, knowing that he can get out of a bad situation by divorce. Where divorce is impossible, the parties are compelled to practice many virtues to maintain a union which usually constitutes their only chance at matrimony.

c) Besides rendering needless that prudent care in the selection of one's partner which so serious a step demands, the possibility of divorce actually incites to crime. If a person is anxious to get a divorce, the sole legal grounds for which are the commission of a crime, he will willingly enough commit that crime.

3. *Divorce militates against the good of society.*

Since the family is the fundamental organic unit of the State, the well-being of the State depends in large measure upon the well-being of the family.

Divorce promotes discord in families; tends to restrict the birth rate; incites to crime; prevents the proper training of future citizens; belittles the practice of self-control, patience, faithfulness, and other virtues, which in the citizen are of estimable value to the State.

736. The foregoing argument proves that as a *general rule* matrimony should be dissolved only by death. Two arguments prove that this is a universal, ironclad rule admitting of no exceptions.

1. In practice it would be impossible to limit divorces only to grave and exceptional cases. *Either divorce will be granted for every reason or it must never be granted.* This is a matter of all or none. The only way that the indissolubility of marriage can be maintained is by absolute indissolubility. If one loophole is allowed, inevitably, like the first breaching of a dike, the whole barrier will be swept away. In little more than one hundred years, the legal reasons for divorce have multiplied enormously; whereas formerly divorce could be had only by a special act of parliament for the reason of adultery, it is now to be had for the asking. Give men an inch and they take a mile. The scholastic writers who held that our position on divorce could not be proved from the unaided light of reason, would have changed their opinion if they had seen the proceedings of a Mexican or Parisian divorce court or the spectacle of States competing with one another to make divorce as easy as possible so as to attract the tourist divorce trade.

2. The main reason for divorce in an exceptional case is relief for the victim of an indissoluble tie. However, under a system of divorce — and there would inevitably be a system, for divorce cannot remain an exceptional and isolated phenomenon — the number of victim cases

would not be fewer but infinitely greater and the chief victim would be the woman, the weaker party. The evils which follow from divorce affect the whole of society; those incidental upon indissolubility are purely personal and do not affect society at large, any more than do the pains of the sick in a hospital. Now matrimony has as its end the good of the race; this end determines its characteristic of indissolubility, which may not be altered or impaired because of accidental hardships to the individual. Hence the common good reasonably demands that individuals bear the trials incidental to an indissoluble tie rather than let loose upon society the vast evils entailed by divorce.

IV. THE ORIGIN OF MATRIMONY

737. The problem of the origin of conjugal society presents two questions. The first may be framed thus: *What cause determined that such an institution should exist?* Evolutionary writers say that it originated in the same sort of paternal and maternal instinct to protect one's young and hence to live together as that which keeps male and female chimpanzee together.[43] This instinct was the root of a habit: in time it grew into a custom imposing moral obligation, which — in the language of those who offer this explanation — means that public opinion would disapprove of, and public authority would punish the husband who abandons wife and children.

738. We again deny as a gratuitous assumption the contention that man has ever been other than a rational animal. Whether man ever had subhuman ancestors is beside the point; we are establishing the specific law of rational animals, and in that law we find a need for conjugal society. That public sentiment is not the constitutive norm of morality, that moral law does not originate in mere mores and customs, we have disposed of in general ethics. Hence conjugal society is not an accidental but convenient arrangement which men luckily stumbled upon and got themselves accustomed to. It is not the result of chance or human experimentation. It is something divinely appointed. From the preceding sections in which we proved conjugal society to be natural and necessary, it is clear that it originated in a command of the Natural Law. God, then, the Legislator of that law, is the Author of conjugal society. As Universal Ruler and Provider, He

---

[43] Herbert Spencer's explanation is typical. See *Principles of Sociology*, Vol. I, pp. 621–640. Cf. also Edward Westermarck, *The History of Human Marriage*, Vol. I, p. 26 ff. London, Macmillan, 1921.

has in view the over-all good of the race — its proper conservation and increase — and has chosen conjugal society as the sole fitting means to this end. In order that His divine purpose be adequately realized and this instrument for human good be made use of, God implants in men and women a strong desire to enter the married state and presents to their reason the truth that their chief hope of temporal felicity lies therein. The fact that some persons listen to the prompting of nature and marry, while others flout it by homosexuality or like excesses, does not interest us now. Our concern is to show that conjugal society is a divinely established institution.

739. The second question which the problem of the origin of matrimony presents is this: *What cause produces every actual conjugal society?* Is there a direct divine intervention in the setting up of each conjugal union according to the homely adage that marriages are made in heaven? Obviously not: there are no signs of such divine intervention. Besides, it would be bordering on the impious to blame God for the folly of so many mismated marriages. It is the way of God with men to indicate the general pattern of essential human institutions and then to leave it to the discretion and choice of men to fill in the particulars. Since, then, men and women are not born married, how are they brought together, what causes the union of each particular married couple? To answer, we must distinguish between (a) the historic origin and (b) the juridic origin of each particular union.

A. Historic Origin

740. Every conjugal union has some factual beginning. Some accidental and variable set of facts culminated in this man's marriage to this woman. These antecedent facts in the main fall into two general patterns: one, called a courtship, wherein the man with more or less assiduity woos his prospective bride; the other, and more customary in human history, a nuptial agreement wherein parents or other parties arrange the union. What these diverse facts may have been or now are, is for the social historian to say. At present we are not directly concerned with these facts except to say that they are merely dispositive and not the causative factors in the resultant union.

B. Juridic Origin

Since the conjugal union is a true society, its creation means the endowing of the parties concerned with obligations and rights which they previously did not possess. A conjugal society is a moral person possessing a definite juridic standing. What in the juridic order is capable of producing the juridic effect of this man's now becoming the husband of this woman? This thing — fact, happening, disposition, legal edict, or whatever it be — will constitute the proximate efficient cause — or better — the juridic cause of every actual conjugal society.

THESIS LIII. The proximate juridic cause of every actual conjugal union can only be the free and mutual consent of a man and a woman.

PROOF

741. Each particular conjugal society must arise from a juridic cause which is in keeping with man's rational nature and with the peculiar character of this society. Such a cause can only be the free and mutual consent of a man and a woman.

1. *This cause must be in keeping with man's nature.* On entering the married state a man disposes of his person for life. Assuredly, the significant act of a man's career whereby he disposes of his person, and that for life, must be a free act. For to be responsible for his person, he must be free in the disposal of it. Second, nature does not determine who is married to whom. Since no individual is compelled to marry, it is left to the free choice of each to enter this society as he chooses and with the partner of his choice.

2. *The cause must be in keeping with the peculiar character of this society.* A union so intimate demands mutual love, which certainly cannot be extorted by force, fear, or command. Second, this state entails tedious burdens which no individual is, *per se,* obliged to assume, much less in the company of this particular partner. Hence the very nature of this society demands that one enter it solely by free choice.

742. N.B. It may not be argued that in the past almost universally, and even now generally among savages, the marriages of women have been arranged by parents or other responsible persons. This fact need not imply that the girl was married against her will. Since she desired matrimony, and since the only way to it was to accept the spouse of her parents' choosing, she would willingly enough acquiesce. If her wishes were not directly consulted, she was not without the means of making her inclination known and her influence felt. Even among savage tribes today, if the girl is unwilling, she is not forced to marry a particular man. Even though parents have married off their children with little consideration of their happiness, and young people have been mated unwillingly, consent is still an essential requisite. These examples are but instances of practice falling short of law. Although many persons lie and steal, it does not follow that there is no moral law against lying and stealing.

743. Corollary. *The marriage rite as the constitutive act of matrimony is a contract.* For this act, consisting in the free and mutual consent of two parties to give and accept rights concerning one and the same object, fulfills the requisite conditions for a valid, bilateral contract.

V. THE MARRIAGE CONTRACT

744. The contract of betrothal must not be confused with the contract of marriage. Betrothal is a mutual promise of marriage, binding in commutative justice, and severable at the will of the parties. It pertains to a *future* giving and acceptance of marital rights. The marriage contract is the mutual handing over of such rights here and now. It is more than a promise to exchange rights; it is the actual exchange of rights, and it is not severable at the will of the parties. We shall now consider the marriage contract in detail in the light of (1) matrimonial consent; (2) the matter of this consent; (3) the parties to the contract; (4) the relation of this contract to other contracts.

A. Matrimonial Consent

745. Consent is so integral a part of the marriage contract that no human power can replace it. If it is wanting, conjugal union is impossible. Matrimonial consent must be (1) genuine, (2) deliberate, (3) mutual, (4) externally manifested, and (5) given by a man and woman capable of making this contract.

1. *Genuine consent* is true agreement; outward pretence of agreement is not consent. A person who has manifested fictitious consent is not married, although positive law rightly considers such a person married until he offers juridical evidence that he did not consent. Fictitious consent, however, may be validated by the proffering of a properly sanating consent. If the withholding of consent was *purely internal,* the marriage contract could be validated by the mere eliciting of true consent, provided the consent of the other party remained. If the withholding of consent was external but *could not be juridically*

proved, an external but private manifestation of consent could validate the contract. If the withholding of consent was external and *could be juridically proved,* an external manifestation of consent, satisfactory to social authority, is required for convalidation.

2. *Deliberate* consent is given with full advertence of the mind and perfect agreement of the will. No one assumes grave obligations without knowing them and being willing to accept them.

3. *Mutual* consent is given by each party because of and with a view to the consent of the other. An onerous bilateral contract requires the agreement of both parties. However, their agreement need not be simultaneous; the consent of one party may be given for the first time, even a long time, after the other party has agreed. If the consent of the first party remains, this delayed consent produces a valid marriage.

4. Consent must be *externally manifested.* The manifestation of agreement is essential in any contract. The Natural Law only requires that each party outwardly signify agreement to the other. However, since the conjugal union is of such importance to society, and since very great evils would arise if this contract were concluded in total secrecy, positive law can and usually does prescribe that this manifestation of agreement accord with a prescribed form, such as the presence of certified witnesses.[44] The Natural Law commands compliance with these forms even when positive law prescribes them under penalty of nullity of contract. However, where compliance with these forms would be impossible and a couple might otherwise be compelled to forego matrimony forever, or for a very long time, the positive law would lapse by *epikeia* and the merely natural form of contract would be permissible.

5. Consent must be given by *a man and woman capable of contracting.* The elements which constitute capability for making the contract will be taken up presently.

Matrimony, like other contracts, is sometimes entered upon under certain conditions. If these conditions are *supplementary* to the marriage contract — modal conditions — they do not affect the matrimonial consent and there is no question of invalidity. If a condition affects matrimonial consent, it may invalidate consent. The validity of one's consent depends on whether the object of one's will act remains a true marriage in the light of the affixed condition, or

---

[44] *Codex Juris Canonici,* 1094.

whether the condition makes the marriage a sham. If the former, consent is valid; if the latter, consent is invalid. If, therefore, one consents only on condition that (*a*) no true right of intercourse be given, or (*b*) only a right to contraceptive intercourse be given, or (*c*) one be at liberty to marry other wives or to break up this union and marry some other person, or (*d*) one be free to commit adultery, his consent is not consent to matrimony. It is dangerous to add any "ands, ifs, or buts" to one's consent: it should be unreserved and unconditional.

B. The Matter of Consent

746. What exactly forms the object of the matrimonial consent, or better, what right does one party transfer to the other in this contract? The man who enters this contract transfers to a woman the exclusive and permanent right to use his body for acts proper to procreate children. By acceptance of this right, the woman is constituted the wife of the man. Similarly, the woman transfers to the man the exclusive and permanent right to use her body for acts proper to procreate children. By acceptance of this right, the man becomes the husband of the woman.

That this alone is the essential object of the matrimonial consent follows from the primary end of matrimony, the procreation and rearing of children. The rights of cohabitation, of mutual love, of a certain community of goods, of the wife to protection and support, and of the husband to obedience, are merely consectaries of this essential point. Cohabitation pertains not to the essence but to the integrity of matrimony; mutual love is the practical condition requisite for the happy outcome of the matrimonial venture; a community of goods is a condition necessary for the reasonable bearing of the obligations of matrimony.

That this right is permanent follows from the indissoluble permanence of this union (§736). That it is an exclusive right follows from monogamistic character of matrimony (§ 731, Cor.). Once this right is mutually exchanged, each party is bound in commutative justice so that any sexual contact with a third party violates justice in a serious matter.

747. To the youthful and inexperienced, the flat statement that a right to carnal intercourse is the primary object of the matrimonial consent, is sometimes a shattering of the pure beauty and romance of marriage. Though this attitude reminds one of Manicheeism, which taught that the flesh is essentially evil, yet it is usually the outcome of a chaste and blameless upbringing. However, a little reflection must show that this act must be in itself good, wholesome, and praiseworthy. It is the ultimate expression of mutual love. It is ordained by God as the sole means of fulfilling a divine purpose. It loses the luster of virtue and lapses into the indecent only through its unholy imitation in the form of fornication, adultery, and contraception.

748. It must be carefully noted that in the exercise of marital rights both parties are absolutely equal. Even though the man is the head of the family, in this fundamental respect he has no priority over his wife. Nor has the wife over the husband, even though the actual burden of childbearing devolves upon her. Neither is subordinate to the other. Each is bound to accede to the other's *serious* request for marital relations so that refusal constitutes a grave violation of justice. The sole causes which excuse from sin in such a refusal are adultery of the other party and grave danger to one's health. Practically speaking, failure to fulfill this fundamental obligation with alacrity and charity are the roots of marital discord and disunion.

Consummation by actual marital relations adds to the married state a certain perfection of rights exercised. Thereby the two are made one flesh. But even before consummation, the contracting parties are truly married. For a couple are married if the man and woman have marital rights in each other's regard. This the ceremony of contract provides. However, in the case of two baptized persons, consummation adds this perfection — absolutely no human authority can sever the bond.

C. Parties to the Consent

749. Parties to consent are a man and a woman physically and juridically capable of matrimony.

1. Physical Capacity

Physical capacity means that each party has (*a*) the age and unimpeded use of reason requisite for true matrimonial consent; (*b*) the ability to perform the human generative act in the natural way. Because of physical incapacity, therefore, the Natural Law excludes from matrimony persons with any of the following six deficiencies:

750. *a*) *Lack of age.* The natural age for matrimony is that age at which a person has sufficient knowledge and discretion to give true matrimonial consent. Positive law usually presumes that a person is not so qualified before the age of puberty and hence prohibits marriage before that age. Canon Law[45] takes the extra precaution of invalidating the attempted marriage of a male before the completion of his sixteenth year and of a female before the completion of her fourteenth year.

751. *b*) *Lack of the use of reason.* Infants or lunatics, intoxicated, drugged, or hypnotized persons are incapable of making a contract.

752. *c*) *Defective knowledge.* A valid contract requires sufficient knowledge of the object of consent. The absence of this knowledge precludes the essential agreement, which is contract. What, then, is that bare minimum of knowledge for lack of which a person is incapable of this contract? From our explanation of the matrimonial consent (§ 745) it follows that one must know at least that matrimony is a permanent society between man and woman for the procreating of children through some sort of bodily communion. It is by no means necessary that one know the precise mode and nature of carnal intercourse, generation, and birth, but one has to know, at least vaguely and in general, that one hands over and acquires a right to some sort of bodily conjunction whence children are begotten and which is peculiar to matrimony. It is confessedly difficult to draw a hard and fast line which would accurately define where sufficient knowledge exists and where an invalidating ignorance begins. Certainly a person would be invalidatingly ignorant who thought matrimony a mere friendly, temporary alliance or the *mere* setting up of a common ménage, or who was totally and absolutely unaware of the need of some kind of corporal intercourse. Positive law — as Canon Law[46] — presumes that this sort of ignorance does not exist after one has reached the age of puberty.

753. *d*) *Mistake,* or error, in this matter, has to do with (1) the person of the other party, or (2) some essential quality of matrimony.

(1) *The person of the other party.* Mistake of person, for instance, John marries Anna thinking her to be Sarah, her twin sister, invalidates consent. It constitutes substantial error. Mistake concerning some quality in the person — as when Mary marries Paul thinking him to be wealthy whereas he is not — does not affect consent. The error is

---

[45] *Codex Juris Canonici,* 1067.
[46] *Ibid.,* 1082, 2.

only accidental. In two cases, however, a mistake of quality is equivalent to a mistake of person. First, the quality may be definitive of the person, as when George marries Marjorie Wilson thinking her to be *The* Marjorie Wilson, President Wilson's daughter. Second, one may marry upon the explicit condition of the existence of a given quality, as when Charles tells Louise that he will marry her provided she is free of venereal disease.

(2) *Some essential quality of matrimony.* In § 752 we have discussed the knowledge essential to consent, but a related and quite knotty question may arise. Unity and indissolubility are essential properties of matrimony. Does ignorance of this truth vitiate consent? For example, a Mohammedan, marrying his first wife, may vaguely hope to take more wives when his financial condition improves; many Americans marry believing in divorce. Do their wrong notions invalidate consent? Usually they do not. Mistaken notions about polygamy and divorce can coexist with true consent because ordinarily these ideas do not affect the will's intention. These persons intend to marry as other people do: the object of their intention is true matrimony, not a simulation of it. When, however, such error *actually* influences consent so that a person agrees upon the express condition that he is entering a marriage terminable by divorce, he does not validly consent.

754. *e) Duress and fear.* Duress is irresistible violence to which one unwillingly submits. It is a bar to any contract. Canon Law[47] safeguards freedom to consent by providing that no marriage is possible between an abductor and a woman forcibly taken or detained with a view to matrimony until such time as she is restored to a place of safety and freedom.

A person who enters matrimony induced by grave fear performs a human act and has true consent, but is such consent sufficient for the matrimonial contract? First, Canon Law[48] declares null from the beginning consent extorted by grave fear arising from a source external to the agent and unjustly inflicted so that one embraces matrimony to escape the threatened evil. Many civil codes have similar prescriptions. But does the Natural Law also invalidate such a consent? There is a sharp cleavage of opinion here. Those who answer in the affirmative say that if an ordinary contract is entered into under pressure of such fear, the contract is later rescindable, but since the

---

[47] *Ibid.,* 1074.   [48] *Ibid.,* 1087, § 1.

matrimonial contract, once validly formed, cannot be rescinded, such consent must be initially invalid. Otherwise, one would suffer an irreparable injury by being morally forced into a permanent state through fear of injustice. On the other hand, it is more reasonably contended that an act elicited even under grave, external, and unjust fear is still a human act, a free choice. Since neither slight fear, nor fear arising from a source internal to the agent, nor just external fear invalidates matrimonial consent, no fear does. Either all fear invalidates a contract or no fear does. Nor may an exception be urged in the case of unjust external fear on the ground that it causes irreparable injury. For one may be led into matrimony by deceitful or even fraudulent misrepresentations and suffer a similar injury, yet no one claims that such consent is initially invalid.

The practical conclusion is that when a nonbaptized person enters matrimony induced by fear in a place where the civil law does not nullify such consent, then by Natural Law such a marriage is to be looked on as valid, according to the maxim that a juridic act is presumed valid unless its invalidity is certainly established.

755. *f*) *Impotence.* Since the right which passes in the matrimonial contract is the right to use one's body for acts proper to procreation, nature must prohibit from matrimony persons incapable of such acts. For if an act is impossible, no right to that act can be given or accepted. The object of contract is nonexistent; hence no contract is possible. Anyone, therefore, who before matrimony is *perpetually* incapable of performing the generative act in the natural way either with this person or with all persons is barred by nature itself from marriage with this person or with all persons. A male has this incapacity if he lacks seed, or the ability to eject seed, or the ability to eject it into the body of a woman. A female is impotent if she cannot receive seed.

Impotence must carefully be distinguished from *sterility* which is inability to generate. Sterility is not a bar to matrimony. This is evident from consideration of the material object of consent which is only the generative act, not generation itself. This ultimately does not depend on the choice of the agent. Nor may one be prohibited from marriage because of impotence unless the disability is clearly certain.

2. *Juridic Capacity*

756. *Juridic capacity* means that a person otherwise physically able is not prevented from matrimony by some juridic obstacle established by Natural or positive law. This juridic obstacle is some external circumstance affecting a person and legally rendering him temporarily or permanently incapable of matrimony.

But this question immediately arises: granted one is mentally and physically fit, why should law specify further requisites. Is not matrimony a private affair and entrance into it but the response of an individual to one of the most primal of human instincts? Since matrimony antedates the State, and since the right to marry is an immediate concession of nature, why should this right be abridged by social authority?

Matrimony, however, is not entirely a private affair. It has such wide-reaching social effects that the well-being of society depends in no small measure upon the well-being of the conjugal union. Since the sexes can consort and propagate in a way that runs counter to the social good, social authority may determine these detrimental circumstances and forbid and even nullify marriage where they are verified.

757. *a)* *Natural juridic capacity.* The Natural Law prohibits matrimony because of (1) consanguinity and (2) an existing marriage tie. A person who attempts to marry despite these impediments contracts an invalid marriage.

(1) *Consanguinity.* Marriage between a parent and a child is unnatural because (*a*) it would destroy the essential relation of inequality between a child and its parent established by nature itself; (*b*) all consanguine marriages tend to be detrimental to the offspring: *a fortiori* these evil consequences would follow from a marriage in which the blood relationship is the closest possible.

Unless it is absolutely necessary to carry on the human race, the marriage of brother and sister is likewise forbidden by nature. That special relation of love and confidence between brother and sister which is of such value to both would be destroyed and turned into a source of evil rather than good if they were free to marry. Unless nature herself forbade all hope of carnal intercourse between offspring of the same parents, the peace and purity of family life would be destroyed. Mentally and bodily defective persons come from such unions. A third reason may be added: the marriage of brother and sister would not establish those new bonds of friendship and relationship which the marriages of unrelated persons provide.

These evils militating against the good of the offspring, the sanctity of family life, and the strengthening of social ties, are found in the marriage of closely related cousins, though of course to a lesser degree. The Natural Law does not prohibit such unions; it is rather left to positive law[49] to regulate them so that these evil effects are prevented.

(2) *An existing marriage tie.* Monogamy is the law of nature. Therefore once a person has entered a valid conjugal union, no human authority can allow him to enter another union until the death of his partner will have severed the existing marital tie.

758. *b) Positive juridic capacity.* Since passing mention has been made of positive law establishing invalidating matrimonial impediments, it is well to make clear the nature of this power and the reason for it. Besides clarifying the conditions under which the Natural Law disqualifies a person from contracting marriage, positive law may determine that there are other conditions wherein matrimony would be harmful to the social good. Since matrimony affects the common good in so many ways, and since the Natural Law is not sufficiently explicit regarding all possible contingencies, there is need of positive legislation to establish, as necessity requires, other impediments and salutary laws that will secure the good estate of matrimony. As we shall presently see (§ 764), matrimony has a naturally sacred and religious character.

Hence any further regulation concerning its essential character must devolve upon religious authority. Therefore it is for the Church to legislate for the marriages of baptized persons, not only because of the naturally religious character of matrimony, but especially because the marriage ceremony of the baptized is a sacrament. To the Church alone is entrusted the care of the sacraments.

It has been contended by some Christian writers who hesitate to give the State its full due, that in the case of nonbaptized persons, the State has no jurisdiction over marriage itself except to clarify and enforce the impediments of the Natural Law. But the need of further legislation for the common good is apparent, and since among the nonbaptized there is no religious authority competent to do this, the task must fall upon the State. However, such civil impediments must, as any other laws, be reasonable, capable of being observed, and promotive of good morals; otherwise, they have no force.

3. Medical Certificates

759. Modern laws require a certificate attesting that one is free from

---

[49] See *Codex Juris Canonici*, 1076, 2.

venereal disease before one may marry. Some of these laws merely prohibit marriage until one is cured; others, declare such marriages null especially if the other party had no knowledge of the existence of the disease. There can be no doubt that the intent of such legislation — the stamping out of these diseases — is admirable. Hence every citizen should co-operate in every lawful manner. But, is such legislation lawful? Is the State competent to make such laws? Must the citizen in conscience obey them?

760. A distinction must be made between marriage laws for the baptized and marriage laws for the unbaptized. As for the baptized, the State has no direct power at all over either marriage itself or the inseparable effects of marriage such as the rights and obligations of the couple, the legitimacy of the children, and parental authority. The reason is twofold: (*a*) marriage is something naturally sacred and falls under the jurisdiction of religious rather than secular authority; (*b*) the Christian marriage contract is a true sacrament and to the Church alone belongs the care of the sacraments. While the State can legislate concerning the *merely* civil effects of Christian marriage, that is, effects separable from marriage itself as dowry, succession to titles and property, it has no power to determine what constitutes a lawful or valid Christian marriage.

Indirectly, as a consequence of some other legal act, the State may affect the marriage of Christians, as when by perpetual imprisonment, the sending of soldiers to war, the segregation of persons infectiously diseased, the State would take away opportunity to marry. By application of the principle of double effect we see that the State may sometimes do this. However, to allow so grave an effect as the curtailment of the right to marry, a proportionately grave cause is always required.

As the guardian of public health, the State may demand examination of prospective spouses, advise remedies, and suggest cures. It may segregate the venereally afflicted for a time *if* segregation is a reasonable means of cure. But the State may not by direct legislative act prohibit or nullify a Christian marriage. This would be usurpation of undue jurisdiction. It would be equivalent to the State saying who could or could not receive any of the other sacraments of the Church.

761. But in making such a law, is not the State merely enunciating the Natural Law? Are not the venereally afflicted obliged by the Natural Law to abstain from marriage? No disease, not even a dreadful disease like leprosy — provided of course it does not induce

impotency — is an impediment in the eyes of the Natural Law. This we gather from the silence of the Church. It is her obligation for the good of Christian matrimony to declare the impediments of the Natural Law, and careful and detailed as her legislation is, she has never said that communicable disease is an impediment. Certainly, if a person who has such a disease were to marry without disclosing the fact to the other party he would do a grave injustice, but if the healthy party were aware of the disease and nevertheless were willing to marry, no natural impediment would exist.

762. Are the baptized obliged in conscience to obey such laws? Prudence certainly demands that where such laws exist the baptized conform to them. They would be bound to submit to an examination and to undertake reasonable means of cure; but if for a pressing reason — say the avoidance of concubinage — a healthy party were willing to marry a syphilitic, the parties could proceed in good conscience. If the marriage were otherwise licit and valid in the eyes of the Church, no civil penalties could morally be inflicted on them for violating this prescription of civil law. Such a marriage could be contracted legitimately as a remedy for concupiscence, the prevention of mortal sin, which is a secondary end of marriage. The physical evils which might follow from such a union to offspring or healthy consort are an immeasurably lesser evil than a single grave sin which such a marriage could prevent. Even the birth of stillborn children does not militate against this principle for it is better, even naturally, to be than never to be at all.

763. We have already shown that the State can establish diriment impediments for the unbaptized. Now a proposed impediment must be adapted to the end in view, and it must promote the moral as well as the physical well-being of society. As for the prophylactic value of such legislation, we must remember it is easy enough to defeat the intent of the law by fraud. Furthermore, an extremely dangerous moral situation can result from the enforcement of such a law, namely, the increase of concubinage. Where such legislation has gone into effect, as in Puerto Rico,[50] an alarming decrease in the number of marriages resulted — there were 13,964 marriages in 1937, but in 1938, the year after the law was passed, there were only 9212.

---

[50] Department of the Interior, Division of Territories and Island Possessions, annual reports of the Commissioner of Health of Puerto Rico.

In New York State[51] in 1937 there were 135,425 marriages; in the first full year after the law became effective there were 104,820.

D. The Relation of Marriage to Other Contracts

764. The marriage contract differs from all other contracts by reason of its (1) end, (2) matter, (3) unalterable terms, and (4) intimate connection with religion.

1. *End.* The end intended by nature in the marriage contract is not primarily the good of the individuals contracting but the good of the race. While persons who enter matrimony consider it the chief source of their temporal happiness, nevertheless this personal good in nature's intent is subordinate to the good of the human race. When this natural order is reversed and the majority of people act as though the primary end of matrimony were the good of the spouses, dire evils inevitably follow. In this misconception are rooted divorce, birth control, and trial marriage.

2. *Matter.* In all other contracts the matter is external and inferior to man. Here the contracting parties dispose of their very persons.

3. *Unalterable terms.* The terms and duration of many contracts are determined by the parties themselves. This is not the case in the marriage contract. This contract sets up a natural institution; and once the contract is formed, the resultant union cannot be dissolved by the mutual consent of the parties, nor can they determine anything contrary to the essential constitution of this union which has already been fixed by the Author of nature and placed beyond the tampering of men.

4. *Intimate connection with religion.* The matrimonial contract is especially related to God because its ultimate end is the procreation of rational beings wherein God concurs in a very special way by the creation of spiritual souls. It initiates conjugal life whose purpose is the increase of immortal beings, destined for eternal beatitude. Besides, the burdens of this state are so heavy that they can reasonably be borne only with the help and solace of religion.

The natural matrimonial contract is not an explicit act of religion;

---

[51] Department of Health, State of New York, Office of Vital Statistics. A further study of statistics of both jurisdictions shows that the people were not long in adjusting themselves to a new situation. In New York State, the number of marriages rose to 132,000 in 1940, and in Puerto Rico to over 19,000. Are we to assume that syphilis was wiped out or that people found ways of getting a clean bill of health?

but, because of its close connection with God's purpose — the procurement of His external glory — it is naturally sacred and holy. However, we know from revelation that the contract between baptized[52] persons has been elevated by Christ to the dignity of a sacrament and thus it becomes an explicit act of supernatural religion.

VI. MATRIMONIAL EVILS

765. Anything which militates against the integrity of matrimony or renders difficult the attainment of its ends is a matrimonial evil. It deprives this institution of a good that should be present. From our discussions of companionate marriage, forced consent, polyandry, polygyny, and divorce, it is evident how these things are destructive of the good of matrimony. Several further points deserve attention.

A. Evils Contrary to the Good of the Spouses

766. Marital love, the rock on which husband and wife build their happiness, is impossible of realization, or if had, is destroyed by certain heedless or sinful acts.

1. *Unwise choice of one's partner.* Passionate haste, which is but a fire of the body, drives into wedlock many young people wholly unsuited to each other. Passion dies and there is no loftier bond to take its place. Young persons ought not to be motivated solely by romantic illusions and physical beauty. To be sensibly realistic, they should ask themselves, What will my dream man be like ten, twenty years from now? How well can we bear the years together? It is an ancient wisdom which says — marry your own kind. This advice has special reference to religion. Marriage intends to make two one flesh, but if there is a profound difference in a couple's philosophy of life — and religion is the basis of a philosophy of life — a complete union of mind and heart is next to impossible. The saddest result of such mismating is that so often the children grow up without any religion.

2. *Selfishness* is at the bottom of domestic quarreling, nagging, the pursuit of habitual sins which, like drunkenness, make family peace impossible. Love is surrender, giving. Not demanding always, always taking. The man or wife who habitually puts self first will certainly fail at marriage.

---

[52] See *Codex Juris Canonici*, 1012, 1.

3. *Adultery* known and uncondoned can be sufficient reason for the perpetual cessation of marital life. It is the heinous rupture of the communion of body whereby two are made one flesh. It is caused by the grudging fulfillment of marriage duties, and desire for variety, excitement, and sensual friendship of a third party. It is not jealousy nor narrow-mindedness but simple common sense which forbids married persons such friendships.

B. Evils Contrary to the Good of the Child

767. Foremost among the evils contrary to the good of the child are abortion and sterilization, which we have already considered. Impediments to the proper rearing of the child are dealt with in the next chapter. Here we come to grips with the foremost moral pest of modern times — contraception or birth control.

1. What Is Birth Control?

768. In general, birth control is planned limitation of offspring. In many periods of human history, for economic or religious reasons, men have desired as numerous a progeny as possible. In a patriarchal economy, agricultural or pastoral, the rearing of children is inexpensive. A man's wealth depends on the number of children who will work for him and his renown upon the descendants who will revere him when he is gone. But as soon as a civilization attains a high peak, children become a personal and economic liability and a tendency to limit the size of the family arises.

769. Thomas Malthus (1766–1834) contended that where the reproductive instinct was uncontrolled, the population increased in geometric proportion (1–2–4–8–16).[53] Since the products of the earth increased only in arithmetic proportion (1–2–3–4–5),[54] the number of births must radically be curbed to prevent overcrowding of population and shortages of food. The remedy he suggested was late marriage and voluntary continence in marriage.[55]

770. In our own time there has been an impressive falling off in the birth rate of all civilized nations. The methods and motives of modern birth control have changed since the time of Malthus. The followers

---

[53] T. R. Malthus, *An Essay on the Principle of Population.* London, Johnson, 1803.
[54] *Ibid.*, Bk. I, Chap. 1, p. 8.
[55] *Ibid.*, Bk. IV, Chaps. 1–2, pp. 483–503.

of Malthus appealed to the common good and advocated chastity and self-restraint. Today, the appeal is based on many motives, economic, social, eugenic, personal, and purely hedonistic. Scarcely any modern advocate of birth control preaches self-restraint but merely what we shall describe as positive contraception.

Controversy has arisen concerning the morality of birth control. To many respectable persons, it is a common sense procedure. To others, an execrable crime. Since there is birth control and birth control, we must determine exactly which kind of birth control defeats the primary end of marriage.

771. *a*) *Does birth control consist in the desire not to have children?* Is the desire "not to have children" intrinsically wrong? Since the obligation to propagate falls directly upon the race and not necessarily upon a particular couple, the answer is *no*. When the race is in danger of extinction and the obligation of propagation directly falls on individual couples, that desire would be wrong.

But is not this a wish opposed to the primary end of marriage and therefore wrong? If a person who intends to have no children goes through a marriage ceremony, and in his matrimonial consent yields no right of intercourse, or fails to grant a perpetual and exclusive right of intercourse, or agrees only to an abuse of intercourse, his consent is invalid. The object of his consent is not true matrimony. A person who wishes matrimony must be willing to accept parenthood. However, the intention of not having children is compatible with valid consent if a person's prevailing intention is to enter the married state and to this intention is joined a subsequent intention either to abuse matrimony by contraception or wholly to refrain from using it. One may validly consent and intend to abuse it, because it is possible to assume obligations which one does not intend to fulfill. This is always grievously wrong. If the intention is not to use matrimony, we must distinguish several different possibilities: (1) The resolution or vow of one party to preserve chastity in matrimony does not invalidate consent provided he gives and accepts matrimonial rights because he can acquire a right even though he does not intend to exercise it. (2) If both parties compact not to use matrimony so that the consent of one is given only on condition that the other agrees to perpetual chastity, their agreement invalidates consent. (3) If both parties agree unconditionally to exchange marital rights and then subjoin to their matrimonial consent the modal condition of not using matrimony, the consent is valid. To marry and intend not to use matrimony is a procedure to be justified only by a most extraordinary reason: matrimony is not the milieu for maintaining chastity.

It is not, then, the intention of having no children which is in itself wrong: the practical evil lies in the choice of illicit means by which this intention is carried out. In the vast majority of cases a person who desires not to have children is on dangerous ground because he is little likely to haggle at illicit means.

772. *b) Is abstention from marital relations wrong?* The effective method of preventing conception is abstention from intercourse. Is it wrong for a couple to abstain?

The obligation which each party assumes is to render the marital debt upon the other's request, but there is no obligation from the nature of the contract to request relations. First, there is no need of a moral obligation because the proximate end intended by nature — sufficient use of generative faculties — is adequately assured by the driving urge to use these faculties and the pleasure attached to their use. Second, requesting relations is a privilege, and no one is *ex se* obliged to use a privilege. Therefore there is no obligation in justice to request relations, although at times one may arise from charity, that is, to prevent a rift of love or to avoid the incontinence of the other party.

A couple, then, may mutually agree to abstain either for a time or even altogether and do no wrong. Far from being wrong, this is justly lauded as virtue.

773. *c) Is it wrong to restrict intercourse to those times when it is most unlikely conception will follow?* The rhythm theory advanced by Latz[56] and others holds that in the menstrual cycle of every woman there is a definite period of sterility which may be accurately computed and forecast. Some medical authorities reject the sterile period: others dispute about the time of its occurrence. Whatever may be the merits of this physiological dispute, it is ethically certain that to confine intercourse to a sterile period is not wrong, because no action intrinsically evil is committed and the intention of avoiding conception is not in itself wrong.

774. *d)* Positive contraception is the prevention of, or the attempt to prevent, the marriage act from issuing in conception. Chemicals

---

[56] John L. Latz, *The Rhythm of Sterility and Fertility in Women.* Chicago, Latz Foundation, 1934.

are used to kill the sperm, or mechanical obstacles or other means are employed to prevent its union with the ovum. This birth control we brand a hideous crime against nature.

2. The Malice of Positive Contraception

THESIS LIV. Every act of positive contraception is intrinsically wrong.

775. Just as lying is a perversion of the faculty of speech, just as masturbation and sodomy are abuses of the sex faculty, so positive contraception is unnatural and is always and everywhere forbidden by the law of nature.

776. This demonstration is of the utmost importance: hence the ultimate basis upon which it rests must be clearly grasped. Let us recall that good is that which is suitable, and nothing is more suitable to a faculty than the natural end for which it was intended. Evil is a deprivation of a good which ought to be present. Perfective good is that which is suitable because it affords the faculty an absent but due perfection or removes a present imperfection. Delectable good is suitable and desirable inasmuch as it is the subjective satisfaction or delight consequent on the attainment of a perfective good. Since nothing so perfects a faculty as the realization of its natural end, this natural end attained is the perfective good of the faculty.

Nature has in view definite perfective goods which man is to attain by use of his faculties. To ensure the sufficient use of these faculties, and thereby the attainment of the fullness of human well-being, nature attaches no inconsiderable delectable good to the use of a faculty. Hence to set a faculty in motion, to enjoy its pleasure, and to allow the action to proceed to its natural term — this is a good and orderly use of the faculty. On the other hand, to set a faculty in motion, to enjoy its delectable good, and then so to distort the act that its natural end is made impossible — this is always evil because it is the deprivation of a good that ought to be present, namely, the possibility of issuing in its natural end. This is a perversion of nature's process, and the gravity of the evil done is measured by the importance of the good which is frustrated.

777. These truths we apply to the sex faculty. The ultimate purpose of the sex faculty is a tremendously important good; and precisely because this ultimate perfective good is not so much a good of the individual as it is a good of the human race, nature has attached to this faculty the most vehement of all sense pleasures. Therefore to set this faculty in motion, to cull the pleasure, and then positively and deliberately to prevent conception, to destroy that ultimate perfective good for which alone the faculty exists, is a foul perversion, an intrinsically disorderly use of the faculty, a frustration of nature in a matter of the utmost moment. The unreason consists not only in the subordination of perfective to delectable good but in the total abolition of the perfective good. If that is not evil, nothing is evil.

PROOF

778. To use an important faculty so as to prevent it from its natural end is intrinsically wrong. But in positive contraception one uses the important faculty of sex so as to prevent it from its natural end. Therefore positive contraception is intrinsically wrong. The major premise of this argument is proved in §§ 776 and 777.

779. Corollary. There are absolutely no circumstances nor motives which ever render the act of contraception excusable. If nature did not condemn the act as such, she would be condoning her own extinction.

780. Though generally the guilt of this act falls equally upon both parties, this crime may be committed so that one party alone sins, as when the man interrupts the act or the woman resorts to lotions after the act. The innocent party has a grave obligation in charity to admonish and to take serious steps to deter the other. If no heed is paid to these warnings, the innocent party does not sin by proceeding with marital relations.

3. Excuses for Birth Control

781. *a) Health motive.* Women are worn out before their time by too frequent childbearing. Births should be more properly spaced for the good both of child and of mother. The American Birth Control League propagandizes with a doleful picture of wan, depressed mothers harried by a brood of noisy children, typified in the letter quoted by Bromley: "We have been married three years and have four children, and I have lost my health. I am so nervous I can hardly do my work. The doctor tells me it is because I have given birth to children too often."[57]

---

[57] Dorothy B. Bromley, *Birth Control: Its Use and Misuse*, p. 16. New York, Harper, 1934.

But this is far from the normal situation. Certainly births ought to be properly spaced and this nature takes care of when the mother herself nurses the child. Of course conception is not impossible during the time of natural nursing but it is exceptional. Apart from the use of contraceptives or abstention, there is usually a natural interval of two years between births — an interval which widens as the woman grows older. Considering the age at which women marry in urban civilization and the incidence of their menopause, one may forecast that their normal expectancy of children will range from four to six — by no means the intolerable burden depicted by the American Birth Control League. It should be noted that among the poor it is not the mere bearing of children which wears out women but the dreadful living conditions they have to endure. The remedy lies not in offering them contraceptive knowledge but in procuring a living wage for the heads of families. Medical science is beginning to return to the position that nature, not man, is the best spacer of births.

After studying 38,087 obstetric patients, Dr. Nicholson J. Eastman[58] of the Johns Hopkins Medical School found these conclusions inescapable: (a) Infants born within two years of a previous viable delivery have at least as low a stillbirth and neonatal mortality as infants born after longer intervals. (b) The longer the interval between births, the more likely the mother is to suffer from some form of hypertensive toxemia of pregnancy. The incidence of this complication is lowest when the interval is twelve to twenty-four months, significantly higher when it is twenty-four to forty-eight, and much higher when it exceeds four years. (c) In patients who had a previous hypertensive toxemia, the likelihood of repetition becomes progressively greater as the intervals become longer.

He found it quite probable that the chances of neonatal mortality increase as the interval widens. His figures were 1.5 per cent for the "Brief" interval group, 2.2 for the "Moderate" interval group, and 2.6 for the "Long" group.

He concludes that physicians recommending child spacing for the health of mother and child often overlook the most potent factor favoring the mother, namely, youth. Child spacing means maternal aging and after the early twenties maternal aging involves greater risks. Whatever advantage is had by a rest period of several years is

[58] N. J. Eastman, "The Effect of the Interval Between Births on Maternal and Fetal Outlook," *American Journal of Obstetrics and Gynecology*, April, 1944, pp. 445-463.

offset and often more than counterbalanced by the aging factor. Youth is a better ally of childbearing than child spacing.

If a woman is able to bear a child every year, her fertility may not be checked by intrinsically wrong means. Nor may such means be resorted to by one who has been told with the utmost certainty that another pregnancy will be fatal to her. Medical directives are not the over-all law of human activity.

One of the principal preoccupations of the advocates of birth control is the recommendation of "safe" contraceptive methods, that is, methods which are not only effective but cause no injury to health. But they carefully conceal the fact that constant use of any contraceptive over a long period is dangerous to health — at least to the woman's. For the female body is intended by nature to absorb the sperm and receive an increase of vitality from that which is the bearer of life. Hence, if the body is constantly excited sexually but starved of the sperm, it is small wonder that physical and psychic disorders result. That such ills result is another indication of the primacy of the moral law, which may not be transgressed with impunity.

782. *b*) *Good of the child motive.* Many parents, otherwise upright and devoted to their duties but without the courage to be continent, practice contraception because they wish fewer children who will be brought up better and left in a more comfortable situation than they were by their parents. But this attitude is really exaltation of material goods above spiritual values.

One or two children will have more material advantages than six — more toys, more amusements, better clothes, more spending money. But normally a large family is a better educative milieu than a small one. A child has better opportunities for development in a large family than in a small one. The larger the number of children, the more closely parents are knit together and the less danger of their separating. To provide for a larger family, man and wife must exercise more moral virtue — more providence, more industry, a graver sense of responsibility, and above all more unselfish devotion. The special effort which they must constantly exert cannot but react favorably upon their children. Hence, these parents will make a better home — better, not in the sense of hardwood floors, refrigerators, and radios, but in the sense of human contact, affection, and moral tone. The father must be alert to provide the means of subsistence; the mother will have neither inclination nor opportunity to spend the best of her time and energy outside the home. Children grow up in an atmosphere of sacrifice; they learn "to wait their turn," to subordinate their whims to the good of all. There is little danger of their being pampered. The rough edges of their character are constantly being worn off in daily interplay by their brothers and sisters.

783. *c*) *The economic motive.* The commonest reason for birth control offered is: "Oh, we would love to have more children but we cannot afford them." Unquestionably the expenses attendant upon childbirth have risen enormously within a generation, and worse, the economic burden of raising children has become increasingly heavier. The reason is not precisely that it costs more to live today, but that everybody is expected to have more. Many wants are artificial; they are demands for so-called necessities which a few years ago were dream luxuries. While the scale of living adapts itself to the average family, unfortunately the average family is now the restricted family. Hence, raising a large family is either beyond the financial resources of the normal parent or the large family tends to become underprivileged.

There should be social co-operation to lessen the expenses of child-birth. Since society has an appreciable stake in the birth of its future citizens, it ought to see to it that these expenses never become an obstacle to a sufficient birth rate.

As to the larger problem of maintenance, two observations are in order. First, society must make it possible for heads of families to secure an income sufficient to support a normal family in human decency. Second, and this is the practical crux of the difficulty, the individual has to solve correctly the problem of every period of high civilization — the problem of choosing between material goods and moral goods. Margaret Sanger pithily puts the problem: "Which would you rather have — a child or a car?"[59] But is it reasonable to seek an increase of material comforts at the price of moral dereliction? As always, so now all larger social and economic problems verge upon the moral, and their ultimate solution is not to be found in rejection of the Natural Law.

The facts of history are plain: a rising birth rate has always been an index of national vigor, and a falling birth rate of national decline.[60] Since wealth is the product of human industry and ingenuity, it cannot

---

[59] See Leclercq, *Marriage and the Family,* p. 215, translator's footnote, 9. New York, Pustet, 1941.

[60] See Rousseau, "Marks of a Good Government," *Social Contract,* Bk. III, c. 9.

come from cutting down the population. This is true even in an industrial civilization which depends on the size of its markets, which in turn depend on the number of nonproductive consumers. Children are the nonproductive consumers and the more the number of children is curtailed, the more markets must shrink. No nation will remain vigorous whose family heads settle down to the enjoyment of comfort instead of devising new sources of subsistence. God gave the earth and all its fullness to man to live upon and He is no niggardly giver. There is an abundant living in the earth for all, and when men use their brains and brawn they obtain it. If Malthus were alive to see the development of the physical sciences, he would not envision a starving human race. Where man falls off, wealth falls off — another indication that the ultimate law of human living is the moral law.

784. *d) The pleasure motive.* This is a very common reason for birth control. Parents can live a pleasant life at a minimum of inconvenience. They can have the pleasures of love and escape its difficult consequences: one or two children, easy to raise and take delight in, rather than six or eight who would be a stone upon one's back. Sex is stamped in bold, harlot colors across the face of contemporaneous life because contraception has opened up to the unmarried a high, wide, and handsome promiscuity.

But there is no greater sign of the softness and imbecility which civilization can generate. The softness is apparent. The Natural Law offers the stern dilemma: be continent, or assume greater responsibilities, worries, and problems. Nevertheless, the easygoing modern evades the law because he loves his comfort. The choice which he makes is imbecility. For the contraceptive addict is the victim of a delusion: he foolishly thinks that here is the one case where a man can have his cake and eat it too. But he forgets two truths. One, that the substantial goods of life — growth in virtue and eternal beatitude — are to be purchased at a price, the endurance of difficulty. The other, that whoever spurns perfective good for the sake of present delight is a fool. Whoever honestly and consistently seeks perfective good must eventually find delight; whoever puts delight first, finishes with neither.

785. Finally, contraception is another instance where reasons of natural goodness, valid and conclusive in themselves, are not enough to persuade men to upright conduct. Only the mind and will, illumined and inspired by supernatural grace, can resist so alluring an evil. One must have supernatural faith to choose between a momentary difficulty and an eternal reward, between the enticement of present convenience and the substantial reality of an eternal punishment; supernatural hope, confidently and blindly to put one's trust in God and appreciate that the same Divine Lawgiver who imposes the burdens of parenthood likewise gives abundant strength to bear them; supernatural charity, to love God and the manifestations of His will above all things seen and unseen.

READINGS

St. Thomas, *Contra Gentiles,* III, 122–126, 136–137; *Supplementum,* QQ. 44–66.

Bonnar, A., O.F.M., *The Catholic Doctor,* pp. 43–71. New York, Kenedy, 1939, 2 ed.

Bouscaren, T. Lincoln, S.J., *Ethics of Ectopic Operations.* Milwaukee, Bruce, 1943, 2 ed.

Cappello, Felix, M., S.J., *De Sacramentis,* Vol. III, *De Matrimonio.* Romae, Universitas Gregoriana, 1933, 3 ed.

Costa Rosetti, Julius, S.J., *Philosophia Moralis,* pp. 430–463. Oeniponte, Rauch, 1886.

Cronin, Michael, *The Science of Ethics,* Vol. II, pp. 388–460. Dublin, Gill, 1909.

Davis, Henry, S.J., *Birth Control Ethics.* New York, Benziger, 1926.

——— *Moral and Pastoral Theology,* Vol. IV, pp. 49–244. New York, Sheed and Ward, 1935.

De Guchteneere, R., *Judgement on Birth Control.* New York, Macmillan, 1931.

Hope, Wingfield, *Life Together.* New York, Sheed and Ward, 1944.

Joyce, George, H., S.J., *Christian Marriage.* London, Sheed and Ward, 1933.

Leclercq, Jacques. *Marriage and the Family,* trans. T. R. Hanley, O.S.B., pp. 1–290. New York, Pustet, 1941.

Leibell, J. F., ed., *Readings in Ethics,* pp. 763–788. Chicago, Loyola University Press, 1926.

Leo XIII, *Arcanum Dei* (encyclical).

McFadden, Charles J., O.S.A., *Medical Ethics for Nurses,* pp. 47–112. Philadelphia, Davis, 1946.

McKevitt, Peter, *The Plan of Society,* pp. 9–41. Dublin, Cahill, 1944.

Moore, Edward A., *The Case Against Birth Control.* New York, Century, 1931.

Pius XI, *Casti Connubii* (encyclical).

Schmiedeler, Edgar, O.S.B., *Marriage and the Family,* pp. 1–54, 80–97. New York, McGraw Hill, 1946.

CHAPTER XXIII

THE FAMILY

786. The primal and simplest of social units, the one closest to life and nature, is the family. Herein man's social needs and tendencies are first, though inadequately, satisfied. The term *family* may apply to the union of (1) husband and wife; (2) parents and children; (3) parents, children, relatives, dependents, and servants dwelling under a common roof. To the last mentioned pertained Aristotle's definition of the family — the association established by nature for supplying man's everyday needs.[1] In the familial union three human relationships stand out: (1) the relationship of husband and wife; (2) the relationship of parents and children; (3) the relationship of master and servant. The first has been discussed in the preceding chapter. The second and third are taken up here with emphasis upon the second as more human and important.

I. PARENTAL SOCIETY

787. Parental society is the moral union of parents and children. It is obvious that this is a natural society, because children are the natural fruit of the conjugal union, the first of natural societies. Our purpose here shall be to determine (1) the adequate end of this society and (2) the chief ways of realizing this end.

A. The End of Parental Society

788. Immediately upon the birth of a child an enormous human want with subsequent human problems arises. Here is a new human being, with the potencies and essential rights of human nature but completely helpless. Since he has a right to go on living and to live as a human being, he must be protected until he can care for himself. He must be taught how men live reasonably so that in time he may live efficiently and reasonably. The process by which he acquires the skill of reasonable living is *education.* It should be noted that educa-

---

[1] *Politics*, Bk. I, 2, 1252 **b.**

tion is not synonymous with schooling. Schools may or may not share in the educative process and, when they do, their contribution is only partial. Education begins at the birth of the child and continues until the child reaches full maturity and is fully prepared for self-direction and further self-development. It is a process of tutelage which gradually fuses into a process of self-perfection.

789. Good education results in the proper and harmonious development of the total youth and renders him capable of living as a man and equipped for the attainment of his final end. Training is an absolute necessity. The blind promptings of natural instinct do not suffice, as in the case of brutes, to lead the child to the proper and skillful use of his distinctively human faculties. This he must acquire from the instruction of others. Those who guide him must see that all his faculties — physical, intellectual, and volitional — receive proportionate attention. None should be neglected lest a disintegrated personality result. Attention, however, should be given to each faculty in proportion to its value to the whole man. The training of the body ought to be duly subordinate to the development of the intellect, which in turn is of less importance than the training of man's will, his supreme faculty. Hence any system of education which ignores moral discipline and religious training is not worthy of the name.

790. The immediate end of education is a competent person, that is, one who in accordance with his natural endowments and place in life discharges his functions as this human being with befitting efficiency and independence. Competence is not to be construed as perfection of the money-making instinct or possession of a haphazard assortment of information. Competence rather is action in accordance with right reason, which supposes possession of right habits and skills. Thus equipped, he can, without unduly leaning on others, live an adequate human life, fulfill his general and particular obligations, and completely take over the task of self-development which should culminate in the attainment of his final end.

791. That every child has a natural right to a good education requires no special proof. It is included in his right to live as a human being. The point of dispute is who has the essential right to educate the individual. One hundred years ago this would have been considered an idle question. Anyone would have answered that by the common consent of mankind this is the task and the right of parents, for the training of children is the principal end of the family.

But because the family has to such a great extent invoked the aid of society in this matter, and exaggerated notions of the right and competency of the State have taken hold in so many places, there is a tendency today to disrupt, by State intervention and monopoly, the order established by nature between parent and child and to give the State rights in education which it cannot have. Communism thus claims the right to take children from parents and raise them in State nurseries and State schools.

THESIS LV. To parents alone belongs the inherent right to educate their children.

792. A most intimate union of souls between parents and children is established by nature and founded on the fact of generation. That this union is natural can be seen from the following facts: (1) the strong love, at first instinctive and later rational, which children have for parents; (2) the unwearied devotion of parents to the interests of their children, the untiring energy to supply, even at the sacrifice of their own personal convenience, all that is necessary for the rearing and development of their offspring; (3) the natural inclination of children to seek the means of their development from their parents alone, spurning the intervention of outsiders. These facts, verifiable every day in the normal family, indicate nature's intent that parents, first and foremost, should be the educators of their children.

PROOF

793. *To parents alone belongs the inherent right to educate,* because:

1. They alone have a right to educate upon whom before all others the Natural Law has imposed an inescapable obligation to educate. For an inescapable obligation to perform a given task carries with it a right to fulfill that obligation. If the obligation falls only on one party, that party alone has the consequent right.

2. Upon parents alone and before all others the Natural Law has imposed the inescapable obligation of educating their children for these reasons:

a) From the fact of generation it is clear that:

(1) By reason of a most peculiar kind of causality, children belong to their parents and in a way that no citizen belongs to the State. Children are part of their parents' bodies, the extension of their parents' personalities. If all created things belong absolutely to God because

of His divine causality, children belong to their parents under God since parents alone are with God cocauses of these children. The care of persons, like the care of things, redounds primarily to those to whom they belong.

(2) Man is responsible for the natural and foreseen results of his free acts. Now since children are in a state of complete physical, intellectual, and moral helplessness because of the generative act of their parents, parents are responsible to provide them a suitable education.

(3) If there is a good absolutely intended by nature (such as the good of education) the natural and special aptitude to attain that good argues to an obligation to do that for which the aptitude is given. Now parents have an aptitude to educate their children, which is shared by no one. This aptitude is founded on their understanding knowledge of them, their selfless love of them, and their vehement inclination to procure their well-being. In education nothing can replace these qualities.

b) There is no indication that the Natural Law has imposed this obligation upon the State or anyone else.

794. Corollary. The essential end of parental society is the good of the child; its secondary end is the well-being of the family itself which arises from the mutual love of all its members and the practice of the domestic virtues. Its remote end is the good of the State which is founded on the family.

795. N.B. I. *An analysis of the right to educate.*

1. The *subject party* is parents and parents alone. The obligation to educate falls on them *in solidum,* that is, if one is lacking or utterly deficient the entire obligation falls on the other. Teachers, tutors, educational officials are the delegates and co-operating assistants of the parents. How much they share in this right depends upon the explicit or implicit delegation of the parents.

2. The *object party* is the child to be trained.

3. The *matter* is all necessary and useful instruments of education such as doctrine, information, and especially discipline — whatever will reasonably promote the true good of the child.

4. The *ground* is the Natural Law imposing on parents an inescapable obligation to care for their children until they can care for themselves.

5. The *title* is the fact of generation. As parents are one principle of generation, so they form one efficient principle of education.

N.B. II. The State has definite rights in education. That this is a subsidiary right will be better shown after the end of the State has been explained.

B. The Means of Education

796. For the task of rearing children successfully parents must have a deep sense of responsibility. Children, as human beings, have an immortal worth; and no matter how much assistance or how many subsidiary agencies parents may summon to their aid, they alone are chargeable with the good or evil upbringing of their children. To acquit themselves of so indefeasible an obligation nature provides the essential means of domestic authority and family affection. Those educational helps which the ordinary family cannot secure of itself are included in our discussion of the State's part in education (cf. § 982 ff.).

THESIS LVI. The Natural Law confers on parents social authority to guide their children to the proper ends of the family. The primacy of this authority resides in the father.

PROOF OF PART I

797. *Nature confers domestic authority upon parents.*

The Natural Law must confer upon every natural society authority for the attainment of that society's end and upon those who alone are capable of wielding it. But the family is a natural society, and in it parents alone are capable of wielding authority. Therefore the Natural Law confers authority upon parents.

PROOF OF PART II

798. *The primacy of domestic authority resides in the father.*

The unity of the family demands that it have one head. The reason is that in the partnership of mother and father one of them must bear the responsibility of making decisions. Natural indications point to the father as being this head, because he generally has the proper qualifications — greater prudence and constancy, greater strength and protective ability. Nature disqualifies the wife for this position because of her natural function of childbearing and her consequent need for protection.

799. Corollary I. *Education is an authoritative process.*

Anyone who knows anything has a right to teach it to another who is willing to listen; but no one has a duty to listen to instruction, much less submit to discipline, unless the one teaching has authority to instruct, compel attention, and exact obedience.

Corollary II. *Children have an obligation of filial reverence to their parents,* as the holders of legitimate authority. As we shall presently see, all human authority is a participation in the divine authority. Reverence is inward and outward respect whereby one recognizes the superior excellence of another and fears to offend against that excellence.

Corollary III. *Children and wives have an obligation of obedience.*

C. Familial Obedience

1. Wives

800. The Natural Law commands wives to obey their husbands in everything that pertains to the reasonable conduct of the family and is compatible with her dignity as a human being and a wife. She is a beloved companion, not a child or a slave. If in some cases the wife has more influence than the husband, the Natural Law is not necessarily overturned. Because of this man's incapacity or this woman's outstanding capacity such an arrangement may be the only one that makes for peace and security in a particular family.

While the civil law and especially social custom today give married women a social and economic freedom they never enjoyed before, nevertheless this so-called emancipation of women should never be such that "the husband suffers the loss of his wife, the children of their mother, and the home and whole family of an ever watchful guardian."[2] There are but few remains of that ancient Christian chivalry whereby men once elevated their wives to a pedestal as queen and mistress of the household. She was looked on as better than man — more religious, more moral, more God-fearing and was deferred to accordingly. Modern woman, somewhat after the fashion of the dog in Æsop's fable who saw in the water the reflection of himself carrying a bone, is snapping after delusive emancipation; and if she completely descends from the regal throne she once enjoyed to go down into the hurly-burly of everyday life to contend with men for a false equality, she will get hurt. And badly. "She will soon be reduced to the old state of slavery (if not in appearance, certainly in reality), and become as amongst the pagans the mere instrument of men."[3]

---

[2] Pius XI, Encyclical on Christian Marriage.   [3] *Ibid.*

2. Children

801. From the fact of parental authority it follows inevitably that children must obey their parents. Only the obedient child is the educated child. Parading under a variety of names, for example, progressive education, there is a modern trend which would tone down the place of authority in education and which looks askance at absolute obedience as breeding inhibitions and dwarfing the child's personality. Let us distinguish truth from falsity in parental authority.

802. *a*) It is possible to tyrannize children. To prevent such action, the motive of any command should be the child's good, not the selfish convenience of parent or teacher. No child should be overwhelmed with a torrent of do's and don't's. A command to be genuine must be reasonable, but all reasonable commands should be carried out. The youngest child should be made to see that disobedience is never tolerated.

803. *b*) Because the child is incapable of self-direction, it must be guided to its true good; but some have a mistaken notion of the child's true good. The child's true good is ultimately a supernatural good; and since all men are tainted by original sin, a child will have great difficulty in recognizing its true good. It is absurd to give children the initiative in their education, because they lack that supernatural gift of integrity whereby lower appetites are completely subordinate to reason. Hence left to their own whims and fancies, they become the victims of their own blind pride and concupiscences. All education must transcend the natural and realistically appreciate the downward trend of a nature debased by sin. The uninhibited child is usually a willful, spoiled, undisciplined brat. As children advance toward maturity, a larger initiative and greater freedom must be accorded them; but to deal with elementary or high school pupils as though they were matriculated in a university is a woeful lack of realism.

804. *c*) Even though there is danger of suppression of good tendencies or even of cruelty on the part of unworthy parents, correction has its essential place in child training. And correction *necessarily* implies corporal punishment. For all authority must have the power of coercion, physical as well as moral. The younger child in many ways is inclined to act like an animal rather than a rational being. When he persists in acting irrationally by continued disobedience, physical pain is the only effective corrective. Spare the rod and spoil the child is as true today as it was in Solomon's time.

805. *d*) To issue commands that advance the child's true welfare and prudently to enforce them requires of parents a loving understanding of the child as an individual. They must recognize that each child is a unique personality, different from all others and possessing differing capacities, hopes, and problems. Parents must be willing to give time and attention to things which primarily are of interest to the child. This demands eternal vigilance, thorough knowledge of his comings and goings, especially of his companions. It may be injected here that too early and too free a mingling of the sexes is bad. Nature isolates young boys to themselves — so also immature girls. This wall of separation should not be artificially broken down, for thereby sexual desires may be awakened too early and grave harm will result since a long period of time must elapse before these stirrings can be satisfied by marriage.

The supreme test of parental wisdom is adolescence. In this period of growth intellect is awakening, habits though still fluid are in the process of hardening, the freedom of manhood is just around the corner. It is no longer possible completely to possess children as in earlier years, to do all their thinking and deciding for them. If they are confronted with freedom and responsibility too suddenly, they may not be able to cope with the situation. Pre-eminent skill is needed to guide them over what are often the rough waters of their late 'teens into the assured ability to think and act as adults.

806. Here again we must depart from the field of ethics and have recourse to the supernatural. For mere considerations of natural goodness and merely natural helps are insufficient to heal the wounds of original and actual sin. Divine grace is the ultimate remedy. Hence the child must be taught to live a sacramental life, to practice not merely the natural virtues of prudence, justice, temperance, and fortitude but also the supernatural virtues of faith, hope, and charity. His moral training should be intertwined with the cultivation of supernatural religion, which should have first place in the home. The effective means of accomplishing this is personal example.

807. Filial obedience, however, is limited both as to scope and duration. The end of parental authority — the good of the child — determines the scope of obedience. Hence a child must not obey when commanded to do what is patently sinful. The choice of a *fixed* state in life is also outside the parent's command. Parents may not forbid their children to embrace the true faith. Nor even to enter religion or to marry. Children are obliged to seek the advice and counsel of their parents and sometimes to defer temporarily such a step because of parental indigence; but since the permanent conduct of their adult life is involved, the choice must ultimately be their own. Therefore, when youth is capable of self-direction, parental authority ceases. The child is emancipated; his education is finished. If civil law does not specify the precise time when this is effected, it surely happens when he leaves the paternal home to assume his place in life. Should he remain in the paternal home after he has attained his majority, he is still subject to his father in what pertains to domestic order.

D. Family Affection

808. Authority in the family must be tempered by love. Between members of a family exists a special kind of love — piety. While a son's obligation to obey ceases in time, his obligation of love, reverence, and gratitude never does. The love which parents have for children should be well ordered and efficacious. It is *well ordered* when it is (*a*) impartial — unreasonable partiality toward a favorite may offend against distributive justice — and (*b*) when it seeks both the spiritual and temporal good of the children in due proportion. Parental love is *efficacious* when it actually procures for the children the goods which befit them. For love is not sentimentality but good will manifested in deeds. The first of such deeds on the part of the father is providing the means of living for wife and children. The spiritual welfare of the children must be given precedence over any material advantage. Those parents are guilty of serious wrong who, for the sake of enhancing their social prestige, or making influential "contacts," or otherwise advancing their worldly prospects, send their children to schools where their supernatural faith is endangered and their eternal beatitude imperiled. When parents grow old and cannot support themselves, piety demands that their children take care of them. Brothers and sisters have a similar obligation of assisting one another in grave need.

II. SERVANT SOCIETY

809. Servant society is the union existing between the blood members of a family and their domestic servants; parents, children, and domestics constitute the family in the completest sense. A domestic, then, is an outsider who agrees to serve a family upon condition of sharing proportionately in the advantages of that family. He differs from a workman laboring for the employer in that the workman is not admitted into the family of his employer.

810. *Is servant society natural?* This society is not natural in the sense that the conjugal union is, that is, it does not fulfill an imperative need of nature. Nor may it be called natural with reference to a situation in which the domestic is a slave or serf, something less than a man, the chattel of a master. However, we may call servant society natural in the sense that the Natural Law countenances it because in a human way it answers a mutual need constantly present among men, namely, (*a*) of parents for domestic assistance and (*b*) of persons of small means for a living which they could scarcely otherwise provide for themselves.

That this mutual need will perdure seems clear enough. Because of the number of children, the importance of their other occupations, their age, or physical disability, many family heads will always require assistance in the orderly conduct of their home. Although numerous household goods formerly produced by familial labor are now procured outside the home, and while modern inventions have made domestic work far less difficult, the need of help in the home will never completely disappear. So too, because of personal inclination, dearth of initiative, lack of training, or opportunity for more lucrative situations, there will always be those who gravitate toward domestic work.

Servants may contract to work for the family but remain outside the family circle or they may make their home with the family as members of the family. In either case there are advantages and disadvantages for both parties. The chief advantage of the first arrangement is that the worker retains his independence and can have a family of his own. In the latter arrangement there is a fuller and more human relation of man to man, of a member of the family to the head of that family.

811. In the servant-master relation, the chief tie binding the parties is commutative justice. The master is obliged to give his servant a just wage and a commensurate living. Those holes in garrets and odd corners which until quite recent times were provided as sleeping quarters for servants could scarcely measure up to the requirements of a decent living. The servant, on the other hand, obliges himself to make an adequate return of service — both as to the time, quality, and quantity of his labor.

But a more human tie — a tie of piety — binds them. The master should act as a father who takes a human interest in the physical and spiritual welfare of those in his care, treats them with paternal kindliness, endeavors to correct their moral defects, sees to it that they fulfill their religious duties, provides for their old age after they have given him a lifetime of service. On their part, servants owe their master a quasi-filial reverence; loyalty and fidelity in looking after the interest of the family which goes beyond the mere letter of a contract; and obedience not only in the matter of service but also of personal conduct.

One of the most fruitful causes of industrial unrest is that nothing of this more human relationship has been carried over into the relationships between employer and employees.

READINGS

St. Thomas, *Summa Theologica,* II–II, 101, 104, 105.

Aristotle, *Politics,* Bk. 1, cc. 3–13.

Cahill, E., S.J., *The Framework of the Christian State,* pp. 350–376. Dublin, Gill, 1932.

Cathrein, Victor, S.J., *Philosophia Moralis,* pp. 368–378. Friburgi Brisgoviae, Herder, 1915, 10 ed.

Costa Rossetti, Julius, S.J., *Philosophia Moralis,* pp. 463–503. Oeniponte, Rauch, 1886.

Devas, Charles S., *Political Economy,* pp. 168–182. London, Longmans Green, 1910, 3 ed.

Haas, Francis J., *Man and Society,* pp. 108–152. New York, Appleton-Century, 1930.

Jarrett, Bede, O.P., *Social Theories of the Middle Ages,* pp. 31–93. Westminster, Md., Newman, 1942.

Leclercq, Jacques, *Marriage and the Family,* pp. 291–387, trans. T. R. Hanley, O.S.B. New York, Pustet, 1941.

Messner, J., *Social Ethics,* trans. J. J. Doherty, pp. 283–317. St. Louis, Herder, 1949.

Osgniach, Augustine, O.S.B., *The Christian State,* pp. 265–273. Milwaukee, Bruce, 1943.

Ostheimer, Anthony, *The Family.* Washington, Catholic University Press, 1939.

Pius XI, *Representanti in Terra* (On the Christian Education of Youth — encyclical).

Plato, *The Laws.* Passim.

Schmiedeler, Edgar, O.S.B., *Marriage and the Family,* pp. 56–267. New York, McGraw Hill, 1946.

CHAPTER XXIV

THE STATE

812. Man's social needs and capacities find their first and most natural outlet in conjugal society whence the family naturally results. Although the family is the basic social unit, it is not adequate to care for all human needs. Therefore, another and more perfect social organization is necessary.

The history of man testifies how by natural growth the family — parents, children, servants, dependents, and blood relations all dwelling together under one family head — expands into the village, the village into the sept or clan, the clan into a tribe, and from the tribe emerges the State, the ultimate and perfect unit. The historical evolution of the State is of little consequence to us except to note that the family antedates it and was in possession of rights and liberties before any actual States came into being. We now investigate the prescriptions of the Natural Law concerning the ultimate social unit or perfect society.

813. A perfect society is one which seeks a good common to all men and possesses the adequate means of attaining such an end. Since artificial societies do not strive after an *adequately* human good, they are imperfect. Though the family seeks such a good it is imperfect in that it has not within itself a sufficiency of means to attain such an end. We shall demonstrate that the State is a perfect society in both respects. However, we may take for granted that it is the ultimate social unit.

814. Before discussing the nature and essential functions of the State, let us, omitting all points of controversy, describe it in a way acceptable to all. By a State we mean not just a body of rulers — a government — but an organic community, both governors and governed, who occupy a given territory and under some independent polity or form of rulership seek by public action an adequate human good.

No one would say that mere local juxtaposition suffices to give a people the unity of a State. Such unity can derive only from a common social bond, a common authority without which there is no social striving for a common good, no social organization. This authority must be self-sufficient and independent; otherwise this is not an ultimate social unit. Hence it is not a State; for all agree that in the present economy the State is the ultimate unit. A given group that is not independent is simply part of an organization which is independent. The need for a proper territory of its own follows from the need to be independent.

All of which seems to agree with Aristotle's definition that a State is the union of families and villages in a complete and self-sufficient life.[1]

I. IS THE STATE A NATURAL SOCIETY?

815. The first problem to be solved is whether the State is a natural institution, an institution prescribed by the Author of nature, or whether it is merely a human invention like a business partnership, a device hit upon by men to be set up and perhaps destroyed as they choose.

As we have shown (§ 697), Hobbes held that the State is an artificial invention, the product of a human compact. Rousseau accepts the main contention of Hobbes adding his own peculiar embroideries. According to the French philosopher, "the most ancient of all societies and the only one that is natural, is the family."[2] Before the State appeared, man lived in a state of nature — he was a noble savage, living an idyllic life by streams and woodland fastnesses, completely free and subordinate to no one. Whenever life in that state becomes impossible, men have to band together in some form of association. The instrument which sets up this association is a social contract whereby each man agrees to give up all his rights to govern and protect himself on the condition that all the others do the same. "At once, in place of the individual personality of each contracting party, this act of association creates a moral and collective body . . . receiving from this act its unity, its common identity, its life and its will. This public person so formed by the union of all other persons formerly

---

[1] *Politics,* Bk. I, 2, 1252b.
[2] *Social Contract,* Bk. I, Chap. 2.

took the name of *city* and now takes that of *Republic or body politic*."[3]

816. According to communism (§ 521), the State is unnatural because it arose from the need of the exploiting classes to keep the exploited masses subservient and will die out when all class distinctions have been abolished. "The State, which is in truth only organized coercion, has inevitably risen at a certain degree of development of society when the latter was divided into irreconcilable classes and could no longer subsist without some power placed above them and separated from them."[4]

THESIS LVII. The State is a natural society.

PROOF

817. The State is a *natural society,* because:

1. Men have an aptitude, an urge, and a compelling need to form states.

a) Aptitude. Men not only desire the fullness of the good life but they have a native ability to band together and procure it. Men have a mutual benevolence whereby they can wish that good to all who are willing to co-operate. They have a natural endowment for such co-operation: they have a power of communication, an inclination to obey authority, and some the ability to command.

b) Natural urge. While man is naturally a social being, his needs and aptitudes can only be imperfectly satisfied in domestic life. Therefore to realize fully his potentialities he is urged to form another and more perfect social organization. The survivors of the mutiny on "The Bounty" who set up a commonwealth on their dot of land in the waste of an ocean exemplify the fact that, where a number of families must live together, the very order of human existence impels them to set up a superfamilial organization.

c) Natural need. The State is a morally necessary means to the full temporal happiness of man. The family normally cannot supply for its members everything physical, intellectual, and moral required for their proper growth and development. Thus the ordinary family is unable to protect itself from serious violence and make itself secure in the stable enjoyment of its rights. Innumerable other advantages — physical,

---

[3] *Ibid.,* Bk. I, Chap. 6.
[4] V. I. Lenin, "Karl Marx," *Encyclopedie Russe.* See also V. I. Lenin, *State and Revolution,* p. 8. New York, International Publishers, 1932.

intellectual, moral, and aesthetic — are simply impossible without the fullest measure of social intercourse. Therefore since the family is not sufficient unto itself, families must band themselves together into States to secure the full measure of human perfection or it will not be obtained.

2. Aptitudes, needs, and urges so universally verified, so closely related to human welfare must be traceable to an appetite of human nature seeking a natural good. Such an appetite must be satisfied by a natural institution.

Corollary. The Natural Law commands men to establish States.

II. THE SPECIFIC END OF THE STATE

818. A few men like Haller[5] have said the State has no specific, distinctive end. However, since the State is a natural, not an artificial entity, it must have a natural end prescribed by the Author of nature. For nature does nothing in vain.

819. As a natural thing it is different from every other natural unit physical or moral. Its natural end is common to all States, because as natural institutions they have a common essential statehood. Hence Montesquieu[6] is wrong when he says that each State has its own specific purpose which differs from that of other States and has in common with others merely the general purpose of its own conservation. Self-preservation cannot constitute a distinctive end because this is common to too many things which differ essentially.

Since the State is a true society, its distinctive end will be some particular sort of a common good. It is agreed that this particular good be called the Public Good. What is this Public Good for whose attainment States exist?

A. The Totalitarian View

820. The State is a superentity, adequately distinct from and superior to the citizen or any collection of citizens. The individual was made for the State, not the State for the citizen. The Public Good, then, will not be the advantage of men but solely the good estate of this superentity.

---

[5] Charles L. de Haller, *Restauration de la Science Politique*, Vol. I, Chap. XVII, pp. 552, 554. Lyon, Russand, 1824.

[6] Baron de Montesquieu, *The Spirit of the Laws*, trans. Nugent-Pritchard, Bk. XI, Chap. IV, p. 181, Vol. I. New York, Appleton, 1900.

Thus Plato held as a supreme but admittedly unrealizable ideal a commonwealth wherein absolutely everything was possessed in common.[7] So complete is the communization he demanded that Marxism, compared to it, appears as a species of rugged individualism. This commonwealth was "a greater man" to which each citizen was totally subordinate as the hand or foot is to the whole body. This "greater man" has an end similar to that of the individual, namely, to live according to virtue.

Hobbes' conception of the Great Leviathan, an accumulation of irresistible force and the origin of morality, laws, and rights, has given fresh impetus to the totalitarian idea in modern days. Some pantheists like Schelling[8] and Hegel[9] have gone to the extreme of identifying the State with God — the State is the absolute being, the all-sufficient one whose end is itself.

The form which totalitarianism has taken today is that of national socialism and communism. National socialism, whether known as nazism or fascism, holds up the nation or race as the absolute being whose end is its own conservation, development, glory, and aggrandizement. It is subject to no law but its own making: the citizen is, does, and has as the nation prescribes.

As national socialism subjugates the citizen to the glory of the nation, communism would subjugate the individual to humanity. In the evolution of humanity toward the millennium of pure communism (§ 528), the State is but a passing phase, an evil to be gotten

---

[7] *Republic,* Bk. V, 458.

[8] Friederich W. J. von Schelling, *Neue Deduktion des Naturrechts.* See his *Sämmtleche Werke,* Vol. I, pp. 247–280. Stuttgart, 1856. See also *System des transcendentalen Idealismus* in the same set, Vol. III, p. 583.

[9] Georg W. F. Hegel, *Grundlinien der Philosophie des Rechts.* See his *Werke,* Vol. 8, Nos. 257–272. Berlin, 1833. In No. 258 he says: "The State in and for itself, is the ethical totality, the actualization of freedom: and actual freedom is the absolute end. The State is the spirit that dwells in the world and realizes itself in the world through consciousness, while in nature the spirit actualizes itself only as its own other, as dormant spirit. Only when present as consciousness, knowing itself as existing objectivity, is this spirit the State. When reasoning about freedom one must not start from the individual consciousness, but only from the essential nature of self consciousness, for whether one knows it or not, this essence still realizes itself as an independent power in which the single individuals are only moments; it is the course of God through the world that constitutes the State. Its ground is the power of Reason actualizing itself as will. When conceiving the State, one must not think of particular States, not of particular institutions, but one must much rather contemplate the *Idea,* God as actual on earth, alone."

rid of. But the present masters of the Soviets soft-pedal this piece of pure Marxism.

THESIS LVIII. The Natural Law forbids that any State be an end completely unto itself.

PROOF

821. *The State cannot be an end unto itself,* because:

1. A means to the good of individual men cannot be its own end. For what is a means to something else, cannot be self-sufficing.

2. Nature intends the State to be a means to the good of individual men. The State has only a temporal existence. It has no immortal soul, nor a life hereafter, nor an eternal destiny. In the hierarchy of objective values it is something less than individual men. All things less than men are means to the good of men.

822. **Corollary I.** The Public Good must be something which redounds to the real good of individual men.

Corollary II. There is scarcely any social doctrine more repulsive to one's sense of human dignity, more degradive of the worth of human personality, more productive of suffering and bloodshed, than the dictum that man exists for an omnipotent State which can do with him as it wills.

Granted, then, that the Public Good must afford advantages to individuals, how many of these advantages are there and what are they? How broad or narrow is the scope of the Public Good? The precise answer to this question will be a summary statement of the natural functions of the State. Of the three answers given, the first interprets the scope of the Public Good very narrowly, the second very broadly, and the third moderately.

B. The Laissez-Faire View

823. Laissez-faire is the opposite of totalitarianism: it is individualism run wild. Beyond preserving external order and liberty by protecting itself and securing the individual rights of the citizen, the State has no further function. It may not interfere with the individual in securing the good life for himself.

Kant originated this view and he arrived at it from his notion of rights. Maintaining a complete cleavage between an internal moral order and an external juridical order, he claimed that the State, as the external force, had nothing to do with morality; its end was to procure and safeguard such external conditions that the rights and liberties of all might harmoniously coexist (cf. § 444). Hence it exists to prohibit those external acts which would disturb that harmony of liberty. Nothing more.

The economic liberals of the Manchester School adopted the Kantian view since it fitted in so well with their dream that society would reach an ideal state of prosperity if there were complete free trade and unlimited competition. For them the State is a benign policeman whose beat is restricted to the guardianship of commutative justice. There is no such thing as social justice — that would be plain socialism.

THESIS LIX. The purpose of the State cannot be restricted to mere safeguarding of the juridic order.

824. The pernicious effects of this doctrine we have already noted (§§ 540–544). Liberalism really means the State must stand by while the little man is exploited by the big man. The atrocious evils of industrial slavery were the inevitable consequences of the laissez-faire doctrine.

PROOF

825. 1. Liberalism is an insufficient declaration of the purpose of a natural institution. It is absurd that a natural institution have but a negative function — the prevention of violations of commutative justice. As the family has a positive function of providing for the welfare of its members, *a fortiori* must the State wherein man expects to realize completely his social tendencies. The positive function of the State is set forth in § 833.

2. Since the State may create rights, for example, a share in the goods of a distantly related intestate, set up corporations, and so on, its function cannot be the mere safeguarding of rights.

3. It is the common conviction of men that the State has a wider and ampler function.

C. The Paternalistic State

826. As the old-fashioned father provided his family with the means of life, so the State directly cares for its citizens from cradle to grave. As children have turned to their fathers for the things they need, adults should now consider that the State owes them a living.

The old conviction that a man should face the world and wrest a living from it should be modified: a large part of that responsibility can be transferred to the State, which is to secure him against the age-old fears of sickness, poverty, unemployment, pauperism in old age. Hence the State undertakes to guarantee the individual proper prenatal care, a decent creche, a happy childhood, an education, remunerative employment, recreation, hospitalization when ill, a sufficient pension when he reaches sixty — all this without too much embarrassing consideration of personal co-operation and deserving. When nature has handicapped him by physical weakness or lack of talent, the State will come to his aid with special assistance that will level him with his fellow citizens. As social evolution has taken from paternal power its right of life and death, the office of family priest, so now in great measure the State will take over its job of family protector and provider.

827. A bright new world is being blueprinted wherein all the old scourges of mankind will be absent. State action is to produce a land flowing with milk and honey, suspiciously similar to the communistic millennium. Precious little mention is made of any increase of moral goodness — of valor, endurance, self-sacrifice, faith, hope, or love of God.

The delusion in paternalism is twofold, namely, that mankind can be so renovated by direct State action that the effects of original sin will be eradicated and that man lives by bread alone.

828. The reality of paternalism is this: at best it is a benevolent socialism. For if the State is to take direct care of its citizens, it must have that measure of control over them demanded by socialism. At worst it is a fraud whereby those who currently hold governmental power in a democracy hope to establish themselves therein indefinitely. An individual or a group can hold power indefinitely if it can destroy those sound safeguards which a democratic people possess against unlimited governmental control, that is, their fundamental political liberties. Hence the people are to be cozened into surrendering these liberties upon the specious promise of economic security. An ancient device, it has succeeded before in the twilight days of a dying democracy — the Roman populace gave up their liberties upon the assurance of bread and games.

THESIS LX. The Natural Law forbids the State to take direct, complete, and perpetual care of its citizens.

829. We do not deny that some measure of direct and perpetual care is involved in the safeguarding of the juridic order, which we shall prove to be the first purpose of the State. Nor is it unreasonable that in a grave crisis such as earthquake, flood, or war a State should temporarily take over complete care of its citizens. However, a great part of the citizenry being perpetually dependent for its livelihood on a direct subvention from the State is a sure sign of a diseased commonwealth. It entails the overthrow of the order of human life established by nature.

PROOF

830. The State cannot have a purpose which if realized would make the citizen less a man. If the State were to take direct, complete, and perpetual care of its citizens, they would be made worse men. Paternalism would be destructive of the moral fiber of citizens indirectly and directly.

1. *Indirectly* paternalism would tremendously lessen the value and importance of the family. Every indication of nature is that the *family first* is to take care of its young, sick, and aged. To transfer this duty to the State as a prime obligation is to destroy a natural function of the family. If the family is weakened, harm will inevitably come to the individual.

It is argued that since the family has not taken adequate care of its sick and aged, the State must. It is true that if a family is unable to provide for itself, the State should come to the rescue. But the State must not directly intervene until every reasonable private means has been resorted to and none has been successful. Put a living wage at the disposal of family heads and the family can and will care for its sick and aged. And better than the State.

2. *Directly* paternalism would be destructive of the moral integrity of the individual. Nature intends that the adult be self-directive and self-providing; but if the State assures him that his needs will be satisfied, he will not develop a sense of responsibility and it will not be necessary for him to practice befitting human virtue. Inevitably paternalism begets laziness, shirking of duty, and an inhuman sense of dependence. There would be little need for providence, thrift, and courage in the face of difficulty.

831. Corollary I. The State must not do for the citizen what he can reasonably do for himself.

Corollary II. No government owes its citizens a living. We shall prove, however, that each citizen owes the government his support.

Corollary III. The State should not inject itself into matters which pertain strictly to the Individual Good. For it to do so means ultimately harm to the Public Good.

832. N.B. Paternalism interferes with the operation of the sanctions of the Natural Law: in order to procure the means to lavish such benefits on its citizens, the State must take from the alert, provident, and thrifty, who are thereby penalized for their success by being compelled to support the shiftless and improvident.

"If any man will not work, neither let him eat."[10] This is both inspired writing and a dictum of the Natural Law. A situation in which a man is permitted to squander his earnings in prosperous times and neglect to provide for the leaner years ahead because he is sure of direct State aid, is an encouragement to foolish living and ultimately a burden upon the more restrained and virtuous. Truly the State ought to protect the common people — who necessarily are of limited means — from the exactions of a monied power but this must not be done by handicapping talent and industry and rewarding ineptitude and sloth. It is quite absurd to imagine that nature has delegated the State, as it were, to follow up after her and compensate the mediocre and dull witted for nature's initial but uneven distribution of her gifts.

D. *The Scholastic View of the State's Purpose*

833. Most scholastics steer a middle course between the narrow concept of the Public Good according to laissez–faire and the exaggerations of the paternalistic State. For them two elements compose the Public Good. They are peace and public prosperity.

1. *Peace* is tranquillity of the juridic order. The outstanding purpose of the State is the maintenance of commutative justice, making individuals and families secure in the peaceful possession and exercise of their natural rights. It is impossible for a man to realize his potentialities if most of his energies are consumed in the defense of himself or his family. To live and develop as a man he requires an atmosphere of security which can be provided only by a State itself secure from

---

[10] 2 Thessalonians 3:10.

internal and external disturbance. Our federal Constitution aptly expresses this purpose in its preamble: "to establish justice, insure domestic tranquillity, provide for the common defense."

2. *Public prosperity.* Prosperity, in general, means an abundance or at least a stable sufficiency of those things required for man's *temporal well-being*. This includes not only material goods such as food, clothing, shelter, property, personal freedom, and physical and mental health but also immaterial goods such as good reputation, culture, and moral and religious training. Prosperity does not so much consist in having many things but in having the right things chief among which are a material competence and the moral virtues. A very clear distinction should be made between private and public prosperity.

a) *Private prosperity* is the possession by the individual of a sufficiency of requisite goods. Private well-being is an individual — at most a family concern and the securing of it is the chief temporal preoccupation of each individual or family head.

b) *Public prosperity* refers to the sum total of those helps and facilities which must be available to put private well-being within reach of all: it is an abundance of social, economic, and industrial *opportunities* which will fairly and equitably provide all classes of citizens sufficient opportunity to use their initiative and industry and thus secure a desirable competence for themselves. The State does not assume responsibility for each one's individual good, nor should it, as a father does his children, endow its citizens with the goods of prosperity, but it ought to offer all a fair chance of self-help.

Since neither the individual nor the family is all sufficient, co-operative effort must supply whatever else is needed for human welfare. This is summed up by the term, *social opportunity*. The manner, measure, and mode of social opportunity to be provided by the State will depend on many factors of time, place, climate, custom, level and complexity of economic development. But every State, no matter how rude and barbarous, must, over and above the defense of the juridic order, provide its members with some measure of collective opportunity. In an industrial civilization such as ours, the State may be said to have achieved one goal of public prosperity when it has produced a general situation wherein every man able and willing to work can find employment and by his industry secure for himself and his own a decent sufficiency of temporal advantages.

This aspect of the State's purpose is touched upon in our federal Constitution by the words: "promote the general welfare and secure the Blessings of Liberty to ourselves and our Posterity."

THESIS LXI. The specifying and proximate end of the State is the public good of peace and public prosperity.

PROOF

834. 1. The proximate and specific end of the State is some good to obtain which men by natural impulse unite into States and which they can neither efficiently nor permanently obtain outside the State. Since the State is a natural society, nature intends it to be the answer to definite human needs. Therefore its specifying end will be that particular good which fulfills these needs. When it is asked what men naturally seek in the State, the correct answer will be a statement of the natural purpose or specifying end of the State.

2. *In virtue of a natural impulse men unite in States because*

a) *primarily* they wish to be secure as regards their persons and homes and in the enjoyment of their rights. They want peace.

b) *secondarily* they desire the means of self-betterment. Preserving their rights and independence, normal men wish, relying on their own effort, to have the advantage of opportunities for physical, intellectual, and moral advancement — opportunities made possible only by co-operative effort. Such opportunities we call *public prosperity*.

3. *Outside the State neither permanently nor efficiently can be realized*

a) peace and security in one's rights. If the State is destroyed, anarchy and confusion result.

b) innumerable opportunities for human development. The progress of mankind has been achieved through the peaceful intercommunication of men. Without the State this has been and will be impossible. By the institution of the family man can manage to live, but without the institution of the State he could never live well.

835. Corollary I. This end — peace and the public welfare — is the measure of the fitness and reasonableness of all the State's functions and activities.

Corollary II. When a given society by and large is no longer capable of promoting peace and the public welfare it automatically ceases to be a State.

III. THE FORMAL CAUSE OF THE STATE

836. Having established the most important of all truths about the State, namely its ultimate specific purpose, we now examine its remaining causes. We shall touch briefly on its formal and material causes, and more fully on its efficient cause.

In § 693 and the following it was proved that the formal cause of any society is a moral juridic bond. According to this principle, the formal cause of the conjugal union is the peculiar bond of mutual love and justice binding man to wife and wife to man. The members of a family are welded into familial unity by the social bond of love, piety, and commutative justice. A State is formally made a State not by civil authority but by the social bond of civic justice uniting a plurality of families into the civic union.

837. *What is this social bond of civic justice?* Civic justice is a species of social justice, which is that over-all obligation obliging individuals and moral persons to promote a common good. This common good may be that of the marital union, of the family, of the State, or of all men united in one fellowship. While a common good primarily means the good estate of a society as such, it secondarily includes the welfare of all and each.

If the common good in question is that of peace and public prosperity, the ordination unto that good is from civic justice. This ordination derives from the relation of citizens toward the State and their obligation to do whatever the public good requires of them. Inasmuch as this obligation of citizens is prescribed by law, natural and positive, we call it the obligation of *legal justice.* Conversely, civic justice is the obligation resting on the heads of the State to administer distributive justice. Therefore, the obligations of citizens to uphold the State by observing legal justice and of the State to promote the general and individual welfare by observing distributive justice, plus the rights which these forms of justice are designed to protect, constitute the bond of civic justice. The equality which this sort of justice envisions is that of the citizen toward the public good and in turn, of the public good toward the citizen. Hence the total complexus of rights and duties flowing from civic justice constitute that social bond which is the formal cause of the State.

IV. THE MATERIAL CAUSE OF THE STATE

838. The material cause of a society is the plurality which is socially united, that is, those component parts upon which the juridic bond of society directly and immediately falls. In the conjugal union, the family, and like simple societies, the material element is always individual physical persons.

Is the same thing true in the State? There are two opinions. According to one — which has behind it the practice of the past few centuries — the material element of the State is the mass of individual citizens. This view is called either the *theory of social atomism,* or the *mechanistic theory of society.* According to the first explanation individuals are bound together in the State in much the same way as atoms in a mass of matter. According to the second explanation the State is a mechanical contrivance of many wheels and cogs — the individual citizens — which are geared together and are powered by a central motor — social authority. Nothing stands between the individual and the supreme authority of the State.

839. The opposite view considers the State an organism, that is, an entity similar to a living body composed of various organs, each of which has a distinct function, and all of whom are oriented to the good of the whole. In an organic society there is a graded hierarchy of social units, one dependent on the other but each flourishing with an autonomous life and function of its own. Hence, the *citizen is not the material element of the State* but some imperfect society is, the family, the municipality, or the province, depending on the complexity of the State's development. Aristotle, whose ideal was the city-state, defines the State as the union of several villages in a single complete and self-sufficing community.[11] By villages he explicitly means households or enlarged families — children, grandchildren, and the like.

As States expand there is an increase in the number of political sub-units having some measure of autonomy under the supreme authority of the State. Yet no matter how large the State grows, men always have the natural tendency to satisfy their first political needs by local self-government. Where States are large and economic problems complex, private or semipublic associations founded on men's work or profession will arise. The purpose of such occupational groups —

---

[11] *Politics,* Bk. I, 2, 1252b.

which are not mere labor unions but associations of all, employers and employees, engaged in the same occupations — ideally is the common interest of all in that group, sought of course in harmony with the common public good. The State should foster such associations, grant them sufficient authority to advance their purposes and to make amicable arrangements with similar associations. These were once called guilds; now their proponents call them corporations. A State which has subordinate societies — municipalities, corporations, and families — leading a vigorous and efficient social life of their own, is *organized;* it leads a truly organic life. If subordinate societies are merely tolerated and most of their functions absorbed by the State, that State is not said to be *organized* but merely *administered.*

840. The atomistic view of the State must be rejected. It first arose as a corollary of the eighteenth-century doctrine of the rights of man and economic liberalism. It led at first to rugged individualism, that overemphasis upon individual freedom which in practice means that the strong and cunning are entitled to full opportunity to oppress the weak. Some react to the evils of economic liberalism by an appeal to socialism; others call upon government to regulate all the relations of the individual to the State. This is that interventionism now practiced by present-day democracies. In either case the final result is that all intermediate social units having been destroyed or absorbed by the State, the State must needlessly interfere in the private concerns of its citizens and thus assume a bewildering and impossible burden.

841. Very aptly Pius XI writes: "Things have come to such a pass that the highly developed social life which once flourished in a variety of prosperous institutions organically linked with each other, has been damaged and all but ruined, leaving thus virtually only the individual and the State. Social life has lost entirely its organic form. The State, now encumbered with all the burdens once borne by associations rendered extinct by it, is in consequence submerged and overwhelmed by an infinity of affairs and duties. . . . It is an injustice, a grave evil and a disturbance of right order for a higher and larger organization to arrogate to itself functions that can be efficiently performed by smaller and lower bodies. This is a fundamental principle of social philosophy, unshaken and unchangeable. . . . Of its very nature the true aim of all social activity should be to help individual units of the social body but never to destroy or absorb them."[12]

---

[12] *Quadragesimo Anno.*

"The State should leave to these smaller groups the settlement of business of minor importance. It will thus carry out with greater freedom, power and success the tasks belonging to it, because it alone can effectively accomplish these, directing, watching, stimulating and restraining. . . . Let those in power be convinced that the more . . . a graded hierarchical order exists between the various subsidiary organizations, the more excellent will be both the authority and the efficiency of the social organization as a whole and the happier and more prosperous the condition of the State."[13]

842.

THESIS LXII. The material cause of the State is the family. Between the family and the State other subordinate societies should be hierarchically arranged.

PROOF OF PART I

843. *The material cause of the State is the family.* The State is composed either of a union of individuals or a union of families. It is not composed of a union of individuals. In the obvious economy of nature, there are only three social units — the individual, the family, and the State. Nature directs the individual to the family union, the family unto the State. To say that individuals are immediately directed by nature to the State, means that nature decrees the social extinction of the family.

Corollary. The bond of civic justice falls *per se* and immediately upon the heads of families; only *per accidens* upon independent, unmarried persons. Children are immediately subject to paternal authority; mediately to civil authority.

PART II

844. *Between the family and the State other subordinate societies should be hierarchically arranged.* In the organic concept of the State, the State is a moral organism. Now an organism is a living structure made up of distinct parts, each having its separate function, joined one to the other by a unifying vital principle so that all work unto the good of the whole body.

The State as a moral organism will be made up of heterogeneous

---

[13] *Ibid.*

and autonomous parts arranged in a hierarchical order based on social function and united by an intrinsic social principle — conspiration toward the common public good.

Lest confusion result, besides the obvious difference of physical and moral union, these further differences between a physical and a moral organism should be noted. In living bodies the parts have only an *apparent* autonomy and they exist *entirely* for the sake of the body and hence their activity is pointed *directly* to the good of the body. In the State, the parts have real autonomy and all have their particular ends; some of them, that is, the human persons, have an *existence which is independent* of the State and in some respects work only *indirectly* for the common good.

Where life is simple and social needs few, the organic structure of the State will be crude and correspondingly simple. There may be no need of other societies except the family and State. Where the community is large and human needs are diverse and complicated, other subordinate societies, notably locally self-governing bodies and occupational groups, ought to be formed. As Pius XI expresses it: "For as nature induces those who dwell in close proximity to unite into municipalities, so those who practise the same trade or profession, economic or otherwise, combine into vocational groups. These groups in a true sense autonomous, are considered by man to be, if not essential to civil society, at least its natural and spontaneous development."[14]

PROOF OF PART II

845. The Natural Law demands organic structure of the State because that type of organization better promotes the common good.

1. It makes for a more flourishing condition of the family since it does not interfere with the family head in matters which are strictly of private concern.

2. The smaller items of the social good are better promoted by individuals organized in small groups in which they take an intelligent interest.

3. The heads of the State, freed from the minutiae of smaller business, have the leisure and energy to promote the over-all interests of the community.

---

[14] *Ibid.*

V. THE EFFICIENT CAUSE OF THE STATE

846. Having seen that the formal cause of the State is the moral bond of civic justice and the material cause the aggregation of families to be civilly united, we seek now the efficient cause of the State.

In the physical order an efficient cause is an agent whose physical action unites the formal cause to the material cause thus producing the new being. Applying this analogously to the moral entity of the State, we ask, What agent brings together the formal and material elements, that is, imposes on the aggregated families the bond of civic justice so that they are transformed into a State?

However, there is danger of confusion in such terminology since the State is a moral, not a physical, thing. Hence the question is better phrased as follows: *What is the proximate juridic cause of any actually existent State?* A similar question was raised in § 739 and the following concerning the conjugal union.

847. To avoid ambiguity it must be recalled that we have already proved that the State originates in a dictate of the Natural Law. The present issue does not concern Hobbes, Rousseau, the communists, or any who ascribe to a positivistic or evolutionary view of the origin of the State; it pertains solely to philosophers who admit a Natural Law and a natural origin of the State. The point of dispute here may be obscured for two reasons. The first reason is failure to distinguish the question of the origin of the State from that of the origin of political authority. To those who maintain that political authority is the formal cause of the State, these two questions must necessarily be one. To those of us who hold civic justice to be the formal cause of the State, two distinct though intimate questions are involved. Hence we shall deal first with the origin of the State and then with the origin of political authority. The second reason for misunderstanding is failure to distinguish between a juridic cause and an historic cause which is merely dispositive. Nor is this question one of idle speculative interest; very practical moral consequences depend upon the settlement of this point.

848. A *juridic cause* is one which *validly* produces a real effect in the juridic order. Since the juridic order is the total assemblage of justice, rights, and juridic duties, a juridic effect will be some right, some duty, or a complex combination of both which is granted, abolished, suspended, or modified. Statehood is a juridic effect, for with its establishment there begins to exist a tremendous aggregation of rights and duties which were nonexistent beforehand. Hence our question is, *What creative thing in the realm of right and justice produces the juridic effect of statehood?*

849. This cause is always twofold: one ultimate, the other proximate. The ultimate ground of every right and duty is always some law. Hence *some law is always the primary juridic cause of any juridic effect.* In the case of the State, the cause is the Natural Law commanding families to unite in the civic union. This we have proved in § 815 and the following against Hobbes and all who claim the State is an artificial device of man.

But no law creates a concrete right or duty in some particular subject without the intervention of some contingent fact. Such a fact in virtue of law actuates in the concrete a definite juridic effect. With reference to the creation of a right, we have called this fact a *title.* This fact or title is a juridic cause, though secondary and proximate.

Our question reduces itself to this, What secondary and proximate juridic cause operating in virtue of the Natural Law can create a State; what fact or facts constitute a valid title to statehood? Note the term, "valid title." We are not asking what facts *actually* lead men to form States. This is an historical question. Our difficulty is purely ethical, namely, what are the fact or facts which ought to be present *legitimately* to induce statehood?

850. Scholastics give two general answers.

1. The sole fact of value in the eyes of the Natural Law to found a State is the consent, at least tacit, of the multitude.

2. While the consent of the multitude is sometimes the proximate juridic cause of the State, this is the exceptional case. Many other facts may constitute title to statehood. It is usually the very force of circumstances which demands the establishment of the State without any reference to the consent of the multitude. Since the formal cause of the State is public authority, the same fact which designates the holder of this authority is likewise the juridic cause determining the origin of the State. Chief among such facts, as cited by the proponents of this theory, are the following:

a) Propagation from one family stem. The State naturally grew out of the family. It grew in size and importance so that its needs could no longer be satisfied by mere domestic organization. For this, political organization was gradually substituted. As the patriarch was head of the family organization he naturally assumed the headship of the nascent State.

b) Natural ability of the territorial proprietor. A number of unrelated people occupy the same territory controlled by one proprietor. Gradually the need of a protector against hostile outsiders, of a judge to settle their disputes, of a lawgiver to direct their economy calls for political organization, the setting up of a ruler. Since no one else has qualifications comparable to those of the proprietor, he is naturally designated as the wielder of authority and his assumption of civil rule brings the State into being.

c) Victory in a just war. Factually many States rose from the power of the sword. If the victory was won by one who had justly entered the war, he could afterward rightly subject to himself the vanquished for reasons of just compensation, of self-defense, of military security, of provision against future harm.

Our criticism of this view is: (1) there is a confusion of historical cause with juridical cause; (2) the alleged ethnographic, historical, economic, or military facts may well have disposed the people to become apt material for the fullness of the civic bond, but (3) apart from consent they cannot *validly* induce the status of civil society.

851. *Concerning our first observation.* Cronin argues for this second position very acutely when he writes: "The head of the village community became imperceptibly, as the community expanded and took on wider and wider functions, the head of the State. Henceforth his authority was more than domestic; it became political as well. And in this way and not through compact, political authority came first to be vested in the supreme ruler in the case of most States. Such is the testimony of history and of all recent sociological inquiry into the origin of political rule amongst primitive peoples. Here is no trace of anything in the nature of a social compact. The first political rulers derived their authority at a time when such a compact would have been unthinkable, a period when any attempt to superimpose upon the family or tribal organization based upon the tie of blood another organization based upon a wholly different principle, viz., popular election to power, would have been exceedingly difficult, if not impossible. And yet in those days the rulers of States wielded the scepter on titles as legitimate and with an authority quite as effective and convincing as any ruler of the present day."[15]

---

[15] *The Science of Ethics*, Vol. II, p. 503.

852. This citation argues that history shows one principal cause of the State. Therefore this had to be a juridic cause, that is, the patriarch assumed rule; he could not have done wrong in so acting. Now a similar investigation into the history of marriage might reveal few traces of the consent of the parties to be married; it might show that the vast majority of marriages were arranged by parents who were little concerned about the consent of their offspring. Such a fact, if proved to be a fact, would not overthrow the ethical conclusion that consent alone is capable of forming the conjugal union. We would not conclude that parental arrangement was the juridic cause of matrimony but simply that whoever did not give his consent was not validly married. So too, even if history affords small evidence of consent in the formation of States, this fact would not rule out the moral necessity of consent. For ethics is not the record of how men *have acted* but a pattern of how they *ought* to.

853. One may question whether scientific history confirms the facts to be such as alleged by Cronin. As far as prehistoric peoples are concerned, we can only conjecture: examined with sufficient scrutiny, the nations known to history do furnish enough evidence to the effect that consent entered into their founding. But even if the facts are as cited; even if the patriarch did everywhere assume political authority, the ethical question is, *Was he justified in doing so without the consent of the heads of the families under him?* Suarez argues: "The son by the attainment of reason, liberty and adult age is emancipated, freed from paternal power and becomes *sui juris*. Wherefore if he has his own family he has his own domestic authority over it equal to that which his father has over his family; nor is he obliged by the very nature of things to form one civic union with his father; nor from the very nature of things does any higher sort of jurisdiction lie between them."[16] The adult who is free of another becomes subject to him only by willingly agreeing to it. Certainly the fact could well have been that the only practicable thing for the children and the grandchildren of the patriarch to do was to agree to his political rule. They may even have had a moral obligation to agree. But suppose one or other did not? Would the patriarch have been justified in forcing them? He could not, because antecedent to their political subjection to him he did not have political coercive power over them.

---

[16] *De Opere Sex Dierum*, Bk. V, Chap. VII, No. 14.

Hence if he compels his rule by force, his authority rests on force, and as we shall show, force of itself cannot beget political authority.

Concerning our second observation. One must not imagine that by "the multitude" we mean a mere mass or unorganized conglomeration of people; rather we have reference to an aggregation of families composing something approximating a moral unity, almost but not perfectly united in the civic union.

There is quite a deep juridic gulf between the status of one large family or collection of families living in the same neighborhood and that of statehood. In that initial stage the authority of family head suffices. As the family grows into the sept or clan, as the unrelated families are bound closer together by intermarriage, trade, religion, or self-defense, their public problems become more complicated and the people must develop a further organization of life to solve them. Historically it was a gradual process: the occasional acceptance of a judge to settle their disputes, or of a war chief for defense, then of a priest for permanent religious guidance, of a spokesman to represent their interests before other groups and make commercial deals in their name. As each step was taken, custom cemented it: prudence demanded its permanency. Not that they originally had before them a complete design of civic order outlined by some philosopher toward which they consciously strove; but out of their own and their ancestors' experiences handed on by tradition, they worked out an economic, military, and juridical organization whose ultimate term was a self-sufficient community, a State, a juridic existence essentially different in its duties and rights from that whence the evolution began.

854. Many factors assisted in this upward process. The blood tie, the family organization, the authority of family heads, common language, religious rites, the outstanding ability of certain persons to serve the public interest, the fact that one group was subjugated by another — these in varying measure played an influencing or disposing part in the end result that these families formed with these other families a self-sufficing community. As the full scope of statehood emerged, as the superfamilial authority took on more and more of the attributes of sovereignty, and the family heads submitted more and more to a common public rule the sole juridic factor making the distinctive steps of the process *legitimate* could only have been the agreement of the family heads involved. Perhaps force did play a vastly greater part than willing agreement. That does not matter ethically, because mere might creates no juridical effects.

THESIS LXIII. The proximate cause of any actually existing State can only be the consent, at least tacit, of the multitude.

855. By a multitude we understand here a somewhat organized group of families, apt material to become a civic organization and looked at, at least conceptually, prior to its assumption of the *total* civic bond whereby it is fashioned into this particular State.

By consent we mean the free agreement whereby families accept in general the duties and rights necessary to constitute a sovereign State no matter how small. To be valid this agreement must be physically free though it may not always be morally free, for circumstances may be such as to produce an imperative command of the Natural Law obliging these people to unite into this State.

It is easy to understand how a man and woman consent to form the conjugal union but how a similar consent on the part of the multitude operates to produce the State may not be easy to grasp. A multitude is more complex: it requires more time for agreement.

856. There is no difficulty understanding explicit consent, either oral or written, such as that had in the formation of the American Republic. Consent is certainly manifested by cheerful subordination to, and co-operation with, public authority. Consent may be complete and spontaneous or it may come about gradually, in other words, all the people may consent at the same time, or group after group may yield its consent only over a considerable period of time. The people may consent to the entirety of the bond, as would be the case now; or they may only gradually assume the obligations of civil life, as in primitive times. Indirect consent may be shown by readiness to accept a definite person or group as ruler: tacit consent is shown by the omission of all protest and repudiation when such action would have been effective or a matter of duty. Hence whether it be expressed or tacit, direct or indirect, we can best denominate this necessary element as *natural consent*.

This consent, however, is worlds apart from the Social Contract of Hobbes and Rousseau. These differences will be more evident after we have investigated the origin of political authority.

PROOF

857. 1. The proximate juridic cause of the State is that fact which in virtue of the Natural Law validly produces the State by imposing the bond of civic justice on the multitude. For the multitude is transformed into a State when it is bound not precisely by ties of friendship, blood, or commutative justice but solely by the bond of civic justice. As the ultimate cause of the State is the Natural Law, so its proximate cause is some fact imposing civic justice on the people and approved of by the Natural Law.

2. The sole fact which may validly produce this effect is the consent, at least tacit, of the multitude. For a group of families not as yet formally constituting a State to have the bond of civic justice imposed on it the Natural Law requires their consent.

a) Their consent is required, because:

1) Just as nature does not designate who is married to whom so, *before the actual formation of the State,* neither does nature designate the members of a definite State. Hence, antecedent to the rise of a State, each man is politically free and independent of others. Adults possessing the use of reason and free will unite into States because they see that such unions are morally necessary and because they intend to reap the benefits of such association. Such an intention is explicit or implicit consent.

2) If the multitude does not freely assume the bond of civic justice when a State is formed, it is forcibly imposed on them. There is no other possibility. But force cannot create those social rights which constitute the State. In the juridic order force may protect and repair a right: it cannot produce a valid and positive effect.

3) Of its very nature the bond of civic justice demands the agreeing of many wills toward the common public good. But an agreement is necessarily consent. Since the object of agreement here is a common good, this consent must be a free consent. The reason is that, in order that a man, hitherto not obligated to seek a good in which *others* are to share, now be obliged to do so, he should freely agree to it.

b) Nothing further is required. Once men have agreed to strive after the common public good, they have assumed the bond of civic justice and the State is formally constituted.

READINGS

Arès, Richard, S.J., *What Is Corporative Organization?* trans. T. P. Fay, S.J. St. Louis, Central Bureau, 1940.

Aristotle, *Politics*, Bk. I, cc. 1–2; Bk. II; Bk. VII, cc. 1–12.

Bruehl, Charles, *The Pope's Plan for Social Reconstruction*, pp. 225–306. New York, Devin Adair, 1939.

Burgess, John, W., *The Foundations of Political Science*, pp. 3–93. New York, Columbia, 1933.

Cathrein, Victor, S.J., *Philosophia Moralis*, pp. 379–425. Friburgi Brisgoviae, Herder, 1915, 10 ed.

Costa Rossetti, Julius, S.J., *Philosophia Moralis*, pp. 574–593. Oeniponte, Rauch, 1866.

Cronin, Michael, *The Science of Ethics*, pp. 461–503. Dublin, Gill, 1909.

Dawson, Christopher, *Religion and the Modern State*, pp. 129–154. New York, Sheed and Ward, 1936.

Gettell, Raymond G., *Political Science*, pp. 17–115. Boston, Ginn, 1933.

Guenechea, Joseph, S.J., *Principia Juris Politici*, pp. 5–133, Vol. I. Romae, Universitas Gregoriana, 1938.

Haas, Francis J., *Man and Society*, pp. 178–185. New York, Appleton-Century, 1930.

Hoare, F. R., *The Papacy and the Modern State*. London, Burns, Oates, Washbourne, 1940.

Hoffman, Ross, *The Organic State*. New York, Sheed and Ward, 1939.

Leo XIII, *Immortale Dei* (encyclical).

MacIver, R. M., *The Modern State*, pp. 3–45. Oxford, Clarendon, 1926.

Macksey, C., S.J., *De Ethica Naturali*, pp. 461–562. Romae, Universitas Gregoriana, 1914.

Messner, J., *Social Ethics*, trans. J. J. Doherty, pp. 463–504. St. Louis, Herder, 1949.

McGovern, William M., *From Luther to Hitler*. Boston, Houghton, Mifflin, 1941.

McKevitt, Peter, *The Plan of Society*, pp. 124–133. Dublin, Cahill, 1944.

Plato, *The Republic*. Passim.

Rommen, Heinrich A., *The State in Catholic Thought*, pp. 248–358. St. Louis, Herder, 1945.

Ruland, Ludwig, *Morality and the Social Order*, pp. 160–179, trans. T. A. Rattler, O.S.A. St. Louis, Herder, 1942.

Ryan-Boland, *Catholic Principles of Politics*, pp. 29–42, 102–139. New York, Macmillan, 1940.

Scott, James B., *Law, the State and the International Community*, Vol. II, pp. 173–238. New York, Columbia, 1939.

Suarez, *De Opere Sex Dierum*, V, 7.

CHAPTER XXV

THE AUTHORITY OF THE STATE

858. Since some scholastics hold that authority is the formal cause of the State, to them the question of the origin of the State is identified with the question of the origin of political authority. Though we do not admit that the State is formally constituted by authority, nevertheless, these two questions are so closely interwoven that an adequate discussion of the nature of the State is impossible without consideration of the nature and origin of authority.

859. *What is political authority?* It is the legitimate power of the State to direct and compel its members to co-operate toward the attainment of the common public good. This is the power of sovereignty, an authority which is supreme, one, total, and constant.

1. *Supremacy.* Every self-sufficient political entity is an independent State and the authority of every independent State originates of itself; it is not derived from any political superior; it is above every political agency within the State; it extends to the plenary control of its own internal and external affairs. However, this supremacy does not imply freedom from natural and divine positive law.

2. *Unity.* Being supreme and independent, every State is one. While there may be many subordinate agencies within the State possessing some measure of authority, there can be only one which is supreme. This the unity of the State demands. There will be as many States as there are supreme authorities. The unity of sovereignty does not demand that it be inseparably attached to one person or one group.

3. *Totality.* This supreme power is a total power, that is to say, it consists in *all* the rights and power which any State must have to achieve the purposes of the State.

4. *Constancy.* Sovereignty is finally a constant quantity. Its *legitimate* power is the same in every State, large or small, ancient or modern. Just as the totality of parental power never fluctuates so that parents

today have as much *parental* authority as in the days of Abraham, so too the content of sovereignty does not change. Rickaby, however, says there is "far more authority in the England of today than in the England of the Heptarchy."[1] Now the amount of authority may appear to fluctuate because strong rulers sometimes go beyond the just limits of their authority and weak rulers fail to use their power to the full. This is obvious. But it may not be so obvious that new and variegated needs, new social tendencies and aspirations do not add to sovereignty powers which it never had in simple, less socially conscious ages. Each power which the State now exercises — provided of course it is legitimate — was always there, but there may have been no need to *exercise* it in this specific way. New circumstances do not confer fresh powers but merely summon the exercise of old powers in a new way. Should civilized States lapse into barbarism, sovereignty would lose none of its powers. It would merely mean that the occasion to exercise many specific powers which a complicated civilization now demands would no longer be present.

I. THE ORIGIN OF AUTHORITY

860. A most general question is proposed here. We are not asking from what particular source this king or president, this parliament or congress received its authority, for we are not as yet interested in the person or persons who hold authority. Our inquiry is more fundamental: whence comes State authority as such? Is it from men or God?

A. Ultimate Origin

861. According to materialistic evolutionary doctrine, humanity is in a process of unending evolution which is governed by inflexible, ironclad laws operating with physical necessity. At the proper time and in the required state of development, civil authority directly and totally proceeded from humanity. According to communism, authority — the State which is only the armed might of the capitalist parading under legal forms — arose from the need of the exploiting classes to keep the masses in subjection (cf. § 521). According to another evolutionary variant, authority rose out of public opinion enforcing tribal customs and taboos.

THESIS LXIV. Supreme political authority has an ultimate divine origin.

---

[1] *Catholic Encyclopedia*, "Authority," Vol. II, p. 138.

PROOF

862. 1. That is ultimately from God which exists because of a peremptory command of the Natural Law. Since God is the Supreme Legislator who speaks through the Natural Law, whatever that law commands, is the command of God.

2. Supreme political power exists because of a peremptory command of the Natural Law. States must exist because they are demanded by the Natural Law for human welfare. Therefore, an essential property of the State, civil authority, is likewise demanded by the Natural Law.

B. Immediate Origin

863. That authority comes from God may be explained in a variety of ways. He could be merely the *mediate* author. First, He could be the mediate author by giving men a general impulse toward it and a wide authorization to do whatever conduces to social welfare. Then, in virtue of this impulse and fortified with this permission, men hit upon authority as an instrument of social betterment. God sanctions it. Thus the Church by a general grant of divine power may erect such corporations or take whatever steps may more readily conduce to man's eternal welfare. In virtue of this delegation She has instituted sacramentals and set up religious orders. Is the same true of the State and its authority?

864. Second, in a much vaguer and more general way God could allow men to solve their human difficulties in the manner that seems good to them and give His approval to whatever does not contravene His explicit law. Thus, after the Black Sox scandal of 1919, the owners of the big league baseball teams formulated a code for organized baseball and set up Commissioner Landis with complete power to keep baseball clean. Now one could hardly say that the rules of organized baseball and the power of Commissioner Landis were from God — this is true only in the remote sense that God approves what is sensible and decent.

865. The contractualists explain the origin of political authority in almost parallel terms. The great writers among them — Hobbes, Rousseau, Locke — believed in God. God is in the background of their social scheme, but to them authority is *immediately from men:* it is a concession yielded by men willing to be ruled; it is divine only very remotely.

According to Hobbes, society arose from a compact men made among themselves for self-preservation and peace. However, even in society men are still vain, contentious, revengeful, and self-seeking. Hence a mere covenant does not suffice to keep men peaceable and orderly, because "covenants without the sword are but words and of no strength to secure a man."[2] There must be some visible power to keep them in awe and tie them by fear of punishment to the performance of their agreements. Hobbes thus evolves his argument: "The agreement of men is by covenant only, which is artificial; and therefore it is no wonder if there be somewhat else required, besides covenant, to make their agreement constant and lasting: which is a common power to keep them in awe. . . .

"The only way to erect such a common power . . . is, to confer all their power and strength on one man, or upon one assembly of men, that may reduce all their wills by plurality of voices, unto one will; which is as much as to say, to appoint one man or assembly of men, to bear their person; and everyone to own, and acknowledge himself to be the author of whatsoever he that so beareth their person, shall act or cause to be acted, in those things which concern the common peace and safety; and therein to submit their wills, every one to his will, and their judgments to his judgment. This is more than consent, or concord: it is a real unity of them all, in one and the same person, made by covenant of every man with every man, in such a manner, as if every man should say to every man, *I authorize and give up my right of governing myself, to this man or to this assembly of men, on this condition, that thou give up thy right to him, and authorize all his actions in like manner*. This done, the multitude so united in one person, is called a commonwealth. . . . This is the generation of that great Leviathan, or rather, to speak more reverently, of that *mortal god*, to which we owe under the *immortal God*, our peace and defense. For by this authority, given him by every particular man in the commonwealth, he hath the use of so much power and strength conferred on him, that by terror thereof, he is enabled to perform the wills of them all, to peace at home, and mutual aid against their enemies abroad. And in him consisteth the essence of the commonwealth; which, to define it, is one person, of whose acts a great multitude, by mutual covenants one with another, have made themselves every one the author, to the end he may use the strength and

---

[2] *Leviathan*, Chap. XIII. See Molesworth's English edition, Vol. III, p. 154.

means of them all, as he shall think expedient, for their peace and common defense."[3]

866. The question which most furiously agitated political thinkers of the eighteenth century was that of the Social Contract. Its greatest protagonist, Rousseau, borrowed the idea from Hobbes and popularized it, explaining it, like Hobbes, as an artificial instrument of human association created by formal agreement of individual men whence proceeds the State and political authority. Their reasons for their conclusion, however, differ. Hobbes arrives at a Social Contract because he was obsessed by the brutish selfishness of men. Rousseau, however, concludes to it because he sees in it the only answer to this difficulty: man must finally associate with other men in society, but how can he do this and still retain his liberty? "The problem," he says, "is to find some form of association which will defend and protect with the whole common force the person and goods of each associate, and in which each, while uniting himself with all, may still obey himself alone, and remain as free as before."[4] The answer is a formal compact whose terms are in essence these: "Each of us puts his person and all his power in common under the supreme direction of the common will, and, in our corporate capacity, we receive each member as an indivisible part of the whole."[5] Each and every man by totally alienating himself and his rights to the community has created a general will of which he is an inseparable part. This general will is *Authority,* the Sovereign. Since his will is an indivisible part of the general will, and since he is at one with the Sovereign People, in obeying the general will the individual is still obeying himself.

The contractualist opinion is thus summarized: individuals had a natural liberty and rights over their own acts; when by formal agreement they yielded this power to the community, political authority arose. Posterity is ever after bound by this contract. Authority, therefore, immediately arose from the will of man.

867. We repudiate this and any other explanation of sovereignty which attributes to it a merely human origin, immediate or remote. Certainly, since mere artificial societies derive totally from the arbitrary will of man, the directive authority they possess emanates from a human source. Thus, since a school is not a natural institution, it

---

[3] *Ibid.,* Chap. XVII. See Molesworth's English edition, Vol. III, pp. 157–158.
[4] *Social Contract,* Bk. I, Chap. VI.
[5] *Ibid.*

receives its authority over its pupils from the explicit or implicit delegation of parents. But in natural societies — the marital union, the family, and the State — the case is different. The authority exercised therein is totally divine. It is in no way the composite resultant of many human choices; it may not be construed as the general will of many agreeing to obey it nor as the accumulated might and right of many men.

THESIS LXV. In the erection of any given State the original possessor of supreme political authority receives it directly and immediately from God.

868. God does not merely approve of political authority or only will it to exist through man's direct contriving. He is its *immediate cause,* that is to say, whenever a new State arises and hence a new authority comes into being, it is God who directly confers this authority upon its first possessor without the mediation of any man. Certainly the intervention of man is required for the erection of the State; but once a new State begins to be, authority derives from no man or collection of men but directly from God. The same is true of parental authority. Human activity is required for a man and woman to become parents; but once parental society is formed by the birth of children, the parents receive authority over their children not from any human source whatever but directly from God.

PROOF

869. That power comes solely and immediately from God which (1) must be present in the State whether man wills it or not; (2) cannot be augmented or diminished by human power; (3) contains prerogatives which no individual or collection of individuals possesses. Such is political authority because:

1. To will the existence of the State and to will it not to have authority is a contradiction, for the absence of authority is the dissolution of the State. Second, God alone provides those things which are essential and indispensable to a natural institution.

2. The specific powers which attach to sovereignty are determined not by human choice but by the natural end of the State. For men to add to these powers is to induce tyranny, a needless restriction of the liberties of citizens. To diminish these powers is to deprive a natural

institution of a means necessary to its end. This no man may legitimately do.

3. One of the specific powers of sovereignty is the right to punish and that even with death. But no individual, as such, has a right to punish a fellow man. He has a right of self-defense or of exacting restitution but never of punishment: punishment is the prerogative of a superior. *A fortiori,* the individual cannot punish with death. Therefore the right of the sword, which belongs to the State (Thesis LXXIV), could not have come from any collection of individuals.

870. Corollary I. The person or group that wields legitimate civil authority holds the place of God and can exact obedience in those things which fall within the scope of civil jurisdiction.

Corollary II. Those subject to such jurisdiction have an obligation in conscience to obey. The precise limits of this duty will be discussed later.

II. THE PRIMARY DEPOSITARY OF POLITICAL AUTHORITY

871. Granted that God is the immediate Author of authority in natural societies, the next question is, Who is the recipient of that authority? It is clear that in the conjugal union nature designates the husband and in parental society the parents — the natural social head (Thesis LVI). What of the State? Who is the first natural possessor of political authority in the State? Three opinions are offered.

A. The Patriarchal Theory

872. According to those who hold that popular consent is not necessary for the legitimate erection of the State (§ 850), authority is immediately conferred by God upon that person, physical or moral, demonstrated by the practical exigencies of the case, to have the greatest natural capacity to rule. This superior aptitude consists not only of personal qualifications but especially of social standing and prestige.[6] It rests upon some prior right which may be that (*a*) of the patriarch to govern his family; (*b*) of the proprietor of the land these people inhabit; (*c*) of the victor in a just war; (*d*) of a benefactor who has conferred notable benefits upon a people. Patriarchal dignity is pre-eminent and primordial among all such social qualifications. If no special individual stands out as the

---

[6] Cathrein, *Philosophia Moralis,* p. 399. Friburgi Brisgoviae, Herder, 1915, 10 ed.

natural candidate to rule, popular choice is resorted to. However, this choice is not a conferral of authority; it is the designation of the one upon whom God immediately bestows power to rule.

B. The Theory of the Divine Right of Kings

873. While some vague outline of this theory may have been voiced by one or other medieval emperor in his struggle with the papacy, this theory was the logical outgrowth of the action of Henry VIII of England, who arrogated to the crown of England all authority, both temporal and spiritual. It was first given articulate form by James I.[7] This theory claims for monarchy what is true of sovereignty in the abstract, that is, the sum of its power is constant and comes from God antecedent to, and irrespective of, the popular will. Just as parents receive authority over their children directly and immediately from God, so does the monarch in the beginning of the State. The mode of designation, however, is different. Parents are holders of authority by the natural designation of God; the monarch by the positive intervention of God, which is had either by a special act of God, as in the case of Saul, or through a permanent institution willed by God, such as election or hereditary succession. Such an institution is not a title or juridic cause of kingly power but a mere condition which designates the person upon whom God immediately confers authority. The totality of sovereign power rests in the king, who may call whom he chooses for assistance, yet his power is indivisible and forever inseparable from him and his successors by divine appointment. Thus is claimed for the temporal sovereign what is true of the spiritual monarch, the pope.

874. The first and second theories agree in this: in every case God directly and immediately confers authority not upon the people but upon the rulers. They differ in this: according to the second theory, God designates the ruler by positive means — his special intervention; according to the first theory the rulers are designated by natural means.

C. The People

875. Authority first descends to the whole people united in the bonds of civic justice.

THESIS LXVI. In the beginning of every State, God confers

---

[7] James I of England, "The Trew Law of Free Monarchies," *The Workes of the Most High and Mightie Prince, James etc.*, pp. 193–210. London, Barker, 1616.

authority upon the whole people united in the bonds of civic justice. The people may and generally ought to transfer the actual function of ruling to one person or one group.

876. There is nothing novel in the doctrine set forth in Theses LXIII and LXVI. It represents the universally accepted teaching of the scholastics from the Middle Ages[8] to the nineteenth century — whose popular expression is found in the sentence, *Vox populi est vox Dei.* The early schoolmen took this over from the Roman legists who thus explained the origin of Roman imperial power. Suarez, with whom most of all this doctrine is identified, calls it certain and common.[9]

877. Some modern scholastics, among whom are a number of avowed monarchists, condemn any explanation of authority which involves what they term a pact and which we name a consent. The word *pact* seems to be limited to an explicit contract. However, there is more than an issue of words here. Of course, they concede that our theory of consent differs vastly from the pact of the contractualists. The main points of difference are these: (*a*) to us, the State is a natural society and we have a moral obligation to form it; to the contractualists the State is artificial and there was no moral obligation involved in its institution; (*b*) to us, many of the individual's rights come from God and nature; to the contractualists, from the Social Contract; (*c*) to us, authority comes immediately from God; to the contractualists, solely from the will of many individuals; (*d*) to us, once authority is transferred to a ruler, he has the right to exact obedience and his authority cannot easily and arbitrarily be recalled; to Rousseau authority so essentially and inalienably belongs to the people that they give a ruler only what they choose which they may recall at will — rulers are only paid agents of the Sovereign People; (*e*) to us, authority may take any concrete form which will promote the general welfare; to Rousseau, the only legitimate form is that of perfect democracy.

878. However, we do agree with the contractualists that the State owes its proximate origin to a social agreement and that political authority resides primarily in the whole people. Hence, something of the taint of Jacobinism, Encyclopedism, and revolutionary horror inevitably attaches to the theory of consent. It opens the door to civil disobedience, sedition, and rebellion. But any doctrine may be mis-

---

[8] Alfred O'Rahilly, "The Sovereignty of the People," *Studies,* March, 1921, pp. 43–46.
[9] *De Legibus,* III, c. II, 3.

interpreted and abused. So too is the opinion of our adversaries, and it may well be asked if greater woe has not been wrought among men by the abuse of their doctrine than of ours. However, the issue will not be settled by a relative weighing of extrinsic consequences but upon the inherent soundness of either contention.

Returning to the position established in Thesis LXIII that States arise from the consent of the multitude, we further hold that when men thus unite in the bonds of civic justice, the Natural Law concedes to the moral power so created — the Commonwealth — all rights and powers necessary for the life and function of a State. Among these necessary powers are organization and actual government.

879. *The power of organization includes the powers* (*a*) to organize the State under a definite form of rulership of its own choice; (*b*) to select individuals in whom governmental functions are to reside stably; (*c*) to determine the stable limitations of these powers by reservation of power to the community, and establish the mode of succession to these powers; (*d*) to govern the community *ad interim* either directly or by the appointment of provisional rulers; (*e*) to reorganize the government whenever a prior government disintegrates or permanently fails to function for the common good, or in new times and circumstances fails to meet the exigencies of the common good; (*f*) to be the authentic judge of conditions requiring reorganization. These are constituent powers, plenary authority to enact a fundamental law upon which governmental activity is to be based.

880. *The power of actual government* is the actual direction of the State unto the common public good by competent executive, legislative, and judicial power in conformity with the fundamental law of the land.

881. Our position is that at the beginning of the State's existence both the authority to organize and to govern devolves upon the community civilly united. If the people choose to set up a purely democratic form of government then, they retain and themselves exercise all the powers of political authority.

But a pure democracy is a virtual impossibility. Only in an exceedingly small community could it work. Therefore it is almost universally necessary for the people to hand over to some individual or group the actual function of government. Thus they entrust the governing powers to appointed rulers, but retain the organizing powers for the emergency of reorganization.

882. The rulers so accepted are the secondary subjects of authority. Their authority comes mediately from God, immediately from the community. Whenever for any valid reason this secondary subject has ceased to exist, it belongs to the community to select another such secondary depositary.

The people agree to this transfer in the same way they consent to assume the bond of civic justice. This consent may be explicit, either oral or written. It may be tacit and virtual, that is, by co-operation with, or acceptance of, a given ruler, by failure to protest against a regime when a protest would be in order. The consent may be spontaneous — even instantaneous — or it may be gradual, being drawn out over a relatively long period of time. The actual transfer is accomplished whenever the people agree to set up or accept some particular political regime other than a pure democracy.

883. *When this transfer is made, may the people attach certain conditions to the exercise of such authority?*

1. They may not delimit that which is essential to effective government. They necessarily transfer sufficient jurisdiction so that the established rulers have the necessary legislative, executive, and judicial authority. Above all, rulers have a full right to exact obedience; the people have an obligation to obey.

2. They cannot arbitrarily recall power transferred. The welfare of the people demands that sovereignty be stable. Therefore, once a regime is established, so long as it remains a functioning government attaining the ends of government, it cannot be cast aside. A government is always presumed to be operative until it manifestly becomes a permanent hindrance to the attainment of the ends of the State.

884. Therefore we reject the contention of Rousseau that after a government is set up the people remain their own governors, and rulers are but their salaried lackeys. For Rousseau rulers are bound to carry out each and every mandate of the Sovereign People and are removable at their will. He thought that the people should meet at definite periods established by law and "the moment the people is legitimately assembled as a sovereign body, the jurisdiction of the government wholly lapses, the executive power is suspended and the person of the meanest citizen is as sacred and inviolable as that of the first magistrate."[10] At these assemblies two questions should always

---

[10] *The Social Contract*, Bk. III, Chap. XIV.

be considered and voted on separately. The first is, "Does it please the Sovereign to preserve the present form of government?" The second is, "Does it please the people to leave its administration in the hands of those who are actually in charge of it?"[11] Apart from the physical impossibility of ever assembling all the people (except in a tiny city-state) to act as Sovereign, Rousseau is wrong on two counts: (a) a constant and arbitrary recall of authority once granted militates against peace and stability in the State; (b) the people do give authority to their rulers, but the essence of authority means that the one possessing it has a true right to command and that the people have an obligation to obey. You cannot keep that which you give away. Therefore, while rulers *become* such by the consent of the governed, they do not require the consent of the governed to *exercise* the function of ruling. Thus we interpret the phrase of the Declaration of Independence, "Governments are instituted among men, deriving their just power from the consent of the governed."

885. Provided, then, there is no essential impairment of the function of rulership, the people may attach to their transfer of power such conditions as these:

1. A fundamental constitution either in the form of a written document or of immemorial custom may provide how the function of sovereignty is to operate: whether sovereignty shall reside in one person, one group or several groups; what the mode of succession to these powers shall be; what relations shall be maintained among the chief bodies of the government.

2. The people may reserve to themselves the ultimate decision concerning certain specific issues, such as declaring war and changing the fundamental constitution.

PROOF OF PART I

886. *In the beginning of every State, God confers authority upon the whole people civilly united.*

First proof.

1. Those particulars of social welfare which nature has not prescribed are to be settled by the free agreement of the social members. For it is inadmissible that one man or group should impose its view on others by force or fraud when nature has left the issue to be settled by men.

---

[11] *Ibid.*, Bk. III, Chap. XVIII.

2. Nature sets up no man as natural ruler, nor does she command any particular form of government. There are absolutely no indications that nature has given political authority to any individual before the creation of a State or that nature prefers one form of government to another (§ 896).

3. Hence the ruler and form of government are decided by the agreement of men. But these decisions would be impossible unless political authority resided first in the whole people. The choice of a ruler and form of government is a fundamental exercising of authority. Hence the fact that the people may do this *legitimately* argues to their prior possession of authority.

Second proof.

1. The primary recipient of authority is the one upon whom first and necessarily rests the obligation of attaining the ends of the State. An obligation to attain an end must necessarily carry with it a right to the necessary means. Now authority is the most essential means to the common good. Hence whoever has the primary obligation of attaining the common good, has the first right to authority.

2. The prime obligation of striving for the common good rests upon the whole people civilly united because:

a) The nature of the State demands this. The moral person, the State, which tends to the common good is not a fragment of that society, for example, a body of rulers, but all the members united in the bonds of civic justice.

b) Whenever visible authority has ceased, the people not only can but must reconstitute it and establish another regime. This they could not do unless the obligation of attaining the common good rested primarily with them.

887. N.B. Ryan is incorrect when he says an original grant of authority to the people is unnecessary for their welfare.[12] Our argument shows it is necessary in order that the people may choose a form of government; that they reconstitute government when an old one falls to pieces; that they may legitimately reserve to themselves some portion of sovereignty. This reservation serves also this salutary purpose: it is a constant reminder to rulers that they are the bearers of a public trust to be managed not for their personal advantage but for the good of all the people. Nothing is more inimical to the welfare of the people

---

[12] Ryan-Boland, *Catholic Principles of Politics*, p. 83. New York, Macmillan, 1941.

than the failure to perceive that the State is for them, not they for the State.

PROOF OF PART II

888. *The people generally ought to transfer the actual function of sovereignty to one person or group* because the general welfare demands this. Except in a very small community it is impossible for the whole people to propose, enact, and execute the requisite laws. No large body of people could efficiently function as a ruler.

Corollary. Lincoln's words about democracy in a true sense may also be applied to government in general: *governments are of the people, for the people, and by the people.* The first, because the State *is* the people; hence, the rulers of a people *ought* to be of the people they rule. The second, because the State is *for* the people. The end of the State is the promotion of *people's* welfare. The worth of any State is measured by the human progress and achieved perfections of its people. The third, because it is from their consent that the power of sovereignty immediately flows.

READINGS

Costa Rossetti, Julius, S.J., *Philosophia Moralis,* pp. 593–661. Oeniponte, Rauch, 1886.

Guenechea, Joseph, S.J., *Principia Juris Politici,* Vol. I, pp. 134–173. Romae, Universitas Gregoriana, 1938.

Haas, Francis J., *Man and Society,* pp. 186–194. New York, Appleton-Century, 1930.

Hoffman, Ross, *The Will to Freedom.* New York, Sheed and Ward, 1935.

Macksey, Charles B., S.J., *Sovereignty and Consent.* New York, America Press, 1920.

Maritain, Jacques, *Scholasticism and Politics,* pp. 89–117. New York, Macmillan, 1940.

Rommen, Heinrich A., *The State in Catholic Thought,* pp. 371–476. St. Louis, Herder, 1945.

Ryan-Boland, *Catholic Principles of Politics,* pp. 43–101, 179–193. New York, Macmillan, 1940.

Simon, Yves, *Nature and Function of Authority.* Milwaukee, Marquette, 1940.

Suarez, *De Opere Sex Dierum,* V, 3; *De Legibus,* III, cc. 1–4.

CHAPTER XXVI

THE CONSTITUTION OF A STATE

889. Once a people agree to accept a particular body of rulers by implicit or explicit transfer of authority, they have government, exercising actual sovereignty and guiding the whole State to its appointed ends. A constitution, no matter how crude, underlies every government. No government is without one, for by a constitution we do not mean merely a written document, agreed to by a sovereign, wherein he agrees to respect certain liberties of his people and follow a definite pattern in his rule. We give it a broader meaning. For our purposes we may call a constitution a fundamental system of governmental principles which indicate the general form government shall take by designating those who shall hold the highest offices, prescribing the mode of their selection or creation, defining the quality and extent of governmental action, and marking the relation of the individual with regard to his government. We shall discuss the notion of a constitution touching briefly on (1) the form of government and (2) the mode of succeeding to governmental power; and treating more extensively (3) governmental activity and (4) the citizen's relation to government.

I. THE FORM OF GOVERNMENT

890. By a government we understand that officially accepted and legitimate person, individual or moral, to whom the function of actual sovereignty is entrusted. In the history of the human race there has been a great variety of governments. Hence, ancient and modern political writers have occupied themselves with discussing what the best form of government is. However, the ethician is concerned with discovering what form of government the Natural Law commands or forbids or permits.

Some distinguish governments on the basis of the mode by which

466

the chief magistrate is selected, that is, election or hereditary succession; the diffusion of governmental powers; or the existence or nonexistence of a written constitution. No division, however, is more fundamental and goes more cleanly to the heart of things than that of Aristotle, which is based upon the number of persons who share in rule. During the nineteenth century there was a movement which discredited Aristotle's division as unscientific and inadequate but it came to nothing. Aristotle's is still the best because it best performs the essential functions of a good division — it resolves the thing to be studied into its simplest elements.

891. "The true forms of government," says Aristotle, "are those in which the one, or the few, or the many, govern with a view to the common interest."[1] Hence there are three simple forms: (1) *monarchy,* in which the whole sovereignty rests in one person; (2) *aristocracy,* in which it resides in a small class; (3) *democracy,* in which it is exercised by the collectivity of the citizens. This last form Aristotle designates by a more generic name, a polity or constitution. "But governments," he continues, "which rule with a view to private interest, whether of the one, or the few, or the many are a perversion . . . . the perversions are these: of kingship, *tyranny;* or aristocracy, *oligarchy;* of constitutional government, *democracy.*"[2] Since democracy has a different connotation in modern usage, for that perverted form of popular rule which Aristotle called democracy we substitute the word ochlocracy, or *mob rule.*

892. All known forms of government either directly fall into one of these simple classes or as *mixed forms* exhibit some variant of one or other or all three. The variations of absolute monarchy, pure aristocracy, and direct democracy are many and differ according to the manner in which the powers of sovereignty — legislative, executive, and judicial — are separated and allocated partly to the one, partly to the few, and partly to the many. Thus governments may be called limited monarchies which follow this pattern: the executive power rests in a hereditary king; judicial power principally in the king to whom the judges are subject, secondarily and partially in the people who serve as jurymen; legislative power partially in an aristocracy represented by an Upper House, partially in the people represented in a Lower House. That has been called a consular form of govern-

[1] *Politics,* Bk. III, 7, 1279a.
[2] *Ibid.,* 1279b.

ment in which legislative power resides either in the people themselves or in them through their representatives; or partly in a favored class and partly in the people; and the executive and judicial functions are vested in a consul. That is called a representative democracy in which the executive power belongs to one directly or indirectly chosen by the people; the legislative power, to representatives of the people; and the judicial power, to appointees of the executive approved of by the legislative body. To call one government a democracy merely because its chief executive is elected and another a monarchy solely because he is a hereditary king is not a very helpful distinction. The fundamental question is, Where is the preponderance of governmental power?

893. *Congressional government* calls for the strict cleavage of legislative, executive, and judicial powers. The idea of separation seems to have been first suggested by Montesquieu,[3] and the conscious purpose underlying it is the prevention of tyranny arising from an accumulation of unrestrained power in one person or group. One group makes the laws, one person administers them, and a third group judges according to them. By a carefully arranged system of checks each counterweights the power of the other. At the core of the system is an executive with real power: he is, independent of, and not chosen by, a legislature which in turn cannot be dissolved before the expiration of its constitutional term.

894. *Congressional government* rests upon the principle of diffusion of power; *cabinet government* upon the principle of concentration of power. A cabinet is a small college of ministers who are the heads of the chief departments of governmental administration. It is immediately responsible to the legislature from which it is selected by the majority party of that body. Whenever it ceases to have the confidence of the legislature, it is forced to resign; when it voluntarily resigns, the legislature is dissolved and new elections are held. It is rightly called the *government,* because it does the real governing of the State. While there is a nominal executive, he is but a figurehead, although he is a person of great dignity as the personal representative of the nation. Power resides in the cabinet, because it directly controls all administration as the supreme *acting executive,* and since cabinet members are also members of the legislature —

---

[3] Baron de Montesquieu, *The Spirit of the Laws,* Bk. XI, cc. X–XX.

indeed the chief men of the majority party — the cabinet controls the legislation as well.

895. <u>Congressional government is the modern and logical outgrowth of the federal concept of the State; cabinet government is the product of the unitary type of State.</u> By the latter is meant a State containing a single supreme government which alone controls all governmental activity and from which every minor agency of government derives its authority. <u>Examples are England, France, and Italy,</u> where the authority of municipalities, counties, and provinces is immediately derived from, and directly subordinate to, one central government. The federal State is a collection of semisovereignties under one supreme government: the authority of the semisovereignties is not usually derived from the central government and in many matters of purely internal interests it is completely independent of the central government. The constituent parts are rightly called semisovereignties, because there are certain matters wherein they are sovereign and to that extent may be called sovereign States but in many other matters — foreign relations — they depend on the central government. Historically the federal State has arisen from a fusion of several smaller independent States into one larger State with the result that the combining States retained something of their former jurisdiction. <u>The United States of America and the German Reich of 1871 are outstanding examples of the federal State.</u>

896. To our question, What kind of a government does the Natural Law command? we find the proponents of the theory of the divine right of kings saying the only legitimate form of government is monarchy. Rousseau makes the same claim for direct democracy.[4]

THESIS LXVII. The Natural Law neither commands nor forbids monarchy, aristocracy, or democracy but allows any form of government which is capable of attaining the ends of the State.

---

[4] Although Rousseau says: "Were there a people of gods, their government would be democratic. So perfect a government is not for men" (*Social Contract,* Bk. III, Chap. IV). Yet one must note the meaning he gives to the word *government.* In his theory, the real sovereign is always the whole people and "a government" is merely a body of administrators (Bk. III, Chap. I) selected by and directly accountable to its sovereign. The Sovereign People should meet at frequent and regular intervals to make laws and demand an accounting of their government (Bk. III, Chap. XII–XIV). This they are to do themselves, *not through representatives* (Chap. XV).

PART I

897. The Natural Law does not demand any of these forms of government, because there are no natural signs indicating nature's intent. Nor does the Natural Law forbid any of them, for the experience of the race testifies that States have functioned well under all three forms.

PART II

898. *The Natural Law allows any form of government which is capable of attaining the ends of the State.* What conduces to a natural good is allowed by the Natural Law. But any form of government capable of attaining the ends of the State conduces to a natural good. Therefore the Natural Law allows any form of government capable of attaining the ends of the State.

Corollary. The Natural Law forbids any form of government that operates for the private interest of rulers to the neglect of the common good of all.

899. N.B. I. *What constitutes the best form of government* is a question that belongs to political science. Two remarks will suffice here. First, the best government for any particular people is that which works best for them in terms of their traditions, economic situation, level of civilization, peculiarity of temperament, and the like. Second, if we take the average run of peoples and circumstances, that form will work best which is most responsive to enlightened public opinion. This is possible only where a large and articulate middle class is found. As Aristotle says, "The best political community is formed by citizens of the middle class, and those States are likely to be well administered in which the middle class is large and stronger if possible than both the other classes . . . great then is the fortune of a State in which the citizens have a moderate and sufficient property."[5]

N.B. II. Once a form of government has been set up and accepted, *it may not be lightly changed.* For the constant turmoil consequent upon frequent change would render impossible the ends of the State. Therefore a change is to be made only when a very grave evil is to be corrected or when the true progress of the State imperatively calls for it. Zigliara[6] says the power to make this change does not

---

[5] *Politics,* Bk. IV, 9, 1295b.

[6] T. M. Zigliara, *Summa Philosophica,* Vol. III, *Jus Naturae,* L. II, c. 2, a. 8, p. 263. Lugduni, 1889.

rest upon the people alone nor the rulers alone but the whole society. This is generally true, though in a rare instance a radical change may be made even against the will of erstwhile rulers (see § 922).

II. TITLES TO AUTHORITY

900. In setting forth the form of government, every constitution makes clear who shall hold supreme authority. The next question is, How does one validly come to have authority?

The ground of authority has already been stated: it is the law of nature demanding the State and with it authority. A *title to authority* is some fact which demonstrates the existence of authority in this particular person or group rather than in another. What, then, are the facts which the Natural Law considers a good title to authority? As in the case of property titles, we distinguish several which are subordinate from one which is primordial, so here we have a number which are proximate and one that is fundamental.

A. Proximate Titles

901. 1. *Legitimate succession* is an entry upon the authority of a predecessor in the mode and manner prescribed by the constitution. This may be by designation on the part of the predecessor, by heredity, or by election. It is presumed that the prescriptions of the constitution are consonant with right reason.

2. *Victory in a just war.* A very rare case may be verified where a justly aggrieved people finds that absolutely the sole way to its own peace and security is to deprive a hostile neighbor of its independence and assume rule over it.

3. *Prescription.* By fraud or violence, a usurper may oust the legitimate government and, though the beginnings of his rule are unlawful, he may in time become the legitimate ruler. The transition from an illegitimate *de facto* government to a *de jure* government is in this wise: (*a*) peaceful possession and efficient use of authority; (*b*) absence of all probable hope of restoring the old government without convulsing the realm.

A people must have some government; and when there is actually only one, though it be illegitimate, they are bound to co-operate with it at least in what pertains to public order and ordinary administration. When this rule has become firmly established and is actually attaining the ends of the State so that the only way to restore the old government is by public upheaval and civil war, then the rights of the old government cede to the right of the community to a peaceable existence. The public welfare is of more importance than the right of an individual, family, or party to rule. When, then, the return of the old government has become morally impossible, the *de facto* government has become legitimized.

B. Fundamental Title

902. The validity of the foregoing facts to establish authority in a particular ruler must rest ultimately upon the *permanent consent of the people*. This is a demand of the Natural Law, not a mere toleration or approval. The reasons are the same as those which show that consent is the juridic cause of the State and that the people are the primary depositary of authority. Cronin, who rejects this position, makes these significant concessions: "First we admit that the consent of the people is the best of all titles. Secondly, where consent is wanting over a long period, its absence might suffice to make a certain form of government wholly impossible, in which case a ruler might be bound to abdicate for the sake of the public good. Thirdly, the development of the republican ideal and the increasing power of the masses in the modern State are gradually rendering the consent of the governed more and more indispensable, at least as a condition of rightful rule. Fourthly, any wide acceptance, by existing rulers, of this principle of popular consent as the only title of political authority might itself confer upon the people the right of originating the form of government, which, once obtained, could not then be lawfully removed from them without their consent."[7]

Although many governments in the past have not reposed on the people's consent, the truth that they *ought to* is gradually becoming more apparent. We repeat that the State is the people; that their notion of what practically constitutes the common good most nearly approaches it; that nothing could be a greater hindrance to the common good than a government to which the people permanently refuse to give their consent.

There is no contradiction in saying that victory in a just war is a proximate title and consent the fundamental title. Thus no one will deny the right of an outraged people to destroy a pernicious foreign

---

[7] *The Science of Ethics*, Vol. II, p. 538. New York, Benziger, 1922, 2 ed.

government and substitute one of their choice as the Allies did to the Nazi Government in 1945. Ultimately, however, the government for the subjugated will become such that they have an obligation to accept it as did the English in Norman times or, where the victor disregards the good of the subjugated so that consent is unreasonable, his government must go, as happened to the English yoke in Eire.

READINGS

St. Thomas, *De Regimine Principum*, Lib. 1, cc. 2–6.

Anderson, William, *American Government*, pp. 87–130. New York, Holt, 1938.

Aristotle, *Politics*, Bk. III, cc. 6–18; Bk. IV.

Burgess, John W., *The Foundations of Political Science*, pp. 113–147. New York, Columbia, 1933.

Cahill, E., S.J., *The Framework of the Christian State*, pp. 476–483. Dublin, Gill, 1932.

Chandler, Albert R., *The Clash of Political Ideals*. New York, Appleton-Century, 1940.

Fortescue, Sir John, *The Governance of England*, ed. Charles Plummer. Oxford, Clarendon, 1885.

Gettell, Ray G., *Political Science*, pp. 239–253. Boston, Ginn, 1933.

Guenechea, Joseph, S.J., *Principia Juris Politici*, Vol. I, pp. 173–220. Romae, Universitas Gregoriana, 1938.

Johnson, F. E., ed., *Foundations of Democracy*. New York, Harper, 1947.

MacIver, R. M., *The Modern State*, pp. 338–362. Oxford, Clarendon, 1926.

Maitland, F. W., *The Constitutional History of England*. Cambridge, University Press, 1934.

McIlwain, F. W., *Constitutionalism*. Ithica, Cornel, 1940.

Meyer, Theodore, S.J., *Institutiones Juris Naturalis*, Vol. II, pp. 426–479. Friburgi Brisgoviae, Herder, 1900.

Oakeshott, Michael, *The Social and Political Doctrines of Contemporary Europe*, pp. 3–42. Cambridge, University Press, 1939.

Ogg and Ray, *Introduction to American Government*, pp. 1–21. New York, Appleton-Century, 1945, 8 ed.

Shotwell, James T., ed., *Governments of Continental Europe*, pp. 3–43, 339–345. New York, Macmillan, 1942.

CHAPTER XXVII

THE FUNCTIONS OF GOVERNMENT

903. Concerning the quality and extent of governmental action, the question arises, What must a government *do* in order to attain the ends of the State? The question is twofold: (*a*) what must the State do for its own people; (*b*) how must it act toward other States? The first question is answered in this and the three following chapters; the second in our treatment of international ethics.

Since authority is the power to direct and compel toward the public good, no government could direct its citizens without the power to issue directives — which is legislative power. Nor could it compel without the power to enforce its directives, which entails executive and judicial power. The functions of a government, then, are explained in terms of its legislative, executive, and judicial powers.

I. LEGISLATIVE POWER

904. Two inquiries are of moment: first, the nature; and, second, the extent of the State's power to make laws. The extent of this power is the subject of the two following chapters. In this chapter we shall consider the nature of legislative power.

905. To be a law a legislative edict must appeal to reason and embody the sensible and reasonable means of attaining some social objective. Anything inept, stupid, silly, or frivolous could not be a prescription of right reason. On this point no controversy is possible.

The law of the State must do more than appeal to reason by advising or suggesting. It must also appeal to the will and embody some kind of compulsion which obliges men to accept it. Every social regulation implies some kind of obligation. In artificial societies obligation can only be hypothetical; for instance, if a person consistently disregards the essential rules of an athletic club or a benevolent association, he is asked to leave. The understanding is that a man must either keep the rules or resign. But a man cannot quit the State. He must live under some government. In the law of the State the note of obligation is clear, peremptory, and apodictic. What is the nature of this compelling force? Is it the physical power of the State to enforce its will, or is it something of nobler substance? Does it impose moral obligation so that a person who disregards the law of the State is not only liable to coercion but also incurs moral guilt?

One hundred and fifty years ago this would have seemed an idle question. All men would have answered that State law can impose an obligation on one's conscience. But the doctrine of Kant, cleaving the juridic from the moral order and denying that the law of the State has morally binding force, gave the initial impetus to a different philosophy of law which is widely prevalent today and is held by persons of quite different moral complexion. A number of causes have accelerated the acceptance of this philosophy. We comment on three of them.

906. 1. *The prevalence of a materialistic view of life.* People who do not hold that man has an immortal soul and that there is a life hereafter cannot logically admit moral obligation binding conscience. If in their personal lives they substitute personal whim, expediency, or external respectability for rigorous and universally binding laws of conduct, their motive for keeping the civil law can only be fear of punishment by the State. Their attitude is: break the law if you can do so profitably and without detection, but be careful of unpleasant publicity and trouble with the police.

907. 2. *The practice of the purely secular and sometimes atheistic State.* Many modern States have become so secularized that they repudiate religious obligation binding themselves, and a few States have even tried to extirpate religion. Consequently the opinion has arisen that as public religion is nonexistent so too is public morality. It is said that the State does not consider itself bound by moral principles; that it follows a policy of expedience and utility. Hence the citizen may deal with the State in the same manner, that is, even though he may have to be moral in his private conduct, no moral tie binds him to keep the law of the State. Many people argue that legislators now have no intention of binding them morally, that some expressly repudiate such a notion and rely on heavy sanctions, public opinion, and efficient law enforcement to make their laws work.

908. 3. *The theory of Holmes.* Few men have had an influence on modern law comparable to that of Oliver Wendell Holmes, who held a philosophy of crude, frank, and brutal force. He was a sceptic to whom truth is completely relative and subjective. He defines truth as "the system of his intellectual limitations."[1] The test of truth for him is "a present or imagined future majority in favor of our view."[2] Hence he can boast, "To have doubted one's own first principles is the mark of a civilized man."[3] Law and morals are absolutely distinct. He wishes that "every word of moral significance could be banished from the law altogether."[4] Force is the final arbiter: he says, "Deep seated preferences cannot be argued about . . . and therefore, when differences are sufficiently far reaching, we try to kill the other man rather than let him have his way."[5] Morality is not based upon the will of a personal God and has no absolute or objective validity for "our system of morals is a body of imperfect social generalizations expressed in terms of emotion."[6] Moral principles are prejudices, that is, judgments made in advance of experience. Morals are reducible to taste so that the morally good is what Holmes likes, the morally evil what he dislikes. Holmes's approval or disapproval of Lesbian practices falls into the same moral category as liking or disliking sugar in one's coffee.[7] Tastes are due to one's environment. Although tastes keep changing, they have this practical importance that, when individuals or groups refuse to conform to the tastes of the dominant group, that is, the persons possessing the greater physical force, the holders of these dominant tastes simply put the screws on the nonconformers.[8]

Man is only a cosmic ganglion he repeats, not a being of absolute worth. He sees "no reason for attributing to man a significance in kind from that which belongs to a baboon or grain of sand."[9] The only thing worth while in life is functioning, the struggle to live. "I know of no true measure of men except the total of human energy

---

[1] Oliver W. Holmes, *Collected Legal Papers*, p. 310. New York, Harcourt Brace, 1920.

[2] *Ibid.*

[3] *Ibid.*, p. 307.

[4] *Ibid.*, p. 179.

[5] *Ibid.*, p. 312.

[6] *Ibid.*, p. 306.

[7] *Holmes-Pollock Letters*, Vol. I, p. 105, ed. M. D. Howe. Cambridge, Mass., Harvard, 1941.

[8] Oliver W. Holmes, "Natural Law," *Harvard Law Review*, 1918, Vol. 32, p. 42.

[9] *Holmes-Pollock Letters*, Vol. II, p. 252.

they embody. . . . The final test of this energy is battle in some form."[10] Human life has little sanctity: a man may easily be sacrificed in the interest of the State. The ultimate arbiter of all life is physical force so that when men disagree thoroughly and irreconcilably the final *ratio decidendi* is, in Holmes's own words, "We don't like it and we shall kill you if we can."[11]

Therefore the only binding force of law is physical force applied through the courts to bad men, namely, those who act contrary to the changing tastes of the dominant group. The sole semblance of legal principle is public policy. To Holmes public policy is any end which the dominant forces of the community desire so intensely as to brook no opposition to its accomplishment.[12] The clever jurist, then, is the one who can predict the shape of tomorrow's tastes and public policy. It is upon these conclusions that *legal realists* are building a jurisprudence devoid of any notion of moral obligation.

THESIS LXVIII. Civil Law not only urges a moral obligation when it declares the Natural Law, but even in matters left indifferent by the Natural Law it may impose obligation binding in conscience.

PROOF OF PART I

909. *By declaring the Natural Law civil law imposes moral obligation,* because:

1. Whatever declares the Natural Law must impose moral obligation.

2. The State can authentically declare the Natural Law for some authority among men must have this power. If the State lacked it, it would be unable to make any laws.

PROOF OF PART II

910. *Even in indifferent matters civil law may impose moral obligation.*

In the first part we treated of *necessary* laws. When the State defines crimes, outlines fundamental obligations, or confirms certain rights it is merely enunciating the Natural Law and the consequent obligation comes directly from the Natural Law. In the second part we pass to

---

[10] Oliver W. Holmes, *Holmes' Speeches,* p. 73. Boston, Little Brown, 1934.

[11] *Justice Oliver Wendell Holmes, His Book Notices and Uncollected Letters,* ed. H. C. Shriver, p. 187. New York, Central Book, 1936.

[12] *Ibid.,* pp. 187–188.

the more proper field of human legislation, namely, those laws which are not necessary but *useful* for the common good. In general ethics we termed these determinative laws. Not only declarative laws but also determinative laws impose obligation. Thus, although the Natural Law does not determine whether the public good must be served by a publicly owned telegraph system or one privately owned — since either could be equally useful to the community — if the legislator chooses a publicly owned system, then, even though a citizen thinks a privately owned system more useful, he would be morally obliged to accept the publicly owned system.

911. Thus, Part II is proved as follows:

1. A precept of the Natural Law commands man to obey the State within the proper field of its jurisdiction. As reason dictates that children must in conscience obey their parents, so reason likewise tells men that they must live under public authority and obey it. If there is widespread disregard of civil authority, social chaos results, and the promotion of human welfare becomes impossible.

2. The State's jurisdiction embraces many matters undeclared by the Natural Law. The nature of the State demands that it regulate matters which are not only necessary but also useful to the public good.

912. N.B. I. The proposition may be proved by two other reasons. (*a*) Since authority is from God, laws made in virtue of divine authority are a participation in Natural and eternal law and hence bind with similar force. (*b*) Since civil law supplements the Natural Law, it has the same *ultimate* purpose, namely, the proper direction to man's last end. Therefore it ought to operate in the manner in which the Natural Law operates, that is, by moral, not physical, necessity. Law which operates with moral necessity imposes moral obligation.

N.B. II. The fact that legislators do not explicitly advert to moral obligation when they frame a law does not prove that they wish to exclude moral obligation. Their intention is to make a true law with all the binding power which law carries.

N.B. III. The stark brutality of Holmes's doctrine on civil law is a remorselessly logical consequence of a modern jurist's erroneous view of man's nature.

N.B. IV. We have proved that, in general, disobedience to the State is wrong; that civil law can impose an obligation in conscience.

A further question is, Does absolutely every law of the State bind the conscience of the citizen? This question will be solved in §§ 924–927.

II. VALID CIVIL LAW

913. What is a true law? Under what conditions does a legislative decree have the force of law and bind the conscience?

THESIS LXIX. To impose obligation, civil law must proceed from legitimate authority and be just, possible, and properly promulgated.

For a law to be valid certain conditions must be fulfilled on the part of the legislator, the matter of the law, and the promulgation of the law.

914. 1. The *legislator* must have legitimate authority over both the citizens and the matter for which he legislates. Thus the laws which Russia made in 1940 to break up the estates of Eastern Poland were invalid, because Russia had no jurisdiction over the Poles. Similarly, the laws of the Emperor Joseph II regulating divine worship in the Austrian Empire were invalid, because the State has no jurisdiction in purely religious matters.

PROOF OF PART I

915. *To impose obligation civil law must proceed from legitimate authority* because imposition of obligation is restriction of man's free will. Only legitimate authority can restrict man's freedom. Man as man has no power to bind his fellow man: all men are by nature independent. Therefore, men must have authority in order to impose their will on other men.

916. 2. *The matter must be just.* The law must always ordain a prescription of right reason. No law may contradict the Natural Law. Thus an edict forbidding a father to bequeath money to his children would be void. Nor may civil law contradict divine positive law as did the laws of England which forbade the Mass. Negatively, civil law must not contravene the law of any higher authority. Positively, it must be either necessary or useful to the common good. Frivolous or silly measures, or measures which benefit only the ruler or a small class, cannot be valid laws.

PROOF OF PART II

917. To *impose obligation the civil law must be just.* To impose obligation the civil law must be based on the Natural Law (cf. § 249). But what is based on the Natural Law must be just. Therefore to impose obligation the civil law must be just.

918. 3. *The matter must be possible,* that is, physically and morally capable of execution by the people. Observance of civil law must not place too heavy a burden on the subject as did the old laws of imprisonment for debt. The great principle is *ad impossible nemo tenetur* — you cannot do the impossible. Therefore, heroic actions cannot generally be the object of human precept though they are sometimes the object of divine precept. Impossibility of fulfillment must be judged by concrete circumstances of place, time, climate, education, tradition, and national temperament. Thus the American draft law of 1940 could never have been enacted in 1812.

To be reasonable and possible law ought to be based on the customs of the people. This gives law its permanency. Rickaby says: "A law is no fleeting, occasional rule of conduct, suited to meet some passing emergency or superficial disturbance. The reason for a law lies deep down, lasting and widespread in the nature of the governed. . . . Every law is made for all time and lives on with the life of the community for whom it is enacted, forever, unless it is either expressly or implicitly repealed. A law in a community is like a habit in an individual, an accretion to nature, which abides as part of the natural being, and guides henceforth the course of natural action. This analogy holds especially of those laws, which are not enacted all of a sudden — and such are rarely the best laws — but grow upon the people with gradual growth unmarked like a habit by the repetition of acts, in the way of immemorial custom."[13]

PROOF OF PART III

To impose obligation civil law must be possible of observance. A law makes an action or its omission necessary, but an action or an omission which is not possible cannot become necessary.

919. 4. *Promulgation.* If law is to produce its effect, it must be so authentically manifested that the people can know that it binds

---

[13] Joseph Rickaby, S.J., *Moral Philosophy,* pp. 126–127. London, Longmans Green, 1919.

them. Therefore, to give his enactment the final force of law, the lawgiver must provide that the people certainly know that the law exists, what it means, and what its binding force is. The mode of promulgation depends on the fundamental constitution of each State.

PROOF OF PART IV

To impose obligation civil law must be properly promulgated. A law must serve as a guide to the social actions of the people which is impossible without due promulgation.

920. Corollary I. *Any edict which fulfills these conditions is a valid law without reference to popular acceptance.* If a constitution so provides, certain proposals may not *become law* until after popular ratification. This indicates that in this instance the people are part of the lawmaking body. But once a law has been duly established and promulgated it does not rest with the people to obey it or not as they choose. A legitimate command has been issued to them and a command necessarily calls for obedience. Acceptance or rejection of a law by the people after promulgation has no effect upon its validity.

If a law is generally disregarded by the majority of the people, these conclusions seem to follow: (*a*) the legislator may quietly allow the law to lapse. This would not be an instance of direct popular authority over established law but of tacit revocation by the lawgiver. (*b*) They certainly commit a fault who after the first promulgation of the law disobey it. When, however, the greater part of the people disobey it and it has not as yet been fully revoked, an individual person is excused from keeping it because observance in these circumstances becomes too great a burden. Suarez says, "The private observance of such a law no longer pertains to the common good."[14] (*c*) Usually widespread nonacceptance of a law is a sign that it originally had some nullifying defect.

III. UNJUST LAWS AND REBELLION

921. A law which certainly fails in any of the above-mentioned conditions is not a law but a species of violence. However, in case of doubt as to the validity of a law the *presumption always favors the existence of the law*. This presumption the common welfare demands.

---

[14] *De Legibus*, III, c. XIX, 13.

What procedure is to be followed concerning an obviously invalid law?

1. *If it is morally impossible to obey,* that is, if obedience would impose too great a burden, a person is not held. If, however, the law is susceptible of division and a man can perform a part, he is not excused from the whole.

2. *If it commands what is contrary to the Natural Law or divine positive law,* a person is obliged to disregard it. A person must obey God rather than man. Thus, parents would have to disobey a law forbidding them to give religious instruction to their children under eighteen years of age.

3. *If it unjustly deprives a man of goods or rights,* he is justified in disobeying and resisting it by all legal means. However, for the sake of avoidance of a worse evil, prudence may dictate submission to such a law. As the seriousness of the attack upon his rights increases so likewise do the lawful means of resisting injustice. Resistance, however, must always be proportioned to the sacredness of the right to be safeguarded, the good to be accomplished, and the resultant disturbance. What limits does reason indicate in resistance to government?

4. *May a man resort to armed force?* He may, if the conditions of blameless self-defense against unjust aggression are verified. The law of self-preservation and protection admits of no exception. As a son may strike a drunken father in order to save his life when no other means of protection are available, so likewise in order to save himself from death, mutilation, apostasy from religion, and dangers of equal gravity, a citizen may forcibly defend himself against his government. Since a private person has this right, he may be assisted by his fellow citizens in vindicating it if a just proportion exists between the good to be effected and the evil of armed disturbance.

What begins as a measure of collective self-defense may issue in the successful vindication of rights against a tyrant. But there is a clear distinction between armed defense of rights and rebellion, which is the endeavor to oust an existing government. One, however, readily leads to the other. The ruler's government is subverted unless those who make the resistance perish as happened in the case of Cromwell and Charles I, the American colonies and George III. Therefore the question of rebellion arises.

922. 5. *May armed resistance proceed to rebellion?*

a) Rebellion or the attempt to overthrow a *legitimate* government is always and everywhere wrong. Defining this crime St. Thomas says, "And therefore because sedition is opposed to a special good, namely, the unity and peace of the people, it is a special sin."[15] He concludes, "Since sedition is an unjust struggle against the common good of the State it is always a mortal sin."[16] A government may abuse its power to rule and still retain a right to the submission of subjects. If every abuse of authority gave citizens a right to rebel, civil order would be at an end. For this reason St. Thomas condemns it. Another reason may be added, namely, the power to rule comes from God, and as long as government retains that jurisdiction, an attempt to overthrow it is defiance of divine authority.

b) *May abuse of power constitute forfeiture of it?* Some authors argue that, although abuse of authority does not destroy authority, yet it could be lost if the abuse is so great as to destroy the title upon which authority rests. They say that title to rule is lost if the ruler has gotten his authority by election or compact and if the conditions stipulated in the contract with the people have been grossly violated: if authority comes directly from God to the ruler, title to rule could never be lost. Since this last condition is true only of the Church and the Roman Pontiff, and since we have shown that the ultimate title of all civil rule is the permanent consent of the people, we might conclude that abuse of authority which destroys the title of consent on which it rests is possible. But this is a cumbersome argument: appeal to titles of rule or broken coronation oaths is unnecessary.

It is simpler to invoke the general welfare as a means of proving that a government may be overthrown. A government ceases to be a government when it substantially ceases to direct the people to the common good. When a government becomes habitually and intolerably tyrannical, when it loses sight of the common good and pursues private interests to the manifest detriment of the people, or when from weakness, inertia, or corruption it is incapable of ruling, it ceases to be a legitimate government.

When, therefore, the common good is no longer realizable under a government, it is lawful to overthrow it, if the following conditions are fulfilled: (*a*) All legal and pacific means must have been tried to amend it without success. (*b*) Reasonable hope must exist that the

---

[15] *Sum. Theol.*, II–II, 2, 42, a. 1.
[16] *Ibid.*, a. 2.

endeavor will be successful and not engender worse evils. (c) The judgment concerning a government's incompetency is made not merely by private persons or a party but by the saner and better part of the people so that it may be considered the judgment of the community as a whole.

St. Thomas says, "A tyrannical regime is not just because it is not ordered to the common good but to the private good of the ruler. . . . Hence the assailing of such a regime has not the malice of sedition; unless perchance the assailing of the typrannical regime is so unwise that the people suffer more harm from the consequent disturbance than they did from the tyrannical government. Rather is the tyrant seditious who fosters discord and sedition among the people that he may the more safely dominate: for that is tyrannical since it is ordained to the personal good of the ruler to the hurt of the people."[17] What St. Thomas calls a tyrannical regime we have called illegitimate.

IV. PENAL LAWS

923. In Section I of this chapter we proved that civil laws bind the conscience. We shall now consider what the quality and quantity of this moral obligation is.

1. *May civil laws bind under penalty of serious wrong?* They may if the matter is grave and the legislator intends grave obligation. That his intention is such is taken for granted unless he explicitly declares the obligation to be slight.

2. *May serious laws bind only under venial wrong?* All moralists agree that they may if the lawgiver so intends. He cannot, though, impose grave obligation if the matter is slight.

3. *May one violate a true civil law without committing a moral wrong?* Practically all moralists now answer affirmatively. Three reasons are offered.

a) The secular lawgiver may sometimes realize his purpose without binding the conscience of his subjects. Relying on the readiness of his subjects to obey, the vigilance and efficiency of his means of enforcement, the sanctions he attaches to the law, and a fear of incurring these, he is able to promote the common good in certain eventualities without burdening one's conscience to conform to his edict.

b) Many citizens of upright conscience are persuaded that it is

---

[17] *Sum. Theol.*, II–II, 2, 42, a. 2, ad 3.

possible to transgress the letter of some laws without wrongdoing; as we shall see, custom is the best interpreter of the law.

c) Laws are so numerous that if every conscious violation of a civil law directly entailed wrong, an intolerable burden would be placed on men's consciences.

924. Civil law may be divided, therefore, into *preceptive laws,* whose observance or nonobservance bind the conscience and *merely penal laws* whose observance or nonobservance do not bind the conscience. The problem is divided into three topics of inquiry: (*a*) the nature of purely penal law; (*b*) the criteria for recognizing penal law; (*c*) the number of penal laws.

A. The Nature of Purely Penal Law

925. At the heart of the difficulty lies the statement of Suarez that every law must impose moral obligation.[18] Every divine law imposes moral obligation because, first, this is the sole kind of obligating force which the Unseen Legislator chooses to exert on men. The Unseen Legislator relies on no visible instruments to enforce His commands. Second, divine law deals only with things which *immediately* order men to their last end the binding force of which is solely moral obligation.

Do all human laws impose moral obligation? Ecclesiastical law does because, first, the end of the Church is procuring the final end of men; second, the Church eschews any resort to force. Is the same true of civil law? Following Suarez[19] many authors say that all laws must impose *some* moral obligation. They then define a purely penal law as one whose morally binding force is disjunctive or hypothetical.

926. Disjunctive obligation is obligation that falls either upon the content of the law or upon acceptance of the penalty provided for violation. But it does not seem reasonable to suppose that the lawgiver offers the subject the choice of keeping the law or paying the penalty. The lawgiver cannot be said to be indifferent to the observance of law. He must desire its observance. Hypothetical obligation means that the lawgiver places no moral obligation on the content of law but solely on acceptance of the penalty if the law is broken. Nor does this explanation seem reasonable, because according to it the legislator puts moral obligation on the penalty which is the less important part of

---

[18] *De Legibus,* I, c. XIV, 7.
[19] *Ibid.,* III, c. XXVII, 3.

the law and puts no moral obligation on the content — the really important part.

927. In either explanation moral obligation is whittled away to the vanishing point. There is no moral obligation to keep the precept of the law; one is not obliged to give himself up after violating the law; he may legally defend himself against conviction, and, if convicted, he may escape if he does so without violence. Since so little obligation would remain, Ryan is inclined to discard the notion of purely penal law in favor of another principle which, according to him, would obtain much better observance of law without imposing intolerable burdens. He says, "According to this principle one may distinguish between the letter of a statute and its spirit, between the end at which it is directed and the means specified in its language."[20] He implies that, although the law retains its moral force, one may act contrary to its letter and commit no moral wrong because one's act does not endanger the end for which the law was made.

928. Defending the notion of a purely penal law, Vermeersch[21] boldly and more reasonably says that it is a law which binds under threat of juridic guilt and punishment but involves no moral guilt. It is contained solely within the external forum and does not touch the inner forum of conscience. Its obligating force is only juridic. It is purely juridic law.

But is not this explanation the Kantian separation of justice from morals? It is not. Kant's mistake was divorcing *all* justice, especially natural justice, from morality and reducing *all* justice to the purely physical and external. Why should we fear to admit an underlying partial truth in Kant's exaggeration, namely, that there are aspects of legal justice which do not directly enter the realm of conscience? How often does a man, parking his car in the wrong direction, really do wrong morally?

Kant denied that the juridic order as such had anything to do with morality (cf. § 444). We admit that justice belongs to the moral order. Then it is retorted that any law of the moral order must impose an obligation in conscience. This is the whole point at issue. It is a reasonable contention that a law may belong to the moral order in two ways: (*a*) as necessary to the common good it imposes obligation in conscience because the lawgiver must invoke his total power to bind;

---

[20] *Catholic Principles of Politics*, p. 189.
[21] *Theologia Moralis*, 3 ed., Vol. I, n. 172; in ed. of 1922, Vol. I, n. 169.

(*b*) as merely helpful to the common good it imposes no obligation in conscience because *the lawgiver does not choose to invoke his total power to bind.* Such law would be moral in that it proceeds from legitimate authority and appeals to reason and will, but not in that it produces obligation in conscience. It is possible for the lawgiver to refrain from an appeal to conscience for two reasons. First, because this is done in religious orders whose laws do not bind under pain of sin. Here the lawgiver prefers to appeal to good will and generosity rather than to impose a burden in conscience. Second, if the lawgiver can impose merely venial obligation if the matter is grave, why can he not denude his law of all moral obligation? He ought to do so sometimes because he has such efficient means of enforcement that he can attain the end of certain laws — the mere external order of the commonwealth — without appeal to moral obligation. He would be unreasonable and would overburden the consciences of his subjects if he sanctioned some laws more strongly than necessary.

If, then, it is objected that such prescriptions ought not to be called laws because the name "law" belongs only to that which imposes an obligation in conscience, the dispute is purely verbal. For the reality is that legislative enactments exist, the violation of which entails no direct sin.

B. *Criteria for Recognizing Purely Penal Law*

929. To differentiate between a prescriptive and a purely penal law it would be easy if one could directly learn the mind of the lawgiver, but in these days of parliamentary legislation this is impossible. One can use only indirect criteria.

Certainly those laws are prescriptive which (*a*) declare and confirm the Natural Law; (*b*) define, create, or extinguish rights and duties in commutative justice; (*c*) immediately promote the common good.

One may judge the penal character of law by a number of tests. (*a*) *The matter of the law* should first be considered. This may be relatively unimportant or have little or no bearing on morals or deal with the mere policing of external order. However, one ought not to conclude that all traffic laws are merely penal. We may judge the character of law (*b*) *from the interpretation which good citizens put upon it,* or (*c*) *from the prevailing philosophy of law* which is current among lawyers, jurists, and legislators. (*d*) Laws which declare acts to be invalid unless certain technicalities are complied with are looked on as merely penal. (*e*) If there is a vast disproportion between the penalty threatened and the violation, or if the penalty is considered a kind of compensation for the violation (fines for avoiding customs' duties), these laws are generally considered penal.

C. Number of Penal Laws

930. When it is asked how many penal laws there are, there is a great difference in the answers. European moralists incline to enlarge the number; Americans to restrict it. No general answer can be given, but merely one that is true for a particular jurisdiction. To judge, therefore, whether the laws of Maryland or the United States are preceptive or penal, one must have recourse to the above-mentioned principles of interpretation and form his judgment.

V. THE MEANING AND DURATION OF THE LAW

931. To determine quality, quantity, and duration of moral obligation under law, one must first know the meaning of the law. Hence, a law, like an insurance policy, should be read in an authentic copy. This ordinary people seldom do: they obtain their information third or fourth hand. In reading a law it should be noted first whether it is addressed to and so obligates public officials or the people at large. The next consideration is what the words of the law mean.

932. 1. *Interpretation* is the attempt to learn the mind and intention of the lawgiver. Since this is conveyed in his words, and since a sound interpretation of legal words demands good faith and common sense, his words are to be understood in the sense in which he used them, that is, according to their natural contextual meaning. One must assume that he is using words to convey rather than to conceal thought. *Verba ita sunt intellegenda ut res magis valeat quam pereat.* Technical words are to be understood in their scientifically accepted sense. When doubt arises as to the meaning of a law three courses are open. (*a*) The first is recourse to the lawgiver himself. The meaning which he gives is *authentic interpretation*. It has the same force as law itself. If sovereignty is divided, the power of giving an authentic interpretation rests sometimes with the legislative body, sometimes with the judiciary. In the United States it is the function of the supreme courts. (*b*) The second method of learning the meaning of the law is recourse to the learned in the law. The meaning given by lawyers and jurists is *doctrinal interpretation*. Its value depends on the learning and experience of the person interpreting. (*c*) Finally, there is *customary interpretation,* or the meaning which the law receives from the practice and conduct of the people. Moralists have always held that custom is the best interpreter of law. Since custom manifests what the people spontaneously do and what arises from natural social evolution, it should be held as the measure of the people's capacity for social co-operation and as that which is most suitable for the common good. It should receive, therefore, the approval of the lawgiver. If it does, it is authentic interpretation. However, modern lawgivers and courts do not admit the force of custom or usage either to induce or abrogate juridic obligations. "Evidence of usage is never admissible to oppose or alter a general principle or rule of law so as . . . to make the legal right and liabilities of the party *other than they are by law*."[22] A usage of trade is not a real exception to this rule because even that must be "known, certain, reasonable and *not* contrary to law."[23] The reason for this attitude is probably because jurisdictions are so vast and people so heterogeneous that it is difficult to determine what true customs are. The disfavor which custom finds in modern law is another indication of the purely juristic character of much of it.

933. 2. *Epikeia* is a mode of interpreting a law whereby an individual judges that it does not apply to this particular case so that he may act contrary to its letter. It is a kind of equity, the equitable adjustment of private good to the overdifficult demands of law. Laws are meant for the common good. When literal compliance with a law becomes detrimental to the common good, it ceases to oblige. It may happen that a preceptive course of action good and useful in most circumstances becomes harmful in others. Since the lawgiver cannot foresee and write into the law all the instances that it will touch, he proposes it in terms which cover the generality of cases. When, then, keeping the law harms the common good, the lawgiver is rightly understood not to wish the observance of the letter of the law. Thus law may forbid the carrying of arms, but if the life of a person is closely sought by an enemy, one may well suppose that the lawgiver intends that the innocent party should take arms and defend himself. For epikeia to be valid, one must be able to elicit with prudent certitude this judgment

---

[22] *Bouvier's Law Dictionary,* "Custom," p. 261.
[23] *Ibid.*

— this is the mind the legislator would have had if he had foreseen this case.

934. In the Natural Law there is no room for epikeia. Since the Divine Lawgiver has foreseen every possible contingency, there are no circumstances in which one may act contrary to the Natural Law. In ecclesiastical law, not only when observance of law is morally impossible but also when it causes special hardship, the lawgiver is rightly regarded as not wishing the law to press too burdensomely on the individual. Irritating laws are an exception, namely, those which nullify acts performed contrary to their prescription. If doubt arises concerning the pertinence of an irritating law, recourse must be had to the lawgiver who has power to *dispense,* that is, to relax the law in favor of an individual. If recourse is impossible, a person may rightly argue that a doubtful law does not oblige.

The attitude of the civil law is quite different. No court would entertain a plea of epikeia, except in a rare instance in which keeping the letter of the law would evidently and immediately impugn public policy. Civil lawgivers wish exceptions to their laws kept to the barest minimum. Even if observance works hardship on the individual, they think it better that the law be observed for the sake of example to the community. No power exists in the United States to dispense from law: the sole remedy is for the legislature to make a new law. This attitude is another indication of the purely juristic character of many modern laws.

935. 3. *Duration of law*. It was stated in § 918 that a law ought to be stable and lasting. Constant changing of laws is harmful to the community because it makes custom impossible, and custom is the great bulwark of observance of the law. A law, therefore, should be changed only when it becomes manifestly harmful or when an evidently more useful statute should replace it.

A law binding in conscience totally ceases, first, by express repeal or introduction of contrary law; second, when the end for which it was levied has totally ceased for the community. The law then becomes useless, and the useless is unreasonable. Thus on account of an epidemic all public gatherings are forbidden; once the epidemic is over the prohibition lapses. Finally, contrary custom tolerated by the lawgiver abrogates law.

The civil law holds that a law is in force until it has been repealed or replaced.

READINGS

Anderson, William, *American Government,* pp. 223–258. New York, Holt, 1938.

Aristotle, *Politics,* Bk. V, 1–9.

Ferree, William, S.M., *The Act of Social Justice.* Washington, Catholic University Press, 1942.

Ford, John, S.J., "Fundamentals of Holmes' Juristic Philosophy," *Fordham Law Review,* Vol. II, No. 3, Nov. 1942, pp. 255–278.

Haas, Francis J., *Man and Society,* pp. 195–215. New York, Appleton-Century, 1930.

LeBuffe-Hayes, *Jurisprudence,* pp. 148–199. New York, Fordham, 1938, 3 ed.

Leo XIII, Encyclical Letter, *Diuturnum.*

Lucey, Francis, S.J., "Natural Law and American Legal Realists," *Georgetown Law Journal,* Vol. 30, No. 3, April, 1942, pp. 493–533.

MacIver, R. M., *The Modern State,* pp. 149–220. Oxford, Clarendon, 1926.

McIlwain, C. H., ed., *The Political Works of James I,* pp. xv-cxi. Cambridge, Mass., Harvard, 1918.

Shotwell, James T., ed., *Governments of Continental Europe,* pp. 140–176. New York, Macmillan, 1940.

Suarez, *De Legibus,* III, cc. 9, 12, 13, 16, 22, 24, 31; V, cc. 2, 3, 7; VI, cc. 1, 7, 10.

────── *De Bello,* Sect. VIII.

CHAPTER XXVIII

THE SCOPE OF CIVIL LEGISLATION

936. Having examined the nature of civil legislation, we now inquire into the particular things concerning which the civil power should legislate. The scope of civil legislation derives from the double purpose of the State. From its primary obligation to insure peace, *protective* legislation is deduced; from its secondary obligation to promote the general welfare, *promotive* legislation is deduced.

I. PROTECTIVE LEGISLATION

937. *Protection of the State.* The first right which the State is to defend, not so much by specific legislation as by its executive arm, is its own right to existence. For the State, as for the individual, the first law is self-preservation. That it must legislate against sedition is clear from § 922. That it may wage war against unjustly aggressive nations will be treated in § 1091.

938. *Protection of citizens.* The State must protect the natural private rights of individuals, families, and legitimate associations of individuals. Life, limb, and health of individuals must be safeguarded not only from the malice of other men but also from the untoward acts of inanimate agencies. A man's person must be secure from seizure and violation. A man must be free to acquire property, gain a livelihood, enter contracts, marry, set up and regulate a family. Good name must be safe from calumny and detraction. Persons must be free to worship God as conscience dictates. They must be protected from unusual inducements to vice and from the scandal of immoral teachings and publications. Private societies and associations may call upon the State to protect them in the legitimate pursuit of their proper ends. If the State were powerless to accomplish these tasks, it could not preserve the order essential for social life. Therefore the State has the following legislative powers. (1) It is competent to determine natural rights and the limits of their exercise. For example, it may fix the legal relations of man and wife, parents and children: it may determine the mode of acquiring, holding, and transmitting property as well as contractual rights and obligations. (2) The State may define and punish crime. (3) It may remove public obstacles to the exercise of private rights. For example, it may legislate against fraudulent labor contracts or offer special protection to weaker groups whose rights may be unduly endangered. (4) It may resolve disputes by erection of proper tribunals. (5) Finally, the State may determine the public duties, privileges, and relations of its citizens.

These things the State must enact into law and carry out if it is to exist at all. Woodrow Wilson called these functions constituent: they are not optional with governments for they are the very bonds of society.[1]

In individual ethics we studied extensively the existence and scope of man's chief private rights with the exception of the right to a livelihood. This right has been reserved for detailed discussion at this point because it can be understood better as a social problem and it especially requires State protection.

A. Right to a Livelihood

939. In a broad sense, a livelihood is the more or less secure possession of the means of living. That the means of life should be available to men, follows from the right to live. Immunity from excessive anxiety in the matter is not a strict right, for mortal man is merely on his way to final perfection. Since the probationary nature of life compels man to work out his salvation in fear and trembling, he may not say that he has a right to freedom from economic or any form of anxiety. Security is a coveted situation of well-being and comfort and is, therefore, variable and subjective. Livelihood, therefore, in the strict sense, means that a man has within reach of his diligence and prudence material means necessary for decent living.

940. A man may acquire the means of living either by (1) *endowment*, private or public; (2) *dependence* on a master or upon charity; (3) *exercise of his faculties*. Concerning the first, we have already established that inheritance is a natural title to property (§ 572 ff.).

---

[1] Woodrow Wilson, *The State*, pp. 613–614. Boston, Heath, 1911, rev. ed.

The right to inherit, however, is not unlimited. A wise testator will remember that for some persons enormous inherited wealth is a ready avenue to frivolous and immoral living. Unchecked inheritance can lead to the accumulation of national wealth in the hands of a few powerful families to the detriment of the people at large. For the public good, then, the State may levy inheritance taxes, graduated to the size of the inheritance, but never in the measure which nullifies right of inheritance. The State endows persons only for past or prospective public service as in the case of a royal family or men of distinguished merit. Persons who are endowed with a living are but a small minority.

941. Concerning the second class, we have already seen that even limited slavery deserves to be reprobated (§ 504). The abnormal and unfortunate, the mentally or physically deficient cannot make a living for themselves and must depend on others. They depend, first, upon their own families; if this help is insufficient, then upon private charity. Since now these sources of help are inadequate, the major burden of supporting the unfortunate devolves upon the State. It is a task that must be done, and since other agencies are inadequate, it goes by default to the State. In meeting this obligation, however, the State must eschew monopolizing action which would dry up charitable feeling, responsibility, and initiative among private persons.

942. Since the vast majority of men fall into the last class, working for a living by bodily or mental toil is of momentous importance both for the individual and the common good.

THESIS LXX. Every man has a right to remunerative work if he can live only by such work.

By living we understand not merely keeping body and soul together but living in a human way.

PROOF

Every man has a right to the necessary means of living. But to live as a man, remunerative work is usually absolutely necessary. Therefore, a man has a right to remunerative work if he can live only by work.

943. A man has two alternatives as far as work is concerned: either he works independently and himself reaps the products of his labor, or he makes a contract with another person in which he hands over his productive labors and receives a wage in exchange.

The chief moral concern of the independent worker — the farmer, merchant, entrepreneur, professional man, and the like — should be observance of commutative justice; in particular, he should be careful to render a just equivalent in goods or services for income received. The law of just price especially applies to him. Since in this class are found the more able or at least the more fortunate and usually the shrewder and more industrious, there is no great danger that they will fail to gain a livelihood. Hence, social action to secure a livelihood for them has seldom been necessary, except occasionally in the case of farmers for whose benefit a legal price of farm products has been established or subsidies granted. The socialistic tendency is to eliminate all independent workers. The evil of such action has been dwelt upon. Since the widest possible distribution of property among private owners constitutes a strong bulwark of an enduring State, that legislation would be unsocial which would make taxes so high that small businesses could not operate, or which would make all professional men salaried servants of the State.

The bulk of men are dependent workers. In medieval times the dependent worker lived by status; that is, a person was born into a fixed social and economic position and although he had little opportunity of rising from his status, he was economically secure in what he had. Having surrendered the security of status with its fixed but certain income, modern man takes his energies into the commodity market and bargains with an employer for the best possible return in exchange. To make a living, then, he must secure (*a*) adequate remuneration and (*b*) sufficient remunerative work must be available.

B. Remuneration

944. To gain a living the workman has two alternatives: he may be a partner or an employee. If he is a partner, he shares both the profits and the losses, and assumes commensurate share of commercial risk. If he is an employee, he has no general responsibility, and for services rendered receives at regular frequent intervals an agreed wage. At present, real partnership is impractical for the vast majority of workmen because they cannot afford the risk of partnership; they have no capital to cushion losses and they need money at frequent intervals.

945. Concerning the employer-employee system wherein the employer assumes the risks, takes the net profit, and gives the worker a regular wage the main moral question is, *What constitutes a just contract between employer and employee.* After the marriage contract, the wage contract is the most important. It is the basis of modern economy: it underlies most problems of social unrest.

The requisites of a just contract between employer and employees are three: (1) both parties must be free to enter it; (2) the employer must give a wage equivalent to service rendered; (3) the employee must render service commensurate with wages received.

946. The first requisite requires no discussion. We begin, then, with the question of a just wage. Since labor capacity is a marketable commodity we must find its true exchange value. In an ethical treatise one cannot state the just price of any marketable ware in a precise computation of dollars and cents. Therefore, in this discussion a *principle* of natural equity must be sought which a person may apply to a concrete wage situation in order to discover whether a just wage is being paid. The inquiry is restricted to the normal adult male who regularly gives up his full working day to an employer.

We have seen that exchange value depends fundamentally upon utility, proximately upon the common estimation of those who buy and sell the commodity in question (§ 607 ff.). What, then, is the value of a man's labor capacity and how do people estimate it?

THESIS LXXI. The minimum just wage of the adult male is the family wage.

947. There is an universal conviction, at least among all working people, that a man ought to receive a wage sufficient to support a family. Does an explanation of this conviction exist in the science of morality? When we examine the fundamental worth of human labor we perceive it to have a very special value, differing from the value of commodities about which men generally bargain. Human labor has a double worth, one intrinsic to the worker himself, the other extrinsic to the hirer of that labor.

948. *The intrinsic value of human labor.* There is something very noble about human labor because it shares the dignity of the human person. Man has an eternal destiny toward which he moves by fulfilling his moral obligations. This he cannot do unless he acquires the material necessities of living. The means given him as a free being for securing a living are his mental and physical energies. Hence a man's labor capacity has definite intrinsic value to himself: it is the natural means by which he is to live as a man. Between a man's work and the satisfaction of his needs there is an immediate relation. This, then, is a just equation: labor capacity equals human needs supplied in a human way.

The needs of the normal adult male extend to many more goods than those necessary for individual well-being and development. It is nature's intent that he be the head of a family. To this nature vehemently urges him, and once he has a family, nature lays upon him the inescapable duty of nurturing it. His dependents also are to live a human life. The workman, therefore, must supply his family at least with decent frugal comfort. Today human living will include (1) decent habitation with privacy, sanitation, and ordinary conveniences; (2) wholesome food; (3) sufficient rest and leisure to enjoy family life; (4) reasonable recreation for health of mind and body; (5) a small surplus for emergencies such as sickness or death. In the concrete, the aggregate of these things vary according to circumstances of time, place, custom, and civilization.

949. Justice, therefore, is not satisfied if an employer, considering merely the extrinsic utility to himself of a workman's labor, fails to pay a family wage. He sins against commutative justice because he fails to satisfy for the *full* value of the labor which he accepts; he sins also against social justice whenever injustice against families is so widespread, that the public good suffers notable detriment.

PROOF

950. *The family wage is due in commutative justice.* Commutative justice demands that a workman receive a wage equivalent to the total value of his labor.

1. The total value of a workman's labor includes not only extrinsic value to an employer but primarily intrinsic value to the workman. His labor is the means nature gives him to live as a man.

2. The only wage which compensates for intrinsic value of labor is one that supplies a workman's needs as a family head. Nature intends the adult male to be a family head and to provide for its present and future needs. Unless the family head does this, he is not living as a man.

951. *The family wage is due in social justice.* If a family wage is not generally available, a workman has a choice of (1) not getting married; (2) drastically limiting his family; (3) having a family of insufficient means. All three are contrary to the social good.

1. It is morally detrimental for both individuals and State if many young and vigorous men are prevented from marrying.

2. A serious curtailment of the birth rate is obviously bad for the State. Curtailment of offspring usually involves positive contraception.

3. If the income of the family head is insufficient, either some of the essentials of life must be foregone, or this income must be supplemented by labor on the part of the wife and children or by relief. It is bad for society if many families must forego essentials of human living because health, education, or morality will suffer. Dire poverty is a common breeding ground of crime. If economic necessity compels a wife to work outside her home, her duties to the home will suffer. If immature children are compelled to work long hours, their health may be affected and they may be deprived of a suitable education. Dependence on relief ought never to be a normal and constant thing in any family. Finally, a community of workmen receiving a family wage is the true backbone of industrialized civilization because they provide a steady market for consumable goods.

952. Corollary I. The fact that a workman agrees to take less than a living wage does not make the contract just. If sheer necessity presses him to accept an unfair contract, he is a victim of injustice. The employer who offers less than a living wage with a take-it-or-leave-it attitude is taking unfair advantage of his own superior economic situation.

Corollary II. The principle of minimum wage holds for married and unmarried alike. The essential value of labor is present even though *per accidens* the workman does not exercise his right to marry. In practice it would be impossible to discriminate without creating deep discontent. The younger unmarried men should be in a safe economic position to marry when the opportunity presents itself. They should be able to save against the heavy initial expense of matrimony. The economic advantage of the older unmarried men could be balanced by special taxes.

Corollary III. For those who are able but unwilling to work the sanction of the Natural Law should be allowed to operate, namely, if a man will not work neither let him eat. That provident and industrious people should be compelled to support professional loafers is contrary to natural equity.

Corollary IV. The employer has an equal right in commutative justice to receive from the workman an honest day's work. This question is treated in the next section.

C. *Equity to the Employer*

953. In many discussions on the wage contract the workman's obligation is ignored. It is assumed that the employee gives a just return for salary received. It is true that he has usually done so. The normal man has the capacity to do a good day's work. This work will be valuable to the employer if the employer has selected a profitable type of business, runs it efficiently, fits the workman to the work for which he is qualified and sees to it that he does what is expected of him. Therefore, since the employer has consistently been the stronger party to the contract, he has been quite able to exact his right. It is, however, possible that he may be prevented from exacting his right by the unjust demands of labor unions.

954. Besides exacting specified quality and quantity of work the employer's rights are claimed to be (*a*) reasonable profit, and (*b*) direction or management. As to the first, the underlying supposition is that some profit exist. The reasonableness of profit has been proved in our rejection of socialism (§ 536). It is a gross exaggeration of the rights of workmen to claim that profits of industry, except those required to repair and replace capital goods, belong to workmen. Workers are only a partial cause of profits gained.

955. In a simple arrangement in which one or a few individuals are both owner and manager, the principles, "The thing perishes to the owner" and "The thing increases to the owner," are clearly applicable. This situation is a private affair of commutative justice, which may be tempered by an employer's knowledge of the needs, merits, or sudden hardships of his employees. The old moralists defined reasonable profit in these circumstances as that which is necessary to maintain the employer in his state of life. This definition is no longer helpful because one may doubt if there are now *fixed* states in life. State in life is generally proportioned to income, but the fact that a man begins life with a yearly income of ten thousand dollars is no pressing reason why he must always enjoy that income. The better definition would seem to be that reasonable profit compensates the businessman for these factors: (*a*) financial risk undertaken; (*b*) cost of educational preparation; (*c*) foresight, ingenuity, courage, and industry which must be exercised to make the enterprise efficient. To evaluate these factors on a specific percentage basis would be impossible. Many variable circumstances of unforeseen loss and occasional good luck enter into business. One may conclude, therefore, that the small businessman who has done justice to his associates and customers, has given his employees a living wage, and has paid his taxes may cheerfully pocket all net profit, be it much or little.

956. Today, however, the situation is not quite so simple. The modern corporation presents many complications. Thousands of stockholders are the owners. But the owners do not manage: management is in the hands of a small, powerful group whose equity in a business is often negligible. Thousands are employed who are totally unknown to ownership and for the most part to management. Since many of these corporations are spread through many localities and dominate the economic lives of many thousands, their fortunate or unfortunate condition affects the common public good. Although they are private societies in name, they are semipublic in fact. Hence the laws of social justice should to a greater or less extent govern their operation.

Their co-operative purpose is making money, and to this end three distinguishable elements contribute essential shares: (*a*) ownership, which makes the effort possible by risking its capital; (*b*) management, which supplies intelligent direction; (*c*) labor, which supplies the rest by faithful and efficient execution of direction. Who, then, should benefit by the goods and money socially produced? Equity indicates that benefits belong to those who help to produce them and in proportion to the value of their contribution. Injustice has been done in this respect, for sometimes stockholders have received no dividends and workers have not been paid adequate wages. Who, then, shall estimate the value of the contribution of ownership, management, and labor? If the decision rested with ownership alone or management alone or labor alone, each would be grossly biased in its own favor. The only recourse is free and equitable agreement. Equity would be destroyed if one party abused the strength of its position to secure more than its rightful share. If the execution of the agreement, or unforeseen circumstances tend to the detriment of any of the parties, a new contract should be drawn. In determining the terms of a new contract each party should have a *proportionate voice*. One of the chief functions of occupational groups described in the Appendix would be the insuring of justice in such contracts. If occupational groups do not exist, or if private agreements cannot be reached, the State, as impartial arbiter, may legislate to regulate prices, wages, and profits. It is undesirable that the State should do this, however, except in grave emergencies.

957. An employer may say that to him the value of a man's work does not equal the wage which he should have to pay. The employer is free not to hire such a person, but if he hires him he should pay a living wage. The man's labor has that value to himself, and in the contract of sale price is not to be determined by the buyer alone. The employer may continue to object that the prices he receives in his business do not allow him to pay a living wage. The answer is that wages of labor should be a primary charge upon merchandise so that prices received do not determine wages but wages paid should determine prices to be asked.

958. Regarding employers who habitually pay less than a living wage several comments are pertinent. (*a*) Employers who take large profits from their business and leave less than a living wage for their employees are maintaining a species of economic slavery. (*b*) If the reason why employers fail to pay a living wage is that they could not otherwise maintain their businesses, several different cases must be distinguished. (1) If this inability is due to temporary reverses, owners and employees could agree to take a proportionate loss until business revives. (2) If this inability is permanent, due to poor management, lack of enterprise and efficient methods, that employer ought to go out of business. No man's profits should be founded on injustice. (3) If a business does not make enough to pay living wages because it is overwhelmed with *unjust* burdens of tariffs and taxes, or because it is compelled to sell its products at unjustly low prices, they who cause such conditions — whether monopolists, financial leaders, or lawmakers — are guilty of grievous wrong. If private initiative cannot remedy the situation — and usually it cannot — the social good demands that governmental regulation provide conditions which make it possible for an honest business to operate at reasonable profit and pay a living wage. This practical ideal every government in an industrial age should unceasingly labor to achieve.

959. If profit still shows after a firm has paid a living wage, has given reasonable dividends, and has reserved funds for replacement of capital goods and future needs, may the workers claim a share in it? If all the items mentioned have been taken care of justly and efficiently, no further profit should be possible. But if in extraordinarily fortunate circumstances such profit exists, workers may claim a share, *if they have been admitted to partnership*. Except for a few persons with considerable savings to invest in their own firm, workers are not now partners; but the way to some type of partnership could be opened to them. This could be effected through an occupational group which would regulate the rewarding of faithful service. Both individual firms and business in general would benefit because hope of real reward would stimulate more interest in work, and would offer more incentive to loyalty and fidelity.

960. The second alleged right of the employer is *management*. In the simple arrangement of an owner superintending his business, the owner has an unimpeachable right to conduct his affairs without interference from his employees. This is an immediate deduction from the nature of ownership which is the plenary control of an object in one's own interest in *accordance with law*. This last phrase — so often neglected — means that in his management the employer must respect the rights which Natural and positive law give employees such as freedom from hazard to life and limb and human working conditions. The workman receives a voice in management only when he is admitted to partnership.

Many of the economic evils spoken of in individual ethics (§ 516) arise from the divorce of ownership from management. The body corporate of stockholders often never manages the business which it owns. Pius XI has called attention to this fact: "Immense power and despotic economic domination is in the hands of a few and these few are frequently not the owners but only the trustees and directors of invested funds who administer them at their good pleasure."[2] The surface evils of these abuses may be removed by legislative action but the true remedy lies deeper, namely, in a more corporative organization of society and especially in development of democratically operated vocational groups.

D. Means of Securing Workers Rights

961. The living wage is the most important but not the only

---

[2] *Quadragesimo Anno.*

aspect of the right to a livelihood. Closely allied are the questions of employment and working conditions. First, sufficient remunerative work must be constantly available. For if a man has a living wage for six months and is idle six months, his living is meager. Second, the surroundings of one's work must have an elemental human decency: they should not impair bodily, mental, or moral well-being.

Who is obliged to procure for a man a decent, steady job with a living wage? The economic liberalists answered, "the workman alone." The liberalist was right to the extent that this obligation is primarily individual, but he was completely wrong in denying its social aspect. Society has an obligation to the workman. The good or evil condition of the State is in proportion to its economic well-being which can be secured only by harmonious interplay of many social factors chief among which are wages and employment. In fact, economic well-being is no longer a mere national concern; it is international, as the world-wide stagnation of the early thirties proved. Therefore the State must maintain wages and employment at a healthy level. This obligation was ignored by the society dominated by the economic liberals. Consequently, the workman, as weaker party to the wage contract, had to accept an unjust bargain. To obtain justice he endeavored to lift himself to a position of bargaining equality with his employer. He used three means: labor unions, strikes, and labor legislation.

E. Labor Unions

962. A *labor union* is an association of workmen whose purpose is to safeguard and promote the industrial rights of workmen. Since the individual is powerless to bargain with an employer on a basis of equality, collective action is resorted to. All the workmen of a given plant or craft or industry unite into a corporate whole which bargains with the employer on behalf of all.

The economic children of Adam Smith and Jeremy Bentham forbade such unions. Although associations of employers, professional men, and other classes might flourish, unions of laboring men were condemned by courts as conspiracies.[3] Many Victorians looked askance at the union as a manifestation of socialistic spirit. A tremendous struggle ensued for the recognition of the union principle. This was

---

[3] Arthur M. Schlesinger, *The Age of Jackson,* pp. 166, 194, Boston, Little Brown, 1945.

not a mere contest of words carried on in newspapers or debating halls but one of broken heads and copious bloodshed. Positive law, like the National Labor Relations Act of the United States, formally recognized the labor union and enjoined employers from interfering with workmen's right to organize and bargain collectively. The underlying ethical principle is simple.

THESIS LXXII. Labor unions are legitimate associations. Their aims and methods should conduce to the general welfare of society.

PROOF OF PART I

963. Whoever has a right to an end also has the right to the just and necessary means to that end. Workers have a right to a livelihood and labor unions are at present just and necessary means to that end.

1. It is eminently just and in accord with man's social nature for individuals to band together to obtain a common natural right by collective action.

2. Unions are necessary means because without them workmen have been helpless and did not achieve a decent livelihood.

PART II

964. Labor unions were a long time coming into their own. Having won emphatic recognition from the law and a place of real power, they ought not now abuse that power. It would be a sad mistake if their conduct served as an illustration of the old adage, Put a beggar on horseback and he will ride to the devil. Although the primary end of a labor union is the good of its membership, this end must be achieved in a manner that preserves the rights of employers and public.

Such is the downward trend of human nature, wounded by sin, that most amazing evils have grown up in the wake of labor unions. Some unions have gotten into the hands of racketeers and have become tools of extortion from public, employers, and workers. Leaders have entrenched themselves in power, conducted the union for their own personal advantage, imposed unjust burdens upon employers, and under pretext of upholding union regulations have outraged common sense. To the sore injustice of owners, unions have waged jurisdictional disputes and called needless strikes. They have been utterly indifferent to the rights of employers so that employees, knowing that they could not be discharged, have failed to do proper work. Decidedly, there have been good unions and bad unions.

PROOF OF PART II

965. 1. Associations upon which in large measure depend economic peace should be conducted with a view to the general interests of the community at large. For society is an organism wherein the good condition of a part should be subordinated to the general well-being of the whole.

2. Labor unions are such associations. They may be private in name but they are public in fact. A large percentage of the population is dependent on their honest and efficient functioning. In so far as they fail to secure justice for their membership and override just claims of employers and public, so will economic peace or strife result.

966. N.B. I. Labor unions ought to be incorporated and subjected to reasonable regulation. Fitting responsibility can thus be placed upon them. As far as possible, democratic procedures in the conduct of union affairs should be mandatory. An accounting of funds should be made to the membership. Excessive fees should be abolished. Unionism's greatest need is honest and statesmanlike leadership.

N.B. II. Has the individual worker an obligation to belong to a labor union? He is not obliged to join a racketeering union or one which is a cloak for subversive activity. If an honest union is available he ought to join it for two reasons. First, the livelihood of all workmen depends on their power of collective bargaining and this in turn depends on union organization. Second, since labor benefits derive from union organization, it would not be fair for an individual to have the advantages of the union and yet refuse to share its responsibilities.

N.B. III. *Ought the State enact into law the Closed Shop (100 per cent union shop) and the Checkoff (compulsory collection of union dues by employers)?* Although the individual has an obligation to join a good union, this obligation is inoperative until evil unions have been eliminated and the rights of employers made more secure. Furthermore, the labor union is a temporary device, a stepping stone to a more perfect socioeconomic organization described in the Appendix.

F. Strikes

967. Before the law came to rescue the workman he was left alone
to fight his own battles. To obtain justice he had to resort to compulsion. This took the form of a strike, which is a concerted stoppage
of work by some or all the employees in an establishment or industry,
along with an appeal to public opinion, in order to enforce the assent
of employers to specific demands of workmen. Since an idle plant
means loss, the practical issue is whether the owner can operate despite the cessation of work by the employees. On the other hand, can
the workers efficiently prevent the employer from operating?

To pose the moral issue we distinguish three kinds of strikes, direct,
sympathetic, and general. The *direct strike* is the walkout of workmen
laboring under the same industrial grievance. The *sympathetic strike*
is the walkout of workmen who themselves have no grievance but
who wish by their strike to help other workmen who are striking.
The *general strike* is the universal walkout of all workmen in the
State.

The strike is a form of passive violence and a species of industrial
war. Where many workers are involved and the struggle is protracted,
the strike is only little less serious than civil disturbance, which has
often accompanied it in the past. Hence the same set of principles
which govern the morality of war apply to the strike.

1. Direct Strike

968. In view of the evils resulting from strikes to employers, workmen, and the public, may strikes be morally justified? The first
problem is, *Is the strike intrinsically evil?* The elements of the strike
are three, quitting of work, concerted quitting of work, appeal to
public opinion. (*a*) *Quitting of work* is not immoral because a workman may stop working for an employer unless he has a definite contract to render service for a specified period. This is seldom true of
the modern workman. (*b*) In a *concerted quitting of work,* organization and combination do not add an immoral element. What
men may lawfully do individually, they may do collectively. If
owners have made specific terms with a labor union to the effect
that the union refrain from strikes for a definite period of time,
to strike during that time while the owners are keeping their part
of the bargain is a serious violation of commutative justice. (*c*) *Appeal*

to public opinion is reasonable. If one refrains from abuse and slander, he has every right to present to the public the justice of his cause.

969. Therefore the strike is not in itself immoral, and workmen may be justified in striking if the following conditions are fulfilled.

a) *They must have a true grievance.* To permit the evils consequent upon the strike, a proportionately justifying cause must exist. Workmen have a right to collective bargaining, human wages, decent hours and working conditions. These are coactive rights to be defended when necessary by the passive pressure of the strike. But no union is justified in striking for trivial reasons: apart from *serious* denial of right, the strike is unjustifiable. Jurisdictional strikes, for instance, are an outrage upon employers and public.

b) *All other means of remedying the grievance must have been resorted to in vain.* If the dispute can be settled by gentler means, for instance, by direct negotiations, arbitration, or remedial legislation, the union is morally bound to use these means.

c) *There must be sound prospects of success, and the good to be achieved must outweigh the evils to be endured by employer, public, and workmen themselves.* If resultant evils to the community over-balance advantages to be won by workmen striking, they are obliged not to strike but they must seek their purposes by more peaceful means. This is true of policemen, firemen, and the like with whose uninterrupted service the public good is closely linked.

d) *The means chosen to promote the strike must be legitimate.* No matter how just their cause and long standing their grievance, work-men may not resort to injustice to achieve their ends. Injustice outlaws the sit-down strike and use of violence.

970. *a*) The sit-down strike is unjust because it is theft of the owner's plant. Courts which tolerate this practice abet grievous wrong.

b) Use of violence introduces two considerations. (1) *May strikers compel fellow workers to join the strike?* As one workman has a right to quit and strike, so another who judges his best interest lies in continuing to work, or is not convinced of the justice or opportune-ness of the strike, is exercising his natural right to work. Moral suasion can be used on him but never force. When strikers violently attempt to prevent nonstrikers from working they become *aggressors.* They are not resorting to force in defense of their own rights, but they are violently assaulting the right of others to work.

(2) *May strikers violently keep off strikebreakers?* The strikebreaker

by taking a vacated job is also exercising the right to work. If his new employer has been just to the strikers, the strikebreaker's action is legitimate. If the strikers are right, the strikebreaker becomes a co-operator in the employer's injustice, but the strikers cannot use violence to keep him off nor to stop the employer from operating. Forceful defense even of private right is first entrusted to the State. To oppose employers and strikebreakers with force is to cause civil disturbance.

It may be said that strikers, who may not prevent an employer from bringing in strikebreakers and continuing to operate, have little chance of succeeding. This conclusion scarcely fits the facts; but even if it were true, it would not alter the moral question. One may not use unlawful means to attain any laudable purpose.

2. Sympathetic Strike

971. Some authors have vehemently condemned every form and instance of the sympathetic strike. But such a sweeping condemnation is hardly justified. We distinguish a variety of cases.

a) Workmen employed in the same plant as the strikers may strike out of sympathy if they are convinced the strikers are right. They ought not passively to assist an unjust employer in his injustice against other workmen.

b) Concerning workmen employed in different firms, each case must be decided on its particular merits. In certain cases this principle of charity may apply, namely, a group of men may be aided by their fellow workers in that which they may do in defense of right. However, in order to exercise charity toward their fellow workers, satisfied workers cannot be unjust to their employers. The mere fact that workers are striking is no guarantee that they are necessarily right. Hence to rush to the defense of other workmen without investigating the justice of their cause cannot be defended. As a nation may not go to war unless it is certain of the justice of its cause, so no body of workmen may strike unless certain of the justice of their action. If no investigation is made concerning the original dispute, sympathetic strikers are comparable to persons who rashly proceed to act without pausing to consider the morality of their actions.

3. The General Strike

972. Stoppage of all work would be disastrous to the common good, resulting in immediate danger to life, limb, security, and the very process of life. No possible benefits to workingmen would justify such an upheaval of society. The general strike is one of the instruments of international communism for fomenting world revolution. Its purpose is dispossession of all owners of productive goods and the theft of their properties.

973. Strikes are a crude and not too efficient remedy for industrial injustice. As J. F. Cronin says: "The aftermath of a long bitter struggle . . . is unpleasant, no matter who wins the strike. If the union succeeds it is likely to adopt in retaliation an autocratic, suspicious and un-co-operative attitude. If the strike is broken, the workers become sullen, resentful."[4] Before the enactment of labor legislation, strikes may have been an evil to be tolerated. The good sought by strikes is better obtained by appeal to public opinion and through public opinion to law. Strikes and violence only weaken the force of legitimate appeal. The process of law and remedial legislation is a slower but more reasonable and eventually a more effective method of obtaining industrial justice than the direct action of strikes. Since a strike, like war, is the last resort of self-defense, once sufficient legislation that safeguards workmen's right to a livelihood is honestly enforced, their right to strike becomes latent.

G. Labor Legislation

974. The most intelligent employers have recognized that their primary asset is a contented and satisfactory working force and hence have voluntarily offered their workers satisfactory conditions.

For the most part, however, concessions from employers have been forced. Official labor has aimed at solidifying the gains of particular workmen and has endeavored to make them available to all workers by translating them into law of the land.

This difficulty arises. May the State pass labor legislation or is labor legislation a trespass upon strictly private rights? Because the pestilential influence of economic liberalism still affects so many people, many legislators make grudging assent to labor laws. They tolerate them because they consider them a trend of the times, not because they see any moral or social principle underlying them. The principle is this: the State must protect natural rights; and if

---

[4] John F. Cronin, *Economics and Society,* p. 217. New York, American Book Co., 1939.

particular classes of individuals experience special difficulty in securing
a right, they are entitled to special protection from the State. Since
the workman has a right to livelihood and to live as a man in his
work, and since his weakness has often made him the victim of
injustice, he is entitled to special protection from the State. Furthermore, from the standpoint of the general welfare, one can hardly
say the State has a sound economy when a goodly proportion of the
populace lacks a decent living.

975. In protective legislation of this kind, the State may not despoil
employers, nullify genuine property rights, nor make the common
good subservient to the clamor of workers. The interest of no class
should dominate the State, neither army, management, nor labor: the
common good is above all class interest.

The State has not overstepped the bounds of justice by legalizing
unions and upholding the right of collective bargaining, nor by putting
a ceiling on hours and a floor under wages. These measures have done
something to bring a living wage within reach of workmen but the
awful specter of unemployment has not been removed. Partial allevia-
tion of this problem has been attempted by direct relief laws and
unemployment compensation, but so far no modern state has permanently solved the difficulty.

The fundamental reason for this failure is that the solution of the
problem does not primarily belong to the State. It is given to the State
to solve because now, on account of the atomization of society, no
other social institution is capable of dealing with it. However, the
whole problem of livelihood could more easily be dealt with by
occupational groups whose nature is explained in the Appendix.

II. PROMOTIVE LEGISLATION

976. In the concrete it is sometimes difficult to draw a hard and
fast line between protective and promotive legislation. One type of legislation merges into the other: elements of both may enter the same
law. In the preceding section of this chapter we saw that legislation
may be initiated for the protection of strict right, for example, the
right to livelihood, and once the right is secured, promotive legislation
may introduce additional benefits. By protective legislation the State
makes secure the essential rights without which persons do not live
a human life. By promotive legislation it seeks to enhance the good
life. The notion if not the name of protective legislation is negative,

for it forbids the spoliation of right: the notion of promotive legislation is positive, for it advances some social good.

The area of human goods extends in ever widening circles from an inner core of strict right to further desirable things, not strictly necessary but conducive to human betterment. In the physical order, once men are sure of life, health, a living, and the like, they may think of improved medical service, recreational facilities, better housing, faster transportation and communication. In the intellectual order provisions may be made for greater facilities for the dissemination of truth and more educational and aesthetic opportunities. In the moral order, legislation may promote the practice of greater virtue, the enrichment of personality, the standing and influence of religion. The possibilities of human advancement, though not infinite, are indeed very great.

977. What part may the State have in social advance? The State may initiate, foster, or take over any project for human betterment if two conditions are fulfilled. First, its action must be socially necessary or useful. An act of the State is socially necessary when the common good demands it and the State alone can perform it; it is socially useful when it promotes the common good and the State can perform it more efficiently than any private agency; it is socially harmful when the State supplants and absorbs legitimate private endeavor. Second, the State must grant all the citizens equal access to this benefit. Unless all citizens share, the common good is subordinated to private or class interest.

It is impossible to discuss every item that may fall into the category of promotive legislation — which is properly the field of political science and sociology. We shall take up, however, a most important topic which illustrates not only the promotive function of the State but also the manner in which its function fuses with its protective role.

Public Education

978. Every modern civilized State gives careful attention to, and expends enormous sums on, every phase of education. In the United States few industries possess the trained personnel, or have such a funded investment in lands, buildings, and equipment, or make annual expenditures comparable to those of the public school system. Extreme care and attention is given to the planning and future expansion of the State's part in education. Very great good or proportionate evil will come to future generations from the way in which these programs are executed. Therefore, it is of the utmost importance that the State's philosophy of education be in accord with the Natural Law.

On account of the educational policy of totalitarian States, a new philosophy of education is receiving wider acceptance. This philosophy holds that nothing limits the action of the State in education but its own good pleasure. A steadily mounting tide of State encroachment upon exclusively private domain is being accepted as normal: too many people think that they are helpless to resist the ground swell of universal statism.

The basic part which t'.e Natural Law gives the State in education already has been stated when it was proved that the essentials of education belong to parents. Therefore the role of the State is sub-ordinate to parental right and duty. The State's educational function, then, is deduced from the primary rights of parents and its own protective and promotive duty.

THESIS LXXIII. The State has the duty of safeguarding the right of children to receive an education from their parents and providing parents with the means of education when their own resources are inadequate. It must likewise remove public hin-drances to education such as subversive teachings and unusual incitements to vice. Although the State has a right to demand that the common good be suitably provided for in the training of youth, nevertheless State monopoly of education is unnecessary and unjust.

979. State educational policy depends on the double end of the State.

1. The primary duty of the State is to *safeguard the rights* of its members. In the field of education the following rights undoubtedly exist: (*a*) The child has from nature a right to receive proper preparation for life. (*b*) Parents have from nature an exclusive obligation and right to educate their children. (*c*) The Church has a charter from God to teach His revelation and a mandate to insist with Christian parents that their children be instructed in the faith and formed to Christian morality. These rights the State must protect but it may not enumerate teaching among its necessary, natural functions because, first, by Natural Law this function belongs to parenthood alone; second, the State has not received as has the Church a divine mandate to teach.

2. The secondary duty of the State is to supply for the common

good what private initiative and effort is unable to effect. Hence, when schools become necessary instruments of education, and when parents are unable to supply these themselves, the State must come to their aid. In conducting schools, however, the State is only the agent and delegate of parents, whose primary rights it may not absorb.

For reasons of the common good, the State has a right to exact a certain amount of learning, culture, or technical skill from its citizens and may require parents to provide this for their children. But this right does not warrant the State to set up an exclusive educational monopoly.

PART I

980. *The State has the duty of safeguarding the right of children to receive an education from their parents.* In order to protect the child's right when parents are neglectful, the State must compel parents to fulfill their obligation. This does not mean that as soon as parental neglect is discovered the State may take over the care of children. The State must first bring pressure to bear upon the parents to acquit themselves of their task. Only after parents have shown themselves manifestly incompetent or evil, and when no resources of private charity are available to rescue the child, only then may the State as a last resort assume full responsibility for the child's upbringing. For public assistance should not be sought if private remedies are available.

It must be stressed that children not only have a right to an education but especially to receive that education from their parents. For no human agency, private or public, not even the State or the Church, may interfere with the essential order established by nature between parent and child.

PROOF OF PART I

981. If children have an inalienable right to an education and if parents alone have the function of imparting it, then in the event of neglect or interference, the State must protect the educational rights both of children and of parents. But children have an inalienable right to an education and parents alone have the right to impart it. Therefore the State has the duty of safeguarding the right of children to receive an education from their parents.

PART II

982. *The State has the duty of providing parents with the means of education when their own resources are inadequate.* Although education is primarily and directly a domestic duty, it may become secondarily and indirectly a matter of public concern. First, the quality of the home product necessarily affects the common good. Second, parents may laudably desire for their children training which they cannot furnish without social co-operative action.

Until quite recent times general education was a purely domestic matter. The preparation for life which a child received depended upon the good will and resources of the head of the family. This is still the situation in many places.

Within the past one hundred years, public opinion in western civilization recognized illiteracy as detrimental to the common good, and decided that a common elementary intellectual training should be made available to all future citizens. This policy necessitated the erection and organization of a vastly increased number of schools. The feasible and efficient way to provide these new instruments of common education was public taxation. Hence, in the civilized world our complicated system of public schools arose.

983. As Part I of this thesis is a practical application of the principle that the prime function of the State is to protect the rights of its members, so the ethical principle of Part II is this: If individual effort is insufficient to procure some human good, the common effort of the State supplies the want. Therefore, if and when schooling and schools become necessary for training the young, and families cannot supply these schools, then the State ought to provide schools and teachers in a way suited to the needs and legitimate wishes of parents. Public assistance, however, must be only of such kind and measure as to supply for a genuine private deficiency. Where privately conducted schools are sufficient and function efficiently, public schools are not needed and should not be built.

PROOF OF PART II

984. The State has a duty to supply means necessary for public welfare which private initiative cannot supply. But private initiative sometimes cannot supply schools and schooling necessary for the public welfare. Therefore the State has the duty of supplying them whenever private initiative is insufficient.

PART III

985. *The State has the duty of removing public hindrances to education such as subversive teachings and public incitements to vice.*

This particular duty of the State in the field of education follows from the obligation of the State to promote the common welfare and from a correct understanding of what constitutes the common welfare.

It is absurd to say that the State has no concern about the morals of its citizens, or that morality is strictly a private affair. It is true that many human acts have no public aspect but many acts do affect society. No man lives in a social vacuum or in moral isolation; good and evil example touches everyone both as individuals and as citizens. Hence, the State is to promote morality at least to the extent of removing gross scandals and incitements to evil that allure the ordinary person. Since youth is especially susceptible to wrongdoing, it is deserving of special public protection. The State, therefore, should aim at producing such a moral tone in society that parents do not find unusual difficulties but are rather assisted in the moral training of their children.

986. At this point we might give thought to the question of *State censorship*. Liberalism has made censorship a hated word, a word which carries obnoxious connotations. But what does the word really mean? A censor is one who authoritatively designates as right or wrong private or public words or acts of others, permitting the right, suppressing the wrong. Are there circumstances in which the State is a legitimate censor? Although no one questions the right of State censorship in war, and many persons have applauded the State's abuse of this right, there is a furious outcry against censorship of teaching.

The issue, then, is this: Where do teaching and incitements to vice touch the common welfare and how is the regulation of them to be reconciled with private right?

987. 1. *Teaching.* Concerning the deposit of faith, it is clear that God's revealed word and the truths necessarily connected therewith are completely outside the province of any secular power. These truths have been especially entrusted by God to the keeping of the Church. The teaching of nonrevealed truth may affect the general welfare from the point of view both of the individual and the State.

a) False teachings affect the individual. It has been proved that the Natural Law forbids man to inflict moral injury upon his neighbor (§ 507). To indoctrinate one's neighbor with pernicious principles of conduct is to do him moral injury, because such indoctrination seriously and directly interferes with the prosecution of his last end. In the case of children, the injury is even graver because fundamental errors ingrained during childhood usually defy all later attempts at eradication.

b) False teachings affect the State. Errors concerning social intercourse, the nature and function of the State, and natural religion are directly harmful to the welfare and stability of the State. It has, therefore, a right to protect itself against error which is likely to produce civil disorder and chaos.

Since State and individual have a right to be immune from moral injury, the State, as guardian of right, may and ought to suppress teachings which *seriously* violate these rights.

988. *But are not freedom of the press, freedom of speech, and freedom of teaching fundamental rights of the individual which no State may abrogate?* Since there are no sky-blue rights, every right is limited by the just counterclaims of other persons. Hence, the right to speak, teach, and write freely must necessarily be limited by the right of individual and State to be protected from error. Freedom may easily degenerate into license. The object of freedom may only be the true and the good. To call moral evil and falsity the objects of freedom is a perversion. When, therefore, the pursuit of such a perversion works extensive harm to others and imperils the common welfare, the civil power may lawfully interfere.

Hence an editor, writer, or teacher has no more permission to write, say, or teach anything he pleases, than he has in his private or public conduct to act as he pleases. As moral goodness should be the norm of his conduct, so truth alone should be the norm of his intellectual utterances. Thought and its expression, of themselves, deserve no greater freedom than any other kind of activity. The State may prevent a radical from assassinating its king; why may it not suppress the writings of a pamphleteer advocating the same? The State may stop a man from having two wives; why may it not prevent him from publishing a book favoring the practice? Mrs. Bertrand Russell[5]

---

[5] Mrs. Bertrand Russell, *The Right to be Happy,* Chap. VI, pp. 260–261. Garden City, 1927.

advocating free love can work greater mischief to the State than the private vices of a public official.

989. But who is to judge the truth or falsity of the utterances of a writer or teacher? Academic freedom claims that the writer or teacher alone is the competent judge. A false principle is involved in this answer, namely, no objective norm of moral or any kind of truth exists, and all truth is subjective. If we apply this principle universally very great harm must come to society. The evidence of harm is before us today. Certainly where truth is elusive, where only probabilities may be found, where merely the better or more expedient thing is at issue, all men must be allowed widest freedom of expression. But not all truth is elusive: there are plain objective dictates of the Natural Law upon which rest the foundations of civic order. The common welfare can be seriously imperiled by writings and teachings counter to the Natural Law. These the State may and ought to suppress. To deny that the State can correctly define pernicious teachings is tantamount to denying the State the power of enunciating the Natural Law; it is to infer that the State has not the knowledge requisite for making any law.

Censorship is a right which a government (like the autocracy of the tsars or its totalitarian successor) may easily abuse by tyrannically suppressing all criticism of its acts and by branding as subversive any theory of rule contrary to that by which it operates. But neither the possibility nor the fact of abuse destroys the reality of right: they merely indicate the need of restraint in the exercise of right.

990. 2. *Other public impediments to sound rearing.* Every age has its peculiar public dangers to youth. Our age must cope with indecent dress; pornographic motion pictures; licentious art and theatrical exhibitions; easy access to drugs, intoxicating liquor, houses of debauch; lack of parental supervision; broken homes. The dangers which threaten youth may vary, but the principle concerning them remains, namely, the State is bound to suppress public impediments to the virtue of youth, the removal of which is possible and would not create greater evil.

PROOF OF PART III

991. The State is obliged to defend itself and its members from moral injury. But subversive teachings and public incitement to vice inflict moral injury both on the State and its youth. Therefore the

State is obliged to suppress subversive teachings and public incitement to vice.

PART IV

992. *The State has a right to demand that the common good be suitably provided for in the training of youth.* As the promoter of the common welfare the State may make definite claims in the educational field. Thus in troubled periods the existence of the State may absolutely require military training. The State may rightfully insist on this; for example, in medieval England sons of knights had to learn to fight on horseback, sons of commoners were required to learn to use the long bow. On this latter point there was reiterated legislation. A nation whose welfare depends on an efficient navy may insist that many of its youth be trained in navigation and similar arts. Modern civilized States demand a certain minimum of intellectual culture; for instance, all children are expected to know how to read, write, and use simple arithmetic processes. Many nations insist that future citizens be imbued with the spirit of the nation; have some knowledge of its past, its traditions, its chief laws and institutions; and foster genuine love for, and devotion to, the true interests of their country.

PROOF OF PART IV

993. The State may command whatever genuinely advances the common welfare. But the suitable preparation of youth for their responsibilities as citizens genuinely advances the common welfare. Therefore, the State may command suitable preparation of youth for their responsibilities as citizens.

PART V

994. *State monopoly of education is unnecessary and unjust.* Since the State furnishes means of education which parents cannot, the danger arises that, having assumed the major financial burden of schooling, the State will also monopolize education, according to the adage that whoever pays the piper calls the tune.

Because the State has an appreciable stake in the correct formation of future citizens, one may erroneously conclude that the State is by nature an educator; that it has an exclusive right to form the young, to say who shall or shall not engage in the profession of teaching, to determine the skills and doctrines to be taught and the textbooks to be used; that all children must attend State schools.

A totalitarian regime always institutes a dictatorship over education. The reason is plain. Not even such a government may completely flout public opinion. Rather it must shape public opinion to its own bent, and nothing is more effective than domination of young minds.

PROOF

995. State monopoly of education is (*a*) *unnecessary* because it involves the State in needless tasks; it is (*b*) *unjust* because it is an invasion of private right.

1. *Needless tasks.* Whole classes of citizens are willing and able to manage the education of their children without help from the State. In private educational institutions adequate provisions can be made for public interests because, if a parent is normally responsible, he will see to it that his children are trained in citizenship and learn to love their country. If he refuses to do so, the State has ample means to compel him other than taking over all education.

2. *Invasion of private right.* The State cannot assume a monopoly of education without overriding prior rights of parents. Nature intends parents to have an exclusive and inalienable right to educate. Their inalienable right arises from the exclusive responsibility which they must absolutely fulfill. The violation of this right is a serious offense against commutative justice.

996. N.B. A State monopoly would also violate the Church's right and hinder its task of teaching God's revelation. As an independent and perfect society, the Church in no way depends on the State for its essential activities. In accordance with the divine command given it to teach, it may found schools and all institutions of learning helpful to its purpose. To claim that it may do so only by sufferance of the State is a serious perversion of right order.

Corollary. Appeals for State assistance in education should be made only when parental and private resources are inadequate.

READINGS

Anderson, William, *American Government,* pp. 493–590. New York, Holt, 1938.

Aristotle, *Politics,* Bk. VII, 13–17.

Bruehl, Charles, *The Pope's Plan for Social Reconstruction,* pp. 182–213. New York, Devin Adair, 1939.

Devas, Charles S., *The Key to the World's Progress*, pp. 114–131. New York, Wagner, 1923.

Husslein, Joseph, S.J., *Democratic Industry*. New York, Kenedy, 1919.

────── *The Christian Social Manifesto*. Milwaukee, Bruce, 1931.

Jarrett, Bede, O.P., *Social Theories of the Middle Ages*, pp. 1–30. Westminster, Md., Newman, 1942.

Jones and Vanderbosch, eds., *Readings in Citizenship*, pp. 329–429. New York, Macmillan, 1932.

Leo XIII, Encyclical Letter, *Rerum Novarum.*

MacIver, R. M., *The Modern State*, pp. 250–281. Oxford, Clarendon, 1926.

Nell-Breuning, Oswald von, S.J., *Reorganization of Social Economy*, ed. B. W. Dempsey, S.J. Milwaukee, Bruce, 1936.

Parsons, Wilfrid, S.J., *Which Way Democracy*, pp. 192–218. New York, Macmillan, 1939.

Pius XI, Encyclical Letter, *Quadragesimo Anno.*

Ryan, John A., *A Living Wage*. New York, Macmillan, 1906.

Ryan, John A., and Husslein, Joseph, S.J., *The Church and Labor*. New York, Macmillan, 1920.

Smith, William J., S.J., *Spotlight on Labor Unions*. New York, Duell, Sloan and Pearce, 1946.

Sturzo, Luigi, *Nationalism and Internationalism*, pp. 131–173. New York, Roy, 1946.

Toner, Jerome L., *The Closed Shop*. Washington, American Council on Public Affairs, 1944.

CHAPTER XXIX

THE EXECUTIVE AND JUDICIAL POWERS

997. No one can deny that a government possesses legislative, executive, and judicial powers. However, because of occasional but inevitable overlapping of these functions, but more so because of dislike of analytical and traditional classifications and worship of the "empirical and positive," there is a modern tendency to substitute the terms "social control and public service" for the old-fashioned terms, "legislative, executive, and judicial functions." However, as in the case of Aristotle's divisions of government, this classic classification stands up because it resolves governmental power into its simplest elements and separates things objectively distinct. "Social control and public service" are favorite terms with authors who regard collectivism as the sole desirable form of government.

998. Whether these powers ought to be separated in practice or kept united in one person or governing body is easily settled in ethics. The Natural Law neither commands nor forbids separation of powers because efficient government is possible under either arrangement. Whether separation or concentration, and how much of either, is better for this particular State will depend upon many circumstances chief of which are political maturity and historic background. The chief argument for concentration is efficiency. The argument for separation is that it is the safest means of preventing tyranny.

999. In a State where the three powers are separated, from several points of view the legislative power is the most important. It may be called the mind of the State. By its laws it creates specific moral obligation among citizens and establishes general norms binding the executive and judiciary. A State cannot exist without good laws.

But from the viewpoint of actual realization of the State's end, the executive power is paramount. The best of laws which are not made to work are of little avail. In a crisis the very existence of the State will depend upon the sheer strength of the executive arm. It is worthy of note that great dignity attaches to the supreme executive as the historic successor of the monarch in whom all power once was vested. The executive, then, may be called the will of the State — its concentrated compelling force. Its most primitive function is maintenance of order among its citizens and protection against foreign aggression. Its most inclusive duty is to carry into effect the laws of the legislature and the decisions of the judiciary.

I. THE EXECUTIVE POWER

1000. Executive functions fall into three classes: diplomatic, military, and administrative. (*a*) *Diplomatic* action is conduct of official business with other States. (*b*) *Military* activity includes whatever pertains to the defense of the State. (*c*) *Administrative* activity is a catchall term referring to all governmental activities which are not strictly legislative or judicial, diplomatic or military. By administration the executive not merely enforces the law without which there can be no orderly civil life, but also provides those public services necessary for public prosperity.

1001. It is usually conceded that the supreme executive office should be held by one person according to the axiom, "To deliberate is the function of many, to act of one." The individual executive cannot pass on his responsibilities; he must stand or fall upon his own performance. A plural executive, however, has functioned efficiently, for example, in Switzerland. In cabinet government, where the prime minister is but *primus inter pares,* the real executive is the entire cabinet.

1002. If a separation of powers is constitutionally required, an overlapping and interchange of legislative and administrative power is inevitable. Since legislation cannot provide for every detail, the administration must be empowered to make ordinances which have practically the effect of law. The executive must have wide power, especially in the time of war. On the other hand, through its committees, the legislature investigates administrators, holds them to an accounting, and, if the committee is permanent, makes itself the ultimate source of authority in the matter. Finally, the laws which actually govern will not include all that are found in statute books but merely those which are enforced. In large measure, laws are made in their enforcement.

1003. In determining the outstanding obligations of the executive, we must distinguish the executive who is total sovereign, or monarch, from the executive who does not possess legislative and judicial supremacy. According to the theory that the monarch is the fount of all authority in the State, he is not subject to any positive law of his own or his predecessor's making. For one cannot simultaneously and under the same circumstances be both superior and subject. According to the same theory, therefore, he is bound only by the Natural Law which compels him to devote himself to the common good even at the expense of his own happiness. Hence came the notion, felicitously phrased by Selden[1] and immortalized by the masterful exposition of Blackstone,[2] that the king can do no wrong. The original meaning is that the monarch is above all positive human law. However, not even the most intransigent defender of the divine right of kings would ever have interpreted the phrase in the words of Sophocles: "Kings are happy in many things but mainly in this that they can do and say whatever they please."[3] Even the monarch must keep the Natural Law. Later the phrase came to mean that as the unbiased distributor of justice, the king cannot constitutionally be supposed capable of injustice. The sole remnant of this idea found in American jurisprudence is the concept that the government is not liable for the wrongful or unauthorized acts of its officers: you cannot sue the government without its consent.

1004. But is the monarch really free of positive law? It is undeniably true that the spiritual monarch, the pope, is above all purely ecclesiastical law, but it ought not absolutely be said that the secular monarch is free of civil law. First, even the most absolute monarchs have been subject to the immemorial customs of their realms. Second, the primary depositary of sovereign powers is the people themselves. Since the monarch's authority is delegated, it is subject to the limitations contained in the original grant of power. Third, the common good may demand the monarch's good example, that is, since he is the visible symbol of the entire State, his conduct ought to represent all individuals keeping the law. His actions, however, are not review-

---

[1] John Selden, *Opera Omnia*, "Table Talk," in Vol. III, Part II, p. 2038. Londini, Wilkins, 1726.

[2] Sir William Blackstone, *Commentaries on the Laws of England*, Bk. I, Chap. 7, II (246).

[3] *Antigone*, 506–507.

able by courts of his creation: he is accountable only to the people civilly united.

1005. A monarch is feasible in a State which is in the process of development. In a mature nation, however, one rightly expects separation of powers and the limited executive. The obligations of the limited executive are summarized in the phrase — carry out the law. The obligation is negative, for he may never violate law in the pursuit of governmental business. To do so renders him guilty of malfeasance. The positive aspect of the executive's obligations consists in accomplishing that which the law demands to be done. If a particular situation is not covered by positive enactment, the Natural Law must guide the executive. In pursuit of diplomatic and military duties, especially in time of war, he requires reasonable latitude of action.

II. THE NATURE OF JUDICIAL POWER

1006. In the concrete, complete and absolute separation of legislative, executive, and judicial powers is impossible. The reason is that government is a practical science and an art with a single aim — advancement of the common good — and hence its three co-ordinate powers constitute one brotherhood working side by side with mutual toleration and co-operation.

Thus, when the executive vetoes a proposed law, or the supreme judiciary invalidates a law, each is exercising legislative power. When the legislature passes a bill of attainder, it acts in a judicial capacity. At times some executive commissions in the United States exercise all three functions. In England, Parliament has become the ultimate depositary of all governmental powers. It makes the laws; it appoints the ministers who exercise the executive power; its House of Lords is the last court of judicial appeal.

1007. Because of this interchange of governmental functions, some authors today say that it is impossible to define the three powers with rigid accuracy. Their essential differences, however, are quite discernible to one who has learned to recognize when one branch of government is exercising a function which theoretically belongs to another. Marshall said, "the legislature makes the law, the executive enforces the law, and the judiciary construes the law."[4]

---

[4] Henry Wheaton, *Reports of Cases Argued and Adjudged in The Supreme Court of the United States,* Bk. VI, Vol. 10, Wayman *vs.* Southard, 46, p. 43. Newark, N. J., Lawyers' Co-operative Publishing Co., 1882.

The primary end of the State is maintenance of the juridic order. This it does, first, by enunciating the general norms of justice. This action is legislation. Second, it pronounces justice in the concrete, that is, when the dispute of sufficient importance arises, the State decides with which of the disputants right and justice lie. This is the exercise of *judicial power,* which is ability authoritatively to resolve a complaint that law or justice has been violated in some particular.

1008. Marshall's emphasis upon the judiciary's power to construe the law led him to the far-reaching conclusion that final explanation of the law is to be sought not from the mind and intention of the legislator but in the interpretation of the judge. Pushed to its logical conclusion, this doctrine means that the law is what the courts determine it to mean, and unless the legislator by subsequent law can overturn judicial sentences, the judiciary becomes the master of the State. To have the final word on what the law means is effectively to be a lawmaker. The power, therefore, which the American judiciary has assumed of invalidating acts of legislature is truly a legislative function. The State may be satisfied that the judiciary play this part, but one must not therefore confuse it with the essential function of judicial power. St. Augustine aptly remarks: "Once laws are established and sanctioned, it must not be allowed to the judge to judge them but to judge according to them."[5]

Disputes requiring judicial solution are reduced to two categories: (*a*) cases in which a petitioner seeks against injustice a remedy to be found chiefly in the *Natural Law;* (*b*) cases in which the remedy against injustice is sought in *established positive law.* The first are handled in courts of equity, the second in courts of law.

1009. 1. *Courts of Equity.* The term *equity* has two meanings in the moral sciences.

a) Among moralists it means the same as ἐπιείκεια, or benign interpretation which indicates that the law does not urge in this instance. St. Thomas speaks of the special virtue of equity. "Legislators," he says, "keep their minds on what usually happens and frame their law for that; yet in some cases the keeping of the law is against the equality of justice and the common good. In such cases it is evil to abide by the law and good to overlook the words of the law and follow the course dictated by a regard for justice and public expediency.

---

[5] *De Vera Religione,* XXXI, 58.

And this is the end of equity."[6] Equity, then, is the tempering of positive law to meet the requirements of universal justice. St. Thomas also says, "Legal justice is directed according to equity. Hence equity is a kind of higher rule of human acts."[7]

b) Among lawyers equity means that natural, evenhanded justice which should exist between contending parties. Among lawyers the term arose from cases which formal positive law did not embrace and to decide which the judge had to resort to natural justice. If, on account of mode of procedure, mandatory regulations, or for any other reason, courts of law are unable to grant a remedy against injustice, a petitioner has recourse to a court of equity.

The main concern of those who administer justice in any court ought not to be forms of law but equality of justice. Justice ought not to be defeated by technicalities. Legalism is a poor substitute for justice. Too often legalism has been the refuge of scoundrels.

1010. 2. *Courts of law* include all other regularly established tribunals whose function is to determine whether customary or statute law has been violated. In these courts, although private persons at times accuse others of violations of commutative justice, the pre-eminent petitioner is the State accusing citizens of violations of legal justice. Since the end of the State's action is the infliction of penalty for violating the law, the fundamental question arises, *By what right may the State punish?*

III. POWER OF PUNISHMENT

1011. St. Thomas says that the acts of law are four, namely, to command, to prohibit, to permit, and to punish.[8] While the majority of men have admitted that punishment is a legitimate function of civil authority, there have been vociferous dissents from time to time especially today. Man's increasing sensitiveness tends to result in the avoidance of every kind of pain. Thus the theory which holds that moral evil is bodily disease contends that the evildoer should be cured but not punished. We are also told that once a bad act is done, to punish is only to add one evil to another. Abuses of punishment and stupid modes of punishment are pointed to as arguments for the abolition of all punishment. Some social historians decry it as a nasty

---

[6] *Sum. Theol.*, II–II, 120, 1.   [7] *Ibid.*, II–II, 120, 2.   [8] *Ibid.*, I–II, 92, 2.

form of revenge, a survival of primitive retaliation. Upon what basis of reason, then, does punishment stand?

1012. *Punishment is the authoritative deprivation of good, operating on some wrongdoer against his will, in order to wipe out a fault committed.* Although anyone can reward, the right to punish belongs only to authority: it is an essential means to the purposes of authority. Punishment is essentially the withdrawal of good from one whose evil act has shown him unworthy of that good. When punishment is inflicted it is not willed as an evil to the person punished but as a good — a requisite for the maintenance of order. When the evildoer willingly assumes a penalty for his fault, he is not undergoing punishment but he offers satisfaction. Only the unwilling are punished. Every punishment must be for a fault already committed: it cannot be inflicted merely to prevent a future fault. The essence of retributive justice is, No fault, no punishment.

1013. The justification of punishment is found in its purpose, which is the inviolable maintenance of the good of which law is the expression and guardian. The end of punishment is practically the same as the end of sanction, for punishment is the application of sanction. Laws are buttressed by sanctions to prevent violation. Once a law is broken, punishment must follow; otherwise sanction loses its power to protect law. Second, once the offender is punished, he is inclined to correct himself and keep the law lest punishment be repeated. Civil law, however, does not intend the amendment of the delinquent primarily for his own good but for the common good — the good estate of law observance. Finally, every true exception to law, if tolerated, becomes a precedent, and precedent tends to perpetuate itself and become the rule. Hence every act against law is destructive of law so that the common good must demand the enforcement of law. Enforcement is to be achieved not only by preventive measures — the threat of punishment if the law is broken — but after a law has been broken, law must demonstrate that it does not tolerate that act. Order demands the cancellation and undoing of a violation of the law. This cannot be done by pretending that what actually happened did not happen but by concrete proof to the lawbreaker that he cannot profit by such conduct. Self-preservation demands that law exact such expiation. It is just that they who choose evil should have evil as their portion.

1014. Civil authority should concern itself chiefly with devising and so administering punishment that the best possible observance of law will result. It should look to the deterring and corrective value of a penal code. The expiatory aspects of punishment are usually too much for the imperfect justice of men. In the main, this may safely be left to the perfect knowledge and justice of God.

IV. CAPITAL PUNISHMENT

1015. Justice requires that the State punish no more severely than the good to be obtained requires. How far may the State go? Since death is the severest of all temporal penalties, does the State possess the power of taking life for crime?

From the most ancient times it has been taken for granted that the State possesses the power of the sword. The codes of ancient peoples known to history and the customs of primitive peoples now surviving make provision for this form of punishment, although there is no unanimity as to the reasons for inflicting it.

In Genesis we read, "Whosoever shall shed man's blood, his blood shall be shed: for man was made to the image of God."[9] In the Mosaic law death was mandatory for homicide, willful assault upon one's father or mother, cursing one's parents, manstealing, bestiality. A significant sentence occurs in the book of Exodus, "Wizards thou shalt not suffer to live."[10] A wizard or witch is one who is so bent on attaining some purpose that he sells himself to the powers of evil and thereby becomes an enemy of the whole human race.

1016. The old codes mention only a few atrocious crimes as deserving of death, but it usually happened that in the course of time these laws were interpreted to include many other offenses. Thus in the oldest days of Rome parricide alone was punishable by death but gradually other crimes were similarly dealt with through the device of calling them parricide. Western Europe, whose jurisprudence was founded in Roman law and usage, witnessed a similar multiplication of causes for the death penalty, until in the reign of George III, Blackstone could lament that one hundred and sixty actions were deemed worthy of death by English law.[11] Thus one could be hanged for cutting down a tree, robbing a rabbit warren, stealing from a dwelling goods worth forty shillings or from a shop goods worth five

---

[9] Gen. 9:6.
[10] Exodus 22:18.
[11] *Commentaries on the Laws of England*, Bk. IV, Chap. I, p. 18.

shillings, counterfeiting the stamps used in the sale of perfumes, and the like.

With the growth of the liberal idea a clamor arose for the removal of the abuses of the death penalty. Much was done to debrutalize criminal codes. Modern sentimentalism, however, has gone a step farther and demands complete abolition of the death penalty. The arguments for abolition are familiar enough, and some States have acceded to the demand.

THESIS LXXIV. The State has the right to punish some criminals with death.

1017. By inflicting irreparable damage or by committing acts of horrendous malice, criminals may become completely harmful to the social body. They may, then, be cut off from society upon the same principle that one excises a gangrenous member from the body. As the Natural Law gives the individual a right in certain circumstances to kill an unjust aggressor, so the State must have a like right of defense against atrocious crime. This right is necessary for the preservation and well-being of the State. Even in those jurisdictions where capital punishment has been abolished by statute, the right of sovereignty to inflict this punishment has not been destroyed: it has merely become latent. This right is a power which no government can totally renounce. It is impossible to imagine the articles of war of any nation which do not contain death penalties. Beccaria[12] says that death penalties may be invoked in time of tremendous upheaval but never in peace. The experience of the race says that the need of capital punishment exists both in war and peace.

PROOF

1018. The State has a right to every action which (*a*) is not intrinsically evil and is both (*b*) expedient and (*c*) strictly necessary for the maintenance of the State.

1. The execution of certain criminals is *not intrinsically evil*. The taking of human life is not always wrong. Otherwise one could not adequately defend himself against unjust attack. What is always wrong is the taking of *innocent* life on human authority.

2. *Capital punishment is expedient* at least in the case of willful

---

[12] Cesare B. Beccaria, *An Essay on Crimes and Punishments,* Chap. XXVIII, p. 76, trans. unknown. Dublin, Exshaw, 1777, 5 ed.

murder. There are two reasons. (*a*) A crime which inflicts irreparable damage requires the ultimate of punishment. The canon of Rhadamanthus quoted by Aristotle says, "If a man have done to him what he has done to others that is the straight course of justice."[13] (*b*) So convinced are the majority of people of the justice of executing murderers that where there is no law to that effect, the people either make their own lynch law or engage in blood feuds.

3. *Capital punishment is strictly necessary.* (*a*) It is necessary for the protection of society against incorrigibly dangerous malefactors and enemies of the State. Neither banishment nor life imprisonment will always be effective. (*b*) The motives inciting to atrocious crime — revenge, jealousy, greed, and lust — are constantly present in society. Hence the abiding need for a counterpoise. The only suitable counterpoise is the knowledge that the crime will be followed by swift conviction and death. A death penalty which is enforced does keep these crimes to a minimum. There are very few homicides in Great Britain as compared to the United States. Murder is punished by death in Great Britain but in the United States only an infinitesimal number of the persons guilty of homicide ever pay the death penalty. "In 1938 only eighty-four cases of homicide were known to the police (in Britain). In thirty the murderers committed suicide, leaving fifty-four cases to be solved. Thirty-seven were convicted or found insane, ten were acquitted usually on the ground that the act did not constitute murder."[14]

READINGS

St. Thomas, *De Regimine Principum,* Lib. 1, cc. 7–15.
Anderson, William, *American Government,* pp. 172–204, 591–674. New York, Holt, 1938.
Aristotle, *Politics,* Bk. V, 10–12.
Garofalo, Baron Raffaele, *Criminology,* trans. R. W. Millar, pp. 372–382. Boston, Little Brown, 1914.
Gettell, Ray. G., *Political Science,* pp. 325–364. Boston, Ginn, 1933.
Guenechea, Joseph, S.J., *Principia Juris Politici,* Vol. II, pp. 144–181. Romae, Universitas Gregoriana, 1939.
Murray-Flynn, *Social Problems,* pp. 441–562. New York, Crofts, 1938.
Ogg and Ray, *Introduction to American Government,* pp. 239–315, 419–451. New York, Appleton-Century, 1938, 6 ed.

---

[13] *Ethics,* V. 5, 1132b.
[14] A. L. Goodhart, in the *Outpost,* No. 64, Aug., 1945.

Ruland, Ludwig, *Morality and the Social Order,* trans. T. A. Rattler, O.S.A., pp. 100–114. St. Louis, Herder, 1942.

Shotwell, James T., ed., *Governments of Continental Europe,* pp. 105–139, 177–202. New York, Macmillan, 1940.

Suarez, *Disputatio* LII, *De Judiciaria Christi Potestate,* ed. Berton, Vol. XIX, pp. 997–1009.

CHAPTER XXX

THE DUTIES OF CITIZENS

1019. In the foregoing description of the responsibilities of government, we have sketched the rough outlines of distributive justice, that is, the good which is due from the State to its members. We turn now to the correlative of distributive justice, to that which members owe the State.

We shall call members of the State *citizens.* Without entering into any of the technical differences known to particular codes between subjects, citizens, naturalized foreigners, resident aliens, and the like, we understand by a citizen a person who owes primary allegiance to the laws of a given State and is entitled to its minimal civic privileges. We say "primary allegiance" because, when a citizen is absent from his own State, he generally owes a secondary allegiance to the laws of the place where he resides. We say "minimal civic privileges" because, although all citizens may not equally participate in civic life by voting, sitting on juries, being eligible for public office, and the like, yet there is a least common denominator of civic standing. If a person falls below this level, as does a slave and felon, he is not a citizen. Certainly all who are born within the territorial jurisdiction of a given State and permanently reside there ought to have citizenship rights, except those whose criminal conduct justly forfeits them.

1020. *Patriotism,* which Samuel Johnson once caustically defined as the last refuge of a scoundrel,[1] is the summary name epitomizing the relations of citizen to State. The bond is piety. This is readily understandable if a State is small and its members are one's own kind and blood. Even though the modern State is much more than the family outgrown, the same relation of piety exists between it and its citizens. For as piety binds man to the family, the first of natural societies,

---

[1] Boswell's *Life of Johnson,* April 7, 1775.

so also it ties him to the State, which is the perfect natural society.

Patriotism is not blind, unreasoning sentiment, nor is it such preference for one's own people which begets contempt for outsiders. It is not prejudice nor bias which regards one's own way of life as necessarily superior to that of all foreigners; which ridicules all strange customs; which considers one's own national acts upright and honorable but those of one's enemy vile and immoral. To one belligerent the indiscriminate bombing of his cities is barbarity — the slaughter of innocents — but his own tenfold retaliation on the enemy is the laudable act of a crusader. Nor is patriotism jingoism, the truculent nonsense that one's nation can dominate whom it pleases, that it is a swan to whom the other nations are so many geese. Rather it is the *well-ordered love of one's State and of one's fellow citizens.* Here the object of love is not one's native soil: some persons might find it impossible to love the dirty streets, the noise, and smokestacks of their native city. The object of love is primarily one's fellow citizens; it is also the moral person, the State. Some people have said that it is impossible to love an abstraction. That impossibility fades before the cold fact that men do — even by dying for it. Like all real love, this love must include benevolence and beneficence. That is a pernicious and immoral patriotism which proclaims, My country, right or wrong. This sentiment presupposes that national welfare, convenience, and prestige are above all moral law; that the State, dealing with other States, has moral license to do whatever it has the force or guile to accomplish. This attitude is one of the scourges of modern life. It has substituted the State for God and the worship of country for religion. Well-ordered love remains within the bounds of reason. What reason dictates to the State in its conduct with other States will be dealt with in the next chapter.

1021. As piety in the family comprises both justice and charity, it includes the same in the State. The good which the citizen strictly owes the State is laid down by *legal* or civic justice. It is aptly called legal justice because law prescribes what the welfare of the State demands of individuals. It may also be called *civic* justice so as to distinguish the common good peculiar to the State from that of the family or the human race at large. The duties of the true patriot are not limited to that which law prescribes: he will come forward, as occasion demands, and freely give of his own to the common need. This is a kind of social charity.

In their civic capacity all members of the State are either public officials or private citizens. In what particulars of legal justice and social charity does the Natural Law bind both classes to advance the welfare of the State?

I. THE PUBLIC OFFICIAL

1022. In a broad sense the public official is a person who regularly performs some public service. In this sense a fireman or policeman would be called a public official. In the strict sense, a public official is a person who has been permanently (as opposed to transiently) invested by law with *authority* to perform some function of government. All public officials have authority — power to impose obligation — and most of them formally enter upon it by taking an oath to exercise it faithfully. Inasmuch as a public official is bound to serve the public welfare he is a *servant of the people;* inasmuch as in a legislative, executive, or judicial capacity he can create, declare, or impose moral obligation he is not a servant but a *lawful superior of the people.*

The over-all obligation of the public official is fulfillment of the duties of his office prescribed by positive and *Natural* Law. This requires not merely punctilious observance of the letter of positive law but intelligent effort to grasp its spirit and attain the purpose which it intends. Hence every official must have latitude of discretion to fit the imperfection of positive law to the requirements of natural justice. He should be convinced that the State and all officers of government are bound by the Natural Law, and that the laws of morality, not mere expediency and legality, should govern his official acts. He should abhor the sentiment, attributed by a biographer to Justice Holmes, that moral conceptions do not belong in a court of law.[2]

The demands of legal justice fall most heavily upon the public official: to him opportunities for exercising social charity more readily occur. To serve the common good, therefore, as the Natural Law indicates, he must measure up to the following requirements.

1023. 1. *The public official must subordinate his private interests to public welfare,* that is, in his official capacity the public good should be his paramount concern. His official acts must be motivated not by

---

[2] Catherine D. Bowen, *Yankee from Olympus,* p. 388. Boston, Little Brown, 1944.

personal but public considerations. He ought not to create useless jobs in order to take care of relatives, friends, or political hangers-on. In the selection of necessary help, he ought not, for personal or party reasons, choose people so incompetent that they would not give the State an adequate return for salary received. He may not use public money nor the official working time of civil servants to secure his re-election or advance party interests. The personal advantages of office, such as salary, perquisites, prestige, and the like, should be only incidental, not primary considerations. He is unfit for public trust who seeks or uses public office primarily as a means of advancing his fortunes or satisfying his desire for power.

1024. 2. The public official must be *incorruptible*. Corruption is stealing public funds, receiving bribes for acting unjustly, seeking gifts, moneys, or advantages other than lawful salary for performance of public duties. Even if this last form of graft may not always be forbidden by positive law, it constitutes grave temptation to partiality, warped judgment, and undue bias in favor of "benefactors." Hence the Natural Law forbids (*a*) special gifts taken by compact to do some just and legal act (the official has already contracted so to act and cannot twice sell that for which he has already contracted); (*b*) any gift or advantage calculated to influence his official acts and be an obstacle to the equitable discharge of his duties.

The official who defrauds the State or an individual of what belongs to them in *commutative justice* owes restitution. A bribe given for an act which the official is bound by his office to perform must be restored for the reason stated above.

On the restoration of bribes there is a curiosity of casuistry that may not be passed over. A probable opinion holds that a judge who takes a bribe for the passage of an unjust sentence may keep it once he has passed the venal sentence. "The reason is that the judge has fulfilled his part of the evil contract and has actually given the briber something which he (the briber) looked upon as worth the money he paid."[3] This opinion is unacceptable. First, let us suppose that a judge at the same sitting gave two judgments, one just and the other unjust, for both of which he has been bribed. Both acts were evil, the second more so than the first. Because the first sentence was just, he would be obliged to restore the bribe. Because the second sentence

[3] Edwin F. Healey, S.J., *Moral Guidance*, pp. 290–291. Chicago, Loyola University Press, 1942.

was unjust, he would be, according to this opinion, in a better moral situation regarding that bribe than regarding the first bribe; for he would have no obligation of restoring the second bribe. The worse act would produce less inconvenient consequences. Therefore by violating commutative justice the bribed judge would be better off *morally* than by observing justice. But this conclusion contradicts the truth that one may not violate the moral law and morally profit thereby even *accidentally*. Second, the doctrine of evil contract, explained in § 591, cannot apply here. When we admit that a person — say a prostitute — may keep the price of an evil act bargained for, we presuppose that the evildoer has some measure of exclusive dominion over the thing or service rendered, and is not disposing of what belongs to another. Here the venal judge is not selling personal service but *public justice*. It is not his to bargain for. Hence he may no more keep the price of perverted justice than he may pocket the price of public lands which he might fraudulently sell.

1025. 3. The official must be *impartial*. Since the official bears the majesty of the State, he must act toward his fellow citizens as the State is bound to act. Now the State stands to its members in a twofold role: custodian of commutative justice and dispenser of public helps. In relation to the State as custodian of justice, all citizens are equal and their rights deserve equal protection. Hence persons who approach an official on business pertaining to commutative justice are to be treated with exact justice, without discrimination, prejudice, favoritism, or partiality. The official cannot be a respecter of persons: exemptions and favors given to friends are so many declensions from justice.

When question arises of the sharing of common benefits, equality before the law does not mean that one person is to receive the same as another. What a person is to receive by way of distributive justice, depends on his need and deserving. The strong and wealthy, who are well able to look after themselves, require no special protection but the poor and ignorant, whose rights are liable to be curtailed by their stronger and less scrupulous neighbors, usually do. Legislators, therefore, ought to bear in mind that there is a constant need for setting up legal barriers to prevent the exploitation of the little man by a monied power. The distribution of bonuses and rewards ought to be made upon a basis of merit and service rendered to the State.

1026. 4. The official must be *diligent,* that is, he must give to public responsibilities the energy and time which their importance requires. By oath of office he has contracted so to act. A person who renders decisions affecting the public good should do so only after commensurate investigation and reflection. It is a pernicious custom to allot public office, as a prize for service rendered a victorious political party, to a person who may turn over the real burden of his office to some deputy and himself be free to pursue his own personal, financial, and political interests. When a "political job" becomes synonymous with sinecure, the public weal is bound to suffer. An official who does that for which he has no authority and which is contrary to law is guilty of *malfeasance*. When he does that for which he has authority but does it in a wrongful or injurious manner, he commits *misfeasance*. When he fails to do what the law commands him to do, he may be punished for *nonfeasance*.

1027. 5. The official must have *knowledge* adequate to his responsibilities. Although honesty and common sense may suffice in certain county or municipal jobs, greater and more technical knowledge is required of public officials charged with greater responsibilities. The reason is that the functions of the State have grown in complexity with the increased complexity of modern life; its action extends into more and more details of life so that human well-being has become more dependent than ever before upon the folly or wisdom of the State's activities. Although a public servant need not be a sociological, economic, or financial expert, he must have a sound social philosophy and fundamental grasp of the major problems facing the people. This he cannot have without a certain minimum of technical knowledge. Bills have too often been drawn up by an interested lobby and turned over for passage to legislators who could not evaluate them upon their intrinsic worth.

II. THE PRIVATE CITIZEN

A. Obedience to Law

1028. The first obligation of the private citizen is obedience to every just law, and the presumption is — until rebutted by positive proof — that all laws are just. By law the State commands the contribution which the individual is to make to the common good. The State's power to command necessarily implies the individual's obligation to obey.

What virtue does the citizen sin against who violates the law of the State? If the violated law is *declarative positive law,* that is a declaration or clearer elucidation of the Natural Law, that virtue is violated whose practice this law demands. Whoever violates the State's law against libel, rape, assault, and the like sins against commutative justice — the husband who fails to support his family sins against piety and commutative justice. These laws are positive only in their mode of proposal and can never be merely penal laws.

All other laws — *determinative positive law* — bind in virtue of legal justice and will be directly binding in conscience or merely penal according to the norms set down in §923 and the following.

1029. Some particular laws may give rise to problems of conscience. First among these we note *laws of compulsory military service.* In time of war or grave danger of war they are gravely binding because they then express the Natural Law commanding citizens to preserve the State. May a person evade them in time of peace? He may not fraudulently evade them, that is, by lying or bribery. If however, he can avoid service by nonsinful means he is free to do so, because such laws in peacetime are generally an obstacle to the common good. They impose too great a burden and in the long run they are incitements to war.

1030. The second type of law which may cause problems of conscience is the tax law. The citizen has an immediate obligation from the Natural Law to support the State financially. The reason is that the State cannot operate without money and since it can get a sufficiency only from its citizens, they must supply it. Every citizen, therefore, in proportion to his financial capacity owes monetary contribution to the State. Positive law must clarify this natural obligation, determine capacity to pay, and fix the manner, amount, and time of each one's contribution. This is done by the ordinary tax laws of a nation. A person, therefore, who consistently flouts tax laws and evades all payment of taxes offends against piety. Usually this is a serious offense for he simply fails to support the State.

With what exactness does tax legislation enunciate the Natural Law? The answer depends upon the justice of the law and the intention of the legislator. If the tax law is just, it binds in conscience except in the instances when the legislator intends merely penal law.

1031. With respect to the first condition, a tax law is just if it is required by the common good. Justice means that the State may not be *excessive* in its demands. The State should conduct its business with reasonable efficiency: it should not undertake tasks which do not fall within its competence. When the State seeks too much revenue, it is asking for that to which it has no claim. Taxes fall on persons or on things. Hence a person should be taxed in proportion to his ability to pay. It is distributive justice that from him who has much, much be required. In choosing things to tax, the State should observe a like proportion of distributive justice. Luxuries should be taxed before necessities. The materials of one business should not be singled out rather than those of another, but each industry and its materials should be taxed upon a basis of cost to the State or exempted because of benefits conferred. Thus automobiles are taxed because of the roads maintained for them: private schools should be exempt because of public service rendered. The norm for choosing an object of taxation should not be the ease of collecting the tax or lack of opposition to it, but equitable distribution of civic burden.

1032. The second condition depends on whether modern governments intend their tax laws to be merely penal. Because a person is disgruntled with government, disapproves of its political principles, or imagines that it discriminates against members of his party, race, or religion, he may not conclude that all its tax laws are merely penal. Unless the government clearly spurns an appeal to conscience, the presumption is for an appeal to conscience.

1033. Certain facts of modern life, however, seem to rule out this presumption. First, tremendous penalties are often attached to tax evasion. Second, taxes are collected with cold efficiency. The government does not wait to collect some taxes from the citizen but compels the employer to deduct taxes from one's salary before the employee even receives it. Third, there is the complexity and multiplicity of tax law. Some tax laws are so involved that a layman often requires expert advice to know how to obey them. Tax laws are so numerous that it is impossible to accuse anyone of violating the Natural Law by failure to pay taxes. Every person pays many taxes; perhaps not overt taxes but certainly hidden ones. For everyone is a consumer. Every consumer of goods and services pays hidden taxes, because sellers of these things have so raised prices that the buyer always absorbs the tax charges of the seller. A package of cigarettes which costs six cents to produce and market could be profitably sold for eight or nine cents. When the smoker pays fifteen cents for them, he is paying taxes. On account of income taxes, sales taxes, luxury taxes, corporation taxes, surplus profit taxes, social security taxes there are few money transactions which do not contain a hidden tax payment.

1034. The whole matter is admittedly obscure. Moral difficulties concerning observance of positive law can sometimes be solved by appeal to interpretation. Here no authentic interpretation exists: the secular State has never said through legislature or courts that it does not intend an appeal to conscience. Doctrinal interpretation helps little, for moralists are far from agreeing on this thorny question. Custom, which is the best interpreter of law, in this country and on this point is nonexistent. There was a time when men of upright conscience regarded as binding in conscience those taxes which were of long standing and which people paid without protest. But the flood of new taxes, the conviction that the government is asking too much, the sight of wholesale evasions, the increased number of persons who repudiate moral obligation in the matter — all this causes good men to doubt the morally binding force of even those taxes about which their fathers never doubted. Men of upright conscience are in a minority. If, then, the majority of their fellow citizens have shrugged off the moral obligation of a positive law, it would be unjust to say that the minority are still bound to observe it under pain of wrong. A plausible case, therefore, can be made for the position that tax laws are merely penal.

1035. From these doubts this seems to appear as true: the conscientious man is convinced that in general he is obliged in conscience to pay taxes because he cannot disregard the admonition of Scripture: "Render to all their due, tribute to whom tribute is due, taxes to whom taxes are due."[4] He is convinced that if by and large he meets his tax assessments, he may without guilt evade one or another tax when chance allows, provided he does not resort to fraud, bribery, or lying. He likens himself to the habitual train rider, that is, if occasionally he gets a free ride, it has been more than compensated for by all the fare he has *already paid*.

1036. Since taxes bind in conscience, *must the evader of taxes make restitution?* If the obligation of paying taxes is from commutative justice, the answer is in the affirmative; if it is only from legal justice, the answer is *no*. Some authors hold for commutative justice and

---

4 Rom. 13:7.

restitution. Since we may not presume but must certainly prove obligation to exist, the burden of proof rests upon the claimants for restitution. Their proofs are not convincing. Some authors seem to think that whenever money is involved, the matter automatically pertains to commutative justice.[5] This is not true. In this case, the money demanded by the State does not belong to it until it has been collected. Before collection the State has a *jus ad rem* to it: only after collection does it have a *jus in re*. A *jus ad rem* does not found a title to restitution. Furthermore, appeal is made to an implied contract between the government and the people. Perhaps in feudal days there was an explicit contract by which the prince pledged himself to conduct the government and the people promised him support, but, since feudalism is dead, no evidence of a natural contract so binding government and people can be adduced.

1037. There are two instances, however, wherein the tax evader owes restitution. First, he owes restitution if he bribes a tax collector. The collector has an explicit contract to collect, and, if he deliberately fails to take what is due, he violates his contract and owes restitution to the State in the amount which he failed to collect. The briber has formally co-operated in the act of injustice. Hence upon him and the corrupt official rests *in solidum* the obligation of making restitution. If the official cannot or will not make restitution, the entire burden falls upon the briber.

Second, the tax evader must make restitution if the amount he fails to pay is so great that it causes the tax rate to go up. Because he has failed to pay his share, others must pay more. His wrongful act has injured them. The Natural Law requires that he undo the harm done to them.

1038. *When does the obligation to pay taxes begin?* In times of great distress the good citizen will spontaneously offer of his goods to the common cause, but ordinarily the tax obligation does not begin until a person has received an official bill from the State. It is the common understanding that the officials of the State are to fix the definite sum which each person is to pay: only after this has been determined does the obligation to pay begin.

But is one obliged in conscience to volunteer information concerning his taxable property, for example, must a man in the absence of

---

[5] Ryan-Boland, *Catholic Principles of Politics*, p. 201. New York, Macmillan, 1940.

specific request tell the government that his income is now such that he is liable for income tax? Some authors say that he is[6] so obliged because (*a*) the law commands him to give this information, and (*b*) not to tell is equivalent to nonpayment. This conclusion is overrigid. It asks too much of human nature. It is the common understanding of upright men that it is for the government to discover this information by itself. Certainly this provision of the income-tax law is purely penal, for men obey it simply because of the heavy penalties for disobedience.

1039. In making declarations of taxable goods a person must be strictly truthful. To pretend that an incomplete declaration is a complete declaration is a lie; if the declaration be attested to by oath, a person commits perjury. It is claimed that, if a custom generally prevails of minimizing one's taxable goods, one who follows such a practice does not violate veracity.[7] This statement may easily be misunderstood. It is correct if it refers to a *genuine custom,* in other words, if the practice of minimizing is truly general and tacitly accepted by the government. In that case, an actual income of ten thousand dollars is expected to be reported, say, as eight thousand dollars and whoever makes such a declaration is truthfully responding to the mind of the questioner. The statement, however, is incorrect if there is no genuine custom and it is quite problematic whether such a custom is ever established. And before it would be established, a great deal of lying and perjury would have been done.

It is most odious that the State compels its citizens to swear to the truth of income-tax returns. Here the secularized State is playing the game of "Heads I win, tails you lose." In many instances the modern State abjures its own natural obligation of religion but in this case it invokes religion for its own financial profit. Swearing to income-tax returns is unnecessary because the matter is not serious enough to demand invocation of religion. Besides, it is scandal of the weak, for it needlessly exposes too many people to the proximate occasion of perjury.

B. Reverence

1040. Superior excellence demands that it be recognized and that, as occasion offers, some outward token of submission to it be accorded.

---

[6] *Ibid.,* p. 203.

[7] Vermeersch, *Theologia Moralis,* Vol. II, No. 567, *editio prima.*

This is reverence. The State has in regard to its citizens superior excellence because it can impose moral obligation on them. Reverence, therefore, is due from citizens to the symbols representing the State's majesty and the public officials sharing in the State's authority.

In a democracy people are inclined to minimize or even reject this duty. The democratic citizen often takes the attitude that he is just as good a man as any public official; that the official has been voted into his job by his fellow citizens, and, as a servant of the public, has no claim to extraordinary consideration. This is a false understanding of civic equality. A private citizen is not the civic equal of a public official: the latter is his superior. Because the official is a bearer of public authority, he is entitled, even though at heart he is a rascal, to esteem and respect for the office which he holds.

C. Civic mindedness

1041. Law observance and reverence do not quit the patriot of civic duty. Charity dictates that he give of himself and his goods to the State in its needs, provided he does not grievously burden himself thereby. There is evident room for social charity in times of calamity and extraordinary need. When war, pestilence, famine, earthquake, fire, flood, sedition, and the like, are seriously menacing the State, the good citizen comes forward unasked to contribute his share to warding off the danger. Patriotism, however, is not a garment to be put on for intermittent occasions and then, like a military uniform, to be laid away in moth balls until the next emergency. Daily, enduring need exists in the State which legislation can never supply, namely, need for constant social activity on the part of citizens. Other things being equal, the State is sound and flourishing in proportion to the active share which citizens take in public life. Its good condition depends on well-informed, vigilant, and publicly active citizens.

As a man must devote time, thought, and energy to his family, so, truly to deserve the name of good man, every citizen must give of himself to the State. Whoever merely refrains from breaking the law is a good citizen only in a negative way. If he never bothers about public interests he scarcely contributes his full share to the common good. Private apathy eventually spells public decay. Hence the good citizen ought to be civic minded or *public spirited,* that is, he should have constant interest in, and manifest practical devotion to, the welfare of the State.

1. Knowledge of Public Affairs

1042. To be public spirited a citizen must have *some knowledge of public life and affairs.* No one can take a fitting and helpful part in community life unless he has a practical knowledge of the fundamental law of the land. This knowledge should extend to the basic institutions and spirit of the State; to an evaluation of the outstanding characters in public life; to something more than hazy notions about the large contemporaneous problems with which legislation must grapple. An intelligent grasp of the trends and needs of the times is required in a a democracy for two reasons: first, democracy is government by public opinion; for wise rule, public opinion must be enlightened. Second, democracy summons its citizens to share in government; hence the uninformed person is an inefficient citizen.

2. Vigilance

1043. The public-spirited citizen is *vigilant.* He observes the course of government and is courageous to protest, when protestation will avail, against incompetence or corruption in government. He is jealous of any infringement of the natural, civil, and political rights which government guarantees him as man and citizen. His natural rights to life, liberty, marriage, property, good name, freedom of conscience have already been established. They do not come from the State nor can the State take them away. There is no need of explicit reference to them in the fundamental law of the State, because one takes for granted that the State exists to protect them.

1044. By *civil rights* we mean freedom and immunities explicitly confirmed to the citizen by statute or fundamental law whose immediate purpose is the welfare of the individual. In the amendments to the Constitution of the United States are enumerated the chief civil rights of American citizens. They are freedom of religion, of speech, of the press, of peaceable assembly; the right to keep and bear arms in accordance with the laws of the states; freedom from the billeting of soldiers in private homes in times of peace; freedom from punishment by bill of attainder or *ex post facto* law; recourse to the writ of habeas corpus under ordinary circumstances; security against unreasonable searches, seizures, and warrants; the right to a hearing before a grand jury in all federal cases involving serious crime; immunity from double jeopardy for the same offense and from acting as witness against oneself; the right not to be deprived of life, liberty, or property without due process of law; the right to just compensation for the taking of private property for public use; the right in criminal cases to a speedy and public trial by jury, to be confronted by witnesses and obtain witnesses, and to the assistance of counsel for defense; the right in civil cases involving more than twenty dollars to a trial by jury; freedom from excessive bail and fines, from cruel and unusual punishments, from involuntary servitude except as a punishment for crime; the right to the equal protection of the laws in all states, to enjoy the privileges and immunities of all the states, to be protected against laws impairing the obligation of contracts, to sue and be sued in the courts, and to a republican form of government. It is explicitly stated in the ninth amendment that the enumeration of certain rights in the Constitution shall not be construed to deny or disparage other rights retained by the people.

Although maintenance of civil rights redounds first to the benefit of individuals, nothing more surely makes for security and stability of the State. That State will always be vigorous in which individual liberty flourishes. Nowhere are citizens more ready to defend the State than in a land where tyranny is impossible.

Political rights exist not for the individual but for the public good. They consist in the capacity of private citizens to participate in government. They are not strictly rights but rather privileges, as we shall explain below.

3. Use of Political Privileges

1045. The public-spirited citizen *makes constant use of his political privileges*. Political privilege is a favor, over and above one's strict civil right, permanently granted by sovereignty to the citizen. The favor is sometimes an exemption from the common law granted to an individual or group but it is usually a concession of a direct or indirect share in governing given to the whole body of citizenry. As subject to law, the citizen has no natural right to make or administer law but once law allows participation, he rightly considers this his political right.

1046. *Jury service* is a political privilege. The patriotic citizen when summoned to it does not shirk it on the mere plea of private business. This contribution to public life he ought to make even at the cost of some private inconvenience.

A jury is a body of men sworn to declare the existence or non-existence of the essential *facts* under dispute in a judicial process. The juryman must be impartial and disinterested. Hence, if a person has a bias in a given case, or has already formed an opinion concerning it, he should not serve in that case. The law itself disbars from the jury kindred and dependents of litigants.

The juryman's verdict should be based on evidence presented, but this does not mean that justice should be abandoned for the sake of legality. In criminal cases, if the evidence leaves reasonable doubt of the defendant's guilt, the juryman must vote for acquittal, unless he has private and certain knowledge of a defendant's guilt whose acquittal would bring great harm to the State. If evidence convicts the defendant, the juryman may acquit if he has private knowledge of innocence. In either case the private knowledge must be certitude, not feeling or unfounded intuition. In civil suits, if evidence is inconclusive, he must favor the party whose right is more probable. If there is equal probability in a case involving possession of a right or good, he should generally favor the possessor.

1047. Furthermore, the public-spirited citizen *always votes*. Today voting is a serious duty. Whether a nation will have good or bad laws, an upright or corrupt administration depends on the voters. Extremely grave issues are laid before them. An indifferent and apathetic electorate is an invitation to tyranny. A person, therefore, who is able to vote but never votes, is guilty of serious omission. In particular cases where serious issues are involved, a proportionately grave inconvenience is required to excuse from wrongdoing a person who does not vote.

The motive of every vote should be the public welfare. In casting his ballot, the citizen should never be swayed by personal profit, mere whim, religious or racial bias but solely by consideration of which of the conflicting issues or candidates is better for city, state, or nation. Although political parties serve a useful civic purpose, their interests should be kept subordinate to the public good.

1048. The voter should learn to evaluate candidates and to recognize who among them has the qualities necessary for public life. To be elected, a candidate should possess three qualities: correct principles of government, aptitude for public life, and public integrity. The policies of a candidate must give clear indication of promoting peace and prosperity in the community. An honest man, who has false notions of the domination of one class in society or of the omnicompetence of government, can do more civic harm than a venal politician whose theories of government accord with the Natural Law. A candidate must have or be able to acquire efficiency in handling public business. There are intelligent and upright men who, because they totally lack political sense, could not succeed in public office. The candidate must give promise of serving the public faithfully, industriously, and beneficially. A man's private vices do not necessarily render him unfit for public office. Although it is likely that a man, immoral in his private actions, will also be immoral in the public acts, there have been able kings, legislators, and administrators whose private lives were far from edifying but whose public service was almost irreplaceable.

4. Social Charity

1049. Finally, *social charity* will suggest that, without assuming too heavy a burden and in the measure which his personal obligations permit, the public-spirited citizen give time, thought, personal service, or material resources to private or semipublic institutions which truly alleviate the sufferings of the needy or promote civic betterment.

READINGS

Anderson, William, *American Government,* pp. 293–436. New York, Holt, 1938.

Aristotle, *Politics,* Bk. III, 1–5.

Cahill, E., S.J., *The Framework of the Christian State,* pp. 484–538. Dublin, Gill, 1932.

Connell, F. J., C.SS.R., *Morals in Politics and Professions,* pp. 1–114. Westminster, Md., Newman, 1946.

Davis, Henry, S.J., *Moral and Pastoral Theology,* Vol. II, pp. 88–90; Vol. IV, pp. 339–351. New York, Sheed and Ward, 1936.

Gettell, Ray. G., *Political Science,* pp. 255–323. Boston, Ginn, 1933.

Guenechea, Joseph, S.J., *Principia Juris Politici,* Vol. II, pp. 302–393. Romae, Universitas Gregoriana, 1939.

Jones and Vanderbosch, eds., *Readings in Citizenship,* pp. 195–264. New York, Macmillan, 1932.

Leo XIII, *Sapientiae Christianae* and *Libertas Humana* (encyclicals).

Maritain, Jacques, *Scholasticism and Politics,* pp. 194–224. New York, Macmillan, 1940.

Meyer, Theodore, S.J., *Institutiones Juris Naturalis,* Vol. II, pp. 638–703. Friburgi Brisgoviae, Herder, 1900.

Noldin-Schmidt, *Summa Theologiae Moralis,* Vol. II, Nos. 313–324. Oeniponte, Rauch, 1938.

Philosophical Studies of the American Philosophical Association, Vol. I. "The Philosophy of James Wilson," pp. 19–141. Washington, The Catholic University Press.

Ritchie, David, *Natural Rights,* pp. 210–262. London, Swann Sonnenschein, 1895.

Ross, J. Elliot, *Christian Ethics,* pp. 315–331. New York, Devin Adair, 1938.

Ryan and Boland, *Catholic Principles of Politics,* pp. 194–216. New York, Macmillan, 1940.

Suarez, *De Legibus,* V, 13–18.

Vann, Gerald, O.P., *Morals Makyth Man,* pp. 142–156. London, Longmans Green, 1938.

Vermeersch, A., S.J., *Theologia Moralis,* Vol. II, Nos. 566–573. Bruges, Beyaert, 1924.

Wright, John J., *National Patriotism in Papal Teaching,* pp. 3–93. Westminster, Md., Newman, 1943.

CHAPTER XXXI

STATE AND STATE

1050. Having examined the mutual relations of the State and its citizens, the next point for study is the conduct of States with respect to one another. Although the State has been defined it will help in our consideration of international problems if we further refine the concept of statehood and express statehood in terms of adequate inter-State relations. Since the State is a moral person, in fact the outstanding moral person, we put the problem thus: What is required and is sufficient to constitute an International Person?

I. THE INTERNATIONAL PERSON

A. What Is an International Person?

1051. According to Holland, "The normal international person is a State which not only enjoys full external sovereignty, but is also a recognized member of the family of nations. States which vary from this type either by being defective in sovereignty, or by having no place in the family of nations, are abnormal international persons."[1] By the family of nations he means the Christian nations and those others which the Christian nations choose to admit within their circle.

1052. Holland's first condition, plenitude of sovereignty, is absolutely necessary for every International Person. To be capable of adequate relations with the self-sufficient social units of the world, a State must itself have political self-sufficiency. This is sovereignty which means that the State is accountable to no superior political body either in relations with its own citizens (internal sovereignty) or in relations with other States (external sovereignty). All authorities agree that the State is a perfect society — the socially self-sufficient unit in the

---

[1] Thomas Holland, *Jurisprudence*, p. 395. Oxford, Clarendon, 1937, 13 ed.

temporal sphere. Any political body, therefore, which lacks something of internal or external sovereignty, fails in self-sufficiency and is not to be accounted as capable of adequate relations with those units which possess full sovereignty.

The second proffered requisite for international standing, membership in the group of nations which has inherited the Christian tradition, we reject. The western nations are so secularized that they are only nominally Christian. The nineteenth-century notion of a *restricted* comity of nations has been abandoned. All that the Natural Law demands for international relationship is plentitude of sovereignty. Every sovereign State is capable of international intercourse, and in justice and in charity should be accorded corresponding standing.

1053. There are political societies, like nascent colonies, which are incapable of exercising full sovereignty. A weak State may conceivably turn to a stronger State for real protection and in return give over to its protector direction of its foreign affairs. Other States have renounced sovereignty to become members of a Federal Union. Since these societies do not have plentitude of sovereignty, they are neither *de facto* nor *de jure* international persons; they are not upon a footing of international equality with sovereign States; they do not have the international rights and duties of sovereign States. *Therefore the international person is each State that possesses full sovereignty.*

1054. When the world is at peace the number of *de facto* sovereign States can be accurately computed. But does this number represent an objectively just situation? The international scene is a curious melange of justice and injustice, of principle and expediency. Hence several interrelated problems arise: (1) Does each sovereign State include in its membership all the groups and only the groups which should rightly form this civic union? (2) Ought some political societies which do not now possess full sovereignty be accorded it and treated as fully competent Internation-Persons? The first problem deals with the Theory of Nationalism and the Rights of Minorities; the second with suppressed and protected States.

B. The Theory of Nationalism

1055. In the nineteenth century the doctrine of nationalism was evolved especially by Italian writers like Mancini.[2] The theory distin-

---

[2] P. S. Mancini, *"Della Nationalita come Fondamento del Dritto delle genti,"* in his *Dritto Internazionale Prelegioni,* pp. 5–64. Napoli, Marghieri, 1873.

guishes between *population,* or those persons actually subject to a particular government, and *nationality,* a large group of persons characterized by special traits of body and mind, and united by similar language, customs, and ancestry. A population may consist of several nationalities or parts of nationalities, as Austria did before 1914. A nationality may be divided among several populations as were the Poles before 1914. According to this theory, a population is an artificial unit; a nationality is the sole natural unit. According to the extreme statement of the theory every nationality has a right to form a State which will include all the members and only the members of that nationality, the rights of all other States notwithstanding. For example, all people of Italian nationality subject to France, Italy, and Switzerland should be incorporated into one purely Italian national State. State and nationality must be coterminous. Hardly anyone, however, would now defend the doctrine in this form. A modified version contends that, if international agreements are not violated, each nationality, capable of autonomy, may demand it when it judges autonomy necessary for national purposes and when it has the strength to effect it. Its ability to accomplish this must be left to the trial of arms.

1056. *The principle of nationality is not a precept of the Natural Law.* Nature does not indicate that only those people who spring from a common stock should be united in one State. There are three reasons for our denial. First, we have proved that consent is the sole juridic cause of the State. Nationality, therefore, can be, at most, a remote cause, that is, a factor dispositive to consent, but it is by no means so overwhelming a factor that it must always demand consent. There can be stronger dispositive factors to consent than nationality, namely, local proximity, mutual need, common history, long-enduring habits of acting together. Second, nationality is often so vague and uncertain that it cannot constitute the determining norm of who should belong to a given State. Who can adequately distinguish and classify all the nationalities? Third, the principle advanced is provocative of perpetual discord. To put this theory into effect would disrupt peace everywhere. The change could not be effected without universal war. Some nationalities are so hopelessly spread out and intermingled with others that separation and relocation could not be humanely effected. Some nationalities are too small to constitute a sovereign State: others, which have never constituted a State, may yet be incapable of self-rule. Finally, even if the nationalities could be distinguished and separated too many old ties would be rudely severed, too many claims to lands and cities would still be bandied about; and so the delimitations of nationalities would still remain so vague that no one could guarantee that this new arrangement of States would be any more productive of concord than that which obtains at present.

C. Rights of Minorities

1057. A situation may exist in which a nationality is morally obliged to remain attached to the State of which it now forms part, for example, Scotland to the Kingdom of Great Britain. Separation would mean general war, entail economic ruin of the separated nationality, foment civil wars, seriously prejudice the rights of the rump State, and the like. However, while retaining its old allegiance and ancient loyalty, the nationality has a right to preserve its language, customs, and national characteristics. These things are an estimable good which all men rightly prize. This right, however, ought not to be so exaggeratedly exercised as to inflict grave injury on the State of which it forms part.

Above all, such a nationality has a right to equitable treatment at the hands of the dominant group. "Dominant" is an invidious word suggesting a stronger party which exploits a weaker party. In no State should there be a dominant group in that sense: all groups have an equal right to share in the benefits of the State.

D. Suppressed States

1058. Although nationalism makes exaggerated claims and is provocative of disturbance, it does express valid protest against many existing injustices. There are nationalities, clearly distinguishable, which have inhabited easily definable areas for centuries, and which once constituted sovereign States. Their sovereignty was violently taken away by some more powerful State acting in its own selfish interests. Ought sovereignty be restored to such suppressed nationalities?

1059. The answer must rest on two ultimate principles, namely, consent and human welfare. If a suppressed nationality is located close to the dominant nation, if the political ties binding them are of long standing as in the case of the Welsh and the English, if forcible suppression is happily ended and human welfare is being promoted by their union, the people *de facto* consent. They are obliged to. Nationality has in it a fair amount of vanity and romanticism. It is silly for a people, because of "old forgotten things and battles long ago," to sigh for a chimerical independence. For time has healed the breach between conqueror and conquered and made of them a united population. This, however, is the rarer instance.

1060. The more usual case is this. Distance separates the two parties; the loss of sovereignty is of fairly recent date; the subordinate people are economically exploited; they are not permitted to make vital decisions affecting their welfare; their legitimate national aspirations are thwarted as inimical to the interests of the dominant State. The victims of such an arrangement do not consent but grudgingly bear a foreign yoke because they must. They rightly aspire to be masters in their own house, because *a given people is usually the best judge and the most efficient procurer of its own welfare.* We may say of States what is true of individuals, namely, no one takes better care of a person than himself.

1061. The assertion that a small nation is better off under the tutelage of a great power is usually hypocrisy — an excuse for imperialism. Conquering nations do not move in on a helpless State nor annex the territory of a beaten foe because they desire to improve the lot of their new subjects. The conqueror is avid for more territory, more power, more prestige, more sources of profit. The little nation has something the big nation wants — the site of a canal, oil, a naval base, rare metals — and the big nation is going to have it. Since transportation and communication are so highly developed, and since most peoples have access to sources of knowledge and technical skill, the vast majority of suppressed and protected States, released from the domination of their "protectors," could attain economic and governmental self-sufficiency. The claim that these people have no capacity for self-rule means that they lack military strength to fight off aggressors. But the time is more than ripe for peaceable peoples to be able to exist without dread of unjust aggression.

II. THE EXISTENCE OF INTERNATIONAL LAW

1062. In international relations States have, in the main, followed the same pattern of conduct as individuals. Among States as among individuals, there is the same desire for self-preservation; the same inclination to exalt oneself; the same bullying of the weak by the strong. We find among the States some courtesy, kindliness, and helpfulness; occasional outbursts of furious passion, hatred, bloodletting, and revenge; the inevitable aftermath of suspicion, envy, and abiding distrust. The consistent difference is that nations are harder, less humane to one another than individuals are.

One wonders if we are not now on the downward slope of a peak of civilization. For several centuries the nations were trying to act more humanely to one another. Until 1914, it seemed that they were on the point of formulating a code of equitable conduct, valid not merely toward civilized nations but toward all peoples. Justice, charity, and equity were to become virtues of governments as well as of individuals. A court of international arbitration was set up at The Hague. "International law" was a commonplace word in men's mouths. But since 1914 manifest symptoms of a return to pagan modes of international intercourse have been too painfully numerous. The two bloodiest and most destructive of all mankind's wars have been fought, and in them has been reverified the mournful plaint of the pagan world, *Vae victis!* Between 1914 and 1945 so many millions of men have been slain on battlefields or wantonly starved, shot, hanged, or butchered, men have heaped such wholesale horrors on their fellow men, that Christianity finds no parallel for it.

1063. This inhumanity is the consequence of two causes which, underneath the shell of civilization, have constantly been at work. The first cause is the individual's repudiation of supernatural faith. From this has followed, as night the day, repudiation of the moral code inculcated by Christian faith. When G. B. Chisholm, Deputy Minister of National Health of Canada, in a public address in the city of Washington ridicules the very concept of right and wrong and blames the psychic disorders, frustrations, and wars of men upon the teaching of moral ideas,[3] a disease long festering in the body social has erupted to the surface.

The second cause is worse, namely, national greed for economic wealth and lust for domination. Justice and amity receive lip service, but meantime nations assault, despoil, and dominate other nations and justify their actions by an unguent of soft words, greasily spread upon their own national consciences, and blandly offered to the world in complete and pious justification. From international competition this formula may be derived: There is no law above the sovereign

---

[3] An address before the William Alanson White Psychiatric Foundation, reported in the *Baltimore Sun*, Oct. 24, 1945.

State. The State may do whatever it wishes, provided it is strong enough to succeed. Ancient Carthage, Babylon, and Persia could appreciate this ethic. Christianity has always taught the opposite; but since the time of Machiavelli, both theory and practice have borne, with increasing acceleration, the nations to the position that sovereign power knows no limit but the counterforce of its neighbors. Although we may not state it in blunt words, there are no real moral commands and prohibitions to give sovereignty pause. Can we wonder that the relations of States, now completely secularized, have become so chaotic, arbitrary, and lawless?

One, therefore, must seriously ask again: Does the law of nature bind the State? Does moral obligation effectively touch the State?

THESIS LXXV. Every State both in regard to its own citizens and to other states is subject to the Natural Law.

The point at issue may be expressed in two ways: (1) *Does the moral person, the State, have moral obligations?* (2) *Must persons who act officially for the State conform their public actions to the Natural Moral Law?* The proofs that follow are offered to answer both questions.

FIRST PROOF

1064. The activities of a natural society, both as regards its own members and other natural societies, are governed by the Natural Law.

Since natural societies originate in the Natural Law and since their main outlines are laid down in that same law, it would be absurd to say that in their *activities* they are free of that law.

We have already shown the principal *natural* duties which the State has regarding its citizens. When one State deals with another State, one body of men is holding intercourse with another body of men. The intercourse of men with men must be controlled by the Natural Law.

Since the State is a natural society, both its internal and external activity is regulated by the Natural Law.

1065. N.B. I. It would be puerile to object that, since in the strict sense obligation can bind only an individual will, the State can have no moral obligations. It is quite correct to speak of moral persons having obligations, for example, a corporation must be humane to its workers, or municipalities must redeem their bonds. It is also understood that ultimately the fulfillment of such obligations devolves upon some particular man or men.

N.B. II. The denial of the subordination of the State to the Natural Law generally arises from a misconception of State sovereignty. Sovereignty means that each State is the political equal of every other, that in the sphere of *temporal* social jurisdiction the State has no superior. It does not mean that the State is free of *all* law but of the law of another State. Despite its political sovereignty, the State is a contingent, not an absolute, thing. Like every other contingent thing it must be subject to a law higher than itself. If men, who are of immortal value, are so subject, the State, which is only a means to man's temporal perfection, must likewise be subject.

SECOND PROOF

1066. If men, acting for the State, were not obliged to conform their public actions to the Natural Law, some deliberate acts of men would be free of moral law. But no deliberate acts of men are free of moral law. Of its nature each human act advances or hinders a man in regard to his last end. Since the Natural Law is the directive to that end, it must direct *all* of man's human acts. Therefore no deliberate act can stand outside the competence of the Natural Law. It is absurd to imagine that men can avoid the commands and prohibitions of the Natural Law by the device of association. Positive law may be evaded by technicalities, but there are no loopholes in the Natural Law. If there were, the Divine Legislator would lack foresight and efficiency. Hence, whenever men act for the State, their public acts must conform to the Natural Law.

Corollary. *A natural international law exists.* As the Natural Law indicates the general outlines of individual conduct, it likewise governs the intercourse of State with State.

1067. *What is international law?* In general, international law is the sum of rules which sovereign States ought to observe in their intercourse with one another. It is not to be confused with *Jus Gentium,* or Law of Nations. In Roman jurisprudence and early scholastic terminology *Jus Gentium* referred to those obvious tenets of positive law which are practically the same in the codes of particular States. They are those easily recognizable and immediate applications of the Natural Law which men cannot help but deduce and incorporate into their law.[4] While some of them apply to the intercourse of nations as such, most of them concern the relations of man to man and State to citizens. International law is rather *Jus inter Gentes*.

Some authors distinguish between public international law, which has been described above, and private international law, that is, the system of adjudicating rights of individuals in cases in which different jurisdictions are involved. The term, private international law, is really a misnomer and is better known in jurisprudence as conflict of laws.

1068. What is of moment is the distinction between positive and natural international law. (*a*) *Positive international law* is that body of rules which, by the express or tacit *agreement* of the nations concerned, governs their inter-State acts. It is the outgrowth of the customs of nations, international treaties, State acts which in the lapse of time have been accepted as precedents and binding upon the Christian nations. (*b*) *Natural international law* consists of laws which immediately flow from the nature of the State and whose validity in no wise depends upon State agreement or acceptance. Upon this law depend all positive agreements binding the nations.

III. THE CONTENT OF NATURAL INTERNATIONAL LAW

1069. What does the Natural Law command, forbid, and allow the nations in their intercourse with one another? Although the State is not an individual and hence some individual obligations do not apply to it; and although the State has a peculiar responsibility which no individual has and hence has rights which the individual does not need: nevertheless, the general laws of human conduct — the demands of justice and charity — must govern inter-State action. We shall treat first of international justice; then of international charity.

A. International Justice

1070. A *natural juridical international order* must exist because States are subject to the Natural Law, and the Natural Law immediately confers rights upon each State as upon a moral person with a natural end to attain and a natural function to perform. To preserve and develop its moral personality, rights are essential to each State. Since natural rights flow from the very essence of statehood,

---

[4] See *Sum. Theol.*, I–II, 95, 4; Suarez, *De Legibus*, Lib. II, c. 17.

each State has equal natural rights. Since each State has the same end and function, no reason could possibly be assigned why one State should not have the same rights as any other. The natural juridic order upon the international level lies in the recognition and maintenance of these rights. What are they?

1. *National Existence*

1071. Once a people have made their political organization self-sufficient, they have become a State. As soon as a State begins to exist, it acquires from nature a right to continue in existence, just as a newborn individual has a natural right to continue to live. The reason is that the new State is a natural institution, and hence a necessary means to the human welfare of this people. As in the case of the individual, so for the State existence is the first good. Since *de facto* it is a State, it acquires a right to be recognized and treated as such by other States.

Since statehood is *sovereignty* — social self-sufficiency and political independence — the State's right of self-preservation means *the maintenance of unimpaired sovereignty.* This involves four principles.

1072. *a)* The independent existence of a State may not be destroyed by another State. History, however, is so much the record of the rise and fall, the appearance and disappearance of States. That most nations have been liquidated by violence is clear, because only two reasons justify loss of independence: (1) a State may agree to merge with another State or States, for example, thirteen independent commonwealths agreed in 1789 to form the United States; (2) if the security and existence of one State is constantly menaced by an implacably hostile State, the aggrieved State may as a measure of ultimate self-defense destroy the other in the same legitimate manner as the individual may kill in self-defense. So extreme a situation is seldom realized, but it seems reasonable that the Roman government in Britain in the fourth century of our era would have been justified in destroying the political organization of the Picts and Scots, if they had any, and in subjugating them if it could, since that was the only means of stopping their attacks and tranquilizing Britain.

1073. *b)* Nor may partial but permanent limitations be imposed upon the sovereignty of one State by another. Each State has the inherent right to manage its own internal and external affairs as it thinks best. If it obeys the Natural Law, it is free to set up the constitution it chooses, make laws which suit it, and enter into treaties as it pleases. Every State with sufficient strength maintains this right against the world. Through weakness and through possession of assets coveted by a more powerful nation, a luckless State has been compelled to allow another State a voice in its foreign and even in its domestic policy.

Immunity from such interference is the *right of nonintervention.* It is an immediate corollary from the concept of sovereignty and is ultimately grounded on human welfare: each State's affairs are best cared for by itself.

Is the rule of nonintervention so ironclad as to admit of no exceptions? As the State is not an end in itself so neither is sovereignty: both must yield to the exigence of human welfare. As human welfare demands nonintervention as the general rule, so human welfare sometimes demands an exception to the rule. Theoretically one State may assume a protectorate over another when a protectorate would be a real advantage to the weaker people. In this case the people would willingly enough accept it. Some strong nations are just and generous but not many. Hence, in practice, permanent limitations of sovereignty are unwillingly borne because they are in the interest of the dominant State: rarely is the weaker State helped by the arrangement.

We shall see how one State may *temporarily* intervene in the affairs of another in discussing charity among nations.

1074. *c) Territorial integrity.* In general, no nation may take over part of another nation's territory or population. The number of actual unjust annexations is incalculable. Outside of the struggle for economic advantage, nothing is so provocative of friction among the nations as lust for territory.

1075. *d) Freedom from fomentation of sedition.* Since civil war can be at times a more serious threat to national existences than external aggression, no nation may stir up discord in another. Every nation is entitled to its own peaceful life as the primary aim of its existence.

2. *Respect*

1076. Just as a man is entitled to the honor which should be accorded his human dignity, so a State deserves proportionate honor and courtesy from all other States. The reason is the excellence of the moral person, the State. Application of this principle is found chiefly in treatment of the State's official representatives in foreign lands. In a lesser degree it also applies to certain chosen symbols of the State, notably its flag. The customs which have spontaneously grown up in this connection evidence men's inclination to obey the Natural Law when no special difficulty is involved.

3. Self-Development

1077. Since the individual has a right to improve and perfect himself, the State has the same right, otherwise the State could not fulfill its natural end — the promotion of public prosperity. The State, therefore, has a right to any means of self-improvement which does not injure another State. In substance this right involves access to means of full human living, freedom of communication, increase of dominion.

1078. a) *Access to means of full human living.* If a people did not have or could not readily obtain a secure supply of the necessaries of life, they would not form a State, for they would lack elemental economic self-sufficiency. Hence it is taken for granted that each State has the means of subsistence. But if a State wishes to make progress, it may need materials, notably minerals. Since the bounty of nature has been intended for the whole human race, no single nation or combination of nations may monopolize the raw wealth of the earth and fix prohibitory prices which put desirable goods beyond the reach of less fortunate nations. Economic monopoly is the real sore spot in international relations. From the envy of the have-nots for the haves arise modern wars. Nor will peace become permanent merely because a present combination of nations is strong enough to beat down the frenzied efforts of virile but impecunious nations to get a place in the sun. Lasting peace is possible only upon a foundation of equitable economic opportunity among the nations.

1079. b) *Freedom of communication.* Nations that wall themselves off from international intercourse quickly cease to make progress. Interchange of goods and ideas is the essential requisite for advancement. No State, therefore, may be prevented from friendly intercourse with the nations of the earth. So also a State would ordinarily do wrong which refused communication with the outside world or forbade it to its subjects. The right of intercourse, however, does not include a strict "Right of Legation," that is, a duty existing in all other States of receiving its official representatives. A nation refusing to receive the ambassadors of another country may violate charity but not justice.

This right also includes the peaceable use of the natural means of communication — the high seas and the common airways.

1080. *c*) *Increase of dominion.* Dominion here does not have reference to proprietary dominion. It is obvious that the State may do what the individual may, namely, own property and increase it.

Increase of dominion is the extension of a State's jurisdiction over any new territory which is not already subject to another State. Occupation is a good title both of proprietary dominion and of jurisdiction. For its occupation to be valid, the State must fulfill three conditions. (1) By a *public* act the State must lay claim to the land. The private act of a citizen who discovers it and makes some of it his private possession is not sufficient. (2) The State must effectively control the land. Mere discovery and claim are not enough: what it cannot control does not pass into its jurisdiction. (3) The land must belong to no other State, barbarous or civilized. If barbarous people are settled on the land and have their own self-sufficient polity, they constitute a legitimate State even though it is not reckoned among the family of nations. No civilized State is justified in forcing foreign jurisdiction upon it. The right of a barbarous State to exist is as good as that of a civilized State. *There is no such thing as naked right of conquest:* force cannot of itself found a right. The legitimate mode of exercising the right to increase dominion is colonization.

1081. *Colonization.* A colony is a group of citizens who have left their own land to people another and whose government is subject to the mother country. Where a colony is established on land which is merely overrun by nomads, the colonizing power must not make it impossible for the nomads to live. If a colony is set up in a land which heretofore was too sparsely inhabited to have a government, the rights of the aboriginal inhabitants to their *private* holdings in land and the like must be respected. Even though their titles are not recorded in a courthouse, they are as valid as those recognized among civilized men.

The status and powers of a colonial government are determined by the mother country. As the colony increases and its need for the protection of the mother country decreases, the management of its affairs may more and more be left to itself. As a son in the family ultimately achieves emancipation from paternal rule, so a colony, fully self-sustaining, is entitled to complete independence when it chooses to exercise it.

4. *Treaties*

1082. A *treaty* is a public contract between two or more sovereign States. It is quite distinct from a private contract between States, for example, the purchase by the Chinese Government of the Brazilian legation buildings in London. As private persons may exchange rights by contract so may States. Treaty making is but an expansion of the right of intercourse.

To bind a nation, a treaty must be an act of the Sovereign. Constitutional law determines where the treaty-making power lies in a government.

Treaties derive their binding power from the Natural Law alone. No agencies of positive international law exist upon which treaties could depend for binding force, interpretation, execution, or reparation. It is, therefore, a general precept of the Natural Law that *agreements made among the nations must be kept.* They bind in commutative justice.

1083. Practically the same requirements for validity and liceity hold for treaties as for private contracts (§ 582 ff.). The outstanding difference between treaties and private contracts is that the individual can appeal to a court to declare an agreement invalid or even to rescind a contract initially good, but the State cannot. No court exists competent to invalidate treaties. Must, then, a State absolutely observe every treaty which it signs? Let us distinguish between treaties willingly and unwillingly entered upon.

1084. *a) May a State refuse to honor a treaty which it has been compelled to accept?* In general, it may not be left to a State later to repudiate, on the score of no consent, a treaty which it had been forced to accept. The reason is that, if this practice were allowed, there would be no end of contention and perhaps of wars among the nations. Our conclusion is demanded by the over-all common good of the nations. Hence, if the terms of the treaty are just, the unwilling signatory is clearly bound to fulfill them. If the injustice is only doubtful, the treaty likewise must be observed. However, if the terms are palpably unjust, no treaty exists no matter how solemn the formalities which inaugurated it. The reason is that what is unjust cannot be the object of any contract. The oppressor State is morally obliged to renounce its claims under the agreement and to repair all injury effected by it. The aggrieved State has no obligation in commutative justice to fulfill its part. Hence, if it can avoid performance without provoking war, it is justified in doing so. If it cannot do so without disturbing international peace, the common good demands that the unjust agreement be kept, especially if the issues involved are not of paramount importance. However, a State's obligations to the fellowship of nations cannot ask too much of it, for example, to observe terms which would lead to loss of independence, acute misery of its people, or spoliation of the fundamental means of development.

1085. *b*) *May a State void a treaty which it has freely entered into?* Treaties cease to bind for the same reasons that private contracts lapse: mutual consent, impossibility of performance, extinction of one party, and the like. The question which arises here is whether there are any circumstances in which a State may lawfully denounce a treaty initially valid and remaining such to the moment of its repudiation?

According to Cronin[5] there is one and only one circumstance wherein a nation may upon its own initiative declare itself freed of treaty obligation, namely, when an implied condition, necessary to impose obligation at the time the treaty is made, no longer holds good. He cites two examples: (1) when one party has substantially failed to live up to its part, the other party may declare itself free of all obligation; (2) when fulfillment would involve loss of independence for one party — unless the treaty was meant to hold even in such a contingency.

5. *Self-Defense*

1086. The above-mentioned rights must be capable of defense; otherwise they are useless. When, then, any of them are violated or are in danger of infringement, a State may protect its interests by protest, negotiation, arbitration, severance of diplomatic relations, an embargo of trade. *May it resort to violence?* Certainly if national territory is suddenly and wantonly invaded by hostile force, the citizens themselves, even in the absence of an official armed force, may, if they are able, repel the invader. This is an instance of collective self-defense. The full issue here is, *May one nation go to war with another?*

6. *War*

1087. *War* is the violent attempt of one nation or part of a nation to impose its will upon another similar group. It is *civil war* when

---

[5] Michael Cronin, *The Science of Ethics*, Vol. II, pp. 658–661. Dublin, Gill, 1909.

the contention is carried on by armed forces within the same nation. There is scarcely anything more destructive of the ends of the State. It is the primary duty of any government to prevent and suppress all civil war. According to international custom, whenever rebels are not only in possession of an army but have a civil political organization sufficient to be responsible for armed forces and quasi-governmental acts, they may be recognized as *belligerents,* that is, capable of waging war according to its accepted laws. The effect of such a declaration is that henceforth the rebels are not to be dealt with as mutineers or pirates; the parent country is freed from all responsibility for what happens within the insurgent lines; neutrals may enter into commercial relations with them. Civil wars never begin by a formal declaration of war but by the interruption of regular administration through insurrection.

Among ancient and modern civilized peoples, international war, that is, war between *sovereign States,* has regularly been initiated by a formal proclamation of hostilities. *Does the Natural Law prohibit or allow a declaration of war?*

1088. If war is intrinsically evil, the Natural Law must forbid it. The immediate object of warlike effort is the destruction of the armed forces of one's adversary which inevitably involves taking human life. Taking human life is not in itself evil; otherwise God could not ordain it in the ordinary course of nature. Nor is taking human life upon human authority intrinsically evil, for it may be justified in personal self-defense or public execution. From its end of work, therefore, war is not condemned. The morality of war is to be determined from motive and circumstances.

On the score of motive we distinguish war of aggression and war of defense. (*a*) *War of aggression* is the violent endeavor to deprive another people of independence, territory, or the like, for the sake of increasing one's own power and prestige. (*b*) *War of defense* is the forceful protection of national rights.

a) *Aggressive War*

THESIS LXXVI. The Natural Law forbids all wars of aggression.

PROOF

1089. (1) The Natural Law forbids the unreasonable suppression of the rights of any State. For nature which grants these rights would contradict itself if it did not forbid all undue interference with them.

(2) War of aggression is unreasonable suppression of the rights of the assaulted State. It is violent trespass upon that State's right to a peaceful existence. The only reasonable use of force against an equal is protection and reparation of right.

Corollary. Except for the one instance noted in §1072 a right of conquest does not exist.

1090. N.B. It is the hypocritical custom of civilized (?) aggressors to conceal their international assaults with such euphemisms as, "preventive defense," "punitive expeditions," "the white man's burden." There must still exist an appreciable temporal utility to moral principles; otherwise modern imperialists would not so assiduously try to disguise their aggressions in the borrowed plumage of virtue.

b) *Defensive War*

THESIS LXXVII. Under certain conditions the Natural Law allows a nation a war of defense.

1091. The same fundamental principles which apply to the use of force by the individual in defense of individual rights we apply here, making due allowance for the difference between individual and nation. For a declaration of war or the initiation of hostilities to be justified, these four conditions must be fulfilled.

1092. (1) War must be an act of *Sovereign Authority*. As we shall show, the only justification of war is legitimate defense of the State. Hence war may be initiated only by the supreme authority in a nation. No individual or subordinate authority may declare war on foreign nationals.

1093. (2) War must be an act of *legitimate self-defense*. Not every right of the State is important enough to justify war. The right to be defended must be of surpassing importance. War is too frightfully serious, too fraught with dreadful consequences for all parties involved, ever to be lightly invoked. Two rights alone measure up to this requirement, namely, independent existence and legitimate development. If a State's independence is in danger, if by unjust means it is being economically strangled to death or prevented from emerging from economic servitude, if its territorial integrity is threatened in a large way, it may go to war. Since war is so horrible, a nation may not fight on account of wounded national honor or injustices done to a few citizens abroad. Nor is *mere* punishment an adequate reason.

No sovereign State has a right to punish another State, because punishment is the prerogative of a superior. *A fortiori,* it is immoral to fight for more territory; for national revenge or increase of power, profit, and prestige; for balance of power; for the sake of interfering in the internal affairs of a neighbor.

The defense of right here postulated clearly implies that the complaining State is not at the same time doing wrong to its prospective adversary. If it is, the two States are simultaneously the victims and the perpetrators of mutual injustice. The aggrieved nation is justified in going to war only when it has clean hands and has itself ceased from all acts of injustice.

1094. (3) There must be *moral certainty* that a State's essential rights are in danger. As a judge may not condemn a man to death unless he is certain of guilt, so a State may not cast the die for war unless it is certain of the justice of its cause. Mere probability of attack is not enough. Since there is a certainly existing obligation to respect the rights of other States and an ever-pressing duty arising from the common good of all nations not to disrupt the peace, there is no room here for the application of probabilism. If, however, all the conditions of just war are verified, the injured State — as in the case of personal assault — need not passively await the military attack of its adversary but may itself strike the first blow.

1095. (4) *War must be the last resort.* Every peaceable means of settling the dispute must first have been tried sincerely and assiduously. Only when no other means are available is violence a justifiable means of safeguarding right. The principle of *proportionate evil* must be fully invoked. Not only must the right to be defended outweigh the evils of war, but government must beforehand ponder all the chances of war. It would be wrong to embark even on a just war without fair prospect of success. And even a successful war may leave a nation worse off than if it had refrained from fighting and tolerated certain injustices. In many wars both the victors and the vanquished suffer irreparably.

PROOF

1096. 1. The Natural Law allows the uniquely necessary means of protecting essential rights if this means is not evil in itself. Otherwise the grant of right is illusory.

2. That defensive war is not in itself evil is proved in § 1088. In

certain circumstances war can be absolutely the only way to maintain the right to independence or the essential means of development.

1097. Since one may never immediately co-operate in an immoral act; since bearing arms is immediate co-operation in war; and since a war may or may not be immoral according to the justice of the cause that is upheld, the moral question arises, Before an individual takes up arms, how *certain* must he be of the justice of the side for which he intends to fight?

A person may fight for a nation other than his own from a motive of charity, that is, for a nation which is justly defending its rights and which needs all possible assistance. Mere romantic preference for one side or love of excitement are insufficient reasons. A volunteer must always investigate and be *morally certain* of the justice of the cause for which he fights.

Concerning persons who fight for their own country, different cases must be distinguished.

1. Conscripts and soldiers already in the army when war begins may legitimately presume that their country is right. The justice or injustice of a war will not usually be evident to the common soldier. Nor is he obliged to investigate because such investigation, even if possible, would lead to nothing. When they doubt, they may resolve their doubt by giving their country the benefit of the doubt. Hence they are to obey their commanders. If, however, they are convinced of the injustice of the war, they may not inflict damage on the enemy. Their right of personal self-defense remains, however. The practical solution of the situation is a request for noncombatant service.

2. Whoever volunteers to serve must first satisfy himself that the cause is just.

3. If a State has foolishly or unjustly gone to war, and is in danger of destruction, the State may call upon all citizens to ward off the peril and all competent citizens are obliged to obey.

4. A person who contends that participation in any war is always immoral is deceived. However, if his conscience is invincibly erroneous and he is summoned to active military service, he must follow his conscience and decline active part in the war.

The obligations of individuals may be summarized thus: (*a*) Statesmen, legislators, and volunteers for a foreign army must be *morally certain* of the justice of their acts. (*b*) When the country declares war, the ordinary man may give it the benefit of any doubt, because full information is not available to him, and because his country is most seriously endangered by the mere fact of war.

c) *The Conduct of War*

1098. It is one thing to go to war for a just cause. It is quite another to try to win a war through immoral practices. Once a war starts one cannot say that all is fair in war.

THESIS LXXVIII. In the prosecution of war the Natural Law forbids every action intrinsically evil.

PROOF

Actions intrinsically evil are always and everywhere wrong and hence forbidden by the Natural Law. Therefore they are also forbidden even in the prosecution of a just war.

Corollary. No State may do what is intrinsically evil even to save itself from total destruction.

The chief particular moral problems arising from war are now considered.

(1) *Use of Violence*

1099. The moral principle governing every use of violence is that *a person should use no more violence than is requisite to make his right secure*. To go beyond that point is to be guilty of unjust aggression. There is a limit to the quality and quantity of violence, even in war. As for quality, a State may not employ weapons which inflict useless and excessive suffering. Weapons are tools of defense intended to crush the aggression of an enemy, not to inflict pain for the sake of pain. By positive agreement the majority of the nations have agreed not to use poisons, poisonous gases, and bacteria. The over-all good of the human race is an added reason for the observance of this convention. As for quantity of violence, once an individual enemy is incapable of resistance through wounds, sickness, lack of weapons, and the like, or is genuinely willing to surrender, violence against him must cease. To kill a wounded or surrendered enemy is murder. To refuse to take prisoners is, equivalently, murder except when an enemy feigns surrender the more easily to inflict damage. In that case soldiers may take every precaution to insure their safety. Prisoners must be humanely treated and when peace is concluded they must be returned to their homes.

1100. Must the old distinction between combatants and noncombatants still be maintained? This distinction is practically denied by the modern concept of *total* war. According to it wars are no longer fought merely by the military but by entire nations in which all citizens contribute to the war effort. According to the theory of total war, a woman working in a war plant is injuring the enemy as much as a flame thrower at the front: total organization has made a warring nation a unified fighting machine engaged in single combat with a similar adversary. As in a personal death struggle all blows are legitimate, so in war any injury done the body social of the enemy is a laudable act.

1101. This view does not square with all the facts. No nation is capable of absolutely total mobilization for war. Wars are fought not by abstract entities but by groups of individuals and in each group there must be innumerable persons — children, sick, old persons — who are incapable of any kind of efficient violence. Since they cannot possibly be aggressors, no violence may be directed at them. A real and practicable distinction between a combatant and a noncombatant must be recognized.

1102. Cronin bases the distinction upon the difference between actual and potential aggression, saying that combatants are "all those who are engaged in actual aggression."[6] Potential aggressors are not combatants. The distinction is quite valid as far as it goes, but in view of recent developments one must further refine the concept of actual aggression. Actual co-operation in aggression may be immediate or remote. Are all remote co-operators combatants? If so, then practically the entire working population becomes combatants. This conclusion is inadmissible.

1103. A *combatant is one who immediately co-operates in military effort and is thereby liable to military attacks.* Two essentials are involved, namely military effort and immediate co-operation. Military effort is force under the control of competent authority. Since war is an act of the State and imputable to the State, particular warlike acts must also be State acts and controlled by authority. The State may not summon forth any and every kind of violence against an enemy, especially that which it cannot direct. To do so is ineffectual and immoral. To summon forth indiscriminate violence against an enemy is immoral because it is encouragement to perpetrate every sort of

---

[6] Michael Cronin, *Science of Ethics,* Vol. II, p. 669. Dublin, Gill, 1909.

crime, and it eventually tends to the dissolution of society's bonds. A combatant, then, is first, one who is authorized to fight as are all members of the armed services. The unauthorized person who kills an enemy combatant, except in self-defense, is an assassin. Without authority his act is not the act of the State. A combatant is also any civilian who temporarily or permanently renders *immediate* aid to military effort. Persons who do so permanently ought to be aggregated to the armed forces. Civilians, who intensively but only remotely and indirectly promote military effort, are not to be classified as combatants and their persons and homes may not become the objects of direct attack. They may not be directly attacked for two reasons. First, direct attack is out of proportion to the indirect violence which they offer the enemy. They are not immediately attacking the person of their enemies; therefore, their persons should be immune from direct attack. Second, to allow direct attack upon such persons is a dangerous threat to the whole human race. Such persons may be effectively prevented from doing war work by bombing the factories in which they work; by destroying the raw materials, means of transportation and communication, and the like, which they use; by taking them prisoner, but *not by a directly aimed attack upon their person.*

1104. Positive international agreement has sharply defined combatants as all those persons and only those persons who belong to the armed forces. By the same agreement they should wear distinguishing marks of their service. The good of mankind and the imperative need to halt the downward trend to modern barbarism demand that these conventions be kept.

While authorities may disagree as to who shall be classified as combatants, no one denies that the direct killing of a noncombatant, except for proved crime, is murder.

1105. *Bombing.* It is a legitimate act of war to bomb directly any military target. The term, military target, includes not only armed personnel and purely military installations, but roads, railways, every kind of communication and transportation, factories, warehouses, government buildings — anything which directly subserves a military purpose. Killing noncombatants in air raids may never be directly willed but only permitted according to the principles of double effect. To bomb a purely civilian area for the sake of terrorizing the enemy into subjection is merely mass murder.

An open city is one which contains nothing of direct military value.

Hence it is immune from air attack. If, however, a belligerent disperses his factories among private homes and uses these as arsenals of war, they automatically become legitimate military targets.

1106. The moral difficulty concerns *area bombing*. In bombing a large area where military and nonmilitary objectives stand next to each other, it will often be impossible to take precautions against hitting nonmilitary targets. Such is the lamentable chance of war. If it is possible to take these precautions, there is a strict moral obligation to do so, for noncombatants have definite rights that must be respected. To take no precautions to avoid hitting churches, hospitals, schools, historical monuments, civilian homes when such precautions are militarily possible, is equivalent to direct attack. Such indiscriminate bombing is immoral. So also is the blanket order to raze a large city.

1107. What is the morality of dropping a single *atomic bomb* which devastates a tremendous area? The answer will depend upon what is in that area. For the act to be good, the area must contain a preponderance of particular military objectives and the military good to be effected must be proportioned to the damage done to noncombatants. To consider atomic bombing merely as an act of total war, as the body blow of one global giant against another, is to forget the pertinent human rights of many thousands of persons. To attack an overwhelmingly civil population with this weapon is simply the direct slaughter of thousands of innocent people. Nor may the action be justified on the ground of bringing war to a speedy end. The best of ends never justifies immoral means.

The introduction of such terrible weapons returns us to our most fundamental issue — the use of violence. Is there a moral obligation to refrain from such stupendous violence? Should the making of such weapons be stopped?

If use of certain weapons becomes a direct threat to the existence of the human race or certainly entails return to barbarism, all nations are obliged to forego use of such weapons and an individual nation would have to suffer abridgment of its rights rather than let loose such calamities on the human race. But this threat does not exist at present.

Can destructive weapons be produced which could imperil all men? If so, the Natural Law must forbid their use, for the over-all good of the human race has precedence over the good of any nation. Such a situation is a possibility, not a present actuality.

There can be no moral obligation on man to cease delving into the secrets of nature on the ground that new discoveries may be misused. We may not put limits to intellectual investigation. Because more and more stupendous forms of violence may be discovered, the moral obligation of being master of that violence grows apace. This mastery can be achieved only by man learning to live with man. It is injustice which he must conquer rather than sink his knowledge of atomic energy to the bottom of the sea.

(2) *Enemy Property*

1108. Since a most effective mode of national defense is to deprive one's enemy of the sinews of war, it is legitimate for the State to seize or destroy any public or private property of the enemy that has a military value. *Property which has no military value must be left untouched.* It should be carefully noted that what is conceded by the Natural Law is *a right of use in self-defense.* These uses are reduced to two: seizure and destruction.

(*a*) *Seizure of enemy property.* The right to take and use enemy property does not by *Natural Law* include the right of permanent possession. Holland[7] is wrong when he calls enemy property a *res nullius,* a thing which may be occupied. The reason is that no kind of force — not even military force — may found a title of ownership or of any kind of right. By *Natural Law,* therefore, when hostilities end, all seized properties automatically revert to their former owners: the enemies' right of use has lapsed.

But must we not recognize a right of booty and prize? From ancient times soldiers have acted as though all enemy goods become the property of the captor and have endeavored to keep what they forcibly took. Agreements among the nations, however, have clarified the issue, and upon *agreements* now in force rests the right of booty and prize. A careful distinction is made between public and private property.

Whenever *public* immovable property falls into the hands of the enemy, he has the use and usufruct of the same. Movable public property is simply appropriated by the enemy occupier. What is taken on land is booty; on sea, is a prize. Title vests not in the individual captors but in the sovereign. He, however, may transfer

---

[7] Thomas Holland, *Jurisprudence,* p. 216. Oxford, Clarendon, 1937, 13 ed.

something of his right to his military in order to encourage them. In the case of prizes, title does not pass until a prize court has passed a sentence of condemnation. Treaties may provide special immunity for churches, museums, works of art, and the like.

It is forbidden to take *private* property except in "cases dictated by the necessary operations of war." When private property is requisitioned it must be paid for or a receipt given, to be honored later by one's own government or the enemy. Combatants who appropriate things for their *personal gain* are looters. Trophies or souvenirs are not loot.

(*b*) *Destruction of enemy property.* Whatever has military value to the enemy is liable to destruction. After property has been destroyed in war, is there an obligation of restitution? If a man uses another's property to save his life and that property is damaged, the user owes nothing in strict justice, for his use has been just. So if a belligerent *in a just war* destroys enemy property he owes no reparations. An unjust belligerent, victor or loser, owes reparations according to his ability to pay.

(3) *Rights of Neutrals*

1109. *The rights of neutrals must be respected.* A neutral is a State which maintains peaceful relations with States at war among themselves. Its duty to remain impartial means that it must refrain from immediate military aid to either party and prevent within its jurisdiction any such act on the part of anyone whatever. What constitutes immediate military aid is more clearly defined in positive international agreements. On the other hand, no belligerent may repudiate treaties made with a neutral, move troops across its territory, engage in battle in its territorial waters, interfere with a neutral's *peaceful* intercourse with other belligerents. However, the right of intercourse of a neutral with a belligerent is restricted by positive agreement in the following respects: a neutral must respect a factual blockade; its ships carrying contraband of war are subject to seizure; private ships may be subjected to search for contraband.

A nation fighting a just war may be joined, from motives of charity, by any other nation. A just belligerent, however, may not solicit aid by promises which are unjust to fulfill. To induce a neutral into an unjust declaration of war is to co-operate immediately in its guilt.

(4) Reprisal

1110. A *reprisal* in positive law is the act of a State (or of an individual authorized by his State) whereby it forcibly seizes the property or otherwise diminishes the right of another State as satisfaction for a claim in justice denied the former by the latter. It is not necessarily a warlike act. A reprisal in war is any evil which a belligerent visits upon its enemy in retaliation for damage sustained. It is human nature to give back what one gets. If nationals of one State meet with cruel and barbarous treatment from the enemy, is the State justified in doing as the enemy has done? If the enemy's act has been a violation of the Natural Law such as torturing prisoners or slaying wounded, the State on its part may not violate the Natural Law. Even if winning the war depended on such conduct, it may never be allowed. Two wrongs will never make a right. If the enemy act has been merely the violation of a treaty, for example, not to use privateers, the other State is freed from observing that treaty.

It is murder to take hostages from a civilian population and execute them because unidentifiable persons are making clandestine attacks upon the enemy occupier. Envoys and hostages may not be slain even when the enemy has done so. It is always wrong to put *innocent* people to death.

(5) Lying

1111. *Lying is as wrong in war as in peace.* There is, however, a recognizable difference between lying and legitimate deception of the enemy. To fabricate atrocity stories and father them upon the enemy in order to rouse world opinion against him is a serious injustice.

(6) Blockade

1112. *Blockade* is a legitimate means of subduing enemy troops. "If civilians suffer, it is not intended that they should suffer; it is their misfortune, and is due to the fortune of a just war that they happen to be in the same place as their army."[8]

---

[8] Henry Davis, *Moral and Pastoral Theology*, Vol. II, p. 122. New York, Sheed and Ward, 1936.

(7) *Terms of Peace*

1113. *The terms of peace must be just.* Since the only justifying reason for war is vindication of right, once that has been fully secured, the victor must rest. To impose harsh terms which take away necessary rights of a beaten nation is injustice, for even in military defeat a nation retains rights. After a just war the victor may claim compensation for damages sustained, yet his bill for reparations may not condemn the people of the losing side to misery. Both justice and charity demand that the victor follow a policy of live and let live.

(8) *Punishment of Enemies*

1114. *May the victor punish the vanquished,* that is, both the nation as a whole and individual enemies guilty of offenses against the victor? Since punishment is one of the four acts of law,[9] no punishment is permissible which does not rest on the authority of law. Three sources of authority to punish are conceivable: positive law, the *Jus Gentium,* and the Natural Law.

The source cannot be positive law because no visible authority superior to the State exists. Suarez[10] found the justification of international punishments in the *Jus Gentium* — those conclusions from the Natural Law which medieval Christian nations agreed should govern their inter-State acts. The moral force of the *Jus Gentium* depends upon consent. Remove consent and a formerly accepted practice is no longer permissible. During the two centuries prior to 1945, however, the nations by contrary doctrine and practice withdrew consent, thereby invalidating this former tenet of the *Jus Gentium.* Modern jurisprudence has been totally positivistic, rejecting the Natural Law upon which the *Jus Gentium* rests. It has taught the absolute sovereignty of the State, rejected custom, and accepted as internationally binding only explicit agreements. In the Hague Conventions the nations agreed that certain punitive measures are permissible *in the actual conduct of war,* for example, spies may be hanged and franc-tireurs may be shot. But concerning punishments to be inflicted after war is concluded, every modern international convention is completely silent. In practice the heads of nations and the

---

9 *Sum. Theol.,* I–II, 92, 2.
10 *De Legibus,* II, XIX, 8.

commanders of armies have been untouchable. No court would assume jurisdiction over a foreign sovereign unless he voluntarily submitted to it not would it try foreign nationals who do not reside within its territory without the consent of their own government. Prior to World War I, the termination of war automatically meant an amnesty for all persons who might be charged with wrongful acts of war.[11] At the end of World War I the Allies gave the German government a list of German citizens to be handed over to the Allies for trial. The German government replied that compliance with the demand was abdication of its sovereignty. It proposed instead to try these persons in a special court of its own. The Allies accepted the proposal as in keeping with current international procedure.

The trials at Nuremberg and elsewhere at the end of World War II were a complete cleavage from all modern precedent. By explicit convention, or by future imitation of the precedent, the nations can signify their agreement to such procedure.

1115. In the absence of implicit or explicit agreement, does the Natural Law immediately confer authority to punish? Suarez[12] denies this but DeLugo,[13] Vitoria,[14] and other sixteenth-century Scholastics assert it. Let us examine the concept of punishment. Punishment is reasonable only as a deterrent, a correction, and an expiation of guilt. It is inflicted on the guilty to prevent further crime, to change their evil disposition, and to restore the order disturbed by their violation of right. The fullness of this power resides in visibly constituted authority in regard to its own natural subjects. Is the defeated nation equally subjected to it?

It is clearly subject to the deterrent and corrective power which every State possesses for the prevention and reparation of international injustices. In the successful vindication of its rights the wronged nation may take measures which will effectively prevent the enemy from repeating his wrong. The victorious State may strip the enemy of the means of future aggression, put individuals to death if the future safety of the State certainly warrants it, and, as an ultimate resort, totally destroy the enemy government and subject the people to itself (cf. § 1072). "If the victor deals with persons who are alien to

---

[11] Charles G. Fenwick, *International Law*, p. 582. New York, D. Appleton-Century, 1934.

[12] *Ibid.*

[13] *De Justitia et Jure*, Disp. X, Sect. II, n. 81.

[14] *De Jure Belli*, No. 19, No. 57.

humanity and religion, these he may rightfully compel to change conduct which is contrary to nature."[15] The Natural Law must give such authority as necessary to right living among men.

1116. But the heart of punishment is expiation. Appalling wrongs demand expiation. Who may exact it? In the extraordinary instance cited above where the victor acts as national sovereign toward the vanquished, he may try individuals for violations of existing international or municipal law, or deliver them to another State for trial in the place where the crime was committed. Apart from these circumstances, does the Natural Law grant the victor authority to exact satisfaction? DeLugo holds that in the absence of civil authority even a private person may assume the role of punisher.[16] Bellarmine says: "A prince who has just cause for war bears the character of judge with regard to another prince who has injured him."[17] Does right reason necessarily demand the grant of such authority? Once the victor is amply secure in his right, does orderly living demand that he be allowed to exact satisfaction? With due reverence for the great authority of the opposite opinion, we submit that such a grant of authority would be destructive of reasonable living. First, the Natural Law does not grant an equal authority over another equal without the latter's consent. Second, no one, individual or nation, is a good judge in his own case. As both accuser and judge, the victor lacks the disinterested calm necessary to hold impartially the scales of justice between himself and a fellow disputant. Just punishments are seldom devised in anger or by interested parties. Third, the victor is too prone to exceed the due measure of natural vindictive justice: the vanquished will consider themselves outraged and when opportunity serves, will strike back for revenge. Thus strife and contention multiply. "Vengeance is mine: I will repay, saith the Lord."[18] This warning applies to nations as well as to individuals.

1117. It will be objected that this doctrine restricts too much the scope of human punishment, that international criminals may easily escape justice. Before answering let us note that the sole issue is expiation. We stated above the right of a just and victorious State to

---

[15] Alberici Gentilis, *De Jure Belli*, Lib. III, C. XI, p. 558. Hanoviae, Haeredes Antonii, 1612.

[16] *Loc. cit.*

[17] *Disputationum Roberti Bellarmini Tomus Secundus. De Laicis,* C. XV, p. 667. Ingolstadii, Adami Sartorii, 1601.

[18] Romans 12:19.

deter and correct its enemy (§ 1115). To the objection, two answers are possible. First, in the absence of an international agreement to punish, it is wiser to leave these criminals to the Supreme Legislator whose justice will be adequate, because otherwise there will be no end of vengeance among the nations. The old pagan precedent which Christian chivalry once stamped out will be revived, that is, whenever a war is lost the losers are enslaved and their leaders put to death. If hope of honorable peace exists, a government may yield before bringing utter ruin on the nation; but if the leaders know their lives are forfeit by defeat, war must assume the ferocity and desperation of a death struggle between wild beasts. Second, the prevalence of international criminals is proof that international justice must be organized positively. The order of daily life forbids the individual to punish his assailants and compels him to seek redress from visibly constituted authority. The nations should follow a similar procedure. When individuals constitute themselves natural ministers of divine retribution, civic order perishes. Because the nations have been doing this on an international scale, peace has been but a preparation for war. Only an international authority, having jurisdiction over the inter-State acts of the nations should legislate against and punish international crime. This international authority does not now exist but it should be created (cf. § 1123 ff.).

B. International Charity

1118. Many persons who admit the relation of natural justice among States deny the existence of a duty of international charity. However, just as charitable obligation binds individuals, so it binds groups. Group life and group action do not strip men of their essential human characteristics and needs. As the needs which one individual cannot supply for himself ought to be charitably supplied by other individuals, so similarly group needs are to be supplied by other groups. Men remain men as members of a nation.

THESIS LXXIX. The Natural Law commands States to exercise charity toward other States.

PROOF

1119. 1. The practice of charity is essential to human well-being. If it is not exercised, men in need lack a human living. Man lives a social life in order that his needs may be supplied by other men.

2. States are obliged to practice that which is essential to human living. Hence they fail in their natural function of supplying a completely human life to the needy when they neglect charity.

3. States do not satisfy this obligation by practicing charity merely to their own members. To restrict charity to one's own people, is to deny the true basis of charity, namely, possession of a common nature and destiny. If there is a duty of charity to some men, there is a duty of charity toward all men.

1120. The general rule of international charity finds a number of particular applications.

1. A nation fighting a righteous war may be aided by another nation.

2. *Immigration.* Nations which have living space and resources to spare ought not to close their doors against all foreigners, especially people from nations which are overcrowded and have limited resources. It is interesting to note that Japan has a population of 70,000,000 and an area roughly equal to that of California.[18] The prudent charity of all nations could provide reasonable remedies for situations of this kind. If they did, we would have fewer wars.

3. *Tariffs.* In protecting one's own financial and industrial security one nation may not exact excessively high dues or enter into commercial agreements with a favored few which deprive many other nations of equitable opportunities to secure raw materials, set up needed industries, or market their products. As in the individual State one class may not make laws which benefit this class to the hurt of other classes, so in international dealings a combination of States ought not enter into cartels which permanently impoverish less fortunate States. Justice as well as charity may thus be violated. The intricate problems here involved can be settled only when all nations sit down in conference and draw up economic agreements which give a fair chance to all. The nations form one human family.

1121. 4. *Intervention.* The liberals of the nineteenth century proclaimed an absolute rule of nonintervention which permitted of no exception, namely — no outsider, individual or nation, may interfere in the internal affairs of a sovereign State for any reason whatever. This principle doubtless arose as a protest against the Holy Alliance, a combination of European powers bent on defeating any attempt to

---

[19] California has an area of 158,693 square miles, and in 1940 it had a population of 7,000,000; Japan has an area of 147,702 square miles and in 1940 it had a population of 70,000,000.

overthrow monarchy in any country. Nonintervention, however, is too narrow an understanding of sovereignty and, when adhered to rigidly, violates true charity. Sovereignty is not an end in itself; it is but a means to human welfare. Hence the rights of sovereignty must be tempered by considerations of the human welfare of the people in whose interest sovereignty exists. If one State has been long and grievously afflicted by another, if the people are revolting against intolerable tyranny, if a State is vainly trying to suppress a revolt injurious to national or international welfare, if a State has been convulsed by endless anarchy — in a word, if a people are overwhelmed by a tremendous evil which is definite, certain, and irremediable by themselves, they may call upon outsiders, individuals or States, to help them. These outsiders have an obligation in charity to assist, if assistance does not bring upon them evils of similar magnitude.

The fact that this principle of charity has been and may again be abused does not refute its existence, nor does the difficulty of deciding when it actually applies. The existence of inhuman and irremediable evil can be determined with certitude. It remains only that the intervening State have an upright motive, which is the good of the people in need. The mode and duration of intervention must likewise be determined by the same unselfish motive.

1122. 5. *Patriotism and internationalism.* No State develops real patriotism by encouraging either disdain for all foreigners or hatred for a particular rival. It is wrong for a father to encourage or even to allow his children constantly to disparage or cherish enmity for his neighbor's children. Likewise in a State, unreasonable ill feeling for foreigners should positively be discouraged. It is true that the State cannot control the thinking and private conversation of its citizens. Nevertheless, no acts of the State should lend approval to uncharitableness; officials should promote sentiments of good will toward all nations; the citizen in his formative years should be taught that he is a member not only of this nation but also of the whole human race. Patriotism which does not develop into sane internationalism is defective. Certainly that isolationism is to be reprobated which disclaims any real connection with, or social obligation to, the rest of the world. A man is naturally a member not only of a family and a nation, but also of that larger society, the human race.

IV. INTERNATIONAL SOCIETY JURIDICALLY ORGANIZED

1123. Social justice defines human obligations to all natural societies. Among natural societies must we include the race at large? We gave an indirect answer to this question when we proved the existence of social obligations toward the human race flowing from the Natural Law. This argument is to the effect that *natural* social obligations toward the race are impossible if the race is not a natural society. However, to present the problem more directly we make two assertions.

1. *The race is a natural unit.* All men are united by common nature and destiny. The biological sciences show that man is a species distinct from all other things. With startling clarity and simplicity revelation manifests the extent and depth of that unity. The word of God reveals that all men have a single origin in one common pair of parents; that all men were tainted with original sin in the fall of their first parents; that all have been redeemed by the death of Christ and all are summoned to a place in the Church, the Mystical Body of Christ.

2. *This natural unit is potentially and inchoatively one society.* All the elements of a functioning society, save one, are present: namely, a plurality, which is the nations of the world; a common end, which is temporal happiness to be attained by all States and the ultimate satisfaction of human sociability; a partial conspiration toward this end by many men of good will; the common bond of *natural* international duties. All that is lacking is *juridical organization* with authority to direct and compel the nations to co-operate unto the common good of all. *Must this final step be taken?* Is there a moral obligation binding the States to constitute positive international authority and to obey it?

THESIS LXXX. The States are now obliged to create a positive international authority with legislative, executive, and judicial power to regulate the international acts of all nations.

1124. Every kind of social obligation does not apply at all times in history. In primeval times the only social obligations which a man had pertained to his family. At that time the familial organization was all that men required or were capable of managing. After families had grown into patriarchal septs and tribes, the need of a superfamilial organization became apparent. The State, which had not been thought of, gradually became a necessity. The clans and tribes who lived in the same territory could have no lasting peace and chance of progress unless they organized a political union. As the idea of the State and its need and function became clear, the heads of families little by little surrendered to the political sovereignty of the State many of their responsibilities and prerogatives.

1125. For countless generations the State has been the ultimate unit in social organization. For centuries the story of the race was a record of the scattering of men across the earth into remote regions whence communication and contact with many others was impossible. In that isolated situation men had no need of an organization over and above the State. Let it be noted that the outstanding contribution of the State to human progress was *intra*national peace. The instrument was law. By subjecting the individual to visible authority in his dealings with other men, dissension, blood, and tumult gave way to comparative peace and order.

1126. But now the uninhabited parts of the earth have been occupied, and the old isolating barriers have disappeared, because modern transportation and communication have made all nations neighbors to one another. As a result, the international needs, contacts, and interdependencies of all States have increased a thousandfold. Unfortunately, however, these relations have not been subjected to competent authority: the impress of compelling law has not been made upon them. The ultimate arbiter of international disputes has not been law but force. From this lack of law has flowed with lamentable acceleration widespread misery. Whenever the Natural Law is inadequate it must be supplemented by positive law. Since the mere precepts of the Natural Law have failed to effect order in so increasingly important a department of human activity, human welfare cries out for the creation of a visible social authority which will submit to law the international acts of all States. As the social acts of individuals are subject to the law of the State, so the international acts of States themselves must become subject to positive international law.

1127. Since law can come only from legitimate authority, the nations must consent to establish international authority. To be effective, this authority must be able not merely to suggest and advise but to make and enforce laws governing inter-State activity. To be a social authority, it must have legislative, executive, and judicial power. The erection of this authority will involve on the part of the nations the surrender of some of their sovereignty. Retaining supreme control of purely domestic matters, the State would hand over to this supra-national authority ultimate control of foreign affairs. Unlimited national sovereignty is not an end in itself. It is less than man and hence for man. When it ceases to promote human welfare it must give way to an arrangement that will.

The fact is that the national State in many respects has ceased to be self-sufficient. Acute human problems have arisen because political readjustments have not yet been made to fit the factual situation. Of course the national sovereignties are loathe to part with anything of their power, but so too in the days of the nascent State, heads of families did not like to yield anything to the tribal king.

PROOF

1128. States are obliged to do that which the welfare of their people imperatively demands. The welfare of all peoples demands positive international authority capable of regulating the international acts of all nations. In the present system of unlimited national sovereignties the welfare neither of particular peoples nor of the whole human race is sufficiently provided for.

1. *The welfare of individual nations is at stake.* It is an anachronism to say that today each nation is adequately self-sufficient. First, when international war arises what single nation can isolate the war or maintain a strict neutrality or when attacked adequately protect its people? Second, economically and financially no nation can get along without the co-operation of the rest of the world.

2. *The welfare of the human race is at stake.* The important social acts of man require regulation and supervision by positive law; otherwise social life is impossible. Ample regulation on local, regional, and national levels is provided by State law. On the international level reign lawlessness and chaos. So long as international relations did not deeply affect the daily lives of men, lack of positive international authority was of small consequence. But now, thanks to transportation, communication, and modernized industry, the economic life of the world is one. Unfortunately, however, international commerce and finance are conducted as undercover war. When the tension becomes too great, world-wide war results.

Grave political injustice, such as denial of self-rule, diminution of the sovereignty of weaker nations, rape of territories, are maintained by force. These injustices, coupled with national jealousies and economic rivalries, are the seeds of potential conflict. But no court of international justice exists in which these disputes may be resolved. The sole arbitrament to date has been war. So frightfully devastating have become the weapons of war that the very existence of the race will be endangered by further development and use of them. With more deadly gases, easier diffusion of bacteria, and more destructive atomic bombs in prospect, international war must be eliminated. State authority embodied in the law of national kings did suppress petty war: the only hope of eliminating or at least lessening the frequency of international war is international authority and law.

READINGS

Beales, A. C. F., *The Catholic Church and International Order.* New York, Penguin Books, 1942.

Cronin, Michael, *Science of Ethics,* Vol. II, pp. 633–679. Dublin, Gill, 1909.

De la Bedoyere, Michael, *Christian Crisis.* New York, Macmillan, 1942.

De Martini, Raymond, O.F.M., *The Right of Nations to Expand by Conquest.* Washington, Catholic University Press, 1947.

Eppstein, John, *The Catholic Tradition of the Law of Nations.* Washington, 1935.

Fenwick, Charles G., *International Law.* New York, Appleton-Century, 1924.

Gonella, Guido, *A World to Reconstruct,* trans. T. Lincoln Bouscaren, S.J., pp. 101–335. Bruce, Milwaukee, 1944.

Haas, Francis J., *Man and Society,* pp. 262–271. New York, Appleton-Century, 1940.

Hayes, Carlton J. H., *Essays on Nationalism.* New York, Macmillan, 1937.

Jarrett, Bede, O.P., *Social Theories of the Middle Ages,* pp. 181–212. Westminster, Md., Newman, 1942.

Kent, James, *Commentaries on American Law,* Vol. I, Part 1, Lect. I–IX.

Leibell, J. F., ed., *Readings in Ethics,* pp. 1010–1073. Chicago, Loyola, 1926.

Liberatore, Matt., S.J., *Institutiones Philosophiae,* Vol. III, pp. 369–406. Neapoli, Giannini, 1871, *ed. quinta.*

Meyer, Theodore, S.J., *Institutiones Juris Naturalis,* Vol. II, pp. 736–838. Friburgi Brisgoviae, Herder, 1900.

Moon, P. T., *Syllabus on International Relations.* New York, Macmillan, 1925.

Parsons, Wilfrid, S.J., *Which Way Democracy,* pp. 246–293. New York, Macmillan, 1939.

Plater, Charles, S.J., *Primer of Peace and War.* London, King, 1915.

Rommen, Heinrich A., *The State in Catholic Thought,* pp. 615–735. St. Louis, Herder, 1945.

Ryan and Boland, *Catholic Principles of Politics,* pp. 217–271. New York, Macmillan, 1940.

Scott, James B., *Law, the State and the International Community,* Vol. II, pp. 241–335. New York, Columbia, 1939.

Sturzo, Luigi, *Nationalism and Internationalism,* pp. 174–308. New York, Roy, 1946.

Suarez, *De Legibus,* II, 17–20.

——— *De Bello,* in Berton's edition, Vol. XII, pp. 737–763.

Taparelli, d'Azeglio, S.J., *Essai Theorique de Droit Naturel Basè sur les Faits,* Tom. III, Lib. 6. Paris, Casterman, 1857.

Watt, Lewis, S.J., *Pope Pius XII on World Order.* Oxford, 1940.

Wright, John J., *National Patriotism in Papal Teaching,* pp. 193–328. Westminster, Md., Newman, 1943.

OCCUPATIONAL GROUPS

When treating of the organic nature of the State in § 839 we spoke of occupational, or vocational groups. A more detailed explanation of their nature, function, and benefit is in order. In the past occupational groups have assured men their livelihood. They could do so again. Furthermore, they would help in solving the grave economic-moral problem of today and would ease the burden of grievously overladen government.

I. THE NATURE OF AN OCCUPATIONAL GROUP

It accords with man's social instincts freely to form societies the better to achieve a desirable end. Since a man's job is of such consuming importance, it is natural that those who have the common interest of the same kind of work combine to protect their livelihood and improve themselves in their work. Such a combination of men would be an occupational group. There is no advantage in haggling over the name to give it: call it occupational or vocational. By the reality we mean a *spontaneously organized, semipublic, autonomous society, intermediate between the family and the State, composed of absolutely all who engage in the same type of labor, trade, or profession, whose purpose is the economic well-being and professional excellence of its members.*

This organization must be established by the people themselves. It may not be superimposed on them by the State. For then it would be artificial and lack that natural development it must have if it is to serve men's economic needs. As an arm of the State, it would only be doing administrative work in the name of the State; and State administration of economics is at all hazards to be avoided. To succeed, this society must be nonpolitical; otherwise it can never perform the autonomous social function of which it is capable.

The occupational group must be semipublic, that is, it is not to be a private society like a labor union. Since its purpose is to secure economic order, justice, and peace for its members — a good which so closely touches the common good — it should have a public character, but since rule would remain in the hands of private citizens, we call it semipublic.

As the municipality has a certain competence and autonomy in political matters which it receives by charter from the State, so this association should be constituted by the State as a corporation and given autonomy and responsibility in the economic order. Its general task would be to produce economic order within the State and to establish and enforce rules to which a man must conform if he wishes to follow a given occupation.

At this suggestion economic liberals raise a keening howl: this corporation would be the death of individual initiative. We agree that it would be the death of unreasonable initiative, as is all law and regulation, but it is time that unsocial and unreasonable activities in the economic field were strongly curbed and economic activity brought back to where it belongs — to the service of society. The occupational group means giving economics that discipline without which orderly activity is impossible. A man does not have to be a doctor, but if he elects to be one, he ought to conform to the ethics of the profession. No one has to live in New York City, but whoever chooses it as his residence must obey the city ordinances. So also if a man wishes to become a printer or manufacturer of textiles, should he not conform to norms governing the printing and textile businesses? But this is fascism, the liberals cry. There is a big difference between fascism and this. Fascism is discipline imposed from without; this discipline is from within, voluntarily agreed to by the members of the group. No sane person denies the chaos of the economic world. Discipline alone will replace that chaos with order, and who can better say what disciplined order in the printing and textile businesses is than the common voice of those who work at them every day?

The immediate end of a corporation will be the good estate of a particular occupation, for example, the healthy condition of the shipping industry. Its ultimate end is the economic welfare and professional betterment of its members. These purposes are realized when the members enjoy a satisfactory economic and professional standing, that is, a real livelihood and a status proportionate to their function and merits; when harmony exists within individual firms, that is, when both employers and employees co-operatively work together for the good of the firm; when order prevails among the firms within the organization.

The corporation also stresses the professional consideration of a job well done. Men are happy at their work when they take a pride in it, ambition to excel at it, and thereby serve the community. The corporation can perform a mighty service by giving trade and business something of the stature of a profession. The primary purpose of the great liberal professions, medicine, law, and the sacred ministry, is service of the community. Personal financial considerations are secondary, because, if a man serves the community, he is assured a decent living. Is it possible that business be raised to an approximate level? The root evil of business is that its total motive is gain. Service to the community scarcely gets lip service. Why could not these values be more proportionately adjusted? Selling clothes and providing amusement are a service to the community — not so noble as healing pain but an appreciable service. Why could not the social and hence the moral aspect of these activities be duly considered by their purveyors? If they did so, women's swimming suits and stage productions would seldom be a pitfall to entrap the peccable onlooker. When pride in one's work and service to the community are considered almost as important as personal gain, that greed which knows no bounds is strongly shackled. Tie down greed, and economic evils tend to disappear.

II. THE FUNCTION OF AN OCCUPATIONAL GROUP

Depending on the size of a country, each occupation would be organized locally, regionally, and nationally. To each corporation the State would grant jurisdiction which is economic and social. (*a*) *Economic* jurisdiction means authority to put order into the production and distribution of goods and services by adapting them to the needs of consumers. (*b*) *Social* jurisdiction means regulation of the professional conduct of the members. Within its proper sphere the corporation could regulate, administer, discipline, and represent. Once the occupations are properly organized, harmony and co-ordination must be established between them. This could be done by a general economic council composed of representatives of all of them.

This body would be competent to advise the State upon economic matters of national importance, but it would not constitute an economic congress parallel to the political congress. It would be nonpolitical and never dominate the State, because government must be aloof from, and above, every interest but the common good.

The cry goes up, This is a Planned Economy. Assuredly, every activity must follow some pattern if it is to achieve its end. Digestion and reproduction, for example, obey rather rigid laws of nature. So also economics must follow some kind of reasoned planning. If chaos is not to continue, there must be economic planning. It will be done. Who is to do it? Leaders of finance, bureaucrats, or democratically controlled occupational groups united in a supreme economic council? The world has had too woeful an experience with the economic decisions of the rugged individualists who control the credit of the world. Sufficient has already been said about the undesirability of State-planned economy. The fumbling attempts of bureaucrats to regulate daily economic life during World War II has shown that they seldom have the technical experience nor the mental viewpoint requisite to make practicable judgments in these matters. As the horse's shoes are still best put on by the blacksmith, they are best capable of making economic decisions whose daily lives are immersed in these things and whose living immediately depends thereon.

III. BENEFITS OF OCCUPATIONAL GROUPS

Society today labors under three major handicaps: (*a*) lack of economic order; (*b*) social injustices; (*c*) need of organic social life. The occupational groups will not bring on the millennium, but in all three difficulties they have a notable contribution to offer.

a) Occupational groups will produce *economic order*. No better solution to the anarchy of production has yet been offered. If production is controlled by social need and not unlimited profit, production becomes more stable and employment steadier. An end will be put to unbridled competition with its unholy offspring of monopolistic gouging. While this system imposes reasonable supervision of private enterprise, supervision will be done by those closest to business and hence most competent to do it wisely. Occupational groups will prevent the calamity of the destruction of private enterprise.

One of the bitterest complaints against the prevailing system is the over-all control of business and industry by anonymous and irresponsible finance. After asserting that control of wealth has gotten into the hands of a few directors of invested funds, Pius XI says: "This power becomes particularly irresistible when exercised by those who, because they hold and control money, are able also to govern credit and determine its allotment, for that reason supplying, so to speak, the life blood to the entire economic body, and grasping, as it were, in their hands the very soul of production, so that no one dare breathe against their will. This accumulation of power, the characteristic note of the modern economic order, is a natural result of limitless free competition, which permits the survival of those who are the strongest, which often means those who fight most relentlessly, pay least heed to the dictates of conscience."[1]

In a corporative arrangement the mere fact that a man has available capital will not suffice to put him into a business. Since the corporation itself will determine who engages in the business, how much is to be produced, and what is reasonable profit, it will be impossible for a man to go into an industry looking for large quick returns: he will be able to do business only on the terms which the corporation establishes. Money will be the servant of industry; industry will no longer be the servant of money. Unlimited opportunities for investment and unlimited competition will no longer exist.

b) Occupational groups will help remove *social injustices*. Unlimited competition offers tremendous prizes of very great wealth to a few persons with the inevitable consequence that many people fail to get a living. Hence arises a proletarian class, that is, large masses of workers without productive wealth and economically dependent on a small class owning all the instruments of production. The corporation would scale down the size of the prizes at the top so as to permit all the members of the corporation a living. This would mean the gradual disappearance of the proletariat. Since the little man would make a living wage and would be secure against unemployment, he could, if he is thrifty and progressive, rise to a status of small ownership and a share in the profits.

Social classes based upon possessions are now hostilely arrayed against each other: capital against labor, employer against employee. The corporation would not be *against* anyone but *for* all its membership.

---

[1] *Quadragesimo Anno.*

This would accomplish two things. First, with enormous profits no longer possible to a few persons, tremendous contrasts of extreme wealth and utter dependence would not be normal.

Second, amicable co-operation would be demanded of all, because all employers and employees would belong to the same organization. This fact would result in the due recognition of the part which labor plays in the production of wealth. The stigma attaching to labor would be removed and a man's social status would not depend on his possessions but on the value of his social function to society.

c) Occupational groups will offer *social organization*. With each corporation functioning under a supreme economic council, dependent on civil authority, the State would have the organic form which it now lacks and a tremendous weight of needless tasks would be lifted from government. Each business and industry would take care of its own personnel by providing cultural and recreational opportunities, unemployment insurance, old age pensions, and all the other desiderata of modern sociology. The State would then be free to regain its natural function of supreme arbiter and dispenser of justice. It would no longer take sides; it would be neither prolabor nor procapital, but the impartial guardian of the good of all.

INDEX

Abortion: contrary to the end of matrimony, 406; defined, 254; indirect, 255; therapeutic, 255

Abrogation of Natural Law, 112

Abstinence, 148

Academic freedom, 516 f

Acceptance in contracts, 310 ff

Accession, 303

Act: deliberate, 30; human, *see* Human act; intellectual, 143; involuntary, 30; moral, *see* Moral act; semideliberate, 31; source of habit, 141 f; voluntary, 29 ff; will, *see* Will act

Activity, social, 365

Adoration, 174

Adultery, 406

Aggressive war always wrong, 564 ff

Aggressor: death of, 247; foetus not an, 254

Agnosticism, 167

Agrarian socialism, 266

Agreement: cause of contract, 313 ff; in contracts, 308 ff; object of, 312 f; parties to, 316

Aleatory contracts, 325 ff

Altruism, 50 f, 182

Ambition, 158

American Journal of Obstetrics and Gynecology, birth spacing, 411

Anarchism, 364

Anarcho-syndicalists, 266

Anger: control of, 192 f; an irascible passion, 36; vice of, 157

Animals have no rights, 237

Antithesis of Marxism, 269

Appetite: concupiscible, 147; elicited, 15; innate, 15; irascible, 147; natural, 62

Arduous good, 149

Aristippus, pleasure the highest good, 17, 49

Aristocracy, 467

Aristotle: all men fear something, 158; canon of Rhadamanthus, 530; definition of family, 416; definition of good, 43; definition of State, 428, 440; definition of virtue, 142; Eudaemonia, 45 f; excellence of human activity, 21; expenses for worship, 158; formation of habits, 141; forms of government, 467; four causes, 4; happiness an act of speculative intellect, 22; how man should live, 20 f; on intemperance, 157; on the just man, 152; love stems from self, 182; on the magnanimous man, 150 ff; on man bereft of social ties, 368; man's end, 13; man needs pleasure, 348; mean of virtue, 143; motives of friendship, 260; Plato's doctrine on universals, 64 *n;* slavery justified, 256; strong middle class, 470

Arnobius, 377

Arnold, M., definition of religion, 166

Art an intellectual virtue, 145

Atheism: of communism, 270 f; discussed, 166 ff

Atomic bomb, 571

Augustine, Plato's doctrine of universals, 64 *n*

Authority: alone can punish, 527; establishment of positive, 581 ff; in family, 420 f; necessary to society, 364; not formal cause of society, 365; political, *see* Political authority; unity of, 365

Autonomous reason: as the norm of morals, 56 ff; not source of obligation, 80

Avebury, Lord, religion of primitives, 118

Backbiting, 259

Bakunin, M., rejects authority, 363

Barmine, A.: communism unproductive, 279; inefficiency of socialistic production, 283 *n*

Beatitude: sanction of the Natural Law, 100; *see also* Happiness

Beccaria, C., no death penalties in peace, 529

Bellarmine, on punishment in war, 577

Belligerent, 564